THE COLLECTED WORKS OF C. S. LEWIS

The Collected Works of

C. S. LEWIS

The Pilgrim's Regress

Christian Reflections

God in the Dock

Inspirational Press • New York

Previously published in three separate volumes:

THE PILGRIM'S REGRESS, copyright © 1933, 1943 by Clive Staples Lewis.
Illustrations copyright © 1981 by Michael Hague.
CHRISTIAN REFLECTIONS, copyright © 1967 by The Executors of the Estate of
C.S. Lewis.
GOD IN THE DOCK, copyright © 1970 by The Trustees of the Estate of C.S. Lewis.

First Inspirational Press edition published in 1996.

Inspirational Press
A division of Budget Book Service, Inc.
386 Park Avenue South
New York, NY 10016

Inspirational Press is a registered trademark of Budget Book Service, Inc.

Published by arrangement with Wm. B. Eerdmans Publishing Co.

Library of Congress Catalog Card Number: 96-77958

ISBN: 0-88486-151-1

Text design by Hannah Lerner.

Printed in the United States of America.

CONTENTS

The Pilgrim's Regress

An Allegorical Apology for Christianity
Reason and Romanticism

Illustrated by Michael Hague

CONTENTS

3

Book Eight: AT BAY

Book Nine: ACROSS THE CANYON

Book Ten: THE REGRESS

List of Illustrations

As cold waters to a thirsty soul,
so is good news from a far country.
                                        —Proverbs

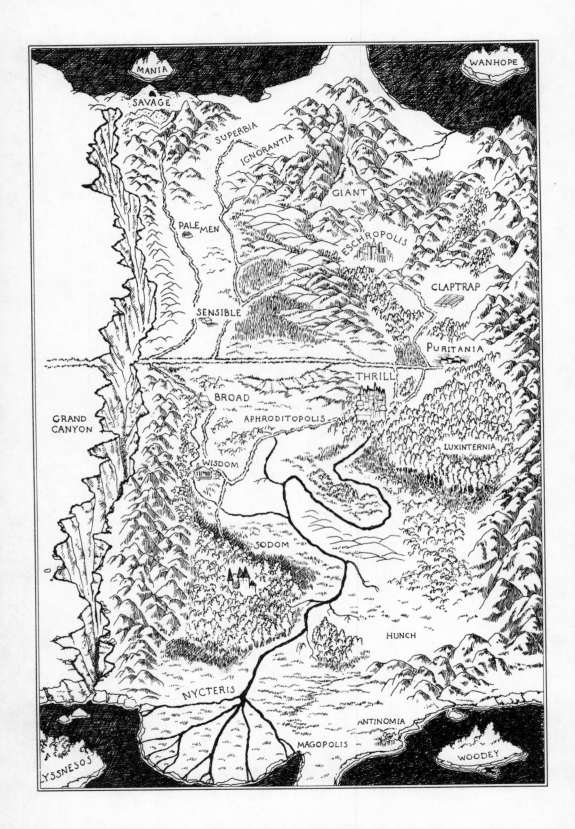

Book One
THE DATA

This every soul seeketh and for the sake of this doth all her actions,
having an inkling that it is; but what it is she cannot sufficiently
discern, and she knoweth not her way, and concerning this she hath no
constant assurance as she hath of other things.
Plato

Whose souls, albeit in a cloudy memory, yet seek back their good,
but, like drunk men, know not the road home.
Boethius

Somewhat it seeketh, and what that is directly it knoweth not, yet
very intentive desire thereof doth so incite it, that all other known
delights and pleasures are laid aside, they give place to the search of
this but only suspected desire.
Hooker

I

The Rules

I DREAMED OF A BOY who was born in the land of Puritania and his name was John. And I dreamed that when John was able to walk he ran out of his parents' garden on a fine morning on to the road. And on the other side of the road there was a deep wood, but not thick, full of primroses and soft green moss. When John set eyes on this he thought he had never seen anything so beautiful; and he ran across the road and into the wood, and was just about to go down on his hands and knees and to pull up the primroses by handfuls, when his mother came running out of the garden gate, and she also ran across the road, and caught John up, and smacked him soundly and told him he must never go into the wood again. And John cried, but he asked no questions, for he was not yet at the age for asking questions. Then a year went past. And then, another fine morning, John had a little sling and he went out into the garden and he saw a bird sitting on a branch. And John got his sling ready and was going to have a shot at the bird, when the cook came running out of the garden and caught John up and smacked him soundly and told him he must never kill any of the birds in the garden.

'Why?' said John.

'Because the Steward would be very angry,' said cook.

'Who is the Steward?' said John.

'He is the man who makes rules for all the country round here,' said cook.

'Why?' said John.

'Because the Landlord set him to do it.'

'Who is the Landlord?' said John.

'He owns all the country,' said the cook.

'Why?' said John.

And when he asked this, the cook went and told his mother. And his mother sat down and talked to John about the Landlord all afternoon: but John took none of it in, for he was not yet at the age for taking it in. Then a year went past, and one dark, cold, wet morning John was made to put on new clothes. They were the ugliest clothes that had ever been put upon him, which John did not mind at all, but they also caught him under the chin, and were tight under the arms which he minded a great deal, and they made him itch all over. And his father and mother took him out along the road, one holding him by each hand (which was uncomfortable, too, and very unnecessary), and told him they were taking him to see the Steward. The Steward lived in a big dark house of stone on the side of the road. The father and mother went in to talk to the Steward first, and John was left sitting in the hall on a chair so high that his feet did not reach the floor. There were other chairs in the hall where he could have sat in comfort, but his father had told him that the Steward would be angry if he did not sit absolutely still and be very good: and John was beginning to be afraid, so he sat still in the high chair with his feet dangling, and his clothes itching all over him, and his eyes starting out of his head. After a very long time his parents came back again, looking as if they had been with the doctor, very grave. Then they said that John must go in and see the Steward too. And when John came into the room, there was an old man with a red, round face, who was very kind and full of jokes, so that John quite got over his fears, and they had a good talk about fishing tackle and bicycles. But just when the talk was at its best, the Steward got up and cleared his throat. He then took down a mask from the wall with a long white beard attached to it and suddenly clapped it on his face, so that his appearance was awful. And he said, 'Now I am going to talk to you about the Landlord. The Landlord owns all the country, and it is *very*, *very* kind of him to allow us to live on it at all—very, very kind.' He went on repeating 'very kind' in a queer sing song voice so long that John would have laughed, but that now he was beginning to be frightened again. The Steward then took down from a peg a big card with small print all over it, and said, 'Here is a list of all the things the Landlord says you must not do. You'd better look at it.' So John took the card: but half the rules seemed to forbid things he had never heard of, and the other half forbade things he was doing every day and could not imagine not doing: and the number of the rules was so enormous that he felt he could never remember them all. 'I hope,' said the Steward, 'that you have not already broken any of the rules?' John's heart began to thump, and his eyes bulged more and more, and he was at his wit's end when the Steward took the mask off and looked at John with his real face and said, 'Better tell a lie, old chap, better tell a lie. Easiest for all concerned,' and popped the mask on his face all in a flash. John gulped and said quickly, 'Oh, no sir.' 'That is just as well,' said the Steward through the mask. 'Because, you know, if you did break any of them and the Landlord got to know of it, do you know what he'd do to you?' 'No, sir,' said John: and the Steward's eyes seemed to be twinkling dreadfully through the holes of the mask. 'He'd take you and shut you up for ever and ever in a black hole full of snakes and scorpions as large as lobsters—for ever and ever. And besides that, he is such a kind, good man, so very, very kind, that I am sure you would never *want* to displease him.' 'No, sir,' said John, 'But, please, sir . . .' 'Well,' said the Steward. 'Please, sir, supposing I did break one, one little one, just by accident, you know. Could nothing stop the snakes and lobsters?' 'Ah! . . .' said the Steward; and then he sat down and talked for a long time, but John could not understand a single syllable. However, it all ended with pointing out that the Landlord was quite extraordinarily kind and good to his tenants, and would certainly torture most of them to death the moment he had the slightest pretext. 'And you can't blame him,' said the Steward. 'For after all, it *is* his land, and it is so very good of him to let us live here at all—people like us, you know.' Then the Steward took off the mask and had a nice, sensible chat with John again, and gave him a cake and brought him out to his father and mother. But just as they were going he bent down and whispered in John's ear, 'I shouldn't bother about it all too much if I were you.' At the same time he slipped the card of the rules into John's hand and told him he could keep it for his own use.

II
The Island

NOW THE DAYS and the weeks went on again, and I dreamed that John had
little peace either by day or night for thinking of the rules and the black hole full of
snakes. At first he tried very hard to keep them all, but when it came to bed-time
he always found that he had broken far more than he had kept: and the thought of
the horrible tortures to which the good, kind Landlord would put him became such
a burden that next day he would become quite reckless and break as many as he
possibly could; for oddly enough this eased his mind for the moment. But then after
a few days the fear would return and this time it would be worse than before because of the dreadful number of rules that he had broken during the interval. But
what puzzled him most at this time was a discovery which he made after the rules
had been hanging in his bedroom for two or three nights: namely, that on the other
side of the card, on the back, there was quite a different set of rules. There were so
many that he never read them all through and he was always finding new ones.
Some of them were very like the rules on the front of the card, but most of them
were just the opposite. Thus whereas the front of the card said that you must be
always examining yourself to see how many rules you had broken, the back of the
card began like this:

Rule 1.—Put the whole thing out of your head
        The moment you get into bed.

Or again, whereas the front said that you must always go and ask your elders what
the rule about a certain thing was, if you were in the least doubt, the back said:

Rule 2.—Unless they saw you do it,
        Keep quiet or else you'll rue it.

And so on. And now I dreamed that John went out one morning and tried to play
in the road and to forget his troubles; but the rules kept coming back into his head
so that he did not make much of it. However, he went on always a few yards further till suddenly he looked up and saw that he was so far away from home that he
was in a part of the road he had never seen before. Then came the sound of a musical
instrument, from behind it seemed, very sweet and very short, as if it were one
plucking of a string or one note of a bell, and after it a full, clear voice—and it
sounded so high and strange that he thought it was very far away, further than a

---

1. *John saw an island where tall
enchanters, bearded to their feet, sat in
green chairs among the forests.*

star. The voice said, Come. Then John saw that there was a stone wall beside the road in that part: but it had (what he had never seen in a garden wall before) a window. There was no glass in the window and no bars; it was just a square hole in the wall. Through it he saw a green wood full of primroses: and he remembered suddenly how he had gone into another wood to pull primroses, as a child, very long ago—so long that even in the moment of remembering the memory seemed still out of reach. While he strained to grasp it, there came to him from beyond the wood a sweetness and a pang so piercing that instantly he forgot his father's house, and his mother, and the fear of the Landlord, and the burden of the rules. All the furniture of his mind was taken away. A moment later he found that he was sobbing, and the sun had gone in: and what it was that had happened to him he could not quite remember, nor whether it had happened in this wood, or in the other wood when he was a child. It seemed to him that a mist which hung at the far end of the wood had parted for a moment, and through the rift he had seen a calm sea, and in the sea an island, where the smooth turf sloped down unbroken to the bays, and out of the thickets peeped the pale, small-breasted Oreads, wise like gods, unconscious of themselves like beasts, and tall enchanters, bearded to their feet, sat in green chairs among the forests. But even while he pictured these things he knew, with one part of his mind, that they were not like the things he had seen—nay, that what had befallen him was not seeing at all. But he was too young to heed the distinction: and too empty, now that the unbounded sweetness passed away, not to seize greedily whatever it had left behind. He had no inclination yet to go into the wood: and presently he went home, with a sad excitement upon him, repeating to himself a thousand times, 'I know now what I want.' The first time that he said it, he was aware that it was not entirely true: but before he went to bed he was believing it.

III
The Eastern Mountains

JOHN HAD A disreputable old uncle who was the tenant of a poor little farm beside his father's. One day when John came in from the garden, he found a great hubbub in the house. His uncle was sitting there with his cheeks the colour of ashes. His mother was crying. His father was sitting very still with a solemn face. And there, in the midst of them, was the Steward with his mask on, John crept round to his mother and asked her what the matter was.

'Poor Uncle George has had notice to quit,' she said.

'Why?' said John.

'His lease is up. The Landlord has sent him notice to quit.'

'But didn't you know how long the lease was for?'

'Oh, no, indeed we did not. We thought it was for years and years more. I am sure the Landlord never gave us any idea he was going to turn him out at a moment's notice like this.'

'Ah, but it doesn't need any notice,' broke in the Steward. 'You know he always retains the right to turn anyone out whenever he chooses. It is very good of him to let any of us stay here at all.'

'To be sure, to be sure,' said the mother.

'That goes without saying,' said the father.

'I'm not complaining,' said Uncle George. 'But it seems cruelly hard.'

'Not at all,' said the Steward. 'You've only got to go to the Castle and knock at the gate and see the Landlord himself. You know that he's only turning you out of here to make you much more comfortable somewhere else. Don't you?'

Uncle George nodded. He did not seem able to get his voice.

Suddenly the father looked at his watch. Then he looked up at the Steward and said:

'Well?'

'Yes,' said the Steward.

Then John was sent up to his bedroom and told to put on the ugly and uncomfortable clothes; and when he came downstairs, itching all over, and tight under the arms, he was given a little mask to put on, and his parents put masks on too. Then I thought in my dream that they wanted to put a mask on Uncle George, but he was trembling so that it would not stay on. So they had to see his face as it was; and his face became so dreadful that everyone looked in a different direction and pretended not to see it. They got Uncle George to his feet with much difficulty, and then they all came out on to the road. The sun was just setting at one end of the road, for the road ran east and west. They turned their backs on the dazzling western sky and there John saw ahead of them the night coming down over the eastern mountains. The country sloped down eastward to a brook, and all this side of the brook was green and cultivated: on the other side of the brook a great black moor sloped upward, and beyond that were the crags and chasms of the lower mountains, and high above them again the bigger mountains: and on top of the whole waste was one mountain so big and black that John was afraid of it. He was told that the Landlord had his castle up there.

They trudged on eastward, a long time, always descending, till they came to the brook. They were so low that the sunset behind them was out of sight. Before them, all was growing darker every minute, and the cold east wind was blowing out of the darkness, right from the mountain tops. When they had stood for a little, Uncle George looked round on them all once or twice, and said, 'Oh, dear! Oh, dear!' in a funny small voice like a child's. Then he stepped over the brook and began to walk away up the moor. It was now so dark and there were so many ups and downs in the moorland that they lost sight of him almost at once. Nobody ever saw him again.

'Well,' said the Steward, untying his mask as they turned homeward. 'We've all got to go when our time comes.'

'That's true,' said the father, who was lighting his pipe. When it was lit he turned to the Steward and said: 'Some of those pigs of George's have won prizes.'

'I'd keep 'em if I were you,' said the Steward. 'It's no time for selling now '

'Perhaps you're right,' said the father

John walked behind with his mother.

'Mother.'

'Well, dear?'

'Could any of us be turned out without notice like that any day?'

'Well, yes. But it is very unlikely.'

'But we *might* be?'

'You oughtn't to be thinking of that sort of thing at your age.'

'Why oughtn't I?'

'It's not healthy. A boy like you.'

'Mother.'

'Yes?'

'Can *we* break off the lease without notice too?'

'How do you mean?'

'Well, the Landlord can turn us out of the farm whenever he likes. Can we leave the farm whenever we like?'

'No, certainly not.'

'Why not?'

'That's in the lease. We must go when he likes, and stay as long as he likes.'

'Why ?'

'I suppose because he makes the leases.'

'What would happen if we did leave?'

'He would be very angry.'

'Would he put us in the black hole?'

'Perhaps.'

'Mother.'

'Well, dear?'

'Will the Landlord put Uncle George in the black hole?'

'How dare you say such a thing about your poor uncle? Of course he won't.'

'But hasn't Uncle George broken all the rules?'

'Broken all the rules? Your Uncle George was a very good man.'

'You never told me that before,' said John.

IV
Leah for Rachel

THEN I TURNED OVER in my sleep and began to dream deeper still: and I dreamed that I saw John growing tall and lank till he ceased to be a child and became a boy. The chief pleasure of his life in these days was to go down the road and look through the window in the wall in the hope of seeing the beautiful Island. Some days he saw it well enough, especially at first, and heard the music and the voice. At first he would not look through the window into the wood unless he had heard the music But after a time both the sight of the Island, and the sounds, became very rare. He would stand looking through the window for hours, and seeing the wood, but no sea or Island beyond it, and straining his ears but hearing nothing except the wind in the leaves. And the yearning for that sight of the Island and the sweet wind blowing over the water from it, though indeed these themselves had given him only yearning, became so terrible that John thought he would die if he did not have them again soon. He even said to himself, 'I would break every rule on the card for them if I could only get them. I would go down into the black hole for ever if it had a window from which I could see the island.' Then it came into his head that perhaps he ought to explore the wood and thus he might find his way down to the sea beyond it: so he determined that the next day, whatever he saw or heard at the window, he would go through and spend the whole day in the wood. When the morning came, it had been raining all night and a south wind had blown the clouds away at sunrise, and all was fresh and shining. As soon as he had had his breakfast John was out on the road. With the wind and the birds, and country carts passing, there were many noises about that morning, so that when John heard a strain of music long before he had reached the wall and the window—a strain like that which he desired, but coming from an unexpected quarter—he could not be absolutely certain that he had not imagined it. It made him stand still in the road for a minute, and in my dream I could hear him thinking—like this: 'If I go after that sound—away off the road, up yonder—it is all luck whether I shall find anything at all. But if I go on to the window, there I *know* I shall reach the wood, and there I can have a good hunt for the shore and the Island. In fact, I shall *insist* on finding it. I am determined to. But if I go a new way I shall not be able to insist: I shall just have to take what comes.' So he went on to the place he knew and climbed through the window into the wood. Up and down and to and fro among the trees he walked, looking this way and that: but he found no sea and no shore, and indeed no end to the wood in any direction. When it came to the middle of the day he was so hot that he sat down and fanned himself. Often, of late, when the sight of the Island had been withheld, he had felt sad and despairing: but what he felt now was more like anger. 'I must have it,' he kept on saying to himself, and then, 'I must have something.' Then it occurred to him that at least he had the wood, which he would once have loved, and that he had not given it a thought all morning. Very well, thought John, I will enjoy the wood: *I will* enjoy it. He set his teeth and wrinkled his forehead and sat still until the sweat rolled off him in an effort to enjoy the wood. But the more he tried the more he felt that there was nothing to enjoy. There was the grass and there were the trees: 'But what am I to *do* with them?' said John. Next it came into his head that he might perhaps get the old feeling—for what, he thought, had the Island ever given him but a *feeling*?—by imagining. He shut his eyes and set his teeth again and made a picture of the Island in his mind: but he could not keep his attention on the picture because he wanted all the time to watch some other part of his mind to see if the *feeling* were beginning. But no feeling began: and then, just as he was opening his eyes he heard a voice speaking to him. It was quite close at hand, and very sweet, and not at all like the old voice of the wood. When he looked round he saw what he had never expected, yet he was not surprised. There in the grass beside him sat a laughing brown girl of about his own age, and she had no clothes on.

'It was me you wanted,' said the brown girl. 'I am better than your silly Islands.'

And John rose and caught her, all in haste, and committed fornication with her in the wood.

V
Ichabod

AFTER THAT JOHN WAS always going to the wood. He did not always have his pleasure of her in the body, though it often ended that way: sometimes he would talk to her about himself, telling her lies about his courage and his cleverness. All that he told her she remembered, so that on other days she could tell it over to him again. Sometimes, even, he would go with her through the wood looking for the sea and the Island, but not often. Meanwhile the year went on and the leaves began to fall in the wood and the skies were more often grey: until now, as I dreamed, John had slept in the wood, and he woke up in the wood. The sun was low and a blustering wind was stripping the leaves from the branches. The girl was still there and the appearance of her was hateful to John: and he saw that she knew this, and the more she knew it the more she stared at him, smiling. He looked round and saw how small the wood was after all—a beggarly strip of trees between the road and a field that he knew well. Nowhere in sight was there anything that he liked at all.

'I shall not come back here,' said John. 'What I wanted is not here. It wasn't you I wanted, you know.'

'Wasn't it?' said the brown girl 'Then be off. But you must take your family with you.'

With that she put up her hands to her mouth and called. Instantly from behind every tree there slipped out a brown girl: each of them was just like herself: the little wood was full of them.

'What are these?'

'Our daughters,' said she. 'Did you not know you were a father? Did you think I was barren, you fool? And now, children,' she added, turning to the mob, 'go with your father.'

Suddenly John became very much afraid and leaped over the wall into the road. There he ran home as fast as he could.

VI

Quem Quaeritis in Sepulchro? Non est Hic

FROM THAT DAY FORTH until he left his home John was not happy. First of all the weight of all the rules that he had broken descended upon him: for while he was going daily to the wood he had almost forgotten the Landlord, and now suddenly the whole reckoning was to pay. In the second place, his last sight of the Island was now so long ago that he had forgotten how to wish for it even, and almost how to set about looking for it. At first he feared to go back to the window in the wall, lest he should meet the brown girl: but he soon found that her family were so constantly with him that place made no difference. Wherever he sat down to rest on a walk, there sooner or later, there would be a little brown girl beside him. When he sat of an evening with his father and mother, a brown girl, visible only to him, would sidle in and sit at his feet: and sometimes his mother would fix her eyes on him and even ask him what he was staring at. But most of all they plagued him whenever he had a fit of fright about the Landlord and the black hole. It was always the same. He would wake one morning full of fear, and take down his card and read it—the front of it—and determine that today he would really begin to keep the rules. And for that day he would, but the strain was intolerable. He used to comfort himself by saying, It will get more easy as I go on. To-morrow it will be easier. But to-morrow was always harder, and on the third day it was worst of all. And on that third day when he crept away to bed, tired to death and raw in his soul, always he would be sure to find a brown girl waiting for him there: and on such a night he had no spirit to resist her blandishments.

But when he perceived that no place was more, or less, haunted than another, then he came sidling back to the window in the wall. He had little hopes of it. He visited it more as a man visits a grave. It was full winter now, and the grove was naked and dark, the trees dripped in it, and the stream—he saw now that it was little more than a gutter—was full of dead leaves and mud. The wall, too, was broken where he had jumped over it. Yet John stood there a long time, many a winter evening, looking in. And he seemed to himself to have reached the bottom of misery.

One night he was trudging home from it, when he began to weep. He thought of that first day when he had heard the music and seen the Island: and the longing, not now for the Island itself, but for that moment when he had so sweetly longed for it, began to swell up in a warm wave, sweeter, sweeter, till he thought he could bear no more, and then yet sweeter again, till on the top of it, unmistakably, there came the short sound of music, as if a string had been plucked or a bell struck once. At the same moment a coach had gone past him. He turned and looked after it, in time to see a head even then being withdrawn from the window: and he thought he heard a voice say, Come. And far beyond the coach, among the hills of the western horizon, he thought that he saw a shining sea, and a faint shape of an Island, not much more than a cloud. It was nothing compared with what he had seen the first time: it was so much further away. But his mind was made up. That night he waited till his parents were asleep, and then, putting some few needments together, he stole out by the back door and set his face to the West to seek for the Island.

Book Two
THRILL

---

*Thou shalt not make to thyself any graven image, nor the likeness of
anything that is in the heaven above.*
Exodus

*The soul of man, therefore, desiring to learn what manner of things
these are, casteth her eyes upon objects akin to herself, whereof none
sufficeth. And then it is that she saith, With the Lord and with the
things whereof I spoke, there is nothing in that likeness; what then is it
like? This is the question, oh son of Dionysius, that is the cause of all
evils—or rather the travail wherein the soul travaileth about it.*
Plato[1]

*Following false copies of the good, that no
Sincere fulfillment of their promise make.*
Dante

*In hand she boldly took
To make another like the former dame,
Another Florimell in shape and look
So lively and so like that many it mistook.*
Spenser

---

1. Some think it wrongly attributed to him.

I
Dixit Insipiens

STILL I LAY DREAMING in bed, and looked, and I saw John go plodding along the road westward in the bitter black of a frosty night. He walked so long that the morning broke. Then presently John saw a little inn by the side of the road and a woman with a broom who had opened the door and was sweeping out the rubbish. So he turned in there and called for a breakfast, and while it was cooking he sat down in a hard chair by the newly-lit fire and fell asleep. When he woke the sun was shining in through the window and there was his breakfast laid. Another traveller was already eating: he was a big man with red hair and a red stubble on all his three chins, buttoned up very tight. When they had both finished the traveller rose and cleared his throat and stood with his back to the fire. Then he cleared his throat again and said:

'A fine morning, young sir.'

'Yes, sir,' said John.

'You are going West, perhaps, young man?'

'I—I think so.'

'It is possible that you don't know me.'

'I am a stranger here.'

'No offence,' said the stranger. 'My name is Mr. Enlightenment, and I believe it is pretty generally known. I shall be happy to give you my assistance and protection as far as our ways lie together.'

John thanked him very much for this and when they went out from the inn there was a neat little trap waiting, with a fat little pony between the shafts: and its eyes were so bright and its harness was so well polished that it was difficult to say which was twinkling the keener in the morning sunshine. They both got into the trap and Mr. Enlightenment whipped up the fat little pony and they went bowling along the road as if nobody had a care in the world. Presently they began to talk.

'And where might you come from, my fine lad?' said Mr. Enlightenment.

'From Puritania, sir,' said John.

'A good place to leave, eh?'

'I am so glad you think that,' cried John. 'I was afraid—'

'I hope I am a man of the world,' said Mr. Enlightenment. 'Any young fellow who is anxious to better himself may depend on finding sympathy and support in me. Puritania! Why, I suppose you have been brought up to be afraid of the Landlord.'

'Well, I must admit I sometimes *do* feel rather nervous.'

'You may make your mind easy, my boy. There is no such person.'

'There is no Landlord?'

'There is absolutely no such thing—I might even say no such *entity*—in existence. There never has been and never will be.'

'And is this absolutely certain?' cried John; for a great hope was rising in his heart.

'Absolutely certain. Look at me, young man. I ask you—do I look as if I was easily taken in?'

'Oh, no,' said John hastily. 'I was just wondering, though. I mean—how did they all come to think there was such a person?'

'The Landlord is an invention of those Stewards. All made up to keep the rest of us under their thumb: and of course the Stewards are hand in glove with the police. They are a shrewd lot, those Stewards. They know which side their bread is buttered on, all right. Clever fellows. Damn me, I can't help admiring them.'

'But do you mean that the Stewards don't believe it themselves?'

'I dare say they do. It is just the sort of cock and bull story they would believe. They are simple old souls most of them—just like children. They have no knowledge of modern science and they would believe anything they were told.'

John was silent for a few minutes. Then he began again:

'But how do you *know* there is no Landlord?'

'Christopher Columbus, Galileo, the earth is round, invention of printing, gunpowder! !' exclaimed Mr. Enlightenment in such a loud voice that the pony shied.

'I beg your pardon,' said John.

'Eh?' said Mr. Enlightenment.

'I didn't quite understand,' said John.

'Why, it's as plain as a pikestaff,' said the other. 'Your people in Puritania believe in the Landlord because they have not had the benefits of a scientific training. For example, I dare say it would be news to you to hear that the earth was round—round as an orange, my lad!'

'Well, I don't know that it would,' said John, feeling a little disappointed. 'My father always said it was round.'

'No, no, my dear boy,' said Mr. Enlightenment, 'you must have misunderstood him. It is well known that everyone in Puritania thinks the earth flat. It is not likely that I should be mistaken on such a point. Indeed, it is out of the question. Then again, there is the palaeontological evidence.'

'What's that?'

'Why, they tell you in Puritania that the Landlord made all these roads. But that is quite impossible for old people can remember the time when the roads were not nearly so good as they are now. And what is more, scientists have found all over the country the traces of *old* roads running in quite different directions. The inference is obvious.'

John said nothing.

'I said,' repeated Mr. Enlightenment, 'that the inference was obvious.'

'Oh, yes, yes, of course,' said John hastily, turning a little red.

'Then, again, there is anthropology.'

'I'm afraid I don't know—'

'Bless me, of course you don't. They don't mean you to know. An anthropologist is a man who goes round your backward villages in these parts, collecting the odd stories that the country people tell about the Landlord. Why, there is one village where they think he has a trunk like an elephant. Now anyone can see that that couldn't be true.'

'It is very unlikely.'

'And what is better still, we know how the villagers came to think so. It all began by an elephant escaping from the local zoo; and then some old villager—he was probably drunk—saw it wandering about on the mountain one night, and so the story grew up that the Landlord had a trunk.'

'Did they catch the elephant again?'

'Did who?'

'The anthropologists.'

'Oh, my dear boy, you are misunderstanding. This happened long before there were any anthropologists.'

'Then how do they know?'

'Well, as to that . . . I see that you have a very crude notion of how science actually works. To put it simply—for, of course, you could not understand the *technical* explanation—to put it simply, they know that the escaped elephant must have been the source of the trunk story because they know that an escaped snake must have been the source of the snake story in the next village—and so on. This is called the inductive method. Hypothesis, my dear young friend, establishes itself by a cumulative process: or, to use popular language, if you make the same guess often enough it ceases to be a guess and becomes a Scientific Fact.'

After he had thought for a while, John said:

'I think I see. Most of the stories about the Landlord are probably untrue; therefore the rest are probably untrue.'

'Well, that is as near as a beginner can get to it, perhaps. But when you have had a scientific training you will find that you can be quite certain about all sorts of things which now seem to you only probable.'

By this time the fat little pony had them several miles, and they had come to a place where a by-road went off to the right. 'If you are going West, we must part here,' said Mr. Enlightenment, drawing up. 'Unless perhaps you would care to come home with me. You see that magnificent city?' John looked down by the by-road and saw in a flat plain without any trees a huge collection of corrugated iron huts, most of which seemed rather old and rusty.

'That,' said Mr. Enlightenment, 'is the city of Claptrap. You will hardly believe me when I say that I can remember it as a miserable village. When I first came here it had only forty inhabitants: it now boasts a population of twelve million, four hundred thousand, three hundred and sixty-one souls, who include, I may add, the majority of our most influential publicists and scientific popularizers. In this unprecedented development I am proud to say that I have borne no small part: but it is no mock modesty to add that the invention of the printing press has been more important than any merely personal agency. If you would care to join us—'

'Well, thank you.' said John, 'but I think I will keep to the main road a little longer.'

He got out of the trap and turned to bid good-bye to Mr. Enlightenment. Then a sudden thought came into his head, and he said:

---

2. *John got out of the trap and turned to bid good-bye to Mr. Enlightenment.*

'I am not sure that I have really understood all your arguments, sir. Is it absolutely certain that there is no Landlord?'

'Absolutely. I give you my word of honour.'

With these words they shook hands. Mr. Enlightenment turned the pony's head up the by-road, gave it a touch with the whip, and in a few moments was out of sight.

II

The Hill

THEN I SAW JOHN bounding forward on his road so lightly that before he knew it he had come to the top of a little hill. It was not because the hill had tired him that he stopped there, but because he was too happy to move. 'There is no Landlord,' he cried. Such a weight had been lifted from his mind that he felt he could fly. All round him the frost was gleaming like silver; the sky was like blue glass; a robin sat in the hedge beside him: a cock was crowing in the distance. 'There is no Landlord.' He laughed when he thought of the old card of rules hung over his bed in the bedroom, so low and dark, in his father's house. 'There is no Landlord. There is no black hole.' He turned and looked back on the road he had come by: and when he did so he gasped with joy. For there in the East, under the morning light, he saw the mountains heaped up to the sky like clouds, green and violet and dark red; shadows were passing over the big rounded slopes, and water shone in the mountain pools, and up at the highest of all the sun was smiling steadily on the ultimate crags. These crags were indeed so shaped that you could easily take them for a castle: and now it came into John's head that he had never looked at the mountains before, because, as long as he thought that the Landlord lived there, he had been afraid of them. But now that there was no Landlord he perceived that they were beautiful. For a moment he almost doubted whether the Island could be more beautiful, and whether he would not be wiser to go East, instead of West. But it did not seem to him to matter, for he said, 'If the world has the mountains at one end and the Island at the other, then every road leads to beauty, and the world is a glory among glories.'

At that moment he saw a man walking up the hill to meet him. Now I knew in my dream that this man's name was Mr. Vertue, and he was about of an age with John, or a little older.

'What is the name of this place?' said John.

'It is called Jehovah-Jirah,' said Mr. Vertue.

Then they both turned and continued their journey to the West. After they had gone a little way Mr. Vertue stole a glance at John's face and then he smiled a little.

'Why do you smile?' said John.

'I was thinking that you looked very glad.'

'So would you be if you had lived in the fear of a Landlord all your life and had just discovered that you were a free man.'

'Oh, it's that, is it?'

'You don't believe in the Landlord, do you?'

'I know nothing about him—except by hearsay like the rest of us.'

'You wouldn't like to be under his thumb.'

'Wouldn't like? I wouldn't *be* under anyone's thumb.'

'You might have to, if he had a black hole.'

'I'd let him put me in the black hole sooner than take orders if the orders were not to my mind.'

'Why, I think you are right. I can hardly believe it yet—that I need not obey the rules. There's that robin again. To think that I could have a shot at it if I liked and no one would interfere with me!'

'Do you want to?'

'I'm not sure that I do,' said John, fingering his sling. But when he looked round on the sunshine and remembered his great happiness and looked twice at the bird, he said, 'No, I don't. There is nothing I want less. Still—I could if I liked.'

'You mean you could if you chose.'

'Where's the difference?'

'All the difference in the world.'

III
A Little Southward

I THOUGHT THAT JOHN would have questioned him further, but now they came in sight of a woman who was walking slower than they so that presently they came up with her and wished her good-day. When she turned, they saw that she was young and comely, though a little dark of complexion. She was friendly and frank, but not wanton like the brown girls, and the whole world became pleasanter to the young men because they were travelling the same way with her. But first they told her their names, and she told them hers, which was Media Halfways.

'And where are you travelling to, Mr. Vertue?' she asked.

'To travel hopefully is better than to arrive,' said Vertue.

'Do you mean you are just out for a walk, just for exercise?'

'Certainly not,' said Vertue, who was becoming a little confused. 'I am on a pilgrimage. I must admit, now that you press me, I have not a very clear idea of the end. But that is not the important question. These speculations don't make one a better walker. The great thing is to do one's thirty miles a day.'

'Why?'

'Because that is the rule.'

'Ho-ho!' said John. 'So you *do* believe in the Landlord after all.'

'Not at all. I didn't say it was the Landlord's rule.'

'Whose is it then?'

'It is my own rule. I made it myself.'

'But why?'

'Well, that again is a speculative question. I have made the best rules I can. If I find any better ones I shall adopt them. In the meantime, the great thing is to have rules of some sort and to keep them.'

'And where are *you* going?' said Media, turning to John.

Then John began to tell his companions about the Island, and how he had first seen it, and was determined to give up everything for the hope of finding it.

'Then you had better come and see my father,' said she. 'He lives in the city of Thrill, and at the bottom of this hill there is a turn to the left which will bring us there in half an hour.'

'Has your father been to the Island? Does he know the way?'

'He often talks about something very like it.'

'You had better come with us, Vertue,' said John, 'since you do not know where you are going and there can be no place better to go than the Island.'

'Certainly not,' said Vertue. 'We must keep to the road. We must keep on.'

'I don't see why,' said John.

'I dare say you don't,' said Vertue.

All this time they were going down the hill, and now they came to a little grassy lane on the left which went off through a wood. Then I thought that John had a little hesitation: but partly because the sun was now hot and the hard metal of the road was becoming sore to his feet, and partly because he felt a little angry with Vertue, and most of all because Media was going that way, he decided to turn down the lane. They said good-bye to Vertue, and he went on his way stumping up the next hill without ever looking back.

IV
Soft Going

WHEN THEY WERE in the lane they walked more gently. The grass was soft under their feet, and the afternoon sun beating down on the sheltered place made it warm. And presently they heard a sound of sweet and melancholy chimes.

'Those are the bells of the city,' said Media.

As they went on they walked closer together, and soon they were walking arm in arm. Then they kissed each other: and after that they went on their way kissing and talking in slow voices, of sad and beautiful things. And the shadow of the wood and the sweetness of the girl and the sleepy sound of the bells reminded John a little bit of the Island, and a little bit of the brown girls.

'This is what I have been looking for all my life,' said John. 'The brown girls were too gross and the Island was too fine. This is the real thing.'

'This is Love,' said Media with a deep sigh. 'This is the way to the *real* Island.'

Then I dreamed that they came in sight of the city, very old, and full of spires and turrets, all covered with ivy, where it lay in a little grassy valley, built on both sides of a lazy, winding river. And they passed the gate in the ruinous old city wall and came and knocked at a certain door and were let in. Then Media brought him in to a darkish room with a vaulted roof and windows of stained glass, and exquisite food was brought to them. With the food came old Mr. Halfways. He was a gliding gentleman with soft, silver hair and a soft, silver voice, dressed in flowing robes: and he was so solemn, with his long beard, that John was reminded of the Steward with his mask on. 'But it is much better than the Steward,' thought John, 'because there is nothing to be afraid of. Also, he doesn't need a mask: his face is really like that.'

V

Leah for Rachel

AS THEY ATE John told him about the Island.

'You will find your Island here,' said Mr. Halfways, looking into John's eyes.

'But how can it be here in the middle of the city?'

'It needs no place. It is everywhere and nowhere. It refuses entry to none who asks. It is an Island of the Soul,' said the old gentleman. 'Surely even in Puritania they told you that the Landlord's castle was within you?'

'But I don't want the castle,' said John. 'And I don't believe in the Landlord.'

'What is truth?' said the old man. 'They were mistaken when they told you of the Landlord: and yet they were not mistaken. What the imagination seizes as beauty must be truth, whether it existed before or not. The Landlord they dreamed to find, we find in our hearts: the Island you seek for, you already inhabit. The children of that country are never far from their fatherland.'

When the meal was ended the old gentleman took a harp, and at the first sweep of his hand across the strings John began to think of the music that he had heard by the window in the wall. Then came the voice: and it was no longer merely silver sweet and melancholy like Mr. Halfways' speaking voice, but strong and noble and full of strange over-tones, the noise of the sea, and of all birds, and sometimes of wind and thunder. And John began to see a picture of the Island with his eyes open: but it was more than a picture, for he sniffed the spicy smell and the sharp brine of the sea mixed with it. He seemed to be in the water, only a few yards from the sand of the Island. He could see more than he had ever seen before. But just as he had put down his feet and touched a sandy bottom and was beginning to wade ashore, the song ceased. The whole vision went away. John found himself back in the dusky room, seated on a low divan, with Media by his side.

'Now I shall sing you something else,' said Mr. Halfways.

'Oh, no,' cried John, who was sobbing. 'Sing the same again. Please sing it again.'

'You had better not hear it twice in the same evening. I have plenty of other songs.'

'I would die to hear the first one again,' said John.

'Well, well, said Mr. Halfways, 'perhaps you know best. Indeed, what does it matter? It is as short to the Island one way as another.' Then he smiled indulgently and shook his head, and John could not help thinking that his talking voice and talking manner were almost silly after the singing. But as soon as the great deep wail of the music began again it swept everything else from his mind. It seemed to him that this time he got more pleasure from the first few notes, and even noticed delicious passages which had escaped him at the first hearing; and he said to himself, 'This is going to be even better than the other. I shall keep my head this time and sip all the pleasure at my ease.' I saw that he settled himself more comfortably to listen and Media slipped her hand into his. It pleased him to think that they were going to the Island together. Now came the vision of the Island again: but this time it was changed, for John scarcely noticed the Island because of a lady with a crown on her head who stood waiting for him on the shore. She was fair, divinely fair. 'At last,' said John, 'a girl with no trace of brown.' And he began again to wade ashore holding out his arms to embrace that queen: and his love for her appeared to him so great and so pure, and they had been parted for so long, that his pity for himself and her almost overwhelmed him. And as he was about to embrace her the song stopped.

'Sing it again, sing it again,' cried John. 'I liked it better the second time.'

'Well, if you insist,' said Mr. Halfways with a shrug. 'It is nice to have a really appreciative audience.' So he sang it the third time. This time John noticed yet more about the music. He began to see how several of the effects were produced and that some parts were better than others. He wondered if it were not a trifle too long. The vision of the Island was a little shadowy this time, and he did not take much notice of it. He put his arm round Media and they lay cheek to cheek. He began to wonder if Mr. Halfways would never end: and when at last the final passage closed, with a sobbing break in the singer's voice, the old gentleman looked up and saw how the young people lay in one another's arms. Then he rose and said:

'You have found your Island—you have found it in one another's hearts.'

Then he tiptoed from the room, wiping his eyes.

VI

Ichabod

'MEDIA, I LOVE YOU,' said John.

'We have come to the *real* Island,' said Media.

'But oh, alas!' said he, 'so long our bodies why do we forbear?'

'Else a great prince in prison lies,' sighed she.

'No one else can understand the mystery of our love,' said he.

At that moment a brisk, hobnailed step was heard and a tall young man strode into the room carrying a light in his hand. He had coal-black hair and a straight mouth like the slit in a pillar-box, and he was dressed in various kinds of metal wire. As soon as he saw them he burst into a great guffaw. The lovers instantly sprang up and apart.

'Well, Brownie,' said he, 'at your tricks again?'

'Don't call me that name,' said Media, stamping her foot. 'I have told you before not to call me that.'

The young man made an obscene gesture at her, and then turned to John, 'I see that old fool of a father of mine has been at you?'

'You have no right to speak that way of father,' said Media. Then, turning to John, her cheeks flaming, her breast heaving, she said, 'All is over. Our dream—is shattered. Our mystery—is profaned. I would have taught you all the secrets of love, and now you are lost to me for ever. We must part. I shall go and kill myself,' and with that she rushed from the room.

VII

Non est Hic

'DON'T BOTHER ABOUT HER,' said the young man. 'She has threatened that a hundred times. She is only a brown girl, though she doesn't know it.'

'A brown girl!' cried John. 'And your father . . .'

'My father has been in the pay of the Brownies all his life. He doesn't know it, the old chuckle-head. Calls them the Muses, or the Spirit, or some rot. In actual fact, he is by profession a pimp.'

'And the Island?' said John.

'We'll talk about it in the morning. Ain't the kind of Island you're thinking of. Tell you what. I don't live with my father and my precious sister. I live in Eschropolis and I am going back to-morrow. I'll take you down to the laboratory and show you some *real* poetry. Not fantasies. The real thing.'

'Thank you very much,' said John.

Then young Mr. Halfways found his room for him and the whole of that household went to bed.

VIII
Great Promises

GUS HALFWAYS WAS the name of Mr. Halfway's son. As soon as he rose in the morning he called John down to breakfast with him so that they might start on their journey. There was no one to hinder them, for old Halfways was still asleep and Media always had breakfast in bed. When they had eaten, Gus brought him into a shed beside his father's house and showed him a machine on wheels.

'What is this?' said John.

'My old bus,' said young Halfways. Then he stood back with his head on one side and gazed at it for a bit: but presently he began to speak in a changed and reverent voice.

'She is a poem. She is the daughter of the spirit of the age, What was the speed of Atalanta to her speed? The beauty of Apollo to her beauty?'

Now beauty to John meant nothing save glimpses of his Island, and the machine did not remind him of his Island at all: so he held his tongue.

'Don't you see?' said Gus. 'Our fathers made images of what they called gods and goddesses; but they were really only brown girls and brown boys whitewashed —as anyone found out by looking at them too long. All self-deception and phallic sentiment. But here you have the real art. Nothing erotic about *her*, eh?'

'Certainly not,' said John, looking at the cog-wheels and coils of wire, 'it is certainly not at all like a brown girl.' It was, in fact, more like a nest of hedgehogs and serpents.

'I should say not,' said Gus. 'Sheer power, eh? Speed, ruthlessness, austerity, significant form, eh? Also' (and here he dropped his voice) 'very expensive indeed.'

Then he made John sit in the machine and he himself sat beside him. Then he began pulling the levers about and for a long time nothing happened: but at last there came a flash and a roar and the machine bounded into the air and then dashed forward. Before John had got his breath they had flashed across a broad thoroughfare which he recognized as the main road, and were racing through the country to the north of it—a flat country of square stony fields divided by barbed wire fences. A moment later they were standing still in a city where all the houses were built of steel.

---

3. *The old gentleman looked up and saw how the young people lay in one another's arms.*

Book Three
THROUGH DARKEST ZEITGEISTHEIM

---

*And every shrewd turn was exalted among men . . . and simple
goodness, wherein nobility doth ever most participate, was mocked away
and clean vanished.*
Thucydides

*Now live the lesser, as lords of the world,
The busy troublers. Banished is our glory,
The earth's excellence grows old and sere.*
Anon

*The more ignorant men are, the more convinced are they that their
little parish and their little chapel is an apex to which civilization and
philosophy has painfully struggled up.*
Shaw

I
Eschropolis

THEN I DREAMED THAT he led John into a big room rather like a bathroom: it was full of steel and glass and the walls were nearly all window, and there was a crowd of people there, drinking what looked like medicine and talking at the tops of their voices. They were all either young, or dressed up to look as if they were young. The girls had short hair and flat breasts and flat buttocks so that they looked like boys: but the boys had pale, egg-shaped faces and slender waists and big hips so that they looked like girls—except for a few of them who had long hair and beards.

'What are they so angry about?' whispered John.

'They are not angry,' said Gus; 'they are talking about Art.'

Then he brought John into the middle of the room and said:

'Say! Here's a guy who has been taken in by my father and wants some real hundred per cent music to clean him out. We had better begin with something neo-romantic to make the transition.'

Then all the Clevers consulted together and presently they all agreed that Victoriana had better sing first. When Victoriana rose John at first thought that she was a schoolgirl: but after he had looked at her again he perceived that she was in fact about fifty. Before she began to sing she put on a dress which was a sort of exaggerated copy of Mr. Halfways' robes, and a mask which was like the Steward's mask except that the nose had been painted bright red and one of the eyes had been closed in a permanent wink.

'Priceless!' exclaimed one half of the Clevers, 'too Puritanian.'

But the other half, which included all the bearded men, held their noses in the air and looked very stiff. Then victoriana took a little toy harp and began. The noises of the toy harp were so strange that John could not think of them as music at all. Then, when she sang, he had a picture in his mind which was a little like the Island, but he saw at once that it was not the Island. And presently he saw people who looked rather like his father, and the Steward and old Mr. Halfways, dressed up as clowns and doing a stiff sort of dance. Then there was a columbine, and some sort of love-story. But suddenly the whole Island turned into an aspidistra in a pot and the song was over.

'Priceless,' said the Clevers.

'I hope you liked it,' said Gus to John.

'Well,' began John doubtfully, for he hardly knew what to say: but he got not further, for at that moment he had a very great surprise. Victoriana had thrown her mask away and walked up to him and slapped him in the face twice, as hard as she could.

'That's right,' said the Clevers, 'Victoriana has *courage*. We may not all agree with you, Vikky dear, but we admire your courage.'

'You may persecute me as much as you like,' said Victoriana to John. 'No doubt to see me thus with my back to the wall, wakes the hunting lust in you. You will always follow the cry of the majority. But I will fight to the end. So there,' and she began to cry.

'I am extremely sorry,' said John. 'But—'

'And *I know* it was a good song,' sobbed Victoriana, 'because all great singers are persecuted in their lifetime—and I'm per-persecuted—and therefore I *must* be a great singer.'

'She has you there,' said the Clevers, as Victoriana left the laboratory.

'You mustn't mind her being a little bitter,' said Gus. 'She is so temperamental and sensitive, and she has suffered a great deal.'

'Well, I must admit,' said one of the Clevers, 'now that she had gone, that I think that stuff of hers rather *vieux jeu*.'

'Can't stand it myself,' said another.

'I think it was *her* face that needed slapping,' said a third.

'She's been spoiled and flattered all her life,' said a fourth. 'That's what's the matter with her.'

'Quite,' said the rest in chorus.

II
A South Wind

'PERHAPS,' SAID GUS, 'someone else would give us a song.'

'I will,' cried thirty voices all together: but one cried much louder than the others and its owner had stepped into the middle of the room before anyone could do anything about it. He was one of the bearded men and wore nothing but a red shirt and a cod-piece made of the skins of crocodiles: and suddenly he began to beat on an African tom-tom and to croon with his voice, swaying his lean, half-clad body to and fro and staring at them all, out of eyes which were like burning coals. This time John saw no picture of an Island at all. He seemed to be in a dark green place full of tangled roots and hairy vegetable tubes: and all at once he saw in it shapes moving and writhing that were not vegetable but human. And the dark green grew darker, and a fierce heat came out of it: and suddenly all the shapes that were moving in the darkness came together to make a single obscene image which dominated the whole room. And the song was over.

'Priceless,' said the Clevers. 'Too stark! Too virile.'

John blinked and looked round; and when he saw all the Clevers as cool as cu-

cumbers, smoking their cigarettes and drinking the drinks that looked like medi-
cines, all as if nothing remarkable had happened, he was troubled in his mind; for
he thought that the song must have meant something different to them, and 'If so,'
he argued, 'what very pure-minded people they must be.' Feeling himself among
his betters, he became ashamed.

'You like it, *hein*?' said the bearded singer.

'I—I don't think I understood it,' said John.

'I make you like it, *hein*,' said the singer, snatching up his tom-tom again. 'It was
what you *really* wanted all the time.'

'No, no,' cried John. 'I know you are wrong there. I grant you, that—that sort of
thing—is what I always *get* if I think too long about the Island. But it can't be what
I *want*.'

'No? Why not?'

'If it is what I wanted, why am I so disappointed when I get it? If what a man
really wanted was food, how could he be disappointed when the food arrived? As
well, I don't understand—'

'What you not understand? I explain to you.'

'Well, it's like this. I thought that you objected to Mr. Halfways' singing because
it led to brown girls in the end.'

'So we do.'

'Well, why is it better to lead to black girls in the beginning?'

A low whistle ran round the whole laboratory. John knew he had made a horrible blunder.

'Look here,' said the bearded singer in a new voice, 'what do you mean? You
are not suggesting that there is anything of that kind about my singing, are you?'

'I—I suppose—perhaps it was my fault,' stammered John.

'In other words,' said the singer, 'you are not yet able to distinguish between art
and pornography!' and advancing towards John very deliberately, he spat in his
face and turned to walk out of the room.

'That's right, Phally,' cried the Clevers, 'serve him right.'

'Filthy-minded little beast,' said one.

'Yah! Puritanian!' said a girl.

'I expect he's impotent,' whispered another.

'You mustn't be too hard on him,' said Gus. 'He is full of inhibitions and everything he says is only a rationalization of them. Perhaps he would get on better with
something more formal. Why don't you sing, Glugly?'

III
Freedom of Thought

GLUGLY INSTANTLY ROSE. She was very tall and as lean as a post: and her mouth was not quite straight in her face. When she was in the middle of the room, and silence had been obtained. she began to make gestures. First of all she set her arms a-kimbo and cleverly turned her hands the wrong way so that it looked as if her wrists were sprained. Then she waddled to and fro with her toes pointing in. After that she twisted herself to make it look as if her hip bone was out of joint. Finally she made some grunts, and said:

'Globol obol oogle ogle globol gloogle gloo,' and ended by pursing up her lips and making a vulgar noise such as children make in their nurseries. Then she went back to her place and sat down.

'Thank you very much,' said John politely.

But Glugly made no reply, for Glugly could not talk, owing to an accident in infancy.

'I hoped you liked it,' said young Halfways.

'I didn't understand her.'

'Ah,' said a woman in spectacles who seemed to be Glugly's nurse or keeper, 'that is because you are looking for beauty. You are still thinking of your Island. You have got to realize that satire is the moving force in modern music.'

'It is the expression of a savage disillusionment,' said someone else.

'Reality has broken down,' said a fat boy who had drunk a great deal of the medicine and was lying flat on his back, smiling happily.

'Our art *must* be brutal,' said Glugly's nurse.

'We lost our ideals when there was a war in this country,' said a very young Clever, 'they were ground out of us in the mud and the flood and the blood. That is why we have to be so stark and brutal.'

'But, look here,' cried John, 'that war was years ago. It was your fathers who were in it: and they are all settled down and living ordinary lives.'

'Puritanian! Bourgeois!' cried the Clevers. Everyone seemed to have risen.

'Hold your tongue,' whispered Gus in John's ear. But already someone had struck John on the head, and as he bowed under the blow someone else hit him from behind.

'It was the mud and blood,' hissed the girls all round him.

'Well,' said John, ducking to avoid a retort that had been flung at him, 'if you are really old enough to remember that war, why do you pretend to be so young?'

'We are young,' they howled; 'we are the new movement; we are the revolt.'

'We have got over humanitarianism,' bellowed one of the bearded men, kicking John on the kneecap.

'And prudery,' said a thin little old maid trying to wrench his clothes off from the neck. And at the same moment six girls leaped at his face with their nails, and he was kicked in the back and the belly, and tripped up so that he fell on his face, and hit again as he rose, and all the glass in the world seemed breaking round his head as he fled for his life from the laboratory. And all the dogs of Eschropolis joined in the chase as he ran along the street, and all the people followed pelting him with ordure, and crying:

'Puritanian! Bourgeois! Prurient!'

IV
The Man Behind the Gun

WHEN JOHN COULD RUN no further he sat down. The noise of the pursuers had died away and, looking back, he could see no sign of Eschropolis. He was covered with filth and blood, and his breathing hurt him. There seemed to be something wrong with one of his wrists. As he was too tired to walk he sat still and thought for a while. And first he thought that he would like to go back to Mr. Halfways. 'It is true,' he said, 'that if you listened to him too long it would lead you to Media—and she *had* a trace of brown in her. But then you had a glimpse of the Island first. Now the Clevers took you straight to brown girls—or worse—without even a glimpse of the Island. I wonder would it be possible to keep always at the Island stage with Mr. Halfways? Must it always end like that?' Then it came into his head that after all he did not want Mr. Halfways' songs, but the Island itself: and that this was the only thing he wanted in the world. And when he remembered this he rose very painfully to continue his journey, looking round for the West. He was still in the flat country, but there seemed to be mountains ahead, and above them the sun was setting. A road ran towards them: so he began to limp along it. Soon the sunset disappeared and the sky was clouded over and a cold rain began.

When he had limped about a mile he passed a man who was mending the fence of his field and smoking a big cigar. John stopped and asked him if he knew the way to the sea.

'Nope,' said the man without looking up.

'Do you know of any place in this country where I could get a night's lodging?'

'Nope,' said the man.

'Could you give me a piece of bread?' said John.

'Certainly not,' said Mr. Mammon, 'it would be contrary to all economic laws. It would pauperize you.' Then, when John lingered, he added, 'Move on. I don't want any loiterers about here.'

John limped on for about ten minutes. Suddenly he heard Mr. Mammon calling out to him. He stopped and turned round.

'What do you want?' shouted John.

'Come back,' said Mr. Mammon.

John was so tired and hungry that he humbled himself to walk back (and the way seemed long) in the hope that Mammon had relented. When he came again to the place where they had talked before, the man finished his work without speaking and then said:

'Where did you get your clothes torn?'

'I had a quarrel with the Clevers in Eschropolis.'

'Clevers?'

'Don't you know them?'

'Never heard of them.'

'You know Eschropolis?'

'Know it? I *own* Eschropolis.'

'How do you mean?'

'What do you suppose they live on?'

'I never thought of that.'

'Every man of them earns his living by writing for me or having shares in my land. I suppose the "Clevers" is some nonsense they do in their spare time—when they're not beating up tramps,' and he glanced at John. Then he resumed his work.

'You needn't wait,' he said presently.

V

Under Arrest

THEN I TURNED ROUND and immediately began to dream again and I saw John plodding westward in the dark and the rain, in great distress, because he was too tired to go on and too cold to stop. And after a time there came a north wind that drove the rain away and skinned the puddles with ice and set the bare boughs clashing in the trees, And the moon came out. Now John looked up with his teeth chattering and saw that he was entering into a long valley of rocks with high cliffs on the right and the left. And the far end of the valley was barred with a high cliff all across except for one narrow pass in the middle. The moonlight lay white on this cliff and right amidst it was a huge shadow like a man's head. John glanced over his shoulder and saw that the shadow was thrown by a mountain behind him, which he had passed in the darkness.

It was far too cold for a man to stay still in the wind, and I dreamed of John going stumblingly forward up the valley till now he had come to the rock-wall and was about to enter the pass. But just as he rounded a great boulder and came full in sight of the pass he saw some armed men sitting in it by a brazier; and immediately they sprang up and barred his way.

'You can't pass here,' said their leader.

'Where can I pass?' said John.

'Where are you going to?'

'I am going to find the sea in order to set sail for an Island that I have seen in the West.'

'Then you cannot pass.'

'By whose orders?'

'Do you not know that all this country belongs to the Spirit of the Age?'

'I am sorry,' said John, 'I didn't know. I have no wish to trespass, I will go round some other way. I will not go through his country at all.'

'You fool,' said the captain, 'you are in his country *now*. This pass is the way out of it, not the way into it. He welcomes strangers. His quarrel is with runaways.' Then he called to one of his men and said, 'Here, Enlightenment, take this fugitive to our Master.'

A young man stepped out and clapped fetters upon John's hands: then putting the length of chain over his own shoulder and giving it a jerk he began to walk down the valley dragging John after him.

VI
Poisoning the Wells

THEN I SAW THEM going down the valley, the way John had come up, with the moon full in their faces: and up against the moon was the mountain which had cast the shadow, and now it looked more like a man than before.

'Mr. Englightenment,' said John at last. 'Is it really you?'

'Why should it not be?' said the guard.

'You looked so different when I met you before.'

'We have never met before.'

'What? Did you not meet me at the inn on the borders of Puritania and drive me five miles in your pony trap?'

'Oh, *that?*' said the other. 'That must have been my father, old Mr. Enlightenment. He is a vain and ignorant old man, almost a Puritanian, and we never mention him in the family. I am Sigismund Enlightenment and I have long since quarrelled with my father.'

They went on in silence for a bit. Then Sigismund spoke again.

'It may save trouble if I tell you at once the best reason for not trying to escape: namely, that there is nowhere to escape to.'

'How do you know there is no such place as my Island?'

'Do you wish very much that there was?'

'I do.'

'Have you never before imagined anything to be true because you greatly wished for it?'

John thought for a little, and then he said, 'Yes.'

'And your Island is *like* an imagination—isn't it?'

'I suppose so.'

'It is just the sort of thing you *would* imagine merely through wanting it—the whole thing is very suspicious. But answer me another question. Have you ever—ever once yet—had a vision of the Island that did not end in brown girls?'

'I don't know that I have. But they weren't what I wanted.'

'No. What you wanted was to have them, and with them, the satisfaction of feeling that you were good. Hence the Island.'

'You mean—'

'The Island was the pretence that you put up to conceal your own lusts from yourself.'

'All the same—I was disappointed when it ended like that.'

'Yes. You were disappointed at finding that you could not have it both ways. But you lost no time in having it the way you could: you did not reject the brown girls.'

They went on in silence for a time and always the mountain with its odd shape grew bigger in front of them; and now they were in its shadow. Then John spoke again, half in his sleep, for he was very tired

'After all, it isn't only my Island. I might go back—back East and try the mountains.'

'The mountains do not exist.'

'How do you know?'

'Have you ever been there? Have you ever seen them except at night or in a blaze of sunrise?'

'No. '

'And your ancestors must have enjoyed thinking that when their leases were out they would go up to the mountains and live in the Landlord's castle—It is a more cheerful prospect than going—nowhere.'

'I suppose so.'

'It is clearly one more of the things people *wish* to believe.'

'But do we never do anything else? Are all the things I see at this moment there only because I wish to see them?'

'Most of them,' said Sigismund. 'For example—you would like that thing in front of us to be a mountain; that is why you think it is a mountain.'

'Why?' cried John. 'What is it?'

And then in my nightmare I thought John became like a terrified child and put his hands over his eyes not to see the giant; but young Mr. Enlightenment tore his hands away and forced his face round and made him see the Spirit of the Age where it sat like one of the stone giants, the size of a mountain, with its eyes shut. Then Mr. Enlightenment opened a little door among the rocks and flung John into a pit made in the side of a hill, just opposite the giant, so that the giant could look into it through its gratings.

'He will open his eyes presently,' said Mr. Enlightenment. Then he locked the door and left John in prison.

VII
Facing the Facts

JOHN LAY IN HIS fetters all night in the cold and stench of the dungeon. And when morning came there was a little light at the grating, and, looking round, John saw that he had many fellow prisoners, of all sexes and ages. But instead of speaking to him, they all huddled away from the light and drew as far back into the pit, away from the grating, as they could. But John thought that if he could breathe a little fresh air he would be better, and he crawled up to the grating. But as soon as he looked out and saw the giant, it crushed the heart out of him: and even as he looked, the giant began to open his eyes and John, without knowing why he did it, shrank from the grating. Now I dreamed that the giant's eyes had this property, that whatever they looked on became transparent. Consequently, when John looked round into the dungeon, he retreated from his fellow prisoners in terror, for the place seemed to be thronged with demons. A woman was seated near him, but he did not know it was a woman, because, through the face, he saw the skull and through that the brains and the passages of the nose, and the larynx, and the saliva moving in the glands and the blood in the veins: and lower down the lungs panting like sponges, and the liver, and the intestines like a coil of snakes. And when he averted his eyes from her they fell on an old man, and this was worse for the old man had a cancer. And when John sat down and drooped his head, not to see the horrors, he saw only the working of his own inwards. Then I dreamed of all these creatures living in that hole under the giant's eye for many days and nights. And John looked round on it all and suddenly he fell on his face and thrust his hands into his eyes and cried out, 'It is the black hole. There may be no Landlord, but it is true about the black hole. I am mad. I am dead. I am in hell for ever.'

VIII
Parrot Disease

EVERY DAY A JAILOR brought the prisoners their food, and as he laid down the dishes he would say a word to them. If their meal was flesh he would remind them that they were eating corpses, or give them some account of the slaughtering: or, if it was the inwards of some beast, he would read them a lecture in anatomy and show the likeness of the mess to the same parts in themselves—which was the more easily done because the giant's eyes were always staring into the dungeon at dinner time. Or if the meal were eggs he would recall to them that they were eating the menstruum of a verminous fowl, and crack a few jokes with the female prisoner. So he went on day by day. Then I dreamed that one day there was nothing but milk for them, and the jailor said as he put down the pipkin:

'Our relations with the cow are not delicate—as you can easily see if you imagine eating any of her other secretions.'

Now John had been in the pit a shorter time than any of the others: and at these words something seemed to snap in his head and he gave a great sigh and suddenly spoke out in a loud, clear voice:

'Thank heaven! Now at last I know that you are talking nonsense.'

'What do you mean?' said the jailor, wheeling round upon him.

'You are trying to pretend that unlike things are like. You are trying to make us think that milk is the same sort of thing as sweat or dung.'

'And pray, what difference is there except by custom?'

'Are you a liar or only a fool, that you see no difference between that which Nature casts out as refuse and that which she stores up as food?'

'So Nature is a person, then, with purposes and consciousness,' said the jailor with a sneer. 'In fact, a Landlady. No doubt it comforts you to imagine you can believe that sort of thing'; and he turned to leave the prison with his nose in the air.

'I know nothing about that,' shouted John after him. 'I am talking of what happens. Milk does feed calves and dung does not.'

'Look here,' cried the jailor, coming back, 'we have had enough of this. It is high treason and I shall bring you before the Master.' Then he jerked John up by his chain and began to drag him towards the door; but John, as he was being dragged, cried out to the others, 'Can't you see it's all a cheat?' Then the jailor struck him in the teeth so hard that his mouth was filled with blood and he became unable to speak: and while he was silent the jailor addressed the prisoners and said:

'You see he is trying to argue. Now tell me, someone, what is argument?'

There was a confused murmur.

'Come, come,' said the jailor. 'You must know your catechisms by now. You, there' (and he pointed to a prisoner little older than a boy whose name was Master Parrot), 'what is argument?'

'Argument,' said Master Parrot, 'is the attempted rationalization of the arguer's desires.'

'Very good,' replied the jailor, 'but you should turn out your toes and put your hands behind your back. That is better. Now: what is the proper answer to an argument providing the existence of the Landlord?'

'The proper answer is, "You say that because you are a Steward."'

'Good boy. But hold your head up. That's right. And what is the answer to an argument proving that Mr. Phally's songs are just as brown as Mr. Halfways'?'

'There are two only generally necessary to damnation,' said Master Parrot. 'The first is, "You say that because you are a Puritanian," and the second is, "You say that because you are a sensualist."'

'Good. Now just one more. What is the answer to an argument turning on the belief that two and two make four?'

'The answer is, "You say that because you are a mathematician." '

'You are a very good boy,' said the jailor. 'And when I come back I shall bring you something nice. And now for *you*,' he added, giving John a kick and opening the grating.

IX
The Giant Slayer

WHEN THEY CAME out into the air John blinked a little, but not much, for they were still only in a half-light under the shadow of the giant, who was very angry, with smoke coming from his mouth, so that he looked more like a volcano than an ordinary mountain. And now John gave himself up for lost, but just as the jailor had dragged him up to the giant's feet, and had cleared his throat, and begun 'The case against this prisoner—' there was a commotion and a sound of horse's hoofs. The jailor looked round, and even the giant took his terrible eyes off John and looked round: and last of all, John himself looked round too. They saw some of the guard coming towards them leading a great black stallion, and in it was seated a figure wound in a cloak of blue which was hooded over the head and came down concealing the face.

'Another prisoner, Lord,' said the leader of the guards.

Then very slowly the giant raised his great, heavy finger and pointed to the mouth of the dungeon.

---

4. *The giant bent forward in his chair and looked at Reason.*

'Not yet,' said the hooded figure. Then suddenly it stretched out its hands with the fetters on them and made a quick movement of the wrists. There was a tinkling sound as the fragments of the broken chain fell on the rock at the horse's feet: and the guardsmen let go the bridle and fell back, watching. Then the rider threw back the cloak and a flash of steel smote light into John's eyes and on the giant's face. John saw that it was a woman in the flower of her age: she was so tall that she seemed to him a Titaness, a sun-bright virgin clad in complete steel, with a sword naked in her hand. The giant bent forward in his chair and looked at her.

'Who are you?' he said.

'My name is Reason,' said the virgin.

'Make out her passport quickly,' said the giant in a low voice. 'And let her go through our dominions and be off with all the speed she wishes.'

'Not yet,' said Reason. 'I will ask you three riddles before I go, for a wager.'

'What is the pledge? said the giant.

'Your head,' said Reason.

There was silence for a time among the mountains.

'Well,' said the giant at last, 'what must be, must be. Ask on.'

'This is my first riddle,' said Reason. 'What is the colour of things in dark places, of fish in the depth of the sea, or of the entrails in the body of man?'

'I cannot say,' said the giant.

'Well,' said Reason. 'Now hear my second riddle. There was a certain man who was going to his own house and his enemy went with him. And his house was beyond a river too swift to swim and too deep to wade. And he could go no faster than his enemy. While he was on his journey his wife sent to him and said, "You know that there is only one bridge across the river: tell me, shall I destroy it that the enemy may not cross; or shall I leave it standing that you may cross?" What should this man do?'

'It is too hard for me,' said the giant.

'Well,' said Reason. 'Try now to answer my third riddle. By what rule do you tell a copy from an original?'

The giant muttered and mumbled and could not answer, and Reason set spurs in her stallion and it leaped up on to the giant's mossy knees and galloped up his foreleg, till she plunged her sword into his heart. Then there was a noise and a crumbling like a landslide and the huge carcass settled down: and the Spirit of the Age became what he had seemed to be at first, a sprawling hummock of rock.

Book Four
BACK TO THE
ROAD

---

*Doth any man doubt, that if there were taken out of men's minds
vain opinions, flattering hopes, false valuations, imaginations as one
would, and the like: but it would leave the minds of a number of men
poor shrunken things: full of melancholy and indisposition, and
unpleasing to themselves?*
Bacon

I
Let Grill Be Grill

THE GUARDS HAD FLED. Reason dismounted from her horse and wiped her sword clean on the moss of the foot hills which had been the giant's knees. Then she turned to the door of the pit and struck it so that it broke and she could look into the darkness of the pit and smell the filth.

'You can all come out,' she said.

But there was no movement from within: only, John could hear the prisoners wailing together and saying:

'It is one more wish-fulfilment dream: it is one more wish-fulfilment dream. Don't be taken in again.'

But presently Master Parrot came to the mouth of the pit and said, 'There is no good trying to fool us. Once bit twice shy.' Then he put out his tongue and retired.

'This psittacosis is a very obstinate disorder,' said Reason. And she turned to mount the black horse.

'May I come with you, lady?' said John.

'You may come until you are tired,' said Reason.

II
Archtype and Ectype

IN MY DREAM I saw them set off together, John walking by the lady's stirrup: and I saw them go up the rocky valley where John had gone on the night of his capture. They found the pass unguarded and it gave back an echo to the horse's hoofs and then in a moment they were out of the mountain country and going down a grassy slope into the land beyond. There were few trees and bare, and it was cold: but presently John looked aside and saw a crocus in the grass. For the first time for many days the old sweetness pierced through John's heart: and the next moment he was trying to call back the sound of the birds wheeling over the Island and the green of the waves breaking on its sand—for they had all flashed about him but so quickly that they were gone before he knew. His eyes were wet.

He turned to Reason and spoke.

'You can tell me, lady. Is there such a place as the Island in the West, or is it only a feeling of my own mind?'

'I cannot tell you,' said she, 'because you do not know.'

'But you know.'

'But I can tell you only what *you* know. I can bring things out of the dark part of your mind into the light part of it. But now you ask me what is not even in the dark of your mind.'

'Even if it were only a feeling in my own mind, would it be a bad feeling?'

'I have nothing to tell you of good and bad.'

'I mean this,' said John. 'And this you can tell me. Is it true that it must always end in brown girls, or rather, that it really *begins* from brown girls? They say it is all a pretence, all a disguise for lust.'

'And what do you think of that saying?'

'It is very like that,' said John. 'Both are sweet, Both are full of longing. The one runs into the other. They *are* very alike.'

'Indeed they are,' said the lady. 'But do you not remember my third riddle?'

'About the copy and the original? I could not understand it.'

'Well, now you shall. The people in the country we have just left have seen that your love for the Island is very like your love for the brown girls. Therefore they say that one is a copy of the other. They would also say that you have followed me because I am like your mother, and that your trust in me is a copy of your love for your mother. And then they would say again that your love for your mother is a copy of your love for the brown girls; and so they would come full circle.'

'And what should I answer them?'

'You would say, perhaps one is a copy of the other. But which is the copy of which?'

'I never thought of that.'

'You are not yet of an age to have thought much,' said Reason. 'But you must see that if two things are alike, then it is a further question whether the first is copied from the second, or the second from the first, or both from a third?'

What would the third be?'

'Some have thought that all these loves were copies of our love for the Landlord.'

'But surely they have considered that and rejected it. Their sciences have disproved it.'

'They could not have, for their sciences are not concerned at all with the general relations of this country to anything that may lie East of it or West of it. They indeed will tell you that their researches have proved that if two things are similar, the fair one is always the copy of the foul one. But their only reason to say so is that they have already decided that the fairest things of all—that is the Landlord, and, if you like, the mountains and the Island—are a mere copy of *this* country. They pretend that their researches lead to that doctrine: but in fact they assume that doctrine first and interpret their researches by it.'

'But they have reasons for assuming it.'

'They have none, for they have ceased to listen to the only people who can tell them anything about it.'

'Who are they?'

'They are younger sisters of mine, and their names are Philosophy and Theology.'

'Sisters! Who is your father?'

'You will know sooner than you wish.'

And now the evening was falling and they were near a little farm, so they turned in there and asked a night's lodging of the farmer, which was readily given them.

III
Esse Is Percipi

NEXT MORNING THEY continued their journey together. In my dream I saw them go through a country of little hills where the road was always winding to conform to the lie of the valleys: and John walked at the lady's stirrup. The fetter of his hands had broken at the moment when she killed the giant, but the handcuffs were still on his wrists. One half of the broken chain hung down from each hand. There was a greater mildness in the air this day and the buds were fully formed in the hedges.

'I have been thinking, lady,' said John, 'of what you said yesterday and I think I understand that though the Island is very like the place where I first met the brown girl, yet she might be the shadow and the Island the reality. But there is one thing that troubles me.'

'What is that?' said Reason.

'I cannot forget what I have seen in the giant's prison. If we are really like that inside, whatever we imagine must be abominable however innocent it looks. It may be true in general that the foul thing is not always the original and the fair thing not always the copy. But when we have to do with human imaginations, with things that come out of *us*, surely then the giant is right? There at least it is much more likely that whatever seems good is only a veil for the bad—only a part of our skin that has so far escaped the giant's eyes and not yet become transparent.'

'There are two things to be said about that,' replied the lady, 'and the first is this. Who told you that the Island was an imagination of yours?'

'Well, you would not assure me that it was anything real.'

'Nor that it was not.'

'But I must think it is one or the other.'

'By my father's soul, you must *not*—until you have some evidence. Can you not remain in doubt?'

'I don't know that I have ever tried.'

'You must learn to, if you are to come far with me. It is not hard to do it. In Eschropolis, indeed, it is impossible, for the people who live there have to give an opinion once a week or once a day, or else Mr. Mammon would soon cut off their food. But out here in the country you can walk all day and all the next day with an unanswered question in your head: you need never speak until you have made up your mind.'

'But if a man wanted to know so badly that he would die unless the question was decided—and no more evidence turned up.'

'Then he would die, that would be all.'

They went on in silence for a while.

'You said there were two things to say,' said John. 'What was the second?'

'The second was this. Did you think that the things you saw in the dungeon were *real*: that we really are like that?'

'Of course I did. It is only our skin that hides them.'

'Then I must ask you the same question that I asked the giant. What is the colour of things in the dark?'

'I suppose, no colour at all.'

'And what of their shape? Have you any notion of it save as what could be seen or touched, or what you could collect from many seeings and touchings?'

'I don't know that I have.'

'Then do you not see how the giant has deceived you?'

'Not quite clearly.'

'He showed you by a trick what our inwards *would* look like if they were visible. That is, he showed you something that is not, but something that would be if the world were made all other than it is. But in the real world our inwards are invisible. They are not coloured shapes at all, they are feelings. The warmth in your limbs at this moment, the sweetness of your breath as you draw it in, the comfort in your belly because we breakfasted well, and your hunger for the next meal— these are the reality: all the sponges and tubes that you saw in the dungeon are the lie.'

'But if I cut a man open I should see them in him.'

'A man cut open is, so far, not a man: and if you did not sew him up speedily you would be seeing not organs, but death. I am not denying that death is ugly: but the giant made you believe that life is ugly.'

'I cannot forget the man with the cancer.'

'What you saw was unreality. The ugly lump was the giant's trick: the reality was pain, which has no colour or shape.'

'Is that much better?'

'That depends on the man.'

'I think I begin to see.'

'Is it surprising that things should look strange if you see them as they are not? If you take an organ out of a man's body—or a longing out of the dark part of a man's mind—and give to the one the shape and colour, and to the other the self-consciousness, which they never have in reality, would you expect them to be other than monstrous?'

'Is there, then, no truth at all in what I saw under the giant's eyes?'

'Such pictures are useful to physicians.'

'Then I really am clean,' said John. 'I am not—like those.'

Reason smiled. 'There, too,' she said, 'there is truth mixed up with the giant's conjuring tricks. It will do you no harm to remember from time to time the ugly sights inside. You come of a race that cannot afford to be proud.'

As she spoke John looked up, in doubt of her meaning: and for the first time since he came into her company he felt afraid. But the impression lasted only for a moment. 'Look,' said John, 'here is a little inn. Is it not time that we rested and ate something?'

IV
Escape

IN THE WARMTH of the afternoon they went on again, and it came into John's mind to ask the lady the meaning of her second riddle.

'It has two meanings,' said she, 'and in the first the bridge signifies Reasoning. The Spirit of the Age wishes to allow argument and not to allow argument.'

'How is that?'

'You heard what they said. If anyone argues with them they say that he is rationalizing his own desires, and therefore need not be answered. But if anyone listens to them they will then argue themselves to show that their own doctrines are true.'

'I see. And what is the cure for this?'

'You must ask them whether any reasoning is valid or not. If they say no, then their own doctrines, being reached by reasoning, fall to the ground. If they say yes, then they will have to examine your arguments and refute them on their merits: for if some reasoning is valid, for all they know, your bit of reasoning may be one of the valid bits.'

'I see,' said John. 'But what was the second interpretation?'

'In the second,' said Reason, 'the bridge signifies the giant's own favourite doctrine of the wish-fulfilment dream. For this also he wishes to use and not to use.'

'I don't see how he wishes *not to* use it.'

'Does he not keep on telling people that the Landlord is a wish-fulfilment dream?'

'Yes; surely that is true—the only true thing he did say.'

'Now think. Is it really true that the giant and Sigismund, and the people in Eschropolis, and Mr. Halfways, are going about filled with a longing that there should be a Landlord, and cards of rules, and a mountain land beyond the brook, with a possibility of a black hole?'

Then John stood still on the road to think. And first he gave a shake of his shoulders, and then he put his hands to his sides, and then he began to laugh till he was almost shaken to pieces. And when he had nearly finished, the vastness and impudence and simplicity of the fraud which had been practised came over him all again, and he laughed harder. And just when he had nearly recovered and was beginning to get his breath again, suddenly he had a picture in his mind of Victoriana and Glugly and Gus Halfways and how they would look if a rumour reached them that there *was* a Landlord and he was coming to Eschropolis. This was too much for him, and he laughed so hard that the broken chains of the Spirit of the Age fell off his wrists altogether. But all the while Reason sat and watched him.

'You had better hear the rest of the argument,' she said at last. 'It may not be such a laughing matter as you suppose.'

'Oh, yes—the argument,' said John, wiping his eyes.

'You see now the direction in which the giant does *not* want the wish-fulfilment theory used?'

'I'm not sure that I do,' said John.

'Don't you see what follows if you adopt his own rules?'

'No,' said John, very loudly: for a terrible apprehension was stealing over him.

'But you must see,' said Reason, 'that for him and all his subjects *disbelief* in the Landlord is a wish-fulfilment dream.'

'I shall not adopt his rules.'

'You would be foolish not to have profited *at all* by your stay in his country,' said Reason. 'There is some force in the wish-fulfilment doctrine.'

'Some, perhaps, but very little.'

'I only wanted to make it clear that whatever force it had was in favour of the Landlord's existence, not against it—specially in your case.'

'Why specially in mine?' said John sulkily.

'Because the Landlord is the thing you have been most afraid of all your life. I do not say that any theory should be accepted because it is disagreeable, but if any should, then belief in the Landlord should be accepted first.'

As Reason said these words they had reached the top of a little hill, and John begged for a halt, being out of breath. He looked back and saw beyond the green, rolling country the dark line of mountains which was the frontier of the giant's land: but behind them, and far bigger, rose the old mountains of the East, picked out in the rays of the declining sun against a dark sky. They seemed no smaller than when John had looked at them long ago from Puritania.

'I do not know where you are leading me,' he said at last, 'and among all these winding roads I have lost my sense of direction. As well, I find the pace of your horse fatiguing. If you will excuse me, I think I will henceforth pursue my journey alone.'

'As you wish,' said Reason. 'But I would strongly advise you to take this turn to the left.'

'Where does it go to?' asked John suspiciously.

'It takes you back to the main road,' said Reason.

'That will do well enough,' said John. 'And now, lady, give me your blessing before I go.'

'I have no blessing to give,' said the Virgin. 'I do not deal in blessings and cursings.'

Then John bade her good-bye and took the road she had pointed out to him. As soon as she was out of sight, I dreamed that he put down his head and ran; for the silly fellow supposed that she might follow him. And he continued running until he found that he was going up a hill—a hill so steep that it left him no breath for running—and at the very top his road cut into another which ran left and right along the ridge. Then John looked one way along it to the East and the other way along it to the West, and saw that it was indeed the main road. He stayed for a minute to mop his brow. Then he turned to the right, with his face towards the setting sun, and resumed his journey.

Book Five

THE GRAND
CANYON

Not by road and foot nor by sail and ocean
Shalt thou find any course that reaches
The world beyond the North.
Pindar

The ephemerals have no help to give. Behold them;
They are deedless and cripple, like to
A dream. The kind of mortals
Is bound with a chain and their eyes are in darkness.
Aeschylus

Alas, what can they teach and not mislead,
Ignorant of themselves, of God much more,
And how the world began, and how man fell.
Milton

I
The Grand Canyon

THE MAIN ROAD SOON began to ascend and after a short climb John found himself on a bleak tableland which continued to rise before him, but at a gentler angle. After he had walked a mile or so he saw the figure of a man ahead, outlined against the setting sun. At first the figure stood still: then it took a few paces to the left and to the right as if in indecision. Then it turned about to face him, and to his surprise hailed him as an old acquaintance. Because of the light in his face John could not at first see who it was, and they had joined hands before he knew that it was Vertue.

'What can have delayed you?' cried John. 'I thought by your pace when I left you that you would have been a week's journey ahead of me by now.'

'If you think that,' said Vertue, 'your way must have been easier than mine. Have you not crossed mountains?'

'I came through a pass,' said John.

'The main road took them without a bend,' said Vertue. 'And I often made scarcely ten miles a day. But that does not signify: I have learned something of climbing and sweated off a good deal of soft flesh. What has really delayed me is this—I have been here for several days.'

With that he motioned John to proceed and they went forward together to the brow of the slope. Then I saw John start back a pace or so with a cry, for he had found that he stood on the edge of a precipice. Then presently he re-approached it with caution and looked.

He saw that the road ran up without warning to the edge of a great gorge or chasm and ended in the air, as if it had been broken off. The chasm might be seven miles wide and as for its length, it stretched southward on his left and northward on his right as far as he could see. The sun shining in his face cast all the further side into shadow, so that he could not see much of it clearly. It seemed to him, however, a rich country from the verdure and the size of the trees.

'I have been exploring the cliffs,' said Vertue. 'And I think we could get half-way down. Come a little nearer. You see that ledge?'

'I have a very poor head for heights,' said John.

'That one,' said Vertue, pointing to a narrow strip of greenery a thousand feet below them.

'I could never reach it.'

'Oh, you could reach *that* easily enough. The difficulty is to know what happens beyond it. I am inclined to think that it overhangs: and though we could get down to it, I am not sure that we could get back if the rest of the descent was impracticable.'

'Then it would be madness to trust ourselves so far.'

'I don't know about that. It would be in accordance with the rule.'

'What rule?'

'The rule is,' said Vertue, 'that if we have one chance out of a hundred of surviving, we must attempt it: but if we have none, absolutely none, then it would be self-destruction, and we need not.'

'It is no rule of mine,' said John.

'But it is. We all have the same set of rules, really, you know.'

'If it is a rule of mine, it is one that I cannot obey.'

'I don't think I understand you,' said Vertue. 'But of course you may be such a bad climber that *you* wouldn't have even one chance . . . that would make a difference, I allow.'

Then a third voice spoke.

'You have neither of you any chance at all unless I carry you down.'

Both the young men turned at the sound. An old woman was seated in a kind of rocky chair at the very edge of the precipice.

'Oh, it's you, Mother Kirk, is it?' said Vertue, and added in an undertone to John, 'I have seen her about the cliffs more than once. Some of the country people say she is second-sighted, and some that she is crazy.'

'I shouldn't trust her,' said John in the same tone. 'She looks to me much more like a witch.' Then he turned to the old woman and said aloud: 'And how could you carry us down, mother? We would be more fit to carry you.'

'I could do it, though,' said Mother Kirk, 'by the power that the Landlord has given me.'

'So you believe in the Landlord, too?' said John.

'How can I not, dear,' said she, 'when I am his own daughter-in-law?'

'He does not give you very fine clothes,' said John, glancing at the old woman's country cloak.

'They'll last my time,' said the old woman placidly.

'We ought to try her,' whispered Vertue to John. 'As long as there is any chance we are not allowed to neglect it.' But John frowned at him to be silent and addressed the old woman again.

'Do you not think this Landlord of yours is a very strange one?' he said.

'How so?' said she.

'Why does he make a road like this running up to the very edge of a precipice— unless it is to encourage travellers to break their necks in the dark?'

'Oh, bless you, he never left it like that,' said the old woman. 'It was a good road all round the world when it was new, and all this gorge is far later than the road.'

'You mean,' said Vertue, 'that there has been some sort of catastrophe.'

'Well,' said Mother Kirk, 'I see there will be no getting you down tonight, so I may as well tell you the story. Come and sit down by me. You are neither of you so wise that you need be ashamed of listening to an old wives' tale.'

II
Mother Kirk's Story

WHEN THEY WERE SEATED, the old woman told the following story:—
'You must know that once upon a time there were no tenants in this country at all, for the Landlord used to farm it himself. There were only the animals and the Landlord used to look after them, he and his sons and daughters. Every morning they used to come down from the mountains and milk the cows and lead out the sheep to pasture. And they needed less watching, for all the animals were tamer then; and there were no fences needed, for if a wolf got in among the flocks he would do them no harm. And one day the Landlord was going home from his day's work when he looked round on the country, and the beasts, and saw how the crops were springing, and it came into his head that the whole thing was too good to keep to himself. So he decided to let the country to tenants, and his first tenant was a young married man. But first the Landlord made a farm in the very centre of the land where the soil was the best and the air most wholesome, and that was the very spot where you are sitting now. They were to have the whole land, but that was too much for them to keep under cultivation. The Landlord's idea was that they could work the farm and leave the rest as a park for the time being: but later they could divide the park up into holdings for their children. For you must know that he drew up a very different lease from the kind you have nowadays. It was a lease in perpetuity on his side, for he promised never to turn them out; but on their side, they could leave when they chose, as long as one of their sons was there, to take the farm on, and then they could go up to live with him in the mountains. He thought that would be a good thing because it would broaden the minds of his own mountain children to mix with strangers. And they thought so too. But before he put the tenants in possession there was one thing he had to do. Up to this time the country had been full of a certain fruit which the Landlord had planted for the refreshment of himself and his children, if they were thirsty during the day as they worked down here. It was a very good fruit and up in the mountains they say it is even more plentiful: but it is very strong and only those who are mountain-bred ought to eat it, for only they can digest it properly. Hitherto, while there were only beasts in the land, it had done no harm for these mountain-apples to be growing in every thicket; for you know that an animal will eat nothing but what is good for it. But now that there were to be men in the land, the Landlord was afraid that they might do themselves an injury; yet it was not to be thought of that he should dig up every sapling of that tree and make the country into a desert. So he decided that it was best to be frank with the young people, and when he found a great big mountain-apple tree growing in the very centre of the farm he said, "So much the better. If they are to learn sense, they may as well learn it from the beginning: and if they will not, there's no help for it. For if they did not find mountain-apples on the farm, they would soon find them somewhere else." So he left the apple tree standing,

and put the man and his wife into their farm: but before he left them he explained the whole affair to them—as much of it could be explained—and warned them on no account to eat any of the apples. Then he went home. And for a time the young man and his wife behaved very well, tending the animals and managing their farm, and abstaining from the mountain-apples; and for all I know they might never have done otherwise if the wife had not somehow made a new acquaintance. This new acquaintance was a landowner himself. He had been born in the mountains and was one of our Landlord's own children, but he had quarrelled with his father and set up on his own, and now had built up a very considerable estate in another country. His estate marches, however, with this country: and as he was a great land-grabber he always wanted to take this bit in—and he has very nearly succeeded.'

'I've never met any tenants of his,' said John.

'Not tenants in chief, my dear,' said the old woman. 'And so you didn't know them. But you may have met the Clevers, who are tenants of Mr. Mammon: and he is a tenant of the Spirit of the Age: who holds directly of the Enemy.'

'I am sure the Clevers would be very surprised,' said John, 'to hear that they had a Landlord at all. They would think this enemy, as you call him, no less a superstition than *your* Landlord.'

'But this is how business is managed,' said Mother Kirk. 'The little people do not know the big people to whom they belong. The big people do not intend that they should. No important transference of property could be carried out if all the small people at the bottom knew what was really happening. But this is not part of my story. As I was saying, the enemy got to know the farmer's wife: and, however he did it, or whatever he said to her, it wasn't long before he persuaded her that the one thing she needed was a nice mountain-apple. And she took one and ate it. And then—you know how it is with husbands—she made the farmer come round to her mind. And at the moment he put out his hand and plucked the fruit there was an earthquake, and the country cracked open all the way across from North to South: and ever since, instead of the farm, there has been this gorge, which the country people call the Grand Canyon. But in my language its name is *Peccatum Adae*.'

III
The Self-Sufficiency of Vertue

'AND I SUPPOSE,' said John sourly, 'the Landlord was so annoyed that it was he who invented the rules and the black hole?'

'The story is not quite so simple as that,' said the old woman, 'so many things happened after the eating of the apple. For one thing, the taste created such a craving in the man and the woman that they thought they could never eat enough of it; and they were not content with all the wild apple trees, but planted more and more, and grafted mountain-apple on to every other kind of tree so that every fruit should have a dash of that taste in it. They succeeded so well that the whole vegetable system of the country is now infected: and there is hardly a fruit or a root in the land—certainly none this side of the canyon—that has not a little mountain-apple in it. You have never tasted anything that was quite free from it.'

'And what has that got to do with the card of rules?' said John.

'Everything,' said Mother Kirk. 'In a country where all the food is more or less poisoned—but some of it very much less than more—you need very complicated rules indeed to keep healthy.'

'Meanwhile,' said Vertue, 'we are not getting on with our journey.'

'I will carry you down in the morning, if you like,' said Mother Kirk. 'Only mind you, it is a dangerous place, and you must do exactly as I tell you.'

'If the place is so dangerous—' began John, when Vertue, who had been struck by the woman's last words, suddenly broke in:

'I am afraid it is no use, mother,' he said; 'I cannot put myself under anyone's orders. I must be the captain of my soul and the master of my fate. But thank you for your offer.'

'You are right,' said John hastily, and added in a whisper. 'The old creature is clearly insane. Our real business is to explore this chasm North and South until we find some place where the descent *is* practicable.'

Vertue had risen.

'We are thinking, mother,' he said, 'that we should like to make sure for ourselves that there is no place where we cannot get down without being carried. You see my own legs have served me so far—and I should not like to start being carried now.'

'It will do you no harm to try,' answered Mother Kirk. 'And I should not wonder if you find a way down. Getting up the other side is another question, to be sure; but perhaps we shall meet again when it comes to that.'

By this time it was quite dark. The two young men bade good night to the woman and drew back along the main road to discuss their plans. Two by-roads branched off from it about a quarter of a mile from the precipice: and as that which went to the north seemed rather the better, and also pointed a little backward and away from the cliffs (which John was anxious not to skirt in the darkness), they turned northward. It was a fine starlit night and grew colder as they proceeded.

IV
Mr. Sensible

WHEN THEY HAD WALKED rather more than a mile John drew Vertue's attention to a light a little back from the road: and I saw them follow it till they came to a gateway and after that to a door, and there they knocked.

'Whose house is this?' said Vertue when the servant opened to them.

'This is Mr. Sensible's house,' said the servant. 'And if you are benighted travellers he will receive you gladly.'

Then he brought them into a room where a lamp was burning clearly, but not very brightly, and an old gentleman was seated by a blazing wood fire with his dog at his feet and his book on his knees and a jig-saw puzzle at one side of him spread out on a wooden frame, and on the other a chessboard with the pieces set for a problem. He rose to greet them very cordially but not hastily.

'You are very welcome, gentlemen,' said Mr. Sensible. 'Pray come and warm yourselves. Drudge' (and here he called to the servant) 'make some supper ready for three: the usual supper, Drudge. I shall not be able to offer you luxury, gentlemen. The wine of my own country, cowslip wine, shall be your drink. It will be rough to your palates, but to mine the draught that I owe to my own garden and my own kitchen will always have a flavour beyond Hippocrene. The radishes, also of my own growing, I think I may venture to praise. But I see by your looks that I have already betrayed my foible. I confess that my garden is my pride. But what then? We are all children, and I reckon him the wisest among us that can make most sport out of the toys suitable to that condition, without seeking to go beyond it. *Regum oequabit opes animis.* Contentment, my friends, contentment is the best riches. Do not let the dog tease you, sir. He has mange. Down, Rover! Alas, Rover! thou little knowest that sentence is passed upon thee.'

'You are surely not going to destroy him, sir?' said John.

'He begins to ail,' said Mr. Sensible. 'And it would be foolish to keep him longer. What would you? *Omnes eodem cogimur.* He has lain in the sun and hunted fleas enough, and now, poor fellow, he must go *quo dives Tullus et Ancus.* We must take life on the terms it is given us.'

'You will miss your old companion.'

'Why, as to that you know, the great art of life is to moderate our passions. Objects of affection are like other belongings. We must love them enough to enrich our lives while we have them—not enough to impoverish our lives when they are gone. You see this puzzle here. While I am engaged on it it seems to me of sovereign importance to fit the pieces together: when it is done I think of it no more: and if I should fail to do it, why I would not break my heart. Confound that Drudge. Hi! whoreson, are we to wait all night for our supper?'

'Coming, sir,' said Drudge from the kitchen.

'I think the fellow goes to sleep over his pots and pans,' said Mr. Sensible, 'but let us occupy the time by continuing our conversation. Good conversation I reckon among the finer sweets of life. But I would not include diatribe or lecturing or persistent discussion under that head. Your doctrinaire is the bane of all talk. As I sit here listening to your opinions—*nullius addictus*—and following the ball wherever it rolls, I defy system. I love to explore your minds *en deshabille.* Nothing comes amiss—*j'aime le jeu, l'amour, les livres, la musique, la ville et la champagne—enfin tout!* Chance is, after all, our best guide—need I call a better witness than the fortunate cast of the dice which has brought you beneath my roof to-night?'

'It wasn't exactly chance,' said Vertue, who had been restlessly waiting to speak. 'We are on a journey and we are looking for a way to cross the Grand Canyon.'

'*Haud equidem invideo,*' said the old gentleman. 'You do not insist on my accompanying you?'

'We hadn't thought of it,' said John.

'Why then I am very willing that you should go!' cried Mr. Sensible with a burst of melodious laughter. 'And yet to what end? I often amuse myself with speculating on that curious restlessness in the mind which drives us, specially in youth, to climb up a mountain merely in order that we may then climb down, or to cross the seas in order that we may pay an inn-keeper for setting before us worse cheer than we might eat in our own house. *Caelum non animum mutamus.* Not that I would repress the impulse, you understand, any more than I would starve any other part of my nature. Here again, the secret of happiness lies in knowing where to stop. A moderate allowance of travelling—enough to quiet, without satiating, a liberal curiosity—is very well. One brings back a few rarities to store in one's inner cabinet against a dull day. But the Grand Canyon—surely a modest tour along the cliffs on this side of it would give you much the same sort of scenery, and save your necks.'

'It wasn't scenery we were looking for,' said John. 'I am trying to find the Island in the West.'

'You refer, no doubt, to some aesthetic experience. There again—I would not urge a young man to shut his eyes to that sort of thing. Who has not felt immortal longings at the lengthening of the shadow or the turning of the leaf? Who has not stretched out his hands for the ulterior shore? *Et ego in Arcadia!* We have all been fools once—aye, and are glad to have been fools too. But our imaginations, like our appetites, need discipline: not, heaven help us, in the interest of any transcendental ethic, but in the interests of our own solid good. That wild impulse must be tasted, not obeyed. The bees have stings, but we rob them of their honey. To hold all that urgent sweetness to our lips in the cup of one perfect moment, missing no faintest ingredient in the flavour of its μονόχρονος ἡδονή, yet ourselves, in a sense, unmoved—this is the true art. This tames in the service of the reasonable life even those pleasures whose loss might seem to be the heaviest, yet necessary, price we paid for rationality. Is it an audacity to hint that for the corrected palate the taste of the draught even owes its last sweetness to the knowledge that we have wrested it from an unwilling source? To cut off pleasures from the consequences and conditions which they have by nature, detaching, as it were, the precious phrase from its irrelevant context, is what distinguishes the man from the brute and the citizen from the savage. I cannot join with those moralists who inveigh against the Roman emetics in their banquets: still less with those who would forbid the even more beneficent contraceptive devices of our later times. That man who can eat as taste, not nature, prompts him and yet fear no aching belly, or who can indulge in Venus and fear no impertinent bastard, is a civilized man. In him I recognize Urbanity—the note of the centre.'

'Do you know of any way across the canyon?' said Vertue abruptly.

'I do not,' said their host, 'for I have never made inquiries. The proper study of mankind is man, and I have always left useless speculations alone. Suppose that there were a way across, to what purpose should I use it? Why should I scramble down this side and up the other to find after my labours the same soil still beneath me and the same heaven above? It would be laughable to suppose that the country beyond the gorge can be any different from the country on this side of it. *Eadem sunt omnia semper.* Nature had already done all she can for our comfort and amusement, and the man who does not find content at home will seek it vainly abroad. Confound that fellow! Drudge! ! Will you bring us our supper or do you prefer to have every bone in your body broken?'

'Coming, sir,' said Drudge from the kitchen.

'There might be different *people* on the other side of the canyon,' suggested John in the momentary pause that followed.

'That is even less likely,' said Mr. Sensible. 'Human nature is always the same. The dress and the manners may vary, but I detect the unchanging heart beneath the shifting disguises. If there are men beyond the canyon, rest assured that we know them already. They are born and they die: and in the interval between they are the same lovable rascals that we know at home.'

'Still,' said John, 'you can't really be certain that there is no such place as my Island. Reason left it an open question.'

'Reason!' exclaimed Mr. Sensible. 'Do you mean the mad woman who goes riding about the country dressed up in armour? I trust that when I spoke of the reasonable life you did not think that I meant anything under *her* auspices? There is a strange confusion in our language here, for the reasonableness which I commend has no more dangerous enemy than Reason. Perhaps I should drop the use of the name altogether, and say that my deity is not reason but *le bon sens.*'

'What is the difference?' said Vertue.

'Sense is easy, Reason is hard. Sense knows where to stop with gracious inconsistency, while Reason slavishly follows an abstract logic whither she knows not. The one seeks comfort and finds it, the other seeks truth and is still seeking. *Le bon sens* is the father of a flourishing family: Reason is barren and a virgin. If I had my way I should clap this Reason of yours in the bridewell to pursue her meditations in the straw. The baggage has a pretty face, I allow: but she leads us from our true aim—joy, pleasure, ease, content, whate'er the name! She is a fanatic who has never learned from my master to pursue the golden mean, and, being a mortal, to think mortal thoughts. *Auream quisquis*—'

'It is very odd that you should say that,' interrupted Vertue, 'for I also was brought up on Aristotle. But I think my text must have differed from yours. In mine, the doctrine of the Means does not bear the sense you have given it at all. He specially says that there is no excess of goodness. You cannot go too far in the right direction. The line that we should follow may start from a middle point in the base of a triangle: but the further off the apex is, the better. In that dimension—'

'*Do manus!*' broke out Mr. Sensible. 'Spare us the rest, young man. We are not at a lecture, and I readily admit that your scholarship is more recent than mine. Philosophy should be our mistress, not our master: and the pursuit of a pedantic accuracy amidst the freedom of our social pleasures is as unwelcome as—'

'And the bit about thinking mortal thoughts,' continued Vertue, whose social experience, as I dreamed, was not extensive, 'the bit about mortal thoughts was quoted by Aristotle to say that he disagreed with it. He held that the end of mortal life was to put on immortality as much as might be. And he also said that the most useless of studies was the noblest.'

'I see you are letter-perfect, young man,' said Mr. Sensible, with a rather chilly smile, 'and I am sure these pieces of information, if repeated to your teachers, would win the applause they deserve. Here, if you will forgive me, they are a little out of place. A gentleman's knowledge of the ancient authors is not that of a pedant: and I think you have misunderstood the place which philosophy ought to hold in the reasonable life. We do not memorize *systems*. What system can stand? What system does not leave us with the old refrain—*que sais-je*? It is in her power to remind us of the strangeness of things—in the brown charm of her secluded meditations—above all, in her decorative function—that philosophy becomes instrumental to the good life. We go to the Porch and the Academy to be spectators, not partisans. Drudge! !'

'Dinner is served, sir,' said Drudge, appearing at the door.

Then I dreamed that they went into the dining-room and so to table.

V
Table Talk

THE COWSLIP WINE CAME with the oysters. It was a little rough, as the old gentleman had prophesied, and the glasses were so very small that Vertue drained his at once. John was afraid that there might be no more to come and therefore dallied over his, partly because he feared that he might put his host out of countenance and partly because he disliked the taste. But his precautions were needless, for with the soup came sherry.

'*Dapibus mensas onerabat inemptis*!' said Mr. Sensible. 'I hope that this wild garden vintage is not unpleasing to an unspoiled palate.'

'You don't mean to say that you have vines?' exclaimed John.

'I was referring to the cowslip wine,' said Mr. Sensible. 'I hope to have some good vines soon, but at present I still rely a little on my neighbours. Is this our own sherry, Drudge?'

'No sir,' said Drudge. 'This is that lot that Mr. Broad sent.'

'Halibut!' said John. 'You surely don't—'

'No,' said Mr. Sensible. 'Sea fish, I confess, I must get from my friends on the coast.'

As the meal went on, John's good manners forbade him to make further inquiries, and when a salad came with one or two very small radishes in it he was positively relieved that his host should be able to claim them as his own produce ('His humble sauce a radish or an egg,' said Mr. Sensible). But in my dream I was privileged to know the sources of the whole meal. The cowslip wine and the radishes were home-grown; the joint had been a present from Mr. Mammon: the entrées and savouries came from Eschropolis: the champagne and ices from old Mr. Halfways. Some of the food was part of the stores which Mr. Sensible had taken over when he came to live there, from his predecessors who had occupied this house before him: for on that tableland, and especially to the North of the main road, the air is so light and cold that things keep for a long time. The bread, the salt, and the apples had been left by Epicurus who was the builder of the house and its first inhabitant. Some very fine hock had belonged to Horace. The claret and also (as I remember) most of the silver, were Montaigne's. But the port, which was one in a thousand and the best thing on that table, had once belonged to Rabelais, who in his turn had it as a present from old Mother Kirk when they were friends. Then I dreamed that after dinner old Mr. Sensible stood up and made a little speech in Latin thanking the Landlord for all they had received.

'What?' said John. 'Do you believe in the Landlord?'

'No part of our nature is to be suppressed,' said Mr. Sensible. 'Least of all a part that has enshrined itself in beautiful traditions. The Landlord has his function like everything else as one element in the good life.'

Then presently Mr. Sensible, who was turning very red, fixed his eyes intently on John and repeated:

'As one element. As one element.'

'I see,' said John, and there was a long silence.

'As well,' began Mr. Sensible with great energy some ten minute later, 'it is part of good manners. Ἀθανάτους μὲν πρῶτα θεούς νόμῳ ὡς διάχειται—Τίμα. My dear Mr. Vertue, my dear young friend, your glass is quite empty. I mean absolutely empty. *Cras ingens iterabimus.*'

There was another and longer pause. John began to wonder whether Mr. Sensible were not asleep, when suddenly Mr. Sensible said with great conviction:

'*Pellite cras ingens tum-tum* νόμῳ ὡς διάχειται.'

Then he smiled at them and finally went to sleep. And presently Drudge came in looking old and thin and dirty in the pale morning light—for I thought that the dawn was just then beginning to show through the chinks of the shutters—to carry his master to bed. Then I saw him come back and lead the guests to their beds. And then the third time I saw him come back into the dining-room and pour out the remains of the claret into a glass and drink it off. Then he stood for a moment or so blinking his red eyes and rubbing his bony, stubbly chin. At last he yawned and set about tidying the room for breakfast.

VI
Drudge

I DREAMED THAT JOHN awoke feeling cold. The chamber in which he lay was luxuriously furnished and all the house was silent, so that John thought it would be useless to rise, and he piled all his clothes on him and tried to sleep again. But

he only grew colder. Then he said to himself, 'Even if there is no chance of breakfast, I may save myself from freezing by walking about': so he rose and huddled
on all his clothes and went down into the house, but the fires were not yet lit. Finding the back door open he went out. It was full morning of a grey sunless day. There
were dark clouds, fairly low, and as John came out one snowflake fell at his feet,
but no more. He found that he was in Mr. Sensible's garden, but it was more of a
yard than a garden. A high wall ran all about it and all within the wall was dry,
brown earth, with a few stony paths. Dibbling the earth with his foot, John found
that the soil was only half an inch deep: under it was solid rock. A little way from
the house he found Drudge down on his hands and knees scraping together what
seemed to be a little pile of dust, but it was in fact the soil of the garden. The little
pile had been got together at the cost of leaving the rock uncovered for a big circle—
like a bald patch—all round Drudge.

'Good morning, Drudge,' said John. 'What are you making?'

'Radish beds, sir.'

'Your master is a great gardener.'

'Talks about it, sir.'

'Does he not work in the garden himself?'

'No, sir.'

'It is a poor soil here. Does he manage to feed himself on his own produce in a good
year?'

'Feeds me on it, sir.'

'What does the garden grow—besides radishes?'

'Nothing, sir.'

John passed on to the end of the garden and looked over the wall, which was lower
here. He drew back with a little start for he found that he was looking down an abyss:
the garden was perched on the edge of the Grand Canyon. Below John's feet, at the
bottom of the gorge, lay the forest, and on the opposite side he saw a mixture of wood
and cliff. The cliffs were all shaggy with trailing and hanging greenery, and streams, rendered immovable to sight by their distance, came down from the land beyond. Even on
that cold morning the farther side looked richer and warmer than his own.

'We must get out of this,' said John. At that moment Drudge called to him.

'I shouldn't lean on that wall, sir,' he said. 'There's frequent landslides.'

'Landslides?'

'Yes, sir. I've rebuilt that wall a dozen times. The house used to be right out
there—half-way across the gorge.'

'The canyon is getting wider, then?'

'At this point, sir. In Mr. Epicurus' time—'

'You have been employed here under other masters, then?'

'Yes, sir. I've seen a good many of them. Whoever has lived here has always
needed me. Choregia they used to call me in the old days, but now they just call
me Drudge.'

'Tell me about your old masters,' said John.

'Mr. Epicurus was the first. Mental case he was, poor gentleman: he had a chronic
fear of the black hole. Something dreadful. I never had a better employer, though.

Nice, kind, quiet-spoken sort of a man. I was very sorry when he went down the cliff—'

'Goodness me!' exclaimed John. 'Do you mean that some of your masters have lost their lives in these landslides?'

'Most of them, sir.'

At that moment a leonine roar came from one of the upper windows of the house. 'Drudge! Son of a bitch! Hot water.'

'Coming, sir,' said Drudge, rising very deliberately from his knees and giving a finishing pat to his heap of dust. 'I shall be leaving here soon,' he continued to John. 'I am thinking of going further North.'

'Further North?'

'Yes, sir. There are openings with Mr. Savage up in the mountains. I was wondering if you and Mr. Vertue were going that way—'

'Drudge!!' bellowed Mr. Sensible's voice from the house.

'Coming, sir,' said Drudge, beginning to untie two pieces of string with which he had confined his trousers beneath his knees. 'So you see, Mr. John, I should be greatly obliged if you would allow me to travel with you.'

'Drudge! Am I to call you again?' shouted Mr. Sensible.

'Coming, sir. If you was to agree I would give Mr. Sensible notice this morning.'

'We are certainly going North for a bit,' said John. 'And I should have no objection, provided Mr. Vertue agrees.'

'Very kind of you, I am sure, sir,' said Drudge. Then he turned and walked slowly into the house.

VII
The Gaucherie of Vertue

MR. SENSIBLE WAS NOT in good humour when they met at breakfast. 'That ungrateful blockhead of a servant of mine is leaving me in the lurch,' he said, 'and for the next few days we must shift for ourselves. I fear I am a wretched cook. Perhaps, Vertue, you would indulge me so far as to take the cooking on yourself until I get a new man? I dare say you could enable the three of us to live a very tolerable sort of picnic life for three days?'

The two young men informed him that they were continuing their journey after breakfast.

'This,' said Mr. Sensible, 'is getting really serious. Do you mean to say that you are going to desert me? I am to be reduced to absolute solitude—deprived of the common decencies of life—compelled to spend my day in menial offices? Very well, sir. I am unacquainted with modern manners: no doubt this is the way in which young men return hospitality.'

'I beg your pardon, sir,' said Vertue. 'I had not seen it in that light. I will certainly act as your servant for a day or so if you wish it. I had not understood that it would be such a burden to you to cook for yourself. I don't remember that you said anything about servants when you were outlining the good life last night.'

'Why, sir,' said Mr. Sensible. 'When I outline the principles of the steam engine I do not explicitly state that I expect fire to burn or the laws of gravity to operate. There are certain things that one always takes for granted. When I speak of the art of life I presuppose the ordinary conditions of life which that art utilizes.'

'Such as wealth,' said Vertue.

'A competence, a competence,' said Mr. Sensible.

'And health, too?' said Vertue.

'Moderate health,' said Mr. Sensible.

'Your art, then,' said Vertue, 'seems to teach men that the best way of being happy is to enjoy unbroken good fortune in every respect. They would not all find the advice helpful. And now, if Drudge will show me his scullery, I will wash up the breakfast things.'

'You may save yourself the trouble, sir,' said Mr. Sensible drily. 'I cannot pretend to your intensity, and I do not choose to be lectured at the breakfast table. When you have mixed more with the world you will learn not to turn the social board into a schoolroom. In the meantime, forgive me if I feel that I should find your continued society a little fatiguing. Conversation should be like the bee which darts to the next flower before the last has ceased swaying from its airy visit: you make it more like a wood beetle eating its way through a table.'

'As you wish,' said Vertue, 'but how will you do?'

'I shall shut up the house,' said Mr. Sensible, 'and practise αὐτάρχεια in a hotel until I have fitted this place up with such mechanical devices as will henceforth render me wholly independent. I see that I have let myself get behind the times. I should have listened more to certain good friends of mine in the city of Claptrap who have kept abreast of modem invention. They assure me that machinery will soon put the good life beyond the reach of chance: and if mechanism alone will not do it I know a eugenist who promises to breed us a race of peons who will be psychologically incapable of playing me a trick like this of Drudge's.'

So it fell out that all four left the house together. Mr. Sensible was astonished to find that Drudge (who parted from his employer very civilly) was accompanying the young men. He only shrugged his shoulders, however, and said, 'Vive la bagatelle! You have stayed in my house which is called Thelema, and its motto is Do what you will. So many men, so many minds. I hope I can tolerate anything except intolerance.' Then he went his way and they saw him no more.

Book Six

NORTHWARD ALONG THE CANYON

For being unlike the magnanimous man, they yet ape him; and that in such particulars as they can.
Aristotle

Much of the soul they talk, but all awry,
And in themselves seek virtue.
Milton

I do not admire the excess of some one virtue unless I am shewn at the same time the excess of the opposite virtue. A man does not prove his greatness by standing at an extremity, but by touching both extremities at once and filling all that lies between them.
Pascal

Contempt is a well-recognized defensive reaction.
I. A. Richards

I
First Steps to the North

'IT IS OF NO USE keeping to the road,' said Vertue. 'We must explore the cliff-edge as we go along and make trial descents from point to point.'

'Begging your pardon, sir,' said Drudge, 'I know these parts very well and there is no way down, at least within thirty miles. You'll miss nothing by keeping to the road for to-day at any rate.'

'How do you know?' asked Vertue. 'Have you ever tried?'

'Oh, bless you, yes,' said Drudge. 'I've often tried to get across the canyon when I was a youngster.'

'Clearly we had better follow the road,' said John.

'I do not feel quite satisfied,' said Vertue. 'But we can always take the cliffs on the way back. I have an idea that if there is a way down it will be at the extreme north where this gorge opens on the sea: or failing everything, we might manipulate the mouth of the gorge by boat. In the meantime I dare say we might do worse than press on by road.'

'I quite agree,' said John.

Then I saw the three set forward on a more desolate march than I had yet beheld. On every side of them the tableland seemed perfectly flat, but their muscles and lungs soon told them that there was a slight but continuous rise. There was little vegetation—here a shrub, and there some grass: but the most of it was brown earth and moss and rock, and the road beneath them was stone. The grey sky was never broken and I do not remember that they saw a single bird: and it was so bleak that if they stopped at any time to rest, the sweat grew cold on them instantly.

Vertue never abated his pace and Drudge kept even with him though always a respectful yard behind: but I saw that John grew footsore and began to lag. For some hours he was always inventing pretexts to stop and finally he said, 'Friends, it is no use, I can go no further.'

'But you must,' said Vertue.

'The young gentleman is soft, sir, very soft,' said Drudge. 'He is not used to this sort of thing. We'll have to help him along.'

So they took him, one by each arm, and helped him along for a few hours. They found nothing to eat or drink in the waste. Towards evening they heard a desolate voice crying 'Maiwi-maiwi,' and looked up, and there was a seagull hanging in the currents of the wind as though it sauntered an invisible stair towards the low rain-clouds.

'Good!' cried Vertue. 'We are nearing the coast.'

'It's a good step yet, sir,' said Drudge. 'These gulls come forty miles inland and more in bad weather.'

Then they plodded on for many more miles. And the sky began to turn from sunless grey to starless black. And they looked and saw a little shanty by the road-side and there they knocked on the door.

II
Three Pale Men

WHEN THEY WERE let in they found three young men, all very thin and pale, seated by a stove under the low roof of the hut. There was some sacking on a bench along one wall and little comfort else.

'You will fare badly here,' said one of the three men. 'But I am a Steward and it is my duty according to my office to share my supper with you. You may come in.' His name was Mr. Neo-Angular.

'I am sorry that my convictions do not allow me to repeat my friend's offer,' said one of the others. 'But I have had to abandon the humanitarian and egalitarian fallacies.' His name was Mr. Neo-Classical.

'I hope,' said the third, 'that your wanderings in lonely places do not mean that you have any of the romantic virus still in your blood.' His name was Mr. Humanist.

John was too tired and Drudge too respectful to reply: but Vertue said to Mr. Neo-Angular, 'You are very kind. You are saving our lives.'

'I am not kind at all,' said Mr. Neo-Angular with some warmth. 'I am doing my duty. My ethics are based on dogma, not on feeling.'

'I understand you very well,' said Vertue. 'May I shake hands with you?'

'Can it be,' said the other, 'that you are one of us? You are a Catholic? A scholastic?'

'I know nothing about that,' said Vertue, 'but I know that the rule is to be obeyed because it is a rule and not because it appeals to my feelings at the moment.'

'I see you are not one of us,' said Angular, 'and you are undoubtedly damned. *Virtutes paganorum splendida vitia.* Now let us eat.'

Then I dreamed that the three pale men produced three tins of bully beef and six biscuits, and Angular shared his with the guests. There was very little for each and I thought that the best share fell to John and Drudge, for Vertue and the young Steward entered into a kind of rivalry who should leave most for the others.

'Our fare is simple,' said Mr. Neo-Classical. 'And perhaps unwelcome to pal-ates that have been reared on the kickshaws of lower countries. But you see the perfection of form. This beef is a perfect cube: this biscuit a true square.'

'You will admit,' said Mr. Humanist, 'that, at least, our meal is quite free from any lingering flavour of the old romantic sauces.'

'Quite free,' said John, staring at the empty tin.

'It's better than radishes, sir,' said Drudge.

'Do you *live* here, gentlemen?' said Vertue when the empty tins had been removed.

'We do,' said Mr. Humanist. 'We are founding a new community. At present we suffer the hardships of pioneers and have to import our food: but when we have brought the country under cultivation we shall have plenty—as much plenty as is needed for the practice of temperance.'

'You interest me exceedingly,' said Vertue. 'What are the principles of this community?'

'Catholicism, Humanism, Classicism,' said all three.

'Catholicism! Then you are all Stewards?'

'Certainly not,' said Classical and Humanist.

'At least you all believe in the Landlord?'

'I have no interest in the question,' said Classical.

'And I,' said Humanist, 'know perfectly well that the Landlord is a fable.'

'And I,' said Angular, 'know perfectly well that he is a fact.'

'This is very surprising, said Vertue. 'I do not see how you have come together, or what your common principles can possibly be.'

'We are united by a common antagonism to a common enemy,' said Humanist. 'You must understand that we are three brothers, the sons of old Mr. Enlightenment of the town of Claptrap.'

'I know him,' said John.

'Our father was married twice,' continued Humanist. 'Once to a lady name Epichaerecacia, and afterwards to Euphuia. By his first wife he had a son called Sigmund who is thus our step-brother.'

'I know him too,' said John.

'We are the children of his second marriage,' said Humanist.

'Then,' cried Vertue, 'we are related—if you care to acknowledge the kinship. You have probably heard that Euphuia had a child before she married your father. I was that child—though I confess that I never discovered who my father was and enemies have hinted that I am a bastard.'

'You have said quite sufficient,' replied Angular. 'You can hardly expect that the subject should be agreeable to us. I might add that my office, if there were nothing else, sets me apart even from my legitimate relations.'

'And what about the common antagonism?' said John.

'We were all brought up,' said Humanist, 'by our step-brother in the university at Eschropolis, and we learned there to see that whoever stays with Mr. Halfways must either come on to Eschropolis or else remain at Thrill as the perpetual minion of his brown daughter.'

'You had not been with Mr. Halfways yourselves, then?' asked John.

'Certainly not. We learned to hate him from watching the effect which his music had on other people. Hatred of him is the first thing that unites us. Next, we discovered how residence in Eschropolis inevitably leads to the giant's dungeon.'

'I know all about that too,' said John.

'Our common hatred therefore links us together against the giant, against Eschropolis, and against Mr. Halfways.'

'But specially against the latter,' said Classical.

'I should rather say,' remarked Angular, 'against half-measures and compromises of all sorts—against any pretence that there is any kind of goodness or decency, any even tolerable temporary resting place, on this side of the Grand Canyon.'

'And that,' said Classical, 'is why Angular is for me, in one sense, *the* enemy, but, in another, *the* friend. I cannot agree with his notions about the other side of the canyon: but just because he relegates his delusions to the *other* side, he is free to agree with me about this side and to be an implacable exposer (like myself) of all attempts to foist upon us any transcendental, romantical, optimistic trash.'

'My own feeling,' said Humanist, 'is rather that Angular is with me in guarding against any confusion of the *levels* of experience. He *canalizes* all the mystical non-sense—the *sehnsucht* and *Wanderlust* and Nympholepsy—and transfers them to the far side: that prevents their drifting about on this side and hindering our real function. It leaves us free to establish a really tolerable and even comfortable civilization here on the plateau; a culture based alike on those truths which Mr. Sensible acknowledges and on those which the giant reveals, but throwing over both alike a graceful veil of illusion. And that way we shall remain human: we shall not become beasts with the giant nor abortive angels with Mr. Halfways.'

'The young gentleman is asleep, sir,' said Drudge: and indeed John had sunk down some time ago.

'You must excuse him,' said Vertue. 'He found the road long to-day.'

Then I saw that all six men lay down together in the sacking. The night was far colder than the night they passed in Mr. Sensible's house: but as there was here no pretence of comfort and they lay huddled together in the narrow hut, John slept warmer here than at Thelema.

III
Neo-Angular

WHEN THEY ROSE in the morning John was so footsore and his limbs ached so that he knew not how to continue his journey. Drudge assured them that the coast could not now be very far. He thought that Vertue could reach it and return in a day and that John might await him in the hut. As for John himself, he was loth to burden hosts who lived in such apparent poverty: but Mr. Angular constrained him to stay, when he had explained that the secular virtue of hospitality was worthless, and care for the afflicted a sin if it proceeded from humanitarian sentiment, but that he was obliged to act as he did by the rules of his order. So, in my dream, I saw Drudge and Vertue set out northwards alone, while John remained with the three pale men.

In the forenoon he had a conversation with Angular.

'You believe, then,' said John, 'that there is a way across the canyon?'

'I know there is. If you will let me take you to Mother Kirk she will carry you over in a moment.'

'And yet, I am not sure that I am not sailing under false colours. When I set out from home, crossing the canyon was never in my thoughts—still less was Mother Kirk.'

'It does not matter in the least what was in your thoughts.'

'It does, to me. You see, my only motive for crossing, is the hope that something I am looking for may be on the other side.'

'That is a dangerous, subjective motive. What is this something?'

'I saw an Island—'

'Then you must forget it as soon as you can. Islands are the Halfways' concern. I assure you, you must eradicate every trace of that nonsense from your mind before I can help you.'

'But how can you help me after removing the only thing that I want to be helped to? What is the use of telling a hungry man that you will grant him his desires, provided there is no question of eating?'

'If you do not *want* to cross the canyon, there is no more to be said. But, then, you must realize where you are. Go on with your Island, if you like, but do not pretend that it is anything but a part of the land of destruction this side of the canyon. If you are a sinner, for heaven's sake have the grace to be a cynic too.'

'But how can you say that the Island is all bad, when it is longing for the Island, and nothing else, that has brought me this far?'

'It makes no difference. All on this side of the canyon is much of a muchness. If you confine yourself to this side, then the Spirit of the Age is right.'

'But this is not what Mother Kirk said. She particularly insisted that some of the food was much less poisonous than the rest.'

'So you have met Mother Kirk? No wonder that you are confused. You had no business to talk to her except through a qualified Steward. Depend upon it, you have misunderstood every word she said.'

'Then there was Reason, too. She refused to say that the Island was an illusion. But perhaps, like Mr. Sensible, you have quarrelled with Reason.'

'Reason is divine. But how should you understand her? You are a beginner. For you, the only safe commerce with Reason is to learn from your superiors the dogmata in which her deliverances have been codified for general use.'

'Look here,' said John. 'Have you ever seen my Island?'

'God forbid.'

'And you have never heard Mr. Halfways either.'

'Never. And I never will. Do you take me for an escapist?'

'Then there is at least one object in the world of which I know more than you. I *tasted* what you call romantic trash; you have only talked about it. You need not tell me that there is a danger in it and an element of evil. Do you suppose that I have not felt that danger and that evil a thousand times more than you? But I know also that the evil in it is not what I went to it to find, and that I should have sought nothing and found nothing without it. I know this by experience as I know a dozen things about it which of you betray your ignorance as often as you speak. Forgive me if I am rude: but how is it possible that you can advise me in this matter? Would you recommend a eunuch as confessor to a man whose difficulties lay in the realm of chastity? Would a man born blind be my best guide against the lust of the eye? But I am getting angry. And you have shared your biscuit with me. I ask your pardon.'

'It is part of my office to bear insults with patience,' said Mr. Angular.

IV
Humanist

IN THE AFTERNOON Mr. Humanist took John out to show him the garden, by whose produce, in time, the new culture was to become self-supporting. As there was no human, or indeed animal, habitation within sight, no wall or fence had been deemed necessary but the area of the garden had been marked out by a line of stones and sea-shells alternately arranged: and this was necessary as the garden would else have been indistinguishable from the waste. A few paths, also marked by stones and shells, were arranged in a geometrical pattern.

'You see,' said Mr. Humanist, 'we have quite abandoned the ideas of the old romantic landscape gardeners. You notice a certain severity. A landscape gardener would have had a nodding grove over there on the right, and a mound on the left, and winding paths, and a pond, and flowerbeds. He would have filled the obscurer parts with the means of sensuality—the formless potato and the romantically irregular cabbage. You see, there is nothing of the sort here.'

'Nothing at all,' said John.

'At present, of course, it is not very fruitful. But we are pioneers.'

'Do you ever try *digging* it?' suggested John.

'Why, no,' said Mr. Humanist, 'you see, it is pure rock an inch below the surface, so we do not disturb the soil. That would remove the graceful veil of illusion which is so necessary to the *human* point of view.'

V
Food from the North

LATE THAT EVENING the door of the hut opened and Vertue staggered in and dropped to a sitting position by the stove. He was very exhausted and it was long before he had his breath to talk. When he had, his first words were:

'You must leave this place, gentlemen. It is in danger.'

'Where is Drudge?' said John.

'He stayed there.'

'And what is this danger?' asked Mr. Humanist.

'I'm going to tell you. By the by, there's no way over the gorge northward.'

'We have been on a fool's errand, then,' said John, 'ever since we left the main road.'

'Except that now we know,' replied Vertue. 'But I must eat before I can tell my story. To-night I am able to return our friends' hospitality,' and with that he produced from various parts of his clothing the remains of a handsome cold pie, two bottles of strong beer and a little flask of rum. For some time there was silence in the hut, and when the meal was finished and a little water had been boiled so that each had a glass of hot grog, Vertue began his story.

VI
Furthest North

'IT IS ALL LIKE this as far as the mountains—about fifteen miles—and there is nothing to tell of our journey except rock and moss and a few gulls. The mountains are frightful as you approach them, but the road runs up to a pass and we had not much difficulty. Beyond the pass you get into a little rocky valley and it was here that we first found any signs of habitation. The valley is a regular warren of caves inhabited by dwarfs. There are several species of them, I gather, though I only distinguished two—a black kind with black shirts and a red kind who call themselves Marxomanni. They are all very fierce and apparently quarrel a good deal but they all acknowledge some kind of vassalage to this man Savage. At least they made no difficulty in letting me through when they heard that I wanted to see him—beyond insisting on giving me a guard. It was there I lost Drudge. He said he had come to join the red dwarfs and would I mind going on alone. He was just the same up to the end—civil as ever—but he was down one of their burrows and apparently quite at home before I could get in a word. Then my dwarfs took me on. I didn't care for the arrangements much. They were not men, you know, not dwarf men, but real dwarfs—trolls. They could talk, and they walk on two legs, but the structure must be quite different from ours. I felt all the time that if they killed me it wouldn't be murder, any more than if a crocodile or a gorilla killed me. It *is* a different species— however it came there. Different faces.

'Well, they kept taking me up and up. It was all rocky zig-zags, round and round. Fortunately, I do not get giddy. My chief danger was the wind whenever we got on a ridge—for of course my guides, being only some three feet high, did not offer it the same target. I had one or two narrow escapes. Savage's nest is a terrifying place. It is a long hall like a barn and when I first caught sight of it—half-way up the sky from where they were leading me—I thought to myself that wherever else we were going it could not be *there*; it looked so inaccessible. But on we went.

'One thing you must get into your heads is that there are caves all the way up, all inhabited. The whole mountain must be honeycombed. I saw thousands of the dwarfs. Like an ant-hill—and not a man in the place except me.

'From Savage's nest you look straight down to the sea. I should think it is the biggest sheer drop on any coast. It was from there that I saw the mouth of the gorge. The mouth is only a lowering of the cliff: from the lowest part of the opening it is still thousands of feet to the sea. There is no conceivable landing. It is no use to anyone but sea-gulls.

'But you want to hear about Savage. He sat on a high chair at the end of his barn— a very big man, almost a giant. When I say that I don't mean his height: I had the same feeling about him that I had about the dwarfs. That doubt about the *species*. He was dressed in skins and had an iron helmet on his head with horns stuck in it.

'He had a woman there, too, a great big woman with yellow hair and high cheek-bones. Grimhild her name is. And the funny thing is that she is the sister of an old friend of yours, John. She is Mr. Halfways' elder daughter. Apparently Savage came down to Thrill and carried her off: and what is stranger still, both the girl and the old gentleman were rather pleased about it than otherwise.

'As soon as the dwarfs brought me in, Savage rapped on the table and bellowed out, "Lay the board for us men," and she set about laying it. He didn't say anything to me for a long time. He just sat and looked and sang. He had only one song and he was singing it off and on all the time I was there. I remember bits of it.

> 'Wind age, wolf age,
> Ere the world crumbles:
> Shard age, spear age,
> Shields are broken. . . .

'Then there was another bit began:

> 'East sits the Old'Un
> In Iron-forest;

Feeds amidst it
Fenris' children. . . .

I sat down after a bit, for I did not want him to think I was afraid of him. When the food was on the table he asked me to have some, so I had it. He offered me a sweet drink, very strong, in a horn, so I drank it. Then he shouted and drank himself and said that mead in a horn was all he could offer me at present: "But soon," he said, "I shall drink the blood of men from skulls." There was a lot of this sort of stuff. We ate roast pork, with our fingers. He kept on singing his song and shouting. It was only after dinner that he began to talk connectedly. I wish I could remember it all. This is the important part of my story

'It is hard to understand it without being a biologist. These dwarfs *are* a different species and an older species than ours. But, then, the specific variation is always liable to reappear in human children. They revert to the dwarf. Consequently, they are multiplying very fast; they are being increased both by ordinary breeding among themselves and also from without by those hark-backs or changelings. He spoke of lots of sub-species besides the Marxomanni—Mussolimini, Swastici, Gangomanni. . . . I can't remember them all. For a long time I couldn't see where he himself came in.

'At last he told me. He is breeding and training them for a descent on this country. When I tried to find out why, for a long time he would only stare at me and sing his song. Finally—as near as I could get it—his theory seemed to be that fighting was an end in itself.

'Mind you, he was not drunk. He said that he could understand old-fashioned people who believed in the Landlord and kept the rules and hoped to go up and live in the Landlord's castle when they had to leave this country. "They have something to live for," he said. "And if their belief was true, their behaviour would be perfectly sensible. But as their belief is not true, there remains only one way of life fit for a man." This other way of life was something he called Heroism, or Master-Morality, or Violence. "All the other people in between," he said, "are ploughing the sand." He went on railing at the people in Claptrap for ages, and also at Mr. Sensible. "These are the dregs of man," he said. "They are always thinking of happiness. They are scraping together and storing up and trying to *build*. Can they not see that the law of the world is against them? Where will any of them be a hundred years hence?" I said they might be building for posterity. "And who will posterity build for?" he asked. "Can't you see that it is all bound to come to nothing in the end? And the end may come to-morrow: and however late it comes, to those who look back all their 'happiness' will seem but a moment that has slipped away and left nothing behind. You can't gather happiness. Do you go to bed with any more in hand on the day you have had a thousand pleasures?" I asked if his "Heroism" left anything behind it either: but he said it did. "The excellent deed," he said, "is eternal. The hero alone has this privilege, that death for him is not defeat, and the lamenting over him and the memory is part of the good he aimed for; and

5. *Savage sat on a high chair at the end of his barn—a very big man, almost a giant.*

the moment of battle fears nothing from the future because it has already cast security away."

'He talked a lot like that. I asked him what he thought of the Eschropolitans and he roared with laughter and said: "When the Cruels meet the Clevers there will not be even the ghost of a tug of war." Then I asked him if he knew you three and he laughed louder still. He said that Angular might turn out an enemy worth fighting when he grew up. "But I don't know," he said. "Likely enough he is only an Eschropolitan turned inside-out—poacher turned game-keeper. As for the other pair, they are the last even of the last men." I asked him what he meant. "The men of Claptrap," he said, "may have some excuse for their folly, for they at least still believe that your country is a place where Happiness is possible. But your two friends are madmen without qualification. They claim to have reached rock-bottom, they talk of being disillusioned. They think that they have reached the furthest North—as if I were not here to the North of them. They live on a rock that will never feed man, between a chasm that they cannot cross and the home of a giant to whom they dare not return: and still they maunder of a culture and a security. If all men who try to build are but polishing the brasses on a sinking ship, then your pale friends are the supreme fools who polish with the rest though they know and admit that the ship is sinking. Their Humanism and whatnot is but the old dream with a new name. The rot in the world is too deep and the leak in the world is too wide. They may patch and tinker as they please, they will not save it. Better give in. Better cut the wood with the grain. If I am to live in a world of destruction let me be its agent and not its patient."

'In the end he said: "I will make this concession to your friends. They do live further North than anyone but me. They are more like men than any of their race. They shall have this honour when I lead the dwarfs to war, that Humanist's skull shall be the first from which I drink the blood of a man: and Grimhild here shall have Classical's."

'That was about all he said. He made me go out on the cliffs with him. It was all I could do to keep my footing. He said, "This wind blows straight from the pole; it will make a man of you." I think he was trying to frighten me. In the end I got away. He loaded me with food for myself and you. "Feed them up," he said. "There is not enough blood in them at present to quench the thirst of a dwarfish sword." Then I came away. And I am very tired.'

VII
Fools' Paradise

'I SHOULD LIKE to meet this Savage,' said Angular. He seems to be a very clear-headed man.'

'I don't know about that,' said Humanist. 'He and his dwarfs seem to me to be just the thing I am fighting against—the logical conclusion of Eschropolis against which I raise the banner of Humanism. All the wild atavistic emotions which old Halfways sets free under false pretences—I am not at all surprised that he likes a valkyrie for a daughter—and which young Halfways unmasks, but cherishes when he has unmasked them; where can they end but in a complete abandonment of the *human*? I am glad to hear of him. He shows how necessary I am.'

'I agree,' said John in great excitement. 'But how are you going to fight? Where are your troops? Where is your base of supplies? You can't feed an army on a garden of stones and sea-shells.'

'It is intelligence that counts,' said Humanist.

'It moves nothing,' said John. 'You see that Savage is scalding hot and you are cold. You must get heat to rival his heat. Do you think you can rout a million armed dwarfs by being "not romantic"?'

'If Mr. Vertue will not be offended,' said Classical, 'I would suggest that he dreamed the whole thing. Mr. Vertue is romantic: he is paying for his wish-fulfilment dreams as he will always pay—with a fear-fulfilment dream. It is well-known that nobody lives further North than we.' But Vertue was too tired to defend his story and soon all the occupants of the hut were asleep.

Book Seven
SOUTHWARD
ALONG THE
CANYON

Now is the seventh winter since Troy fell, and we
Still search beneath unfriendly stars, through every sea
And desert isle, for Italy's retreating strand.
But here is kinsman's country and Acestes' land;
What hinders here to build a city and remain?
Oh fatherland, oh household spirits preserved in vain
From the enemy, shall no new Troy arise? Shall no
New Simois there, re-named for Hector's memory, flow?
Rather, come!—burn with me the boats that work us harm!
Virgil

Through this and through no other fault we fell,
Nor, being fallen, bear other pain than this,
—Always without hope in desire to dwell.
Dante

Some also have wished that the next way to their Father's house
were here that they might be troubled no more with either Hills or
Mountains to go over; but the way is the way, and there's an end.
Bunyan

I
Vertue Is Sick

I SAW THE TWO TRAVELLERS get up from their sacking and bid good-bye to their hosts, and set out southwards. The weather had not changed, nor did I ever see any other weather over that part of the country than clouds and wind without rain. Vertue himself was out of sorts and made haste without the spirit of haste. Then at last he opened his mind to his companion and said, 'John, I do not know what is coming over me. Long ago you asked me—or was it Media asked me—where I was going and why: and I remember that I brushed the question aside. At that time it seemed to me so much more important to keep my rules and do my thirty miles a day. But I am beginning to find that it will not do. In the old days it was always a question of doing what I chose instead of what I wanted: but now I am beginning to be uncertain what it is I choose.'

'How has this come about?' said John.

'Do you know that I nearly decided to stay with Savage?'

'With Savage?'

'It sounds like raving, but think it over. Supposing there is no Landlord, no mountains in the East, no Island in the West, nothing but this country. A few weeks ago I would have said that all those things made no difference. But now—I don't know. It is quite clear that all the ordinary ways of living in this country lead to something which I certainly do *not* choose. I know that, even If I don't know what I *do* choose. I know that I don't want to be a Halfways, or a Clever, or a Sensible. Then there is the life I have been leading myself—marching on I don't know where. I can't see that there is any other good in it except the mere fact of imposing my will on my inclinations. And that seems to be good *training*, but training for what? Suppose after all it was training for battle? Is it so absurd to think that that might be the thing we were born for? A fight in a narrow place, life or death;—that must be the final act of will—the conquest of the deepest inclination of all.'

'I think my heart will break,' said John after they had gone many paces in silence. 'I came out to find my Island. I am not high-minded like you, Vertue: it was never anything but sweet desire that led me. I have not smelled the air from that Island since—since—it is so long that I cannot remember. I saw more of it at home. And now my only friend talks of selling himself to the dwarfs.'

'I am sorry for you,' said Vertue, 'and I am sorry for myself. I am sorry for every blade of grass and for this barren rock we are treading and the very sky above us. But I have no help to give you.'

'Perhaps,' said John, 'there are things East and West of this country after all.'

'Do you still understand me so little as that!' cried Vertue, turning on him. 'Things East and West! Don't you see that that is the other fatal possibility? Don't you see that I am caught either way?'

'Why?' said John: and then, 'Let us sit down. I am tired and we have nowhere to hurry to—not now.'

Vertue sat down as one not noticing that he did it.

'Don't you see?' he said. 'Suppose there is anything East and West. How can that give me a motive for going on? Because there is something dreadful behind? That is a threat. I meant to be a free man. I meant to choose things because I chose to choose them—not because I was paid for it. Do you think I am a child to be scared with rods and baited with sugar plums? It was for this reason that I never even inquired whether the stories about the Landlord were true; I saw that his castle and his black hole were there to corrupt my will and kill my freedom. If it was true it was a truth an honest man must not know.'

Evening darkened on the tableland and they sat for a long time, immovable.

'I believe that I am mad,' said Vertue presently. 'The world cannot be as it seems to me. If there is something to go to, it is a bribe, and I cannot go to it: if I can go, then there is nothing to go to.'

'Vertue,' said John, 'give in. For once yield to desire. Have done with your choosing. *Want* something.'

'I cannot,' said Vertue. 'I must choose because I choose because I choose: and it goes on for ever, and in the whole world I cannot find a reason for rising from this stone.'

'Is it not reason enough that the cold will presently kill us here?'

It had grown quite dark and Vertue made no reply.

'Vertue!' said John, and then suddenly again in a louder voice, frightened, 'Vertue!!' But there was no answer. He groped for his friend in the dark and touched the cold dust of the tableland. He rose on his hands and knees and groped all about, calling. But he was confused and could not even find again the place whence he had risen himself. He could not tell how often he might have groped over the same ground or whether he was getting further and further from their resting-place. He could not be still; it was too cold. So all that night he rummaged to and fro in the dark, calling out Vertue's name: and often it came into his head that Vertue had been all along one of the phantoms of a dream and that he had followed a shade.

II
John Leading

I DREAMED THAT MORNING BROKE over the plateau, and I saw John rise up, white and dirty, in the new twilight. He looked all round him and saw nothing but the heath. Then he walked this way and that, still looking, and so for a long time. And at last he sat down and wept: that also for a long time. And when he had wept enough he rose like a man determined and resumed his journey southward.

He had hardly gone twenty paces when he stopped with a cry, for there lay Vertue at his feet. I understood in my dream that during his groping in the darkness he had unwittingly gone further and further from the place where they had first sat down.

In a moment John was on his knees and feeling for Vertue's heart. It beat still. He laid his face to Vertue's lips. They breathed still. He caught him by the shoulder and shook him.

'Wake up,' he cried, 'the morning is here.'

Then Vertue opened his eyes and smiled at John, a little foolishly.

'Are you well?' said John. 'Are you fit to travel?'

But Vertue only smiled. He was dumb. Then John held out his hands and pulled Vertue to his feet: and Vertue stood up uncertainly but as soon as he made a stride he stumbled and fell, for he was blind. It was long before John understood. Then at last I saw him take Vertue by the hand and, leading him, resume their journey to the South. And there fell upon John that last loneliness which comes when the comforter himself needs comforting, and the guide is to be guided.

III
The Main Road Again

THEY FOUND MR. SENSIBLE'S house empty, as John had expected, with the shutters up and the chimneys smokeless. John decided to push on to the main road and then, if the worst came to the worst, they could go to Mother Kirk: but he hoped it would not come to that.

All their journey South had been a descent, from the northern mountains to Mr. Sensible's: but after his house it began to rise again a little to the main road, which ran along a low ridge, so that, when they had gained the road, the country South of it was suddenly all opened before them. At the same moment there came a gleam of sunshine, the first for many days. The road was unfenced to the heath on its northern side, but in its southern side there was a hedge with a gate in it: and the first thing John saw through the gate was a long low mound of earth. He had not been a farmer's son for nothing. Having led Vertue to the bank of the road and seated him, he lost no time in climbing the gate and digging with both hands into the earthern mound. It contained, as he had expected, turnips; and in a minute he was seated by Vertue, cutting a fine root into chunks, feeding the blind man and teaching him how to feed himself. The sun grew warmer every moment. The spring seemed further on in this place, and the hedge behind them was already more green than brown. Among many notes of birds John thought he would distinguish a lark. They had breakfasted well, and as the warmth increased pleasantly over their aching limbs, they fell asleep.

IV
Going South

WHEN JOHN AWOKE his first look was towards Vertue, but Vertue was still sleeping. John stretched himself and rose: he was warm and well, but a little thirsty. It was a four-cross-road where they had been sitting, for the northern road, at which John looked with a shudder, was but the continuation of a road from the South. He stood and looked down the latter. To his eyes, long now accustomed to the dusty flats of the northern plateau, the country southward was as a rich counterpane. The sun had passed noon by an hour or so, and the slanting light freckled with rounded shadows a green land, that fell ever away before him, opening as it sank into valleys, and beyond then into deeper valleys again, so that places on the same level where now he stood, yonder were mountain tops. Nearer hand were fields and hedgerows, ruddy ploughland, winding woods, and frequent farmhouses white among their trees. He went back and raised Vertue and was about to show it all to him when he remembered his blindness. Then, sighing, he took him by the hand and went down the new road.

Before they had gone far he heard a bubbling sound by the roadside, and found a little spring pouring itself into a stream that ran henceforth with the road, now at the left, now at the right, and often crossed their way. He filled his hat with water and gave Vertue to drink. Then he drank himself and they went on, always downhill. The road nestled deeper each half-mile between banks of grass. There were primroses, first one or two, then clustered, then innumerable. From many turns of the road John caught sight of the deeper valleys to which they were descending, blue with distance and rounded with the weight of trees: but often a little wood cut off all remoter prospect.

The first house they came to was a red house, old and ivied, and well back from the road, and John thought it had the look of a Steward's house: as they came nearer, there was the Steward himself, without his mask, pottering about at some light gardening labour on the sunny side of the hedge. John leaned over the gate and asked for hospitality, explaining at the same time his friend's condition.

'Come in, come in,' said the Steward, 'It will be a great pleasure.'

Now I dreamed that this Steward was the same Mr. Broad who had sent a case of sherry to Mr. Sensible. He was about sixty years of age.

V
Tea on the Lawn

'IT IS ALMOST WARM enough to have tea on the lawn,' said Mr. Broad. 'Martha, I think we will have tea on the lawn.'

Chairs were set and all three sat down. On the smooth lawn, surrounded by laurels and laburnum, it was even warmer than in the road, and suddenly a sweet bird-note shot out from the thickets.

'Listen!' said Mr. Broad, 'it is a thrush. I really believe it is a thrush.'

Maidservants in snowy aprons opened the long windows of the library and came over the grass carrying tables and trays, the silver teapot and the stand of cakes. There was honey for tea. Mr. Broad asked John some questions about his travels.

'Dear me,' he said, when he heard of Mr. Savage, 'dear me! I ought to go and see him. And such a clever man, too, by your account . . . it is very sad.'

John went on to describe the three pale men.

'Ah, to be sure,' said Mr. Broad. 'I knew their father very well. A very able man. I owed a good deal to him at one time. Indeed, as a young man, he formed my mind. I suppose I ought to go and see his boys. Young Angular I *have* met. He is a dear, good fellow—a little narrow; I would venture to say, even a little old-fashioned, though of course I wouldn't for the world—the two brothers are doing splendidly I have no doubt. I really *ought* to go and see them. But I am getting on, and I confess it never suits me up there.'

'It is a very different climate from this,' said John.

'I always think it is possible for a place to be *too* bracing. They call it the land of the Tough-minded—tough-skinned would be a better name. If one has a tendency to lumbago—But, dear me, if you have come from there you must have met my old friend Sensible?'

'You know him too?'

'Know him? He is my oldest friend. He is a kind of connection of mine, and then, you know, we are quite near neighbours. He is only a mile north of the road and I am about a mile south of it. I should think I did know him. I have passed many, many happy hours in his house. The dear old man. Poor Sensible, he is ageing fast. I don't think he has ever quite forgiven me for having kept most of my hair!'

'I should have thought his views differed from yours a good deal.'

'Ah, to be sure, to be sure! He is not very orthodox, perhaps, but as I grow older I am inclined to set less and less store by mere orthodoxy. So often the orthodox view means the lifeless view, the barren formula. I am coming to look more and more at the language of the heart. Logic and definition divide us: it is those things which draw us together that I now value most—our common affections, our common delight in this slow pageant of the countryside, our common struggle towards the light. Sensible's heart is in the right place.'

'I wonder,' said John, 'if he treats that servant of his very well.'

'His language is a little bit rough, I suppose. One must be charitable. You young people are so hard. Dear me, I remember when I was a boy myself.... And then a man of Sensible's age suffers a good deal. We are none of us perfect. Will you not have a little more tea?'

'Thank you,' said John, 'but if you can give me some directions I think I would like to continue my journey. I am trying to find an Island in the West—'

'That is a beautiful idea,' said Mr. Broad. 'And if you will trust an older traveller, the seeking is the finding. How many happy days you have before you!'

'And I want to know,' continued John, 'whether it is really necessary to cross the canyon.'

'To be sure you do. I wouldn't for the world hold you back. At the same time, my dear boy, I think there is a very real danger at your age of trying to make these things too definite. That has been the great error of my profession in past ages. We have tried to enclose everything in formulae, to turn poetry into logic, and metaphor into dogma; and now that we are beginning to realize our mistake we find ourselves shackled by the formulae of dead men. I don't say that they were not adequate once: but they have ceased to be adequate for us with our wider knowledge. When I became a man, I put away childish things. These great truths need re-interpretation in every age.'

'I am not sure that I quite understand,' said John. 'Do you mean that I must cross the canyon or that I must not?'

'I see you want to pin me down,' said Mr. Broad, with a smile, 'and I love to see it. I was like that myself once. But one loses faith in abstract logic as one grows older. Do you never feel that the truth is so great and so simple that no mere words can contain it? The heaven and the heaven of heavens ... how much less this house that I have builded.'

'Well, anyway,' said John, deciding to try a new question. 'Supposing a man *did* have to cross the canyon. Is it true that he would have to rely on Mother Kirk?'

'Ah, Mother Kirk! I love and honour her from the bottom of my heart, but I trust that loving her does not mean being blind to her faults. We are none of us infallible. If I sometimes feel that I must differ from her at present, it is because I honour all the more the *idea* that she stands for, the thing she may yet become. For the moment, there is no denying that she has let herself get a little out of date. Surely, for many of our generation, there is a truer, a more acceptable, message in all this beautiful world around us? I don't know whether you are anything of a botanist. If you would care—'

'I want my Island,' said John. 'Can you tell me how to reach it? I am afraid I am not specially interested in botany.'

'It would open a new world to you,' said Mr. Broad. 'A new window on the Infinite. But perhaps this is not in your line. We must all find our own key to the mystery after all. I wouldn't for the world ...'

'I think I must be going,' said John. 'And I have enjoyed myself very much. If I follow this road, shall I find anywhere that will give me a night's lodging in a few miles?'

'Oh, easily,' said Mr. Broad. 'I should be very glad to have you here if you would care to stay. But if not, there is Mr. Wisdom within an easy walk. You will find him a delightful man. I used to go and see him quite often when I was younger, but it is a little too far for me now. A dear, good fellow—a *little* persistent, perhaps . . . I sometimes wonder if he is really quite free from a trace of narrow-mindedness. . . . You should hear what Sensible says about him! But there: we are none of us perfect, and he is a very good sort of man on the whole. You will like him very much.'

The old Steward bade good-bye to John with almost fatherly kindness, and John, still leading Vertue, pursued his journey.

VI
The House of Wisdom

THE STREAM THAT THEY had followed to the Steward's house was now no longer a brook by the roadside, but a river that sometimes approached, sometimes receded from the road, sliding in swift amber reaches and descending silver rapids. The trees grew more thickly hereabouts and were of larger kinds—and as the valley deepened, tiers of forest rose one above the other on each side. They walked in shadow. But far above their heads the sun was still shining on the mountain tops, beyond the forest slopes and beyond the last steep fields, where there were domed summits of pale grass and winding water-glens, and cliffs the colour of doves, and cliffs the colour of wine. The moths were already flying when they reached an open place. The valley widened and a loop of the river made room for a wide and level lawn between its banks and the wooded mountains. Amidst the lawn stood a low, pillared house approachable by a bridge, and the door stood open. John led the sick man up to them and saw that the lamps were already lit within; and then he saw Wisdom sitting among his children, like an old man.

'You may stay here as long as you wish,' he said in answer to John's question. 'And it may be that we shall heal your friend if his sickness is not incurable. Sit and eat, and when you have eaten you shall tell us your story.'

Then I saw that chairs were brought for the travellers and some of the young men of the house carried water to them to wash. And when they had washed, a woman set a table before them and laid on it a loaf, and cheese, and a dish of fruit, with some curds, and butter-milk in a pitcher: 'For we can get no wine here,' said the old man with a sigh.

---

6. *Then they went on together over hills and dales, very fast, in the moonlight.*

When the meal was over there was silence in the house, and John saw that they waited for his story. So he collected himself and cast back in his mind, a long time, in silence; and when at last he spoke he told the whole thing in order, from the first sight he had had of the Island down to his arrival among them.

Then Vertue was led away from John, and he himself was brought into a cell where there was a bed, and a table, and a pitcher of water. He lay on the bed, and it was hard, but not lumpy, and he was immediately in a deep sleep.

VII
Across the Canyon by Moonlight

IN THE MIDDLE of the night he opened his eyes and saw the full moon, very large and low, shining at his window: and beside his bed stood a woman darkly clothed, who held up her hand for silence when he would have spoken.

'My name is Contemplation,' she said, 'and I am one of the daughters of Wisdom. You must rise and follow me.'

Then John rose and followed her out of the house on to the grassy lawn in the moonlight. She led him across it to its westward edge where the mountain began to rise under its cloak of forest. But as they came right up to the eaves of the forest he saw that there was a crack or crevasse in the earth between them and it, to which he could find no bottom, and though it was not very wide, it was too wide to jump.

'It is too wide a jump by day,' said the lady, 'but in the moonlight you can jump it.'

John felt no doubt of her and gathered himself together and leaped. His leap carried him further than he had intended—though he felt no surprise—and he found himself flying over the tree tops and the steep fields, and he never alighted till he reached the mountain top; and the Lady was there by his side.

'Come,' she said, 'we have still far to go.'

Then they went on together over hills and dales, very fast, in the moonlight, till they came to the edge of a cliff, and he looked down and saw the sea below him: and out in the sea lay the Island. And because it was moonlight and night John could not see it so well as he had sometimes seen it, but either for that reason, or for some other, it seemed to him the more real.

'When you have learned to fly further, we can leap from here right into the Island,' said the Lady. 'But for this night, it is enough.'

As John turned to answer her, the Island and the sea and the Lady herself vanished, and he was awake, in daylight, in his cell in the house of Wisdom, and a bell was ringing.

VIII
This Side by Sunlight

ON THE NEXT DAY Mr. Wisdom caused John and Vertue both to sit by him in a porch of his house looking westward. The wind was in the South and the sky was a little clouded and over the western mountains there was a delicate mist, so that they had the air of being in another world, though they were not more than a mile away. And Mr. Wisdom instructed them.

'As to this Island in the West, and those eastern mountains, and as touching the Landlord also and the Enemy, there are two errors, my sons, which you must equally conquer, and pass right between them, before you can become wise. The first error is that of the southern people, and it consists in holding that these eastern and western places are real places—real as this valley is real, and places as this valley is a place. If any such thought lingers in your minds, I would have you root it out utterly, and give no quarter to that thought, whether it threatens you with fear, or tempts you with hopes. For this is Superstition, and all who believe it will come in the end to the swamps and the jungles of the far South, where they will live in the city of Magicians, transported with delight in things that help not, and haunted with terror of that which cannot hurt. And it is part of the same error to think that the Landlord is a real man: real as I am real, man as I am man. That is the first error. And the second is the opposite of it, and is chiefly current to the North of the road: it is the error of those who say that the eastern and western things are merely illusions in our own minds. This also it is my will that you should utterly reject: and you must be on your guard lest you ever embrace this error in your fear of the other, or run to and fro between the two as your hearts will prompt you to do, like some who will be Materialists (for that is the name of the second error) when the story of the black hole frightens them for their lawless living, or even when they are afraid of spectres, and then another day will believe in the Landlord and the castle because things in this country go hard with them, or because the lease of some dear friend is running out and they would gladly hope to meet him again. But the wise man, ruling his passions with reason and disciplined imagination, withdraws himself to the middle point between these two errors, having found that the truth lies there, and remains fixed immovably. But what that truth is you shall learn to-morrow; and for the present this sick man will be cared for, and you who are whole may do as you will.'

Then I saw Mr. Wisdom rise and leave them, and Vertue was taken to another place. John spent the most part of that day walking in the neighbourhood of the house. He crossed the level grass of the valley and came to its western edge where the mountain began to rise under its cloak of forest. But as he came under the forest eaves, he saw that between him and the first trees there was a crack or crevasse in the earth to which he could find no bottom. It was very narrow, but not quite narrow enough to jump. There seemed also to be some vapour rising from it which made the further side indistinct: but the vapour was not so thick nor the chasm so wide but that he could see here a spray of foliage and there a stone with deep moss, and in one place falling water that caught the sunlight. His desire to pass and to go on to the Island was sharp, but not to the degree of pain. Mr. Wisdom's words that the eastern and western things were neither wholly real nor wholly illusion, had spread over his mind a feeling of intent, yet quiet, comfort. Some fear was removed: the suspicion, never before wholly laid at rest, that his wanderings might lead him soon or late into the power of the Landlord, had passed away, and with it the gnawing anxiety lest the Island had never existed. The world seemed full of expectation, even as the misty veil between him and the forest seemed both to cover and discover sublimities that were without terror and beauties without sensuality; and every now and then a strengthening of the south wind would make a moment's clearness and show him, withdrawn in unexpected depth, remote reaches of the mountain valleys, desolate fields of flowers, the hint of snow beyond. He lay down in the grass. Presently one of the young men of the house passed that way and stopped to talk with him. They spoke of this and that, lazily, and at long intervals. Sometimes they discussed the regions further South where John had not been; sometimes, his own travels. The young man told him that if he had followed the road a few miles beyond the valley he would have come to a fork. The left hand turn would lead you, by a long way round, to the parts about Claptrap: the right went on to the southern forests, to the city of the Magicians and the country of Nycteris, 'and beyond that it is all swamp and sugar cane,' said he, 'and crocodiles and venomous spiders until the land sinks away altogether into the final salt swamp which becomes at last the southern ocean. There are no settlements there except a few lake-dwellers. Theosophists and whatnot, and it is very malarial.'

While they were speaking of the parts that John already knew, he asked his informant whether they in the House of Wisdom knew anything of the Grand Canyon or of the way down into it.

'Do you not know?' said the other, 'that we are in the bottom of the canyon here?' Then he made John sit up and showed him the lie of the land. The sides of the valley drew together northward, and at the same time grew more precipitous, so that at last they came together into a great V. 'And that V is the canyon, and you are looking into it end-ways from the southern end. The eastern face of the canyon is gentle and you were walking down into it all day yesterday, though you did not notice it.'

'So I am in the bottom of it already,' said John. 'And now there is nothing to prevent me from crossing it.'

The young man shook his head.

'There is no crossing it,' he said. 'When I told you we were now at the bottom, I meant the lowest point that can be reached by man. The real bottom is, of course, the bottom of this crevasse which we are sitting by: and that, of course—well, it would be a misunderstanding to talk of getting down it. There is no question of crossing or of getting to what you see over there.'

'Could it not be bridged?' said John.

'In a sense there is nothing to bridge—there is nowhere for this bridge to *arrive* at. You must not take literally the show of forest and mountain which we seem to see as we look across.'

'You don't mean that it is an illusion?'

'No. You will understand better when you have been longer with my father. It is not an illusion, it is an appearance. It is a true appearance, too, in a sense. You *must* see it as a mountain-side or the like—a continuation of the world we *do* know—and it does not mean that there is anything wrong with your eyes or any better way of seeing it to which you can attain. But don't think you can get there. Don't think there is any meaning in the idea of you (a man) going "there," as if it were really a place.'

'What? And the Island too! You would have me give up my heart's desire?'

'I would not. I would not have you cease to fix all your desires on the far side, for to wish to cross is simply to be a man, and to lose that wish is to be a beast. It is not desire that my father's doctrine kills: it is only hope.'

'And what is this valley called?'

'We call it now simply Wisdom's Valley: but the oldest maps mark it as the Valley of Humiliation.'

'The grass is quite wet,' said John, after a pause. 'The dew is beginning.'

'It is time that we went to supper,' said the young man.

IX
Wisdom—Exoteric

NEXT DAY, AS BEFORE, Wisdom had John and Vertue into the porch and continued to instruct them:

'You have heard what you are not to think of the eastern and western things, and now let us discover, as far as the imperfection of our faculty allows, what may rightly be thought. And first, consider this country in which we live. You see that it is full of roads, and no man remembers the making of these roads: neither have we any way to describe and order the land in our minds except by reference to them. You have seen how we determine the position of every other place by its relation to the main road: and though you may say that we have maps, you are to consider that the maps would be useless without the roads, for we find where we are on the map by the skeleton of roads which is common to it and to the country. We see that we have just passed such a turn to the right or the left, or that we are approaching such a bend in the road, and thus we know that we are near to some other place on the map which is not yet visible on the countryside. The people, indeed, say that the Landlord made these roads: and the Claptrapians say that we first made them on the map and have projected them, by some strange process, from it to the country. But I would have you hold fast to the truth, that we find them and do not make them: but also that no *man* could make them. For to make them he would need a bird's-eye view of the whole country, which he could have only from the sky. But no man could live in the sky. Again, this country is full of rules. The Claptrapians say that the Stewards made the rules. The servants of the giant say that we made them ourselves in order to restrain by them the lusts of our neighbours and to give a pompous colouring to our own. The people say that the Landlord made them.

'Let us consider these doctrines one by one. The Stewards made them? How then came they to be Stewards, and why did the rest of us consent to their rules? As soon as we ask this question, we are obliged to ask another. How comes it that those who have rejected the Stewards immediately set about making new rules of their own, and that these new rules are substantially the same as the old? A man says, "I have finished with rules: henceforth I will do what I want": but he finds that his deepest want, the only want that is constant through the flux of his appetites and despondencies, his moments of calm and of passion, is to keep the rules. Because these rules are a disguise for his desires, say the giant's following. But, I ask, what desires? Not any and every desire: the rules are frequently denials of these desires. The desire for self-approbation, shall we say? But why should we approve ourselves for keeping the rules unless we already thought that the rules were good? A man may find pleasure in supposing himself swifter or stronger than he really is, but only if he already loves speed or strength. The giant's doctrine thus destroys itself. If we wish to give a seemly colouring to our lusts we have already the idea of the seemly, and the seemly turns out to be nothing else than that which is according to the rules. The want to obey the rules is this presupposed in every doctrine which describes our obedience to them, or the rules themselves, as a self-flattery. Let us turn then to the old tale of the Landlord. Some mighty man beyond this country has made the rules. Suppose he has: then why do we obey them?'

Mr. Wisdom turned to Vertue and said, 'This part is of great concern to you and to your cure,' then he continued:

'There can be only two reasons. Either because we respect the power of the Landlord, and are moved by fear of the penalties and hopes of the rewards with which he sanctions the rules: or else, because we freely agree with the Landlord, because we also think good the things that he thinks good. But neither explanation will serve. If we obey through hope and fear, in that very act we disobey: for the rule which we reverence most, whether we find it in our own hearts or on the Steward's card, is that rule which says that a man must act disinterestedly. To obey the Landlord thus, would be to disobey. But what if we obey freely, because we agree with him? Alas, this is even worse. To say that we agree, and obey because we agree, is only to say again that we find the same rule written in our hearts and obey *that*. If the Landlord enjoins *that*, he enjoins only what we already purposed to do, and his voice is idle: if he enjoins anything else, his voice again is idle, for we shall disobey him. In either case the mystery of the rules remains unsolved, and the Landlord is a meaningless addition to the problem. If he spoke, the rules were there before he spoke. If we and he agree about them, where is the common original which he and we both copy: what is the thing about which his doctrine and ours are both true?

'Of the rules, then as of the roads, we must say that indeed we find them and do not make them, but that it helps us not at all to assume a Landlord for their maker. And there is a third thing also' (here he looked to John) 'which specially concerns you. What of the Island in the West? The people in our age have all but forgotten it. The giant would say that it is, again, a delusion in your own mind trumped up to conceal lust. Of the Stewards, some do not know that there is such a thing: some agree with the giant, denouncing your Island as wickedness: some say that it is a blurred and confused sight from far off of the Landlord's castle. They have no common doctrine: but let us consider the question for ourselves.

'And first I would have you set aside all suspicion that the giant is right: and this will be the easier for you because you have already talked with Reason. They say it is there to conceal lust. But it does not conceal lust. If it is a screen, it is a very bad screen. The giant would make the dark part of our mind so strong and subtle that we never escape from its deceptions: and yet when this omnipotent conjuror has done all that he can, he produces an illusion which a solitary boy, in the fancies of his adolescence, can expose and see through in two years. This is but wild talk. There is no man and no nation at all capable of seeing the Island, who have not learned by experience, and that soon, how easily the vision ends in lust: and there is none also, not corrupted, who has not felt the disappointment of that ending, who has not known that it is the breaking of the vision not its consummation. The words between you and Reason were true. What does not satisfy when we find it, was not the thing we were desiring. If water will not set a man at ease, then be sure it was not thirst, or not thirst only, that tormented him: he wanted drunkenness to cure his dullness, or talk to cure his solitude, or the like. How, indeed, do we know our desires save by their satisfaction? When do we know them until we say, "Ah, *this* was what I wanted"? And if there were any desire which it was natural for man to feel but impossible for man to satisfy, would not the nature of this desire remain to him always ambiguous? If old tales were true, if a man without putting off humanity could indeed pass the frontiers of our country, if he could be, and yet be a man, in that fabled East and fabled West, then indeed at the moment of fruition, the raising of the cup, the assumption of the crown, the kiss of the spouse— then first, to his backward glance, the long roads of desire that he had trodden would become plain in all their winding, and when he found, he would know what it was that he had sought. I am old and full of tears, and I see that you also begin to feel the sorrow that is born with us. Abandon hope: do not abandon desire. Feel no wonder that these glimpses of your Island so easily confuse themselves with viler things, and are so easily blasphemed. Above all, never try to keep them, never try to revisit the same place or time wherein the vision was accorded to you. You will pay the penalty of all who would bind down to one place or time within our country that which our country cannot contain. Have you not heard from the Stewards of the sin of idolatry, and how, in their old chronicles, the manna turned to worms if any tried to hoard it? Be not greedy, be not passionate; you will but crush dead on your own breast with hot, rough hands the thing you loved. But if ever you incline to doubt that the thing you long for is something real, remember what your own experience has taught you. Think that it is a *feeling* and at once the feeling has no value. Stand sentinel at your own mind, watching for that feeling, and you will find—what shall I say?—a flutter in the heart, an image in the head, a sob in the throat: and was *that* your desire? You know that it was not, and that no feeling whatever will appease you, that *feeling*, refine it as you will, is but one more spurious claimant—spurious as the gross lusts of which the giant speaks. Let us conclude then that what you desire is no state of yourself at all, but something, for that very reason, Other and Outer. And knowing this you will find tolerable the truth that you cannot attain it. That the thing should *be,* is so great a good that when you remember "it is" you will forget to be sorry that you can never have it. Nay, anything that you could have would be so much less than this that its fruition would be immeasurably below the mere hunger for this. Wanting is better than having. The glory of any world wherein you can live is in the end appearance: but then, as one of my sons has said, that leaves the world more glorious yet.'

X
Wisdom—Esoteric

THAT DAY JOHN SPENT as he had spent the other, wandering and often sleeping in the fields. In this valley the year came on with seven-leagued boots. To-day the riverside was thick with fritillaries, the kingfisher flew, the dragon-flies darted, and when he sat it was in the shade. A pleasing melancholy rested upon him, and a great indolence. He talked that day with many of the people of the house, and when he went that night to his cell his mind was full of their resigned voices, and of their faces, so quiet and yet so alert, as though they waited in hourly expectation of something that would never happen. When next he opened his eyes moonlight filled his cell; and as he lay waking heard a low whistle from without his window. He put out his head. A dark figure stood in the shadow of the house. 'Come out and play,' said he. At the same time there came a sound of suppressed laughter from an angle of deeper shadow beyond the speaker.

'This window is too high for me to jump from,' said John.

'You forget that it is by moonlight,' said the other, and held up his hands.

'Jump!' he said.

John cast some clothes about him and bounded from the window. To his surprise, he reached the ground with no hurt or shock, and a moment later he found himself progressing over the lawn in a series of great leaps amidst a laughing crowd of the sons and daughters of the house: so that the valley in the moonlight, if any had watched, would have looked like nothing so much as a great salver which had been made into the arena for a troupe of performing fleas. Their dance or race, led them to the dark border of a neighbouring wood and as John tumbled down breathless at the foot of a hawthorn, he heard with surprise all around him the sounds of silver and glass, of hampers opening, and bottles uncorking.

'My father's ideas of feeding are a little strict,' explained his host, 'and we younger ones have found it necessary to supplement the household meals a bit.'

'Here is champagne, from Mr. Halfways,' said one.

'Cold chicken and tongue from Mr. Mammon. What *should* we do without our friends?'

'Hashish from the south. Nycteris sent it up herself.'

'This claret,' said a girl beside him rather shyly, 'is from Mother Kirk.'   .

'I don't think we ought to drink that,' said another voice, 'that is really going a bit too far.'

'No further than your caviare from the Theosophists,' said the first girl, 'and anyway, I need it. It is only this that keeps me alive.'

'Try some of my brandy,' said another voice. 'All made by Savage's dwarfs.'

'I don't know how you can drink that stuff, Karl.[1] Plain, honest food from Claptrap is what you need.'

'So *you* say, Herbert,'[2] retorted a new speaker. 'But some of us find it rather heavy. For me, a morsel of lamb from the Shepherd's Country and a little mint sauce— that is really all you need to add to our Father's table.'

'We all know what you like, Benedict,'[3] said several.

'I have finished,' announced Karl, 'and now for a night with the dwarfs. Anyone come with me?'

'Not there,' cried another. 'I'm going South to-night to the magicians.'

'You had much better not, Rudolph,'[4] said someone. 'A few quiet hours in Puritania with me would be much better for you—much better.'

'Chuck it, Immanuel,'[5] said another. 'You might as well go to Mother Kirk straight away.'

'Bernard[6] does,' said the girl, who had contributed the claret.

By this time the party was rapidly decreasing, for most of the young people, after trying in vain to win converts to their several schemes of pleasure, had bounded off alone, plunging from treetop to treetop, and soon even the thin silvery sound of their laughter had died away. Those who were left swarmed round John soliciting his attention now for this, now for that, amusement. Some sat down beyond

1. Marx   2. Spencer   3. Spinoza   4. Steiner   5. Kant   6. Bosanquet

the shadow of the wood to work out puzzles in the light of the moon: others settled
to serious leap-frog: the more frivolous ran to and fro chasing the moths, wrestling
with and tickling one another, giggling and making giggle, till the wood rang with
their shrill squeals of glee. It seemed to go on for a long time and if there was any
more in that dream John did not remember it when he woke.

XI
Mum's the Word

AT BREAKFAST ON THE following morning John stole many furtive glances
at the sons and daughters of Wisdom, but he could see no sign that they were conscious of having met him in such different guise during the night. Indeed, neither
then, nor at any other time during his stay in the valley, did he find evidence that
they were aware of their nocturnal holidays: and a few tentative questions assured
him that, unless they were liars, they all believed themselves to be living exclusively on the spare diet of the house. Immanuel indeed admitted, as a speculative
truth, that there were such things as dreams, and that he conceivably dreamed
himself: but then he had a complex proof (which John never quite grasped) that no
one could possibly remember a dream: and though his appearance and constitu-
tion were those of a prize-fighter he attributed this all to the excellent quality of
the local fruit. Herbert was a lumpish sort of man who never could muster any
appetite for his meals: but John discovered that Herbert put this down to his liver
and had no notion that he had been stuffing himself with Claptrapian steak and
gravy all night as hard as he could. Another of the family, Bernard by name, was
in radiant health. John had seen him drinking Mother Kirk's wine with great relish
and refreshment by moonlight: but the waking Bernard maintained that Mother
Kirk's wine was merely a bad, early attempt at the admirable barley-water which
his father sometimes brought out on birthdays and great occasions; and 'to this
barley-water,' he said, 'I owe my health. It has made me what I am.' Still less could
John discover, by all the traps that he laid for them, whether the younger members
of the household had any recollection of their nightly leap-frog and other gambols.
He was forced at last to conclude that either the whole thing had been a private
dream of his own or else the secret was very well kept. A little irritation which some
displayed when he questioned them, seemed to favour the second hypothesis.

XII
More Wisdom

WHEN THEY WERE SEATED in the porch, Wisdom continued his discourse.

'You have learned that there are these three things, the Island, the Roads, and the Rules: that they are certainly in some way real and that we have not made them; and further that it does not help us to invent a Landlord. Nor is it possible that there should really be a castle at one end of the world and an island at the other: for the world is round and we are everywhere at the end of the world, since the end of a sphere is its surface. The world is *all* end: but we can never pass beyond that end. And yet these things which our imagination impossibly places as a world beyond the world's end are, we have seen, in some sense real.

'You have told me how Reason refuted the lies of the giant by asking what was the colour of things in dark places. You learned from her that there is no colour without seeing, no hardness without touching: no *body* to say all, save in the minds of those who perceive it. It follows, then, that all this choir of heaven and furniture of earth are imaginations: not your imaginations nor mine, for here we have met in the same world, which could not be if the world was shut up within my mind or yours. Without doubt, then, all this show of sky and earth floats within some mighty imagination. If you ask Whose, again the Landlord will not help you. He is man: make him as great as you will, he still is other than we and his imagining inaccessible to us, as yours would be to me. Rather we must say that the world is not in this mind, or in that, but in Mind itself, in that impersonal principle of consciousness which flows eternally through us, its perishable forms.

'You see how this explains all the questions that have lain on our knees since we began. We find the roads, the reasonable skeleton in the countryside, the guiding-lines that enable us both to make maps and to use them when we have made, because our country is the off-spring of the rational. Consider also the Island. All that you know of it comes at last to this: that your first sight of it was yearning or wanting and that you have never ceased to want that first sight back, as though you wanted a wanting, as though the wanting were the having, and the having a wanting. What is the meaning of this hungry fruition and this emptiness which is the best filling? Surely, it becomes plain when you have learned that no man says "I" in an unambiguous sense. I am an old man who must soon go over the brook and be seen no more: I am eternal Mind in which time and place themselves are contained. I am the Imaginer: I am one of his imaginations. The Island is nothing else than that perfection and immortality which I possess as Spirit eternal, and vainly crave as mortal soul. Its voices sound at my very ear and are further than the stars; it is under my hand and will never be mine: I have it and lo! the very having is the losing:

because at every moment I, as Spirit, am indeed abandoning my rich estate to become that perishing and imperfect creature in whose repeated deaths and births stands my eternity. And I as man in every moment still enjoy the perfection I have lost, since still, so far as I am at all, I am Spirit, and only by being Spirit maintain my short vitality as soul. See how life subsists by death and each becomes the other: for Spirit lives by dying perpetually into such things as we, and we also attain our truest life by dying to our mortal nature and relapsing, as far as may be, into the impersonality of our source: for this is the final meaning of all moral precepts, and the goodness of temperance and justice and of love itself is that they plunge the red heat of our separate and individual passions back in the ice brook of the Spirit, there to take eternal temper, though not endless duration.

'What I tell you is the *evangelium eternum*. This has been known always: ancients and moderns bear witness to it. The stories of the Landlord in our own time are but a picture-writing which show to the people as much of the truth as they can understand. Stewards must have told you—though it seems that you neither heeded nor understood them—the legend of the Landlord's Son. They say that after the eating of the mountain-apple and the earthquake, when things in our country had gone all awry, the Landlord's Son himself became one of his Father's tenants and lived among us, for no other purpose than that he should be killed. The Stewards themselves do not know clearly the meaning of their story: hence, if you ask them how the slaying of the Son should help us, they are driven to monstrous answers. But to us the meaning is clear and the story is beautiful. It is a picture of the life of Spirit itself. What the Son is in the legend, every man is in reality: for the whole world is nothing else than the Eternal thus giving itself to death that it may live— that we may live. Death is life's mode, and the increase of life is through repeated death.

'And what of the rules? You have seen that it is idle to make them the arbitrary commands of a Landlord: yet those who do so were not altogether astray, for it is equally an error to think that they are each man's personal choice. Remember what we have said of the Island. Because I am and am not Spirit, therefore I have and have not my desire. The same double nature of the word "I," explain the rules. I am the lawgiver: but I am also the subject. I, the Spirit, impose upon the soul which I become, the laws she must henceforth obey: and every conflict between the rules and our inclinations is but a conflict of the wishes of my mortal and apparent self against those of my real and eternal. "I ought but I do not wish"—how meaning- less the words are, how close to saying, "I want and I do not want." But once we have learned to say "I, and yet not I, want," the mystery is plain.

'And now your sick friend is almost whole, and it is nearly noon.'

Book Eight
AT BAY

He that hath understanding in himself is best;
He that lays up his brother's wisdom in his breast
Is good, But he that neither knoweth, nor will be taught
By the instruction of the wise—this man is naught.
Hesiod

Persons without education certainly do not want either acuteness or
strength of mind in what concerns themselves, or in things immediately
within their observation; but they have no power of abstraction—they
see their objects always near, never in the horizon.
Hazlitt

I
Two Kinds of Monist

THAT AFTERNOON AS John was walking in the water meadow he saw a man coming towards him who walked blunderingly like one whose legs were not his own. And as the man came nearer he saw that it was Vertue, with his face very pale.

'What,' cried John, 'are you cured? Can you see? Can you speak?'

'Yes,' said Vertue in a weak voice, 'I suppose I can see.' And he leaned heavily on a stile and breathed hard.

'You have walked too far,' said John. 'Are you ill?'

'I am still weak. It is nothing. I shall get my breath in a moment.'

'Sit down by me,' said John. 'And when you have rested we will go gently back to the house.'

'I am not going back to the house.'

'Not going back? You are not fit to travel—and where are you going?'

'I am not fit for anything, apparently,' said Vertue. 'But I must go on.'

'Go on where? You are not still hoping to cross the canyon? Do you not believe what Wisdom has told us?'

'I do. That is why I am going on.'

'Sit down at least for a moment,' said John, 'and explain yourself.'

'It is plain enough!'

'It isn't plain at all.'

Vertue spoke impatiently.

'Did you not hear what Wisdom said about the rules?' he asked.

'Of course I did,' said John.

'Well, then, he has given me back the rules. *That* puzzle is solved. The rules have to be obeyed, as I always thought. I know that now better than I have ever known it before.'

'Well?'

'And didn't you see what all the rest came to? The rules are from this Spirit or whatever he calls it, which is somehow also me. And any disinclination to obey the rules is the other part of me—the mortal part. Does it not follow from that, and from everything else he said, that the real disobedience to the rules begins with being in this country at all? This country is simply *not* the Island, *not* the rules: that is its definition. My mortal self—that is, for all practical purposes, myself—can be defined only as the part of me that is against the rules. Just as the Spirit answers to the Landlord, so this whole world answers to the black hole.'

'I take it all exactly the other way,' said John. 'Rather this world corresponds to the Landlord's castle. Everything is this Spirit's imagination, and therefore everything, properly understood, is good and happy. That the glory of this world in the end is appearance, leaves the world more glorious yet. I quite agree that the rules—the authority of the rules—becomes stronger than ever: but their content must be—well, easier. Perhaps I should say richer—more concrete.'

'Their content must become harsher. If the real good is simply "what is not here" and *here* means simply "the place where the good is not," what can the real rule be except to live here as little as possible, to commit ourselves as little as we can to the system of this world? I used to talk of innocent pleasures, fool that I was—as if anything could be innocent for us whose mere existence is a fall—as if all that a man eats or drinks or begets were not propagated curse.'

'Really, Virtue, this is a very strange view. The effect of Mr. Wisdom's lessons on me has been just the opposite. I have been thinking how much of the Puritanian virus there must still be in me, to have held me back so long from the blameless generosity of Nature's breasts. Is not the meanest thing, in its degree, a mirror of the One; the lightest or the wildest pleasure as necessary to the perfection of the whole as the most heroic sacrifice? I am assured that in the Absolute, every flame even of carnal passion burns on—'

'Can even eating, even the coarsest food and the barest pittance, be justified? The flesh is but a living corruption—'

'There was a great deal to be said for Media after all—'

'I see that Savage was wiser than he knew—'

'It is true she had a dark complexion. And yet—is not brown as necessary to the spectrum as any other colour?'

'Is not every colour equally a corruption of the white radiance?'

'What we call evil—our greatest wickednesses—seen in the true setting is an element in the good. I am the doubter and the doubt.'

'What we call our righteousness is filthy rags. You are a fool, John, and I am going. I am going up into the rocks till I find where the wind is coldest and the ground hardest and the life of man furthest away. My notice to quit has not yet come, and I must be stained a while longer with the dye of our country. I shall still be part of that dark cloud which offends the white light: but I shall make that part of the cloud which is called Me as thin, as nearly not a cloud, as I can. Body and mind shall pay for the crime of their existence. If there is any fasting, or watching, any mutilation or self-torture more harsh to nature than another, I shall find it out.'

'Are you mad?' said John.

'I have just become sane,' said Virtue. 'Why are you staring at me thus? I know I am pale and my pulse beats like a hammer. So much the saner! Disease is better than health and sees clearer, for it is one degree nearer to the Spirit, one degree less involved in the riot of our animal existence. But it will need stronger pains than this to kill the obscene thirst for life which I drank in with my mother's milk.'

'Why should we leave this pleasant valley?' John began, but Virtue cut him short.

'Who spoke of We? Do you think that I asked or expected *you* to accompany me? *You* to sleep on thorns and eat sloes?'

'You don't mean that we are to part?' said John.

'Pah!' said Virtue. 'You could not do the things I intend to do: and if you could, I would have none of you. Friendship—affection—what are these but the subtlest chains that tie us to our present country? He would be a fool indeed who mortified the body and left the mind free to be happy and thus still to affirm—to wallow in— her finite will. It is not this pleasure or that, but *all* that are to be cut off. No knife will cut deep enough to end the cancer. But I'll cut as deep as I can.'

He rose, still swaying, and continued his way over the meadow northward. He held his hand to his side as though he was in pain. Once or twice he nearly fell.

'What are you following me for?' he shouted to John. 'Go back.'

John stopped for a moment, checked by the hatred in his friend's face. Then, tentatively, he went on again. He thought that Vertue's illness had harmed his brain and had some indistinct hope that he might find means to humour him and bring him back. Before they had gone many paces, however, Vertue turned again and lifted a stone in his hand. 'Be off,' he said, 'or I'll throw it. We have nothing to do with one another, you and I. My own body and my own soul are enemies, and do you think I will spare *you*?'

John halted, undetermined, and then ducked, for the other had hurled the stone. I saw them go on like this for some way, John following at a distance, and stopping, and then continuing again, while Vertue every now and then stoned him and reviled him. But at last the distance between them was too great either for voice or stone to carry.

II
John Led

AS THEY WENT ON thus John saw that the valley narrowed and the sides of it grew steeper. At the same time, the crevasse on his left hand which separated him from the western forest, became wider and wider: so that, what with that, and with the narrowing of the valley as a whole, the level piece where they were travelling was constantly diminished. Soon it was no longer the floor of the valley but only a ledge on its eastern side: and the crevasse revealed itself as being not a slot in the floor but the very floor. John saw that he was, in fact, walking on a shelf half-way down one side of the Grand Canyon. The cliff towered above him.

Presently a kind of spur or root of rock came out from the cliff and barred their way—crossing the ledge with a ruin of granite. And as Vertue began to scramble about the bases of this ascent, trying this grip and that to go up. John gained on him and came again within ear-shot. Before he came to the foot of the crags, however, Vertue had begun to climb. John heard his gasping as he struggled from hold to hold. Once he slipped back and left a little trail of blood where the rock skinned his ankle: but he went on again, and soon John saw him stand up, shaking and wiping the sweat out of his eyes, apparently at the top. He looked down and made gestures threateningly, and shouted, but he was too far for John to hear his words. Next moment John leaped aside to save his limbs, for Vertue had sent a great boulder rolling down: and as its thunder ceased echoing in the gorge and John looked up again, Vertue had gone over the spur out of sight and he saw no more of him.

John sat down in the desolate place. The grass here was finer and shorter, such grass as sheep love, which grows in the quiet intervals between the rocks. The windings of the gorge had already shut off the sight of Wisdom's Valley: yet I saw that John had no thought save of going back. There was indeed a confusion of shame and sorrow and bewilderment in his mind, but he put it all aside and held fast to his fear of the rocks and of meeting Vertue, now mad, in some narrow place whence he could not retreat. He thought, 'I will sit here and rest, till I get my wind, and then I will go back. I must live out the rest of my life as best I can.' Then suddenly he heard himself hailed from above. A Man was descending where Vertue had gone up.

'Hi!' shouted the Man. 'Your friend has gone on. Surely you will follow him?'

'He is mad, sir,' said John.

'No madder than you, and no saner,' said the Man. 'You will both recover if only you will keep together.'

'I cannot get up the rocks,' said John.

'I will give you a hand,' said the Man. And he came down till he was within reach of John, and held out his hand. And John grew pale as paper and nausea came upon him.

'It's now or never,' said the Man.

Then John set his teeth and took the hand that was offered him. He trembled at the very first grip he was made to take but he could not go back for they were speedily so high that he dared not attempt the return alone: and what with pushing and pulling the Man got him right up to the top and there he fell down on his belly in the grass to pant and to groan at the pains in his chest. When he sat up the Man was gone.

III
John Forgets Himself

JOHN LOOKED BACK AND turned away with a shudder. All thought of descending again must be put aside at once and for ever. 'That fellow has left me in a nice fix,' he said bitterly. Next, he looked ahead. The cliffs still rose high above him and dropped far below him: but there was a ledge on a level with him, a narrow ledge, ten feet broad at its best and two at its worst, winding away along the cliff till it became but a green thread. His heart failed him. Then he tried to recall the lessons of Mr. Wisdom, whether they would give him any strength. 'It is only myself,' he said. 'It is I myself, eternal Spirit, who drives this Me, the slave, along that ledge. I ought not to care whether he falls and breaks his neck or not. It is not he that is real, it is I—I—I. Can I remember that?' But then he felt so different from the eternal Spirit that he could call it 'I' no longer. 'It is all very well for *him*,' said John, 'but why does he give me no help? I want help. Help.' Then he gazed up at the cliffs and the narrow sky, blue and remote, between them, and he thought of that universal mind and of the shining tranquillity hidden somewhere behind the colours and the shapes, the pregnant silence under all the sounds, and he thought, 'If one drop of all that ocean would flow into me now—if I, the mortal, could but realize that I *am* that, all would be well. I know there is something there. I know the sensuous curtain is not a cheat.' In the bitterness of his soul he looked up again, saying: 'Help. Help. I want Help.'

But as soon as the words were out of his mouth, a new fear, far deeper than his fear of the cliffs, sprang at him from the hiding-place, close to the surface, where it had lain against this moment. As a man in a dream talks without fear to his dead friend, and only afterwards bethinks himself, 'It was a ghost! I have talked with a ghost!' and wakes screaming: even so John sprang up as he saw what he had done.

'I have been *praying*,' he said. 'It is the Landlord under a new name. It is the rules and the black hole and the slavery dressed out in a new fashion to catch me. And I am caught. Who would have thought the old spider's web was so subtle?'

But this was insupportable to him and he said that he had only fallen into a metaphor. Even Mr. Wisdom had confessed that Mother Kirk and the Stewards gave an account of the truth in picture writing. And one must use metaphors. The feelings and the imagination needed that support. 'The great thing,' said John, 'is to keep the intellect free from them: to remember that they *are* metaphors.'

IV
John Finds His Voice

HE WAS MUCH COMFORTED by this idea of metaphor, and as he was now also rested, he began his journey along the cliff path with some degree of timid resolution. But it was very dreadful to him in the narrower places: and his courage seemed to him to decrease rather than to grow as he proceeded. Indeed he soon found that he could go forward at all only by remembering Mr. Wisdom's Absolute incessantly. It was necessary by repeated efforts of the will to turn thither, consciously to draw from that endless reservoir the little share of vitality that he needed for the next narrow place. He knew now that he was praying, but he thought that he had drawn the fangs of that knowledge. 'In a sense,' he said, 'Spirit is not I.

I am it, but I am not the whole of it. When I turn back to that part of it which is not I—that far greater part which my soul does not exhaust—surely that part is to me an Other. It must become, for my imagination, not really "I" but "Thou." A metaphor—perhaps more than a metaphor. Of course there is no need at all to confuse it with the *mythical* Landlord. . . . However I think of it, I think of it inadequately.'

Then a new thing happened to John, and he began to sing: and this is as much of his song as I remember from my dream:

> He whom I bow to only knows to whom I bow
> When I attempt the ineffable name, murmuring *Thou*;
> And dream of Pheidian fancies and embrace in heart
> Meanings, I know, that cannot be the thing thou art.
> All prayers always, taken at their word, blaspheme,
> Invoking with frail imageries a folk-lore dream;
> And all men are idolaters, crying unheard
> To senseless idols, if thou take them at their word,
> And all men in their praying, self-deceived, address
> One that is not (so saith that old rebuke) unless
> Thou, of mere grace, appropriate, and to thee divert
> Men's arrows, all at hazard aimed, beyond desert.
> Take not, oh Lord, our literal sense, but in thy great,
> Unbroken speech our halting metaphor translate.

When he came to think over the words that had gone out of him he began once more to be afraid of them. Day was declining and in the narrow chasm it was already almost dark.

V

Food at a Cost

FOR A WHILE HE went on cautiously, but he was haunted by a picture in his mind of a place where the path would break off short when it was too dark for him to see, and he would step on air. This fear made him halt more and more frequently to examine his ground: and when he went on it was each time more slowly: till at last he came to a standstill. There seemed to be nothing for it but to rest where he was. The night was warm, but he was both hungry and thirsty. And he sat down. It was quite dark now.

Then I dreamed that once more a Man came to him in the darkness and said, 'You must pass the night where you are, but I have brought you a loaf and if you crawl along the ledge ten paces more you will find that a little fall of water comes down the cliff.'

'Sir,' said John. 'I do not know your name and I cannot see your face, but I thank you. Will you not sit down and eat, yourself?'

'I am full and not hungry,' said the Man. 'And I will pass on. But one word before I go. You cannot have it both ways.'

'What do you mean, sir?'

'Your life has been saved all this day by crying out to something which you call by many names, and you have said to yourself that you used metaphors.'

'Was I wrong, sir?'

'Perhaps not. But you must play fair. If its help is not a metaphor, neither are its commands. If it can answer when you call, then it can speak without your asking. If you can go to it, it can come to you.'

'I think I see, sir. You mean that I am not my own man: in some sense I have a Landlord after all?'

'Even so. But what is it that dismays you? You heard from Wisdom how the rules were yours and not yours. Did you not mean to keep them? And if so, can it scare you to know that there is one who will make you able to keep them?'

'Well,' said John, 'I suppose you have found me out. Perhaps I did not fully mean to keep them—not all—or not all the time. And yet, in a way, I think I did. It is like a thorn in your finger, sir. You know when you set about taking it out yourself— you mean to get it out—you know it will hurt—and it does hurt—but somehow it is not very serious business—well, I suppose, because you feel that you always *could* stop if it was very bad. Not that you intend to stop. But it is a very different thing to hold your hand out to a surgeon to be hurt as much as *he* thinks fit. And at *his* speed.'

The Man laughed. 'I see you understand me very well,' He said, 'but the great thing is to get the thorn out.' And then He went away.

VI
Caught

JOHN HAD NO DIFFICULTY in finding the stream and when he had drunk he sat by it and ate. The bread had a rather flat taste which was somehow familiar and not very agreeable, but he was in no position to be dainty. Extreme weariness prevented him from thinking much of the conversation that had just passed. At the bottom of John's heart the stranger's words lay like a cold weight that he must some day take up and carry: but his mind was full of the pictures of cliff and chasm, of wondering about Vertue, and of smaller fears for the morrow and the moment, and, above all, the blessedness of food and of sitting still; and all these jumbled themselves together in an even dimmer confusion till at last he could no longer remember which he had been thinking of the moment before: and then he knew that he was sleeping: and at last he was in deep sleep and knew nothing.

In the morning it was not so. Jump with his first waking thought the full-grown horror leaped upon him. The blue sky above the cliffs was watching him: the cliffs themselves were imprisoning him: the rocks behind were cutting off his retreat: the path ahead was ordering him on. In one night the Landlord—call him by what name you would—had come back to the world, and filled the world, quite full without a cranny. His eyes stared and His hand pointed and His voice commanded in everything that could be heard or seen, even from this place where John sat, to the end of the world: and if you passed the end of the world He would be there too. All things were indeed one—more truly than Mr. Wisdom dreamed—and all things said one word: CAUGHT—Caught into slavery again, to walk warily and on sufferance all his days, never to be alone; never the master of his own soul, to have no privacy, no corner whereof you could say to the whole universe: This is my own, here I can do as I please. Under that universal and inspecting gaze, John cowered like some small animal caught up in a giant's hands and held beneath a magnifying-glass.

When he had drunk and splashed his face in the stream he continued his way, and presently he made this song.

> You rest upon me all my days
> The inevitable Eye,
> Dreadful and undeflected as the blaze
> Of some Arabian sky;
>
> Where, dead still, in their smothering tent
> Pale travellers crouch, and, bright
> About them, noon's long-drawn Astonishment
> Hammers the rocks with light.
>
> Oh, for but one cool breath in seven,
> One air from northern climes,
> The changing and the castle-clouded heaven
> Of my old Pagan times!
>
> But you have seized all in your rage
> Of Oneness. Round about,
> Beating my wings, all ways, within your cage,
> I flutter, but not out.

And as he walked on, all day, in the strength of the bread he had eaten, not daring often to look down into the gulf and keeping his head mostly turned a little inward to the cliff, he had time to turn his trouble over in his mind and discover new sides to it. Above all it grew upon him that the return of the Landlord had blotted out the Island: for if there still were such a place he was no longer free to spend his soul in seeking it, but must follow whatever designs the Landlord had for him. And at the very best it now seemed that the last of things was at least more like a person than a place, so that the deepest thirst within him was not adapted to the deepest nature of the world. But sometimes he comforted himself by saying that this new and real Landlord must yet be very different from him whom the Stewards proclaimed and indeed from all images that men could make of him. There might still hang about him some of that promising darkness which had covered the Absolute.

VII
The Hermit

PRESENTLY HE HEARD a bell struck, and he looked and saw a little chapel in a cave of the cliff beside him; and there sat a hermit whose name was History, so old and thin that his hands were transparent and John thought that a little wind would have blown him away.

'Turn in, my son,' said the hermit, 'and eat bread and then you shall go on your journey.' John was glad to hear the voice of a man among the rocks and he turned in and sat. The hermit gave him bread and water but he himself ate no bread and drank a little wine.

'Where are you going, son?' he said.

'It seems to me, Father, that I am going where I do not wish; for I set out to find an Island and I have found a Landlord instead.'

And the hermit sat looking at him, nodding almost imperceptibly with the tremors of age.

'The Clevers were right and the pale men were right,' said John, thinking aloud, 'since the world holds no allaying for the thirst I was born with, and seemingly the Island was an illusion after all. But I forget, Father, that you will not know these people.'

'I know all parts of this country,' said the hermit, 'and the genius of places. Where do these people live?'

'To the North of the road. The Clevers are in the country of Mammon, where a stone giant is the lord of the soil, and the pale men are on the Tableland of the Tough-Minded.'

'I have been in these countries a thousand times, for in my young days I was a pedlar and there is no land I have not been in. But tell me, do they still keep their old customs?'

'What customs were those?'

'Why, they all sprang from the ownership of the land there, for more than half of the country North of the road is now held by the Enemy's tenants. Eastward it was the giant, and under him Mammon and some others. But westward, on the Tableland, it was two daughters of the Enemy—let me see—yes, Ignorantia and Superbia. They always did impose strange customs on the smaller tenants. I remember many tenants there—Stoics and Manichees, Sparitates, and all sorts. One time they had a notion to eat better bread than is made of wheat. Another time their very nurses took up a strange ritual of always emptying the baby out along with the bath. Then once the Enemy sent a fox without a tail among them and it persuaded them that all animals should be without tails and they docked all their dogs and horses and cows. I remember they were very puzzled how to apply any corresponding treatment to themselves, until at last a wise man suggested that they could cut off their noses. But the strangest custom of all was one that they practised all the time through all their other changes of customs. It was this—that they never set anything to rights but destroyed it instead. When a dish was dirty they did not wash it, they broke it; and when their clothes were dirty they burned them.'

'It must have been a very expensive custom.'

'It was ruinous, and it meant, of course, that they were constantly importing new clothes and new crockery. But indeed they had to import everything for this is the difficulty of the Tableland. It never has been able to support life and it never will. Its inhabitants have always lived on their neighbours.'

'They must always have been very rich men.'

'They always *were* very rich men. I don't think I remember a single case of a poor or a common person going there. When humble people go wrong they generally go South. The Tough-Minded nearly always go to the Tableland as colonists from Mammon's country. I would guess that your pale men are reformed Clevers.'

'In a kind of way I believe they are. But can you tell me, Father, why these Tough-Minded people behave so oddly?'

'Well, for one thing, they *know* very little. They never travel and consequently never learn anything. They really do not know that there are any places outside Mammon's country and their own Tableland—except that they have heard exaggerated rumours about the Southern swamps, and suppose that everything is swamp a few miles South of themselves. Thus, their disgust with bread came about through sheer ignorance. At home in Mammon's country they knew only the standard bread that Mammon makes, and a few sweet, sticky cakes which Mammon imported from the South—the only kind of Southern product that Mammon would be likely to let in. As they did not like either of these, they invented a biscuit of their own. It never occurred to them to walk a mile off the Tableland into the nearest cottage and try what an honest loaf tasted like. The same with the babies. They disliked babies because babies meant to them the various deformities spawned in the brothels of Mammon: again, a moderate walk would have shown them healthy children at play in the lanes. As for their poor noses—on the Tableland there is nothing to smell, good, bad, or indifferent, and in Mammon's land whatever does not reek of scent reeks of ordure. So they saw no good in noses, though five miles away from them the hay was being cut.'

'And what about the Island, Father?' said John. 'Were they equally wrong about that?'

'That is a longer story, my son. But I see it is beginning to rain, so perhaps you may as well hear it.'

John went to the mouth of the cave and looked out. The sky had grown dark while they talked and a warm rain, blotting out the cliffs like a steam, was descending as far as his eye could reach.

VIII
History's Words

WHEN JOHN HAD RETURNED and seated himself, the hermit resumed:

'You may be sure that they make the same mistake about the Island that they make about everything else. But what is the current lie at present?'

'They say it is all a device of Mr. Halfways—who is in the pay of the Brown Girls.'

'Poor Halfways! They treat him very unfairly—as if he were anything more than the local representative of a thing as widespread and as necessary (though, withal, as dangerous) as the sky! Not a bad representative, either, if you take his songs in your stride and use them as they are meant to be used: of course people who go to him in cold blood to get as much *pleasure* as they can, and therefore hear the same song over and over again, have only themselves to thank if they wake in the arms of Media.'

'That is very true, Father. But they wouldn't believe that I had seen and longed for the Island before I met Mr. Halfways—before I ever heard a song at all. They insist on treating it as his invention.'

'That is always the way with stay-at-homes. If they like something in their own village they take it for a thing universal and eternal, though perhaps it was never heard of five miles away; if they dislike something, they say it is a local, backward, provincial convention, though, in fact, it may be the law of nations.'

'Then it is really true that all men, all nations, have had this vision of an Island?'

'It does not always come in the form of an Island: and to some men, if they inherit particular diseases, it may not come at all.'

'But what *is* it, Father? And has it anything to do with the Landlord? I do not know how to fit things together.'

'It comes from the Landlord. We know this by its results. It has brought you to where you now are: and nothing leads back to him which did not at first proceed from him.'

'But the Stewards would say that it was the Rules which come from him.'

'Not all Stewards are equally travelled men. But those who are, know perfectly well that the Landlord has circulated other things besides the Rules. What use are Rules to people who cannot read?'

'But nearly everyone can.'

'No one is born able to read: so that the starting point for all of us must be a picture and not the Rules. And there are more than you suppose who are illiterate all their lives, or who, at the best, never learn to read well.'

'And for these people the pictures are the right thing?'

'I would not quite say that. The pictures alone are dangerous, and the Rules alone are dangerous. That is why the best thing of all is to find Mother Kirk at the very beginning, and to live from infancy with a third thing which is neither the Rules nor the pictures and which was brought into the country by the Landlord's Son. That, I say, is the best: never to have known the quarrel between the Rules and the pictures. But it very rarely happens. The Enemy's agents are everywhere at work, spreading illiteracy in one district and blinding men to the pictures in another. Even where Mother Kirk is nominally the ruler men can grow old without knowing how to read the Rules. Her empire is always crumbling. But it never quite crumbles: for as often as men become Pagans again, the Landlord again sends them pictures and stirs up sweet desire and so leads them back to Mother Kirk even as he led the actual Pagans long ago. There is, indeed, no other way.'

'Pagans?' said John. 'I do not know that people.'

'I forgot that you had travelled so little. It may well be that you were never in the country of Pagus in the flesh, though in another sense, you have lived there all your life. The curious thing about Pagus was that the people there had not heard of the Landlord.'

'Surely, a great many other people don't know either?'

'Oh, a great many *deny* his existence. But you have to be told about a thing before you can deny it. The peculiarity of the Pagans was that they had not been told: or if they had, it is so long ago that the tradition had died out. You see, the Enemy had practically supplanted the Landlord, and he kept a sharp watch against any news from that quarter reaching the tenants.'

'Did he succeed?'

'No. It is commonly thought that he did, but that is a mistake. It is commonly thought that he fuddled the tenants by circulating a mass of false stories about the Landlord. But I have been through Pagus in my rounds too often to think it was quite so simple. What really happened was this: The Landlord succeeded in getting a lot of messages through.'

'What sort of messages?'

'Mostly pictures. You see, the Pagans couldn't read, because the Enemy shut up the schools as soon as he took over Pagus. But they had pictures. The moment you mentioned your Island I knew what you were at. I have seen that Island dozens of times in those pictures.'

'And what happened then?'

'Almost certainly the same thing has happened to you. These pictures woke desire. You understand me?'

'Very well.'

'And then the Pagans made mistakes. They would keep on trying to get the same picture again: and if it didn't come, they would make copies of it for themselves. Or even if it did come they would try to get out of it not desire but satisfaction. But you must know all this.'

'Yes, yes, indeed. But what came of it?'

'They went on making up more and more stories for themselves about the pictures, and then pretending the stories were true. They turned to brown girls and tried to believe that that was what they wanted. They went far South, some of them, and became magicians, and tried to believe it was that. There was no absurdity and no indecency they did not commit. But however far they went, the Landlord was too many for them. Just when their own stories seemed to have completely overgrown the original messages and hidden them beyond recovery, suddenly the Landlord would send them a new message and all their stories would look stale. Or just when they seemed to be growing really contented with lust or mystery mongering, a new message would arrive and the old desire, the real one, would sting them again, and they would say "Once more it has escaped us."'

'I know. And then the whole cycle would begin over again.'

'Yes. But all the while there was one people that could read. You have heard of the Shepherd People?'

'I had been hoping you would not come to that, Father. I have heard the Stewards talk of them and I think it is that more than anything else that sickened me of the whole story. It is so clear that the Shepherd People are just one of these Pagan peoples—and a peculiarly unattractive one. If the whole thing is hobbled by one leg to that special People . . .'

'This is merely a blunder,' said History. 'You, and those whom you trust, have not *travelled*. You have never been in Pagus. nor among the Shepherds. If you had lived on the roads as I have, you would never say that they were the same. The Shepherds could read: that is the thing to remember about them. And because they could read, they had from the Landlord, not pictures but Rules.'

'But who wants Rules instead of Islands?'

'That is like asking who wants cooking instead of dinner. Do you not see that the Pagans, because they were under the enemy, were beginning at the wrong end? They were like lazy schoolboys attempting eloquence before they learn grammar. They had pictures for their eyes instead of roads for their feet, and that is why most of them could do nothing but desire and then, through starved desire, become corrupt in their imaginations, and so awake and despair, and so desire again. Now the Shepherds, because they were under the Landlord, were made to begin at the right end. Their feet were set on a road: and as the Landlord's Son once said, if the feet have been put right the hands and the head will come right sooner or later. It won't work the other way.'

'You know so much, Father,' said John, 'that I do not know how to answer you. But this is all unlike the accounts I have heard of those countries. Surely some of the Pagans did get somewhere.'

'They did. They got to Mother Kirk. That is the definition of a Pagan—a man so travelling that if all goes well he arrives at Mother Kirk's chair and is carried over this gorge. I saw it happen myself. But we define a thing by its perfection. The trouble about Pagus is that the perfect, and in that sense typical, Pagan, is so uncommon there. It must be so, must it not? These pictures—this ignorance of writing—this endless desire which so easily confuses itself with other desires and, at best, remains pure only by knowing what it does *not* want—you see that it is a starting point from which *one* road leads home and a thousand roads lead into the wilderness.'

'But were the Shepherds not just as bad in their own way? Is it not true that they were illiberal, narrow, bigoted?'

'They *were* narrow. The thing they had charge of was narrow: it was the Road. They found it. They sign-posted it. They kept it clear and repaired it. But you must not think I am setting them up against the Pagans. The truth is that a Shepherd is only half a man, and a Pagan is only half a man, so that neither people was well without the other, nor could either be healed until the Landlord's Son came into the country. And even so, my son, you will not be well until you have overtaken your fellow traveller who slept in my cell last night.'

'Do you mean Vertue?' said John.

'That was his name. I knew him though he did not tell me, for I know his family; and his father, whom he does not know, was called Nomos and lived among the Shepherds. You will never do anything until you have sworn blood brotherhood with him: nor can he do anything without you.'

'I would gladly overtake him,' said John, 'but he is so angry with me that I am afraid to come near him. And even if we made it up, I don't see how we could help falling out again. Somehow we have never been able to be quite comfortable together for very long.'

'Of yourselves you never will. It is only a third that can reconcile you.'

'Who is that?'

'The same who reconciled the Shepherds and the Pagans. But you must go to Mother Kirk to find him.'

'It is raining harder than ever,' said John from the mouth of the cave.

'It will not stop to-night,' said Father History. 'You must stay with me till the morning.'

IX
Matter of Fact

'I SEE,' SAID JOHN presently, 'that this question is harder than the Clevers and the pale men suppose. But they were right in distrusting the Island. From all that you have told me, it is a very dangerous thing.'

'There is no avoiding danger in our country,' said History. 'Do you know what happens to people who set about learning to skate with a determination to get no falls? They fall as often as the rest of us, and they cannot skate in the end.'

'But it is more than dangerous. You said it was beginning at the wrong end, while the Shepherd people began at the right end.'

'That is true. But if you are a Pagan by birth or by nature, you have no choice. It is better to begin at the wrong end than not to begin at all. And the most part of men are always Pagans. Their first step will always be the desire born of the pictures: and though that desire hides a thousand false trails it also hides the only true one for them, and those who preach down the desire under whatever pretext—Stoic, Ascetic, Rigorist, Realist, Classicist—are on the Enemy's side whether they know it or not.'

'Then there is always need for the Island?'

'It does not always take the form of an Island, as I have said. The Landlord sends pictures of many different kinds. What is universal is not the particular picture, but the arrival of some message, not perfectly intelligible, which wakes this desire and sets men longing for something East or West of the world; something possessed, if at all, only in the act of desiring it, and lost so quickly that the craving itself becomes craved; something that tends inevitably to be confused with common or even with vile satisfactions lying close to hand, yet which is able, if any man faithfully live through the dialectic of its successive births and deaths, to lead him at last where true joys are to be found. As for the shapes in which it comes, I have seen many in my travels. In Pagus it was sometimes, as I said, an Island. But it was often, too, a picture of people, stronger and fairer than we are. Sometimes it was a picture telling a story. The strangest shape it ever took was in Medium Aevum—that was a master stroke of the Landlord's diplomacy; for of course, since the Enemy has been in the country, the Landlord has had to become a politician. Medium Aevum was first inhabited by colonists from Pagus. They came there at the very worst period in the history of Pagus, when the Enemy seemed to have succeeded completely in diverting all the desires that the Landlord could arouse into nothing but lust. These poor colonists were in such a state that they could not let their fancies wander for a minute without seeing images of black, craving eyes, and breasts, and gnawing kisses. It seemed hopeless to do anything with them. Then came the Landlord's crowning audacity. The very next picture he sent them was a picture of a Lady! Nobody had ever had the idea of a Lady before: and yet a Lady is a woman: so this was a new thing, which took the Enemy off his guard, and yet at the same time it was an old thing—in fact, the very thing which he was reckoning on as his strongest point. He got the shock of his life. The people went mad over the new picture, and made songs that are sung still, and looked away from the picture at the real women around them and saw them quite differently—so that ordinary love for women became, for a time, itself a form of the real desire, and not merely one of the spurious satisfactions offered to it. Of course the Landlord was playing a dangerous game (nearly all his games *are* dangerous) and the Enemy managed to mix up and corrupt the new message—as usual—but not so much as he wished, or as people afterwards said: and before he had recovered himself, one at least[1] of the tenants had carried this new form of the desire right up to its natural conclusion and found what he had really been wanting. He wrote it all down in what he called a *Comedy*.'

'And what about Mr. Halfways?' said John. 'Where did his kind of song begin?'

'That was the last big arrival of new messages that we had,' said History. 'And it happened just before I retired from the world. It was in the land of Mr. Enlightenment, but he was very different then. I do not know any man who has deteriorated so with advancing years. In those days Claptrap had not been built. The Enemy had agents in the country but did not come there often himself: it must have been just about that time that Mammon was taking it over, and building new towns and turning the people out of the fields into the factories. One of the results was a great deal of anaemia—though there were other causes for that too—and weak hearts. This time the Landlord did a curious thing: he sent them pictures of the country they were actually living in—as if he had sent them a number of mirrors. You see, he always does the last thing the Enemy is expecting. And just as the pictures of the Lady in Medium Aevum had made the real women look different, so when men looked at these pictures of the country and then turned to the real landscape, it was all changed. And a new idea was born in their minds, and they saw something—the old something, the Island West of the world, the Lady, the heart's desire—as it were hiding, yet not quite hidden, like something ever more about to be, in every wood and stream and under every field. And because they saw this, the land seemed to be coming to life, and all the old stories of the Pagans came back to their minds and meant more than the Pagans themselves ever knew: and because women also were in the landscape, the old idea of the Lady came back too. For this is part of the Landlord's skill, that when one message has died he brings it to life again in the heart of the next. But out of this third revelation, which they called Romantic, so many songs were made that I cannot remember all of them: and many deeds were done, too, and many, through the usual false starts and disillusions and rebeginnings of desire, found their way home. Your Mr. Halfways is one of the later and weaker followers of that school.'

'I don't think that the history of the Romantic pictures is quite as clear as the other histories. What exactly was the Landlord doing? And what did the Enemy do?'

'I thought you would have seen. This third stroke of policy was in a way one of the greatest. All the previous pictures had been of something that was *not here* in the world around you. This gave the Enemy the chance of making people believe that you *had* it in the picture, and *lacked* it elsewhere—in other words that the picture itself was the thing you wanted. And that, as you know, means idolatry, and then, when the idol disappoints you (as it must) there is an easy passage to all the spurious satisfactions. But this weapon was knocked out of the Enemy's hand when once the thing in the picture was the very same thing that you saw all round you. Even the stupidest tenant could see that you *had* the landscape, in the only sense in

1. Dante

which it could be had, already: and still you *wanted*: therefore the landscape was not what you wanted. Idolatry became impossible. Of course the Enemy when he had recovered himself, found a new method of defence. Just because the new message could not be idolized, it could be easily belittled. The desire awakened thus between the picture and the countryside could be confused with the ordinary *pleasure* that any healthy man feels in moving about out-of-doors: and when it had been so confused, the Enemy could pretend that the Romantics had made a great pother about nothing. And you can imagine that all the people who had not had pictures sent to them, and therefore not felt the desire, and therefore were itching with envy, would welcome this explanation.'

'I see,' said John. 'But still—on your own showing, all these messages get blurred and corrupted in the end, and then, surely, the thing to do is to look out for the new one. These pale men might be quite right to occupy themselves in cleaning away the rubbish of the old revelation. That might be the way to get ready for the next.'

'That is another notion they have which a little travel would soon blow to pieces. They think that the Landlord works like the factories in Claptrap, inventing every day a new machine which supersedes the old. As machines are among the very few things that they do know something about, they cannot help thinking that everything is like them. But this leads them into two mistakes. First of all, they have no conception how slowly the Landlord acts—the enormous intervals between these big changes in his type of picture. And secondly, they think that the new thing refutes and cancels the old, whereas, in reality it brings it to a fuller life. I have never known a case where the man who was engaged in ridiculing or rejecting the old message became the receiver of the new. For one thing it all takes so long. Why, bless my soul, I remember Homer in Pagus ridiculing some of the story pictures: but they had thousands of years to run still and thousands of souls were to get nourishment out of them. I remember Clopinel[1] in Medium Aevum, jeering at the pictures of the Lady before they had reached half his countrymen. But his jeer was no spell to evoke a new message, nor was he helping any cause but the Enemy's.'

X
Archtype and Ectype

THERE WAS A LONG silence in the cave except for the sound of the rain. Then John began once more:

'And yet . . .' he said, 'and yet, Father, I am terribly afraid. I am afraid that the

---

1. Jean de Meung

things the Landlord really intends for me may be utterly unlike the things he has taught me to desire.'

'They will be very unlike the things you imagine. But you already know that the objects which your desire imagines are always inadequate to that desire. Until you have it you will not know what you wanted.'

'I remember that Wisdom said that too. And I understand that. Perhaps what troubles me is a fear that my desires, after all you have said, do not really come from the Landlord—that there is some older and rival Beauty in the world which the Landlord will not allow me to get. How can we *prove* that the Island comes from him? Angular would say it did not.'

'You have proved it for yourself: you have *lived* the proof. Has not every object which fancy and sense suggested for the desire, proved a failure, confessed itself, after trial, not to be what you wanted? Have you not found by elimination that this desire is the perilous seige in which only One can sit?'

'But then,' said John, 'the very quality of it is so—so unlike what we think of the Landlord. I will confess to you what I had hoped to keep secret. It has been with me almost a bodily desire. There have been times . . . I have felt the sweetness flow over from the soul into the body . . . pass through me from head to foot. It is quite true, what the Clevers say. It *is* a thrill—a physical sensation.'

'That is an old story. You must fear thrills, but you must not fear them too much. It is only a foretaste of that which the real Desirable will be when you have found it. I remember well what an old friend of mine in Medium Aevum once said to me— "out of the soul's bliss," he said, "there shall be a flowing over into the flesh."'

'Did he say that? I did not suppose that anyone except the Clevers knew it. Do not laugh at me, Father—or laugh if you will—I am indeed very ignorant and I have listened to people more ignorant still.'

Twilight, hastened by the rain, had fallen on the canyon, and in the cave it was quite dark. John heard the old man moving to and fro and presently there came the flame of a little lamp lighting up his pale birdlike face. He set food for supper before his guest and bade him eat and then sleep.

'Gladly, Father,' said John, 'for I am very tired. I do not know why I have plagued you with questions about the Island. It is all a story of what happened to me long ago. It was long ago that I saw it clearly. The visions, ever since the first one, have grown rarer, the desires fainter. I have been talking as if I still craved it, but I do not think I can find any craving in my heart now at all.'

The old man sat still, nodding a little as before.

Suddenly John spoke again.

'Why should it *wear out* if it is from the Landlord? It doesn't last, you know. Isn't it that which gives away the whole case?'

'Have you not heard men say, or have you forgotten, that it is like human love?' asked the hermit.

'What has that to do with it?'

'You would not ask if you had been married, or even if you had studied generation among the beasts. Do you not know how it is with love? First comes delight:

then pain: then fruit. And then there is joy of the fruit, but that is different again from the first delight. And mortal lovers must not try to remain at the first step: for lasting passion is the dream of a harlot and from it we wake in despair. You must not try to keep the raptures: they have done their work. Manna kept, is worms. But you are full of sleep and we had better talk no more.'

Then I dreamed that John lay down on a hard bed in the cave; and as he lay between waking and sleeping, the hermit, as he thought, lit two candles at the back of the cave on an altar and went to and fro doing and saying his holy things. And on the very borders of sleep John heard him begin to sing, and this was the song:

> My heart is empty. All the fountains that should run
>   With longing, are in me
> Dried up. In all my countryside there is not one
>   That drips to find the sea.
> I have no care for anything thy love can grant
>   Except the moment's vain
> And hardly noticed filling of the moment's want
>   And to be free from pain.
> Oh, thou that art unwearying, that dost neither sleep
>   Nor slumber, who didst take
> All care for Lazarus in the careless tomb, oh keep
>   Watch for me till I wake.
> If thou think for me what I cannot think, if thou
>   Desire for me what I
> Cannot desire, my soul's interior Form, though now
>   Deep-buried, will not die,
> —No more than the insensible dropp'd seed which grows
>   Through winter ripe for birth
> Because, while it forgets, the heaven remembering throws
>   Sweet influence still on earth,
> —Because the heaven, moved moth-like by thy beauty, goes
>   Still turning round the earth.

Book Nine

ACROSS THE CANYON

Sholde nevere whete wexte bote whete fyrste deyde;
And other sedes also, in the same wyse,
That ben leide on louh erthe, ylore as hit were,
And thorwh the grete grace of God, of greyn ded in erthe
Atte last launceth up wher-by we liven alle.
Langland

You will not sleep, if you lie there a thousand years, until you have
opened your hand and yielded that which is not yours to give or to
withhold. You may think you are dead, but it will be only a dream;
you may think you have come awake, but it will still be only a dream.
Open your hand, and you will sleep indeed—then wake indeed.
George MacDonald

You may as well come quiet.
Police Maxim

I
Across the Canyon by the Inner Light

WHEN JOHN OPENED his eyes the day was still far off but there was light in the cave as though from a hundred candles. The hermit lay fast asleep by one wall of the cell as John lay by the other, and between them stood a woman, something like Reason and something like Mother Kirk, very bright.

'I am Contemplation,' she said. 'Rise and come with me.'

'You are not like the Contemplation that I know,' said John.

'It is one of my shadows whom you have met,' said the Lady. 'And there is little good in them and less harm. But rise and come.'

Then John rose and the Lady took him by the hand and led him out on to the ledge before the cave. And the night was still black with thunderous rain, but the Lady and he were in a sphere of light, so that the raindrops as they passed out of the darkness into it became bright like diamonds in the centre of the sphere and iridescent at the circumference. Held by the Lady's hand he crossed the chasm and passed up the glens of the mountains on the other side. When they had travelled a long way (and still the darkness lay everywhere save where they trod) they came to the sea. And they crossed the sea also, gliding a little above the water, and the water also was dark until it reached their light, but within that it was blue as though it lay in Mediterranean sunshine. But presently the surrounding darkness vanished away and the drop of light in which they had journeyed entered an ocean of light and was swallowed up. The sky was visible above them and it seemed to be early morning, for it was cool and dew soaked their feet. And John looked and saw fields going up before him and the light ran down as a river in the midst of the fields, singing with a voice like a river but more articulate and very loud, too bright to look at. There were many people with them. And as John looked round upon the people he saw that they were approaching some high walls and great gates. And, at the shape of the towers clustered above him, a memory, very deeply buried, stirred in his mind, first sweet, then uneasy, then spreading through the pool of his mind in widening circles of dismay, till at last with certainty, inevitable, unbearable, there flashed before him the picture of those turreted crags seen long ago from Puritania at the summit of the Eastern mountains, and he saw where he was—beyond the brook—where Uncle George had vanished—at the Landlord's castle—the good kind Landlord with the black hole. He began to draw his hand out of the Lady's hand. He could not get it free. She was leading him on to the castle gates and all the crowd of people were moving on in the same direction, with a sinister happiness on their faces. He struggled with Contemplation and screamed: and with that and the struggling he awoke.

II
This Side by Lightning

IT WAS NOW PITCH black in the cave. Only the quiet breathing of the hermit recalled to John where he was: and with the first return of the knowledge he was already creeping out of the cave to dare the black night and the narrow ledge, to crawl the skin off his hands and his knees, to do and suffer anything so long as he was going back and not on—on in this direction where the next turning might lead him into the heart of his adversary's power. The rain fell in torrents and thunder echoed among the rocks: but the cool moisture on his back was better than the hot moisture on his forehead. He did not dare to stand up and walk, for the new terrors had not driven out the old, but rather joined with them in a phantasmagoric harmony, so that all in one moment his inner eye saw the black hole full of the spiders and scorpions—the narrow, narrow ledge sloping horribly the wrong way—the drop into the darkness and his own body bounced from crag to crag—the terrible face of Uncle George when the mask would not stay on it. And as the flashes came faster and the thunder followed faster on each flash, a new fear joined the dance: and in each flash the timeless unforgettable sight of the cliffs, lit up from end to end, gave a new edge to the old fear of climbing: and that again brought back the fear of Uncle George's face (so will mine look when I lie broken at the bottom of the gorge), until at last, when the complexity of fears seemed to admit no increase, a sharp, commanding voice out of the darkness suddenly startled him with such a shock that he seemed not to have been frightened till then.

'Back!' said the voice.

John crouched motionless from the balance of fears. He was not even sure that he *could* turn on this bit of the ledge.

'Back,' said the voice, 'or else show that you're the better man.'

The lightning tore open the darkness and flung it to again. But John had seen his enemy. It was Reason, this time on foot, but still mailed, and her sword drawn in her hand.

'Do you want to fight?' she said in the darkness.

John had a wild thought of catching one of the mailed ankles from where he crouched: but when he had a picture of Reason falling into the gulf he could not get it clear of another picture in which he fell with her.

'I can't turn here,' he said: but the steel was at his throat and turn he did. He shuffled along at a surprising speed, still on his hands and knees, till he had passed the cave again. It was no longer a question of plans or of ultimate escape. The hunted animal's impulse to prolong the chase kept him ragingly on the move. The flashes were growing rarer and a star or two showed ahead. Then all of a sudden a wind shook the last raindrops fiercely in his face and there was moonlight all about him. But he drew back with a groan.

III
This Side by the Darkness

WITHIN AN INCH of him he had seen a face. Now a cloud crossed the moon and the face was no longer visible, but he knew that it was still looking at him—an aged, appalling face, crumbling and chaotic, larger than human. Presently its voice began:

'Do you still think it is the black hole you fear? Do you not know even now the deeper fear whereof the black hole is but the veil? Do you not know why they would all persuade you that there is nothing beyond the brook and that when a man's lease is out his story is done? Because, if this were true, they could in their reckoning make me equal to nought, therefore not dreadful: could say that where I am they are not, that while they are, I am not. They have prophesied soft things to you. I am no negation, and the deepest of your heart acknowledges it. Else why have you buried the memory of your uncle's face so carefully that it has needed all these things to bring it up? Do not think that you can escape me; do not think you can call me Nothing. To you I am not Nothing; I am the being blindfolded, the losing all power of self-defence, the surrender, not because any terms are offered, but because resistance is gone: the step into the dark: the defeat of all precautions: utter helplessness turned out to utter risk: the final loss of liberty. The Landlord's Son who feared nothing, feared me.'

'What am I to do?' said John.

'Which you choose,' said the voice. 'Jump, or be thrown. Shut your eyes or have them bandaged by force. Give in or struggle.'

'I would sooner do the first, if I could.'

'Then I am your servant and no more your master. The cure of death is dying. He who lays down his liberty in that act receives it back. Go down to Mother Kirk.'

John looked about him when next the moon shone. The bottom of the chasm was level far below him, and there he saw what seemed a concourse of dark figures. Amidst them they had left an open space, where there was a glimmer as of water: and near the water there was someone standing. It seemed to him that he was waited for, and he began to explore the face of cliff below him. To his surprise it was no longer sheer and smooth. He tried a few footholds and got five feet below the ledge. Then he sat down again, sick. But the kind of fear which he now suffered was cold and leaden: there was no panic in it: and soon he continued his descent.

---

7. On the floor stood Mother Kirk crowned and sceptered; not far from her sat Vertue, mother-naked.

IV
Securus Te Projice

ON THE FLOOR of *Peccatum Adae* stood Mother Kirk crowned and sceptered in the midst of the bright moonlit circle left by the silent people. All their faces were turned towards her, and she was looking eastward to where John slowly descended the cliff. Not far from her sat Vertue, mother-naked. They were both on the margin of a large pool which lay in a semicircle against the western cliff. On the far side of the water that cliff rose sheer to the edge of the canyon. There was deep silence for about half an hour.

At last the small, drooping figure of a man detached itself from the shadow of the crags and advanced towards them through the open moonlight. It was John.

'I have come to give myself up,' he said.

'It is well,' said Mother Kirk. 'You have come a long way round to reach this place, whither I would have carried you in a few moments. But it is very well.'

'What must I do?' said John.

'You must take off your rags,' said she, 'as your friend has done already, and then you must dive into this water.'

'Alas,' said he, 'I have never learned to dive.'

'There is nothing to learn,' said she. 'The art of diving is not to do anything new but simply to cease doing something. You have only to let yourself go.'

'It is only necessary,' said Vertue, with a smile, 'to abandon all efforts at self-preservation.'

'I think,' said John, 'that if it is all one, I would rather jump.'

'It is not all one,' said Mother Kirk. 'If you jump, you will be trying to save yourself and you may be hurt. As well, you would not go deep enough. You must dive so that you can go right down to the bottom of the pool: for you are not to come up again on this side. There is a tunnel in the cliff, far beneath the surface of the water, and it is through that that you must pass so that you may come up on the far side.'

'I see,' thought John to himself, 'that they have brought me here to kill me,' but he began, nevertheless, to take off his clothes. They were little loss to him, for they hung in shreds, plastered with blood and with the grime of every shire from Puritania to the canyon: but they were so stuck to him that they came away with pain and a little skin came with them. When he was naked Mother Kirk bade him come to the edge of the pool, where Vertue was already standing. It was a long way down to the water, and the reflected moon seemed to look up at him from the depth of a mine. He had had some thought of throwing himself in, with a run, the very instant he reached the edge, before he had time to be afraid. And the making of that resolution had seemed to be itself the bitterness of death, so that he half believed the worst must be over and that he would find himself in the water before he knew. But lo! he was still standing on the edge, still on this side. Then a stranger thing came to pass. From the great concourse of spectators, shadowy people came stealing out to his side, touching his arm and whispering to him: and every one of them appeared to be the wraith of some old acquaintance.

First came the wraith of old Enlightenment and said, 'There's still time. Get away and come back to me and all this will vanish like a nightmare.'

Then came the wraith of Media Halfways and said, 'Can you really risk losing me for ever? I know you do not desire me at this moment. But for ever? Think. Don't burn your boats.'

And the wraith of old Halfways said, 'After all—has this anything to do with the Island as you used to imagine it? Come back and hear my songs instead. You *know* them.'

The wraith of young Halfways said, 'Aren't you ashamed? Be a man. Move with the times and don't throw your life away for an old wives' tale.'

The wraith of Sigmund said, 'You know what this is, I suppose. Religious melancholia. Stop while there is time. If you dive, you dive into insanity.'

The wraith of Sensible said, 'Safety first. A touch of rational piety adds something to life: but this salvationist business . . . well! Who knows where it will end? Never accept unlimited liabilities.'

The wraith of Humanist said, 'Mere atavism. You are diving to escape your real duties. All this emotionalism, after the first plunge, is so much *easier* than virtue in the classical sense.'

The wraith of Broad said, 'My dear boy, you are losing your head. These sudden conversions and violent struggles don't achieve anything. We have had to discard so much that our ancestors thought necessary. It is all far easier, far more gracious and beautiful than they supposed.'

But at that moment the voice of Vertue broke in:

'Come on, John,' he said, 'the longer we look at it the less we shall like it.' And with that he took a header into the pool and they saw him no more. And how John managed it or what he felt I did not know, but he also rubbed his hands, shut his eyes, despaired, and let himself go. It was not a good dive, but, at least, he reached the water head first.

V

Across the Canyon

MY DREAM GREW DARKER so that I have a sense, but little clear memory of the things that John experienced both in the pool and in great catacombs, paved sometimes with water, sometimes with stone, and upon winding stairways in the live rocks whereby he and Vertue ascended through the inwards of the mountain to the land beyond *Peccatum Adae.* He learned many mysteries in the earth and passed through many elements, dying many deaths. One thing has come through into my waking memory. Of all the people he had met in his journey only Wisdom appeared to him in the caverns, and troubled him by saying that no man could really come where he had come and that all his adventures were but figurative, for no professed experience of these places could be anything other than mythology. But then another voice spoke to him from behind him, saying:

'Child, if you will, it *is* mythology. It is but truth, not fact: an image, not the very real. But then it is My mythology. The words of Wisdom are also myth and metaphor: but since they do not know themselves for what they are, in them the hidden myth is master, where it should be servant: and it is but of man's inventing. But this is My inventing, this is the veil under which I have chosen to appear even from the first until now. For this end I made your senses and for this end your imagination, that you might see My face and live. What would you have? Have you not heard among the Pagans the story of Semele? Or was there any age in any land when men did not know that corn and wine were the blood and body of a dying and yet living God?'

And not long after that the light and colour, as with the sound of a trumpet, rushed back upon my dreaming eyes, and my ears were full of the sounds of bird and the rustle of leaves, for John and Vertue had come up out of the earth into the green forests of the land beyond the canyon. Then I saw that they were received into a great company of other pilgrims who had all descended like them into the water and the earth and again come up, and now took their march westward along the banks of a clear river. All kinds of men were among them. And during the whole of this part of their journey Reason rode with the company, talking to them at will and not visiting them any longer by sudden starts, nor vanishing suddenly. It was a wonder to John to find so many companions: nor could he conceive how he had failed to run across them in the earlier parts of his journey.

I watched this journey in my dream a long time. At the outset their goal was heard of only by rumours as of something very far off: then, by continuous marching, winding their way among the peaked and valleyed lands, I saw where they came down to the white beaches of a bay of the sea, the western end of the world; a place very ancient, folded many miles deep in the silence of forests; a place, in some sort, lying rather at the world's beginning, as though men were born travelling away from it. It was early in the morning when they came there and heard the sound of the waves; and looking across the sea—at that hour still almost colourless—all these thousands became still. And what the others saw I do not know: but John saw the Island. And the morning wind, blowing off-shore from it, brought the sweet smell of its orchards to them, but rarefied and made faint with the thinness and purity of early air, and mixed with a little sharpness of the sea. But for John, because so many thousands looked at it with him, the pain and the longing were changed and all unlike what they had been of old: for humility was mixed with their wildness, and the sweetness came not with pride and with the lonely dreams of poets nor with the glamour of a secret, but with the homespun truth of folk-tales, and with the sadness of graves and freshness as of earth in the morning. There was fear in it also, and hope: and it began to seem well to him that the Island should be different from his desires, and so different that, if he had known it, he would not have sought it.

VI
Nella Sua Voluntade

HOW IT FARED with the other pilgrims I did not see, but presently a comely person took John and Vertue apart and said that he had been appointed to be their Guide. I dreamed that he was one born in the Mountain and they called him Slikisteinsauga because his sight was so sharp that the sight of any other who travelled with him would be sharpened by his company.

'Thank you,' said John. 'Pray, do we take ship from here?'

But Slikisteinsauga shook his head: and he asked them to look at the Island again and specially to consider the shape of the crags, or the castle (for they could not well see which at that distance) to which it rose at its highest point.

'I see,' said John presently.

'What do you see?' said the Guide.

'They are the very same shape as that summit of the Eastern Mountain which we called the Landlord's castle as we saw it from Puritania.'

'They are not only the same shape. They are the same.'

'How can that be?' said John with a sinking heart, 'for those mountains were in the extreme East, and we have been travelling West ever since we left home.'

'But the world is round,' said the Guide, 'and you have come nearly round it. The Island is the Mountains: or, if you will, the Island is the other side of the Mountains, and not, in truth, an Island at all.'

'And how do we go on from here?'

The Guide looked at him as a merciful man looks on an animal which he must hurt.

'The way to go on,' he said at last, 'is to go back. There are no ships. The only way is to go East again and cross the brook.'

'What must be must be,' said John. 'I deserve no better. You mean that I have been wasting my labour all my life, and I have gone half-round the world to reach what Uncle George reached in a mile or so.'

'Who knows what your uncle has reached, except the Landlord? Who knows what you would have reached if you had crossed the brook without ever leaving home? You may be sure the Landlord has brought you the shortest way: though I confess it would look an odd journey on a map.'

'How does it strike you, friend?' said John to Vertue.

'It cannot be helped,' said Vertue. 'But indeed, after the water and the earth, I thought we had already crossed the brook in a sense.'

'You will be always thinking that,' said the Guide. 'We call it Death in the Mountain language. It is too tough a morsel to eat at one bite. You will meet that brook more often than you think: and each time you will suppose that you have done with it for good. But some day you really will.'

They were all silent for a while.

'Come,' said the Guide at last, 'if you are ready let us start East again. But I should warn you of one thing—the country will look very different on the return journey.'

Book Ten
THE REGRESS

---

*And if, when he returned into the cave, he were constrained once
more to contend with those that had always there been prisoners, in
judgment of the said shadows, would they not mock him, and say of
him that by going up out of the cave he had come down again with
his eyes marred for his pains, and that it was lost labour for any so much
as to try that ascent?*
Plato

*First I must lead the human soul through all the range
Of heaven, that she may learn
How fortune hath the turning of the wheel of change,
How fate will never turn.*
Bernardus Silvestris

*Let us suppose a person destitute of that knowledge which we have from
our senses. . . . Let it be supposed that in his drought he puts golden dust
into his eyes: when his eyes smart, he puts wine into his ears; that in his
hunger, he puts gravel into his mouth; that in pain, he loads himself
with the iron chains; that feeling cold, he puts his feet in the water; that
being frighted at the fire, he runs away from it; that being weary, he
makes a seat of his bread. . . . Let us suppose that some good being came
to him, and showed him the nature and use of all the things that were
about him.*
Law

I
The Same Yet Different

THEN I DREAMED that the Guide armed John and Vertue at all points and led them back through the country they had just been travelling, and across the canyon again into this country. And they came up out of the canyon at the very place where the main road meets it by Mother Kirk's chair. I looked forward in the same direction where they were looking, expecting to see on my left the bare tableland rising to the North with Sensible's house a little way off, and on my right the house of Mr. Broad and the pleasant valleys southward. But there was nothing of the kind: only the long straight road, very narrow, and on the left crags rising within a few paces of the road into ice and mist and, beyond that, black cloud: on the right, swamps and jungle sinking almost at once into black cloud. But, as it happens in dreams, I never doubted that this was the same country which I had seen before, although there was no similarity. John and Vertue came to a stand with their surprise.

'Courage,' said Slikisteinsauga, 'you are seeing the land as it really is. It is long but very narrow. Beyond these crags and cloud on the North it sinks immediately into the Arctic Sea, beyond which again lies the Enemy's country. But the Enemy's country is joined up with ours on the North by a land bridge called the Isthmus Sadisticus and right amid that Isthmus sits the cold dragon, the cold, costive, crustacean dragon who wishes to enfold all that he can get within the curl of his body and then to draw his body tighter round it so as to have it all inside himself. And you, John, when we pass the Isthmus must go up and contend with him that you may be hardened. But on the South, as soon as it passes into these swamps and this other cloud, the land sinks into the Southern Sea: and across that sea also there comes a land bridge, the Isthmus Mazochisticus, where the hot dragon crawls, the expansive, invertebrate dragon whose fiery breath makes all that she touches melt and corrupt. And to her you, Vertue, must go down that you may steal her heat and be made malleable.'

'Upon my soul,' said John, 'I think Mother Kirk treats us very ill. Since we have followed her and eaten her food the way seems twice as narrow and twice as dangerous as it did before.'

'You all know,' said the Guide, 'that security is mortals' greatest enemy.'

'It will do very well,' said Vertue, 'let us begin.'

Then they set out on their journey and Vertue sang this song:

> 'Thou only art alternative to God, oh, dark
> And burning island among spirits, tenth hierarch,
> Wormwood, immortal Satan, Ahriman, alone

Second to Him to whom no second else were known,
Being essential fire, sprung of His fire, but bound
Within the lightless furnace of thy Self, bricked round
To range in the reverberated heat from seven
Containing walls: hence power thou hast to rival heaven.
Therefore, except the temperance of the eternal love
Only thy absolute lust is worth the thinking of.
All else is weak disguisings of the wishful heart,
All that seemed earth is Hell, or Heaven. God is: thou art:
The rest, illusion. How should man live save as glass
To let the white light without flame, the Father, pass
Unstained: or else—opaque, molten to thy desire,
Venus infernal starving in the strength of fire!'

'Lord, open not too often my weak eyes to this.'

II
The Synthetic Man

AS THEY WENT ON, Vertue glanced to the side of the road to see if there were any trace of Mr. Sensible's house, but there was none.

'It is just as it was when you passed it before,' said the Guide, 'but your eyes are altered. You see nothing now but realities: and Mr. Sensible was so near to nonentity—so shadowy even as an appearance—that he is now invisible to you. That mote will trouble your eyes no longer.'

'I am very surprised,' said Vertue, 'I should have thought that even if he was bad he was a singularly solid and four-square kind of evil.'

'All that solidity,' said the Guide, 'belonged not to him but to his predecessors in that house. There was an appearance of temperance about him, but it came from Epicurus. There was an appearance of poetry, but it came from Horace. A trace of old Pagan dignities lingered in his house—it was Montaigne's. His heart seemed warm for a moment, but the warmth was borrowed from Rabelais. He was a man of shreds and patches, and when you have taken from him what was not his own, the remainder equals nought.'

'But surely,' said Vertue, 'these things were not the less his own because he learned them from others.'

'He did not learn them. He learned only catchwords from them. He could talk like Epicurus of spare diet, but he was a glutton. He had from Montaigne the language of friendship, but no friend. He did not even know what these predecessors had really said. He never read one ode of Horace seriously in his life. And for his

Rabelais, he can quote *Do what you will*. But he has no notion that Rabelais gave that liberty to his Thelemites on the condition that they should be bound by Honour, and for this reason alone free from laws positive. Still less does he know that Rabelais himself was following a great Steward of the olden days who said *Habe caritatem et fac quod vis*: and least of all that this Steward in his turn was only reducing to an epigram the words of his Master, when He said, "On these two commandments hang all the law and the prophets."'

III
Limbo

THEN I DREAMED THAT John looked aside on the right hand of the road and saw a little island of willow trees amid the swamps, where ancient men sat robed in black, and the sound of their sighing reached his ears.

'That place,' said the Guide, 'is the same which you called the Valley of Wisdom when you passed it before: But now that you are going East you may call it Limbo, or the twilit porches of the black hole.'

'Who live there?' asked John, 'and what do they suffer?'

'Very few live there, and they are all men like old Mr. Wisdom—men who have kept alive and pure the deep desire of the soul but through some fatal flaw, of pride or sloth or, it may be, timidity, have refused till the end the only means to its fulfillment; taking huge pains, often, to prove to themselves that the fulfillment is impossible. They are very few because old Wisdom has few sons who are true to him, and the most part of those who come to him either go on and cross the canyon, or else, remaining his sons in name, secretely slip back to feed on worse fare than his. To stay long where he lives requires both a strange strength and a strange weakness. As for their sufferings, it is their doom to live for ever in desire without hope.'

'Is it not rather harsh of the Landlord to make them suffer at all?'

'I can answer that only by hearsay,' returned the Guide, 'for pain is a secret which he has shared with your race and not with mine; and you would find it as hard to explain suffering to me as I should find it to reveal to you the secrets of the Mountain people. But those who know best say this, that any liberal man would choose the pain of this desire, even for ever, rather than the peace of feeling it no longer: and that though the best thing is to have, the next best is to want, and the worst of all is not to want.'

'I see that,' said John. 'Even the wanting, though it is pain too, is more precious than anything else we experience.'

'It is as I foresaw, and you understand it already better than I can. But there is this also. The Landlord does not condemn them to lack of hope: they have done that themselves. The Landlord's interference is all on the other side. Left to itself, the desire without the hope would soon fall back to spurious satisfactions, and these souls would follow it of their own free will into far darker regions at the very bottom of the black hole. What the Landlord has done is to fix it for ever: and by his art, though unfulfilled, it is uncorrupted. Men say that his love and his wrath are one thing. Of some places in the black hole you cannot see this, though you can believe it: but of that Island yonder under the willows, you can see it with your own eyes.'

'I see it very well,' said John.

Then the Guide sang:

'God in His mercy made
The fixèd pains of Hell.
That misery might be stayed,
God in His mercy made
Eternal bounds and bade
Its waves no further swell.
God in his mercy made
The fixèd pains of Hell.'

IV
The Black Hole

'THEN THERE IS, after all,' said John, 'a black hole such as my old Steward described to me.'

'I do not know what your Steward described. But there is a black hole.'

'And still the Landlord is "so kind and good"!'

'I see you have been among the Enemy's people. In these latter days there is no charge against the Landlord which the Enemy brings so often as cruelty. That is just like the Enemy: for he is, at bottom, very dull. He has never hit on the one slander against the Landlord which would be really plausible. Anyone can refute the charge of cruelty. If he really wants to damage the Landlord's character, he has a much stronger line than that to take. He ought to say that the Landlord is an inveterate gambler. That would not be true, but it would be plausible, for there is no denying that the Landlord does take risks.'

'But what about the charge of cruelty?'

'I was just coming to that. The Landlord has taken the risk of working the country with free tenants instead of slaves in chain gangs: and as they are free there is no way of making it impossible for them to go into forbidden places and eat forbidden fruits. Up to a certain point he can doctor them even when they have done so, and break them of the habit. But beyond that point—you can see for yourself. A man can go on eating mountain-apple so long that *nothing* will cure his craving for it: and the very worms it breeds inside him will make him more certain to eat more. You must not try to fix the point after which a return is impossible, but you can see that there will be such a point somewhere.'

'But surely the Landlord can do anything?'

'He cannot do what is contradictory: or, in other words, a meaningless sentence will not gain meaning simply because someone chooses to prefix to it the words "the Landlord can." And it is meaningless to talk of forcing a man to do freely what a man has freely made impossible for himself.'

'I see. But at least these poor creatures are unhappy enough: there is no need to add a black hole.'

'The Landlord does not make the blackness. The blackness is there already wherever the taste of mountain-apple has created the vermiculate will. What do you mean by a hole? Something that ends. A black hole is blackness enclosed, limited. And in that sense the Landlord *has* made the black hole. He has put into the world a Worst Thing. But evil of itself would never reach a worst: for evil is fissiparous and could never in a thousand eternities find any way to arrest its own reproduction. If it could, it would be no longer evil: for Form and Limit belong to the good. The walls of the black hole are the tourniquet on the wound through which the lost soul else would bleed to a death she never reached. It is the Landlord's last service to those who will let him do nothing better for them.'

Then the Guide sang;

> 'Nearly they stood who fall;
> Themselves as they look back
> See always in the track
> The one false step, where all
> Even yet, by lightest swerve
> Of foot not yet enslaved,
> By smallest tremor of the smallest nerve,
> Might have been saved.
>
> 'Nearly they fell who stand,
> And with cold after fear
> Look back to mark how near
> They grazed the Sirens' land,
> Wondering that subtle fate,
> By threads so spidery fine,
> The choice of ways so small, the event so great,
> Should thus entwine.
>
> 'Therefore oh, man, have fear
> Lest oldest fears be true,

Lest thou too far pursue
The road that seems so clear,
And step, secure, a hair's
Breadth past the hair-breadth bourne,
Which, being once crossed forever unawares,
Denies return.'

V

Superbia

THEN THEY WENT FURTHER and saw in the rocks beside them on the left what seemed at first sight a skeleton, but as they drew nearer they saw that there was indeed skin stretched over its bones and eyes flaming in the sockets of its skull. And it was scrabbling and puddering to and fro on what appeared to be a mirror; but it was only the rock itself scraped clean of every speck of dust and fibre of lichen and polished by the continued activity of this famished creature.

'This is one of the Enemy's daughters,' said the Guide, 'and her name is Superbia. But when you last saw her, perhaps she wore the likeness of three pale men.'

As they passed her she began to croak out her song.

'I have scraped clean the plateau from the filthy earth,
Earth the unchaste, the fruitful, the great grand maternal,
Sprawling creature, lolling at random and supine
The broad-faced, sluttish helot, the slave wife
Grubby and warm, who opens unashamed
Her thousand wombs unguarded to the lickerous sun.
Now I have scoured my rock clean from the filthy earth,
On it no root can strike and no blade come to birth,
And though I starve of hunger it is plainly seen
That I have eaten nothing common or unclean.

'I have by fasting purged away the filthy flesh,
Flesh the hot, moist, salt scum, the obscenity
And parasitic tetter, from my noble bones.
I have torn from my breasts—I was an udder'd beast—
My child, for he was fleshly. Flesh is caught
By a contagion carried from impure
Generation to generation through the body's sewer
And now though I am barren, yet no man can doubt
I am clean and my iniquities are blotted out.

'I have made my soul (once filthy) a hard, pure, bright
Mirror of steel: no damp breath breathes upon it
Warming and dimming: it would freeze the finger
If any touched it. I have a mineral soul.
Minerals eat no food and void no excrement.
So I, borrowing nothing and repaying
Nothing, neither growing nor decaying,
Myself am to myself, a mortal God, a self-contained
Unwindowed monad, unindebted and unstained.'

John and the Guide were hurrying past, but Vertue hesitated.

'Her means may be wrong,' he said, 'but there is something to be said for her idea of the End.'

'What idea?' said the Guide.

'Why—self-sufficiency, integrity. Not to commit herself, you know. All said and done, there is something foul about all these natural processes.'

'You had better be careful of your thoughts here,' said the Guide. 'Do not confuse Repentance with Disgust: for the one comes from the Landlord and the other from the Enemy.'

'And yet disgust has saved many a man from worse evils.'

'By the power of the Landlord it may be so—now and then. But don't try to play that game for yourself. Fighting one vice with another is about the most dangerous strategy there is. You know what happens to kingdoms that use alien mercenaries.'

'I suppose you are right,' said Vertue, 'and yet this feeling goes very deep. Is it wholly wrong to be ashamed of being in the body?'

'The Landlord's Son was not. You know the verses—"When thou tookest upon thee to deliver man."'

'That was a special case.'

'It was a special case because it was the archtypal case. Has no one told you that that Lady spoke and acted for all that bears, in the presence of all that begets: for this country as against the things East and West: for matter as against form and patiency against agency? Is not the very word Mother akin to Matter? Be sure that the whole of this land, with all its warmth and wetness and fecundity with all the dark and the heavy and the multitudinous for which you are too dainty, spoke through her lips when she said that He had regarded the lowliness of His handmaiden. And if that Lady was a maid though a mother, you need not doubt that the nature which is, to human sense, impure, is also pure.'

'Well,' said Vertue, turning away from Superbia, 'I will think this over.'

'One thing you may as well know,' remarked the Guide, 'whatever virtues you may attribute to the Landlord, decency is not one of them. That is why so few of your national jokes have any point in my country.'

And as they continued their journey, Vertue sang:

'Because of endless pride
Reborn with endless error,

Each hour I look aside
Upon my secret mirror
Trying all postures there
To make my image fair.

'Thou givest grapes, and I,
Though starving, turn to see
How dark the cool globes lie
In the white hand of me,
And linger gazing thither
Till the live clusters wither.

'So should I quickly die
Narcissus-like of want,
But, in the glass, my eye
Catches such forms as haunt
Beyond nightmare, and make
Pride humble for pride's sake.

'Then and then only turning
The stiff neck round, I grow
A molten man all burning
And look behind and know
Who made the lass, whose light makes dark, whose fair
Makes foul, my shadowy form reflected there
That Self-Love, brought to bed of Love may die and bear
Her sweet son in despair.'

VI
Ignorantia

STILL I LAY DREAMING and saw these three continue their journey through that long and narrow land with the rocks upon their left and the swamps on their right. They had much talk on the way of which I have remembered only snatches since I woke. I remember that they passed Ignorantia some miles beyond her sister Superbia and that led the pilgrims to question their Guide as to whether the Ignorance of the Tough-minded and the Clevers would some day be cured. He said there was less chance of that now than there had ever been: for till recently the Northern people had been made to learn the languages of Pagus 'and that meant,' said the

Guide, 'that at least they started no further from the light than the old Pagans themselves and had therefore the chance to come at last to Mother Kirk. But now they are cutting themselves off even from that roundabout route.'

'Why have they changed?' asked one of the others.

'Why did the shadow whom you call Sensible leave his old house and go to practise αὐτάρχεια in a hotel? Because his Drudge revolted. The same thing is happening all over the plateau and in Mammon's country: their slaves are escaping further north and becoming dwarfs, and therefore the masters are turning all their attention to machinery, by which they hope to be able to lead their old life without slaves. And this seems to them so important that they are suppressing every kind of knowledge except mechanical knowledge. I am speaking of the sub-tenants. No doubt the great landowners in the back-ground have their own reasons for encouraging this movement.'

'There must be a good side somewhere to this revolution,' said Vertue. 'It is too solid—it looks too lasting—to be a mere evil. I cannot believe that the Landlord would otherwise allow the whole face of nature and the whole structure of life to be so permanently and radically changed.'

The Guide laughed. 'You are falling into their own error,' he said. 'The change is not radical, nor will it be permanent. That idea depends on a curious disease which they have all caught—an inability to disbelieve advertisements. To be sure, if the machines did what they promised, the change would be very deep indeed. Their next war, for example, would change the state of their country from disease to death. They are afraid of this themselves—though most of them are old enough to know by experience that a gun is no more likely than a toothpaste or a cosmetic to do the things its makers say it will do. It is the same with all their machines. Their labour-saving devices multiply drudgery; their aphrodisiacs make them impotent: their amusements bore them: their rapid production of food leaves half of them starving, and their devices for saving them have banished leisure from their country. There will be no radical change. And as for permanence—consider how quickly all machines are broken and obliterated. The black solitudes will some day be green again, and of all cities that I have seen these iron cities will break most suddenly.'

And the Guide sang:

'Iron will eat the world's old beauty up.
Girder and grid and gantry will arise,
Iron forest of engines will arise,
Criss-cross of iron crotchet. For your eyes
No green or growth. Over all, the skies
Scribbled from end to end with boasts and lies.
(When Adam ate the irrevocable apple, Thou
Saw'st beyond death the resurrection of the dead.)

'Clamour shall clean put out the voice of wisdom,
The printing-presses with their clapping wings,
Fouling your nourishment. Harpy wings,

Filling your minds all day with foolish things,
Will tame the eagle Thought: till she sings
Parrot-like in her cage to please dark kings.
(When Israel descended into Egypt, Thou
Didst purpose both the bondage and the coming out.)

'The new age, the new art, the new ethic and thought,
And fools crying, Because it has begun
It will continue as it has begun!
The wheel runs fast, therefore the wheel will run
Faster for ever. The old age is done,
We have new lights and see without the sun.
(Though they lay flat the mountains and dry up the sea,
Wilt thou yet change, as though God were a god?)'

VII
Luxuria

AFTER THIS, JOHN LOOKED up and saw that they were approaching a concourse of living creatures beside the road. Their way was so long and desolate (and he was footsore too) that he welcomed any diversion, and he cast his eyes curiously upon this new thing. When he was nearer he saw that the concourse was of men, but they lay about in such attitudes and were so disfigured that he had not recognized them for men: moreover, the place was to the south of the road, and therefore the ground was very soft and some of them were half under water and some hidden in the reeds. All seemed to be suffering from some disease of a crumbling and disintegrating kind. It was doubtful whether all the life that pulsated in their bodies was their own: and soon John was certain, for he saw what seemed to be a growth on a man's arm slowly detach itself under his eyes and become a fat reddish creature, separable from the parent body, though it was in no hurry to separate itself. And once he had seen that, his eyes were opened and he saw the same thing happening all round him, and the whole assembly was but a fountain of writhing and reptilian life quickening as he watched and sprouting out of the human forms. But in each form the anguished eyes were alive, sending to him unutterable messages from the central life which survived, self-conscious, though the self were but a fountain of vermin. One old cripple, whose face was all gone but the mouth and eyes, was sitting up to receive drink from a cup which a woman held to his lips. When he had as much as she thought good, she snatched the cup from his hands and went on to her next patient. She was dark but beautiful.

'Don't lag,' said the Guide, 'this is a very dangerous place. You had better come away. This is Luxuria.'

But John's eyes were caught by a young man to whom the witch had just come in her rounds. The disease, by seeming, had hardly begun with him: there was an unpleasant suspicion about his fingers—something a little too supple for joints—a little independent of his other movements—but, on the whole, he was still a well-looking person. And as the witch came to him the hands shot out to the cup, and the man drew them back again: and the hands went crawling out for the cup a second time, and again the man wrenched them back, and turned his face away, and cried out:

> 'Quick! The black, sulphurous, never quenched,
> Old festering fire begins to play
> Once more within. Look! By brute force I have wrenched
> Unmercifully my hands the other way.
>
> 'Quick, Lord! On the rack thus, stretched tight,
> Nerves clamouring as at nature's wrong.
> Scorched to the quick, whipp'd raw—Lord, in this plight
> You see, you see no man can suffer long.
>
> 'Quick, Lord! Before new scorpions bring
> New venom—ere fiends blow the fire
> A second time—quick, show me that sweet thing
> Which, 'spite of all, more deeply I desire.'

And all the while the witch stood saying nothing, but only holding out the cup and smiling kindly on him with her dark eyes and her dark, red mouth. Then, when she saw that he would not drink, she passed on to the next: but at the first step she took, the young man gave a sob and his hands flew out and grabbed the cup and he buried his head in it: and when she took it from his lips clung to it as a drowning man to a piece of wood. But at last he sank down in the swamp with a groan. And the worms where there should have been fingers were unmistakable.

'Come on,' said Vertue.

They resumed their journey, John lagging a bit. I dreamed that the witch came to him walking softly in the marshy ground by the roadside and holding out the cup to him also: when he went faster she kept pace with him.

'I will not deceive you,' she said, 'You see there is no pretence. I am not trying to make you believe that this cup will take you to your Island. I am not saying it will quench your thirst for long. But taste it, none the less, for you are very thirsty.'

But John walked forward in silence.

'It is true,' said the witch, 'that you never can tell when you have reached the point beyond which there is no return. But that cuts both ways. If you can never be certain that one more taste is safe, neither can you be certain that one more taste is fatal. But you can be certain that you are terribly thirsty.'

But John continued as before.

'At least,' said the witch, 'have one more taste of it, before you abandon it for ever. This is a bad moment to choose for resistance, when you are tired and miserable and have already listened to me too long. Taste this once, and I will leave you. I do not promise never to come back: but perhaps when I come again you will be strong and happy and well able to resist me—not as you are now.'

And John continued as before.

'Come,' said the witch. 'You are only wasting time. You know you will give in, in the end. Look ahead at the hard road and the grey sky. What other pleasure is there in sight?'

So she accompanied him for a long way, till the weariness of her importunity tempted him far more than any positive desire. But he forced his mind to other things and kept himself occupied for a mile or so by making the following verses:

> When Lilith means to draw me
> Within her secret bower,
> She does not overawe me
> With beauty's pomp and power,
> Nor, with angelic grace
> Of courtesy, and the pace
> Of gliding ships, comes veiled at evening hour.
>
> Eager, unmasked, she lingers
> Heart-sick and hunger sore
> With hot, dry, jewelled fingers
> Stretched out, beside her door,
> Offering with gnawing haste
> Her cup, whereof who taste,
> (She promises no better) thirst far more.
>
> What moves me, then, to drink it?
> —Her spells, which all around
> So change the land, we think it
> A great waste where a sound
> Of wind like tales twice told
> Blusters, and cloud is rolled
> Always above yet no rain falls to ground.
>
> Across drab iteration
> Of bare hills, line on line,
> The long road's sinuation
> Leads on. The witch's wine,
> Though promising nothing, seems
> In that land of no streams,
> To promise best—the unrelished anodyne.

And by the time he had reached the word *anodyne* the witch was gone. But he had never in his life felt more weary, and for a while the purpose of his pilgrimage woke no desire in him.

VIII
The Northern Dragon

'NOW,' SAID THE GUIDE, 'our time is come.'

They looked at him inquiringly.

'We are come,' said he, 'to that point of the road which lies midway between the two land bridges that I spoke of. The cold dragon is here on our left. and the hot dragon on our right. Now is the time to show what you are made of. Wolf is waiting in the wood southward: in the rocks northward, raven wheeling, in hope of carrion. Behoves you both be on guard quickly. God defend you.'

'Well,' said Virtue. And he drew his sword and slung his shield round from his back. Then he held out his hand first to the Guide, and then to John. 'So long,' he said.

'Go where it is least green,' said Guide, 'for there the ground is firmest. And good luck.'

Virtue left the road and began to pick his way cautiously southward, feeling out the fen-paths. The Guide turned to John.

'Have you any practice with a sword?' he said.

'None, sir,' answered John.

'None is better than a smattering. You must trust to mother-wit. Aim at his belly—an upward jab. I shouldn't try cutting, if I were you: you don't know enough.'

'I will do the best I can,' said John. And then, after a pause: 'There is only one dragon, I suppose. I don't need to guard my back.'

'Of course there is only one, for he has eaten all the others. Otherwise he would not be a dragon. You know the maxim—*serpens nisi sepentem comederit*—'

Then I saw John also settle his gear and step off the road to the left. The ascent began at once, and before he was ten yards from the road he was six feet above it: but the formation of the rocks was such that it was like mounting a huge stair, and was tiring rather than difficult. When he first stopped to wipe the sweat out of his eyes the mist was already so dense that he could hardly see the road beneath him. Ahead the grey darkness shaded quickly into black. Then suddenly John heard a dry, rattling sound in front of him, and a little above. He got a better grip on his sword, and took one pace towards it, listening intently. Then came the sound again: and after that he heard a croaking voice, as of a gigantic frog. The dragon was singing to himself:

'Once the worm-laid egg broke in the wood.
I came forth shining into the trembling wood,
The sun was on my scales, dew upon the grasses,
The cool, sweet grasses and the budding leaves.
I wooed my speckled mate. We played at druery
And sucked warm milk dropping from the goats' teats.

'Now I keep watch on the gold in my rock cave
In a country of stones: old, deplorable dragon,
Watching my hoard. In winter night the gold
Freezes through toughest scales my cold belly.
The jagged crowns and twisted cruel rings
Knobbly and icy are old dragon's bed.

'Often I wish I hadn't eaten my wife,
Though worm grows not to dragon till he eat worm.
She could have helped me, watch and watch about,
Guarding the hoard. Gold would have been the safer.
I could uncoil my weariness at times and take
A little sleep, sometimes when she was watching.

'Last night under the moonset a fox barked,
Woke me. Then I knew I had been sleeping.
Often an owl flying over the country of stones
Startles me, and I think I must have slept.
Only a moment. That very moment a man
Might have come out of the cities, stealing, to get my gold.

'They make plots in the towns to steal my gold.
They whisper of me in a low voice, laying plans,
Merciless men. Have they not ale upon the benches,
Warm wife in bed, singing, and sleep the whole night?
But I leave not the cave but once in winter
To drink of the rock pool: in summer twice.

'They feel no pity for the old, lugubrious dragon.
Oh, Lord, that made the dragon, grant me Thy peace!
But ask not that I should give up the gold,
Nor move, nor die; others would get the gold.
Kill, rather, Lord, the men and the other dragons
That I may sleep, go when I will to drink.'

As John listened to this song he forgot to be afraid. Disgust first, and then pity, chased fear from his mind: and after them came a strange desire to speak with the dragon and to suggest some sort of terms and division of the spoil: not that he desired the gold, but it seemed to him a not all ignoble desire to surround and contain so much within oneself. But while these things passed through his imagination, his body took care of him, keeping his grip steady on the sword hilt, his eyes strained into the darkness, and his feet ready to spring: so that he was not taken by surprise when he saw that in the rolling of the mist above him something else was rolling, and rolling round him to enclose him. But still he did not move. The dragon was paying its body out like a rope from a cave just above him. At first it swayed, the great head bobbing vertically, as a caterpillar sways searching for a new grip with half its length while the other half rests still on the leaf. Then the head dived and went behind him. He kept turning round to watch it, and it led the volume of the dragon's body round in a circle and finally went back into the cave, leaving a loop of dragon all round the man. Still John waited till the loop began to tighten, about on a level with his chest. Then he ducked and came up again with a jab of his sword into the under-side of the brute. It went in to the hilt, but there was no blood. At once the head came twisting back out of the cave. Eyes full of cruelty—cold cruelty without a spark of rage in it—stared into his face. The mouth was wide open— it was not red within, but grey like lead—and the breath of the creature was freezing cold. As soon as it touched John's face, everything was changed. A corselet of ice seemed to be closed about him, seemed to shut in his heart, so that it could never again flutter with panic or with greed. His strength was multiplied. His arms seemed to him iron. He found he was laughing and making thrust after thrust into the brute's throat. He found that the struggle was already over—perhaps hours ago. He was standing unwearied in a lonely place among rocks with a dead reptile at his feet. He remembered that he had killed it. And the time before he had killed it seemed very long ago.

IX
The Southern Dragon

JOHN CAME LEAPING DOWN the rocks into the road, whistling a tune. The Guide came to greet him, but before they had spoken a word they both turned round in wonder at a great cry from the South. The sun had come out so that the whole marsh glittered like dirty copper: and at first they thought that it was the sun upon his arms that made Vertue flash like flame as he came leaping, running, and dancing towards them. But as he drew nearer they saw that he was veritably on fire. Smoke came from him, and where his feet slipped into the bog holes there were

---

8. *Then John ducked and came up again with a jab of his sword into the under-side of the brute.*

little puffs of steam. Hurtless flames ran up and down his sword and licked over his hand. His breast heaved and he reeled like a drunk man. They made towards him, but he cried out:

'I have come back with victory got—
But stand away—touch me not
Even with your clothes. I burn red-hot.

'The worm was bitter. When she saw
My shield glitter beside the shaw
She spat flame from her golden jaw.

'When on my sword her vomit split
The blade took fire. On the hilt
Beryl cracked, and bubbled gilt.

'When sword and sword arm were all flame
With the very heat that came
Out of the brute, I flogged her tame.

'In her own spew the worm died.
I rolled her round and tore her wide
And plucked the heart from her boiling side.

'When my teeth were in the heart
I felt a pulse within me start
As though my breast would break apart.

'It shook the hills and made them reel
And spun the woods round like a wheel.
The grass singed where I set my heel.

'Behemoth is my serving man!
Before the conquered hosts of Pan
Riding tamed Leviathan
Loud I sing for well I can
RESVRGAM and IO PAEAN,
IO, IO, IO, PAEAN!!

'Now I know the stake I played for,
Now I know what a worm's made for!'

X
The Brook

MY DREAM WAS FULL of light and noise. I thought they went on their way sing-ing and laughing like schoolboys. Vertue lost all his dignity, and John was never tired: and for ten miles or so they picked up an old fiddler who was going that way, who played them such jigs and they danced more than they walked. And Vertue invented doggerels to his tunes to mock the old Pagan virtues in which he had been bred.

But in the midst of all this gaiety, suddenly John stood still and his eyes filled with tears. They had come to a little cottage, beside a river, which was empty and ruinous. Then they all asked John what ailed him.

'We have come back to Puritania,' he said, 'and that was my father's house. I see that my father and mother are gone already beyond the brook. I had much I would have said to them. But it is no matter.'

'No matter indeed,' said the Guide, 'since you will cross the brook yourself be-fore nightfall.'

'For the last time?' said Vertue.

'For the last time,' said the Guide, 'all being well.'

And now the day was declining and the Eastern Mountains loomed big and black ahead of them. Their shadows lengthened as they went down towards the brook.

'I am cured of playing the Stoic,' said Vertue, 'and I confess that I go down in fear and sadness. I also—there were many people I would have spoken to. There were many years I would call back, Whatever there is beyond the brook, it cannot be the same. Something is being ended. It is a real brook.

'I am not one that easily flits past in thought
The ominous stream, imagining death made for nought.
This person, mixed of body and breath, to which concurred
Once only one articulation of thy word,
Will be resolved eternally: nor can time bring
(Else time were vain) once back again the self-same thing.
Therefore among the riddles that no man has read
I put thy paradox, Who liveth and was dead.
As Thou hast made substantially, thou wilt unmake
In earnest and for everlasting. Let none take
Comfort in frail supposal that some hour and place
To those who mourn recovers the wished voice and face.
Whom Thy great *Exit* banishes, no after age
Of epilogue leads back upon the lighted stage.
Where is Prince Hamlet when the curtain's down? Where fled
Dreams at the dawn, or colours when the light is sped?

We are thy colours, fugitive, never restored,
Never repeated again. Thou only art the Lord,
Thou only art holy. In the shadowy vast
Of thine Osirian wings Thou dost enfold the past.
There sit in throne antediluvian, cruel kings,
There the first nightingale that sang to Eve yet sings,
There are the irrecoverable guiltless years,
There, yet unfallen, Lucifer among his peers.

'For thou art also a deity of the dead, a god
Of graves, with necromancies in thy potent rod;
Thou art Lord of the unbreathable transmortal air
Where mortal thinking fails: night's nuptial darkness, where
All lost embraces intermingle and are bless'd,
And all die, but all are, while Thou continuest.'

The twilight was now far advanced and they were in sight of the brook. And John said, 'I thought all those things when I was in the house of Wisdom. But now I think better things. Be sure it is not for nothing that the Landlord has knit our hearts so closely to time and place—to one friend rather than another and one shire more than all the land.

'Passing to-day by a cottage, I shed tears
When I remembered how once I had dwelled there
With my mortal friends who are dead. Years
Little had healed the wound that was laid bare.

'Out, little spear that stabs. I, fool, believed
I had outgrown the local, unique sting,
I had transmuted away (I was deceived)
Into love universal the lov'd thing.

'But Thou, Lord, surely knewest Thine own plan
When the angelic indifferences with no bar
Universally loved but Thou gav'st man
The tether and pang of the particular;

'Which, like a chemic drop, infinitesimal,
Plashed into pure water, changing the whole,
Embodies and embitters and turns all
Spirit's sweet water to astringent soul.

'That we, though small, may quiver with fire's same
Substantial form as Thou—nor reflect merely,
As lunar angel, back to thee, cold flame.
Gods we are, Thou has said: and we pay dearly.'

And now they were already at the brook, and it was so dark that I did not see them go over. Only, as my dream ended, and the voice of the birds at my window began to reach my ear (for it was a summer morning), I heard the voice of the Guide, mixed with theirs and not unlike them, singing this song:

> 'I know not, I,
>   What the men together say,
> How lovers, lovers die
>   And youth passes away.
>
> 'Cannot understand
>   Love that mortal bears
> For native, native land
>   —All lands are theirs.
>
> 'Why at grave they grieve
>   For one voice and face,
> And not, and not receive
>   Another in its place.
>
> 'I, above the cone
>   Of the circling night
> Flying, never have known
>   More or lesser light.
>
> 'Sorrow it is they call
>   This cup: whence my lip,
> Woe's me, never in all
>   My endless days must sip.'

Afterword to Third Edition

ON RE-READING THIS BOOK ten years after I wrote it, I find its chief faults to be those two which I myself least easily forgive in the books of other men: needless obscurity, and an uncharitable temper.

There were two causes, I now realise, for the obscurity. On the intellectual side my own progress had been from 'popular realism' to Philosophical Idealism; from Idealism to Pantheism; from Pantheism to Theism; and from Theism to Christianity. I still think this a very natural road, but I now know that it is a road very rarely trodden. In the early thirties I did not know this. If I had had any notion of my own isolation, I should either have kept silent about my journey or else endeavoured to describe it with more consideration for the reader's difficulties. As things were, I committed the same sort of blunder as one who should narrate his travels through the Gobi Desert on the assumption that this route was as familiar to the British public as the line from Euston to Crewe. And this original blunder was soon aggravated by a profound change in the philosophical thought of our age. Idealism itself went out of fashion. The dynasty of Green, Bradley, and Bosanquet fell, and the world inhabited by philosophical students of my own generation became as alien to our successors as if not years but centuries had intervened.

The second cause of obscurity was the (unintentionally) 'private' meaning I then gave to the word 'Romanticism'. I would not now use this word to describe the experience which is central in this book. I would not, indeed, use it to describe anything, for I now believe it to be a word of such varying senses that it has become useless and should be banished from our vocabulary. Even if we exclude the vulgar sense in which a 'romance' means simply 'a love affair' (Peer and Film Star Romance) I think we can distinguish at least seven kinds of things which are called 'romantic'.

1. Stories about dangerous adventure—particularly, dangerous adventure in the past or in remote places—are 'romantic'. In this sense Dumas is a typically 'romantic' author, and stories about sailing ships, the Foreign Legion, and the rebellion of 1745, are usually 'romantic'.

2. The marvellous is 'romantic', provided it does not make part of the believed religion. Thus magicians, ghosts, fairies, witches, dragons, nymphs, and dwarfs are 'romantic'; angels, less so. Greek gods are 'romantic' in Mr. James Stephens or Mr. Maurice Hewlett; not so in Homer and Sophocles. In this sense Malory, Boiardo, Ariosto, Spenser, Tasso, Mrs. Radcliffe, Shelley, Coleridge, William Morris, and Mr. E. R. Eddison are 'romantic' authors.

3. The art dealing with 'Titanic' characters, emotions strained beyond the common pitch, and high-flown sentiments or codes of honour is 'romantic'. (I welcome the growing use of the word 'Romanesque' to describe this type.) In this sense Rostand and Sidney are 'romantic', and so (though unsuccessfully) are Dryden's Heroic Dramas, and there is a good deal of 'romanticism' in Corneille. I take it that Michelangelo is, in this sense, a 'romantic' artist.

4. 'Romanticism' can also mean the indulgence in abnormal, and finally in anti-natural, moods. The *macabre* is 'romantic', and so is an interest in torture, and a love of death. This, if I understand them, is what M. Mario Praz and M. D. de Rougemont would mean by the word. In this sense *Tristan* is Wagner's most 'romantic' opera; Poe, Baudelaire, and Flaubert, are 'romantic' authors; Surrealism is 'romantic'.

5. Egoism and Subjectivism are 'romantic'. In this sense the typically 'romantic' books are *Werther* and Rousseau's *Confessions,* and the works of Byron and Proust.

6. Every revolt against existing civilisation and conventions whether it look forward to revolution, or backward to the 'primitive' is called 'romantic' by some people. Thus pseudo-Ossian, Epstein, D. H. Lawrence, Walt Whitman, and Wagner are 'romantic.'

7. Sensibility to natural objects, when solemn and enthusiastic, is 'romantic.' In this sense *The Prelude* is the most 'romantic' poem in the world: and there is much 'romanticism' in Keats, Shelley, de Vigny, de Musset, and Goethe.

It will be seen, of course, that many writers are 'romantic' on more than one account. Thus Morris comes in my first class as well as my second. Mr. Eddison in my second as well as my third, Rousseau in my sixth as well as my fifth, Shelley in my sixth and fifth, and so on. This may suggest some common root, whether historical or psychological, for all seven: but the real qualitative difference between them is shown by the fact that a liking for any one does not imply liking for the others. Though people who are 'romantic' in different senses may turn to the same books, they turn to them for different reasons, and one half of William Morris's readers do not know how the other half live. It makes all the difference in the world whether you like Shelley because he provides a mythology or because he promises a revolution. Thus I myself always loved the second kind of Romanticism and detested the fourth and fifth kinds; I liked the first very little and the third only after I was grown-up—as an acquired taste.

But what I meant by 'Romanticism' when I wrote the *Pilgrim's Regress*—and what I would still be taken to mean on the title page of this book—was not exactly any one of these seven things. What I meant was a particular recurrent experience which dominated my childhood and adolescence and which I hastily called 'Romantic' because inanimate nature and marvellous literature were among the things that evoked it. I still believe that the experience is common, commonly misunderstood, and of immense importance: but I know now that in other minds it arises under other *stimuli* and is entangled with other irrelevancies and that to bring it into the forefront of consciousness is not so easy as I once supposed. I will now try to describe it sufficiently to make the following pages intelligible.

The experience is one of intense longing. It is distinguished from other longings by two things. In the first place, though the sense of want is acute and even painful, yet the mere wanting is felt to be somehow a delight. Other desires are felt as pleasures only if satisfaction is expected in the near future: hunger is pleasant only while we know (or believe) that we are soon going to eat. But this desire, even when there is no hope of possible satisfaction, continues to be prized, and even to be preferred to anything else in the world, by those who have once felt it. This hunger is better than any other fullness; this poverty better than all other wealth. And thus it comes about, that if the desire is long absent, it may itself be desired, and that new desiring becomes a new instance of the original desire, though the subject may not at once recognise the fact and thus cries out for his lost youth of soul at the very moment in which he is being rejuvenated. This sounds complicated, but it is simple when we live it. 'Oh to feel as I did then!' we cry; not noticing that even while we say the words the very feeling whose loss we lament is rising again in all its old bitter-sweetness. For this sweet Desire cuts across our ordinary distinctions between wanting and having. To have it is, by definition, a want: to want it, we find, is to have it.

In the second place, there is a peculiar mystery about the *object* of this Desire. Inexperienced people (and inattention leaves some inexperienced all their lives) suppose, when they feel it, that they know what they are desiring. Thus if it comes to a child while he is looking at a far off hillside he at once thinks 'if only I were there'; if it comes when he is remembering some event in the past, he thinks 'if only I could go back to those days'. If it comes (a little later) while he is reading a 'romantic' tale or poem of 'perilous seas and faerie lands forlorn', he thinks he is wishing that such places really existed and that he could reach them. If it comes (later still) in a context with erotic suggestions he believes he is desiring the perfect beloved. If he falls upon literature (like Maeterlinck or the early Yeats) which treats of spirits and the like with some show of serious belief, he may think that he is hankering for real magic and occultism. When it darts out upon him from his studies in history or science, he may confuse it with the intellectual craving for knowledge.

But every one of these impressions is wrong. The sole merit I claim for this book is that it is written by one who has proved them all to be wrong. There is no room for vanity in the claim: I know them to be wrong not by intelligence but by experience, such experience as would not have come my way if my youth had been wiser, more virtuous, and less self-centred than it was. For I have myself been deluded by every one of these false answers in turn, and have contemplated each of them earnestly enough to discover the cheat. To have embraced so many false Florimels is no matter for boasting: it is fools, they say, who learn by experience. But since they do at least learn, let a fool bring his experience into the common stock that wiser men profit by it.

Every one of these supposed *objects* for the Desire is inadequate to it. An easy experiment will show that by going to the far hillside you will get either nothing, or else a recurrence of the same desire which sent you thither. A rather more difficult, but still possible, study of your own memories, will prove that by returning to the past you could not find, as a possession, that ecstasy which some sudden reminder of the past now moves you to desire. Those remembered moments were either quite commonplace at the time (and owe all their enchantment to memory) or else were themselves moments of desiring. The same is true of the things described in the poets and marvellous romancers. The moment we endeavour to think out seriously what it would be like if they were actual, we discover this. When Sir Arthur Conan Doyle claimed to have photographed a fairy, I did not, in fact, believe it: but the mere making of the claim—the approach of the fairy to within even that hailing distance of actuality—revealed to me at once that if the claim had succeeded it would have chilled rather than satisfied the desire which fairy literature had hitherto aroused. Once grant your fairy, your enchanted forest, your satyr, faun, wood-nymph and well of immortality *real*, and amidst all the scientific, social and practical interest which the discovery would awake, the Sweet Desire would have disappeared, would have shifted its ground, like the cuckoo's voice or the rainbow's end, and be now calling us from beyond a *further* hill. With Magic in the darker sense (as it has been and is actually practised) we should fare even worse. How if one had gone that way—had actually called for something and it had come? What would one feel? Terror, pride, guilt, tingling excitement . . . but what would all that have to do with our Sweet Desire? It is not at Black Mass or *séance* that the Blue Flower grows. As for the sexual answer, that I suppose to be the most obviously false Florimel of all. On whatever plane you take it, it is not what we were looking for. Lust can be gratified. Another personality can become to us 'our America, our New-found-land'. A happy marriage can be achieved. But what has any of the three, or any mixture of the three, to do with that unnameable something, desire for which pierces us like a rapier at the smell of a bonfire, the sound of wild ducks flying overhead, the title of *The Well at the World's End*, the opening lines of *Kubla Khan*, the morning cobwebs in late summer, or the noise of falling waves?

It appeared to me therefore that if a man diligently followed this desire, pursuing the false objects until their falsity appeared and then resolutely abandoning them, he must come out at last into the clear knowledge that the human soul was made to enjoy some object that is never fully given—nay, cannot even be imagined as given—in our present mode of subjective and spatio-temporal experience. This Desire was, in the soul, as the Siege Perilous in Arthur's castle—the chair in which only one could sit. And if nature makes nothing in vain, the One who can sit in this chair must exist. I knew only too well how easily the longing accepts false objects and through what dark ways the pursuit of them leads us: but I also saw that the Desire itself contains the corrective of all these errors. The only fatal error was to pretend that you had passed from desire to fruition, when, in reality, you had found either nothing, or desire itself, or the satisfaction of some different desire. The dialectic of Desire, faithfully followed, would retrieve all mistakes, head you off from all false paths, and force you not to propound, but to live through, a sort of ontological proof. This lived dialectic, and the merely argued dialectic of my philosophical progress, seemed to have converged on one goal; accordingly I tried to put them both into my allegory which thus became a defence of Romanticism (in my peculiar sense) as well as of Reason and Christianity.

After this explanation the reader will more easily understand (I do not ask him to condone) the bitterness of certain pages in this book. He will realise how the

Post-War period must have looked to one who had followed such a road as mine. The different intellectual movements of that time were hostile to one another; but the one thing that seemed to unite them all was their common enmity to 'immortal longings'. The direct attack carried out on them from below by those who followed Freud or D. H. Lawrence, I think I could have borne with some temper; what put me out of patience was the scorn which claimed to be from above, and which was voiced by the American 'Humanists', the Neo-Scholastics, and some who wrote for *The Criterion*. These people seemed to me to be condemning what they did not understand. When they called Romanticism 'nostalgia' I, who had rejected long ago the illusion that the desired object was in the past, felt that they had not even crossed the *Pons Asinorum*. In the end I lost my temper.

If I were now writing a book I could bring the question between those thinkers and myself to a much finer point. One of them described Romanticism as 'spilled religion'. I accept the description. And I agree that he who has religion ought not to spill it. But does it follow that he who finds it spilled should avert his eyes? How if there is a man to whom those bright drops on the floor are the beginning of a trail which, duly followed, will lead him in the end to taste the cup itself? How if no other trail, humanly speaking, were possible? Seen in this light my ten years' old quarrel both with the counter-Romantics on the one hand and with the sub-Romantics on the other (the apostles of instinct and even of gibberish) assumes, I trust, a certain permanent interest. Out of this double quarrel came the dominant image of my allegory—the barren, aching rocks of its 'North', the foetid swamps of its 'South', and between them the Road on which alone mankind can safely walk.

The things I have symbolised by North and South, which are to me equal and opposite evils, each continually strengthened and made plausible by its critique of the other, enter our experience on many different levels. In agriculture we have to fear both the barren soil and the soil which is irresistibly fertile. In the animal kingdom, the crustacean and the jellyfish represent two low solutions of the problem of existence. In our eating, the palate revolts both from excessive bitter and excessive sweet. In art, we find on the one hand, purists and doctrinaires, who would rather (like Scaliger) lose a hundred beauties than admit a single fault, and who cannot believe anything to be good if the unlearned spontaneously enjoy it: on the other hand, we find the uncritical and slovenly artists who will spoil the whole work rather than deny themselves any indulgence of sentiment or humour or sensationalism. Everyone can pick out among his own acquaintance the Northern and Southern types—the high noses, compressed lips, pale complexions, dryness and taciturnity of the one, the open mouths, the facile laughter and tears, the garrulity and (so to speak) general greasiness of the others. The Northerners are the men of rigid systems whether sceptical or dogmatic, Aristocrats, Stoics, Pharisees, Rigorists, signed and sealed members of highly organised 'Parties'. The Southerners are by their very nature less definable; boneless souls whose doors stand open day and night to almost every visitant, but always with readiest welcome for those, whether Maenad or Mystagogue, who offer some sort of intoxication. The delicious tang of the forbidden and the unknown draws them on with fatal attraction; the smudging of all frontiers, the relaxation of all resistances, dream, opium, darkness, death, and the return to the womb. Every feeling is justified by the mere fact that it is felt: for a Northerner, every feeling on the same ground is suspect. An arrogant and hasty selectiveness on some narrow *a priori* basis cuts him off from the sources of life. In Theology also there is a North and South. The one cries 'Drive out the bondmaid's son', and the other 'Quench not the smoking flax'. The one exaggerates the distinctness between Grace and Nature into a sheer opposition and by vilifying the higher levels of Nature (the real *praeparatio evangelica* inherent in certain immediately sub-Christian experiences) makes the way hard for those who are at the point of coming in. The other blurs the distinction altogether, flatters mere kindliness into thinking it is charity and vague optimisms or pantheisms into thinking that they are Faith, and makes the way out fatally easy and imperceptible for the budding apostate. The two extremes do not coincide with Romanism (to the North) and Protestantism (to the South). Barth might well have been placed among my Pale Men, and Erasmus might have found himself at home with Mr. Broad.

I take our own age to be predominantly Northern—it is two great 'Northern' powers that are tearing each other to pieces on the Don while I write. But the matter is complicated, for the rigid and ruthless system of the Nazis has 'Southern' and swamp-like elements at its centre; and when our age is 'Southern' at all, it is excessively so. D. H. Lawrence and the Surrealists have perhaps reached a point further 'South' than humanity ever reached before. And this is what one would expect. Opposite evils, far from balancing, aggravate each other. 'The heresies that men leave are hated most'; widespread drunkenness is the father of Prohibition and Prohibition of widespread drunkenness. Nature, outraged by one extreme, avenges herself by flying to the other. One can even meet adult males who are not ashamed to attribute their own philosophy to 'Reaction' and do not think the philosophy thereby discredited.

With both the 'North' and the 'South' a man has, I take it, only one concern—to avoid them and hold the Main Road. We must not 'hearken to the over-wise *or* to the over-foolish giant'. We were made to be neither cerebral men nor visceral men, but Men. Not beasts nor angels but Men—things at once rational and animal.

Three other cautions remain to be given. 1. The map on the end leaves has puzzled some readers because, as they say, 'it marks all sorts of places not mentioned in the text.'* But so do all maps in travel books. John's route is marked with a dotted line: those who are not interested in the places off that route need not bother about them. They are a half whimsical attempt to fill in the 'Northern' and 'Southern' halves of the world with the spiritual phenomena appropriate to them. Most of the names explain themselves. *Wanhope* is Middle English for Despair; *Woodey* and *Lyssanesos* mean 'Isle of Insanity'; *Behmenheim* is named, unfairly, after Jakob Boehme or Behmen; *Golnesshire* (Anglo-Saxon *Gál*) is the country of Lechery; in *Trineland* one feels 'in tune with the infinite'; and *Zeitgeistheim*, of course, is the habitat of the *Zeitgeist* or Spirit of the Age. *Naughtstow* is 'a place that is no good at all'. The two military railways were meant to symbolise the double attack from Hell on the two sides of our nature. It was hoped that the roads spreading out from each of the enemy railheads would look rather like claws or tentacles or tentacles reaching out into the country of Man's Soul. If you like to put little black arrows pointing South on the seven Northern roads (in the fashion of the newspaper war maps) and others pointing North on the six Southern roads, you would get a clear picture of the Holy War as I see it. You might amuse yourself by deciding where to put them—a question that admits different answers. On the Northern front, for example, I should represent the enemy in occupation of Cruelsland and Superbia, and thus threatening the Pale Men with a pincer movement. But I don't claim to know; and doubtless the position shifts every day. 2. The name *Mother Kirk* was chosen because 'Christianity' is not a very convincing name. Its defect was that it not unnaturally led the reader to attribute to me a much more definite *Ecclesiastical* position than I could really boast of. The book is concerned solely with Christianity as against unbelief. 'Denominational' questions do not come in. 3. In this afterword the autobiographical element in John has had to be stressed because the source of the obscurities lay there. But you must not assume that everything in the book is autobiographical. I was attempting to generalise, not to tell people about my own life.

C. S. LEWIS

*The map for this edition has been redrawn omitting the shires and the railways—Ed.

Christian Reflections

Edited by
Walter Hooper

CONTENTS

Preface

SHORTLY AFTER HIS conversion in 1929, C. S. Lewis wrote to a friend: 'When all is said (and truly said) about the divisions of Christendom, there remains, by God's mercy, an enormous common ground.'[1] From that time on Lewis thought that the best service he could do for his unbelieving neighbours was to explain and defend the belief that has been common to nearly all Christians at all times—that 'enormous common ground' which he usually referred to as 'mere' Christianity.

He was a thoroughgoing supernaturalist, believing in the Creation, the Fall, the Incarnation, the Resurrection, the Second Coming, and the Four Last Things (death, Judgement, Heaven, Hell). His defence of 'mere' Christianity was colourfully varied, depending on which part of the line needed defending; to that part which seemed thinnest he naturally went, adapting his tactics to suit his audience. Such, I think, is evident from this rather heterogeneous collection of Christian 'Reflections.' These fourteen papers, which I have attempted to arrange chronologically, were composed over the last twenty-odd years of Lewis's life; some were written specifically for periodicals; others, published here for the first time, were read to societies in and around Oxford and Cambridge. There are passages in some of the earlier papers where readers will find anticipations of his later work; but such overlaps are inevitable.

There is not yet available any such thing as *The Complete Works of C. S. Lewis* which a person could buy in a set of uniform volumes. But if the *Works* were obtainable (almost all are easy to secure as separate books) and one were to read from start to finish all the volumes called 'Religious Writings' he would, I think, be struck by what I consider the central premise of all Lewis's theological works—a premise implicit, even, in his books on other subjects. It is that *all* men are immortal.

I think this deserves singular emphasis; not only because it is such an important ingredient in Lewis's understanding of 'mere' (i.e., 'pure') Christianity, but because the fact that men are immortal is news to many people today. And (a point in which Lewis would support me), because most of the modern liberal theologians are so busy being 'relevant' (or whatever else is in fashion) that they make no effective presentation of 'mere' Christianity—the Everlasting Gospel—to those for whom Christ died.

To illustrate this particular feature of orthodox Christianity which Lewis constantly underlined, one need only refer to the well-known *Screwtape Letters*. Lewis himself considered the book's popularity disproportionate to its worth: he liked *Perelandra* best of all his works and thought it worth twenty *Screwtapes*. Still though

---

1. From an unpublished letter to Dom Bede Griffiths, O.S.B. (c. 1933).

he bore a grudge against the book and chafed at having always to be 'the author of *The Screwtape Letters*' on the dustjackets of most of his subsequent books, I never heard him say anything that could be taken as a retraction of its contents.

Screwtape's advice to his nephew, Wormwood, has been read by, and has edified (I expect), millions of readers. But, like many well-known books, it has its debunkers; most of whom debunk it for the same reason. One critic recently wrote: 'With the concentration camps across the Channel and the blitz at home, Screwtape seems to have been aiming at rather small targets and to have been decidedly lacking in the historical imagination . . . Lewis was a better student of the daily scene than he often realized; but less equipped to venture beyond the flaming ramparts of the world.'[1] Another writer, attempting to 'disentangle what is of permanent value . . . from what is ephemeral' in Lewis's works, notes the 'general moral pettiness' of *The Screwtape Letters*, adding that 'In the age which has produced Auschwitz, it is distasteful to have such slight topics associated with human damnation.'[2]

I dare say Lewis would have replied that damnation is far more likely to be distasteful than topics associated with it. But can anything which leads to damnation be 'petty'? Despite the fact that Auschwitz is an almost unparalleled instance of human wickedness and human suffering, it would have been an inappropriate example for Lewis's purpose. It is in one sense, the wrong *kind* of thing: its 'bigness,' so to speak, and uniqueness blunt its usefulness as a universal temptation to sin. Lewis's answer to such critics—his answer to what *Screwtape* is about—is writ plain in Screwtape's caution to the younger devil:

> You will say that these are very small sins; and doubtless like all young tempters, you are anxious to be able to report spectacular wickedness [Auschwitz?]. But do remember, the only thing that matters is the extent to which you separate the man from the Enemy. It does not matter how small the sins are provided that their cumulative effect is to edge the man away from the Light and out into the Nothing. Murder is no better than cards if cards can do the trick. Indeed the safest road to Hell is the gradual one—the gentle slope, soft underfoot, without sudden turnings, without milestones, without signposts.[3]

Because Lewis emphasized the reality of hell, not only in *Screwtape* but in *The Problem of Pain* (specially chapter VIII) and other books, it is often inferred that he was preoccupied with it—simply *wanted* it to be true. This indeed is to misunderstand not only Lewis but the Faith itself. For him the real problem was: so much mercy, yet *still* there is hell. Regardless of what we all wish Christianity were, he knew that this terrible doctrine has the support of Scripture (specially of Our Lord's own words) as well as that of reason: 'If a game is played, it must be possible to lose it.'[4]

I remember one very warm day when Lewis and I were reading in his study that I remarked, rather too loudly: 'Wheew! It's hot as hell !'—'How do *you* know?' came his answer. 'Better not say that.' I knew at once that he referred—more by the tone of his voice than anything else—to hell as the possible destination of some

1. Graham Hough, 'The Screwtape Letters', *The Times* (10 Feb. 1966), p. 15.
2. W. W. Robson, 'C. S. Lewis', *The Cambridge Quarterly*, vol. I (Summer, 1966), p. 253.
3. *The Screwtape Letters*, London: Geoffrey Bles Ltd. (1942), pp. 64–5.
4. *The Problem of Pain*, London: Geoffrey Bles Ltd. (1940), p. 106.

of us. The contemporary preoccupation with 'individual freedom' and 'rights' has deceived so many of us into imagining that we can make up our *own* theology, that Lewis's orthodox belief in a real heaven and hell strikes us as little short of fanatical: 'As there is one Face above all worlds merely to see which is irrevocable joy, so at the bottom of all worlds that face is waiting whose sight alone is the misery from which none who beholds it can recover. And though there [seem] to be, and indeed [are], a thousand roads by which a man could walk through the world, there [is] not a single one which [does] not lead sooner or later either to the Beatific or the Miserific Vision.'[1]

It would not be enough to leave the matter here. From everything that I heard Lewis say, certainly from his writings, I know that the 'Face above all worlds' was to him the most concrete and desirable of all realities. But he never forgot that every human soul would enjoy ultimately a vision either Beatific or Miserific. In a passage from his sermon 'The Weight of Glory', beside which modern liberal theology seems embarrassingly vapid, he strikes at the heart of the matter:

It is a serious thing to live in a society of possible gods and goddesses, to remember that the dullest and most uninteresting person you talk to may one day be a creature which, if you saw it now, you would be strongly tempted to worship, or else a horror and a corruption such as you now meet, if at all, only in a nightmare. All day long we are, in some degree, helping each other to one or other of these destinations. It is in the light of these overwhelming possibilities, it is with the awe and the circumspection proper to them, that we should conduct all our dealings with one another, all friendships, all loves, all play, all politics. There are no *ordinary* people. You have never talked to a mere mortal. Nations, cultures, arts, civilizations—these are mortal, and their life is to ours as the life of a gnat. But it is immortals whom we joke with, work with, marry, snub, and exploit—immortal horrors or everlasting splendours. This does not mean that we are to be perpetually solemn. We must play. But our merriment must be of that kind (and it is, in fact, the merriest kind) which exists between people who have, from the outset, taken each other seriously—no flippancy, no superiority, no presumption. And our charity must be a real and costly love, with deep feeling for the sins in spite of which we love the sinner—no mere tolerance or indulgence which parodies love as flippancy parodies merriment. Next to the Blessed Sacrament itself, your neighbour is the holiest object presented to your senses. If he is your Christian neighbour he is holy in almost the same way, for in him also Christ *vere latitat*—the glorifier and the glorified, Glory Himself, is truly hidden.[2]

I trust that I shall not labour the emphasis Lewis placed on the *either-or* of the Christian faith by recording a couple of snatches from my conversation with him—primarily in order to underline how solid this reality stood for him, not only in the pulpit or in the heat of writing, but in 'the light of common day'.

We were talking one time about a bore whom we both knew, a man who was generally recognized as being almost unbelievably dull. I told Lewis that the man succeeded in interesting me by the very intensity of his boredom. 'Yes,' he said, 'but let us not forget that Our Lord might well have said, "As ye have done it unto one of the least of these my bores, ye have done it unto me." 'There was a twinkle

---

1. *Perelandra*, London: The Bodley Head (1943), p. 126, (tenses altered).
2. 'The Weight of Glory', *Theology*, vol. XLIII (Nov. 1941), pp. 273-74.

in his eye as he said it and we both laughed, yet knowing at the same time that it was no joke. On another occasion I mentioned that I knew of a man's grave, the epitaph on whose tombstone read 'Here lies an atheist, all dressed up but with nowhere to go.' Lewis replied: 'I bet he wishes that were so.'

I should now, before introducing the papers in this book, like to record to Lewis's credit a positive restraint which he put upon all his theological works. As he was minded to write only about 'mere' Christianity, so he steadfastly refused to write about *differences* of belief He knew that discussions (or, more likely, arguments) about differences in doctrine or ritual were seldom edifying. At least he considered it far too dangerous a luxury for himself—far better stick to that 'enormous common ground'.

He made no exception even in his conversation, a fact I know to my own shame. I remember the first (and only) time I mentioned 'low' and 'high' churchmanship in his presence. He looked at me as though I had offered him poison. 'We must *never* discuss that,' he said, gently but firmly. Again, shortly before the publication of *Honest to God* in the United States, the editor of a popular American magazine asked Lewis to write a critique of the book for his columns. Lewis wrote back: 'What would you yourself think of me if I did? . . . A great deal of my utility has depended on my having kept out of dog-fights between professing schools of "Christian" thought. I'd sooner preserve that abstinence to the end.' This 'abstinence' has surely not weakened our conception of the Faith; his salutary single-mindedness has, rather, shown us its balance and true colours such as (I believe) few Christian apologists have succeeded in doing. Lewis, I think, understood very well what diet Our Lord intended when He commanded the Apostle '*Feed* my sheep.'

I am grateful to all those who have permitted me to reprint some of the papers in this book. (1) 'Christianity and Literature' was read to a religious society in Oxford and is reprinted from *Rehabilitations and Other Essays* (Oxford, 1939). (2) The three papers which I have collected under the title 'Christianity and Culture' include only Lewis's part in a controversy which first appeared in the columns of *Theology*. The entire controversy is composed of the following papers:

1. C. S. Lewis, 'Christianity and Culture', *Theology*, vol. XL (March 1940), pp. 166–79.
2. S. L. Bethell and E. F. Carritt, 'Christianity and Culture: Replies to Mr Lewis', *ib.*, vol. XL (May 1940), pp. 356–66.
3. C. S. Lewis, 'Christianity and Culture' (a letter), *ib.*, vol. XL (June 1940), pp. 475–77.
4. George Every, 'In Defence of Criticism', *ib.*, vol. XLI (Sept. 1940), pp. 159–65.
5. C. S. Lewis, 'Peace Proposals for Brother Every and Mr Bethell', *ib.*, vol. XLI (Dec. 1940), pp. 339–48.

I beg the reader to note that 'Christianity and Culture' came fairly early in Lewis's theological corpus. It might best be considered an early step in his spiritual pilgrimage—but certainly not his arrival. Here, instead of spirit progressively irradiating and transforming soul, he seems to envisage a relation between them in strict terms of 'either-or', with soul as Calvin's 'nature' and spirit as his 'grace', and spirit beginning exactly where soul leaves off. Later on he dealt much more profoundly with the relation between soul and spirit in such things as the essay on 'Transposition' and *The Four Loves*. He says, for instance, in 'Transposition':

May we not . . . suppose . . . that there is no experience of the spirit so transcendent and supernatural, no vision of Deity Himself so close and so far beyond all images and emotions, that to it also there cannot be an appropriate correspondence on the sensory level? Not by a new sense but by the incredible flooding of those very sensations we now have with a meaning, a transvaluation, of which we have here no faintest guess?[1]

(3) 'Religion: Reality or Substitute?' is reprinted from the now extinct *World Dominion*, vol. XIX (Sept.-Oct. 1941), except for the autobiographical paragraph 4 and part of paragraph 9 which were added a few years later. (4) The essay on 'Ethics' is published here for the first time. As I have suggested in a footnote (p. 205), I believe this paper to have been written before Lewis's *Abolition of Man* (1943); if I am right, it appears in the correct chronological sequence. (5) *'De Futilitate'* is an address given at Magdalen College, Oxford, during the Second World War at the invitation of Sir Henry Tizard (then President of Magdalen College). It, too, is published for the first time. (6) 'The Poison of Subjectivism' is reprinted from *Religion in Life*, vol. XII (Summer 1943).

(7) 'The Funeral of a Great Myth', published for the first time, may appear an intruder on theological premises. I have included it here because the 'myth' discussed in this essay seems quite obviously to be an outgrowth and development of one of the myths compared to the Christian Faith in Lewis's 'Is Theology Poetry?' (*The Socratic Digest,* No. 3 (1945), pp. 25-35). Its close connection with the *Digest* essay caused me to feel it deserved a place here; it is, also, relevant to the idea of Theism. (8) 'On Church Music' is reprinted from *English Church Music*, vol. XIX (April 1949). Lewis did not himself like hymns and the existence of this paper is entirely owing to the special invitation of his friend, Mr. Leonard Blake, who was editor of *English Church Music* at the time. (9) 'Historicism' originally appeared in *The Month*, vol. IV (October 1950).

(10) The two-part essay on 'The Psalms' is published for the first time. Judging from the handwriting (Lewis wrote all his works by hand), it roughly corresponds in time with the publication of his book, *Reflections on the Psalms* (1958). By the by, Lewis and T. S. Eliot met one another for the first time in 1961 at Lambeth Palace where they worked together on the Archbishops of Canterbury and York's Commission for the Revision of the Psalter. (11) Although two pages of the manuscript of 'The Language of Religion' are lost, the omission, fortunately, does not seriously affect the main argument of the paper. It appears in print for the first time, as does (12) 'Petitionary Prayer: A Problem without an Answer' which was originally read to the Oxford Clerical Society on 8th December 1953. (13) 'Modern Theology and Biblical Criticism' is the title I have given to a paper Lewis read at Westcott House, Cambridge, on 11th May 1959. This is its first publication. (14) 'The Seeing Eye'

---

1. 'Transposition', *Transposition and Other Addresses,* London: Geoffrey Bles Ltd. (1949), p. 20. An expanded version of this essay appears in *Screwtape Proposes a Toast and Other Pieces,* London: Fontana Books (1965).

was originally published in the American periodical, *Show*, vol. III (Feb. 1963) under the title 'Onward, Christian Spacemen'. Lewis so heartily disliked the title which the editors of *Show* gave this piece that I felt justified in re-naming it.

As Lewis did not prepare these essays for publication, I have ventured to add here and there a footnote where references might be useful and to draw attention to other works by Lewis on the same subject. My own notes are enclosed within square brackets in order to prevent their being confused with Lewis's.

My thanks go to Major W. H. Lewis to whom I owe the honour of serving as his late brother's editor. I have received so much help and kindness from Mr Owen Barfield and Dr and Mrs Austin Farrer that I gratefully record my obligation to them. I also express my gratitude to Miss Jackie Gibbs who assisted me with the typing. Finally, it is a pleasure to thank Mr Daryl R. Williams of my College who has so conscientiously corrected the proofs to this book.

Wadham College, Oxford.   WALTER HOOPER
St Michael and All Angels, 1966

Christianity and Literature

WHEN I WAS ASKED to address this society, I was at first tempted to refuse because the subject proposed to me, that of Christianity and Literature, did not seem to admit of any discussion. I knew, of course, that Christian story and sentiment were among the things on which literature could be written, and, conversely, that literature was one of the ways in which Christian sentiment could be expressed and Christian story told; but there seemed nothing more to be said of Christianity in this connection than of any of the hundred and one other things that men made books about. We are familiar, no doubt, with the expression 'Christian Art', by which people usually mean Art that represents Biblical or hagiological scenes, and there is, in this sense, a fair amount of 'Christian Literature'. But I question whether it has any literary qualities peculiar to itself. The rules for writing a good passion play or a good devotional lyric are simply the rules for writing tragedy or lyric in general: success in sacred literature depends on the same qualities of structure, suspense, variety, diction, and the like which secure success in secular literature. And if we enlarge the idea of Christian Literature to include not only literature on sacred themes but all that is written by Christians for Christians to read, then, I think, Christian Literature can exist only in the same sense in which Christian cookery might exist. It would be possible, and it might be edifying, to write a Christian cookery book. Such a book would exclude dishes whose preparation involves unnecessary human labour or animal suffering, and dishes excessively luxurious. That is to say, its choice of dishes would be Christian. But there could be nothing specifically Christian about the actual cooking of the dishes included. Boiling an egg is the same process whether you are a Christian or a Pagan. In the same way, literature written by Christians for Christians would have to avoid mendacity, cruelty, blasphemy, pornography, and the like, and it would aim at edification in so far as edification was proper to the kind of work in hand. But whatever it chose to do would have to be done by the means common to all literature; it could succeed or fail only by the same excellences and the same faults as all literature; and its literary success or failure would never be the same thing as its obedience or disobedience to Christian principles.

I have been speaking so far of Christian Literature *proprement dite*—that is, of writing which is intended to affect us as literature, by its appeal to imagination. But in the visible arts I think we can make a distinction between sacred art, however sacred in theme, and pure iconography—between that which is intended, in the first instance, to affect the imagination and the aesthetic appetite, and that which is meant merely as the starting-point for devotion and meditation. If I were treating the visible arts I should have to work out here a full distinction of the work of art from the icon on the one hand and the toy on the other. The icon and the toy have this in common that their value depends very little on their perfection as artefacts—a shapeless rag may give as much pleasure as the costliest doll, and two sticks tied crosswise may kindle as much devotion as the work of Leonardo.[1] And to make matters more complicated the very same object could often be used in all three ways. But I do not think the icon and the work of art can be so sharply distinguished in literature. I question whether the badness of a really bad hymn can ordinarily be so irrelevant to devotion as the badness of a bad devotional picture. Because the hymn uses words, its badness will, to some degree, consist in confused or erroneous thought and unworthy sentiment. But I mention this difficult question here only to say that I do not propose to treat it. If any literary works exist which have a purely iconographic value and no literary value, they are not what I am talking about. Indeed I could not, for I have not met them.

Of Christian Literature, then, in the sense of 'work aiming at literary value and written by Christians for Christians', you see that I have really nothing to say and believe that nothing can be said. But I think I have something to say about what may be called the Christian approach to literature: about the principles, if you will, of Christian literary theory and criticism. For while I was thinking over the subject you gave me I made what seemed to me a discovery. It is not an easy one to put into words. The nearest I can come to it is to say that I found a disquieting contrast between the whole circle of ideas used in modern criticism and certain ideas recurrent in the New Testament. Let me say at once that it is hardly a question of logical contradiction between clearly defined concepts. It is too vague for that. It is more a repugnance of atmospheres, a discordance of notes, an incompatibility of temperaments.

What are the key-words of modern criticism? *Creative,* with its opposite *derivative; spontaneity,* with its opposite *convention; freedom,* contrasted with *rules.* Great authors are innovators, pioneers, explorers; bad authors bunch in schools and follow models. Or again, great authors are always 'breaking fetters' and 'bursting bonds'. They have personality, they 'are themselves'. I do not know whether we often think out the implication of such language into a consistent philosophy; but we certainly have a general picture of bad work flowing from conformity and discipleship, and of good work bursting out from certain centres of explosive force— apparently self-originating force—which we call men of genius.

Now the New Testament has nothing at all to tell us of literature. I know that there are some who like to think of Our Lord Himself as a poet and cite the parables to support their view. I admit freely that to believe in the Incarnation at all is to believe that every mode of human excellence is implicit in His historical human character: poethood, of course, included. But if all had been developed, the limitations of a single human life would have been transcended and He would not have been a man; therefore all excellences save the spiritual remained in varying degrees

[1. Cf. Lewis's 'How the Few and the Many Use Pictures and Music' in *An Experiment in Criticism* (Cambridge, 1961), pp. 17–18: 'The Teddy-bear exists in order that the child may endow it with imaginary life and personality and enter into a quasi-social relationship with it. That is what "playing with it" means. The better this activity succeeds the less the actual appearance of the object will matter. Too close or prolonged attention to its changeless and expressionless face impedes the play. A crucifix exists in order to direct the worshipper's thought and affections to the Passion. It had better not have any excellencies, subtleties, or originalities which will fix attention upon itself. Hence devout people may, for this purpose, prefer the crudest and emptiest icon. The emptier, the more permeable; and they want, as it were, to pass through the material image and go beyond.']

implicit. If it is claimed that the poetic excellence is more developed than others—say, the intellectual—I think I deny the claim. Some of the parables do work like poetic similes; but then others work like philosophic illustrations. Thus the Unjust Judge is not emotionally or imaginatively like God: he corresponds to God as the terms in a proportion correspond, because he is to the Widow (in one highly specialized respect) as God is to man. In that parable Our Lord, if we may so express it, is much more like Socrates than Shakespeare. And I dread an over-emphasis on the poetical element in His words because I think it tends to obscure that quality in His human character which is, in fact, so visible in His irony, His *argumenta ad homines,* and His use of the *a fortiori,* and which I would call the homely, peasant shrewdness. Donne points out that we are never told He laughed; it is difficult in reading the Gospels not to believe, and to tremble in believing, that He smiled.

I repeat, the New Testament has nothing to say of literature; but what it says on other subjects is quite sufficient to strike that note which I find out of tune with the language of modern criticism. I must begin with something that is unpopular. St Paul tells us (I Cor, xi, 3) that man is the 'head' of woman. We may soften this if we like by saying that he means only man *quâ* man and woman *quâ* woman and that an equality of the sexes as citizens or intellectual beings is not therefore absolutely repugnant to his thought: indeed, that he himself tells us that in another respect, that is 'in the Lord', the sexes cannot be thus separated (*ibid.,* xi, II). But what concerns me here is to find out what he means by Head. Now in verse 3 he has given us a very remarkable proportion sum: that God is to Christ as Christ is to man and man is to woman, and the relation between each term and the next is that of Head. And in verse 7 we are told that man is God's image and glory, and woman is man's glory. He does not repeat 'image', but I question whether the omission is intentional, and I suggest that we shall have a fairly Pauline picture of this whole series of Head relations running from God to woman if we picture each term as the 'image and glory' of the preceding term. And I suppose that of which one is the image and glory is that which one glorifies by copying or imitating. Let me once again insist that I am not trying to twist St Paul's metaphors into a logical system. I know well that whatever picture he is building up, he himself will be the first to throw it aside when it has served its turn and to adopt some quite different picture when some new aspect of the truth is present to his mind. But I want to see clearly the sort of picture implied in this passage—to get it clear however temporary its use or partial its application. And it seems to me a quite clear picture; we are to think of some original divine virtue passing downwards from rung to rung of a hierarchical ladder, and the mode in which each lower rung receives it is, quite frankly, imitation.

What is perhaps most startling in this picture is the apparent equivalence of the woman-man and man-God relation with the relation between Christ and God, or, in Trinitarian language, with the relation between the First and Second Persons of the Trinity. As a layman and a comparatively recently reclaimed apostate I have, of course, no intention of building a theological system—still less of setting up a *catena* of New Testament metaphors as a criticism on the Nicene or the Athanasian creed, documents which I wholly accept. But it is legitimate to notice what kinds of metaphor the New Testament uses; more especially when what we are in search of is not dogma but a kind of flavour or atmosphere. And there is no doubt that this kind of proportion sum—A:B: :B:C—is quite freely used in the New Testament where A and B represent the First and Second Persons of the Trinity. Thus St Paul has already told us earlier in the same epistle that we are 'of Christ' and Christ is 'of God' (iii, 23). Thus again in the Fourth Gospel, Our Lord Himself compares the relation of the Father to the Son with that of the Son to His flock, in respect of knowledge (x, 15) and of love (xv, 9).

I suggest, therefore, that this picture of a hierarchical order in which we are encouraged—though, of course, only from certain points of view and in certain respects—to regard the Second Person Himself as a step, or stage, or degree, is wholly in accord with the spirit of the New Testament. And if we ask how the stages are connected the answer always seems to be something like imitation, reflection, assimilation. Thus in Gal. iv, 19, Christ is to be 'formed' inside each believer—the verb here used (μορφωθῇ) meaning to shape, to figure, or even to draw a sketch. In First Thessalonians (i, 6) Christians are told to imitate St Paul and the Lord, and elsewhere (I Cor. xi, I) to imitate St Paul as he in turn imitates Christ—thus giving us another stage of progressive imitation. Changing the metaphor we find that believers are to acquire the fragrance of Christ, *redolere Christum* (2 Cor. ii, 16): that the glory of God has appeared in the face of Christ as, at the creation, light appeared in the universe (2 Cor. iv, 6); and, finally, if my reading of a much disputed passage is correct, that a Christian is to Christ as a mirror to an object (2 Cor. iii, 18).

These passages, you will notice, are all Pauline; but there is a place in the Fourth Gospel which goes much farther—so far that if it were not a Dominical utterance we would not venture to think along such lines. There (v. 19) we are told that the Son does only what He sees the Father doing. He watches the Father's operations and does the same (ὁμοίως ποιεῖ) or 'copies'. The Father, because of His love for the Son, shows Him all that He does. I have already explained that I am not a theologian. What aspect of the Trinitarian reality Our Lord, as God, saw while He spoke these words, I do not venture to define; but I think we have a right and even a duty to notice carefully the earthly image by which He expressed it—to see clearly the picture He puts before us. It is a picture of a boy learning to do things by watching a man at work. I think we may even guess what memory, humanly speaking, was in His mind. It is hard not to imagine that He remembered His boyhood, that He saw Himself as a boy in a carpenter's shop, a boy learning how to do things by watching while St Joseph did them. So taken, the passage does not seem to me to conflict with anything I have learned from the creeds, but greatly to enrich my conception of the Divine sonship.

Now it may be that there is no absolute logical contradiction between the passages I have quoted and the assumptions of modern criticism: but I think there is so great a difference of temper that a man whose mind was at one with the mind of the New Testament would not, and indeed could not, fall into the language which most critics now adopt. In the New Testament the art of life itself is an art of imitation: can we, believing this, believe that literature, which must derive from real life, is to aim at being 'creative', 'original', and 'spontaneous'. 'Originality' in the New

Testament is quite plainly the prerogative of God alone; even within the triune being of God it seems to be confined to the Father. The duty and happiness of every other being is placed in being derivative, in reflecting like a mirror. Nothing could be more foreign to the tone of scripture than the language of those who describe a saint as a 'moral genius' or a 'spiritual genius' thus insinuating that his virtue or spirituality is 'creative' or 'original'. If I have read the New Testament aright, it leaves no room for 'creativeness' even in a modified or metaphorical sense. Our whole destiny seems to lie in the opposite direction, in being as little as possible ourselves, in acquiring a fragrance that is not our own but borrowed, in becoming clean mirrors filled with the image of a face that is not ours. I am not here supporting the doctrine of total depravity, and I do not say that the New Testament supports it; I am saying only that the highest good of a creature must be creaturely—that is, derivative or reflective—good. In other words, as St Augustine makes plain *(De Civ. Dei* xii, cap. I), pride does not only go before a fall but is a fall—a fall of the creature's attention from what is better, God, to what is worse, itself.

Applying this principle to literature, in its greatest generality, we should get as the basis of all critical theory the maxim that an author should never conceive himself as bringing into existence beauty or wisdom which did not exist before, but simply and solely as trying to embody in terms of his own art some reflection of eternal Beauty and Wisdom. Our criticism would therefore from the beginning group itself with some existing theories of poetry against others. It would have affinities with the primitive or Homeric theory in which the poet is the mere pensioner of the Muse. It would have affinities with the Platonic doctrine of a transcendent Form partly imitable on earth; and remoter affinities with the Aristotelian doctrine of μίμησις and the Augustan doctrine about the imitation of Nature and the Ancients. It would be opposed to the theory of genius as, perhaps, generally understood; and above all it would be opposed to the idea that literature is self-expression.

But here some distinctions must be made. I spoke just now of the ancient idea that the poet was merely the servant of some god, of Apollo, or the Muse; but let us not forget the highly paradoxical words in which Homer's Phemius asserts his claim to be a poet—

Αὐτοδίδακτος δ' εἰμί, θεὸς δέ μοι ἐν φρεσὶν οἴμας
Παντοίας ἐνέφυσεν. (*Od.* xxii, 347.)

'I am self-taught; a god has inspired me with all manner of songs.' It sounds like a direct contradiction. How can he be self-taught if the god has taught him all he knows? Doubtless because the god's instruction is given internally, not through the senses, and is therefore regarded as part of the Self, to be contrasted with such external aids as, say, the example of other poets. And this seems to blur the distinction I am trying to draw between Christian imitation and the 'originality' praised by modern critics. Phemius obviously claims to be original, in the sense of being no other poet's disciple, and in the same breath admits his complete dependence on a supernatural teacher. Does not this let in 'originality' and 'creativeness' of the only kind that have ever been claimed?

If you said: 'The only kind that ought to have been claimed', I would agree; but as things are, I think the distinction remains, though it becomes finer than our first glance suggested. A Christian and an unbelieving poet may both be equally original in the sense that they neglect the example of their poetic forbears and draw on resources peculiar to themselves, but with this difference. The unbeliever may take his own temperament and experience, just as they happen to stand, and consider them worth communicating simply because they are facts or, worse still, because they are his. To the Christian his own temperament and experience, as mere fact, and as merely his, are of no value or importance whatsoever: he will deal with them, if at all, only because they are the medium through which, or the position from which, something universally profitable appeared to him. We can imagine two men seated in different parts of a church or theatre. Both, when they come out, may tell us their experiences, and both may use the first person. But the one is interested in his seat only because it was his—'I was most uncomfortable', he will say. 'You would hardly believe what a draught comes in from the door in that corner. And the people! I had to speak pretty sharply to the woman in front of me.' The other will tell us what could be seen from his seat, choosing to describe this because this is what he knows, and because every seat must give the best view of something. 'Do you know', he will begin, 'the moulding on those pillars goes on round at the back. It looks, too, as if the design on the back were the older of the two.' Here we have the expressionist and the Christian attitudes towards the self or temperament. Thus St Augustine and Rousseau both write *Confessions;* but to the one his own temperament is a kind of absolute (*au moins je suis autre*), to the other it is 'a narrow house too narrow for Thee to enter—oh make it wide. It is in ruins—oh rebuild it.' And Wordsworth, the romantic who made a good end, has a foot in either world and though he practises both, distinguishes well the two ways in which a man may be said to write about himself. On the one hand he says:

> [For] I must tread on shadowy ground, must sink
> Deep, and aloft ascending breathe in worlds
> To which the heaven of heavens is but a veil.[1]

On the other he craves indulgence if

>   with this
> I mix[2] more lowly matter; with the thing
> Contemplated, describe the Mind and Man
> Contemplating; and who and what he was—
> The transitory being that beheld
> This vision.[3]

[1. *The Recluse*, Part I, Book I II. 772–74, from Appendix A in *The Poetical Works of William Wordsworth*, vol. V, ed. E. de Selincourt and Helen Darbishire (Oxford, 1949).]
[2. 'Mix' is, I think, a scribal error for Wordsworth's 'blend' as given in the de Selincourt and Darbishire edition.]
[3. *Op. cit.*, 11. 829–34.]

In this sense, then, the Christian writer may be self-taught or original. He may base his work on the 'transitory being' that he is, not because he thinks it valuable (for he knows that in his flesh dwells no good thing), but solely because of the 'vision' that appeared to it. But he will have no preference for doing this. He will do it if it happens to be the thing he can do best; but if his talents are such that he can produce good work by writing in an established form and dealing with experiences common to all his race, he will do so just as gladly. I even think he will do so more gladly. It is to him an argument not of strength but of weakness that he should respond fully to the vision only 'in his own way'. And always, of every idea and of every method he will ask not 'Is it mine?', but 'Is it good?'

This seems to me the most fundamental difference between the Christian and the unbeliever in their approach to literature. But I think there is another. The Christian will take literature a little less seriously than the cultured Pagan: he will feel less uneasy with a purely hedonistic standard for at least many kinds of work. The unbeliever is always apt to make a kind of religion of his aesthetic experiences; he feels ethically irresponsible, perhaps, but he braces his strength to receive responsibilities of another kind which seem to the Christian quite illusory. He has to be 'creative'; he has to obey a mystical amoral law called his artistic conscience; and he commonly wishes to maintain his superiority to the great mass of mankind who turn to books for mere recreation. But the Christian knows from the outset that the salvation of a single soul is more important than the production or preservation of all the epics and tragedies in the world: and as for superiority, he knows that the vulgar since they include most of the poor probably include most of his superiors. He has no objection to comedies that merely amuse and tales that merely refresh; for he thinks like Thomas Aquinas *ipsa ratio hoc habet ut quandoque rationis usus intercipiatur.* We can play, as we can eat, to the glory of God. It thus may come about that Christian views on literature will strike the world as shallow and flippant; but the world must not misunderstand. When Christian work is done on a serious subject there is no gravity and no sublimity it cannot attain. But they will belong to the theme. That is why they will be real and lasting—mighty nouns with which literature, an adjectival thing, is here united, far over-topping the fussy and ridiculous claims of literature that tries to be important simply as literature. And *a posteriori* it is not hard to argue that all the greatest poems have been made by men who valued something else much more than poetry—even if that something else were only cutting down enemies in a cattle-raid or tumbling a girl in a bed. The real frivolity, the solemn vacuity, is all with those who make literature a self-existent thing to be valued for its own sake. Pater prepared for pleasure as if it were martyrdom.

Now that I see where I have arrived a doubt assails me. It all sounds suspiciously like things I have said before, starting from very different premisses. Is it King Charles's Head? Have I mistaken for the 'vision' the same old 'transitory being' who, in some ways, is not nearly transitory enough? It may be so: or I may, after all be right. I would rather be right if I could; but if not, if I have only been once more following my own footprints, it is the sort of tragi-comedy which, on my own principles, I must try to enjoy. I find a beautiful example proposed in the *Paradiso* (XXVIII) where poor Pope Gregory, arrived in Heaven, discovered that his theory of the hierarchies, on which presumably he had taken pains, was quite wrong. We are told how the redeemed soul behaved; *'di sè medesmo rise'*. It was the funniest thing he'd ever heard.

Christianity and Culture

*'If the heavenly life is not grown up in you, it signifies
nothing what you have chosen in the stead of it, or why you have chosen it.'*
—William Law

AT AN EARLY AGE I came to believe that the life of culture (that is, of intellectual and aesthetic activity) was very good for its own sake, or even that it was the good for man. After my conversion, which occurred in my later twenties, I continued to hold this belief without consciously asking how it could be reconciled with my new belief that the end of human life was salvation in Christ and the glorifying of God. I was awakened from this confused state of mind by finding that the friends of culture seemed to me to be exaggerating. In my reaction against what seemed exaggerated I was driven to the other extreme, and began, in my own mind, to belittle the claims of culture. As soon as I did this I was faced with the question, 'If it is a thing of so little value, how are you justified in spending so much of your life on it?'

The present inordinate esteem of culture by the cultured began, I think, with Matthew Arnold—at least if I am right in supposing that he first popularized the use of the English word *spiritual* in the sense of German *geistlich*. This was nothing less than the identification of levels of life hitherto usually distinguished. After Arnold came the vogue of Croce, in whose philosophy the aesthetic and logical activities were made autonomous forms of 'the spirit' co-ordinate with the ethical. There followed the poetics of Dr I. A. Richards. This great atheist critic found in a good poetical taste the means of attaining psychological adjustments which improved a man's power of effective and satisfactory living all round, while bad taste resulted in a corresponding loss. Since this theory of value was a purely psychological one, this amounted to giving poetry a kind of soteriological function; it held the keys of the only heaven that Dr Richards believed in. His work (which I respect profoundly) was continued, though not always in directions that he accepted, by the editors of *Scrutiny*,[1] who believe in 'a necessary relationship between the quality of the individual's response to art and his general fitness for humane living'. Finally, as might have been expected, a somewhat similar view was expressed by a Christian writer: in fact by Brother Every in *Theology* for March, 1939. In an article entitled 'The Necessity of *Scrutiny*' Brother Every inquired what Mr Eliot's admirers were to think of a Church where those who seemed to be theologically equipped preferred Housman, Mr Charles Morgan, and Miss Sayers, to

---

1. I take *Scrutiny* throughout as it is represented in Brother Every's article. An independent criticism of that periodical is no part of my purpose.

Lawrence, Joyce and Mr E. M. Forster; he spoke (I think with sympathy) of the 'sensitive questioning individual' who is puzzled at finding the same judgements made by Christians as by 'other conventional people'; and he talked of 'testing' theological students as regards their power to evaluate a new piece of writing on a secular subject.

As soon as I read this there was the devil to pay. I was not sure that I understood—I am still not sure that I understand—Brother Every's position. But I felt that some readers might easily get the notion that 'sensitivity' or good taste were among the *notes* of the true Church, or that coarse, unimaginative people were less likely to be saved than refined and poetic people. In the heat of the moment I rushed to the opposite extreme. I felt, with some spiritual pride, that I had been saved in the nick of time from being 'sensitive'. The 'sentimentality and cheapness' of much Christian hymnody had been a strong point in my own resistance to conversion. Now I felt almost thankful for the bad hymns.[1] It was good that we should have to lay down our precious refinement at the very doorstep of the church; good that we should be cured at the outset of our inveterate confusion between *psyche* and *pneuma*, nature and supernature.

A man is never so proud as when striking an attitude of humility. Brother Every will not suspect me of being still in the condition I describe, nor of still attributing to him the preposterous beliefs I have just suggested. But there remains, none the less, a real problem which his article forced upon me in its most acute form. No one, presumably, is really maintaining that a fine taste in the arts is a condition of salvation. Yet the glory of God, and, as our only means to glorifying Him, the salvation of human souls, is the real business of life. What, then, is the value of culture? It is, of course, no new question; but as a living question it was new to me.

I naturally turned first to the New Testament. Here I found, in the first place, a demand that whatever is most highly valued on the natural level is to be held, as it were, merely on sufferance, and to be abandoned without mercy the moment it conflicts with the service of God. The organs of sense (Matt. v, 29) and of virility (Matt. xix, 12) may have to be sacrificed. And I took it that the least these words could mean was that a life, by natural standards, crippled and thwarted was not only no bar to salvation, but might easily be one of its conditions. The text about hating father and mother (Luke xiv, 26) and our Lord's apparent belittling even of His own natural relation to the Blessed Virgin (Matt. xii, 48) were even more discouraging. I took it for granted that anyone in his senses would hold it better to be a good son than a good critic, and that whatever was said of natural affection was implied *a fortiori* of culture. The worst of all was Philippians iii, 8, where something obviously more relevant to spiritual life than culture can be—'blameless' conformity to the Jewish Law—was described as 'muck'.

In the second place I found a number of emphatic warnings against every kind of superiority. We were told to become as children (Matt. xviii, 3), not to be called

---

1. We should be cautious of assuming that we know what their most banal expressions actually stand for in the minds of uneducated, holy persons. Of a saint's conversation Patmore says: 'He will most likely dwell with reiteration on commonplaces with which you were perfectly acquainted before you were twelve years old; but you must . . . remember that the knowledge which is to you a superficies is to him a solid' (*Rod, Root and Flower, Magna Moralia*, xiv).

Rabbi (Matt. xxiii, 8), to dread reputation (Luke vi, 26). We were reminded that few of the σοφοί κατὰ σάρκα—which, I suppose, means precisely the intelligentsia— are called (1 Cor. i, 26); that a man must become a fool by secular standards before he can attain real wisdom (1 Cor. iii, 18).

Against all this I found some passages that could be interpreted in a sense more favourable to culture. I argued that secular learning might be embodied in the Magi; that the Talents in the parable might conceivably include 'talents' in the modern sense of the word; that the miracle at Cana in Galilee by sanctifying an innocent, sensuous pleasure[1] could be taken to sanctify at least a recreational use of culture— mere 'entertainment'; and that aesthetic enjoyment of nature was certainly hallowed by our Lord's praise of the lilies. At least some use of science was implied in St Paul's demand that we should perceive the Invisible through the visible (Rom. i, 20). But I was more than doubtful whether his exhortation, 'Be not children in mind' (I Cor. xiv, 20), and his boast of 'wisdom' among the initiate, referred to anything that we should recognize as secular culture.

On the whole, the New Testament seemed, if not hostile, yet unmistakably cold to culture. I think we can still believe culture to be innocent after we have read the New Testament; I cannot see that we are encouraged to think it important.

It might be important none the less, for Hooker has finally answered the contention that Scripture must contain everything important or even everything necessary. Remembering this, I continued my researches. If my selection of authorities seems arbitrary, that is due not to a bias but to my ignorance. I used such authors as I happened to know.

Of the great pagans Aristotle is on our side. Plato will tolerate no culture that does not directly or indirectly conduce either to the intellectual vision of the good or the military efficiency of the commonwealth. Joyce and D. H. Lawrence would have fared ill in the Republic. The Buddha was, I believe, anti-cultural, but here especially I speak under correction.

St Augustine regarded the liberal education which he had undergone in his boyhood as a *dementia,* and wondered why it should be considered *honestior et uberior* than the really useful 'primary' education which preceded it (*Conf.* I, xiii). He is extremely distrustful of his own delight in church music *(ibid.,* X, xxxiii). Tragedy (which for Dr Richards is 'a great exercise of the spirit')[2] is for St Augustine a kind of sore. The spectator suffers, yet loves his suffering, and this is a *miserabilis insania . . . quid autem mirum cum infelix pecus aberrans a grege tuo et inpatiens custodiae tuae turpi scabie foedarer (ibid.,* III, ii).

St Jerome, allegorizing the parable of the Prodigal Son, suggests that the husks with which he was fain to fill his belly may signify *cibus daemonum . . . carmina poetarum, saecularis sapientia, rhetoricorum pompa verborum* (Ep. xxi, 4).

Let none reply that the Fathers were speaking of polytheistic literature at a time when polytheism was still a danger. The scheme of values presupposed in most imaginative literature has not become very much more Christian since the time of St Jerome. In *Hamlet* we see everything questioned *except* the duty of revenge. In

1. On a possible deeper significance in this miracle, see F. Mauriac, *Vie de Jésus,* cap. 5, *ad fin.*
2. *Principles of Literary Criticism,* p. 69.

all Shakespeare's works the conception of good really operative—whatever the characters may say—seems to be purely worldly. In medieval romance, honour and sexual love are the true values; in nineteenth-century fiction, sexual love and material prosperity. In romantic poetry, either the enjoyment of nature (ranging from pantheistic mysticism at one end of the scale to mere innocent sensuousness at the other) or else the indulgence of a *Sehnsucht* awakened by the past, the distant, and the imagined, but not believed, supernatural. In modern literature, the life of liberated instinct. There are, of course, exceptions: but to study these exceptions would not be to study literature as such, and as a whole. 'All literatures', as Newman has said,[1] 'are one; they are the voices of the natural man . . . if Literature is to be made a study of human nature, you cannot have a Christian Literature. It is a contradiction in terms to attempt a sinless Literature of sinful man.' And I could not doubt that the sub-Christian or anti-Christian values implicit in most literature did actually infect many readers. Only a few days ago I was watching, in some scholarship papers, the results of this infection in a belief that the crimes of such Shakespearian characters as Cleopatra and Macbeth were somehow compensated for by a quality described as their 'greatness'. This very morning I have read in a critic the remark that if the wicked lovers in Webster's *White Devil* had repented we should hardly have forgiven them. And many people certainly draw from Keats's phrase about negative capability or 'love of good and evil' (if the reading which attributes to him such meaningless words is correct) a strange doctrine that experience *simpliciter* is good. I do not say that the sympathetic reading of literature must produce such results, but that it may and often does. If we are to answer the Fathers' attack on pagan literature we must not ground our answer on a belief that literature as a whole has become, in any important sense, more Christian since their days.

In Thomas Aquinas I could not find anything directly bearing on my problem; but I am a very poor Thomist and shall be grateful for correction on this point.

Thomas à Kempis I take to be definitely on the anti-cultural side.

In the *Theologia Germanica* (cap. xx) I found that nature's refusal of the life of Christ 'happeneth most of all where there are high natural gifts of reason, for that soareth upwards in its own light and by its own power, till at last it cometh to think itself the true Eternal Light'. But in a later chapter (xlii) I found the evil of the false light identified with its tendency to love knowledge and discernment more than the object known and discerned. This seemed to point to the possibility of a knowledge which avoided that error.

The cumulative effect of all this was very discouraging to culture. On the other side—perhaps only through the accidental distribution of my ignorance—I found much less.

I found the famous saying, attributed to Gregory, that our use of secular culture was comparable to the action of the Israelites in going down to the Philistines to have their knives sharpened. This seems to me a most satisfactory argument as far as it goes, and very relevant to modern conditions. If we are to convert our hea-

---

1. *Scope and Nature of University Education.* Discourse 8.

then neighbours, we must understand their culture. We must 'beat them at their own game'. But of course, while this would justify Christian culture (at least for some Christians whose vocation lay in that direction) at the moment, it would come very far short of the claims made for culture in our modern tradition. On the Gregorian view culture is a weapon; and a weapon is essentially a thing we lay aside as soon as we safely can.

In Milton I found a disquieting ally. His *Areopagitica* troubled me just as Brother Every's article had troubled me. He seemed to make too little of the difficulties; and his glorious defence of freedom to explore all good and evil seemed, after all, to be based on an aristocratic preoccupation with great souls and a contemptuous indifference to the mass of mankind which, I suppose, no Christian can tolerate.

Finally I came to that book of Newman's from which I have already quoted, the lectures on *University Education*. Here at last I found an author who seemed to be aware of both sides of the question; for no one ever insisted so eloquently as Newman on the beauty of culture for its own sake, and no one ever so sternly resisted the temptation to confuse it with things spiritual. The cultivation of the intellect, according to him, is 'for this world':[1] between it and 'genuine religion' there is a 'radical difference';[2] it makes 'not the Christian . . . but the gentleman', and looks like virtue 'only at a distance';[3] he 'will not for an instant allow' that it makes men better.[4] The 'pastors of the Church' may indeed welcome culture because it provides innocent distraction at those moments of spiritual relaxation which would otherwise very likely lead to sin; and in this way it often 'draws the mind off from things which will harm it to subjects worthy of a rational being'. But even in so doing 'it does not raise it above nature, nor has any tendency to make us pleasing to our Maker'.[5] In some instances the cultural and the spiritual value of an activity may even be in inverse ratio. Theology, when it ceases to be part of liberal knowledge, and is pursued for purely pastoral ends, gains in 'meritoriousness' but loses in liberality 'just as a face worn by tears and fasting loses its beauty'.[6] On the other hand Newman is certain that liberal knowlege is an end in itself; the whole of the fourth Discourse is devoted to this theme. The solution of this apparent antinomy lies in his doctrine that everything, including, of course, the intellect, 'has its own perfection. Things animate, inanimate, visible, invisible, all are good in their kind, and have a *best* of themselves, which is an object of pursuit.'[7] To perfect the mind is 'an object as intelligible as the cultivation of virtue, while, at the same time, it is absolutely distinct from it'.[8]

Whether because I am too poor a theologian to understand the implied doctrine of grace and nature, or for some other reason, I have not been able to make Newman's conclusion my own. I can well understand that there is a kind of goodness which is not moral; as a well-grown healthy toad is 'better' or 'more perfect' than a three-legged toad, or an archangel is 'better' than an angel. In this sense a clever man is 'better' than a dull one, or any man than any chimpanzee. The trouble comes when we start asking how much of our time and energy God wants us to

---

1. *Op. cit.*, VIII, p. 227, in Everyman Edition.　　2. VII, p. 184, 5.　　3. IV, p. 112.　　4. IV, p. 111.
5. VII, p. 180.　　6. IV, p. 100.　　7. IV, p. 113.　　8. IV, p. 114.

spend in becoming 'better' or 'more perfect' in this sense. If Newman is right in saying that culture has *no* tendency 'to make us pleasing to our Maker', then the answer would seem to be, 'None.' And that is a tenable view: as though God said, 'Your *natural* degree of perfection, your place in the chain of being, is my affair: do you get on with what I have explicitly left as your task—righteousness.' But if Newman had thought this he would not, I suppose, have written the discourse on 'Liberal Knowledge its Own End'. On the other hand, it would be possible to hold (perhaps it is pretty generally held) that one of the moral duties of a rational creature was to attain to the highest non-moral perfection it could. But if this were so, then (*a*) The perfecting of the mind would not be 'absolutely distinct' from virtue but part of the content of virtue; and (*b*) It would be very odd that Scripture and the tradition of the Church have little or nothing to say about this duty. I am afraid that Newman has left the problem very much where he found it. He has clarified our minds by explaining that culture gives us a non-moral 'perfection'. But on the real problem—that of relating such non-moral values to the duty or interest of creatures who are every minute advancing either to heaven or hell—he seems to help little. 'Sensitivity' may be a perfection: but if by becoming sensitive I neither please God nor save my soul, why should I become sensitive? Indeed, what exactly is meant by a 'perfection' compatible with utter loss of the end for which I was created?

My researches left me with the impression that there could be no question of restoring to culture the kind of status which I had given it before my conversion. If any constructive case for culture was to be built up it would have to be of a much humbler kind; and the whole tradition of educated infidelity from Arnold to *Scrutiny* appeared to me as but one phase in that general rebellion against God which began in the eighteenth century. In this mood I set about construction.

1. I begin at the lowest and least ambitious level. My own professional work, though conditioned by taste and talents, is immediately motivated by the need for earning my living. And on earning one's living I was relieved to note that Christianity, in spite of its revolutionary and apocalyptic elements, can be delightfully humdrum. The Baptist did not give the tax-gatherers and soldiers lectures on the immediate necessity of turning the economic and military system of the ancient world upside down; he told them to obey the moral law—as they had presumably learned it from their mothers and nurses—and sent them back to their jobs. St Paul advised the Thessalonians to stick to their work (1 Thess. iv, 11) and not to become busybodies (2 Thess. iii, 11) . The need for money is therefore *simpliciter* an innocent, though by no means a splendid, motive for any occupation. The Ephesians are warned to work professionally at something that is 'good' (Eph. iv, 28). I hoped that 'good' here did not mean much more than 'harmless', and I was certain it did not imply anything very elevated. Provided, then, that there was a demand for culture, and that culture was not actually deleterious, I concluded I was justified in making my living by supplying that demand—and that all others in my position (dons, schoolmasters, professional authors, critics, reviewers) were similarly justified; especially if, like me, they had few or no talents for any other career—if their 'vocation' to a cultural profession consisted in the brute fact of not being fit for anything else.

2. But is culture even harmless? It certainly can be harmful and often is. If a Christian found himself in the position of one inaugurating a new society *in vacuo* he might well decide not to introduce something whose abuse is so easy and whose use is, at any rate, not necessary. But that is not our position. The abuse of culture is already there, and will continue whether Christians cease to be cultured or not. It is therefore probably better that the ranks of the 'culture-sellers' should include some Christians—as an antidote. It may even be the duty of some Christians to be culture-sellers. Not that I have yet said anything to show that even the lawful use of culture stands very high. The lawful use might be no more than innocent pleasure; but if the abuse is common, the task of resisting that abuse might be not only lawful but obligatory. Thus people in my position might be said to be 'working the thing which is good' in a stronger sense than that reached in the last paragraph.

In order to avoid misunderstanding, I must add that when I speak of 'resisting the abuse of culture' I do not mean that a Christian should take money for supplying one thing (culture) and use the opportunity thus gained to supply a quite different thing (homiletics and apologetics). That is stealing. The mere presence of Christians in the ranks of the culture-sellers will inevitably provide an antidote.

It will be seen that I have now reached something very like the Gregorian view of culture as a weapon. Can I now go a step further and find any intrinsic goodness in culture for its own sake?

3. When I ask what culture has done to me personally, the most obviously true answer is that it has given me quite an enormous amount of pleasure. I have no doubt at all that pleasure is in itself a good and pain in itself an evil; if not, then the whole Christian tradition about heaven and hell and the passion of our Lord seems to have no meaning. Pleasure, then, is good; a 'sinful' pleasure means a good offered, and accepted, under conditions which involve a breach of the moral law. The pleasures of culture are not intrinsically bound up with such conditions—though of course they can very easily be so enjoyed as to involve them. Often, as Newman saw, they are an excellent diversion from guilty pleasures. We may, therefore, enjoy them ourselves, and lawfully, even charitably, teach others to enjoy them.

This view gives us some ease, though it would go a very little way towards satisfying the editors of *Scrutiny*. We should, indeed, be justified in propagating good taste on the ground that cultured pleasure in the arts is more varied, intense, and lasting, than vulgar or 'popular' pleasure.[1] But we should not regard it as meritorious. In fact, much as we should differ from Bentham about value in general, we should have to be Benthamites on the issue between pushpin and poetry.

4. It was noticed above that the values assumed in literature were seldom those of Christianity. Some of the principal values actually implicit in European literature were described as (*a*) honour, (*b*) sexual love, (*c*) material prosperity, (*d*) pantheistic contemplation of nature, (*e*) *Sehnsucht* awakened by the past, the remote, or the (imagined) supernatural, (*f*) liberation of impulses. These were called 'sub-Christian'. This is a term of disapproval if we are comparing them with Christian values: but if we take 'sub-Christian to mean 'immediately sub-Christian' (i.e., the

1. If this is true, as I should gladly believe but have never seen proved.

highest level of merely natural value lying immediately below the lowest level of spiritual value) it may be a term of relative approval. Some of the six values I have enumerated may be sub-Christian in this (relatively) good sense. For (c) and (f) I can make no defence; whenever they are accepted by the reader with anything more than a 'willing suspension of disbelief ' they must make him worse. But the other four are all two-edged. I may symbolize what I think of them all by the aphorism 'Any road out of Jerusalem must also be a road into Jerusalem.' Thus:

(a) To the perfected Christian the ideal of honour is simply a temptation. His courage has a better root, and, being learned in Gethsemane, may have no honour about it. But to the man coming up from below, the ideal of knighthood may prove a schoolmaster to the ideal of martyrdom. Galahad is the *son* of Launcelot.

(b) The road described by Dante and Patmore is a dangerous one. But mere animalism, however disguised as 'honesty', 'frankness', or the like, is not dangerous, but fatal. And not all are qualified to be, even in sentiment, eunuchs for the Kingdom's sake. For some souls romantic love also has proved a school master.[1]

(d) There is an easy transition from Theism to Pantheism; but there is also a blessed transition in the other direction. For some souls I believe, for my own I remember, Wordsworthian contemplation can be the first and lowest form of recognition that there is something outside ourselves which demands reverence. To return to Pantheistic errors about the nature of this something would, for a Christian, be very bad. But once again, for 'the man coming up from below' the Wordsworthian experience is an advance. Even if he goes no further he has escaped the worst arrogance of materialism: if he goes on he will be converted.

(e) The dangers of romantic *Sehnsucht* are very great. Eroticism and even occultism lie in wait for it. On this subject I can only give my own experience for what it is worth. When we are first converted I suppose we think mostly of our recent sins; but as we go on, more and more of the terrible past comes under review. In this process I have not (or not yet) reached a point at which I can honestly repent of my early experiences of romantic *Sehnsucht*. That they were occasions to much that I do repent, is clear; but I still cannot help thinking that this was my abuse of them, and that the experiences themselves contained, from the very first, a wholly good element. Without them my conversion would have been more difficult.[2]

I have dwelt chiefly on certain kinds of literature, not because I think them the only elements in culture that have this value as schoolmasters, but because I know them best; and on literature rather than art and knowledge for the same reason. My general case may be stated in Ricardian terms—that culture is a storehouse of the best (sub-Christian) values. These values are in themselves of the soul, not the spirit. But God created the soul. Its values may be expected, therefore, to contain some reflection or antepast of the spiritual values. They will save no man. They resemble the regenerate life only as affection resembles charity, or honour resembles virtue, or the moon the sun. But though 'like is not the same', it is better than unlike.

---

1. See Charles Williams, *He Came Down from Heaven*.
2. I am quite ready to describe *Sehnsucht* as 'spilled religion', provided it is not forgotten that the spilled drops may be full of blessing to the unconverted man who licks them up, and therefore begins to search for the cup whence they were spilled. For the drops will be taken by some whose stomachs are not yet sound enough for the full draught.

Imitation may pass into initiation. For some it is a good beginning. For others it is not; culture is not everyone's road into Jerusalem, and for some it is a road out.

There is another way in which it may predispose to conversion. The difficulty of converting an uneducated man nowadays lies in his complacency. Popularized science, the conventions or 'unconventions' of his immediate circle, party programmes, etc., enclose him in a tiny windowless universe which he mistakes for the only possible universe. There are no distant horizons, no mysteries. He thinks everything has been settled. A cultured person, on the other hand, is almost compelled to be aware that reality is very odd and that the ultimate truth, whatever it may be, *must* have the characteristics of strangeness—*must* be something that would seem remote and fantastic to the uncultured. Thus some obstacles to faith have been removed already.

On these grounds I conclude that culture has a distinct part to play in bringing certain souls to Christ. Not all souls—there is a shorter, and safer, way which has always been followed by thousands of simple affectional natures who begin, where we hope to end, with devotion to the person of Christ.

Has it any part to play in the life of the converted? I think so, and in two ways. (*a*) If all the cultural values, on the way up to Christianity, were dim antepasts and ectypes of the truth, we can recognize them as such still. And since we must rest and play, where can we do so better than here—in the suburbs of Jerusalem? It is lawful to rest our eyes in moonlight—especially now that we know where it comes from, that it is only sunlight at second hand. (*b*) Whether the purely contemplative life is, or is not, desirable for any, it is certainly not the vocation of all. Most men must glorify God by doing to His glory something which is not *per se* an act of glorifying but which becomes so by being offered. If, as I now hope, cultural activities are innocent and even useful, then they also (like the sweeping of the room in Herbert's poem) can be done to the Lord. The work of a charwoman and the work of a poet become spiritual in the same way and on the same condition. There must be no return to the Arnoldian or Ricardian view. Let us stop giving ourselves airs.

If it is argued that the 'sensitivity' which Brother Every desires is something different from my 'culture' or 'good taste', I must reply that I have chosen those words as the most general terms for something which is differently conceived in every age—'wit', 'correctness', 'imagination' and (now) 'sensitivity'. These names, of course, record real changes of opinion about it. But if it were contended that the latest conception is so different from all its predecessors that we now have a radically new situation—that while 'wit' was not necessary for a seventeenth-century Christian, 'sensitivity' is necessary for a twentieth-century Christian—I should find this very hard to believe. 'Sensitivity' is a potentiality, therefore neutral. It can no more be an end to Christians than 'experience'. If Philippians i, 9, is quoted against me, I reply that delicate discriminations are there traced to charity, not to critical experience of books. Every virtue is a *habitus*—i.e., a *good* stock response. Dr Richards very candidly recognizes this when he speaks of people 'hag-ridden by their vices *or their virtues*' (*op. cit.*, p. 52, italics mine). But we want to be so ridden. I do not want a sensitivity which will show me how different each temptation to lust or cowardice is from the last, how unique, how unamenable to general rules. A stock response is precisely what I need to acquire. Moral theologians, I believe, tell us to fly at sight from temptations to faith or chastity. If that is not (in Dr Richards' words) a 'stock', 'stereotyped', 'conventional' response, I do not know what is. In fact, the new ideal of 'sensitivity' seems to me to present culture to Christians in a somewhat less favourable light than its predecessors. Sidney's poetics would be better. The whole school of critical thought which descends from Dr Richards bears such deep marks of its anti-Christian origins that I question if it can ever be baptized.

II

To the Editor of *Theology*.

Sir,

Mr Bethell's main position is so important that I hope you will allow me at some future date to deal with it in a full-length argument. For the moment, therefore, I will only say: (1) That I made no reference to his previous paper for the worst of reasons and the best of causes—namely, that I had forgotten it. For this negligence I ask his pardon. On looking back at the relevant number of *Theology*, I see from marginalia in my own hand that I must have read his contribution with great interest; for my forgetfulness I can only plead that a great many things have happened to us all since then. I am distressed that Mr Bethell should suppose himself deliberately slighted. I intended no disrespect to him. (2) That my position 'logically implies . . . total depravity' I deny simply. How any logician could derive the proposition 'Human nature is totally depraved' from the proposition 'Cultural activities do not in themselves improve our spiritual condition', I cannot understand. Even if I had said (which I did not), 'Man's aesthetic nature is totally depraved,' no one could infer 'Man's whole nature is totally depraved' without a glaring transference from *secundum quid* to *simpliciter*. I put it to Mr Bethell that he has used 'logically implies' to mean 'may without gross uncharity rouse the suspicion of'—and that he ought not to use words that way.

To Mr Carritt I reply that my argument assumed the divinity of Christ, the truth of the creeds, and the authority of the Christian tradition, because I was writing in an Anglican periodical. That is why Dominical and patristic sayings have for me more than an antiquarian interest. But though my attribution of authority to Christ or the Fathers may depend on premises which Mr Carritt does not accept, my belief that it is proper to combine my own reasonings with the witness of authority has a different ground, prior to any decision on the question, 'Who is authoritative?' One of the things my reason tells me is that I ought to check the results of my own thinking by the opinions of the wise. I go to authority because reason sends me to it— just as Mr. Carritt, after adding up a column of figures, might ask a friend, known to be a good calculator, to check it for him, and might distrust his own result if his friend got a different one.

I said that culture was a storehouse of the best sub-Christian *values*, not the best sub-Christian *virtues*. I meant by this that culture recorded man's striving for those ends which, though not the true end of man (the fruition of God), have nevertheless some degree of similarity to it, and are not so grossly inadequate to the nature of man as, say, physical pleasure, or money. This similarity, of course, while making it less evil to rest in them, makes the danger of resting in them greater and more subtle.

The salvation of souls is a means to the glorifying of God because only saved souls can duly glorify Him. The thing to which, on my view, culture must be subordinated, is not (though it includes) moral virtue, but the conscious direction of all will and desire to a transcendental Person in whom I believe all values to reside, and the reference to Him in every thought and act. Since that Person 'loves righteousness' this total surrender to Him involves Mr Carritt's 'conscientiousness'. It would therefore be impossible to 'glorify God by doing what we thought wrong'. Doing what we think right, on the other hand, is not the same as glorifying God. I fully agree with Mr Carritt that *a priori* we might expect the production of whatever is 'good' to be one of our duties. If God had never spoken to man, we should be justified in basing the conduct of life wholly on such *a priori* grounds. Those who think God has spoken will naturally listen to what He has to say about the where, how, to what extent, and in what spirit any 'good' is to be pursued. This does not mean that our own conscience is simply negated. On the contrary, just as reason sends me to authority, so conscience sends me to obedience: for one of the things my conscience tells me is that if there exists an absolutely wise and good Person (Aristotle's φρόνιμος raised to the nth) I owe Him obedience, specially when that Person, as the ground of my existence, has a kind of paternal claim on me, and, as a benefactor, has a claim on my gratitude. What would happen if there were an absolute clash between God's will and my own conscience—i.e., if *either* God could be bad *or* I were an incurable moral idiot—I naturally do not know, any more than Mr Carritt knows what would happen if he found absolutely demonstrative evidence for two contradictory propositions.

I mentioned Hooker, not because he simply denied that Scripture contains all things necessary, but because he advanced a proof that it cannot—which proof, I supposed, most readers of *Theology* would remember. 'Text-hunting' is, of course, 'Puritanical', but also scholastic, patristic, apostolic, and Dominical. To *that* kind of charge I venture, presuming on an indulgence which Mr Carritt has extended to me for nearly twenty years, to reply with homely saws: as that an old trout can't be caught by tickling, and they know a trick worth two of that where I come from. Puritan, quotha!

Yours faithfully,
C. S. LEWIS

III

PEACE PROPOSALS FOR BROTHER EVERY AND MR BETHEL

I BELIEVE there is little real disagreement between my critics (Brother Every and Mr Bethell) and myself. Mr Carritt, who does not accept the Christian premises, must here be left out of account, though with all the respect and affection I feel for my old tutor and friend.

The conclusion I reached in *Theology*, March, 1940, was that culture, though not in itself meritorious, was innocent and pleasant, might be a vocation for some, was helpful in bringing certain souls to Christ, and could be pursued to the glory of God. I do not see that Brother Every and Mr Bethell really want me to go beyond this position.

The argument of Mr Bethell's paper in *Theology*, July, 1939 (excluding its historical section, which does not here concern us), was that the deepest, and often unconscious, beliefs of a writer were implicit in his work, even in what might seem the minor details of its style, and that, unless we were Croceans, such beliefs must be taken into account in estimating the value of that work. In *Theology*, May, 1940, Mr Bethell reaffirmed this doctrine with the addition that the latent beliefs in much modern fiction were naturalistic, and that we needed trained critics to put Christian readers on their guard against this pervasive influence.

Brother Every, in *Theology*, September, 1940, maintained that our tastes are symptomatic of our real standards of value, which may differ from our professed standards; and that we needed trained critics to show us the real latent standards in literature—in fact 'to teach us how to read'.

I cannot see that my own doctrine and those of my critics come into direct contradiction at any point. My fear was lest excellence in reading and writing were being elevated into a spiritual value, into something meritorious *per se;* just as other things excellent and wholesome in themselves, like conjugal love (in the sense of *eros)* or physical cleanliness, have, at some times and in some circles been confused with virtue itself or esteemed necessary parts of it. But it now appears that my critics never intended to make any such claim. Bad Taste for them is not itself spiritual evil but the symptom which betrays, or the 'carrier' which circulates, spiritual evil. And the spiritual evil thus betrayed or carried turns out not to be any specifically cultural or literary kind of evil, but false beliefs or standards—that is, intellectual error or moral baseness; and as I never intended to deny that error and baseness were evils nor the literature could imply and carry them, I think that all three of us may shake hands and say we are agreed. I do not mean to suggest that my critics have *merely* restated a platitude which neither I nor anyone else ever disputed. The value of their contribution lies in their insistence that the real beliefs may differ from the professed and may lurk in the turn of a phrase or the choice of an epithet; with the result that many preferences which seem to the ignorant to be simply 'matters of taste' are visible to the trained critic as choices between good and evil, or truth and error. And I fully admit that this important point had been neglected in my essay of March, 1940. Now that it has been made, I heartily accept it. I think this is agreement.

But to test the depth of agreement I would like my critics to consider the following positions. By agreement I mean only agreement in our doctrines. Differences of temper and emphasis between Christian critics are inevitable and probably desirable.

1. Is it the function of the 'trained critic' to discover the latent beliefs and standards in a book, or to pass judgement on them when discovered, or both? I think Brother Every confines the critic's function to discovery. About Mr Bethell I am

not so sure. When he says (*Theology*, May, 1940, p. 360) that we need a minority of trained critics to 'lay bare the false values of contemporary culture' this might mean two things: (*a*) 'To expose the falsity of the values of contemporary culture'; (*b*) 'To reveal what the values of contemoprary culture actually are—and, by the way, I personally think those values false.' It is necessary to clear this up before we know what is meant by a 'trained critic'. Trained in what? A man who has had a literary training may be an expert in disengaging the beliefs and values latent in literature; but the judgement on those beliefs and values (that is, the judgement on all possible human thoughts and moralities) belongs either to a quite different set of experts (theologians, philosophers, casuists, scientists) or else not to experts at all but to the unspecialized 'good and wise man', the φρόνιμος. Now I for my part have no objection to our doing both when we criticize, but I think it very important to keep the two operations distinct. In the discovery of the latent belief we have had a special training, and speak as experts; in the judgement of the beliefs, once they have been discovered, we humbly hope that we are being trained, like everyone else, by reason and ripening experience, under the guidance of the Holy Ghost, as long as we live, but we speak on them simply as men, on a level with all our even-Christians, and indeed with less authority than any illiterate man who happens to be older, wiser, and purer, than we. To transfer to these judgements any specialist authority which may belong to us as 'trained critics' is charlatanism, if the attempt is conscious, and confusion if it is not. If Brother Every (see *Theology*, September, 1940, p. 161) condemns a book because of 'English Liberal' implications he is really saying two things: (*a*) This book has English Liberal implications; (*b*) English Liberalism is an evil. The first he utters with authority because he is a trained critic. In the second, he may be right or he may be wrong; but he speaks with no more authority than any other man. Failure to observe this distinction may turn literary criticism into a sort of stalking horse from behind which a man may shoot all his personal opinions on any and every subject, without ever really arguing in their defence and under cover of a quite irrelevant specialist training in literature. I do not accuse Brother Every of this. But a glance at any modern review will show that it is an ever-present danger.

2. In *Theology*, May, 1940 (p. 359), Mr Bethell speaks of 'some form of biological or economic naturalism' as the unconscious attitude in most popular fiction of today, and cites, as straws that show the wind, the popularity of 'urges' and 'overmastering passions'. Now, fortunately, I agree with Mr Bethell in thinking naturalism an erroneous philosophy: and I am ready to grant, for the purposes of argument, that those who talk about 'urges' do so because they are unconsciously naturalistic. But when all this has been granted, can we honestly say that the *whole* of our dislike of 'urges' is explained, without remainder, by our disagreement with naturalism? Surely not. Surely we object to that way of writing for another reason *as well*— because it is so worn, so facile, so obviously attempting to be impressive, so associated in our minds with dullness and pomposity.[1] In other words, there are two

---

1. Pomp is at times a literary virtue. Pomposity (the unsuccessful attempt at pomp) may, of course, spring from an evil (pride); it may also be the maladroit effort of a humble writer to 'rise' to a subject which he honestly feels to be great.

elements in our reaction. One is the detection of an attitude in the writer which, as instructed Christians and amateur philosophers, we disapprove; the other is really, and strictly, an affair of taste. Now these, again, require to be kept distinct. Being fallen creatures we tend to resent offences against our taste, at least as much as, or even more than, offences against our conscience or reason; and we would dearly like to be able—if only we can find any plausible argument for doing so—to inflict upon the man whose writing (perhaps for reasons utterly unconnected with good and evil) has afflicted us like a bad smell, the same kind of condemnation which we can inflict on him who has uttered the false and the evil. The tendency is easily observed among children; friendship wavers when you discover that a hitherto trusted playmate actually *likes* prunes. But even for adults it is 'sweet, sweet, sweet poison' to feel able to imply 'thus saith the Lord' at the end of every expression of our pet aversions. To avoid this horrible danger we must perpetually try to distinguish, however closely they get entwined both by the subtle nature of the facts and by the secret importunity of our passions, those attitudes in a writer which we can honestly and confidently condemn as real evils, and those qualities in his writing which simply annoy and offend us as men of taste. This is difficult, because the latter are often so much more obvious and provoke such a very violent response. The only safe course seems to me to be this: to reserve our condemnation of attitudes for attitudes universally acknowledged to be bad by the Christian conscience speaking in agreement with Scripture and ecumenical tradition. A bad book is to be deemed a real evil in so far as it can be shown to prompt to sensuality, or pride, or murder, or to conflict with the doctrine of Divine Providence, or the like. The other dyslogistic terms dear to critics (vulgar, derivative, cheap, precious, academic, affected, bourgeois, Victorian, Georgian, 'literary', etc.) had better be kept strictly on the taste side of the account. In discovering what attitudes are present you can be as subtle as you like. But in your theological and ethical condemnation (as distinct from your dislike of the taste) you had better be very un-subtle. You had better reserve it for plain mortal sins, and plain atheism and heresy. For our passions are always urging us in the opposite direction, and if we are not careful criticism may become a mere excuse for taking revenge on books whose smell we dislike by erecting our temperamental antipathies into pseudo-moral judgements.

3. In practical life a certain amount of 'reading between the lines' is necessary: if we took every letter and every remark simply at its face value we should soon find ourselves in difficulties. On the other hand, most of us have known people with whom 'reading between the lines' became such a mania that they overlooked the obvious truth of every situation and lived in the perpetual discovery of mares' nests; and doctors tell us of a form of lunacy in which the simplest remark uttered in the patient's presence becomes to him evidence of a conspiracy and the very furniture of his cell takes on an infinitely sinister significance. Will my critics admit that the subtle and difficult task of digging out the latent beliefs and values, however necessary, is attended with some danger of our neglecting the obvious and surface facts about a book, whose importance, even if less than that of the latent facts, is certainly much higher than zero? Suppose two books A and B. Suppose it can be truly said of A: 'The very style of this book reveals great sensitivity and

honesty, and a readiness for total commitments; excellent raw material for sanctity if ever the author were converted.' And suppose it can be truly said of B: 'The very style of this book betrays a woolly, compromising state of mind, knee-deep entangled in the materialistic values which the author thinks he has rejected.' But might it not also be true to say of book A, 'Despite its excellent latent implications, its ostensible purpose (which will corrupt thousands of readers) is the continued glorification of mortal sin'; and of B, 'Despite its dreadful latent materialism, it does set courage and fidelity before the reader in an attractive light, and thousands of readers will be edified (though much less edified than they suppose) by reading it'? And is there not a danger of this second truth being neglected? We want the abstruse knowledge *in addition to* the obvious: not *instead of* it.

4. It is clear that the simple and ignorant are least able to resist, by reason, the influence of latent evil in the books they read. But is it not also true that this is often balanced by a kind of protection which comes to them through ignorance itself? I base this on three grounds: *(a)* Adults often disquiet themselves about the effect of a work upon children—for example, the effect of the bad elements in *Peter Pan*, such as the desire not to grow up or the sentimentalities about Wendy. But if I may trust my own memory, childhood simply does not receive these things. It rightly wants and enjoys the flying, the Indians, and the pirates (not to mention the pleasure of being in a theatre at all), and just accepts the rest as part of the meaningless 'roughage' which occurs in all books and plays; for at that age we never expect any work of art to be interesting all through. (When I began writing stories in exercise books I tried to put off all the things I really wanted to write about till at least the second page—I thought it wouldn't be like a real grown-up book if it became interesting at once.) *(b)* I often find expressions in my pupils' essays which seem to me to imply a great deal of latent error and evil. Now, since it would, in any case, be latent, one does not expect them to own up to it when challenged. But one does expect that a process of exploration would discover the mental atmosphere to which the expression belonged. But in my experience exploration often produces a conviction that it had, in my pupils' minds, no evil associations, because it had no associations at all. They just thought it was the ordinary way of translating thought into what they suppose to be 'literary English'. Thousands of people arc no more corrupted by the implications of 'urges', 'dynamism', and 'progressive' than they are edified by the implications of 'secular', 'charity', and 'Platonic'.[1] The same process of attrition which empties good language of its virtue does, after all, empty bad language of much of its vice.[2] *(c)* If one speaks to an uneducated man about some of the worst features in a film or a book, does he not often reply unconcernedly, 'Ah . . . they always got to bring a bit of that into a film,' or, 'I reckon they put that in to wind it up like' ? And does this not mean that he is aware, even to excess, of the difference between art and life? He *expects* a certain amount of meaningless nonsense—which

---

1. For example, God forbid that when Mr Bethell (May, 1940, p. 301) uses 'old-fashioned' as a dyslogistic term we should immediately conclude that he really had the garage or dressmaking philosophy (Madam would like the *latest* model) which his words suggest. We know it slipped out by a sort of accident, for which *veniam petimus damusque vicissim.*

2. This applies also to 'bad language' in the popular sense, obscenity or profanity. The custom of such language has its origin in sin, but to the individual speaker it may be mere meaningless noise.

expectation, though very regrettable from the cultural point of view, largely protects him from the consequences of which we, in our sophisticated naivety, are afraid.

5. Finally, I agree with Brother Every that our leisure, even our play, is a matter of serious concern. There is no neutral ground in the universe: every square inch, every split second, is claimed by God and counterclaimed by Satan. But will Brother Every agree in acknowledging a real difficulty about merely recreational reading (I do not include all reading under this head), as about games? I mean that they are serious, and yet, to do them at all, we must somehow do them as if they were not. It is a serious matter to choose wholesome recreations: but they would no longer be recreations if we pursued them seriously. When Mr Bethell speaks of the critic's 'working hours' (May, 1940, p. 360) I hope he means his hours of criticism, not his hours of reading. For a great deal (not all) of our literature was made to be read lightly, for entertainment. If we do not read it, in a sense, 'for fun' and with our feet on the fender, we are not using it as it was meant to be used, and all our criticism of it will be pure illusion. For you cannot judge any artefact except by using it as it was intended. It is no good judging a butter-knife by seeing whether it will saw logs. Much bad criticism, indeed, results from the efforts of critics to get a work-time result out of something that never aimed at producing more than pleasure. There is a real problem here, and I do not see my way through it. But I should be disappointed if my critics denied the existence of the problem.

If any real disagreement remains between us, I anticipate that it will be about my third point—about the distinction there drawn between the real spiritual evil carried or betrayed in a book and its mere faults of taste. And on this subject I confess that my critics can present me with a very puzzling dilemma. They can ask me whether the statement, 'This is tawdry writing', is an objective statement describing something bad in a book and capable of being true or false, or whether it is merely a statement about the speaker's own feelings—different in form, but fundamentally the same, as the proposition 'I don't like oysters.' If I choose the latter, then most criticism becomes purely subjective—which I don't want. If I choose the former then they can ask me, 'What are these qualities in a book which you admit to be in some sense good and bad but which, you keep on warning us, are not "really" or "spiritually" good and bad? Is there a kind of good which is not good? Is there any good that is not pleasing to God or any bad which is not hateful to Him?' And if you press me along these lines I end in doubts. But I will not get rid of those doubts by falsifying the little light I already have. That little light seems to compel me to say that there are two kinds of good and bad. The first, such as virtue and vice or love and hatred, besides being good or bad themselves make the possessor good or bad. The second do not. They include such things as physical beauty or ugliness, the possession or lack of a sense of humour, strength or weakness, pleasure or pain. But the two most relevant for us are the two I mentioned at the beginning of this essay, conjugal *eros* (as distinct from *agape,* which, of course, is a good of the first class) and physical cleanliness. Surely we have all met people who said, indeed, that the latter was *next* to godliness, but whose unconscious attitude made it a *part* of godliness, and no small part? And surely we agree that any good of this second class, however good on its own level, becomes an enemy when it thus assumes demonic pretensions and erects itself into a quasi-spiritual value. As M. de Rougemont has recently told us, the conjugal *eros* 'ceases to be a devil only when it ceases to be a god'. My whole contention is that in literature, in addition to the spiritual good and evil which it carries, there is also a good and evil of this second class, a properly cultural or literary good and evil, which must not be allowed to masquerade as good and evil of the first class. And I shall feel really happy about all the minor differences between my critics and me when I find in them some recognition of this danger—some admission that they and I, and all of the like education, are daily tempted to a kind of idolatry.

I am not pretending to know how this baffling phenomenon—the two kinds or levels of good and evil—is to be fitted into a consistent philosophy of values. But it is one thing to be unable to explain a phenomenon, another to ignore it. And I admit that all of these lower goods ought to be encouraged, that, as pedagogues, it is our duty to try to make our pupils happy and beautiful, to give them cleanly habits and good taste; and the discharge of that duty is, of course, a good of the first class. I will admit, too, that evils of this second class are often the result and symptom of real spiritual evil; dirty finger-nails, a sluggish liver, boredom, and a bad English style, may often in a given case result from disobedience, laziness, arrogance, or intemperance. But they may also result from poverty or other misfortune. They may even result from virtue. The man's ears may be unwashed behind or his English style borrowed from the jargon of the daily press, because he has given to good works the time and energy which others use to acquire elegant habits or good language. Gregory the Great, I believe, vaunted the barbarity of his style. Our Lord ate with unwashed hands.

I am stating, not solving, a problem. If my critics want to continue the discussion I think they can do so most usefully by taking it right away from literature and the arts to some other of these mysterious 'lower goods'—where, probably, all our minds will work more coolly. I should welcome an essay from Brother Every or Mr Bethell on conjugal *eros* or personal cleanliness. My dilemma about literature is that I admit bad taste to be, in some sense, 'a bad thing', but do not think it *per se* 'evil'. My critics will probably say the same of physical dirt. If we could thrash the problem out on the neutral ground of clean and dirty fingers, we might return to the battlefield of literature with new lights.

I hope it is now unnecessary to point out that in denying 'taste' to be a spiritual value, I am not for a moment suggesting, as Mr Bethell thought (May, 1940, p. 357), that it comes 'under God's arbitrary condemnation'. I enjoyed my breakfast this morning, and I think that was a good thing and do not think it was condemned by God. But I do not think myself a good man for enjoying it. The distinction does not seem to me a very fine one.

Religion: Reality or Substitute?

Hebrews X, I. *'The Law having a shadow of good things to come.'*

WE ARE ALL QUITE familiar with this idea, that the old Jewish priesthood was a mere symbol and that Christianity is the reality which it symbolized. It is important, however, to notice what an astonishing, even impudent, claim it must have seemed as long as the temple at Jerusalem was still standing. In the temple you saw real sacrifice being offered—real animals really had their throats cut and their actual flesh and blood were used in the ritual; in Christian assemblies a ceremony with wine and bits of bread was conducted. It must have been all but impossible to resist the conviction that the Jewish service was the reality and the Christian one a mere substitute—wine is so obviously a substitute for blood and bread for flesh! Yet the Christians had the audacity to maintain that it was the other way round—that their innocuous little ritual meal in private houses was the real sacrifice and that all the slaughtering, incense, music, and shouting in the temple was merely the shadow.

In considering this we touch upon the very central region where all doubts about our religion live. Things do look so very much as if our whole faith were a substitute for the real well-being we have failed to achieve on earth. It seems so very likely that our rejection of the World is only the disappointed fox's attempt to convince himself that unattainable grapes are sour. After all, we do not usually think much about the next world till our hopes in this have been pretty well flattened out—and when they are revived we not infrequently abandon our religion. And does not all that talk of celestial love come chiefly from monks and nuns, starved celibates consoling themselves with a compensatory hallucination? And the worship of the Christ child—does it not also come to us from centuries of lonely old maids? There is no good ignoring these disquieting thoughts. Let us admit from the outset that the psychologists have a good *prima facie* case. The theory that our religion is a substitute has a great deal of plausibility.

Faced with this, the first thing I do is to try to find out what I know about substitutes, and the realities for which they are substituted, in general. And I find that I don't know so much as I thought I did. Until I considered the matter I had a sort of impression that one could recognize the difference by mere inspection if one was really honest—that the substitute would somehow betray itself by the mere taste, would ring false. And this impression was, in fact, one of the sources from which the doubts I mentioned were drawing their strength. What made it seem so likely that religion was a substitute was not any general philosophical argument about the existence of God, but rather the experienced fact that for the most of us at most times the spiritual life *tasted so* thin, or insipid, compared with the natural. And I thought that was just what a substitute might be expected to taste like. But after reflection, I discovered that this was not only not an obvious truth but was even contradicted by some of my own experience.

I once knew two bad boys who smoked secretly and stole their father's tobacco. Their father had cigarettes, which he really smoked himself, and cigars—a great many cigars—which he kept for visitors. The boys liked cigarettes very much better than cigars. But every now and then there would come a day when their father had let his supply of cigarettes get so low that the boys thought the theft of even one or two would inevitably be detected. On such days they took cigars instead; and one of them would say to the other: 'I'm afraid we'll have to put up with cigars today', and the other would reply: 'Well, I suppose a cigar is better than nothing.' This is not a fable I'm inventing, but a historical fact that I can vouch for. And here, surely, we have a very good instance of the value to be attached to anyone's first hasty ideas about a reality and a substitute. To these children, a cigar was simply an inferior substitute for a cigarette, a *pis-aller*. And, of course, the boys, at that stage, were quite right about their own feelings: but they would have become ludicrously wrong if they had therefore inferred that cigars, in their own nature, were merely a kind of makeshift cigarette. On that question their own childish experience offered them no evidence: they had to learn the answer from quite different sources, or else to wait until their palates were grown up. And may I add the important moral of the story? One of these boys has been permanently punished by a life-long inability to appreciate cigars.

Here is another example. When I was a boy, gramophone records were not nearly so good as they are now. In the old recording of an orchestral piece you could hardly hear the separate instrument at all, but only a single undifferentiated sound. That was the sort of music I grew up on. And when, at a somewhat later age, I began to hear real orchestras, I was actually disappointed with them, just because you didn't get that single sound. What one got in a concert room seemed to me to lack the unity I had grown to expect, to be not an orchestra but merely a number of individual musicians on the same platform. In fact, I felt it 'wasn't the Real Thing'. This is an even better example than the former one. For a gramophone record is precisely a substitute, and an orchestra the reality. But owing to my musical miseducation the reality appeared to be a substitute and the substitute a reality.

'Substitutes' suggest wartime feeding. Well, there too I have an example. During the last war, as at present, we had to eat margarine instead of butter. When I began doing so I couldn't tell the difference between them. For the first week or so, I would have said, 'You may call the margarine a substitute if you like, but it is actually just as good as the real thing.' But by the end of the war I could never again have mistaken one for the other and I never wanted to see margarine again. This is different from the previous examples because here I started knowing which, in fact, was the substitute. But the point is that mere immediate taste did not at first confirm this bit of knowledge. It was only after long experience that the margarine revealed itself to my senses as the inferior.

But enough of my own experiences. I will turn to a better man, to Milton, and to that scene which I used to think the most grotesque, but now think one of the most profound, in *Paradise Lost*. I mean the part where Eve, a few minutes after her creation, sees herself in a pool of water, and falls in love with her own reflection. Then God makes her look up, and she sees Adam. But the interesting point is that the first sight of Adam is a disappointment; he is a much less immediately attractive object than herself Being divinely guided, Eve gets over this difficult *pons asinorum* and lives to learn that being in love with Adam is more inexhaustible, more fruitful, and even better fun, than being in love with herself. But if she had been a sinner, like ourselves, she would not have made the transition so easily; she also would have passed through the stage of finding the real, external lover a second best. Indeed the region from which this example is drawn illustrates my theme better than almost any other. To the pervert, normal love, when it does not appear simply repulsive, appears at best a mere milk and water substitute for that ghastly world of impossible fantasies which have become to him the 'real thing'. But every department of life furnishes us with examples. The ears that are delighted with jazz cannot quite believe that 'classical music' is anything but a sort of 'vegetarian jazz' (to quote my friend Barfield), and great literature seems to vulgar taste at first a pale reflection of the 'thrillers' or 'triangle dramas' which it prefers.

From all this I want to draw the following conclusion. Introspection is of no use at all in deciding which of two experiences is a substitute or a second best. At a certain stage all those sensations which we should expect to find accompanying the proper satisfaction of a fundamental need will actually accompany the substitute, and *vice versa*. And I want to insist that if we are once convinced of this principle, we should then hold it quite unflinchingly from this moment to the end of our lives. When a witness has once been proved unreliable, turn him out of the court. It is mere waste of time to go sneaking back to his evidence and thinking 'After all' and 'He *did* say'. If immediate feeling has shown itself quite worthless in this matter, then let us never listen to immediate feeling again. If our criterion between a real, and a substituted, satisfaction must be sought somewhere else, then in God's name, seek it somewhere else.

When I say 'somewhere else' I am not yet speaking of Faith or a supernatural gift. What I mean can be shown by an example. If those two bad boys had really wanted to find out whether their view of cigars and cigarettes were correct, there were various things they might have done. They might have asked a grown-up, who would have told them that cigars were actually regarded as the greater luxury of the two, and thus had their error corrected by authority. Or they might have found out by their own researches—that is by buying their smokes instead of stealing them —that cigars were more expensive than cigarettes and thence inferred that they could not in reality be a mere substitute for them. This would have been correction by reason. Finally, they might have practised obedience, honesty, and truthfulness and waited till an age at which they were allowed to smoke—in which case they would have arrived at a more reasonable view about these two ways of preparing tobacco by experience. Authority, reason, experience; on these three, mixed in varying proportions all our knowledge depends. The authority of many wise men in many different times and places forbids me to regard the spiritual world as an illusion. My reason, showing me the apparently insoluble difficulties of materialism and proving that the hypothesis of a spiritual world covers far more of the facts with far fewer assumptions, forbids me again. My experience even of such feeble attempts as I have made to live the spiritual life does not lead to the results which the pursuit of an illusion ordinarily leads to, and therefore forbids me yet again. I am not now saying that no one's reason and no one's experience produce different results. I am only trying to put the whole problem the right way round, to make it clear that the value given to the testimony of any feeling must depend on our whole philosophy, not our whole philosophy on a feeling. If those who deny the spiritual world prove their case on general grounds, then, indeed, it will follow that our apparently spiritual experiences *must* be an illusion; but equally, if we are right, it will follow that they are the prime reality and that our natural experiences are a second best. And let us note that whichever view we embrace, mere feeling will continue to assault our conviction. Just as the Christian has his moments when the clamour of this visible and audible world is so persistent and the whisper of the spiritual world so faint that faith and reason can hardly stick to their guns, so, as I well remember, the atheist too has his moments of shuddering misgiving, of an all but irresistible suspicion that old tales may after all be true, that something or someone from outside may at any moment break into his neat, explicable, mechanical universe. Believe in God and you will have to face hours when it seems *obvious* that this material world is the only reality: disbelieve in Him and you must face hours when this material world seems to shout at you that it is *not* all. No conviction, religious or irreligious, will, of itself, end once and for all this fifth-columnist in the soul. Only the practice of Faith resulting in the habit of Faith will gradually do that.

Have we now got to a position from which we can talk about Faith without being misunderstood? For in general we are shy of speaking plain about Faith as a virtue. It looks so like praising an intention to believe what you want to believe in the face of evidence to the contrary: the American in the old story defined Faith as 'the power of believing what we know to be untrue'. Now I define Faith as the power of continuing to believe what we once honestly thought to be true until cogent reasons for honestly changing our minds are brought before us. The difficulty of such continuing to believe is constantly ignored or misunderstood in discussions of this subject. It is always assumed that the difficulties of faith are intellectual difficulties, that a man who has once accepted a certain proposition will automatically go on believing it till real grounds for disbelief occur. Nothing could be more superficial. How many of the freshmen who come up to Oxford from religious homes and lose their Christianity in the first year have been honestly *argued* out of it? How many of our own sudden temporary losses of faith have a rational basis which would stand examination for a moment? I don't know how it is with others, but I find that mere change of scene always has a tendency to decrease my faith at first— God is less credible when I pray in a hotel bedroom than when I am in College. The society of unbelievers makes Faith harder even when they are people whose opinions, on any other subject, are known to be worthless.

These irrational fluctuations in belief are not peculiar to religious belief. They are happening about all our beliefs all day long. Haven't you noticed it with our thoughts about the war? Some days, of course, there is really good or really bad news, which gives us rational grounds for increased optimism or pessimism. But everyone must have experienced days in which we are caught up in a great wave of confidence or down into a trough of anxiety though there are no new grounds either for the one or the other. Of course, once the mood is on us, we *find* reasons soon enough. We say that we've been 'thinking it over': but it is pretty plain that the mood has created the reasons and not *vice versa.* But there are examples closer to the Christian problem even than these. There are things, say in learning to swim or to climb, which look dangerous and aren't. Your instructor tells you it's safe. You have good reason from past experience to trust him. Perhaps you can even see for yourself, by your own reason, that it is safe. But the crucial question is, will you be able to go on believing this when you actually see the cliff edge below you or actually feel yourself unsupported in the water? You will have no *rational* grounds for disbelieving. It is your senses and your imagination that are going to attack belief. Here, as in the New Testament, the conflict is not between faith and reason but between faith and sight. We can face things which we *know* to be dangerous if they don't look or sound too dangerous; our real trouble is often with things we *know* to be safe but which look dreadful. Our faith in Christ wavers not so much when real arguments come against it as when it *looks* improbable—when the whole world takes on that desolate *look* which really tells us much more about the state of our passions and even our digestion than about reality.

When we exhort people to Faith as a virtue, to the settled intention of continuing to believe certain things, we are not exhorting them to fight against reason. The intention of continuing to believe is required because, though Reason is divine, human reasoners are not. When once passion takes part in the game, the human reason, unassisted by Grace, has about as much chance of retaining its hold on truths already gained as a snowflake has of retaining its consistency in the mouth of a blast furnace. The sort of arguments against Christianity which our reason can be persuaded to accept at the moment of yielding to temptation are often preposterous. Reason may win truths; without Faith she will retain them just so long as Satan pleases. There is nothing we cannot be made to believe or disbelieve. If we wish to be rational, not now and then, but constantly, we must pray for the gift of Faith, for the power to go on believing not in the teeth of reason but in the teeth of lust and terror and jealousy and boredom and indifference that which reason, authority, or experience, or all three, have once delivered to us for truth. And the answer to that prayer will, perhaps, surprise us when it comes. For I am not sure, after all, whether one of the causes of our weak faith is not a secret wish that our faith should *not* be very strong. Is there some reservation in our minds? Some fear of what it might be like if our religion became *quite* real? I hope not. God help us all, and forgive us.

On Ethics

IT IS OFTEN ASSERTED in modern England that the world must return to Christian ethics in order to preserve civilization, or even in order to save the human species from destruction. It is sometimes asserted in reply that Christian ethics have been the greatest obstacle to human progress and that we must take care never to return to a bondage from which we have at last so fortunately escaped. I will not weary you with a repetition of the common arguments by which either view could be supported. My task is a different one. Though I am myself a Christian, and even a dogmatic Christian untinged with Modernist reservations and committed to supernaturalism in its full rigour, I find myself quite unable to take my place beside the upholders of the first view. The whole debate between those who demand and those who deprecate a return to Christian ethics, seems to me to involve presuppositions which I cannot allow. The question between the contending parties has been wrongly put.

I must begin by distinguishing the senses in which we may speak of ethical systems and of the differences between them. We may, on the one hand, mean by an ethical system a body of ethical injunctions. In this sense, when we speak of Stoical Ethics we mean the system which strongly commends suicide (under certain conditions) and enjoins Apathy in the technical sense, the extinction of the emotions: when we speak of Aristotelian ethics we mean the system which finds in Virtuous Pride or Magnanimity the virtue that presupposes and includes all other virtues; when we speak of Christian ethics we mean the system that commands humility, forgiveness, and (in certain circumstances) martyrdom. The differences, from this point of view, are differences of content. But we also sometimes speak of Ethical Systems when we mean systematic analyses and explanations of our moral experience. Thus the expression 'Kantian Ethics' signifies not primarily a body of commands—Kant did not differ remarkably from other men on the content of ethics—but the doctrine of the Categorical Imperative. From this point of view Stoical Ethics is the system which defines moral behaviour by conformity to Nature, or the whole, or Providence—terms almost interchangeable in Stoical thought: Aristotelian ethics is the system of eudaemonism: Christian ethics, the system which, whether by exalting Faith above Works, by asserting that love fulfils the Law, or by demanding Regeneration, makes duty a self-transcending concept and endeavours to escape from the region of mere morality.

It would of course be naive to suppose that there is no profound connection between an ethical system in the one sense and an ethical system in the other. The philosopher's or theologian's theory of ethics arises out of the practical ethics he already holds and attempts to obey; and again, the theory, once formed, reacts on his judgement of what ought to be done. That is a truth in no danger of being neglected by an age so steeped in historicism[1] as ours. We are, if anything, too deeply imbued with the sense of period, too eager to trace a common spirit in the ethical practice and ethical theory, in the economics, institutions, art, dress and language of a society. It must, however, also be insisted that Ethical Systems in the one sense do not differ in a direct ratio to the difference of Ethical Systems in another. The number of actions about whose ethical quality a Stoic, an Aristotelian, a Thomist, a Kantian, and a Utilitarian would agree is, after all very large. The very act of studying diverse ethical theories, as theories, exaggerates the practical differences between them. While we are studying them from that point of view we naturally and, for that purpose, rightly seize on the marginal case where the theoretical difference goes with a contradiction between the injunctions, because it is the *experimentum crucis*. But the exaggeration useful in one inquiry must not be carried over into other inquiries.

When modern writers urge us to return, or not to return, to Christian Ethics, I presume they mean Christian Ethics in our first sense: a body of injunctions, not a theory as to the origin, sanctions, or ultimate significance, of those injunctions. If they do not mean that, then they should not talk about a return to Christian Ethics but simply about a return to Christianity. I will at any rate assume that in this debate Christian Ethics means a body of injunctions.

And now my difficulties begin. A debate about the desirability of adopting Christian Ethics seems to proceed upon two presuppositions. (1) That Christian Ethics is one among several alternative bodies of injunctions, so clearly distinct from one another that the whole future of our species in this planet depends on our choice between them. (2) That we to whom the disputants address their pleadings, are for the moment standing outside all these systems in a sort of ethical vacuum, ready to enter whichever of them is most convincingly recommended to us. And it does not appear to me that either presupposition corresponds at all closely or sensitively to the reality.

Consider with me for a moment the first presupposition. Did Christian Ethics really enter the world as a novelty, a new, peculiar set of commands, to which a man could be in the strict sense *converted*? I say converted to the practical ethics: he could of course be converted to the Christian faith, he could accept, not only as a novelty, but as a transcendent novelty, a mystery hidden from all eternity, the deity and resurrection of Jesus, the Atonement, the forgiveness of sins. But these novelties themselves set a rigid limit to the novelty we can assume in the ethical injunctions. The convert accepted forgiveness of sins. But of sins against what Law? Some new law promulgated by the Christians? But that is nonsensical. It would be the mockery of a tyrant to forgive a man for doing what had never been forbidden until the very moment at which the forgiveness was announced. The idea (at least in its grossest and most popular form) that Christianity brought a new ethical code into the world is a grave error. If it had done so, then we should have to conclude that all who first preached it wholly misunderstood their own message: for all of them, its Founder, His precursor, His apostles, came demanding repentance and

[1. See Lewis's essay on 'Historicism', pp. 243ff.]

offering forgiveness, a demand and an offer both meaningless except on the assumption of a moral law already known and already broken.

It is far from my intention to deny that we find in Christian ethics a deepening, an internalization, a few changes of emphasis, in the moral code. But only serious ignorance of Jewish and Pagan culture would lead anyone to the conclusion that it is a radically new thing. Essentially, Christianity is not the promulgation of a moral discovery. It is addressed only to penitents, only to those who admit their disobedience to the known moral law. It offers forgiveness for having broken, and supernatural help towards keeping, that law, and by so doing re-affirms it. A Christian who understands his own religion laughs when unbelievers expect to trouble him by the assertion that Jesus uttered no command which had not been anticipated by the Rabbis—few, indeed, which cannot be paralleled in classical, ancient Egyptian, Ninevite, Babylonian, or Chinese texts.[1] We have long recognized that truth with rejoicing. Our faith is not pinned on a crank.

The second presupposition—that of an ethical vacuum in which we stand deciding what code we will adopt—is not quite so easily dealt with, but I believe it to be, in the long run, equally misleading. Of course, historically or chronologically, a man need not be supposed to stand outside all ethical codes at the moment when you exhort him to adopt Christian ethics. A man who is attending one lecturer or one physician may be advised to exchange him for another. But he cannot come to a decision without first reaching a moment of indecision. There must be a point at which he feels himself attached to neither and weighs their rival merits. Adherence to either is inconsistent with choice. In the same way, the demand that we should reassume, or refrain from reassuming, the Christian code of ethics, invites us to enter a state in which we shall be unattached.

I am not, of course, denying that some men at some times can be in an ethical vacuum, adhering to no Ethical System. But most of those who are in that state are by no means engaged in deciding what system they shall adopt, for such men do not often propose to adopt any. They are more often concerned with getting out of gaols or asylums. Our question is not about them. Our question is whether the sort of men who urge us to return (or not to return) to Christian Ethics, or the sort of men who listen to such appeals, can enter the ethical vacuum which seems to be involved in the very conception of choosing an ethical code. And the best way of answering this question is (as sometimes happens) by asking another first. Supposing we can enter the vacuum and view all Ethical Systems from the outside, what sort of motives can we then expect to find for entering any one of them?

One thing is immediately clear. We can have no *ethical* motives for adopting any of these systems. It cannot, while we are in the vacuum, be our duty to emerge from it. An act of duty is an act of obedience to the moral law. But by definition we are standing outside all codes of moral law. A man with no ethical allegiance can have

[1. Readers will have already recognized themes in this paper which recall the main argument of Lewis's *Abolition of Man* (Oxford, 1943; Bles, 1946)—a book which is, in my opinion, an all but indispensable introduction to the entire *corpus* of Lewisiana. Though I am unable to establish a date for this paper, my guess is that it anticipates the *Abolition* by a year or so.

On the similarities in various ethical systems, see his 'Illustrations of the *Tao*' (= The Way, or the Natural Law) which forms the Appendix to *The Abolition of Man*.]

no ethical motive for adopting one. If he had, it would prove that he was not really in the vacuum at all. How then does it come about that men who talk as if we could stand outside all moralities and choose among them as a woman chooses a hat, nevertheless exhort us (and often in passionate tones) to make some one particular choice? They have a ready answer. Almost invariably they recommend some code of ethics on the ground that it, and it alone, will preserve civilization, or the human race. What they seldom tell us is whether the preservation of the human race is itself a duty or whether they expect us to aim at it on some other ground.

Now if it is a duty, then clearly those who exhort us to it are not themselves really in a moral vacuum, and do not seriously believe that we are in a moral vacuum. At the very least they accept, and count on our accepting, one moral injunction. Their moral code is, admittedly, singularly poor in content. Its solitary command, compared with the richly articulated codes of Aristotle, Confucius, or Aquinas, suggests that it is a mere residuum; as the arts of certain savages suggest that they are the last vestige of a vanished civilization. But there is a profound difference between having a fanatical and narrow morality and having no morality at all. If they were really in a moral vacuum, whence could they have derived the idea of even a single duty?

In order to evade the difficulty, it may be suggested that the preservation of our species is not a moral imperative but an end prescribed by Instinct. To this I reply, firstly, that it is very doubtful whether there is such an instinct; and secondly, that if there were, it would not do the work which those who invoke instinct in this context demand of it.

Have we in fact such an instinct? We must here be careful about the meaning of the word. In English the word *instinct* is often loosely used for what ought rather to be called appetite: thus we speak of the sexual instinct. *Instinct* in this sense means an impulse which appears in consciousness as desire, and whose fulfilment is marked by pleasure. That we have no instinct (in this sense) to preserve our species, seems to me self-evident. Desire is directed to the concrete—this woman, this plate of soup, this glass of beer: but the preservation of the species is a high abstraction which does not even enter the mind of unreflective people, and affects even cultured minds most at those times when they are least instinctive. But instinct is also, and more properly, used to mean Behaviour as if from knowledge. Thus certain insects carry out complicated actions which have in fact the result that their eggs are hatched and their larvae nourished: and since (rightly or wrongly) we refuse to attribute conscious design and foreknowledge to the agent we say that it has acted 'by instinct'. What that means on the subjective side, how the matter appears, if it appears at all, to the insect, I suppose we do not know. To say, in this sense, that we have an instinct to preserve the human race, would be to say that we find ourselves compelled, we know not how, to perform acts which in fact (though that was not our purpose) tend to its preservation. This seems very unlikely. What are these acts? And if they exist, what is the purpose of urging us to preserve the race by adopting (or avoiding) Christian Ethics? Had not the job better be left to instinct?

Yet again, *Instinct* may be used to denote these strong impulses which are, like the appetites, hard to deny though they are not, like the appetites, directed to concrete physical pleasure. And this, I think, is what people really mean when they speak of an instinct to preserve the human race. They mean that we have a natural, unreflective, spontaneous impulse to do this, as we have to preserve our own offspring. And here we are thrown back on the debatable evidence of introspection. I do not find that I have this impulse, and I do not see evidence that other men have it. Do not misunderstand me. I would not be thought a monster. I acknowledge the preservation of man as an end to which my own preservation and happiness are subordinate; what I deny is that that end has been prescribed to me by a powerful, spontaneous impulse.

The truth seems to me to be that we have such an impulse to preserve our children and grandchildren, an impulse which progressively weakens as we carry our minds further and further into the abyss of future generations, and which, if left to its own spontaneous strength, soon dies out altogether. Let me ask anyone in this audience who is a father whether he has a spontaneous impulse to sacrifice his own son for the sake of the human species in general. I am not asking whether he would so sacrifice his son. I am asking whether, if he did so, he would be obeying a spontaneous impulse. Will not every father among you reply that if this sacrifice were demanded of him and if he made it, he would do so not in obedience to a natural impulse but in hard-won defiance of it? Such an act, no less than the immolation of oneself, would be a triumph over nature.

But let us leave that difficulty on one side. Let us suppose, for purposes of argument, that there really is an 'instinct' (in whatever sense) to preserve civilization, or the human race. Our instincts are obviously in conflict. The satisfaction of one demands the denial of another. And obviously the instinct, if there is one, to preserve humanity, is the one of all others whose satisfaction is likely to entail the greatest frustration of my remaining instincts. My hunger and thirst, my sexual desires, my family affections, are all going to be interfered with. And remember, we are still supposed to be in the vacuum, outside all ethical systems. On what conceivable ground, in an ethical void, on the assumption that the preservation of the species is not a moral but a merely instinctive end, can I be asked to gratify my instinct for the preservation of the species by adopting a moral code? Why should this instinct be preferred to all my others? It is certainly not my strongest. Even if it were, why should I not fight against it as a dipsomaniac is exhorted to fight against his tyrannous desire? Why do my advisers assume from the very outset, without argument, that this instinct should be given a dictatorship in my soul? Let us not be cheated with words. It is no use to say that this is the deepest, or highest, or most fundamental, or noblest of my instincts. Such words either mean that it is my strongest instinct (which is false and would be no reason for obeying it even if it were true) or else conceal a surreptitious re-introduction of the ethical.

And in fact the ethical has been re-introduced. Or, more accurately, it has never really been banished. The moral vacuum was from the outset a mere figment. Those who expect us to adopt a moral code as a means to the preservation of the species have themselves already a moral code and tacitly assume that we have one too. Their starting point is a purely moral maxim *That humanity ought to be preserved.* The introduction of instinct is futile. If you do not arrange our instincts in a hierarchy of comparative dignity, it is idle to tell us to obey instinct, for the instincts are at war. If you do, then you are arranging them in obedience to a moral principle, passing an ethical judgement upon them. If instinct is your only standard, no instinct is to be preferred to another: for each of them will claim to be gratified at the expense of all the rest. Those who urge us to choose a moral code are already moralists. We may throw away the preposterous picture of a wholly unethical man confronted with a series of alternative codes and making his free choice between them. Nothing of the kind occurs. When a man is wholly unethical he does not choose between ethical codes. And those who say they are choosing between ethical codes are already assuming a code.

What, then, shall we say of the maxim which turns out to be present from the beginning—*That humanity ought to be preserved*? Where do we get it from? Or, to be more concrete, where do I get it from? Certainly, I can point to no moment in time at which I first embraced it. It is, so far as I can make out, a late and abstract generalization from all the moral teaching I have ever had. If I now wanted to find authority for it, I should have no need to appeal to my own religion. I could point to the confession of the righteous soul in the Egyptian *Book of the Dead*—'I have not slain men.' I could find in the Babylonian Hymn that he who meditates oppression will find his house overturned. I would find, nearer home in the Elder Edda that 'Man is man's delight.' I would find in Confucius that the people should first be multiplied, then enriched, and then instructed. If I wanted the spirit of all these precepts generalized I could find in Locke that 'by the fundamental law of Nature Man is to be preserved as much as possible'.

Thus from my point of view there is no particular mystery about this maxim. It is what I have been taught, explicitly and implicitly, by my nurse, my parents, my religion, by sages or poets from every culture of which I have any knowledge. To reach this maxim I have no need to choose one ethical code among many and excogitate impossible motives for adopting it. The difficulty would be to find codes that contradict it. And when I had found them they would turn out to be, not radically different things, but codes in which the same principle is for some reason restricted or truncated: in which the preservation and perfection of Man shrinks to that of the tribe, the class, or the family, or the nation. They could all be reached by mere subtraction from what seems to be the general code: they differ from it not as ox from man but as dwarf from man.

Thus far as concerns myself. But where do those others get it from, those others who claimed to be standing outside all ethical codes? Surely there is no doubt about the answer. They found it where I found it. They hold it by inheritance and training from the general (if not strictly universal) human tradition. They would never have reached their solitary injunction if they had really begun in an ethical vacuum. They have trusted the general human tradition at least to the extent of taking over from it one maxim.

But of course in that tradition this maxim did not stand alone. I found beside it many other injunctions: special duties to parents and elders, special duties to my wife and child, duties of good faith and veracity, duties to the weak, the poor and the desolate (these latter not confined, as some think, to the Judaic-Christian texts).

And for me, again, there is no difficulty. I accept all these commands, all on the same authority. But there is surely a great difficulty for those who retain one and desire to drop the rest? And now we come to the heart of our subject.

There are many people in the modern world who offer us, as they say, new moralities. But as we have just seen there can be no moral motive for entering a new morality unless that motive is borrowed from the traditional morality, which is neither Christian nor Pagan, neither Eastern nor Western, neither ancient nor modern, but general. The question then arises as to the reasonableness of taking one maxim and rejecting the rest. If the remaining maxims have no authority, what is the authority of the one you have selected to retain? If it has authority, why have the others no authority? Thus a scientific Humanist may urge us to get rid of what he might call our inherited *Taboo* morality and realize that the total exploitation of nature for the comfort and security of posterity is the sole end. His system clashes with mine, say, at the point where he demands the compulsory euthanasia of the aged or the unfit. But the duty of caring for posterity, on which he bases his whole system, has no other source than that same tradition which bids me honour my parents and do no murder (a prohibition I find in the *Voluspa* as well as in the Decalogue). If, as he would have me believe, I have been misled by the tradition when it taught me my duty to my parents, how do I know it has not misled me equally in prescribing a duty to posterity? Again, we may have a fanatical Nationalist who tells me to throw away my antiquated scruples about universal justice and benevolence and adopt a system in which nothing but the wealth and power of my own country matters. But the difficulty is the same. I learned of a special duty to my own country in the same place where I also learned of a general duty to men as such. If the tradition was wrong about the one duty, on what ground does the Nationalist ask me to believe that it was right about the other? The Communist is in the same position. I may well agree with him that exploitation is an evil and that those who do the work should reap the reward. But I only believe this because I accept certain traditional notions of justice. When he goes on to attack justice as part of my *bourgeois* ideology, he takes away the very ground on which I can reasonably be asked to accept his new communistic code.

Let us very clearly understand that, in a certain sense, it is no more possible to invent a new ethics than to place a new sun in the sky. Some precept from traditional morality always has to be assumed. We never start from a *tabula rasa:* if we did, we should end, ethically speaking, with a *tabula rasa.* New moralities can only be contractions or expansions of something already given. And all the specifically modern attempts at new moralities are contractions. They proceed by retaining some traditional precepts and rejecting others: but the only real authority behind those which they retain is the very same authority which they flout in rejecting others. Of course this inconsistency is concealed; usually, as we have seen, by a refusal to recognize the precepts that are retained as moral precepts at all.

But many other causes contribute to the concealment. As in the life of the individual so in that of a community, particular circumstances set a temporary excess of value on some one end. When we are in love, the beloved, when we are ill, health, when we are poor, money, when we are frightened, safety, seems the only thing worth having. Hence he who speaks to a class, a nation, or a culture, in the grip of some passion, will not find it difficult to insinuate into their minds the fatal idea of some one finite good which is worth achieving at all costs, and building an eccentric ethical system on that foundation. It is, of course, no genuinely new system. Whatever the chosen goal may be, the idea that I should seek it for my class or culture or nation at the expense of my own personal satisfaction has no authority save that which it derives from traditional morality. But in the emotion of the moment this is over-looked.

Added to this, may we not recognize in modern thought a very serious exaggeration of the ethical differences between different cultures? The conception which dominates our thought is enshrined in the word *ideologies,* in so far as that word suggests that the whole moral and philosophical outlook of a people can be explained without remainder in terms of their method of production, their economic organization, and their geographical position. On that view, of course, differences, and differences to any extent, are to be expected between ideologies as between languages and costumes. But is this what we actually find? Much anthropology seems at first to encourage us to answer Yes. But if I may venture on an opinion in a field where I am by no means an expert, I would suggest that the appearance is somewhat illusory. It seems to me to result from a concentration on those very elements in each culture which are most variable (sexual practice and religious ritual) and also from a concentration on the savage. I have even found a tendency in some thinkers to treat the savage as the normal or archetypal man. But surely he is the exceptional man. It may indeed be true that we were all savages once, as it is certainly true that we were all babies once. But we do not treat as normal man the imbecile who remains in adult life what we all were (intellectually) in the cradle. The savage has had as many generations of ancestors as the civilized man: he is the man who, in the same number of centuries, either has not learned or has forgotten, what the rest of the human race know. I do not see why we should attach much significance to the diversity and eccentricity (themselves often exaggerated) of savage codes. And if we turn to civilized man, I claim that we shall find far fewer differences of ethical injunction than is now popularly believed. In triumphant monotony the same indispensable platitudes will meet us in culture after culture. The idea that any of the new moralities now offered us would be simply one more addition to a variety already almost infinite, is not in accordance with the facts. We are not really justified in speaking of different moralities as we speak of different languages or different religions.

You will not suspect me of trying to reintroduce in its full Stoical or medieval rigour the doctrine of Natural Law. Still less am I claiming as the source of this substantial ethical agreement anything like Intuition or Innate Ideas. Nor, Theist though I am, do I here put forward any surreptitious argument for Theism. My aim is more timid. It is even negative. I deny that we have any choice to make between clearly differentiated ethical systems. I deny that we have any power to make a new ethical system. I assert that wherever and whenever ethical discussion begins we find already before us an ethical code whose validity has to be assumed before we can even criticize it. For no ethical attack on any of the traditional precepts can be made except on the ground of some other traditional precept. You can attack the concept of justice because it interferes with the feeding of the masses, but you have taken the duty of feeding the masses from the world-wide code. You may exalt patriotism at the expense of mercy; but it was the old code that told you to love your country. You may vivisect your grandfather in order to deliver your grandchildren from cancer: but, take away traditional morality, and why should you bother about your grandchildren?

Out of these negatives, there springs a positive. Men say 'How are we to act, what are we to teach our children, now that we are no longer Christians?' You see, gentlemen, how I would answer that question. You are deceived in thinking that the morality of your father was based on Christianity. On the contrary, Christianity presupposed it. That morality stands exactly where it did; its basis has not been withdrawn for, in a sense, it never had a basis. The ultimate ethical injunctions have always been premisses, never conclusions. Kant was perfectly right on that point at least: the imperative is categorical. Unless the ethical is assumed from the outset, no argument will bring you to it.

In thus recalling men to traditional morality I am not of course maintaining that it will provide an answer to every particular moral problem with which we may be confronted. M. Sartre seems to me to be the victim of a curious misunderstanding when he rejects the conception of general moral rules on the ground that such rules may fail to apply clearly to all concrete problems of conduct. Who could ever have supposed that by accepting a moral code we should be delivered from all questions of casuistry? Obviously it is moral codes that create questions of casuistry, just as the rules of chess create chess problems. The man without a moral code, like the animal, is free from moral problems. The man who has not learned to count is free from mathematical problems. A man asleep is free from all problems. Within the framework of general human ethics problems will, of course, arise and will sometimes be solved wrongly. This possibility of error is simply the symptom that we are awake, not asleep, that we are men, not beasts or gods. If I were pressing on you a panacea, if I were recommending traditional ethics as a means to some end, I might be tempted to promise you the infallibility which I actually deny. But that, you see, is not my position. I send you back to your nurse and your father, to all the poets and sages and law givers, because, in a sense, I hold that you are already there whether you recognize it or not: that there is really no ethical alternative: that those who urge us to adopt new moralities are only offering us the mutilated or expurgated text of a book which we already possess in the original manuscript. They all wish us to depend on them instead of on that original, and then to deprive us of our full humanity. Their activity is in the long run always directed against our freedom.

De Futilitate

WHEN I WAS ASKED to address you, Sir Henry Tizard suggested that the problem of futility was likely *to* be present to many of your minds. It would have been raised by the disappointment of all those hopes with which the last war closed and the uneasy feeling that the results of the present war may prove equally disappointing. And if I remember rightly he also hinted that the feeling of futility might go even deeper. The eschatological hopes which supported our more remote, and Christian ancestors, and the secular hopes which supported the Revolutionaries or even the Liberals of the last century, have both rather faded out. There is a certain vacuity left: a widespread question as to what all this hustling and crowded life is *about*, or whether indeed it is about anything.

Now in one way I am the worst person in the world to address you on this subject. Perhaps because I had a not very happy boyhood, or perhaps because of some peculiarity in my glands, I am too familiar with the idea of futility to feel the shock of it so sharply as a good speaker on the subject ought to. Early in this war a labouring man who was doing a midnight Home Guard Patrol with another educated man and myself, discovered from our conversation that we did not expect that this war would end wars, or, in general, that human misery would ever be abolished. I shall never forget that man standing still there in the moonlight for at least a whole minute, as this entirely novel idea sank in and at last breaking out 'Then what's the good of the ruddy world going on?' What astonished me—for I was as much astonished as the workman—was the fact that this misgiving was wholly new to him. How, I wondered, could a man have reached the middle forties without ever before doubting whether there *was* any good in the ruddy world going on? Such security was to me unimaginable. I can understand a man coming in the end, and after prolonged consideration, to the view that existence is not futile. But how any man could have taken it for granted beat me, and beats me still. And if there is anyone present whose fear of futility is based solely on such local and temporary facts as the war or the almost equally threatening prospect of the next peace, I must ask him to bear with me while I suggest that we have to face the possibility of a much deeper and more radical futility: one which, if it exists at all, is wholly incurable.

This cosmic futility is concealed from the masses by popular Evolutionism. Speaking to a scientifically trained audience I need not labour the point that popular Evolutionism is something quite different from Evolution as the biologists understand it. Biological Evolution is a theory about how organisms change. Some of these changes have made organisms, judged by human standards, 'better'—more flexible, stronger, more conscious. The majority of the changes have not done so. As J. B. S. Haldane says, in evolution progress is the exception and degeneration the rule. Popular Evolutionism ignores this. For it, 'Evolution' simply means 'improvement'. And it is not confined to organisms, but applied also to moral qualities, institutions, arts, intelligence and the like. There is thus lodged in popular thought the conception that improvement is, somehow, a cosmic law: a conception to which the sciences give no support at all. There is no general tendency even for organisms to improve. There is no evidence that the mental and moral capacities of the human race have been increased since man became man. And there is certainly no tendency for the universe as a whole to move in any direction which we should call 'good'. On the contrary, Evolution—even if it were what the mass of the people suppose it to be—is only (by astronomical and physical standards) an inconspicuous foreground detail in the picture. The huge background is filled by quite different principles: entropy, degradation, disorganization. Everything suggests that organic life is going to be a very short and unimportant episode in the history of the universe. We have often heard individuals console themselves for their individual troubles by saying: 'It will be all the same 100 years hence.' But you can do the like about our troubles as a species. Whatever we do it is all going to be the same in a few hundred million years hence. Organic life is only a lightning flash in cosmic history. In the long run, nothing will come of it.

Now do not misunderstand me. I am not for one moment trying to suggest that this long-term futility provides any ground for diminishing our efforts to make human life, while it lasts, less painful and less unfair than it has been up to date. The fact that the ship is sinking is no reason for allowing her to be a floating hell while she still floats. Indeed, there is a certain fine irony in the idea of keeping the ship very punctiliously in good order up to the very moment at which she goes down. If the universe is shameless and idiotic, that is no reason why we should imitate it. Well brought up people have always regarded the tumbril and the scaffold as places for one's best clothes and best manners. Such, at least, was my first reaction to the picture of the futile cosmos. And I am not, in the first instance, suggesting that that picture should be allowed to make any difference to our practice. But it must make a difference to our thoughts and feelings.

Now it seems to me that there are three lines, and three only, which one can take about this futility. In the first place, you can simply 'take it'. You can become a consistent pessimist, as Lord Russell was when he wrote *The Worship of a Free Man*, and base your whole life on what he called 'a firm foundation of unshakable despair'. You will feed yourself on the Wessex novels and *The Shropshire Lad* and Lucretius: and a very manly, impressive figure you may contrive to be. In the second place you can deny the picture of the universe which the scientists paint. There are various ways of doing this. You might become a Western Idealist or an Oriental Pantheist. In either case you would maintain that the material universe was, in the last resort, not quite real. It is a kind of mirage produced by our senses and forms of thought: Reality is to be sought elsewhere. Or you might say—as Jews, Mohammedans and Christians do, that though Nature is real as far as she goes, still there are other realities, and that by bringing them in you alter the picture so much that it is no longer a picture of futility. Or thirdly, one could accept the scientific picture and try to do something about the futility. I mean, instead of criticizing the universe we may criticize our own feeling about the universe, and try to show that our sense of futility is unreasonable or improper or irrelevant. I imagine this third procedure will seem to you, at any rate to begin with, the most promising. Let us explore it.

I think the most damaging criticism we can level against our own feeling of cosmic futility is this: 'Futility' is the opposite of 'utility'. A machine or plan is futile when it does not serve the purpose for which it was devised. In calling the universe futile, therefore, we are really applying to it a means-and-end pattern of thought: treating it as if it were a thing manufactured and manufactured for some purpose. In calling it futile we are only expressing our naïve surprise at the discovery that basic reality does not possess the characteristics of a human artefact—a thing made by men to serve the purposes of men—and the demand that it should may be regarded as preposterous: it is rather like complaining that a tree is futile because the branches don't happen to come just where we want them for climbing it—or even a stone because it doesn't happen to be edible.

This point of view certainly seems, at first, to have all the bracing shock of common sense, and I certainly believe that no philosophy which does not contain this view as at least one of its elements is at all likely to be true. But taken by itself it will turn out to be rather too simple.

If we push it to its logical conclusion we shall arrive at something like this. The proper way of stating the facts is not to say that the universe is futile, but that the universe has produced an animal, namely man, which can make tools. The long habit of making tools has engendered in him another habit—that of thinking in terms of means and ends. This habit becomes so deeply engrained that even when the creature is not engaged in tool-making it continues to use this pattern of thought—to 'project' it (as we say) upon reality as a whole. Hence arises the absurd practice of demanding that the universe should be 'good' or complaining that it is 'bad'. But such thoughts are *merely* human. They tell us nothing about the universe, they are merely a fact about Man—like his pigmentation or the shape of his lungs.

There is something attractive about this: but the question is how far we can go. Can we carry through to the end the view that human thought is *merely* human: that it is simply a zoological fact about *homo sapiens* that he thinks in a certain way: that it in no way reflects (though no doubt it results from) non-human or universal reality? The moment we ask this question, we receive a check. We are at this very point asking whether a certain view of human thought is true. And the view in question is just the view that human thought is *not* true, not a reflection of reality. And this view is itself a thought. In other words, we are asking 'Is the thought that no thoughts are true, itself true?' If we answer Yes, we contradict ourselves. For if all thoughts are untrue, then this thought is untrue.

There is therefore no question of a total skepticism about human thought. We are always prevented from accepting total skepticism because it can be formulated only by making a tacit exception in favour of the thought we are thinking at the moment—just as the man who warns the newcomer 'Don't trust anyone in this office' always expects you to trust him at that moment. Whatever happens, then, the most we can ever do is to decide that certain types of human thought are 'merely human' or subjective, and others not. However small the class, *some* class of thoughts must be regarded not as mere facts about the way human brains work, but as true insights, as the reflection of reality in human consciousness.

One popular distinction is between what is called scientific thought and other kinds of thought. It is widely believed that scientific thought does put us in touch with reality, whereas moral or metaphysical thought does not. On this view, when we say that the universe is a space-time continuum we are saying something about reality, whereas if we say that the universe is futile, or that men ought to have a living wage, we are only describing our own subjective feelings. That is why in modern stories of what the Americans call 'scientifictional' type—stories about unknown species who inhabit other planets or the depth of the sea—these creatures are usually pictured as being wholly devoid of our moral standards but as accepting our scientific standards. The implication is, of course, that scientific thought, being objective, will be the same for all creatures that can reason at all, whereas moral thought, being merely a subjective thing like one's taste in food, might be expected to vary from species to species.

But the distinction thus made between scientific and non-scientific thoughts will not easily bear the weight we are attempting to put on it. The cycle of scientific thought is from experiment to hypothesis and thence to verification and a new hypothesis. Experiment means sense-experiences specially arranged. Verification involves inference. 'If X existed, then, under conditions Y, we should have the experience Z.' We then produce the conditions Y and Z appears. We thence infer the existence of X. Now it is clear that the only part of this process which assures us of any reality outside ourselves is precisely the inference 'If X, then Z', or conversely 'Since Z, therefore X'. The other parts of the process, namely hypothesis and experiment, cannot by themselves give us any assurance. The hypothesis is, admittedly, a mental construction—something, as they say, 'inside our own heads'. And the experiment is a state of our own consciousness. It is, say, a dial reading or a colour seen if you heat the fluid in the test tube. That is to say, it is a state of visual sensation. The apparatus used in the experiment is believed to exist outside our own minds only on the strength of an inference: it is inferred as the cause of our visual sensations. I am not at all suggesting that the inference is a bad one. I am not a subjective idealist and I fully believe that the distinction we make between an experiment in a dream and an experiment in a laboratory is a sound one. I am only pointing out that the material or external world in general is an inferred world and that therefore particular experiments, far from taking us out of the magic circle of inference into some supposed direct contact with reality, are themselves evidential only as parts of that great inference. The physical sciences, then, depend on the validity of logic just as much as metaphysics or mathematics. If popular thought feels 'science' to be different from all other kinds of knowledge because science is experimentally verifiable, popular thought is mistaken. Experimental verification is not a new kind of assurance coming in to supply the deficiencies of mere logic. We should therefore abandon the distinction between scientific and non-scientific thought. The proper distinction is between logical and non-logical thought. I mean, the proper distinction for our present purpose: that purpose being to find whether there is any class of thoughts which has objective value, which is not *merely* a fact about how the human cortex behaves. For that purpose we can make no distinction between science and other logical exercises of thought, for if logic is discredited science must go down along with it.

It therefore follows that all knowledge whatever depends on the validity of inference. If, in principle, the feeling of certainty we have when we say 'Because A is B therefore C must be D' is an illusion, if it reveals only how our cortex has to work and not how realities external to us must really be, then we can know nothing whatever. I say 'in principle' because, of course, through inattention or fatigue we often make false inferences and while we make them they feel as certain as the sound ones. But then they are always corrigible by further reasoning. That does not matter. What would matter would be if inference itself, even apart from accidental errors, were a merely subjective phenomenon.

Now let me go back a bit. We began by asking whether our feeling of futility could be set aside as a merely subjective and irrelevant result which the universe has produced in human brains. I postponed answering that question until we had attempted a larger one. I asked whether *in general* human thought could be set aside as irrelevant to the real universe and merely subjective. I now claim to have found the answer to this larger question. The answer is that at least one kind of thought— logical thought—cannot be subjective and irrelevant to the real universe: for unless thought is valid we have no reason to believe in the real universe. We reach our knowledge of the universe only by inference. The very object to which our thought is supposed to be irrelevant depends on the relevance of our thought. A universe whose only claim to be believed in rests on the validity of inference must not start telling us that inference is invalid. That would really be a bit too nonsensical. I conclude then that logic is a real insight into the way in which real things have to exist. In other words, the laws of thought are also the laws of things: of things in the remotest space and the remotest time.[1]

This admission seems to me completely unavoidable and it has very momentous consequences.

In the first place it rules out any materialistic account of thinking. We are compelled to admit between the thoughts of a terrestrial astronomer and the behaviour of matter several light-years away that particular relation which we call truth. But this relation has no meaning at all if we try to make it exist between the matter of the star and the astronomer's brain, considered as a lump of matter. The brain may be in all sorts of relations to the star no doubt: it is in a spatial relation, and a time relation, and a quantitative relation. But to talk of one bit of matter as being true about another bit of matter seems to me to be nonsense. It might conceivably turn out to be the case that every atom in the universe thought, and thought truly, about every other. But that relation between any two atoms would be something quite distinct from the physical relations between them. In saying that thinking is not

---

[1. Lewis's best and fullest treatment on the validity of human reasoning appears in the first six chapters of his book *Miracles: A Preliminary Study* (Bles, 1947), especially chapter III, 'The Self-Contradiction of the Naturalist'. He later felt that he had in chapter III confused two senses of *irrational*; this chapter was rewritten and appears in its corrected form in the paper-backed edition of *Miracles* (Fontana Books, 1960).]

matter I am not suggesting that there is anything mysterious about it. In one sense, thinking is the simplest thing in the world. We do it all day long. We know what it is like far better than we know what matter is like. Thought is what we start from: the simple, intimate, immediate *datum*. Matter is the inferred thing, the mystery.

In the second place, to understand that logic must be valid is to see at once that this thing we all know, this thought, this mind, cannot in fact be really alien to the nature of the universe. Or, putting it the other way round, the nature of the universe cannot be really alien to Reason. We find that matter always obeys the same laws which our logic obeys. When logic says a thing must be so, Nature always agrees. No one can suppose that this can be due to a happy coincidence. A great many people think that it is due to the fact that Nature produced the mind. But on the assumption that Nature is herself mindless this provides no explanation. To be the result of a series of mindless events is one thing: to be a kind of plan or true account of the laws according to which those mindless events happened is quite another. Thus the Gulf Stream produces all sorts of results: for instance, the temperature of the Irish Sea. What it does not produce is maps of the Gulf Stream. But if logic, as we find it operative in our own minds, is really a result of mindless nature, then it is a result as improbable as that. The laws whereby logic obliges us to think turn out to be the laws according to which every event in space and time must happen. The man who thinks this an ordinary or probable result does not really understand. It is as if cabbages, in addition to resulting *from* the laws of botany also gave lectures in that subject: or as if, when I knocked out my pipe, the ashes arranged themselves into letters which read: 'We are the ashes of a knocked-out pipe.' But if the validity of knowledge cannot be explained in that way, and if perpetual happy coincidence throughout the whole of recorded time is out of the question, then surely we must seek the real explanation elsewhere.

I want to put this other explanation in the broadest possible terms and am anxious that you should not imagine I am trying to prove anything more, or more definite, than I really am. And perhaps the safest way of putting it is this: that we must give up talking about 'human reason'. In so far as thought is merely human, merely a characteristic of one particular biological species, it does not explain our knowledge. Where thought is strictly rational it must be, in some odd sense, not ours, but cosmic or super-cosmic. It must be something not shut up inside our heads but already 'out there'—in the universe or behind the universe: either as objective as material Nature or more objective still. Unless all that we take to be knowledge is an illusion, we must hold that in thinking we are not reading rationality into an irrational universe but responding to a rationality with which the universe has always been saturated. There are all sorts of different ways in which you can develop this position, either into an idealist metaphysic or a theology, into a theistic or a pantheistic or dualist theology. I am not tonight going to trace those possible developments, still less to defend the particular one which I myself accept. I am only going to consider what light this conception, in its most general form, throws on the question of futility.

As first sight it might seem to throw very little. The universe, as we have observed it, does not appear to be in any sense good as a whole, though it throws up some

particular details which are very good indeed—strawberries and the sea and sunrise and the song of the birds. But these, quantitatively considered, are so brief and
small compared with the huge tracts of empty space and the enormous masses of
uninhabitable matter that we might well regard them as lucky accidents. We might
therefore conclude that though the ultimate reality is logical it has no regard for
values, or at any rate for the values we recognize. And so we could still accuse it of
futility. But there is a real difficulty about accusing it of anything. An accusation
always implies a standard. You call a man a bad golf player because you know what
Bogey is. You call a boy's answer to a sum wrong because you know the right answer. You call a man cruel or idle because you have in mind a standard of kindness or diligence. And while you are making the accusation you have to accept the
standard as a valid one. If you begin to doubt the standard you automatically doubt
the cogency of your accusation. If you are sceptical about grammar you must be
equally sceptical about your condemnation of bad grammar. If nothing is certainly
right, then of course it follows that nothing is certainly wrong. And that is the snag
about what I would call Heroic Pessimism—I mean the kind of Pessimism you get
in Swinburne, Hardy and Shelley's *Prometheus* and which is magnificently summed
up in Housman's line 'Whatever brute and blackguard made the world'. Do not
imagine that I lack sympathy with that kind of poetry: on the contrary, at one time
of my life I tried very hard to write it—and, as far as quantity goes, I succeeded. I
produced reams of it.[1] But there is a catch. If a Brute and Blackguard made the world,
then he also made our minds. If he made our minds, he also made that very standard in them whereby we judge him to be a Brute and Blackguard. And how can
we trust a standard which comes from such a brutal and blackguardly source? If
we reject him, we ought also to reject all his works. But one of his works is this very
moral standard by which we reject him. If we accept this standard then we are really
implying that he is not a Brute and Blackguard. If we reject it, then we have thrown
away the only instrument by which we can condemn him. Heroic anti-theism thus
has a contradiction in its centre. You must trust the universe in one respect even in
order to condemn it in every other.

   What happens to our sense of values is, in fact, exactly what happens to our logic.
If it is a purely human sense of values—a biological by-product in a particular spe-

---

[1. No doubt Lewis is referring to many of the poems in his first book, *Spirits in Bondage: A Cycle of Lyrics* (Heinemann,
1919) which he published under the pseudonym, Clive Hamilton. One of the best examples in the collection is the
following lines from 'Ode for New Year's Day':

> . . . Nature will not pity, nor the red God lend an ear.
> Yet I too have been mad in the hour of bitter paining
> And lifted up my voice to God, thinking that he could hear
> The curse wherewith I cursed Him because the Good was dead.
> But lo ! I am grown wiser, knowing that our own hearts
> Have made a phantom called the Good, while a few years have sped
> Over a little planet . . .
>
> . . . . . .
>
> Ah, sweet, if a man could cheat him ! If you could flee away
> Into some other country beyond the rosy West,
> To hide in the deep forests and be for ever at rest
> From the rankling hate of God and the outworn world's decay !]

cies with no relevance to reality—then we cannot, having once realized this, continue to use it as the ground for what are meant to be serious criticisms of the nature of things. Nor can we continue to attach any importance to the efforts we make towards realizing our ideas of value. A man cannot continue to make sacrifices for the good of posterity if he really believes that his concern for the good of posterity is simply an irrational subjective taste of his own on the same level with his fondness for pancakes or his dislike for Spam. I am well aware that many whose philosophy involves this subjective view of values do in fact sometimes make great efforts for the cause of justice or freedom. But that is because they forget their philosophy. When they really get to work they think that justice is really good—objectively obligatory whether any one likes it or not: they remember their opposite philosophical belief only when they go back to the lecture room. Our sense that the universe is futile and our sense of a duty to make those parts of it we can reach less futile, both really imply a belief that it is not in fact futile at all: a belief that values are rooted in reality, outside ourselves, that the Reason in which the universe is saturated is also moral.

There remains, of course, the possibility that its values are widely different from ours. And in some sense this must be so. The particular interpretation of the universe which I accept certainly represents them as differing from ours in many acutely distressing ways. But there are strict limits to the extent which we can allow to this admission.

Let us go back to the question of Logic. I have tried to show that you reach a self-contradiction if you say that logical inference is, in principle, invalid. On the other hand, nothing is more obvious than that we frequently make false inferences: from ignorance of some of the factors involved, from inattention, from inefficiencies in the system of symbols (linguistic or otherwise) which we are using, from the secret influence of our unconscious wishes or fears. We are therefore driven to combine a steadfast faith in inference as such with a wholesome scepticism about each particular instance of inference in the mind of a human thinker. As I have said, there is no such thing (strictly speaking) as *human* reason: but there is emphatically such a thing as human thought—in other words, the various specifically human conceptions of Reason, failures of complete rationality, which arise in a wishful and lazy human mind utilizing a tired human brain. The difference between acknowledging this and being sceptical about Reason itself, is enormous. For in the one case we should be saying that reality contradicts Reason, whereas now we are only saying that total Reason—cosmic or super-cosmic Reason—*corrects* human imperfections of Reason. Now correction is not the same as mere contradiction. When your false reasoning is corrected you 'see the mistakes': the true reasoning thus takes up into itself whatever was already rational in your original thought. You are not moved into a totally new world; you are given *more* and *purer* of what you already had in a small quantity and badly mixed with foreign elements. To say that Reason is objective is to say that all our false reasonings could in principle be corrected by more Reason. I have to add 'in principle' because, of course, the reasoning necessary to give us absolute truth about the whole universe might be (indeed, certainly would be) too complicated for any human mind to hold it all together or even to keep on attending. But that, again, would be a defect in the human instrument, not in Reason. A sum in simple arithmetic may be too long and complicated for a child's limited powers of concentration: but it is not a radically different kind of thing from the short sums the child *can* do.

Now it seems to me that the relation between our sense of values and the values acknowledged by the cosmic or super-cosmic Reason is likely to be the same as the relation between our attempts at logic and Logic itself. It is, I admit, conceivable that the ultimate Reason acknowledges no values at all: but that theory, as I have tried to show, is inconsistent with our continuing to attach any importance to our own values. And since everyone in fact intends to continue doing so, that theory is not really a live option. But if we attribute a sense of value to the ultimate Reason, I do not think we can suppose it to be totally different from our own sense of value. If it were, then our own sense of value would have to be merely human: and from that all the same consequences would flow as from an admission that the supreme mind acknowledged no values at all. Indeed to say that a mind has a sense of values *totally* different from the only values we can conceive is to say that that mind has we know not what: which is precious near saying nothing particular about it. It would also be very odd, on the supposition that our sense of values is a mere illusion, that education, rationality, and enlightenment show no tendency to remove it from human minds. And at this stage in the argument there is really no inducement to do any of these rather desperate things. The *prima facie* case for denying a sense of values to the cosmic or super-cosmic mind has really collapsed the moment we see that we have to attribute reason to it. When we are forced to admit that reason cannot be merely human, there is no longer any compulsive inducement to say that virtue is purely human. If wisdom turns out to be something objective and external, it is at least probable that goodness will turn out to be the same. But here also it is reasonable to combine a firm belief in the objective validity of goodness with a considerable scepticism about all our particular moral judgements. To say that they all require correction is indeed to say both that they are partially wrong and that they are not merely subjective facts about ourselves—for if that were so the process of enlightenment would consist not in correcting them but in abandoning them altogether.

There is, to be sure, one glaringly obvious ground for denying that any moral purpose at all is operative in the universe: namely, the actual course of events in all its wasteful cruelty and apparent indifference, or hostility, to life. But then, as I maintain, that is precisely the ground which we cannot use. Unless we judge this waste and cruelty to be real evils we cannot of course condemn the universe for exhibiting them. Unless we take our own standard of goodness to be valid in principle (however fallible our particular applications of it) we cannot mean anything by calling waste and cruelty evils. And unless we take our own standard to be something more than ours, to be in fact an objective principle to which we are responding, we cannot regard that standard as valid. In a word, unless we allow ultimate reality to be moral, we cannot morally condemn it. The more seriously we take our own charge of futility the more we are committed to the implication that reality in the last resort is not futile at all. The defiance of the good atheist hurled at an apparently ruthless and idiotic cosmos is really an unconscious homage to something in or behind that cosmos which he recognizes as infinitely valuable and authoritative: for if mercy and justice were really only private whims of his own with no objective and impersonal roots, and if he realized this, he could not go on being indignant. The fact that he arraigns heaven itself for disregarding them means that at some level of his mind he knows they are enthroned in a higher heaven still.

I cannot and never could persuade myself that such defiance is displeasing to the supreme mind. There is something holier about the atheism of a Shelley than about the theism of a Paley. That is the lesson of the Book of Job. No explanation of the problem of unjust suffering is there given: that is not the point of the poem. The point is that the man who accepts our ordinary standard of good and by it hotly criticizes divine justice receives the divine approval: the orthodox, pious people who palter with that standard in the attempt to justify God are condemned. Apparently the way to advance from our imperfect apprehension of justice to the absolute justice is *not* to throw our imperfect apprehensions aside but boldly to go on applying them. Just as the pupil advances to more perfect arithmetic not by throwing his multiplication table away but by working it for all it is worth.

Of course no one will be content to leave the matter just where the Book of Job leaves it. But that is as far as I intend to go to-night. Having grasped the truth that our very condemnation of reality carries in its heart an unconscious act of allegiance to that same reality as the source of our moral standards, we then of course have to ask how this ultimate morality in the universe can be reconciled with the actual course of events. It is really the same sort of problem that meets us in science. The pell-mell of phenomena, as we first observe them, seems to be full of anomalies and irregularities; but being assured that reality is logical we go on framing and trying out hypotheses to show that the apparent irregularities are not really irregular at all. The history of science is the history of that process. The corresponding process whereby, having admitted that reality in the last resort must be moral, we attempt to explain evil, is the history of theology. Into that theological inquiry I do not propose to go at present. If any of you thinks of pursuing it, I would risk giving him one piece of advice. I think he can save himself time by confining his attention to two systems—Hinduism and Christianity. I believe these are the two serious options for an adult mind. Materialism is a philosophy for boys. The purely moral systems like Stoicism and Confucianism are philosophies for aristocrats. Islam is only a Christian heresy, and Buddhism a Hindu heresy: both are simplification inferior to the things simplified. As for the old Pagan religions, I think we could say that whatever was of value in them survives either in Hinduism or in Christianity or in both, and there only: they are the two systems which have come down, still alive, into the present without leaving the past behind them.

But all that is a matter for further consideration. I aim tonight only at reversing the popular belief that reality is totally alien to our minds. My answer to that view consists simply in restating it in the form: 'Our minds are totally alien to reality.' Put that way, it reveals itself as a self-contradiction. For if our minds are totally alien to reality then all our thoughts, including this thought, are worthless. We must, then, grant logic to the reality; we must, if we are to have any moral standards, grant it moral standards too. And there is really no reason why we should not do the same about standards of beauty. There is no reason why our reaction to a beautiful landscape should not be the response, however humanly blurred and partial, to a something that is really there. The idea of a wholly mindless and valueless universe has to be abandoned at one point—i.e., as regards logic: after that, there is no telling at how many other points it will be defeated nor how great the reversal of our nineteenth-century philosophy must finally be.

The Poison of Subjectivism

ONE CAUSE OF MISERY and vice is always present with us in the greed and pride of men, but at certain periods in history this is greatly increased by the temporary prevalence of some false philosophy. Correct thinking will not make good men of bad ones; but a purely theoretical error may remove ordinary checks to evil and deprive good intentions of their natural support. An error of this sort is abroad at present. I am not referring to the Power philosophies of the Totalitarian states, but to something that goes deeper and spreads wider and which, indeed, has given these Power philosophies their golden opportunity. I am referring to Subjectivism.

After studying his environment man has begun to study himself. Up to that point, he had assumed his own reason and through it seen all other things. Now, his own reason has become the object: it is as if we took out our eyes to look at them. Thus studied, his own reason appears to him as the epiphenomenon which accompanies chemical or electrical events in a cortex which is itself the by-product of a blind evolutionary process. His own logic, hitherto the king whom events in all possible worlds must obey, becomes merely subjective. There is no reason for supposing that it yields truth.

As long as this dethronement refers only to the theoretical reason, it cannot be wholehearted. The scientist has to assume the validity of his own logic (in the stout old fashion of Plato or Spinoza) even in order to prove that it is merely subjective, and therefore he can only flirt with subjectivism. It is true that this flirtation sometimes goes pretty far. There are modern scientists, I am told, who have dropped the words *truth* and *reality* out of their vocabulary and who hold that the end of their work is not to know what is there but simply to get practical results. This is, no doubt, a bad symptom. But, in the main, subjectivism is such an uncomfortable yokefellow for research that the danger, in this quarter, is continually counteracted.

But when we turn to practical reason the ruinous effects are found operating in full force. By practical reason I mean our judgement of good and evil. If you are surprised that I include this under the heading of reason at all, let me remind you that your surprise is itself one result of the subjectivism I am discussing. Until modern times no thinker of the first rank ever doubted that our judgements of value were rational judgements or that what they discovered was objective. It was taken for granted that in temptation passion was opposed, not to some sentiment, but to reason. Thus Plato thought, thus Aristotle, thus Hooker, Butler and Doctor Johnson. The modern view is very different. It does not believe that value judgements are really judgements at all. They are sentiments, or complexes, or attitudes, produced in a community by the pressure of its environment and its traditions, and differing from one community to another. To say that a thing is good is merely to express our feeling about it; and our feeling about it is the feeling we have been socially conditioned to have.

But if this is so, then we might have been conditioned to feel otherwise. 'Perhaps', thinks the reformer or the educational expert, 'it would be better if we were. Let us improve our morality.' Out of this apparently innocent idea comes the disease that will certainly end our species (and, in my view, damn our souls) if it is not crushed; the fatal superstition that men can create values, that a community can choose its 'ideology' as men choose their clothes. Everyone is indignant when he hears the Germans define justice as that which is to the interest of the Third Reich. But it is not always remembered that this indignation is perfectly groundless if we ourselves regard morality as a subjective sentiment to be altered at will. Unless there is some objective standard of good, over-arching Germans, Japanese and ourselves alike whether any of us obey it or no, then of course the Germans are as competent to create their ideology as we are to create ours. If 'good' and 'better' are terms deriving their sole meaning from the ideology of each people, then of course ideologies themselves cannot be better or worse than one another. Unless the measuring rod is independent of the things measured, we can do no measuring. For the same reason it is useless to compare the moral ideas of one age with those of another: progress and decadence are alike meaningless words.

All this is so obvious that it amounts to an identical proposition. But how little it is now understood can be gauged from the procedure of the moral reformer who, after saying that 'good' means 'what we are conditioned to like' goes on cheerfully to consider whether it might be 'better' that we should be conditioned to like something else. What in Heaven's names does he mean by 'better'?

He usually has at the back of his mind the notion that if he throws over traditional judgement of value, he will find something else, something more 'real' or 'solid' on which to base a new scheme of values. He will say, for example, 'We must abandon irrational taboos and base our values on the good of the community'—as if the maxim 'Thou shalt promote the good of the community' were anything more than a polysyllabic variant of 'Do as you would be done by' which has itself no other basis than the old universal value judgement he claims to be rejecting. Or he will endeavour to base his values on biology and tell us that we must act thus and thus for the preservation of our species. Apparently he does not anticipate the question, 'Why should the species be preserved?' He takes it for granted that it should, because he is really relying on traditional judgements of value. If he were starting, as he pretends, with a clean slate, he could never reach this principle. Sometimes he tries to do so by falling back on 'instinct'. 'We have an instinct to preserve our species', he may say. But have we? And if we have, who told us that we must obey our instincts? And why should we obey this instinct in the teeth of many others which conflict with the preservation of the species? The reformer knows that some instincts are to be obeyed more than others only because he is judging instincts by a standard, and the standard is, once more, the traditional morality which he claims to be superseding. The instincts themselves obviously cannot furnish us with grounds for grading the instincts in a hierarchy. If you do not bring a knowledge of their comparative respectability *to* your study of them, you can never derive it *from* them.

This whole attempt to jettison traditional values as something subjective and to substitute a new scheme of values for them is wrong. It is like trying to lift yourself by your own coat collar. Let us get two propositions written into our minds with indelible ink.

(1) The human mind has no more power of inventing a new value than of planting a new sun in the sky or a new primary colour in the spectrum.

(2) Every attempt to do so consists in arbitrarily selecting some one maxim of traditional morality, isolating it from the rest, and erecting it into an *unum necessarium*.

The second proposition will bear a little illustration. Ordinary morality tells us to honour our parents and cherish our children. By taking the second precept alone you construct a Futurist Ethic in which the claims of 'posterity' are the sole criterion. Ordinary morality tells us to keep promises and also to feed the hungry. By taking the second precept alone you get a Communist Ethic in which 'production', and distribution of the products to the people, are the sole criteria. Ordinary morality tells us, *ceteris paribus*, to love our kindred and fellow-citizens more than strangers. By isolating this precept you can get either an Aristocratic Ethic with the claims of our class as sole criterion, or a Racialist Ethic where no claims but those of blood are acknowledged. These monomaniac systems are then used as a ground from which to attack traditional morality; but absurdly, since it is from traditional morality alone that they derive such semblance of validity as they possess. Starting from scratch, with no assumptions about value, we could reach none of them. If reverence for parents or promises is a mere subjective by-product of physical nature, so is reverence for race or posterity. The trunk to whose root the reformer would lay the axe is the only support of the particular branch he wishes to retain.

All idea of 'new' or 'scientific' or 'modern' moralities must therefore be dismissed as mere confusion of thought. We have only two alternatives. Either the maxims of traditional morality must be accepted as axioms of practical reason which neither admit nor require argument to support them and not to 'see' which is to have lost human status; or else there are no values at all, what we mistook for values being 'projections' of irrational emotions. It is perfectly futile, after having dismissed traditional morality with the question, 'Why should we obey it?' then to attempt the reintroduction of value at some later stage in our philosophy. Any value we reintroduce can be countered in just the same way. Every argument used to support it will be an attempt to derive from premises in the indicative mood a conclusion in the imperative. And this is impossible.

Against this view the modern mind has two lines of defence. The first claims that traditional morality is different in different times and places—in fact, that there is not one morality but a thousand. The second exclaims that to tie ourselves to an immutable moral code is to cut off all progress and acquiesce in 'stagnation'. Both are unsound.

Let us take the second one first. And let us strip it of the illegitimate emotional power it derives from the word 'stagnation' with its suggestion of puddles and mantled pools. If water stands too long it stinks. To infer thence that whatever stands long must be unwholesome is to be the victim of metaphor. Space does not stink because it has preserved its three dimensions from the beginning. The square on the hypotenuse has not gone mouldy by continuing to equal the sum of the squares on the other two sides. Love is not dishonoured by constancy, and when we wash our hands we are seeking stagnation and 'putting the clock back', artificially restoring our hands to the *status quo* in which they began the day and resisting the natural trend of events which would increase their dirtiness steadily from our birth to our death. For the emotive term 'stagnant' let us substitute the descriptive term 'permanent'. Does a permanent moral standard preclude progress? On the contrary, except on the supposition of a changeless standard, progress is impossible. If good is a fixed point, it is at least possible that we should get nearer and nearer to it; but if the terminus is as mobile as the train, how can the train progress towards it? Our ideas of the good may change, but they cannot change either for the better or the worse if there is no absolute and immutable good to which they can approximate or from which they can recede. We can go on getting a sum more and more nearly right only if the one perfectly right answer is 'stagnant'.

And yet it will be said, I have just admitted that our ideas of good may improve. How is this to be reconciled with the view that 'traditional morality' is a *depositum fidei* which cannot be deserted? The answer can be understood if we compare a real moral advance with a mere innovation. From the Stoic and Confucian, 'Do not do to others what you would not like them to do to you'; to the Christian, 'Do as you would be done by' is a real advance. The morality of Nietzsche is a mere innovation. The first is an advance because no one who did not admit the validity of the old maxim could see reason for accepting the new one, and anyone who accepted the old would at once recognize the new as an extension of the same principle. If he rejected it, he would have to reject it as a superfluity, something that went too far, not as something simply heterogeneous from his own ideas of value. But the Nietzschean ethic can be accepted only if we are ready to scrap traditional morals as a mere error and then to put ourselves in a position where we can find no ground for any value judgements at all. It is the difference between a man who says to us: 'You like your vegetables moderately fresh; why not grow your own and have them perfectly fresh?' and a man who says, 'Throw away that loaf and try eating bricks and centipedes instead.' Real moral advances, in fine, are made *from within* the existing moral tradition and in the spirit of that tradition and can be understood only in the light of that tradition. The outsider who has rejected the tradition cannot judge them. He has, as Aristotle said, no *arche*, no premises.

And what of the second modern objection—that the ethical standards of different cultures differ so widely that there is no common tradition at all? The answer is that this is a lie—a good, solid, resounding lie. If a man will go into a library and spend a few days with the *Encyclopedia of Religion and Ethics* he will soon discover the massive unanimity of the practical reason in man. From the Babylonian *Hymn to Samos*, from the Laws of Manu, the *Book of the Dead*, the Analects, the Stoics, the

Platonists, from Australian aborigines and Redskins, he will collect the same triumphantly monotonous denunciations of oppression, murder, treachery and falsehood, the same injunctions of kindness to the aged, the young, and the weak, of almsgiving and impartiality and honesty. He may be a little surprised (I certainly was) to find that precepts of mercy are more frequent than precepts of justice; but he will no longer doubt that there is such a thing as the Law of Nature. There are, of course, differences. There are even blindnesses in particular cultures—just as there are savages who cannot count up to twenty. But the pretence that we are presented with a mere chaos—though no outline of universally accepted value shows through—is simply false and should be contradicted in season and out of season wherever it is met. Far from finding a chaos, we find exactly what we should expect if good is indeed something objective and reason the organ whereby it is apprehended—that is, a substantial agreement with considerable local differences of emphasis and, perhaps, no one code that includes everything.

The two grand methods of obscuring this agreement are these: First, you can concentrate on those divergences about sexual morality which most serious moralists regard as belonging to positive rather than to Natural Law, but which rouse strong emotions. Differences about the definition of incest or between polygamy and monogamy come under this head. (It is untrue to say that the Greeks thought sexual perversion innocent. The continual tittering of Plato is really more evidential than the stern prohibition of Aristotle. Men titter thus only about what they regard as, at least, a *peccadillo*: the jokes about drunkenness in *Pickwick,* far from proving that the nineteenth-century English thought it innocent, prove the reverse. There is an enormous difference of *degree* between the Greek view of perversion and the Christian, but there is not opposition.) The second method is to treat as differences in the judgement of value what are really differences in belief about fact. Thus human sacrifice, or persecution of witches, are cited as evidence of a radically different morality. But the real difference lies elsewhere. We do not hunt witches because we disbelieve in their existence. We do not kill men to avert pestilence because we do not think pestilence can thus be averted. We do 'sacrifice' men in war, and we do hunt spies and traitors.

So far I have been considering the objections which unbelievers bring against the doctrine of objective value, or the Law of Nature. But in our days we must be prepared to meet objections from Christians too. 'Humanism' and 'liberalism' are coming to be used simply as terms of disapprobation, and both are likely to be so used of the position I am taking up. Behind them lurks a real theological problem. If we accept the primary platitudes of practical reason as the unquestioned premises of all action, are we thereby trusting our own reason so far that we ignore the Fall, and are we retrogressively turning our absolute allegiance away from a person to an abstraction?

As regards the Fall, I submit that the general tenor of scripture does not encourage us to believe that our knowledge of the Law has been depraved in the same degree as our power to fulfil it. He would be a brave man who claimed to realize the fallen condition of man more clearly than St Paul. In that very chapter (Romans 7) where he asserts most strongly our inability to keep the moral law he also asserts most confidently that we perceive the Law's goodness and rejoice in it according to the inward man. Our righteousness may be filthy and ragged; but Christianity gives us no ground for holding that our perceptions of right are in the same condition. They may, no doubt, be impaired; but there is a difference between imperfect sight and blindness. A theology which goes about to represent our practical reason as radically unsound is heading for disaster. If we once admit that what God means by 'goodness' is sheerly different from what we judge to be good, there is no difference left between pure religion and devil worship.

The other objection is much more formidable. If we once grant that our practical reason is really reason and that its fundamental imperatives are as absolute and categorical as they claim to be, then unconditional allegiance to them is the duty of man. So is absolute allegiance to God. And these two allegiances must, somehow, be the same. But how is the relation between God and the moral law to be represented? To say that the moral law is God's law is no final solution. Are these things right because God commands them or does God command them because they are right? If the first, if good is to be *defined* as what God commands, then the goodness of God Himself is emptied of meaning and the commands of an omnipotent fiend would have the same claim on us as those of the 'righteous Lord'. If the second, then we seem to be admitting a cosmic dyarchy, or even making God Himself the mere executor of a law somehow external and antecedent to His own being. Both views are intolerable.

At this point we must remind ourselves that Christian theology does not believe God to be a person. It believes Him to be such that in Him a trinity of persons is consistent with a unity of Deity. In that sense it believes Him to be something very different from a person, just as a cube, in which six squares are consistent with unity of the body, is different from a square. (Flatlanders, attempting to imagine a cube, would either imagine the six squares coinciding, and thus destroy their distinctness, or else imagine them set out side by side, and thus destroy the unity. Our difficulties about the Trinity are of much the same kind.) It is therefore possible that the duality which seems to force itself upon us when we think, first, of our Father in Heaven, and, secondly, of the self-evident imperatives of the moral law, is not a mere error but a real (though inadequate and creaturely) perception of things that would necessarily be two in any mode of being which enters our experience, but which are not so divided in the absolute being of the superpersonal God. When we attempt to think of a person and a law, we are compelled to think of this person either as obeying the law or as making it. And when we think of Him as making it we are compelled to think of Him either as making it in conformity to some yet more ultimate pattern of goodness (in which case that pattern, and not He, would be supreme) or else as making it arbitrarily by a *sic volo, sic jubeo* (in which case He would be neither good nor wise). But it is probably just here that our categories betray us. It would be idle, with our merely mortal resources, to attempt a positive correction of our categories—*ambulavi in mirabilibus supra me.* But it might be permissible to lay down two negations: that God neither *obeys* nor *creates* the moral law. The good is uncreated; it never could have been otherwise; it has in it no shadow of contingency; it lies, as Plato said, on the other side of existence. It is the

Rita of the Hindus by which the gods themselves are divine, the *Tao* of the Chinese from which all realities proceed. But we, favoured beyond the wisest pagans, know what lies beyond existence, what admits no contingency, what lends divinity to all else, what is the ground of all existence, is not simply a law but also a begetting love, a love begotten, and the love which, being between these two, is also immi-nent in all those who are caught up to share the unity of their self-caused life. God is not merely good, but goodness; goodness is not merely divine, but God.

These may seem fine-spun speculations: yet I believe that nothing short of this can save us. A Christianity which does not see moral and religious experience con-verging to meet at infinity, not at a negative infinity, but in the positive infinity of the living yet superpersonal God, has nothing, in the long run, to divide it from devil worship; and a philosophy which does not accept value as eternal and objec-tive can lead us only to ruin. Nor is the matter of merely speculative importance. Many a popular 'planner' on a democratic platform, many a mild-eyed scientist in a democratic laboratory means, in the last resort, just what the Fascist means. He believes that 'good' means whatever men are conditioned to approve. He believes that it is the function of him and his kind to condition men; to create consciences by eugenics, psychological manipulation of infants, state education and mass pro-paganda. Because he is confused, he does not yet fully realize that those who cre-ate conscience cannot be subject to conscience themselves. But he must awake to the logic of his position sooner or later; and when he does, what barrier remains between us and the final division of the race into a few conditioners who stand themselves outside morality and the many conditioned in whom such morality as the experts choose is produced at the experts' pleasure? If 'good' means only the local ideology, how can those who invent the local ideology be guided by any idea of good themselves? The very idea of freedom presupposes some objective moral law which overarches rulers and ruled alike. Subjectivism about values is eternally incompatible with democracy. We and our rulers are of one kind only so long as we are subject to one law. But if there is no Law of Nature, the *ethos* of any society is the creation of its rulers, educators and conditioners; and every creator stands above and outside his own creation.

Unless we return to the crude and nursery-like belief in objective values, we perish. If we do, we may live, and such a return might have one minor advantage. If we believed in the absolute reality of elementary moral platitudes, we should value those who solicit our votes by other standards than have recently been in fashion. While we believe that good is something to be invented, we demand of our rulers such qualities as 'vision', 'dynamism', 'creativity', and the like. If we returned to the objective view we should demand qualities much rarer, and much more beneficial—virtue, knowledge, diligence and skill. 'Vision' is for sale, or claims to be for sale, everywhere. But give me a man who will do a day's work for a day's pay, who will refuse bribes, who will not make up his facts, and who has learned his job.

The Funeral
of a Great Myth

THERE ARE SOME mistakes which humanity has made and repented so often that there is now really no excuse for making them again. One of these is the injustice which every age does to its predecessor; for example, the ignorant contempt which the Humanists (even good Humanists like Sir Thomas More) felt for medieval philosophy or Romantics (even good Romantics like Keats) felt for eighteenth-century poetry. Each time all this 'reaction' and resentment has to be punished and unsaid; it is a wasteful performance. It is tempting to try whether we, at least, cannot avoid it. Why should we not give our predecessors a fair and filial dismissal?

Such, at all events, is the attempt I am going to make in this paper. I come to bury the great Myth of the nineteenth and early twentieth Century; but also to praise it. I am going to pronounce a funeral oration.

By this great Myth I mean that picture of reality which resulted during the period under consideration, not logically but imaginatively, from some of the more striking and (so to speak) marketable theories of the real scientists. I have heard this Myth called 'Wellsianity'. The name is a good one in so far as it does justice to the share which a great imaginative writer bore in building it up. But it is not satisfactory. It suggests, as we shall see, an error about the date at which the Myth became dominant; and it also suggests that the Myth affected only the 'middle-brow' mind. In fact it is as much behind Bridges' *Testament of Beauty* as it is behind the work of Wells. It dominates minds as different as those of Professor Alexander and Walt Disney. It is implicit in nearly every modern article on politics, sociology, and ethics.

I call it a Myth because it is, as I have said, the imaginative and not the logical result of what is vaguely called 'modern science'. Strictly speaking, there is, I confess, no such thing as 'modern science'. There are only particular sciences, all in a stage of rapid change, and sometimes inconsistent with one another. What the Myth uses is a selection from the scientific theories—a selection made at first, and modified afterwards, in obedience to imaginative and emotional needs. It is the work of the folk imagination, moved by its natural appetite for an impressive unity. It therefore treats its *data* with great freedom—selecting, slurring, expurgating, and adding at will.

The central idea of the Myth is what its believers would call 'Evolution' or 'Development' or 'Emergence', just as the central idea in the myth of Adonis is Death and Re-birth. I do not mean that the doctrine of Evolution as held by practising biologists is a Myth. It may be shown, by later biologists, to be a less satisfactory hypothesis than was hoped fifty years ago. But that does not amount to being a Myth. It is a genuine scientific hypothesis. But we must sharply distinguish between Evolution as a biological theorem and popular Evolutionism or Developmentalism which is certainly a Myth. Before proceeding to describe it and (which is my chief business) to pronounce its eulogy, I had better make clear its mythical character.

We have, first of all, the evidence of chronology. If popular Evolutionism were (as it imagines itself to be) not a Myth but the intellectually legitimate result of the scientific theorem on the public mind, it would arise *after* that theorem had become widely known. We should have the theorem known first of all to a few, then adopted by all the scientists, then spreading to all men of general education, then beginning to affect poetry and the arts, and so finally percolating to the mass of the people. In fact, however, we find something quite different. The clearest and finest poetical expressions of the Myth come before the *Origin of Species* was published (1859) and long before it had established itself as scientific orthodoxy. There had, to be sure, been hints and germs of the theory in scientific circles before 1859. But if the mythopoeic poets were at all infected by those germs they must have been very up-to-date indeed, very predisposed to catch the infection. Almost before the scientists spoke, certainly before they spoke clearly, imagination was ripe for it.

The finest expression of the Myth in English does not come from Bridges, nor from Shaw, nor from Wells, nor from Olaf Stapledon. It is this:

> As Heaven and Earth are fairer, fairer far
> Than Chaos and blank Darkness, though once chief;
> And as we show beyond that Heaven and Earth
> In form and shape compact and beautiful,
> In will, in action free, companionship,
> And thousand other signs of purer life;
> So on our heels a fresh perfection treads,
> A power more strong in beauty, born of us,
> And fated to excel us, as we pass
> In glory that old Darkness.

Thus Oceanus, in Keats's *Hyperion*, nearly forty years before the *Origin of Species*. And on the continent we have the *Nibelung's Ring*. Coming, as I do, to bury but also to praise the receding age, I will by no means join in the modern depreciation of Wagner. He may, for all I know, have been a bad man. He may (though I shall never believe it) have been a bad musician. But as a mythopoeic poet he is incomparable. The tragedy of the Evolutionary Myth has never been more nobly expressed than in his Wotan: its heady raptures never more irresistibly than in *Siegfried*. That he himself knew quite well what he was writing about can be seen from his letter to August Rockel in 1854. 'The progress of the whole drama shows the necessity of recognizing and submittmg to the change, the diversity, the multiplicity, the eternal novelty, of the Real. Wotan rises to the tragic height of willing his own downfall. This is all we have to learn from the history of Man—to will the necessary and ourselves to bring it to pass.'

If Shaw's *Back to Methuselah* were really, as he supposed, the work of a prophet or a pioneer ushering in the reign of a new Myth, its predominantly comic tone and its generally low emotional temperature would be inexplicable. It is admirable fun: but not thus are new epochs brought to birth. The ease with which he plays with the Myth shows that the Myth is fully digested and already senile. Shaw is the Lucian or the Snorri of this mythology: to find its Aeschylus or its Elder Edda you must go back to Keats and Wagner.

That, then, is the first proof that popular Evolution is a Myth. In making it Imagination runs ahead of scientific evidence. 'The prophetic soul of the big world' was already pregnant with the Myth: if science has not met the imaginative need, science would not have been so popular. But probably every age gets, within certain limits, the science it desires.

In the second place we have internal evidence. Popular Evolutionism or Developmentalism differs *in content* from the Evolution of the real biologists. To the biologist Evolution is a hypothesis. It covers more of the facts than any other hypothesis at present on the market and is therefore to be accepted unless, or until, some new supposal can be shown to cover still more facts with even fewer assumptions. At least, that is what I think most biologists would say. Professor D. M. S. Watson, it is true, would not go so far. According to him Evolution 'is accepted by zoologists not because it has been observed to occur or . . . can be proved by logically coherent evidence to be true, but because the only alternative, special creation, is clearly incredible'. (Watson, quoted in *Nineteenth Century* (April 1943), 'Science and the B.B.C.') This would mean that the sole ground for believing it is not empirical but metaphysical—the dogma of an amateur metaphysician who finds 'special creation' incredible. But I do not think it has really come to that. Most biologists have a more robust belief in Evolution than Professor Watson. But it is certainly a hypothesis. In the Myth, however, there is nothing hypothetical about it: it is basic fact: or, to speak more strictly, such distinctions do not exist on the mythical level at all. There are more important differences to follow.

In the science, Evolution is a theory about *changes*: in the Myth it is a fact about *improvements*. Thus a real scientist like Professor J. B. S. Haldane is at pains to point out that popular ideas of Evolution lay a wholly unjustified emphasis on those changes which have rendered creatures (by human standards) 'better' or more interesting. He adds: 'We are therefore inclined to regard progress as the rule in evolution. Actually it is the exception, and for every case of it there are ten of degeneration.'[1] But the Myth simply expurgates the ten cases of degeneration. In the popular mind the word 'Evolution' conjures up a picture of things moving 'onwards and upwards', and of nothing else whatsoever. And it might have been predicted that it would do so. Already, before science had spoken, the mythical imagination knew the kind of 'Evolution' it wanted. It wanted the Keatsian and

1. 'Darwinism Today', *Possible Worlds*, p. 28.

Wagnerian kind: the gods superseding the Titans, and the young, joyous, careless, amorous Siegfried superseding the care-worn, anxious, treaty-entangled Wotan. If science offers any instances to satisfy that demand, they will be eagerly accepted. If it offers any instances that frustrate it, they will simply be ignored.

Again, for the scientist Evolution is a purely biological theorem. It takes over organic life on this planet as a going concern and tries to explain certain changes within that field. It makes no cosmic statements, no metaphysical statements, no eschatological statements. Granted that we now have minds we can trust, granted that organic life came to exist, it tries to explain, say, how a species that once had wings came to lose them. It explains this by the negative effect of environment operating on small variations. It does not in itself explain the origin of organic life, nor of the variations, nor does it discuss the origin and validity of reason. It may well tell you how the brain, through which reason now operates, arose, but that is a different matter. Still less does it even attempt to tell you how the universe as a whole arose, or what it is, or whither it is tending. But the Myth knows none of these reticences. Having first turned what was a theory of change into a theory of improvement, it then makes this a *cosmic* theory. Not merely terrestrial organisms but *everything* is moving 'upwards and onwards'. Reason has 'evolved' out of instinct, virtue out of complexes, poetry out of erotic howls and grunts, civilization out of savagery, the organic out of inorganic, the solar system out of some sidereal soup or traffic block. And conversely, reason, virtue, art and civilization as we now know them are only the crude or embryonic beginnings of far better things—perhaps Deity itself—in the remote future. For in the Myth, 'Evolution' (as the Myth understands it) is the formula of *all* existence. To exist means to be moving from the status of 'almost zero' to the status of 'almost infinity'. To those brought up on the Myth nothing seems more normal, more natural, more plausible, than that chaos should turn into order, death into life, ignorance into knowledge. And with this we reach the full-blown Myth. It is one of the most moving and satisfying world dramas which have ever been imagined.

The drama proper is preceded (do not forget the Rheingold here) by the most austere of all preludes; the infinite void and matter endlessly, aimlessly moving to bring forth it knows not what. Then by some millionth, millionth chance—what tragic irony!—the conditions at one point of space and time bubble up into that tiny fermentation which we call organic life. At first everything seems to be against the infant hero of our drama; just as everything always was against the seventh son or ill-used step-daughter in a fairy tale. But life somehow wins through. With incalculable sufferings (the Sorrows of the Volsungs were nothing to it), against all but insuperable obstacles, it spreads, it breeds, it complicates itself; from the amoeba up to the reptile, up to the mammal. Life (here comes our first climax) 'wantons as in her prime'. This is the age of monsters: dragons prowl the earth, devour one another, and die. Then the old irresistible theme of the Younger Son or the Ugly Duckling is repeated. As the weak, tiny spark of life herself began amidst the beasts that are far larger and stronger than he, there comes forth a little, naked, shivering, cowering biped, shuffling, not yet fully erect, promising nothing: the product of another millionth,

millionth chance. His name in this Myth is Man: elsewhere he has been the young Beowulf whom men at first thought a dastard, or the stripling David armed only with a sling against mail-clad Goliath, or Jack the Giant-Killer himself, or even Hop-o'-my-Thumb. He thrives. He begins killing his giants. He becomes the Cave Man with his flints and his club, muttering and growling over his enemies' bones, almost a brute yet somehow able to invent art, pottery, language, weapons, cookery and nearly everything else (his name in another story is Robinson Crusoe), dragging his screaming mate by her hair (I do not exactly know why), tearing his children to pieces in fierce jealousy until they are old enough to tear him, and cowering before the terrible gods whom he has invented in his own image.

But these were only growing pains. In the next act he has become true Man. He learns to master Nature. Science arises and dissipates the superstitions of his infancy. More and more he becomes the controller of his own fate. Passing hastily over the historical period (in it the upward and onward movement gets in places a little indistinct, but it is a mere nothing by the time-scale we are using) we follow our hero on into the future. See him in the last act, though not the last scene, of this great mystery. A race of demi-gods now rule the planet (in some versions, the galaxy). Eugenics have made certain that only demi-gods will now be born: psychoanalysis that none of them shall lose or smirch his divinity: economics that they shall have to hand all that demi-gods require. Man has ascended his throne. Man has become God. All is a blaze of glory. And now, mark well the final stroke of mythopoeic genius. It is only the more debased versions of the Myth that end here. For to end here is a little bathetic, even a little vulgar. If we stopped at this point the story would lack the highest grandeur. Therefore, in the best versions, the last scene reverses all. Arthur died: Siegfried died: Roland died at Roncesvaux. Dusk steals darkly over the gods. All this time we have forgotten Mordred, Hagen, Ganilon. All this time Nature, the old enemy who only seemed to be defeated, has been gnawing away, silently, unceasingly, out of the reach of human power. The Sun will cool—all suns will cool—the whole universe will run down. Life (every form of life) will be banished without hope of return from every cubic inch of infinite space. All ends in nothingness. 'Universal darkness covers all.' True to the shape of Elizabethan tragedy, the hero has swiftly fallen from the glory to which he slowly climbed: we are dismissed 'in calm of mind, all passion spent'. It is indeed much better than an Elizabethan tragedy, for it has a more complete finality. It brings us to the end not of a story, but of all possible stories: *enden sah ich die welt.*

I grew up believing in this Myth and T have felt—I still feel—its almost perfect grandeur. Let no one say we are an unimaginative age: neither the Greeks nor the Norsemen ever invented a better story. Even to the present day, in certain moods, I could almost find it in my heart to wish that it was not mythical, but true.[1] And yet, how could it be?

[1. In a paper read to the Oxford Socratic Club on 'Is Theology Poetry?', Lewis admits that if Christian Theology were only a myth he would not find even it as attractive as the Myth considered in this paper: 'Christianity offers the attraction neither of optimism nor of pessimism. It represents the life of the universe as being very like the mortal life of men on this planet—"of a mingled yarn, good and ill together."' *The Socratic Digest* (1945).]

What makes it impossible that it should be true is not so much the lack of evidence for this or that scene in the drama or the fatal self-contradiction which runs right through it. The Myth cannot even get going without accepting a good deal from the real sciences. And the real sciences cannot be accepted for a moment unless rational inferences are valid: for every science claims to be a series of inferences from observed facts. It is only by such inferences that you can reach your nebulae and protoplasm and dinosaurs and sub-men and cave-men at all. Unless you start by believing that reality in the remotest space and the remotest time rigidly obeys the laws of logic, you can have no ground for believing in any astronomy, any biology, any paleontology, any archaeology. To reach the positions held by the real scientists—which are then taken over by the Myth—you must—in fact, treat reason as an absolute. But at the same time the Myth asks me to believe that reason is simply the unforeseen and unintended by-product of a mindless process at one stage of its endless and aimless becoming. The content of the Myth thus knocks from under me the only ground on which I could possibly believe the Myth to be true. If my own mind is a product of the irrational—if what seem my clearest reasonings are only the way in which a creature conditioned as I am is bound to feel—how shall I trust my mind when it tells me about Evolution? They say in effect 'I will prove that what you call a proof is only the result of mental habits which result from heredity which results from bio-chemistry which results from physics.' But this is the same as saying: 'I will prove that proofs are irrational': more succinctly, 'I will prove that there are no proofs': The fact that some people of scientific education cannot by any effort be taught to see the difficulty, confirms one's suspicion that we here touch a radical disease in their whole style of thought. But the man who does see it, is compelled to reject as mythical the cosmology in which most of us were brought up. That it has embedded in it many true particulars I do not doubt: but in its entirety, it simply will not do. Whatever the real universe may turn out to be like, it can't be like that.

I have been speaking hitherto of this Myth as of a thing to be buried because I believe that its dominance is already over; in the sense that what seem to me to be the most vigorous movements of contemporary thought point away from it. Physics (a discipline less easily mythological) is replacing biology as the science *par excellence* in the mind of the plain man. The whole philosophy of Becoming has been vigorously challenged by the American 'Humanists'. The revival of theology has attained proportions that have to be reckoned with. The Romantic poetry and music in which popular Evolutionism found their natural counterpart are going out of fashion. But of course a Myth does not die in a day. We may expect that this Myth, when driven from cultured circles, will long retain its hold on the masses, and even when abandoned by them will continue for centuries to haunt our language. Those who wish to attack it must beware of despising it. There are deep reasons for its popularity.

The basic idea of the Myth—that small or chaotic or feeble things perpetually turn themselves into large, strong, ordered things—may, at first sight, seem a very odd one. We have never actually seen a pile of rubble turning itself into a house.

But this odd idea commends itself to the imagination by the help of what seem to be two instances of it within everyone's knowledge. Everyone has seen individual organisms doing it. Acorns become oaks, grubs become insects, eggs become birds, every man was once an embryo. And secondly—which weighs very much in the popular mind during a machine age—everyone has seen Evolution really happening in the history of machines. We all remember when locomotives were smaller and less efficient than they are now. These two apparent instances are quite enough to convince the imagination that Evolution in a cosmic sense is the most natural thing in the world. It is true that reason cannot here agree with imagination. These apparent instances are not really instances of Evolution at all. The oak comes indeed from the acorn, but then the acorn was dropped by an earlier oak. Every man began with the union of an ovum and a spermatozoon, but the ovum and the spermatozoon came from two fully developed human beings. The modern express engine came from the *Rocket*: but the *Rocket* came, not from something under and more elementary than itself but from something much more developed and highly organized—the mind of a man, and a man of genius. Modern art may have 'developed' from savage art. But then the very first picture of all did not 'evolve' itself: it came from something overwhelmingly greater than itself, from the mind of that man who by seeing for the first time that marks on a flat surface could be made to look like animals and men, proved himself to excel in sheer blinding genius any of the artists who have succeeded him. It may be true that if we trace back any existing civilization to its beginnings we shall find those beginnings crude and savage: but then when you look closer you usually find that these beginnings themselves come from a wreck of some earlier civilization. In other words, the apparent instances of, or analogies to, Evolution which impress the folk imagination, operate by fixing our attention on one half of the process. What we actually see all round us is a double process—the perfect 'dropping' an imperfect seed which in its turn develops to perfection. By concentrating exclusively on the record or upward movement in this cycle we seem to see 'evolution'. I am not in the least denying that organisms on this planet may have 'evolved'. But if we are to be guided by the analogy of Nature as we now know her, it would be reasonable to suppose that this evolutionary process was the second half of a long pattern—that the crude beginnings of life on this planet have themselves been 'dropped' there by a full and perfect life. The analogy may be mistaken. Perhaps Nature was once different. Perhaps the universe as a whole is quite different from those parts of it which fall under our observation. But if that is so, if there was once a dead universe which somehow made itself alive, if there was absolutely original savagery which raised itself by its own shoulder strap into civilization, then we ought to recognize that things of this sort happen no longer, that the world we are being asked to believe in is radically unlike the world we experience. In other words, all the immediate *plausibility* of the Myth has vanished. But it has vanished only because we have been thinking it will remain plausible to the imagination, and it is imagination which makes the Myth: it takes over from rational thought only what it finds convenient.

Another source of strength in the Myth is what the psychologists would call its 'ambivalence'. It gratifies equally two opposite tendencies of the mind, the tendency to denigration and the tendency to flattery. In the Myth everything is becoming everything else: in fact everything *is* everything else at an earlier or later stage of development—the later stages being always the better. This means that if you are feeling like Mencken you can 'debunk' all the respectable things by pointing out that they are 'merely' elaborations of the disreputable things. Love is 'merely' an elaboration of lust, virtue merely all elaboration of instinct, and so forth. On the one hand it also means that if you are feeling what the people call 'idealistic' you can regard all the nasty things (in yourself or your party or your nation) as being 'merely' the undeveloped forms of all the nice things: vice is only undeveloped virtue, egoism only undeveloped altruism, a little more education will set everything right.

The Myth also soothes the old wounds of our childhood. Without going as far as Freud we may yet well admit that every man has an old grudge against his father and his first teacher. The process of being brought up, however well it is done, cannot fail to offend. How pleasing, therefore, to abandon the old idea of 'descent' from our concocters in favour of the new idea of 'evolution' or 'emergence': to feel that we have risen from them as a flower from the earth, that we transcend them as Keats' gods transcended the Titans. One then gets a kind of cosmic excuse for regarding one's father as a muddling old Mima and his claims upon our gratitude or respect as an insufferable *stamenlied*. 'Out of the way, old fool: it is we who know to forge Nothung !'

The Myth also pleases those who want to sell things to us. In the old days, a man had a family carriage built for him when he got married and expected it to last all his life. Such a frame of mind would hardly suit modern manufacturers. But popular Evolutionism suits them exactly. Nothing *ought* to last. They want you to have a new car, a new radio set, a new everything every year. The new model must always be superseding the old. Madam would like the *latest* fashion. For this is evolution, this is development, this the way the universe itself is going: and 'sales-resistance' is the sin against the Holy Ghost, the *élan vital*.

Finally, modern politics would be impossible without the Myth. It arose in the Revolutionary period. But for the political ideals of that period it would never have been accepted. That explains why the Myth concentrates on Haldane's one case of biological 'progress' and ignores his ten cases of 'degeneration'. If the cases of degeneration were kept in mind it would be impossible not to see that any given change in society is at least as likely to destroy the liberties and amenities we already have as to add new ones: that the danger of slipping back is at least as great as the chance of getting on: that a prudent society must spend at least as much energy on conserving what it has as on improvement. A clear knowledge of these truisms would be fatal both to the political Left and to the political Right of modern times. The Myth obscures that knowledge. Great parties have a vested interest in maintaining the Myth. We must therefore expect that it will survive in the popular press (including the ostensibly *comic* press) long after it has been expelled from educated circles. In Russia, where it has been built into the state religion, it may survive for centuries: for

It has great allies,
Its friends are propaganda, party cries,
And bilge, and Man's incorrigible mind.

But that is not the note on which I would wish to end. The Myth has all these discreditable allies: but we should be far astray if we thought it had no others. As I have tried to show it has better allies too. It appeals to the same innocent and permanent needs in us which welcome Jack the Giant-Killer. It gives us almost everything the imagination craves—irony, heroism, vastness, unity in multiplicity, and a tragic close. It appeals to every part of me except my reason. That is why those of us who feel that the Myth is already dead for us must not make the mistake of trying to 'debunk' it in the wrong way. We must not fancy that we are securing the modern world from something grim and dry, something that starves the soul. The contrary is the truth. It is our painful duty to wake the world from an enchantment. The real universe is probably in many respects less poetical, certainly less tidy and unified, than they had supposed. Man's rôle in it is less heroic. The danger that really hangs over him is perhaps entirely lacking in true tragic dignity. It is only in the last resort, and after all lesser poetries have been renounced and imagination sternly subjected to intellect, that we shall be able to offer them any compensation for what we intend to take away from them. That is why in the meantime we must treat the Myth with respect. It was all (on a certain level) nonsense: but a man would be a dull dog if he could not feel the thrill and charm of it. For my own part, though I believe it no longer, I shall always enjoy it as I enjoy other myths. I shall keep my Cave-Man where I keep Balder and Helen and the Argonauts: and there often re-visit him.

On Church Music

I AM A layman and one who can boast no musical education. I cannot even speak from the experience of a lifelong churchgoer. It follows that Church Music is a subject on which I cannot, even in the lowest degree, appear as a teacher. My place is in the witness box. If it concerns the court to know how the whole matter appears to such as I (not only *laicus* but *laicissimius*) I am prepared to give my evidence.

I assume from the outset that nothing should be done or sung or said in church which does not aim directly or indirectly either at glorifying God or edifying the people or both. A good service may of course have a cultural value as well, but that is not what it exists for; just as, in an unfamiliar landscape, a church may help me to find the points of the compass, but was not built for that purpose.

These two ends, of edifying and glorifying, seem to me to be related as follows. Whenever we edify, we glorify, but when we glorify we do not always edify. The edification of the people is an act of charity and obedience and therefore in itself a glorification of God. But it is possible for a man to glorify God in modes that do not edify his neighbour. This fact confronted the Church at an early stage in her career, in the phenomenon called 'speaking with tongues'. In I Corinthians xiv, St Paul points out that the man who is inspired to speak in an unknown tongue may do very well, as far as he himself is concerned, but will not profit the congregation unless his utterance can be translated. Thus glorifying and edifying may come to be opposed.

Now at first sight to speak with unknown tongues and to sing anthems which are beyond the musical capacity of the people would seem to be very much the same kind of thing. It looks as if we ought to extend to the one the embargo which St Paul places on the other. And this would lead to the forbidding conclusion that no Church Music is legitimate except that which suits the existing taste of the people.

In reality, however, the parallel is not perhaps so close as it seems. In the first place, the mode after which a speech in an unknown tongue could glorify God was not, I suppose, the same as the mode after which learned music is held to do so. It is (to say the least) doubtful whether the speeches in 'tongues' claimed to glorify God by their aesthetic quality. I suppose that they glorified God firstly by being miraculous and involuntary, and secondly by the ecstatic state of mind in which the speaker was. The idea behind Church Music is very different. It glorifies God by being excellent in its own kind; almost as the birds and flowers and the heavens themselves glorify Him. In the composition and highly-trained execution of sacred music we offer our natural gifts at their highest to God, as we do also in ecclesiastical architecture, in vestments, in glass and gold and silver, in well-kept parish accounts, or the careful organization of a Social. And in the second place, the incapacity of the people to 'understand' a foreign language and their incapacity to 'understand' good music are not really the same. The first applies absolutely and equally (except for a lucky accident) to all the members of the congregation. The second is not equally present or equally incurable perhaps in any two individuals. And finally, the alternative to speech in an unknown tongue was speech in a known tongue. But in most discussions about Church Music the alternative to learned music is popular music—giving the people 'what they like' and allowing them to sing (or shout) their 'old favourites'.

It is here that the distinction between our problem and St Paul's seems to me to be the sharpest. That words in a known tongue might edify was obvious. Is it equally obvious that the people are edified by being allowed to shout their favourite hymns? I am well aware that the people like it. They equally like shouting *Auld Lang Syne* in the streets on New Year's Eve or shouting the latest music-hall song in a tap-room. To make a communal, familiar noise is certainly a pleasure to human beings. And I would not be thought to despise this pleasure. It is good for the lungs, it promotes good fellowship, it is humble and unaffected, it is in every way a whole-some, innocent thing—as wholesome and innocent as a pint of beer, a game of darts, or a dip in the sea. But is it, any more than these, a means of edification? No doubt it can be done—all these things can be done—eating can be done—to the glory of God. We have an Apostle's word for it. The perfected Christian can turn all his humblest, most secular, most economic, actions in that direction. But if this is accepted as an argument for popular hymns it will also be an argument for a good many other things. What we want to know is whether untrained communal sing-ing is in itself any more edifying than other popular pleasures. And of this I, for one, am still wholly unconvinced. I have often heard this noise; I have sometimes contributed to it. I do not yet seem to have found any evidence that the physical and emotional exhilaration which it produces is necessarily, or often, of any reli-gious relevance. What I, like many other laymen, chiefly desire in church are fewer, better, and shorter hymns; especially fewer.

The case for abolishing all Church Music whatever thus seems to me far stron-ger than the case for abolishing the difficult work of the trained choir and retain-ing the lusty roar of the congregation. Whatever doubts I feel about the spiritual value of the first I feel at least equally about the spiritual value of the second.

The first and most solid conclusion which (for me) emerges is that both musical parties, the High Brows and the Low, assume far too easily the spiritual value of the music they want. Neither the greatest excellence of a trained performance from the choir, nor the heartiest and most enthusiastic bellowing from the pews, must be taken to signify that any specifically religious activity is going on. It may be so, or it may not. Yet the main sense of Christendom, reformed and unreformed, would be against us if we tried to banish music from the Church. It remains to suggest, very tentatively, the ways in which it can really be pleasing to God or help to save the souls of men.

There are two musical situations on which I think we can be confident that a blessing rests. One is where a priest or an organist, himself a man of trained and delicate taste, humbly and charitably sacrifices his own (aesthetically right) desires and gives the people humbler and coarser fare than he would wish, in a belief (even, as it may be, the erroneous belief) that he can thus bring them to God. The other is where the stupid and unmusical layman humbly and patiently, and above all silently, listens to music which he cannot, or cannot fully, appreciate, in the belief that it somehow glorifies God, and that if it does not edify him this must be his own defect. Neither such a High Brow nor such a Low Brow can be far out of the way. To both, Church Music will have been a means of grace; not the music they have liked, but the music they have disliked. They have both offered, sacrificed, their taste in the fullest sense. But where the opposite situation arises, where the musician is filled with the pride of skill or the virus of emulation and looks with contempt on the unappreciative congregation, or where the unmusical, complacently entrenched in their own ignorance and conservatism, look with the restless and resentful hostility of an inferiority complex on all who would try to improve their taste—there, we may be sure, all that both offer is unblessed and the spirit that moves them is not the Holy Ghost.

These highly general reflections will not, I fear, be of much practical use to any priest or organist in devising a working compromise for a particular church. The most they can hope to do is to suggest that the problem is never a merely musical one. Where both the choir and the congregation are spiritually on the right road no insurmountable difficulties will occur. Discrepancies of taste and capacity will, indeed, provide matter for mutual charity and humility.

For us, the musically illiterate mass, the right way is not hard to discern; and as long as we stick to it, the fact that we are capable only of a confused rhythmical noise will not do very much harm, if, when we make it, we really intend the glory of God. For if that is our intention it follows of necessity that we shall be as ready to glorify Him by silence (when required) as by shouts. We shall also be aware that the power of shouting stands very low in the hierarchy of natural gifts, and that it would be better to learn to sing if we could. If any one tries to teach us we will try to learn. If we cannot learn, and if this is desired, we will shut up. And we will also try to listen intelligently. A congregation in this state will not complain if a good deal of the music they hear in church is above their heads. It is not the mere ignorance of the unmusical that really resists improvements. It is jealousy, arrogance, suspicion, and the wholly detestable species of conservatism which those vices engender. How far it may be politic (part of the wisdom of the serpent) to make concessions to the 'old guard' in a congregation, I would not like to determine. But I do not think it can be the business of the Church greatly to co-operate with the modern State in appeasing inferiority complexes and encouraging the natural man's instinctive hatred of excellence. Democracy is all very well as a political device. It must not intrude into the spiritual, or even the aesthetic, world.

The right way for the musicians is perhaps harder, and I, at any rate, can speak of it with much less confidence. But it seems to me that we must define rather carefully the way, or ways, in which music can glorify God. There is, as I hinted above, a sense in which all natural agents, even inanimate ones, glorify God continually by revealing the powers He has given them. And in that sense we, as natural agents, do the same. On that level our wicked actions, in so far as they exhibit our skill and strength, may be said to glorify God, as well as our good actions. An excellently performed piece of music, as a natural operation which reveals in a very high degree the peculiar powers given to man, will thus always glorify God whatever the intention of the performers may be. But that is a kind of glorifying which we share with 'the dragons and great deeps', with the 'frosts and snows'. What is looked for in us, as men, is another kind of glorifying, which depends on intention. How easy or how hard it may be for a whole choir to preserve that intention through all the discussions and decisions, all the corrections and disappointments, all the temptations to pride, rivalry and ambition, which precede the performance of a great work, I (naturally) do not know. But it is on the intention that all depends. When it succeeds, I think the performers are the most enviable of men; privileged while mortals to honour God like angels and, for a few golden moments, to see spirit and flesh, delight and labour, skill and worship, the natural and the supernatural, all fused into that unity they would have had before the Fall. But I must insist that no degree of excellence in the music, simply as music, can assure us that this paradisal state has been achieved. The excellence proves 'keenness'; but men can be 'keen' for natural, or even wicked, motives. The absence of keenness would prove that they lacked the right spirit; its presence does not prove that they have it. We must beware of the naive idea that our music can 'please' God as it would please a cultivated human hearer. That is like thinking, under the old Law, that He really needed the blood of bulls and goats. To which an answer came, 'Mine are the cattle upon a thousand hills', and 'if I am hungry, I will not tell *thee*.' If God (in that sense) wanted music, He would not tell *us*. For all our offerings, whether of music or martyrdom, are like the intrinsically worthless present of a child, which a father values indeed, but values only for the intention.[1]

[1. Before this article was written, Lewis was invited by the Rev Mr Erik Routley to become a member of the panel of the Hymn Society of Great Britain and Ireland to whom new hymns are submitted in order that their merit might be assessed. As could be expected, Lewis refused. However, his answers to the request are published (with Mr Routley's letters) as 'Correspondence with an Anglican who Dislikes Hymns', The Presbyter, VI, No. 2 (1948) pp. 15–20. (The two letters from Lewis, dated 16 July 1946 and 21 September 1946, are printed over the initials 'A.B.')]

Historicism

'He that would fly without wings must fly in his dreams.'
　　　　　　　　　　　　　—Coleridge

I GIVE THE NAME *Historicism* to the belief that men can, by the use of their natural powers, discover an inner meaning in the historical process. I say *by the use of their natural powers* because I do not propose to deal with any man who claims to know the meaning either of all history or of some particular historical event by divine revelation. What I mean by a Historicist is a man who asks me to accept his account of the inner meaning of history on the grounds of his learning and genius. If he had asked me to accept it on the grounds that it had been shown him in a vision, that would be another matter. I should have said to him nothing. His claim (with supporting evidence in the way of sanctity and miracles) would not be for me to judge. This does not mean that I am setting up a distinction, to be applied by myself, between inspired and uninspired writers. The distinction is not between those who have and those who lack inspiration, but between those who claim and those who do not claim it. With the former I have at present no concern.

I say *an inner meaning* because I am not classifying as Historicists those who find a 'meaning' in history in any sense whatever. Thus, to find causal connections between historical events, is in my terminology the work of a historian not of a historicist. A historian, without becoming a Historicist, may certainly infer unknown events from known ones. He may even infer future events from past ones; prediction may be a folly, but it is not Historicism. He may 'interpret' the past in the sense of reconstructing it imaginatively, making us feel (as far as may be) what it was like, and in that sense what it 'meant', to a man to be a twelfth-century villein or a Roman *eques*. What makes all these activities proper to the historian is that in them the conclusions, like the premises, are historical. The mark of the Historicist, on the other hand, is that he tries to get from historical premises conclusions which are more than historical; conclusions metaphysical or theological or (to coin a word) atheo-logical. The historian and the Historicist may both say that something 'must have' happened. But *must* in the mouth of a genuine historian will refer only to a *ratio cognoscendi*: since A happened B 'must have' preceded it; if William the Bastard arrived in England he 'must have' crossed the sea. But 'must' in the mouth of a Historicist can have quite a different meaning. It may mean that events fell out as they did because of some ultimate, transcendent necessity in the ground of things.

When Carlyle spoke of history as a 'book of revelations' he was a Historicist. When Novalis called history 'an evangel' he was a Historicist. When Hegel saw in history the progressive self-manifestation of absolute spirit he was a Historicist.

When a village woman says that her wicked father-in-law's paralytic stroke is 'a judgement on him' she is a Historicist. Evolutionism, when it ceases to be simply a theorem in biology and becomes a principle for interpreting the total historical process, is a form of Historicism. Keats' *Hyperion* is the epic of Historicism, and the words of Oceanus,

> 'tis the eternal law
> That first in beauty should be first in might,

are as fine a specimen of Historicism as you could wish to find.

The contention of this article is that Historicism is an illusion and that Historicists are, at the very best, wasting their time. I hope it is already clear that in criticizing Historicists I am not at all criticizing historians. It is not formally impossible that a Historicist and a historian should be the same man. But the two characters are in fact very seldom combined. It is usually theologians, philosophers and politicians who become Historicists.

Historicism exists on many levels. The lowest form of it is one that I have already mentioned: the doctrine that our calamities (or more often our neighbours' calamities) are 'judgements'; which here means divine condemnations or punishments. This sort of Historicism sometimes endeavours to support itself by the authority of the Old Testament. Some people even talk as if it were the peculiar mark of the Hebrew prophets to interpret history in this way. To that I have two replies. Firstly, the Scriptures come before me as a book claiming divine inspiration. I am not prepared to argue with the prophets. But if any man thinks that because God was pleased to reveal certain calamities as 'judgements' to certain chosen persons, he is therefore entitled to generalize and read all calamities in the same way, I submit that this is a *non sequitur*. Unless, of course, that man claims to be himself a prophet; and then I must refer his claim to more competent judges. But secondly, we must insist that such an interpretation of history was not the characteristic of ancient Hebrew religion, not the thing which sets it apart and makes it uniquely valuable. On the contrary, this is precisely what it shares with popular Paganism. To attribute calamity to the offended gods and therefore to seek out and punish the offender, is the most natural thing in the world and therefore the worldwide method. Examples such as the plague in *Iliad A* and the plague at the opening of the *Oedipus Tyrannus* come at once to mind. The distinctive thing. the precious peculiarity, of Scripture is the series of divine rebuffs which this naïve and spontaneous type of Historicism there receives; in the whole course of Jewish history, in the Book of Job, in Isaiah's suffering servant (liii), in Our Lord's answers about the disaster at Siloam (Luke xiii, 4) and the man born blind (John ix, 13). If this sort of Historicism survives, it survives in spite of Christianity. And in a vague form it certainly does survive. Some who in general deserve to be called true historians are betrayed into writing as if nothing failed or succeeded that did not somehow deserve to do so. We must guard against the emotional overtones of a phrase like 'the judgement of history'. It might lure us into the vulgarest of all vulgar errors, that of idolizing as the goddess History what manlier ages belaboured as the strumpet Fortune. That would sink us below the Christian, or even the best Pagan, level. The very Vikings and Stoics knew better.

But subtler and more cultivated types of Historicism now also claim that their view is especially congenial to Christianity. It has become a commonplace, as Fr Paul Henri lately remarked in his Deneke lecture at Oxford, to say that Judaic and Christian thought are distinguished from Pagan and Pantheistic thought precisely by the significance which they attribute to history. For the Pantheist, we are told, the content of time is simply illusion; history is a dream and salvation consists in awaking. For the Greeks, we are told, history was a mere flux or, at best, cyclic: significance was to be sought not in Becoming but in Being. For Christianity, on the other hand, history is a story with a well-defined plot, pivoted on Creation, Fall, Redemption, and Judgement. It is indeed the divine revelation *par excellence*, the revelation which includes all other revelations.

That history in a certain sense must be all this for a Christian, I do not deny. In what sense, will be explained later. For the moment, I submit that the contrast as commonly drawn between Judaic or Christian thought on the one hand and Pagan or Pantheistic on the other is in some measure illusory. In the modern world, quite plainly, Historicism has a Pantheistic ancestor in Hegel and a materialistic progeny in the Marxists. It has proved so far a stronger weapon in our enemies' hands than in ours. If Christian Historicism is to be recommended as an apologetic weapon it had better be recommended by the maxim *fas est et ab hoste doceri* than on the ground of any supposedly inherent congeniality. And if we look at the past we shall find that the contrast works well as between Greek and Christian but not as between Christian and other types of Pagan. The Norse gods, for example, unlike the Homeric, are beings rooted in a historical process. Living under the shadow of Ragnarok they are preoccupied with time. Odin is almost the god of anxiety: in that way Wagner's Wotan is amazingly true to the Eddaic original. In Norse theology cosmic history is neither a cycle nor a flux; it is irreversible, tragic epic marching deathward to the drum-beat of omens and prophecies. And even if we rule out Norse Paganism on the ground that it was possibly influenced by Christianity, what shall we do with the Romans? It is quite clear that they did not regard history with the indifference, or with the merely scientific or anecdotal interests, of the Greeks. They seem to have been a nation of Historicists. I have pointed out elsewhere that all Roman epic before Virgil was probably metrical chronicle;[1] and the subject was always the same—the coming-to-be of Rome. What Virgil essentially did was to give this perennial theme a new unity by his symbolical structure. The *Aeneid* puts forward, though in mythical form, what is precisely a reading of history, an attempt to show what the *fata Jovis* were labouring to bring about. Everything is related not to Aeneas as an individual hero but to Aeneas as the Rome-bearer. This, and almost only this, gives significance to his escape from Troy, his *amour* with Dido, his descent into Hades, and his defeat of Turnus. *Tantae molis erat*: all history is for Virgil an immense parturition. It is from this Pagan source that one kind of Historicism descends to Dante. The Historicism of the *De Monarchia*, though skilfully, and of

[1. 'Virgil and the Subject of Secondary Epic', *A Preface to Paradise Lost* (Oxford, 1942), p. 32ff.]

course sincerely, mortised into the Judaic and Christian framework, is largely Roman and Virgilian. St Augustine indeed may be rightly described as a Christian Historicist. But it is not always remembered that he became one in order to refute Pagan Historicism. The *De Civitate* answers those who traced the disasters of Rome to the anger of the rejected gods. I do not mean to imply that the task was uncongenial to St Augustine, or that his own Historicism is merely an *argumentum ad hominem*. But it is surely absurd to regard as specifically Christian in him the acceptance of a *terrain* which had in fact been chosen by the enemy.

The close connection which some see between Christianity and Historicism thus seems to me to be largely an illusion. There is no *prima facie* case in its favour on such grounds as that. We are entitled to examine it on its merits.

What appears, on Christian premises, to be true in the Historicist's position is this. Since all things happen either by the divine will or at least by the divine permission, it follows that the total content of time must in its own nature be a revelation of God's wisdom, justice, and mercy. In this direction we can go as far as Carlyle or Novalis or anyone else. History is, in that sense, a perpetual Evangel, a story written by the finger of God. If, by one miracle, the total content of time were spread out before me, and if, by another, I were able to hold all that infinity of events in my mind and if, by a third, God were pleased to comment on it so that I could understand it, then, to be sure, I could do what the Historicist says he is doing. I could read the meaning, discern the pattern. Yes; and if the sky fell we should all catch larks. The question is not what could be done under conditions never vouchsafed us *in via*, nor even (so far as I can remember) promised us *in patria*, but what can be done now under the real conditions. I do not dispute that History is a story written by the finger of God. But have we the text? (It would be dull work discussing the inspiration of the Bible if no copy of it had ever been seen on earth.)

We must remind ourselves that the word *History* has several senses. It may mean the total content of time: past, present, and future. It may mean the content of the past only, but still the total content of the past, the past as it really was in all its teeming riches. Thirdly, it may mean so much of the past as is discoverable from surviving evidence. Fourthly, it may mean so much as has been actually discovered by historians working, so to speak, 'at the face', the pioneer historians never heard of by the public who make the actual discoveries. Fifthly, it may mean that portion, and that version, of the matter so discovered which has been worked up by great historical writers. (This is perhaps the most popular sense: *history* usually means what you read when you are reading Gibbon or Mommsen, or the Master of Trinity.) Sixthly, it may mean that vague, composite picture of the past which floats, rather hazily, in the mind of the ordinary educated man.

When men say that 'History' is a revelation, or has a meaning, in which of these six senses do they use the word *History?* I am afraid that in fact they are very often thinking of history in the sixth sense; in which case their talk about revelation or meaning is surely unplausible in the extreme. For 'history' in the sixth sense is the land of shadows, the home of wraiths like Primitive Man or the Renaissance or the Ancient-Greeks-and-Romans. It is not at all surprising, of course, that those who stare at it too long should see patterns. We see pictures in the fire. The more indeterminate the object, the more it excites our mythopoeic or 'esemplastic' faculties. To the naked eye there is a face in the moon; it vanishes when you use a telescope. In the same way, the meanings or patterns discernible in 'history' (Sense Six) disappear when we turn to 'history' in any of the higher senses. They are clearest for each of us in the periods he has studied least. No one who has distinguished the different senses of the word *History* could continue to think that history (in the sixth sense) is an evangel or a revelation. It is an effect of perspective.

On the other hand, we admit that history (in Sense One) is a story written by the finger of God. Unfortunately we have not got it. The claim of the practising Historicist then will stand or fall with his success in showing that history in one of the intermediate senses—the first being out of reach and the sixth useless for his purpose—is sufficiently close to history in the first sense to share its revealing qualities.

We drop, then, to history in Sense Two: the total content of past time as it really was in all its richness. This would save the Historicist if we could reasonably believe two things: first, that the formidable omission of the future does not conceal the point or meaning of the story, and, secondly, that we do actually possess history (Sense Two) up to the present moment. But can we believe either?

It would surely be one of the luckiest things in the world if the content of time up to the moment at which the Historicist is writing happened to contain all that he required for reaching the significance of total history. We ride with our backs to the engine. We have no notion what stage in the journey we have reached. Are we in Act I or Act V? Are our present diseases those of childhood or senility? If, indeed, we knew that history was cyclic we might perhaps hazard a guess at its meaning from the fragment we have seen. But then we have been told that the Historicists are just the people who do not think that history is merely cyclic. For them it is a real story with a beginning, a middle, and an end. But a story is precisely the sort of thing that cannot be understood till you have heard the whole of it. Or, if there are stories (bad stories) whose later chapters add nothing essential to their significance, and whose significance is therefore contained in something less than the whole, at least you cannot tell whether any given story belongs to that class until you have at least once read it to the end. Then, on a second reading, you may omit the dead wood in the closing chapters. I always now omit the last Book of *War and Peace*. But we have not yet read history to the end. There might be no dead wood. If it is a story written by the finger of God, there probably isn't. And if not, how can we suppose that we have seen 'the point' already? No doubt there are things we can say about this story even now. We can say it is an exciting story, or a crowded story, or a story with humorous characters in it. The one thing we must not say is what it means, or what its total pattern is.

But even if it were possible, which I deny, to see the significance of the whole from a truncated text, it remains to ask whether we have that truncated text. Do we possess even up to the present date the content of time as it really was in all its richness? Clearly not. The past, by definition, is not present. The point I am trying to make is so often slurred over by the unconcerned admission 'Of course we don't know *everything*' that I have sometimes despaired of bringing it home to other people's minds. It is not a question of failing to know everything: it is a question (at least as regards quantity) of knowing next door to nothing. Each of us finds that in his own life every moment of time is completely filled. He is bombarded every second by sensations, emotions, thoughts, which he cannot attend to for multitude, and nine-tenths of which he must simply ignore. A single second of lived time contains more than can be recorded. And every second of past time has been like that for every man that ever lived. The past (I am assuming in the Historicist's favour that we need consider only the human past) in its reality, was a roaring cataract of billions upon billions of such moments: any one of them too complex to grasp in its entirety, and the aggregate beyond all imagination. By far the greater part of this teeming reality escaped human consciousness almost as soon as it occurred. None of us could at this moment give anything like a full account of his own life for the last twenty-four hours. We have already forgotten; even if we remembered, we have not time. The new moments are upon us. At every tick of the clock, in every inhabited part of the world, an unimaginable richness and variety of 'history' falls off the world into total oblivion. Most of the experiences in 'the past as it really was' were instantly forgotten by the subject himself. Of the small percentage which he remembered (and never remembered with perfect accuracy) a smaller percentage was ever communicated even to his closest intimates; of this, a smaller percentage still was recorded; of the recorded fraction only another fraction has ever reached posterity. *Ad nos vix tenuis famae perlabitur aura.* When once we have realized what 'the past as it really was' means, we must freely admit that most—that nearly all—history (in Sense Two) is, and will remain, wholly unknown to us. And if *per impossibile* the whole were known, it would be wholly unmanageable. To know the whole of one minute in Napoleon's life would require a whole minute of your own life. You could not keep up with it.

If these fairly obvious reflections do not trouble the Historicist that is because he has an answer. 'Of course', he replies, 'I admit that we do not know and cannot know (and, indeed, don't want to know) all the mass of trivialities which filled the past as they fill the present; every kiss and frown, every scratch and sneeze, every hiccup and cough. But we know the important facts.' Now this is a perfectly sound reply for a historian: I am not so clear that it will do for the Historicist. You will notice that we are now already a long way from history in Sense One—the total story written by the finger of God. First, we had to abandon the parts of that story which are still in the future. Now it appears we have not even got the text of those parts which we call 'past'. We have only selections; and selections which, as regards quantity, stand to the original text rather as one word would stand to all the books in the British Museum. We are asked to believe that from selections on that scale men (not miraculously inspired) can arrive at the meaning or plan or purport of the original. This is credible only if it can be shown that the selections make up in quality for what they lack in quantity. The quality will certainly have to be remarkably good if it is going to do that.

'The important parts of the past survive.' If a historian says this (I am not sure that most historians would) he means by 'importance' relevance to the particular inquiry he has chosen. Thus, if he is an economic historian, economic facts are for him important: if a military historian, military facts. And he would not have embarked on his inquiry unless he had some reason for supposing that relevant evidence existed. 'Important' facts, for him, usually do survive because his undertaking was based on the probability that the facts he calls important are to be had. Sometimes he finds he was mistaken. He admits defeat and tries a new question. All this is fairly plain sailing. But the Historicist is in a different position. When he says 'Important facts survive' he must mean by the 'important' (if he is saying anything to the purpose) that which reveals the inner meaning of History. The important parts of the past must for a Hegelian Historicist be those in which Absolute Spirit progressively manifests itself; for a Christian Historicist, those which reveal the purposes of God.

In this claim I see two difficulties. The first is logical. If history is what the Historicist says—the self-manifestation of Spirit, the story written by the finger of God, the revelation which includes all other revelations—then surely he must go to history itself to teach him what is important. How does he know beforehand what sort of events are, in a higher degree than others, self-manifestations of Spirit? And if he does not know that, how does he get his assurance that it is events of that type which manage (what a convenience!) to get recorded?

The second difficulty is obvious, if we think for a moment of the process whereby a fact about the past reaches, or fails to reach, posterity. Prehistoric pottery survives because earthenware is easy to break and hard to pulverize; prehistoric poetry has perished because words, before writing, are winged. Is it reasonable to conclude either that there was no poetry or that it was, by the Historicist's standard, less important than the pottery? Is there a discovered law by which important manuscripts survive and unimportant perish? Do you ever turn out an old drawer (say, at the break-up of your father's house) without wondering at the survival of trivial documents and the disappearance of those which everyone would have thought worth preservation? And I think the real historian will allow that the actual *detritus* of the past on which he works is very much more like an old drawer than like an intelligent epitome of some longer work. Most that survives or perishes survives or perishes by chance: that is, as a result of causes which have nothing to do either with the historian's or the Historicist's interests. Doubtless, it would be possible for God so to ordain these chances that what survives is always just what the Historicist needs. But I see no evidence that He has done so; I remember no promise that He would.

The 'literary' sources, as the historian calls them, no doubt record what their writers for some reason thought important. But this is of little use unless their standards of importance were the same as God's. This seems unlikely. Their standards do not agree with one another nor with ours. They often tell us what we do not greatly want to know and omit what we think essential. It is often easy to see why. Their standard of importance can be explained by their historical situation. So, no doubt, can ours. Standards of historical importance are themselves embedded in history. But then, by what standard can we judge whether the 'important' in some high-flying Hegelian sense has survived? Have we, apart from our Christian faith, any assurance that the historical events which we regard as momentous coincide with those which would be found momentous if God showed us the whole text and deigned to comment? Why should Genghis Khan be more important than the patience or despair of some one among his victims? Might not those whom we regard as significant figures—great scholars, soldiers, and statesmen—turn out to have their chief importance as giving occasion to states of soul in individuals whom we never heard of? I do not, of course, mean that those whom we call the great are not themselves immortal souls for whom Christ died, but that in the plot of history as a whole they might be minor characters. It would not be strange if we, who have not sat through the whole play, and who have heard only tiny fragments of the scenes already played, sometimes mistook a mere super in a fine dress for one of the protagomsts.

On such a small and chance selection from the total past as we have, it seems to me a waste of time to play the Historicist. The philosophy of history is a discipline for which we mortal men lack the necessary data. Nor is the attempt always a mere waste of time: it may be positively mischievous. It encourages a Mussolini to say that 'History took him by the throat' when what really took him by the throat was desire. Drivel about superior races or immanent dialectic may be used to strengthen the hand and ease the conscience of cruelty and greed. And what quack or traitor will not now woo adherents or intimidate resistance with the assurance that his scheme is inevitable, 'bound to come', and in the direction which the world is already taking?

When I have tried to explain myself on this subject in conversation I have sometimes been met by the rejoinder: 'Because historians do not know all, will you forbid them to try to understand what they do know?' But this seems to me to miss the whole point. I have already explained in what sense historians should attempt to understand the past. They may infer unknown events from known, they may reconstruct, they may even (if they insist) predict. They may, in fact, tell me almost anything they like about history except its metahistorical meaning. And the reason is surely very plain. There are inquiries in which scanty evidence is worth using. We may not be able to get certainty, but we can get probability, and half a loaf is better than no bread. But there are other inquiries in which scanty evidence has the same value as no evidence at all. In a funny anecdote, to have heard all except the last six words in which the point lies, leaves you, as a judge of its comic merits, in the same position as the man who has heard none of it. The historian seems to me to be engaged on an inquiry of the first type; the Historicist, on one of the second. But let us take a closer analogy.

Suppose a lost Greek play of which fragments totalling six lines survive. They have survived, of course, in grammarians who quoted them to illustrate rare inflexions. That is, they survive because someone thought them important for some reason, not because they were important in the play as a play. If any one of them had dramatic importance, that is simply a lucky accident, and we know nothing about it. I do not condemn the classical scholar to produce nothing more than a bare text of the fragments any more than I condemn the historian to be a mere annalist. Let the scholar amend their corruptions and draw from them any conclusions he can about the history of Greek language, metre or religion. But let him not start talking to us about the significance of the play as a play. For that purpose the evidence before him has a value indistinguishable from zero.

The example of a defective text might be used in another way. Let us assume a mutilated MS, in which only a minority of passages are legible. The parts we can still read might be tolerable evidence for those features which are likely to be constant and evenly distributed over the whole; for example, spelling or handwriting. On such evidence a palaeographer might, without excessive boldness, hazard a guess about the character and nationality of the scribe. A literary critic would have much less chance of guessing correctly at the purport of the whole text. That is because the palaeographer deals with what is cyclic or recurrent, and the literary critic with something unique, and uniquely developing throughout. It is possible, though not likely, that all the torn or stained or missing leaves were written by a different scribe; and if they were not, it is very unlikely that he altered his graphic habits in all the passages we cannot check. But there is nothing in the world to prevent the legible line (at the bottom of a page)

Erimian was the noblest of the brothers ten

having been followed on the next and now missing page, by something like

As men believed; so false are the beliefs of men.

This provides the answer to a question which may be asked: Does my canon that historical premises should yield only historical conclusions entail the corollary that scientific premises should yield only scientific conclusions? If we call the speculations of Whitehead or Jeans or Eddington 'scienticism' (as distinct from 'science') do I condemn the scientist as much as the Historicist? I am inclined, so far as I can see my way at present, to answer No. The scientist and the historian seem to me like the palaeographer and the literary critic in my parable. The scientist studies those elements in reality which repeat themselves. The historian studies the unique. Both have a defective MS but its defects are by no means equally damaging to both. One specimen of gravitation, or one specimen of handwriting, for all we can see to the contrary, is as good as another. But one historical event, or one line of a poem, is different from another and different in its actual context from what it would be in any other context, and out of all these differences the unique character of the whole is built up. That is why, in my opinion, the scientist who becomes a scientist is in a stronger position than the historian who becomes a Historicist. It may not be very wise to conclude from what we know of the physical universe that 'God is a mathematician': it seems to me, however, much wiser than to conclude anything about His 'judgements' from mere history. *Caveas disputare de occultis Dei judiciis*, says the author of the *Imitation*. He even advises us what antidotes to use *quando haec suggerit inimicus*.

It will, I hope, be understood that I am not denying all access whatever to the revelation of God in history. On certain great events (those embodied in the creeds)

we have what I believe to be divine comment which makes plain so much of their significance as we need, and can bear, to know. On other events, most of which are in any case unknown to us, we have no such comment. And it is also important to remember that we all have a certain limited, but direct, access to History in Sense One. We are allowed, indeed compelled, to read it sentence by sentence, and every sentence is labelled *Now*. I am not, of course, referring to what is commonly called 'contemporary history', the content of the newspapers. That is possibly the most phantasmal of all histories, a story written not by the hand of God but by foreign offices, demagogues, and reporters. I mean the real or primary history which meets each of us moment by moment in his own experience. It is very limited, but it is the pure, unedited, unexpurgated text, straight from the Author's hand. We believe that those who seek will find comment sufficient whereby to understand it in such degree as they need; and that therefore God is every moment 'revealed in history', that is, in what MacDonald called 'the holy present'. Where, except in the present, can the Eternal be met? If I attack Historicism it is not because I intend any disrespect to primary history, the real revelation springing direct from God in every experience. It is rather because I respect this real original history too much to see with unconcern the honours due to it lavished on those fragments, copies of fragments, copies of copies of fragments, or floating reminiscences of copies of copies, which are, unhappily, confounded with it under the general name of *history*.

The Psalms

THE DOMINANT IMPRESSION I get from reading the Psalms is one of antiquity. I seem to be looking into a deep pit of time, but looking through a lens which brings the figures who inhabit that depth up close to my eye. In that momentary proximity they are almost shockingly alien; creatures of unrestrained emotion, wallowing in self-pity, sobbing, cursing, screaming in exultation, clashing uncouth weapons or dancing to the din of strange musical instruments. Yet, side by side with this, there is also a different image in my mind: Anglican choirs, well laundered surplices, soapy boys' faces, hassocks, an organ, prayer-books, and perhaps the smell of new-mown graveyard grass coming in with the sunlight through an open door. Sometimes the one, sometimes the other, impression grows faint, but neither, perhaps, ever quite disappears. The irony reaches its height when a boy soloist sings in that treble which is so beautifully free from all personal emotion the words whereby ancient warriors lashed themselves with frenzy against their enemies; and does this in the service of the God of Love, and himself, meanwhile, perhaps thinks neither of that God nor of ancient wars but of 'bullseyes' and the Comics. This irony, this double or treble vision, is part of the pleasure. I begin to suspect that it is part of the profit too.

How old the Psalms, as we now have them, really are is a question for the scholars. I am told there is one (No. 18) which might really have come down from the age of David himself; that is, from the tenth century B.C. Most of them, however, are said to be 'post exilic'; the book was put together when the Hebrews, long exiled in Babylonia, were repatriated by that enlightened ruler, Cyrus of Persia. This would bring us down to the sixth century. How much earlier material the book took in is uncertain. Perhaps for our present purpose it does not greatly matter. The whole spirit and technique and the characteristic attitudes in the Psalms we have might be very like those of much older sacred poetry which is now lost. We know that they had such poetry; they must have been already famous for that art when their Babylonian conquerors (see No. 137) asked them for a specimen. And some very early pieces occur elsewhere in the Old Testament. Deborah's song of triumph over Sisera in Judges V might be as old as the battle that gave rise to it back in the thirteenth century. If the Hebrews were conservative in such matters then sixth century poems may be very like those of their ancestors. And we know they were conservative. One can see that by leaping forward six centuries into the New Testament and reading the *Magnificat*. The Virgin has something other (and more momentous) to say than the old Psalmists; but what she utters is quite unmistakably a psalm. The style, the dwelling on Covenant, the delight in the vindication of the poor, are all perfectly true to the old model. So might the old model have been true to one yet older. For poetry of that sort did not, like ours, seek to express those things in which individuals differ, and did not aim at novelty. Even if the Psalms we read were all composed as late as the sixth century B.C., in reading them I suspect that we have our hands on the near end of a living cord that stretches far back into the past.

In most moods the spirit of the Psalms feels to me more alien than that of the oldest Greek literature. But that is not an affair of dates. Distance in temper does not always coincide with distance in time. To most of us, perhaps to all of us at most times (unless we are either very uneducated or very holy or, as might be, both) the civilization that descends from Greece and Rome is closer, more congenial, than what we inherit from ancient Israel. The very words and concepts which we use for science, philosophy, criticism, government, grammar, are all Graeco-Roman. It is this, and not Israel, that has made us, in the ordinary sense, 'civilized'. But no Christian can read the Bible without discovering that these ancient Hebrews, generally so remote, may at any moment turn out to be our brothers in a sense in which no Greek or Roman ever was. What a dull, remote thing, for example, the Book of Proverbs seems at a first glance: bearded Orientals uttering endless platitudes as if in a parody of the *Arabian Nights*. Compared with Plato or Aristotle—compared even with Xenophon—it is not *thought* at all. Then, suddenly, just as you are going to give it up, your eye falls on the words, 'If thine enemy be hungry, give him bread to eat, and if he be thirsty give him water to drink' (xxv, 21). One rubs one's eyes. So they were saying that already. They knew that so long before Christ came. There is nothing like it in Greek, nor, if my memory serves me, in Confucius. And this is the sort of surprise we shall often get in the Psalms. These strange, alien figures may at any moment show that, in spiritual descent (as opposed to cultural) it is they, after all, who are our ancestors and the classical nations who are alien. Conversely, in reading the classics we sometimes have the opposite surprise. Those loved authors, so civilized, tolerant, humane, and enlightened, every now and then reveal that they are divided from us by a gulf. Hence the eternal, roguish tittering about pederasty in Plato or the hard pride that makes Aristotle's *Ethics* in places almost comic. We begin to doubt whether any one of them (even Virgil himself) if we could recall him from the dead might not, in the first hour's conversation, let out something that would utterly estrange us.

I do not at all mean that the Hebrews were just 'better' than the Greeks and the Romans. On the contrary we shall find in the Psalms expressions of a cruelty more vindictive and a self-righteousness more complete than anything in the classics. If we ignore such passages and read only a few selected favourite Psalms, we miss the point. For the point is precisely this: that these same fanatic and homicidal Hebrews, and not the more enlightened peoples, again and again—for brief moments—reach a Christian level of spirituality. It is not that they are better or worse than the Pagans, but that they are both better and worse. One is forced to recognize that, in one respect, these alien poets are our predecessors, and the only predecessors we can find in all antiquity. They have something the Pagans have not. They know something of which Socrates was ignorant. This Something does not seem to us to arise at all naturally from what else we can see of their character.

It looks like something that has been given them from outside; in fact, like what it professes to be, a revelation. Their claim to be the 'Chosen' people is strong.

We may, indeed, be surprised at the choice. If we had been allowed to see the world as it was, say, in the fifteenth century B.C., and asked to guess which of the stocks then existing was going to be entrusted with the consciousness of God and with the transmission of that blood which would one day produce a body for the incarnation of God Himself, I do not think many of us would have guessed right. (I think the Egyptians would have been my own favourite.)

A similar strangeness meets us elsewhere. The raw material out of which a thing is made is not always that which would seem most promising to one who does not understand the process. There is nothing hard, brittle, or transparent about the ingredients of glass. Again, to come nearer to the present matter, do not our own personal ancestors, our family, seem at first rather improbable? Later, as we begin to recognize the heredity that works in us, we understand. But surely not at first. What young man feels 'These are exactly the sort of people whose son (or grandson, or descendant) I might be expected to be' ? For usually, in early life, the people with whom one seems to have most in common, the people who share one's interests, the 'men of one's own totem', are not one's relatives, so that the idea of having been born into the wrong family is an attractive myth. (We are delighted when the hero, in *Siegfried,* forces the dwarf to confess that he is not his son.) The thing one is made out of is not necessarily like oneself (still less, like one's idea of that self) and looks at first even more unlike than it really is. It may be so with the origins of our species. The Evolutionists say we descend from 'anthropoids', creatures akin to apes. Is it (at first sight) the descent we would have chosen? If an intelligence such as ours had looked at the prehuman world and been told that one of the species then in existence was to be raised to rational and spiritual status and at last behold its Creator face to face, would he have picked the winner? Not unless it realized the importance of its hand-like paws; just as one would not guess the ingredients of glass unless one knew some chemistry. So we, because of something we do not know, are bewildered to find the ancient Hebrews 'chosen' as they were.

From this point of view there is no better psalm to begin with than No. 109. It ends with a verse which every Christian can at once make his own: the Lord is 'the prisoner's friend', standing by the poor (or friendless) to save him from unjust judges. This is one of the characteristic notes of the Psalms and one of the things for which we love them. It anticipates the temper of the *Magnificat*. It is hardly to be paralleled in Pagan literature (the Greek gods were very active in casting down the proud, but hardly in raising the humble). It will commend itself even to a modern unbeliever of good will; he may call it wishful thinking, but he will respect the wish. In a word, if we read only the last verse we should feel in full sympathy with this psalmist. But the moment we look back at what precedes that verse, he turns out to be removed from us by infinite distances; or, worse still, to be loathsomely akin to that in us which it is the main business of life to purge away. Psalm 109 is as unabashed a hymn of hate as was ever written. The poet has a detailed programme for his enemy which he hopes God will carry out. The enemy is to be placed under a wicked ruler. He is to have 'an accuser' perpetually at his side:

whether an evil spirit, a 'Satan', as our Prayer Book version renders it, or merely a human accuser—a spy, an *agent provocateur*, a member of the secret police (v. 5). If the enemy attempts to have any religious life, this, far from improving his position, must make him even worse: 'let his prayer be turned into sin' (v. 6). And after his death—which had better, please, be early (v. 7)—his widow and children and descendants are to live in unrelieved misery (vv. 8–12). What makes our blood run cold, even more than the unrestrained vindictiveness, is the writer's untroubled conscience. He has no qualms, scruples, or reservations; no shame. He gives hatred free rein—encourages and spurs it on—in a sort of ghastly innocence. He offers these feelings, just as they are, to God, never doubting that they will be acceptable: turning straight from the maledictions to 'Deal thou with me, O Lord God, according unto thy Name: for sweet is thy mercy' (v. 20).

The man himself, of course, lived very long ago. His injuries may have been (humanly speaking) beyond endurance. He was doubtless a hot-blooded barbarian, more like a modern child than a modern man. And though we believe (and can even see from the last verse) that some knowledge of the real God had come to his race, yet he lived in the cold of the year, the early spring of Revelation, and those first gleams of knowledge were like snow drops, exposed to the frosts. For him, then, there may have been excuses. But we—what good can we find in reading such stuff?

One good, certainly. We have here an uninhibited expression of those feelings which oppression and injustice naturally produce. The psalm is a portrait: under it should be written 'This is what you make of a man by ill-treating him.' In a modern child or savage the results might be exactly the same. In a modern, Western European adult—especially if he were a professing Christian—they would be more sophisticated; disguised as a disinterested love of justice, claiming to be concerned with the good of society. But under that disguise, and none the better for it in the sight of God, the feelings might still be there. (I am thinking of a total stranger who forwarded to me a letter written to her in denigration of myself by another total stranger, because, as she said, 'she felt it her duty'.) Now in a case of what we ordinarily call 'seduction' (that is, sexual seduction) we should think it monstrous to dwell on the guilt of the party who yielded to temptation and ignore that of the party who tempted. But every injury or oppression is equally a temptation, a temptation to hatred, and in that sense a seduction. Whenever we have wronged our fellow man, we have tempted him to be such a man as wrote Psalm 109. We may have repented of our wrong: we do not always know if he has repented of his hatred. How do accounts now stand between us if he has not?

I do not know the answer to that question. But I am inclined to think that we had better look unflinchingly at the sort of work we have done; like puppies, we must have 'our noses rubbed in it'. A man, now penitent, who has once seduced and abandoned a girl and then lost sight of her, had better not avert his eyes from the crude realities of the life she may now be living. For the same reason we ought to read the psalms that curse the oppressor; read them with fear. Who knows what imprecations of the same sort have been uttered against ourselves? What prayers have Red men, and Black, and Brown and Yellow, sent up against us to their gods or sometimes to God Himself? All over the earth the White Man's offence 'smells to heaven': massacres, broken treaties, theft, kidnappings, enslavement, deportation, floggings, lynchings, beatings-up, rape, insult, mockery, and odious hypocrisy make up that smell. But the thing comes nearer than that. Those of us who have little authority, who have few people at our mercy, may be thankful. But how if one is an officer in the army (or, perhaps worse, an N.C.O.)? a hospital matron? a magistrate? a prison-warden? a school prefect? a trade-union official? a Boss of any sort? in a word, anyone who cannot be 'answered back'? It is hard enough, even with the best will in the world, to be just. It is hard, under the pressure of haste, uneasiness, ill-temper, self-complacency, and conceit, even to continue intending justice. Power corrupts; the 'insolence of office' will creep in. We see it so clearly in our superiors; is it unlikely that our inferiors see it in us? How many of those who have been over us did not sometimes (perhaps often) need our forgiveness? Be sure that we likewise need the forgiveness of those that are under us.

We may not always receive it. They may not be Christians at all. They may not be far enough on the way to master that hard work of forgiveness which we have set them. Bitter, chronic resentment, unsuccessfully resisted or not resisted at all, may be burning against us: the spirit, essentially, of Psalm 109.

I do not mean that God hears and will grant such prayers as that psalmist uttered. They are wicked. He condemns them. All resentment is sin. And we may hope that those things which our inferiors resent were not really half so bad as they imagine. The snub was unintentional; the high-handed behaviour on the bench was due to ignorance and an uneasy awareness of one's own incapacity; the seemingly unfair distribution of work was not really unfair, or not intended to be; the inexplicable personal dislike for one particular inferior, so obvious to him and to some of his fellows, is something of which we are genuinely unconscious (it appears in our conscious mind as discipline, or the need for making an example). Anyway, it is very wicked of them to hate us. Yes; but the folly consists in supposing that God sees the wickedness in them apart from the wickedness in us which provoked it. They sin by hatred because we tempted them. We have, in that sense, seduced, debauched them. They are, as it were, the mothers of this hatred: we are the fathers.

It is from this point of view that the *Magnificat* is terrifying. If there are two things in the Bible which should make our blood run cold, it is one; the other is that phrase in Revelation, 'The wrath of the lamb'. If there is not mildness in the Virgin Mother, if even the lamb, the helpless thing that bleats and has its throat cut, is not the symbol of the harmless, where shall we turn? The resemblance between the *Magnificat* and traditional Hebrew poetry which I noted above is no mere literary curiosity. There is, of course, a difference. There are no cursings here, no hatred, no self-righteousness. Instead, there is mere statement. He has scattered the proud, cast down the mighty, sent the rich empty away. I spoke just now of the ironic contrast between the fierce psalmists and the choir-boy's treble. The contrast is here brought up to a higher level. Once more we have the treble voice, a girl's voice, announcing without sin that the sinful prayers of her ancestors do not remain entirely unheard; and doing this, not indeed with fierce exultation, yet—who can mistake the tone?— in a calm and terrible gladness.

I am tempted here to digress for a moment into a speculation which may bring ease to us in one direction while it alarms us in another. Christians are unhappily divided about the kind of honour in which the Mother of the Lord should be held, but there is one truth about which no doubt seems admissible. If we believe in the Virgin Birth and if we believe in Our Lord's human nature, psychological as well as physical (for it is heretical to think Him a human body which had the Second Person of the Trinity *instead of* a human soul) we must also believe in a human heredity for that human nature. There is only one source for it (though in that source all the true Israel is summed up). If there is an iron element in Jesus may we not without irreverence guess whence, humanly speaking, it came? Did neighbours say, in His boyhood, 'He's His Mother's Son'? This might set in a new and less painful light the severity of some things He said to, or about, His Mother. We may suppose that she understood them very well.

I have called this a digression, but I am not sure that it is one. Two things link the Psalms with us. One is the *Magnificat,* and one, Our Lord's continued quotations from them, though not, to be sure, from such Psalms as 109. We cannot reject from our minds a book in which His was so steeped. The Church herself has followed Him and steeped our minds in the same book.

In a word, the Psalmists and we are both in the Church. Individually they, like us, may be sometimes very bad members of it; tares, but tares that we have no authority to pull up. They may often be ignorant, as we (though perhaps in different ways) are ignorant, what spirit they are of. But we cannot excommunicate them, nor they us.

I do not at all mean (though if you watch, you will certainly find some critic who says I meant) that we are to make any concession to their ferocity. But we may learn to see the good thing which that ferocity is mixed with. Through all their excesses there runs a passionate craving for justice. One is tempted at first to say that such a craving, on the part of the oppressed, is no very great merit; that the wickedest men will cry out for fair play when you give them foul play. But unfortunately this is not true. Indeed at this very moment the spirit which cries for justice may be dying out.

Here is an alarming example. I had a pupil who was certainly a socialist, probably a Marxist. To him the 'collective', the State, was everything, the individual nothing; freedom, a bourgeois delusion. Then he went down and became a schoolmaster. A couple of years later, happening to be in Oxford, he paid me a visit. He said he had given up socialism. He was completely disillusioned about state-control. The interferences of the Ministry of Education with schools and schoolmasters were, he had found, arrogant, ignorant, and intolerable: sheer tyranny. I could take lots of this and the conversation went on merrily. Then suddenly the real purpose of his visit was revealed. He was so 'browned-off' that he wanted to give up school mastering; and could I—had I any influence—would I pull any wires to get him a job—*in the Ministry of Education*?

There you have the new man. Like the psalmists he can hate, but he does not, like the psalmists, thirst for justice. Having decided that there is oppression he immediately asks: 'How can I join the oppressors?' He has no objection to a world which is divided between tyrants and victims; the important thing is which of these two groups you are in. (The moral of the story remains the same whether you share his view about the Ministry or not.)

There is, then, mixed with the hatred in the psalmists. a spark which should be fanned, not trodden out. That spark God saw and fanned, till it burns clear in the *Magnificat*. The cry for 'judgement' was to be heard.

But the ancient Hebrew idea of 'judgement' will need an essay to itself.

II

The Day of Judgement is an idea very familiar, and very dreadful, to Christians. 'In all times of our tribulation, in all time of our wealth, in the hour of death, and in the day of judgement, Good Lord deliver us.' If there is any concept which cannot by any conjuring be removed from the teaching of Our Lord, it is that of the great separation; the sheep and the goats, the broad way and the narrow, the wheat and the tares, the winnowing fan, the wise and foolish virgins, the good fish and the refuse, the door closed on the marriage feast, with some inside and some outside in the dark. We may dare to hope—some dare to hope—that this is not the whole story, that, as Julian of Norwich said, 'All will be well and all manner of thing will be well.' But it is no use going to Our Lord's own words for that hope. Something we may get from St Paul: nothing, of that kind, from Jesus. It is from His own words that the picture of 'Doomsday' has come into Christianity.

One result of this is that the word 'judgement' in a religious context immediately suggests to us a criminal trial; the Judge on the bench, the accused in the dock, the hope of acquittal, the fear of conviction. But to the ancient Hebrews 'judgement' usually suggested something quite different.

In the Psalms judgement is not something that the conscience-stricken believer fears but something the downtrodden believer hopes for. God 'shall judge the world in righteousness' and 'be a defence for the oppressed' (ix, 8–9). 'Judge me, O Lord', cries the poet of Psalm 35. More surprisingly, in 67 even the 'nations', the Gentiles, are told to 'rejoice and be glad' because God will 'judge the folk righteously'. (Our fear is precisely lest the judgement should be a good deal more righteous than we can bear.) In the jubilant 96th Psalm the very sky and earth are to 'be glad', the fields are to 'be joyful' and all the trees of the wood 'shall rejoice before the Lord' because 'He cometh to judge the earth'. At the prospect of that judgement which we dread there is such revelry as a Pagan poet might have used to herald the coming of Dionysus.

Though our Lord, as I have said, imposed on us the modern, Christian conception of the Day of Judgement, yet His own words elsewhere illuminate the old Hebraic conception. I am thinking of the Unjust Judge in the parable. To most of us, unless we had that parable in mind, the mention of a wicked judge would instantly suggest someone like Judge Jeffries: a roaring, interrupting, bloodthirsty brute, bent on hanging a prisoner, bullying the jury and the witnesses. Our hope is that we shall *not* be judged by him. Our Lord's Unjust Judge is a wholly different character. You want him to judge you, you pester him to judge you. The whole difficulty is to get your case heard. Obviously what Our Lord has in view is not a criminal trial at all but a civil trial. We are looking at 'justice' from the point of view not of a prisoner but of a plaintiff: a plaintiff with a watertight case, if only she could get the defendant into court.

The picture is strange to us only because we enjoy in our own country an un-usually good legal profession. We take it for granted that judges do not need to be bribed and cannot be bribed. This is, however, no law of nature, but a rare achieve-ment; we ourselves might lose it (shall certainly lose it if no pains are taken for its conservation); it does not inevitably go with the use of the English language. Over many parts of the world and in many periods the difficulty for poor and unimpor-tant people has been not only to get their case fairly heard but to get it heard at all. It is their voices that speak in the continual hope of the Hebrews for 'judgement', the hope that some day, somehow, wrongs will be righted.

But the idea is not associated only with courts of law. The 'Judges' who give their name to a most interesting historical book in the Old Testament were not, I gather, so called only because they sometimes exercised what we should consider judicial functions. Indeed the book has very little to say about 'judging' in that sense. Its 'judges' are primarily heroes, fighting men, who deliver Israel from foreign tyrants: giant-killers. The name which we translate as 'judges' is apparently connected with a verb which means to vindicate, to avenge, to right the wrongs of. They might equally well be called champions, avengers. The knight errant of medieval romance who spends his days liberating, and securing justice for, distressed damsels, would almost have been, for the Hebrews, a 'judge'.

Such a Judge—He who will at last do us right, the deliverer, the protector, the queller of tyrants—is the dominant image in the Psalms. There are, indeed, some few passages in which a psalmist thinks of 'judgement' with trembling: 'Enter not into judgement with thy servant: for in thy sight shall no man living be justified' (143, 2), or 'If thou, Lord, wilt be extreme to mark what is done amiss: O Lord, who may abide it?' (130, 3). But the opposite attitude is far commoner: 'Hear the right, O Lord' (17, 1), 'Be thou my Judge' (26, 1), 'Plead thou my cause' (35, 1), 'Give sen-tence with me, O God' (43, 1), 'Arise, thou Judge of the world' (94, 2). It is for jus-tice, for a hearing, far more often than for pardon, that the psalmists pray.

We thus reach a very paradoxical generalization. Ordinarily, and of course cor-rectly, the Jewish and the Christian church, the reign of Moses and the reign of Christ, are contrasted as Law against Grace, justice against mercy, rigour against tenderness. Yet apparently those who live under the sterner dispensation hope for God's judgement while those who live under the milder fear it. How does this come about? The answer, by and large, will be plain to all who have read the Psalms with attention. The psalmists, with very few exceptions, are eager for judgement because they believe themselves to be wholly in the right. Others have sinned against them; their own conduct (as they frequently assure us) has been impeccable. They ear-nestly invite the divine inspection, certain that they will emerge from it with flying colours. The adversary may have things to hide, but they have not. The more God examines their case, the more unanswerable it will appear. The Christian, on the other hand, trembles because he knows he is a sinner.

Thus in one sense we might say that Jewish confidence in the face of judgement is a by-product of Jewish self-righteousness. But that is far too summary. We must consider the whole experience out of which the self-righteous utterances grow: and secondly, what, on a deeper level, those utterances really mean.

The experience is dark and dreadful. We must not call it the 'dark night of the soul' for that name is already appropriate to another darkness and another dread, encountered at a far higher level than (I suppose) any of the psalmists had reached. But we may well call it the Dark Night of the Flesh, understanding by 'the flesh' the natural man. For the experience is not in itself necessarily religious and thousands of unbelievers undergo it in our own time. It arises from natural causes; but it becomes religious in the psalmists because they are religious men.

It must be confessed at the outset that all those passages which paint this Dark Night can be regarded, if we wish, as the expressions of a neurosis. If we choose to maintain that several psalmists wrote in, or on the verge of, a nervous breakdown, our theory will cover all the facts. That is, the psalmists assert as true about their own situation all those things which a patient, in a certain neurotic condition, wrongly believes to be true of his. For our present purpose, I think this does not matter much. Neurosis is a thing that occurs; we may have passed, or may yet have to pass, through that valley. It concerns us to see how certain believers in God behaved in it before us. And neurosis is, after all, a relative term. Who can say that he never touches the fringes of it? Even if the Psalms were written by neurotics, that will not make them wholly irrelevant.

But of course we cannot be at all sure that they were. The neurotic wrongly believes that he is threatened by certain evils. But another man (or the neurotic himself at another time) may be really threatened with those same evils. It may be only the patient's nerves that make him so sure that he has cancer, or is financially ruined, or is going to hell; but this does not prove that there are no such things as cancer or bankruptcy or damnation. To suggest that the situation described in certain psalms must be imaginary seems to me to be wishful thinking. The situation does occur in real life. If anyone doubts this let him consider, while I try to present this Dark Night of the Flesh, how easily it might be, not the subjective impression, but the real situation of any one of the following:

1. A small, ugly, unathletic, unpopular boy in his second term at a thoroughly bad English public school. 2. An unpopular recruit in an army hut. 3. A Jew in Hitler's Germany. 4. A man in a bad firm or government office whom a group of rivals are trying to get rid of. 5. A Papist in sixteenth-century England. 6. A Protestant in sixteenth-century Spain. 7. An African in Malan's Africa. 8. An American socialist in the hands of Senator McCarthy or a Zulu, noxious to Chaka, during one of the old, savage witch-hunts.

The Dark Night of the Flesh can be objective; it is not even very uncommon.

One is alone. The fellow-recruit who seemed to be a friend on the first day, the boys who were your friends last term, the neighbours who were your friends before the Jew-baiting began (or before you attracted Senator McCarthy's attention), even your connections and relatives, have begun to give you a wide berth. No one wishes to be seen with you. When you pass acquaintances in the street they always happen to be looking the other way. 'They of mine acquaintance were afraid of me; and they that did see me without conveyed themselves from me' (31, 13). Lovers, neighbours, kinsmen stand 'afar off' (38, 11). 'I am become a stranger unto my brethren' (69, 8). 'Thou hast put away mine acquaintance far from me: and made me to be abhorred of them' (88, 7). 'I looked also upon my right hand and saw there was no man that would know me' (142, 4).

Sometimes it is not an individual but a group (a religious body or even a whole nation) that has this experience. Members fall off; allies desert; the huge combinations against us extend and harden daily. Harder even to bear than our dwindling numbers and growing isolation, is the increasing evidence that 'our side' is ineffective. The world is turned upside down by bad men and 'What hath the righteous done?', where are our counter-measures? (11, 3). We are 'put to rebuke' (12, 9). Once there were omens in our favour and great leaders on our side. But those days are gone: 'We see not our tokens, there is not one prophet more' (74, 10). England in modern Europe and Christians in modern England often feel like this.

And all round the isolated man, every day, is the presence of the unbelievers. They know well enough what we are believing or trying to believe ('help thou my unbelief') and regard it as total illusion. 'Many one there be that say of my soul, There is no help for him in his God' (3, 2). As if God, supposing He exists, had nothing to do but look after *us*! (10, 14); but in fact, 'There is no God' (14, 1). If the sufferer's God really exists 'let Him deliver him' now! (22, 8). 'Where is now thy God?' (42, 3).

The man in the Dark Night of the Flesh is in everyone else's eyes extremely funny; the stock joke of that whole school or hut or office. They can't see him without laughing: they make faces at him (22, 7). The drunks work his name into their comic songs (69, 12). He is a 'by-word' (44, 15). Unfortunately all this laughter is not exactly honest, spontaneous laughter such as a man with some oddity of voice or face might learn to bear and even, in the end, to join in. These mockers do not laugh *although* it hurts him nor even without caring whether it hurts or not; they laugh *because* it will hurt. Any humiliation or miscarriage of his is jam to them; they crow over him when he's down—'when my foot slipped, they rejoiced greatly against me' (38, 16).

If one had a certain sort of aristocratic and Stoic pride one might perhaps answer scorn with scorn and even (in a sense) rejoice, as Coventry Patmore rejoiced, to live 'in the high mountain air of public obloquy'. If so, one would not be completely in the Dark Night. But the sufferer, for better or worse, is not—or if he once was, is now no longer—that sort of man. The continual taunts, slights, and humiliations (partly veiled or brutally plain according to the *milieu*) get past his defences and under his skin. He is in his own eyes also the object they would make him. He has no come-back. Shame has covered his face (69, 7). He might as well be a dumb man; in his mouth are no reproofs (38, 13). He is 'a worm and no man' (22, 6).

The Language of Religion

I HAVE BEEN asked to talk about religious language and the gist of what I have to say is that, in my opinion, there is no specifically religious language. I admit of course that some things said by religious people can't be treated exactly as we treat scientific statements. But I don't think that is because they are specimens of some special language. It would be truer to say that the scientific statements are in a special language. The language of religion, which we may presently have to distinguish from that of theology, seems to me to be, on the whole, either the same sort we use in ordinary conversation or the same sort we use in poetry, or somewhere between the two. In order to make this clearer, I am afraid I must turn away from the professed subject of my paper for some time and talk about language.

I begin with three sentences (1) It was very cold (2) There were 13 degrees of frost (3) 'Ah, bitter chill it was! The owl, for all his feathers was a-cold; The hare limped trembling through the frozen grass, And silent was the flock in woolly fold: Numb'd were the Beadsman's fingers.' I should describe the first as Ordinary language, the second as Scientific language, and the third as Poetic language. Of course there is no question here of different languages in the sense in which Latin and Chinese are different languages. Two and three are improved uses of the same language used in one. Scientific and Poetic language are two different artificial perfections of Ordinary: artificial, because they depend on skills; different, because they improve Ordinary in two different directions. Notice also that Ordinary could advance a little towards either so that you could pass by degrees into Scientific or Poetic. For 'very cold' you could substitute 'freezing hard' and, for 'freezing hard', 'freezing harder than last night'. That would be getting nearer to the Scientific. On the other hand you could say 'bitterly cold' and then you would be getting nearer the Poetic. In fact you would have anticipated one of the terms used in Keats's description.

The superiority of the Scientific description clearly consists in giving for the coldness of the night a precise quantitative estimate which can be tested by an instrument. The test ends all disputes. If the statement survives the test, then various inferences can be drawn from it with certainty: e.g., various effects on vegetable and animal life can be predicted. It is therefore of use in what Bacon calls 'operation'. We can take action on it. On the other hand it does not, of itself, give us any information about the quality of a cold night, does not tell us what we shall be feeling if we go out of doors. If, having lived all our lives in the tropics, we didn't know what a hard frost was like, the thermometer reading would not of itself inform us. Ordinary language would do that better—'Your ears will ache'—'You'll lose the feeling in your fingers'—'You'll feel as if your ears were coming off.' If I could tell you (which unhappily I can't) the temperature of the coldest water I ever bathed in, it would convey the reality only to the few who had bathed in many temperatures and taken thermometer readings of them. When I tell you 'It was so cold that at first it felt like scalding hot water', I think you will get a better idea of it. And where a scientific statement could draw on no experience at all, like statements about optics made to a student born blind, then, though it might retain its proper virtues of precision, verifiability, and use in operation, it would in one sense convey nothing. Only in one sense, of course. The blind student could, presumably, draw inferences from it and use it to gain further knowledge.

I now turn to the Poetic. Its superiority to Ordinary language is, I am afraid, a much more troublesome affair. I feel fairly sure what it does not consist in: it does not consist either in discharging or arousing more emotion. It may often do one of these things or both, but I don't think that is its *differentia*. I don't think our bit of Keats differs from the Ordinary 'It was very cold' primarily or solely by getting off Keats's chest more dislike of cold nights, nor by arousing more dislike in me. There is, no doubt, some mere 'getting off the chest' in the exclamation 'Ah' and the catachresis 'bitter'. Personally, I don't feel the emotion to be either Keats's or mine. It is for me the imagined people in the story who are saying 'Ah' and 'bitter'; not with the result of making me share their discomfort, but of making me imagine how very cold it was. And the rest is all taken up with pictures of what might have been observed on such a night. The invitation is not to my emotions but to my senses. Keats seems to me to be simply conveying the quality of a cold night, and not imposing any emotions on me (except of course the emotion of pleasure at finding anything vividly conveyed to the imagination). He is in fact giving me all that concrete, qualitative information which the Scientific statement leaves out. But then, of course, he is not verifiable, nor precise, nor of much use for operation.

We must not, however, base our view on a single passage, which may have been unfairly chosen. Let us begin at quite another point. One of the most obvious differences between all the poetry I have ever read and all the straight prose (I say 'straight' to exclude prose which verges on the poetic) is this simple one, hardly ever stated: the poetry contains a great many more adjectives. This is perfectly obvious. From Homer, who never omits to tell us that the ships were black and the sea salt, or even wet, down to Eliot with his 'hollow valley' and 'multi-foliate rose', they all do it. Poets are always telling us that grass is green, or thunder loud, or lips red. It is not, except in bad poets, always telling us that things are shocking or delightful. It does not, in that direct way, attempt to discharge or excite emotion. On the contrary, it seems anxious to bombard us with masses of factual information which we might, on a prose view, regard as irrelevant or platitudinous.

[Here pages 4 and 5 of the manuscript are missing. Page 6 begins as follows :]

[In order to] discharge an emotion it is not necessary that we should make it clear to any audience. By 'expression' I mean that sort of utterance which will make clear to others how we are feeling. There are, of course, any number of intermediate stages between discharge and expression: but perfect expression in the presence of the perfect hearer would enable him to know exactly how you were feeling. To what extent this involves arousing the same emotion, or a replica of it in him—in other words, to what extent the perfect expression would be emotive—I don't know. But I think that to respond to expression is in principle different from having an emotion aroused in one, even though the arousing of some sort of phantom emotion may always be involved. There seems to me to be a difference between understanding another person's fear because he has expressed it well and being actually *infected* by his fear as so often happens. Or again, there seems to be a difference between understanding the feelings of Shakespeare's Troilus before his assignation and being infected by similar feelings, as the writer of pornography intends to infect us.

But the really important point is the third[1] one. Even if Poetic language often expresses emotion and thereby (to some undefined extent) arouses emotion, it does not follow that the expression of emotion is always its sole, or even its chief function. For even in Ordinary language one of the best ways of describing something is to tell what reactions it provoked in us. If a man says, 'They kept their rooms terribly over-heated. Before I'd been in there five minutes, I was dripping', he is usually not concerned, as an end in itself, with giving us autobiographical fact that he perspired. He wants to make us realize how hot it was. And he takes the right way. Indeed in the last resort there is hardly any other way. To say that things were blue, or hard, or cool, or foul-smelling, or noisy, is to tell how they affected our senses. To say that someone is a bore, or a decent chap, or revolting, is to tell how he affected our emotions. In the same way, I think that Poetic language often expresses emotion not for its own sake but in order to inform us about the object which aroused the emotion. Certainly it seems to me to give us such information. Burns tells us that a woman is like a red, red rose, and Wordsworth that another woman is like a violet by a mossy stone half hidden from the eye. Now of course the one woman resembles a rose, and the other a half-hidden violet, not in size, weight, shape, colour, anatomy, or intelligence, but by arousing emotions in some way analogous to those which the flowers would arouse. But then we know quite well what sort of women (and how different from each other) they must have been to do so. The two statements do not in the least reduce to mere expressions of admiration. They tell us what kind of admiration and therefore what kind of woman. They are even, in their own proper way, verifiable or falsifiable: having seen the two women we might say 'I see what he meant in comparing her to a rose' and 'I see what he meant in comparing her to a violet', or might decide that the comparisons were bad. I am not of course denying that there are other love poems (some of Wyatt's, for example) where the poet is wholly concerned with his own emotions and we get no impression of the woman at all. I deny that this is the universal rule.

Finally we have those instances where Poetic language expresses an experience which is not accessible to us in normal life at all, an experience which the poet himself may have imagined and not, in the ordinary sense, 'had'. An instance would be when Asia, in *Prometheus Unbound,* says 'My soul is an enchanted boat.' If anyone thinks this is only a more musical and graceful way of saying 'Gee! this is fine', I disagree with him. An enchanted boat moves without oar or sail to its destined haven. Asia is at that moment undergoing a process of transfiguration, almost of

[1. Apparently referring to an enumeration of points Lewis made in the missing pages.]

apotheosis. Effortless and unimpeded movement to a goal desired but not yet seen is the point. If we were experiencing Asia's apotheosis we should feel like that. In fact we have never experienced apotheosis. Nor, probably, has Shelley. But to communicate the emotion which would accompany it is to make us know more fully than before what we meant by apotheosis.

This is the most remarkable of the powers of Poetic language: to convey to us the quality of experiences which we have not had, or perhaps can never have, to use factors within our experience so that they become pointers to something outside our experience—as two or more roads on a map show us where a town that is off the map must lie. Many of us have never had an experience like that which Wordsworth records near the end of *Prelude* XIII; but when he speaks of 'the visionary dreariness' I think we get an inkling of it. Other examples would be (for me) Marvell's 'green thought in a green shade', and (for everyone) Pope's 'die of a rose in aromatic pain'. Perhaps the most astonishing is in the *Paradiso* where Dante says that as he rose from one sphere of the Ptolemaic universe to the next, he knew that he had risen only by finding that he was moving forward more quickly.[1]

It must be remembered that I have been speaking simply of Poetic language not of poetry. Poetry of course has other characteristics besides its language. One of them is that it is very often fiction; it tells about people who never really lived and events that never really took place. Hence Plato's jibe that the poets are liars. But surely it would be a great confusion to attach the note of fiction to every specimen of Poetic *language*. You just can't tell whether Keats's description is of a winter night that really occurred or of one he imagined. The use of language in conveying the quality of a real place, a person, or thing is the same we should need to convey the quality of a feigned one.

My long, and perhaps tedious, digression on Poetic language is now almost at an end. My conclusion is that such language is by no means merely an expression, nor a stimulant, of emotion, but a real medium of information. Which information may, like any other, be true or false: true as Mr Young[2] on weirs, or false as the bit in *Beowulf* about the dragon sniffing along the path. It often does stimulate emotion, by expressing emotion, but usually in order to show us the object to which such emotion would be the response. A poet, Mr Robert Conquest, has put something like my view:

Observation of real events includes the observer, 'heart' and all;
(The common measurable features are obtained by omitting this part.)
But there is also a common aspect in the emotional
Shared by other members of the species; this is conveyed by 'art'.

The poem combines all these . . .[3]

[1. I cannot find this in the *Paradiso*. It may be, however, a conflation of several passages. See *Paradiso* viii, 13; x, 35; and xiv, 85.]
[2. Lewis is referring, I believe, to the Rev Canon Andrew Young, whose poems, he felt, were something like a combination of Wordsworth and Marvell. An interesting reference to 'weirs' is found in Young's poem, 'The Slow Race'. For discussion on other possibilities see my letter, 'A C. S. Lewis Mystery', *The Spectator* (28 October 1966), p. 546.]
[3. 'Excerpts from a Report to the Galactic Council', *The Listener*, vol. LII (14 October 1954), p. 612.]

Because events, as real events 'really' are and feigned events would 'really' be if they occurred, cannot be conveyed without bringing in the observer's heart and the common emotional reaction of the species, it has been falsely concluded that poetry represented the heart for its own sake, and nothing but the heart.

But I must not go too far. I think Poetic language does convey information, but it suffers from two disabilities in comparison with Scientific. (1) It is verifiable or falsifiable only to a limited degree and with a certain fringe of vagueness. Not all men, only men of some discrimination, would agree, on seeing Burn's mistress that the image of 'a red, red rose' was good, or (as might be) bad. In that sense, Scientific statements are, as people say now, far more easily 'cashed'. But the poet might of course reply that it always will be easier to cash a cheque for 30 shillings than one for 1,000 pounds, that the scientific statements are cheques, in one sense, for very small amounts, giving us, out of the teeming complexity of every concrete reality only 'the common measurable features'. (2) Such information as Poetic language has to give can be received only if you are ready to meet it half-way. It is no good holding a dialectical pistol to the poet's head and demanding how the deuce a river could have hair, or thought be green, or a woman a red rose. You may win, in the sense of putting him to a *non-plus*. But if he had anything to tell you, you will never get it by behaving in that way. You must begin by trusting him. Only by so doing will you find out whether he is trustworthy or not. *Credo ut intelligam* (it is time some theological expression came in) is here the only attitude.

Now, as I see it, the language in which we express our religious beliefs and other religious experiences, is not a special language, but something that ranges between the Ordinary and the Poetical. But even when it begins by being Ordinary, it can usually, under dialectical pressure, be found to become either Theological or Poetical. An example will best show what I mean by this trichotomy. I think the words 'I believe in God' are Ordinary language. If you press us by asking what we mean, we shall probably have to move in one of two directions. We might say 'I believe in incorporeal entity, personal in the sense that it can be the subject and object of love, on which all other entities are unilaterally dependent.' That is what I call Theological language, though far from a first-class specimen of it. In it we are attempting, so far as is possible, to state religious matter in a form more like that we use for scientific matter. This is often necessary, for purposes of instruction, clarification, controversy and the like. But it is not the language religion naturally speaks. We are applying precise, and therefore abstract, terms to what for us is the supreme example of the concrete. If we do not always feel this fully, that, I think, is because nearly all who say or read such sentences (including unbelievers) really put into them much that they know from other sources—tradition, literature, etc. But for that, it would hardly be more information than 'There are 15 degrees of frost' would be to those who had never experienced frost.

And this is one of the great disadvantages under which the Christian apologist labours. Apologetics is controversy. You cannot conduct a controversy in those poetical expressions which alone convey the concrete: you must use terms as definable and univocal as possible, and these are always abstract. And this means that the thing we are really talking about can never appear in the discussion at all.

We have to try to prove *that* God is in circumstances where we are denied every means of conveying *who* God is. It is faintly parallel to the state of a witness who has to try to convey something so concrete as the known character of a friend under cross-examination. Under other conditions he might possibly succeed in giving you a real impression of him; but not under hostile cross-examination. You remember Hamlet's speech to Horatio, 'Horatio thou art e'en as just a man', etc. But you could never have had it in a witness-box.

That, then, is one way in which we could go on from 'I believe in God'—the Theological: in a sense, alien to religion, crippling, omitting nearly all that really matters, yet, in spite of everything, sometimes successful.

On the other hand, you could go on, following the spontaneous tendency of religion, into poetical language. Asked what you meant by God, you might say 'God is love' or 'the Father of lights', or even 'underneath are the everlasting arms'. From what has gone before, you will understand that I do not regard these poetical expressions as merely expressions of emotion. They will of course express emotion in any who utters them, and arouse emotion in any who hears them with belief. But so would the sentence 'Fifty Russian divisions landed in the South of England this morning.' Momentous matter, if believed, will arouse emotion whatever the language. Further, these statements make use of emotion, as Burns makes use of our emotions about roses. All this is, in my view, consistent with their being essentially informative. But, of course, informative only to those who will meet them half way.

The necessity for such poetic expressions is closely connected with the grounds on which they are believed. They are usually two: authority, and religious experience.

Christians believe that Jesus Christ is the Son of God because He said so. The other evidence about Him has convinced them that He was neither a lunatic nor a quack. Now of course the statement cannot mean that He stands to God in the very same physical and temporal relation which exists between offspring and male parent in the animal world. It is then a poetical statement. And such expression must here be necessary because the reality He spoke of is outside our experience. And here once more the religious and the theological procedure diverge. The theologian will describe it as 'analogical', drawing our minds at once away from the subtle and sensitive exploitations of imagination and emotion with which poetry works to the clear-cut but clumsy analogies of the lecture-room. He will even explain in what respects the father-son relationship is *not* analogical to the reality, hoping by elimination to reach the respects in which it is. He may even supply other analogies of his own—the lamp and the light which flows from it, or the like. It is all unavoidable and necessary for certain purposes. But there is some death in it. The sentence 'Jesus Christ is the Son of God' cannot be all got into the form 'There is between Jesus and God an asymmetrical, social, harmonious relation involving homogeneity.' Religion takes it differently. A man who is both a good son and a good father, and who is continually urged to become a better son and a better father by meditation on the Divine Fatherhood and Sonship, and who thus comes in the end to make that Divine relation the norm to which his own human sonship and fatherhood are still merely analogical, is best receiving the revelation. It would be idle to tell such a man that the formula 'is the Son of God' tells us (what is almost zero) that an unknown X is in an unknown respect 'like' the relation of father and son. He has met it half way. Information has been given him: as far as I can see, in the only way possible.

Secondly, there is religious experience, ranging from the most ordinary experiences of the believer in worship, forgiveness, dereliction, and divine help, up to the highly special experiences of the mystics. Through such experience Christians believe that they get a sort of verification (or perhaps sometimes falsification) of their tenets. Such experience cannot be conveyed to one another, much less to unbelievers, except by language which shares to some extent the nature of Poetic language. That is what leads some people to suppose that it can be nothing but emotion. For of course, if you accept the view that Poetic language is purely emotional, then things which can be expressed only in Poetic language will presumably be emotions. But if we don't equate Poetic language with emotional language, the question is still open.

Now it seems to me a mistake to think that our experience in general can be communicated by precise and literal language and that there is a special class of experiences (say, emotions) which cannot. The truth seems to me the opposite: there is a special region of experiences which can be communicated *without* Poetic language, namely, its 'common measurable features', but most experience cannot. To be incommunicable by Scientific language is, so far as I can judge, the normal state of experience. All our sensuous experience is in this condition, though this is somewhat veiled from us by the fact that much of it is very common and therefore everyone will understand our references to it at a hint. But if you have to describe to a doctor any unusual sensation, you will soon find yourself driven to use pointers of the same nature (essentially) as Asia's enchanted boat. An army doctor who suspected you of malingering would soon reduce you to halting and contradictory statements; but if by chance you had not been malingering he would have cut himself off from all knowledge of what might have turned out an interesting case.

But are there, as I have claimed, other experiences besides sensation (and, of course, emotion) which are in this predicament? I think there are. But, frankly, I am now getting into very deep water indeed. I am almost sure I shall fail to make myself clear, but the attempt must be made.

It seems to me that imagining is something other than having mental images. When I am imagining (say, Hamlet on the battlements or Herackles' journey to the Hyperboreans) there are images in my mind. They come and go rapidly and assist what I regard as the real imagining only if I take them all as provisional make-shifts, each to be dropped as soon as it has served its (instantaneous) turn. If any one of them becomes static and grows too clear and full, imagination proper is inhibited. A too lively visual imagination is the reader's, and writer's, bane; as toys, too elaborate and realistic, spoil children's play. They are, in the etymological sense, the *offal* (the off-fall) of imagination: the slag from the furnace. Again, thinking seems to me something other than the succession of linked concepts which we use when we successfully offer our 'thought' to another in argument. That appears to me to be always a sort of translation of a prior activity: and it was the prior activity which alone enabled us to find these concepts and links. The possibility of finding them may be a good test of the value of that previous activity; certainly the only test we have. It would be dangerous to indulge ourselves with the fancy of having valuable profundities within us which (unfortunately) we can't get out. But, perhaps, in others, where we are neutrals, we are sometimes not quite wrong in thinking that a sensible man, unversed in argument, has thought better than his mishandling of his own case suggests. If we lend him a helping hand and he replies 'Of course! That's it. That is what I really meant to say', he is not always a hypocrite. Finally, in all our joys and sorrows, religious, aesthetic, or natural, I seem to find things (almost indescribably) thus. They are *about* something. They are a by-product of the (logically) prior act of *attending to* or *looking towards* something.[1] We are not really concerned with the emotions: the emotions *are* our concern about something else. Suppose that a mother is anxious about her son who is on active service. It is no use going to her with the offer of some drug or hypnotism or spell that would obliterate her anxiety. What she wants is not the cessation of anxiety but the safety of her son (I mean, on the whole. On one particular wakeful night, she might, no doubt, be glad of your magic). Nor is it any use offering her a magic which would prevent her from feeling any grief if her son were killed: what she dreads is not grief but the death of her son. Similarly, it is no use offering me a drug which will give me over again the feelings I had on first hearing the overture *to The Magic Flute.* The feelings, by themselves—the flutter in the diaphragm—are of very mediocre interest to me. What gave them their value was the thing they were about. So in our Christian experiences. No doubt we experience sorrow when we repent and joy when we adore. But these were by-products of our attention to a particular Object.

If I have made myself at all clear (but I probably have not) you see what, for me, it adds up to. The very essence of our life as conscious beings, all day and every day, consists of something which cannot be communicated except by hints, similes, metaphors, and the use of those emotions (themselves not very important) which are pointers to it. I am not in the least talking about the Unconscious as psychologists understand it. At least, though it cannot be fully introspected, this region is, in many of us, very far from unconscious. I say 'in many of us'. But I sometimes wonder whether we may not be survivals. Evolution may not have ceased; and in evolution a species may lose old powers as well as acquire—possibly in order to acquire—new ones. There seem to be people about to whom imagination means only the presence of mental images (not to mention those like Professor Ryle who deny even that); to whom thought means only unuttered speech; and to whom emotions are final, as distinct from the things they are about. If this is so, and if they increase, then all real communications between them and the earlier type of man will finally be impossible.

Something like this may be happening. You remember Wells's *Country of the Blind.* Now its inhabitants, being men, must have descended from ancestors who could see. During centuries a gradual atrophy of sight must have spread through the whole race; but at no given moment, till it was complete, would it (probably)

---

1. *Looking towards* is neither more nor less metaphorical than *attending to.*

have been equally advanced in all individuals. During this intermediate period a very interesting linguistic situation would have arisen. They would have inherited from their unblind ancestors all the visual vocabulary—the names of the colours, words like 'see' and 'look' and 'dark' and 'light'. There would be some who still used them in the same sense as ourselves: archaic types who saw the green grass and perceived the light coming at dawn. There would be others who had faint vestiges of sight, and who used these words, with increasing vagueness, to describe sensations so evanescent as to be incapable of clear discrimination. (The moment at which they begin to think of them as sensations in their own eyeballs, not as externals, would mark an important step.) And there would be a third class who has achieved full blindness, to whom *see* was merely a synonym for *understand* and *dark* for *difficult*. And these would be the vanguard, and the future would be with them, and a very little cross-examination of the archaic type that still saw would convince them that its attempt to give some other meaning to the old visual words was merely a tissue of vague, emotive uses and category mistakes. This would be as clear to them as it is clear to many modern people that Job's words 'But now mine eye hath seen thee: wherefore I abhor myself and repent in dust and ashes' are, and can be, nothing but the expression of an emotion.[1]

As I say, this sometimes crosses my mind. But I am full of doubts about the whole subject, and everything I have said is merely tentative. Perhaps I should also point out that it is not apologetics. I have not tried to prove that the religious sayings are true, only that they are significant: if you meet them with a certain good will, a certain readiness to find meaning. For if they should happen to contain information about real things, you will not get it on any other terms. As for proof, I sometimes wonder whether the Ontological Argument did not itself arise as a partially unsuccessful translation of an experience without concepts or words. I don't think we can initially argue from the *concept* of Perfect Being to its existence. But did they really, inside, argue from the experienced glory that it could not be generated subjectively?

[1. An interesting variation of this same theme is found in Lewis's poem, 'The Country of the Blind', *Poems*, ed. Walter Hooper, (Bles, 1964), pp. 33–34.]

Petitionary Prayer:
A Problem Without an Answer

THE PROBLEM I am submitting to you arises not about prayer in general but only about that kind of prayer which consists of request or petition. I hope no one will think that he is helping to solve my problem by reminding me that there are many other and perhaps higher sorts of prayer. I agree that there are. I here confine myself to petitionary prayer not because I think it the only, or the best, or the most characteristic, form of prayer, but because it is the form which raises the problem. However low a place we may decide to give it in the life of prayer, we must give it some place, unless we are prepared to reject both Our Lord's precept in telling us to pray for our daily bread and His practice in praying that the cup might pass from Him. And as long as it holds any place at all, I have to consider my problem.

Let me make clear at once where that problem does not lie. I am not at all concerned with the difficulty which unbelievers sometimes raise about the whole conception of petitioning God, on the ground that absolute wisdom cannot need to be informed of our desires, or that absolute goodness cannot need to be prompted to beneficence, or that the immutable and impassible cannot be affected by us, cannot be to us as patient to agent. All these difficulties are, no doubt, well worth most serious discussion, but I do not propose to discuss them here. Still less am I asking why petitions, and even the fervent petitions of holy men, are sometimes not granted. That has never seemed to me to be, in principle, a difficulty at all. That wisdom must sometimes refuse what ignorance may quite innocently ask seems to be self-evident.

My problem arises from one fact and one only; the fact that Christian teaching seems at first sight to contain two different patterns of petitionary prayer which are inconsistent: perhaps inconsistent in their theological implications, but much more obviously and pressingly inconsistent in the practical sense that no man, so far as I can see, could possibly follow them both at the same moment. I shall call them the A Pattern and the B Pattern.

The A Pattern is given in the prayer which Our Lord Himself taught us. The clause 'Thy will be done' by its very nature must modify the sense in which the following petitions are made. Under the shadow—or perhaps I should rather say, in the light—of that great submission nothing can be asked save conditionally, save in so far as the granting of it may be in accordance with God's will. I do not of course mean that the words 'Thy will be done' are merely a submission. They should, and if we make progress they will increasingly, be the voice of joyful desire, free of hunger and thirst, and I argue very heartily that to treat them simply as a clause of submission or renunciation greatly impoverishes the prayer. But though they should be something far more and better than resigned or submissive, they must not be less: they must be that *at least.* And as such they necessarily discipline all the succeeding clauses. The other specimen of the A Pattern comes from Our Lord's own example in Gethsemane. A particular event is asked for with the reservation, 'Nevertheless, not my will but thine.'

It would seem from these passages that we are directed both by Our Lord's command and by His example to make all our petitionary prayers in this conditional form; well aware that God in His wisdom may not see fit to give us what we ask and submitting our wills in advance to a possible refusal which, if it meets us, we shall know to be wholly just, merciful, and salutary. And this, I suppose, is how most of us do try to pray and how most spiritual teachers tell us to pray. With this pattern of prayer—the A Pattern—I myself would be wholly content. It is in accordance both with my heart and my head. It presents no theoretical difficulties. No doubt my rebellious will and my turbulent hopes and fears will find plenty of practical difficulty in following it. But as far as my intellect goes it is all easy. The road may be hard but the map is clear.

You will notice that in the A Pattern, whatever faith the petitioner has in the existence, the goodness, and the wisdom of God, what he obviously, even as it were by definition, has not got is a sure and unwavering belief that God will give him the particular thing he asks for. When Our Lord in Gethsemane asks that the cup may be withdrawn His words, far from implying a certainty or even a strong expectation that it will in fact be withdrawn, imply the possibility that it will not be; a possibility, or even a probability, so fully envisaged that a preparatory submission to that event is already being made.

We need not, so far as I can see, here concern ourselves with any special problems raised by the unique and holy Person of Him who prayed. It is enough to point out that if we are expected to imitate Him in our prayers, then, though we are doubtless to pray with faith in one sense, we are not to pray with any assurance that we shall receive what we ask. For real assurance that we shall receive it seems to be incompatible with the act of preparing ourselves for a denial. Men do not prepare for an event which they think impossible. And unless we think refusal impossible, how can we believe granting to be certain?

And, once again, if this were the only pattern of prayer, I should be quite content. If the faith which is demanded of us were always a faith in the goodness of God, a faith that whether granting or denying He equally gave us the best, and never a faith that He would give precisely what we ask, I should have no problem. Indeed, such a submissive faith would seem to me, if I were left to my own thoughts, far better than any confidence that our own necessarily ignorant petitions would prevail. I should be thankful that we were safe from that cruel mercy which the wiser Pagans had to dread, *numinibus vota exaudita malignis.* Even as it is I must often be glad that certain past prayers of my own were not granted.

But of course this is not the actual situation. Over against the A Pattern stands the B Pattern. Again and again in the New Testament we find the demand not for faith in such a general and (as it would seem to me) spiritual sense as I have described but for faith of a far more particular and (as it would seem to me) cruder sort: faith that the particular thing the petitioner asks will be given him. It is as if God demanded of us a faith which the Son of God in Gethsemane did not possess, and which if He had possessed it, would have been erroneous.

What springs first to mind is, of course, the long list of passages in which faith is required to those whom Our Lord healed. Some of these may be, for our present purpose, ambiguous. Thus in Matt. ix, 22, the words 'Your faith has healed you' to the woman with the haemorrhage will be interpreted by some as a proposition not in theology but in medicine. The woman was cured by auto-suggestion: faith in any charm or quack remedy would on that view have done as well as faith in Christ—though, of course, the power in Christ to evoke faith even of that kind might have theological implications in the long run. But such a view, since it will not cover all the instances, had better not be brought in for any, on the principle of Occam's razor. And surely it can be stretched only by extreme efforts to cover instances where the faith is, so to speak, vicarious. Thus the relevant faith in the case of the sick servant (Matt. viii, 13) is not his own but that of his master the Centurion; the healing of the Canaanite child (Matt. xv, 28) depends on her mother's faith.

Again, it might perhaps be maintained that in some instances the faith in question is not a faith that this particular healing will take place but a deeper, more all-embracing faith in the Person of Christ Himself; not, of course, that the petitioners can be supposed to have believed in His deity but that they recognized and accepted His holy, or at the very least, His numinous, character. I think there is something in this view, but sometimes the faith seems to be very definitely attached to the particular gift. Thus in Matt. ix, 28, the blind men are asked not 'Do you believe in Me?' but 'Do you believe that I can do this?' Still, the words are 'that I can' not 'that I will', so we may pass that example over. But what are we to say of Matt. xiv, 31, where Peter is called ὀλιγόπιοτε, because he lost his faith and sank in the waves. I should perhaps say, at this point, that I find no difficulty in accepting the walking on the water as historical. I suspect that the distinction often made between 'Nature' miracles and others seems plausible only because most of us know less about pathology and psychology than about gravitation. Perhaps if we knew all, the Divine suggestion of a single new thought to my mind would appear neither more nor less a 'Nature' miracle than stilling the storm or feeding the five thousand. But that is not a point I wish to raise. I am concerned only with the implications of ὀλιγόπιοτε. For it would seem that St Peter might have had any degree of faith in the goodness and power of God and even in the Deity of Christ and yet been wholly uncertain whether he could continue walking on the water. For in that case his faith would surely have told him that whether he walked or whether he sank he was equally in God's hands, and, submitting himself in the spirit of the Gethsemane prayer, he would have prepared himself, so far as infirmity allowed, to glorify God either by living or by drowning, and his failure, if he failed, would have been due to an imperfect mortification of instinct but not to a lack (in that sense) of faith. The faith which he is accused of lacking must surely be faith in the particular event: the continued walking on water.

All these examples, however, might be dismissed on the ground that they are not, in one strict sense of the word, examples of prayer. Let us then turn to those that are.

Whether you will agree to include Matt. xxi, 21, I don't know. Our Lord there says ἐὰν ἔχητε πίστιν καὶ μὴ διακριθῆτε, 'If you have faith with no hesitations or reservations, you can tell a mountain to throw itself into the sea and it will.' I very much hope that no one will solemnly remind us that Our Lord, according to the flesh, was an Oriental and that Orientals use hyperboles, and think that this has disposed of the passage. Of course Orientals, and Occidentals, use hyperboles, and of course Our Lord's first hearers did not suppose Him to mean that large and highly mischievous disturbances of the landscape would be common or edifying operations of faith. But a sane man does not use hyperbole to mean nothing: by a great thing (which is not literally true) he suggests a great thing which is. When he says that someone's heart is broken he does not mean that this organ is literally fractured, but he does mean that the person in question is in very great anguish. Only a windbag says 'His heart is broken' when he means 'He is somewhat depressed.' And if all Orientals were doomed by the mere fact of being Orientals to be windbags (which of course they are not) the Truth Himself, the Wisdom of the Father, would not and could not have been united with the human nature of an Oriental. (The point is worth making. Some people make allowances for local and temporary conditions in the speeches of Our Lord on a scale which really implies that God chose the time and place of the Incarnation very injudiciously.) Our Lord need not mean the words about the mountain literally; but at the very least they must mean doing some mighty work. The point is that the condition of doing such a mighty work is unwavering, unhesitating faith. Indeed He goes on in the very next sentence to make the same statement without any figures of speech at all: πάντα ὅσα ἂν αἰτήσητε ἐν τῇ προσευχῇ πιστεύοντες λήψεσθε.[1]

Can we even here take πιστεύοντες to mean 'having a general faith in the power and goodness of God'? We cannot. The corresponding passage in Mark,[2] though it adds a new difficulty, makes this point at least embarrassingly plain. The words are πάντα ὅσα προσεύχεσθε καὶ αἰτεῖσθε πιστεύετε ὅτι ἐλάβετε καί ἔσται ὑμῖν. The tense, present or (worse still) aorist, is of course perplexing. I hope someone will explain to us what either might represent in Aramaic. But there is no doubt at all that what we are to believe is precisely that we get 'all the things' we ask for. We are not to believe that we shall get either what we ask or else something far better: we are to believe that we shall get those very things. It is a faith, unwavering faith in that event, to which success is promised.

The same astonishing—and even, to my natural feelings, shocking—promise is repeated elsewhere with additions which may or may not turn out to be helpful for our present purpose.

[1. Matt. xxi, 22: 'And whatever you ask in prayer, you will receive, if you have faith.']
[2. Mark xi, 23–4: 'Truly, I say to you, whoever says to this mountain, "Be taken up and cast into the sea", and does not doubt in his heart, but believes that what he says will come to pass, it will be done for him. Therefore I tell you, whatever you ask in prayer, believe that you receive it, and you will.']

In Matt. xviii, 19, we learn that if two (or two or three) agree in a petition it will be granted. Faith is not explicitly mentioned here but is no doubt assumed: if it were not, the promise would be only the more startling and the further (I think) from the pattern of Gethsemane. The reason for the promise follows: 'For where two or three are gathered together εἰς τὸ ἐμον ὄνομα, there am I in their midst.' With this goes John xiv, 13, 'Whatever you ask in my name, I will do this': not this or something far better, but 'whatever you ask'.

I have discovered that some people find in these passages a solution of the whole problem. For here we have the prayer of the Church (as soon as two or three are gathered together in that Name) and the presence of Christ in the Church: so that the prayer which is granted by the Father is the prayer of the Son, and prayer and answer alike are an operation within the Deity.

I agree that this makes the promises less startling; but does it reconcile them with the A Pattern? And does it reconcile them with the facts? For surely there have been occasions on which the whole Church prays and is refused? I suppose that at least twice in this century the whole Church prayed for peace and no peace was given her. I think, however we define the Church, we must say that the whole Church prayed: peasants in Italy and popes in Russian villages, elders at Peebles, Anglicans in Cambridge, Congregationalists in Liverpool, Salvationists in East London. You may say (though I would not) that some who prayed were not in the Church; but it would be hard to find any in the Church who did not pray. But the cup did not pass from them. I am not, in principle, puzzled by the fact of the refusal: what I am puzzled by is the promise of granting.

And this at once raises a question which shows how frighteningly practical the problem is. *How* did the Church pray? Did she use the A Pattern or the B? Did she pray with unwavering confidence that peace would be given, or did she humbly follow the example of Gethsemane, adding 'If it be Thy will . . . not as I will, but as Thou wilt', preparing herself in advance for a refusal of that particular blessing and putting all her faith into the belief that even if it were denied, the denial would be full of mercy? I am disposed to believe that she did the latter. And was that, conceivably, her ghastly mistake? Was she like the διακρινόμενος, the man of doubtful faith who, as St James tells us,[1] must not suppose that he will receive anything? Have all my own intercessory prayers for years been mistaken? For I have always prayed that the illnesses of my friends might be healed 'if it was God's will', very clearly envisaging the possibility that it might not be. Perhaps this has all been a fake humility and a false spirituality for which my friends owe me little thanks; perhaps I ought never to have dreamed of refusal, μηδὲν διακρινόμενος?

Again, if the true prayer is joined with the prayer of the Church and hers with the prayer of Christ, and is therefore irresistible, was not it Christ who prayed in Gethsemane, using a different method and meeting with denial?

Another attempted solution runs something like this. The promise is made to prayers in Christ's name. And this of course means not simply prayers which end

---

[1. James i, 6–8: 'But let him ask in faith, with no doubting, for he who doubts is like a wave of the sea that is driven and tossed by the wind. For that person must not suppose that a double-minded man, unstable in all his ways, will receive anything from the Lord.']

with the formula 'Through Jesus Christ Our Lord' but prayers prayed in the spirit of Christ, prayers uttered by us when, and in so far as, we are 'in' Him. Such prayers are the ones that can be made with unwavering faith that the blessing we ask for will be given us. And this may be supported (though I suspect it had better not be) from 1 John v, 14, 'Whatever we ask Him according to His will, He will hear us.' But how are we to hold this view and yet avoid the implication (*quod nefas dicere*) that Christ Himself in Gethsemane failed to pray in the spirit of Christ, since He neither used the form which that spirit is held to justify nor received the answer which that spirit is held to insure? As for the Johannine passage, would we dare to produce it in this context before an audience of intelligent but simple inquirers. They come to us (this often happens) saying that they have been told that those who pray in faith to the Christian God will get what they ask: that they have tried it and not got what they asked: and what, please, is our explanation? Dare we say that when God promises 'You shall have what you ask' He secretly means 'You shall have it if you ask for something I wish to give you'? What should we think of an earthly father who promised to give his son whatever he chose for his birthday and, when the boy asked for a bicycle gave him an arithmetic book, then first disclosing the silent reservation with which the promise was made?

Of course the arithmetic book may be better for the son than the bicycle, and a robust faith may manage to believe so. That is not where the difficulty, the sense of cruel mockery, lies. The boy is tempted, not to complain that the bicycle was denied, but that the promise of 'anything he chose' was made. So with us.

It is possible that someone present may be wholly on the side of the B Pattern: someone who has seen many healed by prayer. Such a person will be tempted to reply that most of us are in fact grievously wrong in our prayer-life: that miracles are accorded to unwavering faith: that if we dropped our disobedient lowliness and pseudo-spiritual timidity blessings we never dreamed of would be showered on us at every turn. I certainly would not hear such a person with scepticism, still less with mockery. I believe in miracles, here and now. But if this is the complete answer, then why was the A Pattern of prayer ever given at all?

I have no answer to my problem, though I have taken it to about every Christian I know, learned or simple, lay or clerical, within my own Communion or without. Before closing I have, however, one hesitant observation to make.

One thing seems to be clear to me. Whatever else faith may mean (that is, faith in the granting of the blessing asked, for with faith in any other sense we need not at this point be concerned) I feel quite sure that it does not mean any state of psychological certitude such as might be—I think it sometimes is—manufactured from within by the natural action of a strong will upon an obedient imagination. The faith that moves mountains is a gift from Him who created mountains. That being so, can I ease my problem by saying that until God gives me such a faith I have no practical decision to make; I must pray after the A Pattern because, in fact, I cannot pray after the B Pattern? If, on the other hand, God even gave me such a faith, then again I should have no decision to make; I should find myself praying in the B Pattern. This would fall in with an old opinion of my own that we ought all of us to be ashamed of not performing miracles and that we do not feel this shame enough.

We regard our own state as normal and theurgy as exceptional, whereas we ought perhaps to regard the worker of miracles, however rare, as the true Christian norm and ourselves as spiritual cripples. Yet I do not find this quite a satisfactory solution. I think we might get over the prayer in Gethsemane. We might say that in His tender humility Our Lord, just as He refused the narcotic wine mingled with myrrh, and just as He chose (I think) to be united to a human nature not of iron nerves but to a nature sensitive, shrinking, and unable not to live through torture in advance, so He chose on that night to plumb the depths of Christian experience, to resemble not the heroes of His army but the very weakest camp followers and unfits; or even that such a choice is implied in those unconsciously profound and involuntarily blessed words 'He saved others, Himself He cannot save.' But some discomfort remains. I do not like to represent God as saying 'I will grant what you ask in faith' and adding, so to speak, 'Because I will not give you the faith—not that kind—unless you ask what I want to give you.' Once more, there is just a faint suggestion of mockery, of goods that look a little larger in the advertisement than they turn out to be. Not that we complain of any defect in the goods: it is the faintest suspicion of excess in the advertisement that is disquieting. But at present I have got no further. I come to you, reverend Fathers, for guidance. How am I to pray this very night?

Modern Theology
and Biblical Criticism

THIS PAPER AROSE out of a conversation I had with the Principal[1] one night last term. A book of Alec Vidler's happened to be lying on the table and I expressed my reaction to the sort of theology it contained. My reaction was a hasty and ignorant one, produced with the freedom that comes after dinner.[2] One thing led to another and before we were done I was saying a good deal more than I had meant about the type of thought which, so far as I could gather, is now dominant in many theological colleges. He then said, 'I wish you would come and say all this to my young men.' He knew of course that I was extremely ignorant of the whole thing. But I think his idea was that you ought to know how a certain sort of theology strikes the outsider. Though I may have nothing but misunderstandings to lay before you, you ought to know that such misunderstandings exist. That sort of thing is easy to overlook inside one's own circle. The minds you daily meet have been conditioned by the same studies and prevalent opinions as your own. That may mislead you. For of course as priests it is the outsiders you will have to cope with. You exist in the long run for no other purpose. The proper study of shepherds is sheep, not (save accidentally) other shepherds. And woe to you if you do not evangelize. I am not trying to teach my grandmother. I am a sheep, telling shepherds what only a sheep can tell them. And now I start my bleating.

There are two sorts of outsiders: the uneducated, and those who are educated in some way but not in your way. How you are to deal with the first class, if you hold views like Loisy's or Schweitzer's or Bultmann's or Tillich's or even Alec Vidler's, I simply don't know. I see—and I'm told that you see—that it would hardly do to tell them what you really believe. A theology which denies the historicity of nearly everything in the Gospels to which Christian life and affections and thought have been fastened for nearly two millennia—which either denies the miraculous altogether or, more strangely, after swallowing the camel of the Resurrection strains at such gnats as the feeding of the multitudes—if offered to the uneducated man can produce only one or other of two effects. It will make him a Roman Catholic or an atheist. What you offer him he will not recognize as Christianity. If he holds to what he calls Christianity he will leave a Church in which it is no longer taught and look for one where it is. If he agrees with your version he will no longer call

[1. The Principal of Westcott House, Cambridge, now the Bishop of Edinburgh (The Rt Rev Kenneth Carey).]
[2. While the Bishop was out of the room, Lewis read 'The Sign at Cana' in Alec Vidler's *Windsor Sermons* (S.C.M. Press, 1958). The Bishop recalls that when he asked him what he thought about it, Lewis 'expressed himself very freely about the sermon and said that he thought that it was quite incredible that we should have had to wait nearly 2,000 years to be told by a theologian called Vidler that what the Church has always regarded as a miracle was, in fact, a parable!']

himself a Christian and no longer come to church. In his crude, coarse way, he would respect you much more if you did the same. An experienced clergyman told me that most liberal priests, faced with this problem, have recalled from its grave the late medieval conception of two truths: a picture-truth which can be preached to the people, and an esoteric truth for use among the clergy. I shouldn't think you will enjoy this conception much when you have to put it into practice. I'm sure if I had to produce picture-truths to a parishioner in great anguish or under fierce temptation, and produce them with that seriousness and fervour which his condition demanded, while knowing all the time that I didn't exactly—only in some Pickwickian sense—believe them myself, I'd find my forehead getting red and damp and my collar getting tight. But that is your headache, not mine. You have, after all, a different sort of collar. I claim to belong to the second group of outsiders: educated, but not theologically educated. How one member of that group feels I must now try to tell you.

The undermining of the old orthodoxy has been mainly the work of divines engaged in New Testament criticism. The authority of experts in that discipline is the authority in deference to whom we are asked to give up a huge mass of beliefs shared in common by the early Church, the Fathers, the Middle Ages, the Reformers, and even the nineteenth century. I want to explain what it is that makes me sceptical about this authority. Ignorantly sceptical, as you will all too easily see. But the scepticism is the father of the ignorance. It is hard to persevere in a close study when you can work up no *prima facie* confidence in your teachers.

First then, whatever these men may be as Biblical critics, I distrust them as critics. They seem to me to lack literary judgement, to be imperceptive about the very quality of the texts they are reading. It sounds a strange charge to bring against men who have been steeped in those books all their lives. But that might be just the trouble. A man who has spent his youth and manhood in the minute study of New Testament texts and of other people's studies of them, whose literary experiences of those texts lacks any standard of comparison such as can only grow from a wide and deep and genial experience of literature in general, is, I should think, very likely to miss the obvious things about them. If he tells me that something in a Gospel is legend or romance, I want to know how many legends and romances he has read, how well his palate is trained in detecting them by the flavour; not how many years he has spent on that Gospel. But I had better turn to examples.

In what is already a very old commentary I read that the Fourth Gospel is regarded by one school as a 'spiritual romance', 'a poem not a history', to be judged by the same canons as Nathan's parable, the Book of Jonah, *Paradise Lost* 'or, more exactly, *Pilgrim's Progress*'.[1] After a man has said that, why need one attend to anything else he says about any book in the world? Note that he regards *Pilgrim's Progress*, a story which professes to be a dream and flaunts its allegorical nature by every single proper name it uses, as the closest parallel. Note that the whole epic

[1. Lewis is quoting from an article, 'The Gospel According to St. John', by Walter Lock in *A New Commentary on Holy Scripture, including the Apocrypha*, ed. by Charles Gore, Henry Leighton Goudge, Alfred Guillaume (S.P.C.K, 1928), p. 241. Lock, in turn, is quoting from James Drummond's *An Inquiry into the Character and Authorship of the Fourth Gospel* (Williams and Norgate, 1903).]

panoply of Milton goes for nothing. But even if we leave out the grosser absurdities and keep to *Jonah,* the insensitiveness is crass—*Jonah,* a tale with as few even pretended historical attachments as *Job,* grotesque in incident and surely not without a distinct, though of course edifying, vein of typically Jewish humour. Then turn to John. Read the dialogues: that with the Samaritan woman at the well, or that which follows the healing of the man born blind. Look at its pictures: Jesus (if I may use the word) doodling with his finger in the dust; the unforgettable ἦν δὲ νύξ (xiii, 30). I have been reading poems, romances, vision-literature, legends, myths all my life. I know what they are like. I know that not one of them is like this. Of this text there are only two possible views. Either this is reportage—though it may no doubt contain errors—pretty close up to the facts; nearly as close as Boswell. Or else, some unknown writer in the second century, without known predecessors or successors, suddenly anticipated the whole technique of modern, novelistic, realistic narrative. If it is untrue, it must be narrative of that kind. The reader who doesn't see this has simply not learned to read. I would recommend him to read Auerbach.[1]

Here, from Bultmann's *Theology of the New Testament* (p. 30) is another: 'Observe in what unassimilated fashion the prediction of the parousia (Mk. viii, 38) follows upon the prediction of the passion (viii, 31).'[2] What can he mean? Unassimilated? Bultmann believes that predictions of the parousia are older than those of the passion. He therefore wants to believe—and no doubt does believe—that when they occur in the same passage some discrepancy or 'unassimilation' must be perceptible between them. But surely he foists this on the text with shocking lack of perception. Peter has confessed Jesus to be the Anointed One. That flash of glory is hardly over before the dark prophecy begins—that the Son of Man must suffer and die. Then this contrast is repeated. Peter, raised for a moment by his confession, makes his false step; the crushing rebuff 'Get thee behind me' follows. Then, across that momentary ruin which Peter (as so often) becomes, the voice of the Master, turning to the crowd, generalizes the moral. All His followers must take up the cross. This avoidance of suffering, this self-preservation, is not what life is really about. Then, more definitely still, the summons to martyrdom. You must stand to your tackling. If you disown Christ here and now, He will disown you later. Logically, emotionally, imaginatively, the sequence is perfect. Only a Bultmann could think otherwise.

Finally, from the same Bultmann: 'The personality of Jesus has no importance for the kerygma either of Paul or of John . . . Indeed the tradition of the earliest Church did not even unconsciously preserve a picture of his personality. Every attempt to reconstruct one remains a play of subjective imagination.'[3]

So there is no personality of Our Lord presented in the New Testament. Through what strange process has this learned German gone in order to make himself blind to what all men except him see? What evidence have we that he would recognize

[1. Lewis means, I think, Erich Auerbach's *Mimesis: The Representation of Reality in Western Literature,* translated by Williard R. Trask (Princeton, 1953).]

[2. Rudolf Bultmann, *Theology of the New Testament,* translated by Kendrick Grobel, vol. I (S.C.M. Press, 1952), p. 30.]

[3. *Op. cit.,* p. 35.]

a personality if it were there? For it is Bultmann *contra mundum*. If anything whatever is common to all believers, and even to many unbelievers, it is the sense that
in the Gospels they have met a personality. There are characters whom we know
to be historical but of whom we do not feel that we have any personal knowledge—
knowledge by acquaintance; such are Alexander, Attila, or William of Orange. There
are others who make no claim to historical reality but whom, none the less, we know
as we know real people: Falstaff, Uncle Toby, Mr Pickwick. But there are only three
characters who, claiming the first sort of reality, also actually have the second. And
surely everyone knows who they are: Plato's Socrates, the Jesus of the Gospels, and
Boswell's Johnson. Our acquaintance with them shows itself in a dozen ways. When
we look into the Apocryphal gospels, we find ourselves constantly saying of this
or that *logion*, 'No. It's a fine saying, but not His. That wasn't how He talked.'—just
as we do with all pseudo-Johnsoniana. We are not in the least perturbed by the
contrasts within each character: the union in Socrates of silly and scabrous titters
about Greek pederasty with the highest mystical fervour and the homeliest good
sense; in Johnson, of profound gravity and melancholy with that love of fun and
nonsense which Boswell never understood though Fanny Burney did; in Jesus of
peasant shrewdness, intolerable severity, and irresistible tenderness. So strong is
the flavour of the personality that, even while He says things which, on any other
assumption than that of Divine Incarnation in the fullest sense, would be appallingly
arrogant, yet we—and many unbelievers too—accept Him at His own valuation
when He says 'I am meek and lowly of heart.' Even those passages in the New
Testament which superficially, and in intention, are most concerned with the Divine,
and least with the Human Nature, bring us face to face with the personality. I am
not sure that they don't do this more than any others. 'We beheld His glory, the
glory as of the only begotten of the Father, full of graciousness and reality . . . which
we have looked upon and our hands have handled.' What is gained by trying to
evade or dissipate this shattering immediacy of personal contact by talk about 'that
significance which the early church found that it was impelled to attribute to the
Master'? This hits us in the face. Not what they were impelled to do but what
impelled them. I begin to fear that by *personality* Dr Bultmann means what I should
call impersonality: what you'd get in a D.N.B. article or an obituary or a Victorian
Life and Letters of Yeshua Bar-Yosef in three volumes with photographs.

That then is my first bleat. These men ask me to believe they can read between
the lines of the old texts; the evidence is their obvious inability to read (in any sense
worth discussing) the lines themselves. They claim to see fern-seed and can't see
an elephant ten yards away in broad daylight.

Now for my second bleat. All theology of the liberal type involves at some point—
and often involves throughout—the claim that the real behaviour and purpose and
teaching of Christ came very rapidly to be misunderstood and misrepresented by
His followers, and has been recovered or exhumed only by modern scholars. Now
long before I became interested in theology I had met this kind of theory elsewhere.
The tradition of Jowett still dominated the study of ancient philosophy when I was
reading Greats. One was brought up to believe that the real meaning of Plato had
been misunderstood by Aristotle and wildly travestied by the neo-Platonists, only

to be recovered by the moderns. When recovered, it turned out (most fortunately) that Plato had really all along been an English Hegelian, rather like T. H. Green. I have met it a third time in my own professional studies; every week a clever undergraduate, every quarter a dull American don, discovers for the first time what some Shakespearian play really meant. But in this third instance I am a privileged person. The revolution in thought and sentiment which has occurred in my own lifetime is so great that I belong, mentally, to Shakespeare's world far more than to that of these recent interpreters. I see—I feel it in my bones—I know beyond argument—that most of their interpretations are merely impossible; they involve a way of looking at things which was not known in 1914, much less in the Jacobean period. This daily confirms my suspicion of the same approach to Plato or the New Testament. The idea that any man or writer should be opaque to those who lived in the same culture, spoke the same language, shared the same habitual imagery and unconscious assumptions, and yet be transparent to those who have none of these advantages, is in my opinion preposterous. There is an *a priori* improbability in it which almost no argument and no evidence could counterbalance.

Thirdly, I find in these theologians a constant use of the principle that the miraculous does not occur. Thus any statement put into Our Lord's mouth by the old texts, which, if He had really made it, would constitute a prediction of the future, is taken to have been put in after the occurrence which it seemed to predict. This is very sensible if we start by knowing that inspired prediction can never occur. Similarly in general, the rejection as unhistorical of all passages which narrate miracles is sensible if we start by knowing that the miraculous in general never occurs. Now I do not here want to discuss whether the miraculous is possible. I only want to point out that this is a purely philosophical question. Scholars, as scholars, speak on it with no more authority than anyone else. The canon 'If miraculous, unhistorical' is one they bring to their study of the texts, not one they have learned from it. If one is speaking of authority, the united authority of all the Biblical critics in the world counts here for nothing. On this they speak simply as men; men obviously influenced by, and perhaps insufficiently critical of, the spirit of the age they grew up in.

But my fourth bleat—which is also my loudest and longest—is still to come.

All this sort of criticism attempts to reconstruct the genesis of the texts it studies; what vanished documents each author used, when and where he wrote, with what purposes, under what influences—the whole *Sitz im Leben* of the text. This is done with immense erudition and great ingenuity. And at first sight it is very convincing. I think I should be convinced by it myself, but that I carry about with me a charm—the herb *moly*—against it. You must excuse me if I now speak for a while of myself. The value of what I say depends on its being first-hand evidence.

What forearms me against all these Reconstructions is the fact that I have seen it all from the other end of the stick. I have watched reviewers reconstructing the genesis of my own books in just this way.

Until you come to be reviewed yourself you would never believe how little of an ordinary review is taken up by criticism in the strict sense: by evaluation, praise, or censure, of the book actually written. Most of it is taken up with imaginary histories of the process by which you wrote it. The very terms which the reviewers use in praising or dispraising often imply such a history. They praise a passage as 'spontaneous' and censure another as 'laboured'; that is, they think they know that you wrote the one *currente calamo* and the other *invita Minerva*.

What the value of such reconstructions is I learned very early in my career. I had published a book of essays; and the one into which I had put most of my heart, the one I really cared about and in which I discharged a keen enthusiasm, was on William Morris.[1] And in almost the first review I was told that this was obviously the only one in the book in which I had felt no interest. Now don't mistake. The critic was, I now believe, quite right in thinking it the worst essay in the book; at least everyone agreed with him. Where he was totally wrong was in his imaginary history of the causes which produced its dullness.

Well, this made me prick up my ears. Since then I have watched with some care similar imaginary histories both of my own books and of books by friends whose real history I knew. Reviewers, both friendly and hostile, will dash you off such histories with great confidence; will tell you what public events had directed the author's mind to this or that, what other authors had influenced him, what his over-all intention was, what sort of audience he principally addressed, why—and when—he did everything.

Now I must first record my impression; then, distinct from it, what I can say with certainty. My impression is that in the whole of my experience not one of these guesses has on any one point been right; that the method shows a record of 100 per cent. failure. You would expect that by mere chance they would hit as often as they miss. But it is my impression that they do no such thing. I can't remember a single hit. But as I have not kept a careful record my mere impression may be mistaken. What I think I can say with certainty is that they are usually wrong.

And yet they would often sound—if you didn't know the truth—extremely convincing. Many reviewers said that the Ring in Tolkien's *The Lord of the Rings* was suggested by the atom bomb. What could be more plausible? Here is a book published when everyone was preoccupied by that sinister invention; here in the centre of the book is a weapon which it seems madness to throw away yet fatal to use. Yet in fact, the chronology of the book's composition makes the theory impossible. Only the other week a reviewer said that a fairy tale by my friend Roger Lancelyn Green was influenced by fairy tales of mine. Nothing could be more probable. I have an imaginary country with a beneficent lion in it: Green, one with a beneficent tiger. Green and I can be proved to read one another's works; to be indeed in various ways closely associated. The case for an affiliation is far stronger than many which we accept as conclusive when dead authors are concerned. But it's all untrue nevertheless. I know the genesis of that Tiger and that Lion and they are quite independent.[2]

[1. Lewis's essay on 'William Morris' appears in *Rehabilitations and Other Essays* (Oxford, 1939).]
[2. Lewis corrected this error in the following letter, 'Books for Children', in *The Times Literary Supplement* (28 November 1958), p. 689: 'Sir,—A review of Mr R. L. Green's *Land of the Lord High Tiger* in your issue of 21 November spoke of myself (in passing) with so much kindness that I am reluctant to cavil at anything it contained: but in justice to Mr Green I must. The critic suggested that Mr Green's Tiger owed something to my fairy-tales. In reality this is not so and is chronologically impossible. The Tiger was an old inhabitant, and his land a familiar haunt, of Mr Green's imagination long before I began writing. There is a moral here for all of us as critics. I wonder how much *Quellenforschung* in our studies of older literature seems solid only because those who knew the facts are dead and cannot contradict it?']

Now this surely ought to give us pause. The reconstruction of the history of a text, when the text is ancient, sounds very convincing. But one is after all sailing by dead reckoning; the results cannot be checked by fact. In order to decide how reliable the method is, what more could you ask for than to be shown an instance where the same method is at work and we have facts to check it by? Well, that is what I have done. And we find, that when this check is available, the results are either always, or else nearly always, wrong. The 'assured results of modern scholarship', as to the way in which an old book was written, are 'assured', we may conclude, only because the men who knew the facts are dead and can't blow the gaff. The huge essays in my own field which reconstruct the history of *Piers Plowman* or *The Faerie Queene* are most unlikely to be anything but sheer illusions.[1]

Am I then venturing to compare every whipster who writes a review in a modern weekly with these great scholars who have devoted their whole lives to the detailed study of the New Testament? If the former are always wrong, does it follow that the latter must fare no better?

There are two answers to this. First, while I respect the learning of the great Biblical critics, I am not yet persuaded that their judgement is equally to be respected. But, secondly, consider with what overwhelming advantages the mere reviewers start. They reconstruct the history of a book written by someone whose mother-tongue is the same as theirs; a contemporary, educated like themselves, living in something like the same mental and spiritual climate. They have everything to help them. The superiority in judgement and diligence which you are going to attribute to the Biblical critics will have to be almost superhuman if it is to offset the fact that they are everywhere faced with customs, language, race-characteristics, class-characteristics, a religious background, habits of composition, and basic assumptions, which no scholaship will ever enable any man now alive to know as surely and intimately and instinctively as the reviewer can know mine. And for the very same reason, remember, the Biblical critics, whatever reconstructions they devise, can never be crudely proved wrong. St Mark is dead. When they meet St Peter there will be more pressing matters to discuss.

You may say, of course, that such reviewers are foolish in so far as they guess how a sort of book they never wrote themselves was written by another. They assume that you wrote a story as they would try to write a story; the fact that they would so try, explains why they have not produced any stories. But are the Biblical critics in this way much better off? Dr Bultmann never wrote a gospel. Has the experience of his learned, specialized, and no doubt meritorious, life really given him any power of seeing into the minds of those long dead men who were caught up into what, on any view, must be regarded as the central religious experience of the whole human race? It is no incivility to say—he himself would admit—that he must in every way be divided from the evangelists by far more formidable barriers—spiritual as well as intellectual—than any that could exist between my reviewers and me.

[1. For a fuller treatment on book-reviewing, see Lewis's essay 'On Criticism' in his *Of Other Worlds: Essays and Stories*, ed. Walter Hooper, (Bles, 1966), pp. 43–58.]

My picture of one layman's reaction—and I think it is not a rare one—would be incomplete without some account of the hopes he secretly cherishes and the naive reflections with which he sometimes keeps his spirits up.

You must face the fact he does not expect the present school of theological thought to be everlasting. He thinks, perhaps wishfully thinks, that the whole thing may blow over. I have learned in other fields of study how transitory the 'assured results of modem scholarship' may be, how soon scholarship ceases to be modern. The confident treatment to which the New Testament is subjected is no longer applied to profane texts. There used to be English scholars who were prepared to cut up *Henry VI* between half a dozen authors and assign his share to each. We don't do that now. When I was a boy one would have been laughed at for supposing there had been a real Homer: the disintegrators seemed to have triumphed forever. But Homer seems to be creeping back. Even the belief of the ancient Greeks that the Mycenaeans were their ancestors and spoke Greek has been surprisingly supported. We may without disgrace believe in a historical Arthur. Everywhere, except in theology, there has been a vigorous growth of scepticism about scepticism itself. We can't keep ourselves from murmuring *multa renascentur quae jam cecidere*.

Nor can a man of my age ever forget how suddenly and completely the idealist philosophy of his youth fell. McTaggart, Green, Bosanquet, Bradley seemed enthroned forever; they went down as suddenly as the Bastille. And the interesting thing is that while I lived under that dynasty I felt various difficulties and objections which I never dared to express. They were so frightfully obvious that I felt sure they must be mere misunderstandings: the great men could not have made such very elementary mistakes as those which my objections implied. But very similar objections—though put, no doubt, far more cogently than I could have put them—were among the criticisms which finally prevailed. They would now be the stock answers to English Hegelianism. If anyone present tonight has felt the same shy and tentative doubts about the great Biblical critics, perhaps he need not feel quite certain that they are only his stupidity. They may have a future he little dreams of.

We derive a little comfort, too, from our mathematical colleagues. When a critic reconstructs the genesis of a text he usually has to use what may be called linked hypotheses. Thus Bultmann says that Peter's confession is 'an Easter-story projected backward into Jesus' life-time' (p. 26, *op. cit.*). The first hypothesis is that Peter made no such confession. Then, granting that, there is a second hypothesis as to how the false story of his having done so might have grown up. Now let us suppose—what I am far from granting—that the first hypothesis has a probability of 90 per cent. Let us assume that the second hypothesis also has a probability of 90 per cent. But the two together don't still have 90 per cent., for the second comes in only on the assumption of the first. You have not A plus B; you have a complex AB. And the mathematicians tell me that AB has only an 81 per cent. probability. I'm not good enough at arithmetic to work it out, but you see that if, in a complex reconstruction, you go on thus superinducing hypothesis on hypothesis, you will in the end get a complex in which, though each hypothesis by itself has in a sense a high probability, the whole has almost none.

You must not, however, paint the picture too black. We are not fundamentalists. We think that different elements in this sort of theology have different degrees of strength. The nearer it sticks to mere textual criticism, of the old sort, Lachmann's sort, the more we are disposed to believe in it. And of course we agree that passages almost verbally identical cannot be independent. It is as we glide away from this into reconstructions of a subtler and more ambitious kind that our faith in the method wavers; and our faith in Christianity is proportionately corroborated. The sort of statement that arouses our deepest skepticism is the statement that something in a Gospel cannot be historical because it shows a theology or an ecclesiology too developed for so early a date. For this implies that we know, first of all, that there was any development in the matter, and secondly, how quickly it proceeded. It even implies an extraordinary homogeneity and continuity of development: implicitly denies that anyone could greatly have anticipated anyone else. This seems to involve knowing about a number of long dead people—for the early Christians were, after all, people—things of which I believe few of us could have given an accurate account if we had lived among them; all the forward and backward surge of discussion, preaching, and individual religious experience. I could not speak with similar confidence about the circle I have chiefly lived in myself. I could not describe the history even of my own thought as confidently as these men describe the history of the early Church's mind. And I am perfectly certain no one else could. Suppose a future scholar knew that I abandoned Christianity in my teens, and that, also in my teens, I went to an atheist tutor. Would not this seem far better evidence than most of what we have about the development of Christian theology in the first two centuries? Would he not conclude that my apostasy was due to the tutor? And then reject as 'backward projection' any story which represented me as an atheist before I went to that tutor? Yet he would be wrong. I am sorry to have become once more autobiographical. But reflection on the extreme improbability of his own life— by historical standards—seems to me a profitable exercise for everyone. It encourages a due agnosticism.

For agnosticism is, in a sense, what I am preaching. I do not wish to reduce the sceptical element in your minds. I am only suggesting that it need not be reserved exclusively for the New Testament and the Creeds. Try doubting something else.

Such scepticism might, I think, begin at the very beginning with the thought which underlies the whole demythology of our time. It was put long ago by Tyrrell. As man progresses he revolts against 'earlier and inadequate expressions of the religious idea . . . Taken literally, and not symbolically, they do not meet his need. And as long as he demands to picture to himself distinctly the term and satisfaction of that need he is doomed to doubt, for his picturing will necessarily be drawn from the world of his present experience.'[1]

In one way of course Tyrrell was saying nothing new. The Negative Theology of Pseudo-Dionysius had said as much, but it drew no such conclusions as Tyrrell. Perhaps this is because the older tradition found our conceptions inadequate to God

---

[1. George Tyrrell, 'The Apocalyptic Vision of Christ' in *Christianity at the Cross-Roads* (Longmans, Green & Co., 1909), p. 125.]

whereas Tyrrell finds it inadequate to 'the religious idea'. He doesn't say whose idea. But I am afraid he means Man's idea. We, being men, know what we think: and we find the doctrines of the Resurrection, the Ascension, and the Second Coming inadequate to our thoughts. But supposing these things were the expressions of God's thought?

It might still be true that 'taken literally and not symbolically' they are inadequate. From which the conclusion commonly drawn is that they must be taken symbolically, not literally; that is, wholly symbolically. All the details are equally symbolical and analogical.

But surely there is a flaw here. The argument runs like this. All the details are derived from our present experience; but the reality transcends our experience: therefore all the details are wholly and equally symbolical. But suppose a dog were trying to form a conception of human life. All the details in its picture would be derived from canine experience. Therefore all that the dog imagined could, at best, be only analogically true of human life. The conclusion is false. If the dog visualized our scientific researches in terms of ratting, this would be analogical; but if it thought that eating could be predicated of humans only in an analogical sense, the dog would be wrong. In fact if a dog could, *per impossibile*, be plunged for a day into human life, it would be hardly more surprised by hitherto unimagined differences than by hitherto unsuspected similarities. A reverent dog would be shocked. A modernist dog, distrusting the whole experience, would ask to be taken to the vet.

But the dog can't get into human life. Consequently, though it can be sure that its best ideas of human life are full of analogy and symbol, it could never point to any one detail and say, 'This is entirely symbolic.' You cannot know that everything in the representation of a thing is symbolical unless you have independent access to the thing and can compare it with the representation. Dr Tyrrell can tell that the story of the Ascension is inadequate to his religious idea, because he knows his own idea and can compare it with the story. But how if we are asking about a transcendent, objective reality to which the story is our sole access? 'We know not— oh we know not.' But then we must take our ignorance seriously

Of course if 'taken literally and not symbolically' means 'taken in terms of mere physics', then this story is not even a religious story. Motion away from the earth— which is what Ascension physically means—would not in itself be an event of spiritual significance. Therefore, you argue, the spiritual reality can have nothing but an analogical connection with the story of an ascent. For the union of God with God and of Man with God-man can have nothing to do with space. Who told you this? What you really mean is that we can't see how it could possibly have anything to do with it. That is a quite different proposition. When I know as I am known I shall be able to tell which parts of the story were purely symbolical and which, if any, were not; shall see how the transcendent reality either excludes and repels locality, or how unimaginably it assimilates and loads it with significance. Had we not better wait?

Such are the reactions of one bleating layman to Modern Theology. It is right you should hear them. You will not perhaps hear them very often again. Your parishioners will not often speak to you quite frankly. Once the layman was anxious to hide the fact that he believed so much less than the Vicar: he now tends to hide the fact that he believes so much more. Missionary to the priests of one's own church is an embarrassing rôle; though I have a horrid feeling that if such mission work is not soon undertaken the future history of the Church of England is likely to be short.

The Seeing Eye

THE RUSSIANS, I am told, report that they have not found God in outer space. On the other hand, a good many people in many different times and countries claim to have found God, or been found by God, here on earth.

The conclusion some want us to draw from these data is that God does not exist. As a corollary, those who think they have met Him on earth were suffering from a delusion.

But other conclusions might be drawn:

1. We have not yet gone far enough in space. There had been ships on the Atlantic for a good time before America was discovered.
2. God does exist but is locally confined to this planet.
3. The Russians did find God in space without knowing it, because they lacked the requisite apparatus for detecting Him.
4. God does exist but is not an object either located in a particular part of space nor diffused, as we once thought 'ether' was, throughout space.

The first two conclusions do not interest me. The sort of religion for which they could be a defence would be a religion for savages: the belief in a local deity who can be contained in a particular temple, island or grove. That, in fact, seems to be the sort of religion about which the Russians—or some Russians, and a good many people in the West—are being irreligious. It is not in the least disquieting that no astronauts have discovered a god of that sort. The really disquieting thing would be if they had.

The third and fourth conclusions are the ones for my money.

Looking for God—or Heaven—by exploring space is like reading or seeing all Shakespeare's plays in the hope that you will find Shakespeare as one of the characters or Stratford as one of the places. Shakespeare is in one sense present at every moment in every play. But he is never present in the same way as Falstaff or Lady Macbeth. Nor is he diffused through the play like a gas.

If there were an idiot who thought plays existed on their own, without an author (not to mention actors, producer, manager, stagehands and what not), our belief in Shakespeare would not be much affected by his saying, quite truly, that he had studied all the plays and never found Shakespeare in them.

The rest of us, in varying degrees according to our perceptiveness, 'found Shakespeare' in the plays. But it is a quite different sort of 'finding' from anything our poor friend has in mind.

Even he has in reality been in some way affected by Shakespeare, but without knowing it. He lacked the necessary apparatus for detecting Shakespeare.

Now of course this is only an analogy. I am not suggesting at all that the existence of God is as easily established as the existence of Shakespeare. My point is that, if God does exist, He is related to the universe more as an author is related to a play than as one object in the universe is related to another.

If God created the universe, He created space-time, which is to the universe as the metre is to a poem or the key is to music. To look for Him as one item within the framework which He Himself invented is nonsensical.

If God—such a God as any adult religion believes in—exists, mere movement in space will never bring you any nearer to Him or any farther from Him than you are at this very moment. You can neither reach Him nor avoid Him by travelling to Alpha Centauri or even to other galaxies. A fish is no more, and no less, in the sea after it has swum a thousand miles than it was when it set out.

How, then, it may be asked, can we either reach or avoid Him?

The avoiding, in many times and places, has proved so difficult that a very large part of the human race failed to achieve it. But in our own time and place it is extremely easy. Avoid silence, avoid solitude, avoid any train of thought that leads off the beaten track. Concentrate on money, sex, status, health and (above all) on your own grievances. Keep the radio on. Live in a crowd. Use plenty of sedation. If you must read books, select them very carefully. But you'd be safer to stick to the papers. You'll find the advertisements helpful; especially those with a sexy or a snobbish appeal.

About the reaching, I am a far less reliable guide. That is because I never had the experience of looking for God. It was the other way round; He was the hunter (or so it seemed to me) and I was the deer. He stalked me like a redskin, took unerring aim, and fired. And I am very thankful that that is how the first (conscious) meeting occurred. It forearms one against subsequent fears that the whole thing was only wish fulfilment. Something one didn't wish for can hardly be that.

But it is significant that this long-evaded encounter happened at a time when I was making a serious effort to obey my conscience. No doubt it was far less serious than I supposed, but it was the most serious I had made for a long time.

One of the first results of such an effort is to bring your picture of yourself down to something nearer life-size. And presently you begin to wonder whether you are yet, in any full sense, a person at all; whether you are entitled to call yourself 'I' (it is a sacred name). In that way, the process is like being psycho-analysed, only cheaper—I mean, in dollars; in some other ways it may be more costly. You find that what you called yourself is only a thin film on the surface of an unsounded and dangerous sea. But not merely dangerous. Radiant things, delights and inspirations, come to the surface as well as snarling resentments and nagging lusts.

One's ordinary self is, then, a mere façade. There's a huge area out of sight behind it.

And then, if one listens to the physicists, one discovers that the same is true of all the things around us. These tables and chairs, this magazine, the trees, clouds and mountains are façades. Poke (scientifically) into them and you find the unimaginable structure of the atom. That is, in the long run, you find mathematical formulas.

There are you (whatever YOU means) sitting reading. Out there (whatever THERE means) is a white page with black marks on it. And both are façades. Behind both lies—well, Whatever-it-is. The psychologists, and the theologians, though they use different symbols, equally use symbols when they try to probe the depth behind the façade called YOU. That is, they can't really say 'It is this', but they can say 'It is in some way like this.' And the physicists, trying to probe behind the other façade, can give you only mathematics. And the mathematics may be true about the reality, but it can hardly be the reality itself, any more than contour lines are real mountains.

I am not in the least blaming either set of experts for this state of affairs. They make progress. They are always discovering things. If governments make a bad use of the physicists' discoveries, or if novelists and biographers make a bad use of the psychologists' discoveries, the experts are not to blame. The point, however, is that every fresh discovery, far from dissipating, deepens the mystery.

Presently, if you are a person of a certain sort, if you are one who has to believe that all things which exist must have unity it will seem to you irresistibly probable that what lies ultimately behind the one façade also lies ultimately behind the other. And then—again, if you are that sort of person—you may come to be convinced that your contact with that mystery in the area you call yourself is a good deal closer than your contact through what you call matter. For in the one case I, the ordinary, conscious I, am continuous with the unknown depth.

And after that, you may come (some do) to believe that that voice—like all the rest, I must speak symbolically—that voice which speaks in your conscience and in some of your intensest joys, which is sometimes so obstinately silent, sometimes so easily silenced, and then at other times so loud and emphatic, is in fact the closest contact you have with the mystery; and therefore finally to be trusted, obeyed, feared and desired more than all other things. But still, if you are a different sort of person, you will not come to this conclusion.

I hope everyone sees how this is related to the astronautical question from which we started. The process I have been sketching may equally well occur, or fail to occur, wherever you happen to be. I don't mean that all religious and all irreligious people have either taken this step or refused to take it. Once religion and its opposite are in the world—and they have both been in it for a very long time—the majority in both camps will be simply conformists. Their belief or disbelief will result from their upbringing and from the prevailing tone of the circles they live in. They will have done no hunting for God and no flying for God on their own. But if no minorities who did these things on their own existed I presume that the conforming majorities would not exist either. (Don't imagine I'm despising these majorities. I am sure the one contains better Christians than I am; the other, nobler atheists than I was.)

Space-travel really has nothing to do with the matter. To some, God is discoverable everywhere; to others, nowhere. Those who do not find Him on earth are unlikely to find Him in space. (Hang it all, we're in space already; every year we go a huge circular tour in space.) But send a saint up in a spaceship and he'll find God in space as he found God on earth. Much depends on the seeing eye.

And this is especially confirmed by my own religion, which is Christianity. When I said a while ago that it was nonsensical to look for God as one item within His own work, the universe, some readers may have wanted to protest. They wanted to say, 'But surely, according to Christianity, that is just what did once happen? Surely the central doctrine is that God became man and walked about among other men in Palestine? If that is not appearing as an item in His own work, what is it?'

The objection is much to the point. To meet it, I must readjust my old analogy of the play. One might imagine a play in which the dramatist introduced himself as a character into his own play and was pelted off the stage as an impudent impostor by the other characters. It might be rather a good play; if I had any talent for the theatre I'd try my hand at writing it. But since (as far as I know) such a play doesn't exist, we had better change to a narrative work; a story into which the author puts himself as one of the characters.

We have a real instance of this in Dante's *Divine Comedy*. Dante is (1) the muse outside the poem who is inventing the whole thing, and (2) a character inside the poem, whom the other characters meet and with whom they hold conversations. Where the analogy breaks down is that everything the poem contains is merely imaginary, in that the characters have no free will. They (the characters) can say to Dante only what Dante (the poet) has decided to put into their mouths. I do not think we humans are related to God in that way. I think God can make things which not only—like a poet's or novelist's characters—*seem* to have a partially independent life, but really have it. But the analogy furnishes a crude model of the Incarnation in two respects: (1) Dante the poet and Dante the character are in a sense one, but in another sense two. This is a faint and far-off suggestion of what theologians mean by the 'union of the two natures' (divine and human) in Christ. (2) The other people in the poem meet and see and hear Dante; but they have not even the faintest suspicion that he is making the whole world in which they exist and has a life of his own, outside it, independent of it.

It is the second point which is most relevant. For the Christian story is that Christ was perceived to be God by very few people indeed; perhaps, for a time only by St Peter, who would also, and for the same reason, have found God in space. For Christ said to Peter, 'Flesh and blood have not taught you this.' The methods of science do not discover facts of that order.

Indeed the expectation of finding God by astronautics would be very like trying to verify or falsify the divinity of Christ by taking specimens of His blood or dissecting Him. And in their own way they did both. But they were no wiser than before. What is required is a certain faculty of recognition.

If you do not at all know God, of course you will not recognize Him, either in Jesus or in outer space.

The fact that we have not found God in space does not, then, bother me in the least. Nor am I much concerned about the 'space race' between America and Russia. The more money, time, skill and zeal they both spend on that rivalry, the less, we may hope they will have to spend on armaments. Great powers might be more usefully, but are seldom less dangerously, employed than in fabricating costly objects and flinging them, as you might say, overboard. Good luck to it! It is an excellent way of letting off steam.

But there are three ways in which space-travel will bother me if it reaches the stage for which most people are hoping.

The first is merely sentimental, or perhaps aesthetic. No moonlit night will ever be the same to me again if, as I look up at that pale disc, I must think 'Yes: up there to the left is the Russian area, and over there to the right is the American bit. And up at the top is the place which is now threatening to produce a crisis.' The immemorial Moon—the Moon of the myths, the poets, the lovers—will have been taken from us forever. Part of our mind, a huge mass of our emotional wealth, will have gone. Artemis, Diana, the silver planet belonged in that fashion to all humanity: he who first reaches it steals something from us all.

Secondly, a more practical issue will arise when, if ever, we discover rational creatures on other planets. I think myself, this is a very remote contingency. The balance of probability is against life on any other planet of the solar system. We shall hardly find it nearer than the stars. And even if we reach the Moon we shall be no nearer to stellar travel than the first man who paddled across a river was to crossing the Pacific.

This thought is welcome to me because, to be frank, I have no pleasure in looking forward to a meeting between humanity and any alien rational species. I observe how the white man has hitherto treated the black, and how, even among civilized men, the stronger have treated the weaker. If we encounter in the depth of space a race, however innocent and amiable, which is technologically weaker than ourselves, I do not doubt that the same revolting story will be repeated. We shall enslave, deceive, exploit or exterminate; at the very least we shall corrupt it with our vices and infect it with our diseases.

We are not fit yet to visit other worlds. We have filled our own with massacre, torture, syphilis, famine, dust bowls and with all that is hideous to ear or eye. Must we go on to infect new realms?

Of course we might find a species stronger than ourselves. In that case we shall have met, if not God, at least God's judgement in space. But once more the detecting apparatus will be inadequate. We shall think it just our bad luck if righteous creatures rightly destroy those who come to reduce them to misery.

It was in part these reflections that first moved me to make my own small contributions to science fiction. In those days writers in that genre almost automatically represented the inhabitants of other worlds as monsters and the terrestrial invaders as good. Since then the opposite set-up has become fairly common. If I could believe that I had in any degree contributed to this change, I should be a proud man.[1]

[1. The reference is to Lewis's interplanetary novels, *Out of the Silent Planet, Perelandra* and *That Hideous Strength*. He was probably the first writer to introduce the idea of having *fallen* terrestrial invaders discover on other planets—in his own books, Mars (*Out of the Silent Planet*) and Venus (*Perelandra*)—*unfallen* rational beings who were in no need of redemption and with nothing to learn from us. See also his essay, 'Will We Lose God in Outer Space?' *Christian Herald*, vol. LXXXI (April, 1958), pp. 19, 74–6.]

The same problem, by the way, is beginning to threaten us as regards the dolphins. I don't think it has yet been proved that they are rational. But if they are, we have no more right to enslave them than to enslave our fellow-men. And some of us will continue to say this, but we shall be mocked.

The third thing is this. Some people are troubled, and others are delighted, at the idea of finding not one, but perhaps innumerable rational species scattered about the universe. In both cases the emotion arises from a belief that such discoveries would be fatal to Christian theology. For it will be said that theology connects the Incarnation of God with the Fall and Redemption of man. And this would seem to attribute to our species and to our little planet a central position in cosmic history which is not credible if rationally inhabited planets are to be had by the million.

Older readers will, with me, notice the vast change in astronomical speculation which this view involves. When we were boys all astronomers, so far as I know, impressed upon us the antecedent improbabilities of life in any part of the universe whatever. It was not thought unlikely that this earth was the solitary exception to a universal reign of the inorganic. Now Professor Hoyle, and many with him, say that in so vast a universe life must have occurred in times and places without number. The interesting thing is that I have heard both these estimates used as arguments against Christianity.

Now it seems to me that we must find out more than we can at present know—which is nothing—about hypothetical rational species before we can say what theological corollaries or difficulties their discovery would raise.

We might, for example, find a race which was, like us, rational but, unlike us, innocent—no wars nor any other wickedness among them; all peace and good fellowship. I don't think any Christian would be puzzled to find that they knew no story of an Incarnation or Redemption, and might even find our story hard to understand or accept if we told it to them. There would have been no Redemption in such a world because it would not have needed redeeming. 'They that are whole need not the physician.' The sheep that has never strayed need not be sought for. We should have much to learn from such people and nothing to teach them. If we were wise, we should fall at their feet. But probably we should be unable to 'take it'. We'd find some reason for exterminating them.

Again, we might find a race which, like ours, contained both good and bad. And we might find that for them, as for us, something had been done: that at some point in their history some great interference for the better, believed by some of them to be supernatural, had been recorded, and that its effects, though often impeded and perverted, were still alive among them. It need not, as far as I can see, have conformed to the pattern of Incarnation, Passion, Death and Resurrection. God may have other ways—how should I be able to imagine them?—of redeeming a lost world. And Redemption in that alien mode might not be easily recognizable by our missionaries, let alone by our atheists.

We might meet a species which, like us, needed Redemption but had not been given it. But would this fundamentally be more of a difficulty than any Christian's first meeting with a new tribe of savages? It would be our duty to preach the Gospel to them. For if they are rational, capable both of sin and repentance, they are our brethren, whatever they look like. Would this spreading of the Gospel from earth, through man, imply a pre-eminence for earth and man? Not in any real sense. If a thing is to begin at all, it must begin at some particular time and place; and any time and place raises the question: 'Why just then and just there?' One can conceive an extraterrestrial development of Christianity so brilliant that earth's place in the story might sink to that of a prologue.

Finally, we might find a race which was strictly diabolical—no tiniest spark felt in them from which any goodness could ever be coaxed into the feeblest glow; all of them incurably perverted through and through. What then? We Christians had always been told that there were creatures like that in existence. True, we thought they were all incorporeal spirits. A minor readjustment thus becomes necessary.

But all this is in the realm of fantastic speculation. We are trying to cross a bridge, not only before we come to it, but even before we know there is a river that needs bridging.

God in the Dock

Essays on Theology and Ethics

Edited by
Walter Hooper

CONTENTS

Preface

DR JOHNSON, SPEAKING of an eighteenth-century theologian, remarked that he 'tended to unsettle every thing, and yet settle nothing'.[1] I wonder what the robust Doctor would make of our age: an age in which one sees in most bookshops and Sunday papers the controversial—and, oftentimes, apostate—works of clergy who 'unsettle' every article of the Faith they are ordained and paid to uphold. It is, partly because of this, a pleasure for me to offer as an antidote this new book by C. S. Lewis.

I say 'new' because, though these essays and letters were written over a period of twenty-four years, almost all are published in book-form for the first time. Considering how rapidly theological fashions change, it might be expected that these pieces would already be old stuff. There are, however, I expect, others like myself who are more concerned with whether a book is *true* than whether it was written last week. I believe that Lewis's refusal to compromise, neck or nothing, Heaven or Hell, does not for one moment detract from their relevance to the basic problems which still assail us.

Because of my desire to read everything that Lewis wrote, I undertook the long but happy task of 'excavating' his contributions to ephemeral publications. Now, at last, my years of searching libraries and reading faded newsprint are over. But, more important, I anticipate that the majority of them will have never been seen by most readers, and I hope they will derive as much satisfaction as I do from having them firmly stitched between two boards.

Since these new Lewisiana have been culled from such a wide variety of sources, they make, as might be expected, a very mixed bag. I do not apologize for this because so much of their interest lies in the many different angles from which we are able to view the Christian religion. Lewis never received a penny for most of them. Some of the essays were written simply because he felt the topic badly needed ventilating and the healthy position defending; others at the request of a newspaper or a periodical; there are other pieces, such as the ones from *The Socratic Digest*, which he composed for the purpose of defending the Faith against the attacks of agnostics and atheists.

Because Lewis knew how to adapt his material to suit the audience he was writing for, the essays differ both in length and in emphasis. Nevertheless, all share a particular seriousness. Not 'gloominess', for they sparkle with wit and common sense; but 'seriousness' because of the high stakes which Lewis believed were involved in being a man—a possible son of God or a possible candidate for hell.

During his years as an agnostic, Lewis wanted to know the answers to such questions as why God allows pain, why Christianity—out of all other religions—

---

1. James Boswell, *The Life of Samuel Johnson*, ed. George Birkbeck Hill (Oxford, 1887), vol. II, p. 124.

was held to be the true one, why and if miracles actually happen. As a result, he quite naturally anticipated the questions other men ask. After his conversion in 1931, Lewis, who seldom refused an invitation to speak or write about the Faith, found himself moving in very different circles. He preached to and argued with fellow dons, industrial workers, members of the Royal Air Force, and university students. It was partly due to this varied experience that he came to see why the professional theologians could not make Christianity understandable to most people. As a result, he set himself the task of 'translating' the Gospel into language which men use and understand. He believed that if you found it difficult to answer questions from men of different trades it was probably because 'You haven't really thought it out; not to the end; not to "the absolute ruddy end".'[2]

There were many Christians in Oxford in the early 1940s who, like Lewis, felt that both the *pros* and the *cons* of the Christian religion should be discussed openly. This led to the foundation of the Socratic Club in 1941. Lewis was the obvious person for the presidency, a position he held until he went to Cambridge in 1954. Meetings were (and still are) held every Monday evening in Term. One Monday a Christian would read a paper, to be answered by an unbeliever, and the following Monday an agnostic or atheist would read a paper which was, in turn, answered by a Christian. Lewis had always relished 'rational opposition', and the Socratic Club served as the perfect arena for testing the strengths and weaknesses of his apologetics. One example of the kind of paper he read at the Socratic is 'Religion without Dogma?' which he wrote as a reply to Professor H. H. Price's paper on 'The Grounds of Modern Agnosticism'.

It was difficult for the most able unbeliever to contend with Lewis's formidable logic and immense learning in the Socratic Club. On the other hand, we find him, in his articles in *The Coventry Evening Telegraph* and popular magazines, adapting his language and logic to less educated people. Pieces such as 'Religion and Science' and 'The Trouble with "X". . .', with their lucidity and apt analogies, have unmasked many popular fallacies about the supposed opposition between religion and science, and have led many people to understand what Christianity is about.

Regardless of one's education, it is impossible to decide whether Christianity is true or false if you do not know what it is *about*. And, just as there were many who were totally ignorant of Christianity when Lewis began to write, so there are many today who do not know what the real issue is. It is foolish to pretend. The recent flood of autobiographical explanations why such and such a bishop or parson cannot accept the Christian Faith has, I expect, driven many people into deeper ignorance and also (perhaps) into the despairing belief that it could not be understood however hard one tried.

For Lewis, who believed that to be born meant either an eventual surrender to God or an everlasting divorce from Him, this was a serious matter. One day he and I were speculating as to what would happen if a group of friendly and inquisitive Martians suddenly appeared in the middle of Oxford and asked (those who did not flee) what Christianity is. We wondered how many people, apart from

2. P. 473.

voicing their prejudices about the Church, could supply them with much in the way of accurate information. On the whole, we doubted whether the Martians would take back to their world much that is worth having. On the other hand, 'there is nothing', Lewis argued, 'in the nature of the younger generation which incapacitates them for receiving Christianity'. But, as he goes on to say, 'no generation can bequeath to its successors what it has not got.'[3]

What it has not got. The question as to *why* it has not got it is, obviously, too complex for me to answer. Nevertheless, having been a college chaplain for five years, I can see that much of the ignorance today is rightly attributed by Lewis to 'the liberal writers who are continually accommodating and whittling down the truth of the Gospel'.[4] And what Lewis would most emphatically *not* do is 'whittle down'.

He believed that, regardless of the temporary fashions which our ideas about God and morality pass through, there is nothing which can make the Everlasting Gospel out of date. ('All that is not eternal is eternally out of date.')[5] On the other hand, he believed that our methods of getting the truth across must often vary. Indeed, his own methods vary considerably: but he nowhere attempts to empty God out with the bath-water. For instance, we have from Lewis's pen straightforward apologetical works such as *Mere Christianity* and *The Problem of Pain*, theological satires such as *The Screwtape Letters* and *The Great Divorce*, and (for lack of a better word) his 'concealed' Christianity in the interplanetary novels and the Chronicles of Narnia.

Though Lewis's methods are not acceptable to liberal theologians (see, for example, his 'Rejoinder to Dr Pittenger'), he has probably got more orthodox Christianity into more heads than any religious writer since G. K. Chesterton. His graceful prose, his easy conversational style (almost all his books are written in the first person), his striking metaphors, and love of clarity are, no doubt, chiefly the result of his wide reading, his delight in writing, and his large share of mother wit. But they are more closely related than those who have read only his theological books might imagine to his abilities as a literary critic.

Beginning with his literary criticism and going on to his theological works, one will probably find that the process works the other way round as well. However, the point I particularly want to emphasize is this. Lewis believed that the proper work of a literary critic is to write about the merits and faults of a book, rather than to speculate about the genesis of the book or the author's private life. Though he had a high regard for textual criticism (and lectured on it at one time), he never overlooked the obvious in favour of the hypothetical. Similarly, in his theological works Lewis (who never claimed to be more than a layman writing for other laymen) does not offer ingenious guesses about whether, say, such and such a passage in one of the Gospels was supplied by the early Church long after that Gospel was written, but what the Gospels as we have them do, in fact, say and mean.

The essays in this book which are more or less 'straight' theology fall into two groups. The first contains those in which the primary topic is miracles. Lewis main-

3. Pp. 377, 378.
4. P. 476, 477.
5. C. S. Lewis, *The Four Loves* (London, 1960), ch. vi, p. 156.

tained that the Faith stripped of its supernatural elements could not conceivably be called Christianity. Because the miraculous is too toned down or hushed up today, I feel that his essays on the miraculous are particularly ripe for publication. Though most of what he says about miracles and the self-refutation of Naturalists can be found in his full-length book on *Miracles* (London, 1947; revised, 1960), I believe that the short essays here could have one advantage over the book. They might appeal to readers who have not the leisure to read, or who might get bogged down in, longer works.

The second category is hinted at in the title of this book. 'The ancient man', Lewis wrote, 'approached God (or even the gods) as the accused person approaches his judge. For the modern man the roles are reversed. He is the judge: God is in the dock.'[6] It would be ridiculous to suppose we can easily put *man* back in the dock. Lewis discusses his own methods for attempting this in his essay on 'Christian Apologetics' (the only essay in this volume which has never been published in any form before). 'In my experience', he says in this essay, 'if one begins from the sin that has been one's chief problem during the last week, one is very often surprised at the way this shaft goes home.'[7] Those who have read *Screwtape* will recall numerous instances in which he pinpoints those (seemingly) small sins which, if allowed to grow unchecked, in the end dominate man. As for the essays that follow, I should be surprised if those who read 'The Trouble with "X" . . .' do not have the sensation (which I do) of seeing their reflection in a mirror.

Lewis struck me as the most thoroughly *converted* man I ever met. Christianity was never for him a separate department of life; not what he did with his solitude; 'not even', as he says in one essay, 'what God does with His solitude'.[8] His whole vision of life was such that the natural and the supernatural seemed inseparably combined. Because of this, I have included in this collection his numerous semi-theological essays on topics such as the proposed ordination of women and vivisection. There are also a number of essays such as 'The Humanitarian Theory of Punishment' which could more properly be called ethical. Lastly, because of my concern that nothing be lost, I have added to the back of this book all Lewis's letters on theology and ethics that have appeared in newspapers and magazines.

The absence of moral values is so acutely felt today that it would seem a pity not to make public whatever help is available to our confused and spiritually-starved world. There may be contemporary writers who strike us as more humane, tender, 'original' and up to date than Lewis. But, like the Three Little Pigs, we need, not straw, but firm brick houses. Those who are concerned about the cheap religion and shoddy values so typical of our times will be aware of our immediate need for the antidote which Lewis provides: his realism, his moral rectitude, his ability to see beyond the partial perspectives which limit so many existentialists.

It will be noticed that I have, in the footnotes, given the sources of many of the quotations including the biblical ones. This will, perhaps, seem pedantic to some readers. I may have been at fault, but I hope that there will be some who might be

6. P. 464, 465.
7. P. 364, 365.
8. P. 386.

as grateful to have them as I was to find them. I have also provided in the footnotes translations of the more difficult Latin phrases. This book was prepared with American as well as English readers in mind, and I have included in my footnotes relevant information which is not, I believe, as generally known in the United States as it is here. In order that my notes may be easily distinguished from the author's, I have used * for Lewis's and arabic numerals for mine. Those who compare the texts of the essays published here with their originals will discover, in a few instances, some minor changes. This is because I have Lewis's own published copies of some essays, and where he has made changes or corrections I have followed his emendations. I have also felt it my responsibility to correct obvious errors wherever I have found them.

Though these essays do not fall easily into neat sub-divisions, I have, nevertheless, felt that divisions of some sort would be helpful to the reader. I have, therefore, divided the essays into three parts, conscious while doing so that some of the essays would fit almost as well in one part as they would in another. Part I contains those essays which are clearly theological: Part II contains those which I term semi-theological, and Part III includes those in which the basic theme is ethics. Part IV is composed of Lewis's letters arranged in the chronological order in which they were published.

I am very grateful to the publishers who have allowed me to reprint these essays and letters. I hope they will not think me ungenerous and slovenly if, instead of listing them separately, I acknowledge their permission by citing the original sources of the essays in the list that follows. The sources of the letters are found in Part IV. It is to be understood that all the publishers are English except where I have stated otherwise.

PART I: (1) 'Evil and God' is reprinted from *The Spectator,* vol. CLXVI (7 February 1941), p. 141. (2) 'Miracles' was preached in St Jude on the Hill Church, London, on the 26th November 1942 and appeared in *St Jude's Gazette,* No. 73 (October 1942), pp. 4–7. A shorter and slightly altered version of this sermon was published in *The Guardian* (2 October 1942), p. 316. *The Guardian* was a weekly Anglican newspaper which was founded in 1846 and ceased publication in 1951. (3) 'Dogma and the Universe' was published in two parts in *The Guardian* (19 March 1943), p. 96 and (26 March 1943), pp. 104, 107. The second part originally bore the title 'Dogma and Science'. (4) 'Answers to Questions on Christianity' was first published as a pamphlet by the Electrical and Musical Industries Christian Fellowship, Hayes, Middlesex [1944]. (5) 'Myth Became Fact' first appeared in *World Dominion,* vol. XXII (September-October 1944), pp. 267–70. (6) 'Horrid Red Things' was originally published in the *Church of England Newspaper,* vol. LI (6 October 1944), pp. 1–2. (7) 'Religion and Science' is reprinted from *The Coventry Evening Telegraph* (3 January 1945), p. 4. (8) 'The Laws of Nature' is also from *The Coventry Evening Telegraph* (4 April 1945), p. 4. (9) 'The Grand Miracle' was preached in St Jude on the Hill Church, London, and afterwards published in *The Guardian* (27 April 1945), pp. 161, 165. (10) 'Christian Apologetics', which is published for the first time, was read to an assembly of Anglican priests and youth leaders at the 'Carmarthen

Conference for Youth Leaders and Junior Clergy' at Carmarthen during Easter 1945. (11) 'Work and Prayer' first appeared in *The Coventry Evening Telegraph* (28 May 1945), p. 4. (12) 'Man or Rabbit?' was first published as a pamphlet by the Student Christian Movement in Schools. The pamphlet does not bear a date, but my guess is that it appeared sometime in 1946.

(13) 'On the Transmission of Christianity' is my title for Lewis's Preface to B. G. Sandhurst's *How Heathen is Britain?* (Collins Publishers, 1946), pp. 9–15. (14) 'Miserable Offenders' was preached at St Matthew's Church, Northampton, on the 7th April 1946 and afterwards published by St Matthew's Church in a booklet *Five Sermons by Laymen* (April-May 1946), pp. 1–6. (15) 'The Founding of the Oxford Socratic Club' is my title for Lewis's Preface to *The Socratic Digest*, No. 1 (1942–1943), pp. 3–5. This piece is obviously an intruder in this section, and would more properly fit into Part II. I have chosen, however, to give it the place it has because of its connection with the essay which follows. (16) 'Religion without Dogma?' was read to the Socratic Club on the 20th May 1946 and published as 'A Christian Reply to Professor Price' in *The Phoenix Quarterly*, vol. I, No. 1 (Autumn 1946), pp. 31–44. It was reprinted as 'Religion without Dogma?' in *The Socratic Digest*, No. 4 [1948], pp. 82–94. The 'Reply' which I have appended to this essay is Lewis's answer to Miss G. E. M. Anscombe's article 'A Reply to Mr C. S. Lewis' Argument that "Naturalism" is Self-refuting', both of which appeared in issue No. 4 of *The Socratic Digest*, pp. 15–16 and pp. 7–15 respectively. (17) 'Some Thoughts' was written one evening in The White Horse Inn at Drogheda, Ireland, at the request of the Medical Missionaries of Mary who founded Our Lady of Lourdes Hospital at Drogheda, and was published in *The First Decade: Ten Years of Work of the Medical Missionaries of Mary* (Dublin, At the Sign of the Three Candles [1948]), pp. 91–94. (18) 'The Trouble with "X"...' was first published in the *Bristol Diocesan Gazette*, vol. XXVII (August 1948), pp. 3–6. (19) 'What Are We to Make of Jesus Christ?' is reprinted from *Asking Them Questions*, Third Series, ed. Ronald Selby Wright (Oxford University Press, 1950), pp. 47–53. (20) 'The Pains of Animals: A Problem in Theology' first appeared in *The Month*, vol. CLXXXIX (February 1950), pp. 95–104. I am indebted to Miss M. F. Matthews for permission to include the late Dr C. E. M. Joad's part of this essay. (21) 'Is Theism Important? A Reply' is reprinted from *The Socratic Digest*, No. 5 (1952), pp. 48–51. (22) The 'Rejoinder to Dr Pittenger' first appeared in the columns of the American periodical *The Christian Century*, vol. LXXV (26 November 1958), pp. 1359–61. (23) 'Must Our Image of God Go?' is taken from *The Observer* (24 March 1963), p. 14.

PART II: The first three essays in this part are reprinted from the columns of *The Guardian*. (1) 'Dangers of National Repentance' is from the issue of 15 March 1940, p. 127. (2) 'Two Ways with the Self' is from that of 3 May 1940, p. 215, and (3) 'Meditation on the Third Commandment' from that of 10 January 1941, p. 18. (4) 'On the Reading of Old Books' is my title for Lewis's Preface to St Athanasius' *The Incarnation of the Word of God*, translated by A Religious of C.S.M.V., first published by Geoffrey Bles Ltd. in 1944 and by A. R. Mowbray and Co. Ltd. in 1953. (5) 'Two Lectures' is Lewis's title for an essay originally published as 'Who was Right—Dream Lecturer or Real Lecturer?' in *The Coventry Evening Telegraph* (21 February

1945), p. 4. (6) 'Meditation in a Toolshed' is reprinted from *The Coventry Evening Telegraph* (17 July 1945), p. 4. (7) 'Scraps' originally appeared in the *St James' Magazine* (December 1945), pp. [4–5], which was published by St James' Church, Birkdale, Southport. (8) 'The Decline of Religion' is taken from an Oxford periodical, *The Cherwell*, vol . XXVI (29 November 1946), pp. 8–10. (9) 'Vivisection' was first published as a pamphlet by the New England Anti-Vivisection Society [1947]. (10) 'Modern Translations of the Bible' is a title I have chosen for Lewis's Preface to J. B. Phillips' *Letters to Young Churches: A Translation of the New Testament Epistles* (Geoffrey Bles Ltd., 1947), pp. vii-x.

(11) 'Priestesses in the Church?' was originally published as 'Notes on the Way' in *Time and Tide*, vol . XXIX (14 August 1948), pp. 830–31. (12) 'God in the Dock' is my title for 'Difficulties in Presenting the Christian Faith to Modern Unbelievers', *Lumen Vitae*, vol. III (September 1948), pp. 421–26. (13) 'Behind the Scenes' appeared first in *Time and Tide*, vol. XXXVII (1 December 1956), pp. 1450–51. (14) 'Revival or Decay?' is reprinted from *Punch,* vol. CCXXXV (9 July 1958), pp. 36–38. (15) 'Before We Can Communicate' was published in *Breakthrough*, No. 8 (October 1961), p. 2. (16) 'Cross-Examination' is the title I have chosen for an interview Mr Sherwood E. Wirt of the Billy Graham Association had with Lewis in Magdalene College, Cambridge, on the 7th May 1963. The interview was originally published in two parts under different titles. The first part was called 'I Was Decided Upon', *Decision*, vol. II (September 1963), p. 3, and the second 'Heaven, Earth and Outer Space', *Decision*, vol. II (October 1963), p. 4.

PART III: (1) A shortened form of 'Bulverism' appeared under the title 'Notes on the Way' in *Time and Tide,* vol. XXII (29 March 1941), p. 261. A longer version, which is the one found here, appeared in *The Socratic Digest,* No. 2 (June 1944), pp. 16–20. (2) 'First and Second Things' is Lewis's title for 'Notes on the Way' from *Time and Tide*, vol. XXIII (27 June 1942), pp. 519–20. (3) 'The Sermon and the Lunch' is reprinted from the *Church of England Newspaper,* No. 2692 (21 September 1945), pp. 1–2. (4) 'The Humanitarian Theory of Punishment' first appeared in *20th Century: An Australian Quarterly Review*, vol. III, No. 3 (1949), pp. 5–12. This same journal in vol. VI, No. 2 (1952), pp. 20–26 published Drs Norval Morris and Donald Buckle's 'Reply to C. S. Lewis'. Both pieces were later reprinted in *Res Judicatae*, vol. VI (June 1953), pp. 224–30 and pp. 231–37 respectively. Then followed Professor J. J. C. Smart's 'Comment: The Humanitarian Theory of Punishment' in *Res Judicatae*, vol. VI (February 1954), pp. 368–71, and Lewis's 'On Punishment: A Reply'—that is, a reply to all three men—in *Res Judicatae*, vol. VI (August 1954), pp. 519–23. (5) 'Xmas and Christmas: A Lost Chapter from Herodotus' first appeared in *Time and Tide*, vol. XXXV (4 December 1954), p. 1607. (6) 'What Christmas Means to Me' is reprinted from *Twentieth Century*, vol. CLXII (December 1957), pp. 517–18. (7) 'Delinquents in the Snow' appeared first in *Time and Tide*, vol. XXXVIII (7 December 1957), pp. 1521–22. (8) 'Willing Slaves of the Welfare State' is from *The Observer* (20 July 1958), p. 6. (9) 'We Have No "Right to Happiness"' is the last thing Lewis wrote for publication. It appeared shortly after his death in *The Saturday Evening Post* vol. CCXXXVI (21–28 December 1963), pp. 10, 12.

Finally, as on many previous occasions, I would like to thank Major W. H. Lewis, Mr Owen Barfield, Mr Colin Hardie, Mr Roger Lancelyn Green, Professor John Lawlor and Miss Nan Dunbar for the assistance they have given me in making these Lewis 'excavations' available to others.

Jesus College, Oxford   WALTER HOOPER
May 1970

PART I

1
Evil and God

DR JOAD'S ARTICLE on 'God and Evil' last week[1] suggests the interesting conclusion that since neither 'mechanism' nor 'emergent evolution' will hold water, we must choose in the long run between some monotheistic philosophy, like the Christian, and some such dualism as that of the Zoroastrians. I agree with Dr Joad in rejecting mechanism and emergent evolution. Mechanism, like all materialist systems, breaks down at the problem of knowledge. If thought is the undesigned and irrelevant product of cerebral motions, what reason have we to trust it? As for emergent evolution, if anyone insists on using the word *God* to mean 'whatever the universe happens to be going to do next', of course we cannot prevent him. But nobody would in fact so use it unless he had a secret belief that what is coming next will be an improvement. Such a belief, besides being unwarranted, presents peculiar difficulties to an emergent evolutionist. If things can improve, this means that there must be some absolute standard of good above and outside the cosmic process to which that process can approximate. There is no sense in talking of 'becoming better' if better means simply 'what we are becoming'—it is like congratulating yourself on reaching your destination and defining destination as 'the place you have reached'. Mellontolatry, or the worship of the future, is a *fuddled* religion.

We are left then to choose between monotheism and dualism—between a single, good, almighty source of being, and two equal, uncreated, antagonistic Powers, one good and the other bad. Dr Joad suggests that the latter view stands to gain from the 'new urgency' of the fact of evil. But *what* new urgency? Evil may seem more urgent to us than it did to the Victorian philosophers—favoured members of the happiest class in the happiest country in the world at the world's happiest period. But it is no more urgent for us than for the great majority of monotheists all down the ages. The classic expositions of the doctrine that the world's miseries are compatible with its creation and guidance by a wholly good Being come from Boethius waiting in prison to be beaten to death and from St Augustine meditating on the sack of Rome. The present state of the world is normal; it was the last century that was the abnormality.

This drives us to ask why so many generations rejected Dualism. Not, assuredly, because they were unfamiliar with suffering; and not because its obvious *prima facie* plausibility escaped them. It is more likely that they saw its two fatal difficulties, the one metaphysical, and the other moral.

The metaphysical difficulty is this. The two Powers, the good and the evil, do not explain each other. Neither Ormuzd nor Ahriman can claim to be the Ultimate.

1. C. E. M. Joad, 'Evil and God,' *The Spectator*, vol. CLXVI (31 January 1941), pp. 112–13.

More ultimate than either of them is the inexplicable fact of their being there to-gether. Neither of them chose this *tête-à-tête*. Each of them, therefore, is *conditioned*—finds himself willy-nilly in a situation; and either that situation itself, or some un-known force which produced that situation, is the real Ultimate. Dualism has not yet reached the ground of being. You cannot accept two conditioned and mutually independent beings as the self-grounded, self-comprehending Absolute. On the level of picture-thinking this difficulty is symbolised by our inability to think of Ormuzd and Ahriman without smuggling in the idea of a common *space* in which they can be together and thus confessing that we are not yet dealing with the source of the universe but only with two members contained in it. Dualism is a truncated metaphysic.

The moral difficulty is that Dualism gives evil a positive, substantive, self-consistent nature, like that of good. If this were true, if Ahriman existed in his own right no less than Ormuzd, what could we mean by calling Ormuzd good except that we happened to prefer *him*. In what sense can the one party be said to be right and the other wrong? If evil has the same kind of reality as good, the same autonomy and completeness, our allegiance to good becomes the arbitrarily chosen loyalty of a partisan. A sound theory of value demands something different. It demands that good should be original and evil a mere perversion; that good should be the tree and evil the ivy; that good should be able to see all round evil (as when sane men understand lunacy) while evil cannot retaliate in kind; that good should be able to exist on its own while evil requires the good on which it is parasitic in order to continue its parasitic existence.

The consequences of neglecting this are serious. It means believing that bad men like badness as such, in the same way in which good men like goodness. At first this denial of any common nature between us and our enemies seems gratifying. We call them fiends and feel that we need not forgive them. But, in reality, along with the power to forgive, we have lost the power to condemn. If a taste for cruelty and a taste for kindness were equally ultimate and basic, by what common stan-dard could the one reprove the other? In reality, cruelty does not come from desir-ing evil as such, but from perverted sexuality, inordinate resentment, or lawless ambition and avarice. That is precisely why it can be judged and condemned from the standpoint of innocent sexuality, righteous anger, and ordinate acquisitiveness. The master can correct a boy's sums because they are blunders in arithmetic—in the same arithmetic which he does and does better. If they were not even attempts at arithmetic—if they were not in the arithmetical world at all—they could not be arithmetical mistakes.

Good and evil, then, are not on all fours. Badness is not even bad *in the same way* in which goodness is good. Ormuzd and Ahriman cannot be equals. In the long run, Ormuzd must be original and Ahriman derivative. The first hazy idea of *devil* must, if we begin to think, be analysed into the more precise ideas of 'fallen' and 'rebel' angel. But only in the long run. Christianity can go much further with the Dualist than Dr Joad's article seems to suggest. There was never any question of tracing *all* evil to man; in fact, the New Testament has a good deal more to say about dark superhuman powers than about the fall of Adam. As far as this world is concerned, a Christian can share most of the Zoroastrian outlook; we all live between the 'fell, incensed points'[2] of Michael and Satan. The difference between the Christian and the Dualist is that the Christian thinks one stage further and sees that if Michael is really in the right and Satan really in the wrong this must mean that they stand in two different relations to somebody or something far further back, to the ultimate ground of reality itself. All this, of course, has been watered down in modern times by the theologians who are afraid of 'mythology', but those who are prepared to reinstate Ormuzd and Ahriman are presumably not squeamish on that score.

Dualism can be a manly creed. In the Norse form ('The giants will beat the gods in the end, but I am on the side of the gods') it is nobler by many degrees than most philosophies of the moment. But it is only a half-way house. Thinking along these lines you can avoid Monotheism, and remain a Dualist, only by refusing to follow your thoughts home. To revive Dualism would be a real step backwards and a bad omen (though not the worst possible) for civilization.

2. Shakespeare, *Hamlet*, V. ii, 60.

2

Miracles

I HAVE KNOWN only one person in my life who claimed to have seen a ghost. It was a woman; and the interesting thing is that she disbelieved in the immortality of the soul before seeing the ghost and still disbelieves after having seen it. She thinks it was a hallucination. In other words, seeing is not believing. This is the first thing to get clear in talking about miracles. Whatever experiences we may have, we shall not regard them as miraculous if we already hold a philosophy which excludes the supernatural. Any event which is claimed as a miracle is, in the last resort, an experience received from the senses; and the senses are not infallible. We can always say we have been the victims of an illusion; if we disbelieve in the supernatural this is what we always shall say. Hence, whether miracles have really ceased or not, they would certainly appear to cease in Western Europe as materialism became the popular creed. For let us make no mistake. If the end of the world appeared in all the literal trappings of the Apocalypse,[1] if the modern materialist saw with his own eyes the heavens rolled up[2] and the great white throne appearing,[3] if he had the sensation of being himself hurled into the Lake of Fire,[4] he would continue forever, in that lake itself, to regard his experience as an illusion and to find the explanation of it in psycho-analysis, or cerebral pathology. Experience by itself proves nothing. If a man doubts whether he is dreaming or waking, no experiment can solve his doubt, since every experiment may itself be part of the dream. Experience proves this, or that, or nothing, according to the preconceptions we bring to it.

This fact, that the interpretation of experiences depends on preconceptions, is often used as an argument against miracles. It is said that our ancestors, taking the supernatural for granted and greedy of wonders, read the miraculous into events that were really not miracles. And in a sense I grant it. That is to say, I think that just as our preconceptions would prevent us from apprehending miracles if they really occurred, so their preconceptions would lead them to imagine miracles even if they did not occur. In the same way, the doting man will think his wife faithful when she is not and the suspicious man will not think her faithful when she is: the question of her actual fidelity remains, meanwhile, to be settled, if at all, on other grounds. But there is one thing often said about our ancestors which we must *not* say. We must not say 'They believed in miracles because they did not know the Laws of Nature.' This is nonsense. When St Joseph discovered that his bride was pregnant, he was 'minded to put her away'.[5] He knew enough biology for that.

1. The book of Revelation.
2. *Ibid.*, vi. 14.
3. *Ibid.*, xx. 11.
4. *Ibid.*, xix. 20; xx. 10; xx. 14–15; xxi. 8.
5. Matthew i. 19.

Otherwise, of course he would not have regarded pregnancy as a proof of infidelity. When he accepted the Christian explanation, he regarded it as a miracle precisely because he knew enough of the Laws of Nature to know that this was a suspension of them. When the disciples saw Christ walking on the water they were frightened:[6] they would not have been frightened unless they had known the laws of Nature and known that this was an exception. If a man had no conception of a regular order in Nature, then of course he could not notice departures from that order: just as a dunce who does not understand the normal metre of a poem is also unconscious of the poet's variations from it. Nothing is wonderful except the abnormal and nothing is abnormal until we have grasped the norm. Complete ignorance of the laws of Nature would preclude the perception of the miraculous just as rigidly as complete disbelief in the supernatural precludes it, perhaps even more so. For while the materialist would have at least to explain miracles away, the man wholly ignorant of Nature would simply not notice them.

The experience of a miracle in fact requires two conditions. First we must believe in a normal stability of nature, which means we must recognize that the data offered by our senses recur in regular patterns. Secondly, we must believe in some reality beyond Nature. When both beliefs are held, and not till then, we can approach with an open mind the various reports which claim that this super- or extra-natural reality has sometimes invaded and disturbed the sensuous content of space and time which makes our 'natural' world. The belief in such a supernatural reality itself can neither be proved nor disproved by experience. The arguments for its existence are metaphysical, and to me conclusive. They turn on the fact that even to think and act in the natural world we have to assume something beyond it and even assume that we partly belong to that something. In order to think we must claim for our own reasoning a validity which is not credible if our own thought is merely a function of our brain, and our brains a by-product of irrational physical processes. In order to act, above the level of mere impulse, we must claim a similar validity for our judgments of good and evil. In both cases we get the same disquieting result. The concept of nature itself is one we have reached only tacitly by claiming a sort of *super*-natural status for ourselves.

If we frankly accept this position and then turn to the evidence, we find, of course, that accounts of the supernatural meet us on every side. History is full of them—often in the same documents which we accept wherever they do not report miracles. Respectable missionaries report them not infrequently. The whole Church of Rome claims their continued occurrence. Intimate conversation elicits from almost every acquaintance at least one episode in his life which is what he would call 'queer' or 'rum'. No doubt most stories of miracles are unreliable; but then, as anyone can see by reading the papers, so are most stories of all events. Each story must be taken on its merits: what one must not do is to rule out the supernatural as the one impossible explanation. Thus you may disbelieve in the Mons Angels[7] because you cannot find a sufficient number of sensible people who say they saw them. But if you found a sufficient number, it would, in my view,

6. Matthew xiv. 26; Mark vi. 49; John vi. 19.

be unreasonable to explain this by collective hallucination. For we know enough of psychology to know that spontaneous unanimity in hallucination is very improbable, and we do not know enough of the supernatural to know that a manifestation of angels is equally improbable. The supernatural theory is the less improbable of the two. When the Old Testament says that Sennacherib's invasion was stopped by angels,[8] and Herodotus says it was stopped by a lot of mice who came and ate up all the bowstrings of his army,[9] an open-minded man will be on the side of the angels. Unless you start by begging the question, there is nothing intrinsically unlikely in the existence of angels or in the action ascribed to them. But mice just don't do these things.

A great deal of scepticism now current about the miracles of our Lord does not, however, come from disbelief of all reality beyond nature. It comes from two ideas which are respectable but I think mistaken. In the first place, modern people have an almost aesthetic dislike of miracles. Admitting that God can, they doubt if He would. To violate the laws He Himself has imposed on His creation seems to them arbitrary, clumsy, a theatrical device only fit to impress savages—a solecism against the grammar of the universe. In the second place, many people confuse the laws of nature with the laws of thought and imagine that their reversal or suspension would be a contradiction in terms—as if the resurrection of the dead were the same sort of thing as two and two making five.

I have only recently found the answer to the first objection. I found it first in George MacDonald and then later in St Athanasius. This is what St Athanasius says in his little book *On the Incarnation:* 'Our Lord took a body like to ours and lived as a man in order that those who had refused to recognize Him in His superintendence and captaincy of the whole universe might come to recognize from the works He did here below in the body that what dwelled in this body was the Word of God.' This accords exactly with Christ's own account of His miracles: 'The Son can do nothing of Himself, but what He seeth the Father do.'[10] The doctrine, as I understand it, is something like this:

There is an activity of God displayed throughout creation, a wholesale activity let us say which men refuse to recognize. The miracles done by God incarnate, living as a man in Palestine, perform the very same things as this wholesale activity, but at a different speed and on a smaller scale. One of their chief purposes is that men, having seen a thing done by personal power on the small scale, may recognize, when they see the same thing done on the large scale, that the power behind it is also personal—is indeed the very same person who lived among us two thousand years ago. The miracles in fact are a retelling in small letters of the very same story which is written across the whole world in letters too large for some of us to see. Of that larger script part is already visible, part is still unsolved. In other words, some of the miracles do locally what God has already done universally: others do

---

7. Lewis is referring to the story that angels appeared, protecting British troops in their retreat from Mons, France, on the 26th August 1914. A recent summary of the event by Jill Kitson 'Did Angels appear to British troops at Mons?' is found in *History Makers,* No. 3 (1969), pp. 132–33.
8. II Kings xix. 35.
9. Herodotus, Bk. II, Sect. 141.
10. John v. 19.

locally what He has not yet done, but will do. In that sense, and from our human point of view, some are reminders and others prophecies.

God creates the vine and teaches it to draw up water by its roots and, with the aid of the sun, to turn that water into a juice which will ferment and take on certain qualities. Thus every year, from Noah's time till ours, God turns water into wine. That, men fail to see. Either like the Pagans they refer the process to some finite spirit, Bacchus or Dionysus: or else, like the moderns, they attribute real and ultimate causality to the chemical and other material phenomena which are all that our senses can discover in it. But when Christ at Cana makes water into wine, the mask is off.[11] The miracle has only half its effect if it only convinces us that Christ is God: it will have its full effect if whenever we see a vineyard or drink a glass of wine we remember that here works He who sat at the wedding party in Cana. Every year God makes a little corn into much corn: the seed is sown and there is an increase, and men, according to the fashion of their age, say 'It is Ceres, it is Adonis, it is the Corn-King,' or else 'It is the laws of Nature.' The close-up, the translation, of this annual wonder is the feeding of the five thousand.[12] Bread is not made there of nothing. Bread is not made of stones, as the Devil once suggested to Our Lord in vain.[13] A little bread is made into much bread. The Son will do nothing but what He sees the Father do. There is, so to speak, a family *style*. The miracles of healing fall into the same pattern. This is sometimes obscured for us by the somewhat magical view we tend to take of ordinary medicine. The doctors themselves do not take this view. The magic is not in the medicine but in the patient's body. What the doctor does is to stimulate Nature's functions in the body, or to remove hindrances. In a sense, though we speak for convenience of healing a cut, every cut heals itself; no dressing will make skin grow over a cut on a corpse. That same mysterious energy which we call gravitational when it steers the planets and biochemical when it heals a body is the efficient cause of all recoveries, and if God exists, that energy, directly or indirectly, is His. All who are cured are cured by Him, the healer within. But once He did it visibly, a Man meeting a man. Where He does not work within in this mode, the organism dies. Hence Christ's one miracle of destruction is also in harmony with God's wholesale activity. His bodily hand held out in symbolic wrath blasted a single fig tree;[14] but no tree died that year in Palestine, or any year, or in any land, or even ever will, save because He has done something, or (more likely) ceased to do something, to it.

When He fed the thousands he multiplied fish as well as bread. Look in every bay and almost every river. This swarming, pulsating fecundity shows He is still at work. The ancients had a god called Genius—the god of animal and human fertility, the presiding spirit of gynaecology, embryology, or the marriage bed—the 'genial bed' as they called it after its god Genius.[15] As the miracles of wine and bread

---

11. John ii. 1–11.
12. Matthew xiv. 15–21; Mark vi. 34–44; Luke ix. 12–17; John vi. 1–11.
13. Matthew iv. 3; Luke iv. 3.
14. Matthew xxi. 19; Mark xi. 13–20.
15. For further information on this subject see the chapter on 'Genius and Genius' in Lewis's *Studies in Medieval and Renaissance Literature*, ed. Walter Hooper (Cambridge, 1966), pp. 169–74.

and healing showed who Bacchus really was, who Ceres, who Apollo, and that all were one, so this miraculous multiplication of fish reveals the real Genius. And with that we stand at the threshold of the miracle which for some reason most offends modern ears. I can understand the man who denies the miraculous altogether; but what is one to make of the people who admit some miracles but deny the Virgin Birth? Is it that for all their lip service to the laws of Nature there is only one law of Nature that they really believe? Or is it that they see in this miracle a slur upon sexual intercourse which is rapidly becoming the one thing venerated in a world without veneration? No miracle is in fact more significant. What happens in ordinary generation? What is a father's function in the act of begetting? A microscopic particle of matter from his body fertilizes the female: and with that microscopic particle passes, it may be, the colour of his hair and his great grandfather's hanging lip, and the human form in all its complexity of bones, liver, sinews, heart, and limbs, and pre-human form which the embryo will recapitulate in the womb. Behind every spermatozoon lies the whole history of the universe: locked within it is no small part of the world's future. That is God's normal way of making a man—a process that takes centuries, beginning with the creation of matter itself, and narrowing to one second and one particle at the moment of begetting. And once again men will mistake the sense impressions which this creative act throws off for the act itself or else refer it to some infinite being such as Genius. Once, therefore, God does it directly, instantaneously; without a spermatozoon, without the millenniums of organic history behind the spermatozoon. There was of course another reason. This time He was creating not simply a man, but the man who was to be Himself: the only true Man. The process which leads to the spermatozoon has carried down with it through the centuries much undesirable silt; the life which reaches us by that normal route is tainted. To avoid that taint, to give humanity a fresh start, He once short-circuited the process. There is a vulgar anti-God paper which some anonymous donor sends me every week. In it recently I saw the taunt that we Christians believe in a God who committed adultery with the wife of a Jewish carpenter. The answer to that is that if you describe the action of God in fertilizing Mary as 'adultery' then, in that sense, God would have committed adultery with every woman who ever had a baby. For what He did once without a human father, He does always even when He uses a human father as His instrument. For the human father in ordinary generation is only a carrier, sometimes an unwilling carrier, always the last in a long line of carriers, of life that comes from the supreme life. Thus the filth that our poor, muddled, sincere, resentful enemies fling at the Holy One, either does not stick, or, sticking, turns into glory.

So much for the miracles which do small and quick what we have already seen in the large letters of God's universal activity. But before I go on to the second class— those which foreshadow parts of the universal activity we have not yet seen—I must guard against a misunderstanding. Do not imagine I am trying to make the miracle less miraculous. I am not arguing that they are more probable because they are less unlike natural events: I am trying to answer those who think them arbitrary, theatrical, unworthy of God, meaningless interruptions of universal order. They remain in my view wholly miraculous. To do instantly with dead and baked corn what ordinarily happens slowly with live seed is just as great a miracle as to make bread of stones. Just as great, but a different *kind* of miracle. That is the point. When I open Ovid,[16] or Grimm,[17] I find the sort of miracles which really would be arbitrary. Trees talk, houses turn into trees, magic rings raise tables richly spread with food in lonely places, ships become goddesses, and men are changed into snakes or birds or bears. It is fun to read about: the least suspicion that it had really happened would turn that fun into nightmare. You find no miracles of that kind in the Gospels. Such things, if they could be, would prove that some alien power was invading Nature; they would not in the least prove that it was the same power which had made Nature and rules her every day. But the true miracles express not simply a god, but God: that which is outside Nature, not as a foreigner, but as her sovereign. They announce not merely that a King has visited our town, but that it is *the* King, *our* King.

The second class of miracles, on this view, foretell what God has not yet done, but will do, universally. He raised one man (the man who was Himself) from the dead because He will one day raise all men from the dead. Perhaps not only men, for there are hints in the New Testament that all creation will eventually be rescued from decay, restored to shape and subserve the splendour of re-made humanity.[18] The Transfiguration[19] and the walking on the water[20] are glimpses of the beauty and the effortless power over all matter which will belong to men when they are really waked by God. Now resurrection certainly involves 'reversal' of natural process in the sense that it involves a series of changes moving in the opposite direction to those we see. At death, matter which has been organic, falls back gradually into the inorganic, to be finally scattered and used perhaps in other organisms. Resurrection would be the reverse process. It would not of course mean the restoration to each personality of those very atoms, numerically the same, which had made its first or 'natural' body. There would not be enough to go round, for one thing; and for another, the unity of the body even in this life was consistent with a slow but perplexed change of its actual ingredients. But it certainly does mean matter of some kind rushing towards organism as now we see it rushing away. It means, in fact, playing backwards a film we have already seen played forwards. In that sense it is a reversal of Nature. But, of course, it is a further question whether reversal in this sense is necessarily contradiction. Do we know that the film cannot be played backwards?

Well, in one sense, it is precisely the teaching of modern physics that the film never works backwards. For modern physics, as you have heard before, the universe is 'running down'. Disorganization and chance is continually increasing. There will come a time, not infinitely remote, when it will be wholly run down or wholly

---

16. The reference is to Ovid's (43 B.C.-A.D. 18) *Metamorphoses*.
17. The fairy tales of the brothers, Jacob Ludwig Carl (1785–1863) and Wilhelm Carl (1786–1859) Grimm.
18. E.g., Romans viii. 22: 'We know that the whole creation groaneth and travaileth in pain together until now.'
19. Matthew xvii. 1–9, Mark ix. 2–10.
20. Matthew xiv. 26; Mark vi. 49; John vi. 19.

disorganized, and science knows of no possible return from that state. There must have been a time, not infinitely remote, in the past when it was wound up, though science knows of no winding-up process. The point is that for our ancestors the universe was a picture: for modern physics it is a story. If the universe is a picture these things either appear in that picture or not; and if they don't, since it is an infinite picture, one may suspect that they are contrary to the nature of things. But a story is a different matter; specially if it is an incomplete story. And the story told by modern physics might be told briefly in the words 'Humpty Dumpty was falling.' That is, it proclaims itself an incomplete story. There must have been a time before he fell, when he was sitting on the wall; there must be a time after he had reached the ground. It is quite true that science knows of no horses and men who can put him together again once he has reached the ground and broken. But then she also knows of no means by which he could originally have been put on the wall. You wouldn't expect her to. All science rests on observation: all our observations are taken *during* Humpty Dumpty's fall, because we were born after he lost his seat on the wall and shall be extinct long before he reaches the ground. But to assume from observations taken while the clock is running down that the unimaginable winding-up which must have preceded this process cannot occur when the process is over is the merest dogmatism. From the very nature of the case the laws of degradation and disorganization which we find in matter at present, cannot be the ultimate and eternal nature of things. If they were, there would have been nothing to degrade and disorganize. Humpty Dumpty can't fall off a wall that never existed.

Obviously, an event which lies outside the falling or disintegrating process which we know as Nature, is not imaginable. If anything is clear from the records of Our Lord's appearances after His resurrection, it is that the risen body was very different from the body that died and that it lives under conditions quite unlike those of natural life. It is frequently not recognized by those who see it:[21] and it is not related to space in the same way as our bodies. The sudden appearances and disappearances[22] suggest the ghost of popular tradition: yet He emphatically insists that He is not merely a spirit and takes steps to demonstrate that the risen body can still perform animal operations, such as eating.[23] What makes all this baffling to us is our assumption that to pass beyond what we call Nature—beyond the three dimensions and the five highly specialized and limited senses—is immediately to be in a world of pure negative spirituality, a world where space of any sort and sense of any sort has no function. I know no grounds for believing this. To explain even an atom Schrödinger[24] wants seven dimensions: and give us new senses and we should find a new Nature. There may be Natures piled upon Natures, each supernatural to the one beneath it, before we come to the abyss of pure spirit; and to be in that abyss, at the right hand of the Father, may not mean being absent from any of these Natures—may mean a yet more dynamic presence on all levels. That is why I think

21. Luke xxiv. 13–31, 36–7; John xx. 14–16.
22. Mark xvi. 14; Luke xxiv. 31, 36; John xx. 19, 26.
23. Luke xxiv. 42–3; John xxi. 13.
24. Arthur Schrödinger (1887–1961), the Austrian physicist.

it very rash to assume that the story of the Ascension is mere allegory. I know it sounds like the work of people who imagined an absolute up and down and a local heaven in the sky. But to say this is after all to say 'Assuming that the story is fake, we could thus explain how it arose.' Without that assumption we find ourselves 'moving about in worlds unrealised'[25] with no probability—or improbability—to guide us. For if the story is true then a being still in some mode, though not our mode, corporeal, withdrew at His own will from the Nature presented by our three dimensions and five senses, not necessarily into the non-sensuous and undimensioned but possibly into, or through, a world or worlds of super-sense and super-space. And He might choose to do it gradually. Who on earth knows what the spectators might see? If they say they saw a momentary movement along the vertical plane—then an indistinct mass—then nothing—who is to pronounce this improbable?

My time is nearly up and I must be very brief with the second class of people whom I promised to deal with: those who mistake the laws of Nature for laws of thought and, therefore, think that any departure from them is a self-contradiction, like a square circle or two and two making five. To think this is to imagine that the normal processes of Nature are transparent to the intellect, that we can say why she behaves as she does. For, of course, if we cannot see why a thing is so, then we cannot see any reason why it should not be otherwise. But in fact the actual course of Nature is wholly inexplicable. I don't mean that science has not yet explained it, but may do so some day. I mean that the very nature of explanation makes it impossible that we should even explain why matter has the properties it has. For explanation, by its very nature, deals with a world of 'ifs and ands'. Every explanation takes the form 'Since A, therefore B' or 'If C, then D.' In order to explain any event you have to assume the universe as a going concern, a machine working in a particular way. Since this particular way of working is the basis of all explanation, it can never be itself explained. We can see no reason why it should not have worked a different way.

To say this is not only to remove the suspicion that miracle is self-contradictory, but also to realize how deeply right St Athanasius was when he found an essential likeness between the miracles of Our Lord and the general order of Nature. Both are a full stop for the explaining intellect. If the 'natural' means that which can be fitted into a class, that which obeys a norm, that which can be paralleled, that which can be explained by reference to other events, then Nature herself as a whole is *not* natural. If a miracle means that which must simply be accepted, the unanswerable actuality which gives no account of itself but simply *is*, then the universe is one great miracle. To direct us to that great miracle is one main object of the earthly acts of Christ: that are, as He himself said, Signs.[26] They serve to remind us that the explanations of particular events which we derive *from* the given, the unexplained, the almost wilful character of the actual universe, are not explanations of that char-

25. This is probably a misquotation of Wordsworth's 'Moving about in worlds not realised.' *Intimations of Immortality*, ix, 149.
26. Matthew xii. 39; xvi. 4; xxiv. 24, 30; Mark xiii. 22; xvi. 17, 20; Luke xxi. 11, 25.

acter. These Signs do not take us away from reality; they recall us to it—recall us from our dream world of 'ifs and ands' to the stunning actuality of everything that is real. They are focal points at which more reality becomes visible than we ordinarily see at once. I have spoken of how He made miraculous bread and wine and of how, when the Virgin conceived, He had shown Himself the true Genius whom men had ignorantly worshipped long before. It goes deeper than that. Bread and wine were to have an even more sacred significance for Christians and the act of generations was to be the chosen symbol among all mystics for the union of the soul with God. These things are no accidents. With Him there are no accidents. When He created the vegetable world He knew already what dreams the annual death and resurrection of the corn would cause to stir in pious Pagan minds, He knew already that He Himself must so die and live again and in what sense, including and far transcending the old religion of the Corn King. He would say 'This is my Body.'[27] *Common* bread, miraculous bread, sacramental bread—these three are distinct, but not to be separated. Divine reality is like a fugue. All His acts are different, but they all rhyme or echo to one another. It is this that makes Christianity so difficult to talk about. Fix your mind on any one story or any one doctrine and it becomes at once a magnet to which truth and glory come rushing from all levels of being. Our featureless pantheistic unities and glib rationalist distinctions are alike defeated by the seamless, yet ever-varying texture of reality, the liveness, the elusiveness, the intertwined harmonies of the multidimensional fertility of God. But if this is the difficulty, it is also one of the firm grounds of our belief. To think that this was a fable, a product of our own brains as they are a product of matter, would be to believe that this vast symphonic splendour had come out of something much smaller and emptier than itself. It is not so. We are nearer to the truth in the vision seen by Julian of Norwich, when Christ appeared to her holding in His hand a little thing like a hazel nut and saying, 'This is all that is created.'[28] And it seemed to her so small and weak that she wondered how it could hold together at all.[29]

---

27. Matthew xxvi. 26; Mark xiv. 22; Luke xxii. 19; I Corinthians xi. 24.
28. *Sixteen Revelations of Divine Love,* ed. Roger Hudleston (London, 1927), ch. 5, p. 9.
29. See Letter 3.

3
Dogma and the Universe

IT IS A common reproach against Christianity that its dogmas are unchanging, while human knowledge is in continual growth. Hence, to unbelievers, we seem to be always engaged in the hopeless task of trying to force the new knowledge into moulds which it has outgrown. I think this feeling alienates the outsider much more than any particular discrepancies between this or that doctrine and this or that scientific theory. We may, as we say, 'get over' dozens of isolated 'difficulties', but that does not alter his sense that the endeavour as a whole is doomed to failure and perverse: indeed, the more ingenious, the more perverse. For it seems to him clear that, if our ancestors had known what we know about the universe, Christianity would never have existed at all: and, however we patch and mend, no system of thought which claims to be immutable can, in the long run, adjust itself to our growing knowledge.

That is the position I am going to try to answer. But before I go on to what I regard as the fundamental answer, I would like to clear up certain points about the actual relations between Christian doctrine and the scientific knowledge we already have. That is a different matter from the continual growth of knowledge we imagine, whether rightly or wrongly, in the future and which, as some think, is bound to defeat us in the end.

In one respect, as many Christians have noticed, contemporary science has recently come into line with Christian doctrine, and parted company with the classical forms of materialism. If anything emerges clearly from modern physics, it is that nature is not everlasting. The universe had a beginning, and will have an end. But the great materialistic systems of the past all believed in the eternity, and thence in the self-existence of matter. As Professor Whittaker said in the Riddell Lectures of 1942, 'It was never possible to oppose seriously the dogma of the Creation except by maintaining that the world has existed from all eternity in more or less its present state.'[1] This fundamental ground for materialism has now been withdrawn. We should not lean too heavily on this, for scientific theories change. But at the moment it appears that the burden of proof rests, not on us, but on those who deny that nature has some cause beyond herself.

In popular thought, however, the origin of the universe has counted (I think) for less than its character—its immense size and its apparent indifference, if not hostility, to human life. And very often this impresses people all the more because it is supposed to be a modern discovery—an excellent example of those things which our ancestors did not know and which, if they had known them, would have prevented the very beginnings of Christianity. Here there is a simple historical false-

1. Sir Edmund Taylor Whittaker, *The Beginning and End of the World*, Riddell Memorial Lectures, Fourteenth Series (Oxford, 1942), p. 40.

hood. Ptolemy knew just as well as Eddington[2] that the earth was infinitesimal in comparison with the whole content of space.[3] There is no question here of knowledge having grown until the frame of archaic thought is no longer able to contain it. The real question is why the spatial insignificance of the earth, after being known for centuries, should suddenly in the last century have become an argument against Christianity. I do not know why this has happened; but I am sure it does not mark an increased clarity of thought, for the argument from size is, in my opinion, very feeble.

When the doctor at a post-mortem diagnoses poison, pointing to the state of the dead man's organs, his argument is rational because he has a clear idea of that opposite state in which the organs would have been found if no poison were present. In the same way, if we use the vastness of space and the smallness of earth to disprove the existence of God, we ought to have a clear idea of the sort of universe we should expect if God did exist. But have we? Whatever space may be in itself—and, of course, some moderns think it finite—we certainly perceive it as three-dimensional, and to three-dimensional space we can conceive no boundaries. By the very forms of our perceptions, therefore, we must feel as if we lived somewhere in infinite space. If we discovered no objects in this infinite space except those which are of use to man (our own sun and moon), then this vast emptiness would certainly be used as a strong argument against the existence of God. If we discover other bodies, they must be habitable or uninhabitable: and the odd thing is that both these hypotheses are used as grounds for rejecting Christianity. If the universe is teeming with life, this, we are told, reduces to absurdity the Christian claim—or what is thought to be the Christian claim—that man is unique, and the Christian doctrine that to this one planet God came down and was incarnate for us men and our salvation. If, on the other hand, the earth is really unique, then that proves that life is only an accidental by-product in the universe, and so again disproves our religion. Really, we are hard to please. We treat God as the police treat a man when he is arrested; whatever He does will be used in evidence against Him. I do not think this is due to our wickedness. I suspect there is something in our very mode of thought which makes it inevitable that we should always be baffled by actual existence, *whatever* character actual existence may have. Perhaps a finite and contingent creature—a creature that might not have existed—will always find it hard to acquiesce in the brute fact that it is, here and now, attached to an actual order of things.

However that may be, it is certain that the whole argument from size rests on the assumption that differences of size ought to coincide with differences of value: for unless they do, there is, of course, no reason why the minute earth and the yet smaller human creatures upon it should not be the most important things in a universe that contains the spiral nebulae. Now, is this assumption rational or emotional? I feel, as well as anyone else, the absurdity of supposing that the galaxy could be of less moment in God's eyes than such an atom as a human being. But I notice that I feel no similar absurdity in supposing that a man of five-feet high may be

2. Sir Arthur Stanley Eddington (1882–1944) who wrote *The Expanding Universe* (1933).
3. Ptolemy lived at Alexandria in the 2nd century A.D. The reference is to his *Almagest*, bk. I, ch. v.

more important than another man who is five-feet three and a half—nor that a man may matter more than a tree, or a brain more than a leg. In other words, the feeling of absurdity arises only if the differences of size are very great. But where a relation is perceived by reason it holds good universally. If size and value had any real connexion, small differences in size would accompany small differences in value as surely as large differences in size accompany large differences in value. But no sane man could suppose that this is so. I don't think the taller man *slightly* more valuable than the shorter one. I don't allow a slight superiority to trees over men, and then neglect it because it is too small to bother about. I perceive, as long as l am dealing with the small differences of size, that they have no connexion with value whatsoever. I therefore conclude that the importance attached to the great differences of size is an affair, not of reason but of emotion—of that peculiar emotion which superiorities in size produce only after a certain point of absolute size has been reached.

We are inveterate poets. Our imaginations awake. Instead of mere quantity, we now have a quality—the sublime. Unless this were so, the merely arithmetical greatness of the galaxy would be no more impressive than the figures in a telephone directory. It is thus, in a sense, from ourselves that the material universe derives its power to over-awe us. To a mind which did not share our emotions, and lacked our imaginative energies, the argument from size would be sheerly meaningless. Men look on the starry heavens with reverence: monkeys do not. The silence of the eternal spaces terrified Pascal,[4] but it was the greatness of Pascal that enabled them to do so. When we are frightened by the greatness of the universe, we are (almost literally) frightened by our own shadows: for these light years and billions of centuries are mere arithmetic until the shadow of man, the poet, the maker of myth, falls upon them. I do not say we are wrong to tremble at his shadow; it is a shadow of an image of God. But if ever the vastness of matter threatens to overcross our spirits, one must remember that it is matter spiritualized which does so. To puny man, the great nebula in Andromeda owes in a sense its greatness.

And this drives me to say yet again that we are hard to please. If the world in which we found ourselves were not vast and strange enough to give us Pascal's terror, what poor creatures we should be! Being what we are, rational but also animate, amphibians who start from the world of sense and proceed through myth and metaphor to the world of spirit, I do not see how we could have come to know the greatness of God without that hint furnished by the greatness of the material universe. Once again, what sort of universe do we demand? If it were small enough to be cosy, it would not be big enough to be sublime. If it is large enough for us to stretch our spiritual limbs in, it must be large enough to baffle us. Cramped or terrified, we must, in any conceivable world, be one or the other. I prefer terror. I should be suffocated in a universe that I could see to the end of. Have you never, when walking in a wood, turned back deliberately for fear you should come out at the other side and thus make it ever after in your imagination a mere beggarly strip of trees?

4. Blaise Pascal, *Pensées*, No. 206.

I hope you do not think I am suggesting that God made the spiral nebulae solely or chiefly in order to give me the experience of awe and bewilderment. I have not the faintest idea why He made them; on the whole, I think it would be rather surprising if I had. As far as I understand the matter, Christianity is not wedded to an anthropocentric view of the universe as a whole. The first chapters of Genesis, no doubt, give the story of creation in the form of a folk-tale—a fact recognized as early as the time of St Jerome—and if you take them alone you might get that impression. But it is not confirmed by the Bible as a whole. There are few places in literature where we are more sternly warned against making man the measure of all things than in the Book of Job: 'Canst thou draw out leviathan with an hook? Will he make a covenant with thee? wilt thou take him for a servant? Shall not one be cast down even at the sight of him?'[5] In St Paul, the powers of the skies seem usually to be hostile to man. It is, of course, the essence of Christianity that God loves man and for his sake became man and died. But that does not prove that man is the sole end of nature. In the parable, it was the one lost sheep that the shepherd went in search of:[6] it was not the only sheep in the flock, and we are not told that it was the most valuable—save in so far as the most desperately in need has, while the need lasts, a peculiar value in the eyes of Love. The doctrine of the Incarnation would conflict with what we know of this vast universe only if we knew also that there were other rational species in it who had, like us, fallen, and who needed redemption in the same mode, and that they had not been vouchsafed it. But we know none of these things. It may be full of life that needs no redemption. It may be full of life that has been redeemed. It may be full of things quite other than life which satisfy the Divine Wisdom in fashions one cannot conceive. We are in no position to draw up maps of God's psychology, and prescribe limits to His interests. We would not do so even for a man whom we knew to be greater than ourselves. The doctrines that God is love and that He delights in men, are positive doctrines, not limiting doctrines. He is not less than this. What more He may be, we do not know; we know only that He must be more than we can conceive. It is to be expected that His creation should be, in the main, unintelligible to us.

Christians themselves have been much to blame for the misunderstanding on these matters. They have a bad habit of talking as if revelation existed to gratify curiosity by illuminating all creation so that it becomes self-explanatory and all questions are answered. But revelation appears to me to be purely practical, to be addressed to the particular animal, Fallen Man, for the relief of his urgent necessities—not to the spirit of inquiry in man for the gratification of his liberal curiosity. We know that God has visited and redeemed His people, and that tells us just as much about the general character of the creation as a dose given to one sick hen on a big farm tells it about the general character of farming in England. What we must do, which road we must take to the fountain of life, we know, and none who has seriously followed the directions complains that he has been deceived. But whether there are other creatures like ourselves, and how they are dealt with: whether inanimate matter exists only to serve living creatures or for some other reason:

5. Job xli. 1, 4, 9.
6. Matthew xviii. 12; Luke xv. 4.

whether the immensity of space is a means to some end, or an illusion, or simply the natural mode in which infinite energy might be expected to create—on all these points I think we are left to our own speculations.

No. It is not Christianity which need fear the giant universe. It is those systems which place the whole meaning of existence in biological or social evolution on our own planet. It is the creative evolutionist, the Bergsonian or Shavian, or the Communist, who should tremble when he looks up at the night sky. For he really is committed to a sinking ship. He really is attempting to ignore the discovered nature of things, as though by concentrating on the possibly upward trend in a single planet he could make himself forget the inevitable downward trend in the universe as a whole, the trend to low temperatures and irrevocable disorganization. For entropy is the real cosmic wave, and evolution only a momentary tellurian ripple within it.

On these grounds, then, I submit that we Christians have as little to fear as anyone from the knowledge actually acquired. But, as I said at the beginning, that is not the fundamental answer. The endless fluctuations of scientific theory which seem today so much friendlier to us than in the last century may turn against us tomorrow. The basic answer lies elsewhere.

Let me remind you of the question we are trying to answer. It is this: How can an unchanging system survive the continual increase of knowledge? Now, in certain cases we know very well how it can. A mature scholar reading a great passage in Plato, and taking in at one glance the metaphysics, the literary beauty, and the place of both in the history of Europe, is in a very different position from a boy learning the Greek alphabet. Yet through that unchanging system of the alphabet all this vast mental and emotional activity is operating. It has not been broken by the new knowledge. It is not outworn. If it changed, all would be chaos. A great Christian statesman, considering the morality of a measure which will affect millions of lives, and which involves economic, geographical and political considerations of the utmost complexity, is in a different position from a boy first learning that one must not cheat or tell lies, or hurt innocent people. But only in so far as that first knowledge of the great moral platitudes survives unimpaired in the statesman will his deliberation be moral at all. If that goes, then there has been no progress, but only mere change. For change is not progress unless the core remains unchanged. A small oak grows into a big oak: if it became a beech, that would not be growth, but mere change. And thirdly, there is a great difference between counting apples and arriving at the mathematical formulae of modern physics. But the multiplication table is used in both and does not grow out of date.

In other words, wherever there is real progress in knowledge, there is some knowledge that is not superseded. Indeed, the very possibility of progress demands that there should be an unchanging element. New bottles for new wine, by all means: but not new palates, throats and stomachs, or it would not be, for us, 'wine' at all. I take it we should all agree to find this sort of unchanging element in the simple rules of mathematics. I would add to these the primary principles of morality. And I would also add the fundamental doctrines of Christianity. To put it in rather more technical language, I claim that the positive historical statements made by Christianity have the power, elsewhere found chiefly in formal principles, of receiving, without intrinsic change, the increasing complexity of meaning which increasing knowledge puts into them.

For example, it may be true (though I don't for a moment suppose it is) that when the Nicene Creed said 'He came down from Heaven', the writers had in mind a local movement from a local heaven to the surface of the earth—like a parachute descent. Others since may have dismissed the idea of a spatial heaven altogether. But neither the significance nor the credibility of what is asserted seems to be in the least affected by the change. On either view, the thing is miraculous: on either view, the mental images which attend the act of belief are inessential. When a Central African convert and a Harley Street specialist both affirm that Christ rose from the dead, there is, no doubt, a very great difference between their thoughts. To one, the simple picture of a dead body getting up is sufficient; the other may think of a whole series of biochemical and even physical processes beginning to work backwards. The Doctor knows that, in his experience, they never have worked backwards; but the negro knows that dead bodies don't get up and walk. Both are faced with miracle, and both know it. If both think miracle impossible, the only difference is that the Doctor will expound the impossibility in much greater detail, will give an elaborate gloss on the simple statement that dead men don't walk about. If both believe, all the Doctor says will merely analyze and explicate the words 'He rose.' When the author of Genesis says that God made man in His own image, he may have pictured a vaguely corporeal God making man as a child makes a figure out of plasticine. A modern Christian philosopher may think of a process lasting from the first creation of matter to the final appearance on this planet of an organism fit to receive spiritual as well as biological life. But both mean essentially the same thing. Both are denying the same thing—the doctrine that matter by some blind power inherent in itself has produced spirituality.

Does this mean that Christians on different levels of general education conceal radically different beliefs under an identical form of words? Certainly not. For what they agree on is the substance, and what they differ about is the shadow. When one imagines his God seated in a local heaven above a flat earth, where another sees God and creation in terms of Professor Whitehead's philosophy,[7] this difference touches precisely what does not matter. Perhaps this seems to you an exaggeration. But is it? As regards material reality, we are now being forced to the conclusion that we know nothing about it save its mathematics. The tangible beach and pebbles of our first calculators, the imaginable atoms of Democritus, the plain man's picture of space, turn out to be the shadow: numbers are the substance of our knowledge, the sole liaison between mind and things. What nature is in herself evades us; what seem to naive perception to be the evident things about her, turn out to be the most phantasmal. It is something the same with our knowledge

---

7. Alfred North Whitehead (1861–1947), who wrote, among other works, *Science and the Modern World* (1925) and *Religion in the Making* (1926).

of spiritual reality. What God is in Himself, how He is to be conceived by philosophers, retreats continually from our knowledge. The elaborate world-pictures which accompany religion and which look each so solid while they last, turn out to be only shadows. It is religion itself—prayer and sacrament and repentance and adoration—which is here, in the long run, our sole avenue to the real. Like mathematics, religion can grow from within, or decay. The Jew knows more than the Pagan, the Christian more than the Jew, the modern vaguely religious man less than any of the three. But, like mathematics, it remains simply itself, capable of being applied to any new theory of the material universe and outmoded by none.

When any man comes into the presence of God he will find, whether he wishes it or not, that all those things which seemed to make him so different from the men of other times, or even from his earlier self, have fallen off him. He is back where he always was, where every man always is. *Eadem sunt omnia semper.*[8] Do not let us deceive ourselves. No possible complexity which we can give to our picture of the universe can hide us from God: there is no copse, no forest, no jungle thick enough to provide cover. We read in Revelation of Him that sat on the throne 'from whose face the earth and heaven fled away'.[9] It may happen to any of us at any moment. In the twinkling of an eye, in a time too small to be measured, and in any place, all that seems to divide us from God can flee away, vanish, leaving us naked before Him, like the first man, like the only man, as if nothing but He and I existed. And since that contact cannot be avoided for long, and since it means either bliss or horror, the business of life is to learn to like it. That is the first and great commandment.

8. 'Everything is always the same.'
9. Revelation xx. 11.

4
Answers to Questions
on Christianity

[The answers to questions printed here were given by Lewis at a 'One Man Brains Trust' held on the 18th April 1944 at the Head Office of Electric and Musical Industries Ltd., Hayes, Middlesex. Shorthand notes were made and a typescript was sent to Lewis. He revised it a little, and it was printed in 1944. Mr H. W. Bowen was the question-master.]

Lewis:

I have been asked to open with a few words on Christianity and Modern Industry. Now Modern Industry is a subject of which I know nothing at all. But for that very reason it may illustrate what Christianity, in my opinion, does and does not do. Christianity does *not* replace the technical. When it tells you to feed the hungry it doesn't give you lessons in cookery. If you want to learn *that*, you must go to a cook rather than a Christian. If you are not a professional Economist and have no experience of Industry, simply being a Christian won't give you the answer to industrial problems. My own idea is that modern industry is a radically hopeless system. You can improve wages, hours, conditions, etc., but all that doesn't cure the deepest trouble: i.e., that numbers of people are kept all their lives doing dull repetition work which gives no full play to their faculties. How that is to be overcome, I do not know. If a single country abandoned the system it would merely fall a prey to the other countries which hadn't abandoned it. I don't know the solution: that is not the kind of thing Christianity teaches a person like me. Let's now carry on with the questions.

Question 1.

Christians are taught to love their neighbours. How, therefore, can they justify their attitude of supporting the war?

Lewis:

You are told to love your neighbour as yourself. How do you love yourself? When I look into my own mind, I find that I do not love myself by thinking myself a dear old chap or having affectionate feelings. I do not think that I love myself because I am particularly good, but just because I am myself and quite apart from my character. I might detest something which I have done. Nevertheless, I do not cease to love myself. In other words, that definite distinction that Christians make between hating sin and loving the sinner is one that you have been making in your own case since you were born. You dislike what you have done, but you don't cease to love yourself. You may even think that you ought to be hanged. You may even think that you ought to go to the Police and own up and be hanged. Love is not affectionate feeling, but a steady wish for the loved person's ultimate good as far as it can be obtained. It seems to me, therefore, that when the worst comes to the worst, if you cannot restrain a man by any method except by trying to kill him, then a Christian must do that. That is my answer. But I may be wrong. It is very difficult to answer, of course.

Question 2.

Supposing a factory worker asked you: 'How can I find God?' How would you reply?

Lewis:

I don't see how the problem would be different for a factory worker than for anyone else. The primary thing about any man is that he is a human being, sharing all the ordinary human temptations and assets. What is the special problem about the factory worker? But perhaps it is worth saying this:

Christianity really does two things about conditions here and now in this world:

(1) It tries to make them as good as possible, i.e., to reform them; but also

(2) It fortifies you against them in so far as they remain bad.

If what was in the questioner's mind was this problem of repetition work, then the factory worker's difficulty is the same as any other man confronted with any sorrow or difficulty. People will find God if they consciously seek from Him the right attitude towards all unpleasant things . . . if that is the point of the question?

Question 3.

Will you please say how you would define a practising Christian? Are there any other varieties?

Lewis:

Certainly there are a great many other varieties. It depends, of course, on what you mean by 'practising Christian'. If you mean one who has practised Christianity in every respect at every moment of his life, then there is only One on record— Christ Himself. In that sense there are no practising Christians, but only Christians who, in varying degrees, try to practise it and fail in varying degrees and then start again. A perfect practice of Christianity would, of course, consist in a perfect imitation of the life of Christ—I mean, in so far as it was applicable in one's own particular circumstances. Not in an idiotic sense—it doesn't mean that every Christian should grow a beard, or be a bachelor, or become a travelling preacher. It means that every single act and feeling, every experience, whether pleasant or unpleasant, must be referred to God. It means looking at everything as something that comes from Him, and always looking to Him and asking His will first, and saying: 'How would He wish me to deal with this?'

A kind of picture or pattern (in a very remote way) of the relation between the perfect Christian and his God, would be the relation of the good dog to its master. This is only a very imperfect picture, though, because the dog hasn't reason like its master: whereas we do share in God's reason, even if in an imperfect and interrupted way ('interrupted' because we don't think rationally for very long at a time—it's too tiring—and we haven't information to understand things fully, and our intelligence itself has certain limitations). In that way we are more like God than the dog is like us, though, of course, there are other ways in which the dog is more like us than we are like God. It is only an illustration.

Question 4.

What justification on ethical grounds and on the grounds of social expediency exists for the Church's attitude towards Venereal Disease and prophylaxis and publicity in connection with it?

Lewis:

I need further advice on that question, and then perhaps I can answer it. Can the questioner say which Church he has in mind?

Voice.

The Church concerned is the Church of England, and its attitude, though not written, is implicit in that it has more or less banned all publicity in connection with prophylactic methods of combating Venereal Disease. The view of some is that moral punishment should not be avoided.

Lewis:

I haven't myself met any clergymen of the Church of England who held that view: and I don't hold it myself. There are obvious objections to it. After all, it isn't only Venereal Disease that can he regarded as a punishment for bad conduct. Indigestion in old age may be the result of overeating in earlier life: but no one objects to advertisements for Beecham's Pills. I, at any rate, strongly dissent from the view you've mentioned.

Question 5.

Many people feel resentful or unhappy because they think they are the target of unjust fate. These feelings are stimulated by bereavement, illness, deranged domestic or working conditions, or the observation of suffering in others. What is the Christian view of this problem?

Lewis:

The Christian view is that men were created to be in a certain relationship to God (if we are in that relation to Him, the right relation to one another will follow inevitably). Christ said it was difficult for 'the rich' to enter the Kingdom of Heaven,[1]

---

1. Matthew xix. 23; Mark x. 23; Luke xviii. 24.

referring, no doubt, to 'riches' in the ordinary sense. But I think it really covers riches in every sense—good fortune, health, popularity, and all the things one wants to have. All these things tend—just as money tends—to make you feel independent of God, because if you have them you are happy already and contented in this life. You don't want to turn away to anything more, and so you try to rest in a shadowy happiness as if it could last for ever. But God wants to give you a real and eternal happiness. Consequently He may have to take all these 'riches' away from you: if He doesn't, you will go on relying on them. It sounds cruel, doesn't it? But I am beginning to find out that what people call the cruel doctrines are really the kindest ones in the long run. I used to think it was a 'cruel' doctrine to say that troubles and sorrows were 'punishments'. But I find in practice that when you are in trouble, the moment you regard it as a 'punishment', it becomes easier to bear. If you think of this world as a place intended simply for our happiness, you find it quite intolerable: think of it as a place of training and correction and it's not so bad.

Imagine a set of people all living in the same building. Half of them think it is a hotel, the other half think it is a prison. Those who think it a hotel might regard it as quite intolerable, and those who thought it was a prison might decide that it was really surprisingly comfortable. So that what seems the ugly doctrine is one that comforts and strengthens you in the end. The people who try to hold an optimistic view of this world would become pessimists: the people who hold a pretty stern view of it become optimistic.

Question 6.

Materialists and some astronomers suggest that the solar planetary system and life as we know it was brought about by an accidental stellar collision. What is the Christian view of this theory?

Lewis:

If the solar system was brought about by an accidental collision, then the appearance of organic life on this planet was also an accident, and the whole evolution of Man was an accident too. If so, then all our present thoughts are mere accidents—the accidental by-product of the movement of atoms. And this holds for the thoughts of the materialists and astronomers as well as for anyone else's. But if *their* thoughts—i.e., of Materialism and Astronomy—are merely accidental by-products, why should we believe them to be true? I see no reason for believing that one accident should be able to give me a correct account of all the other accidents. It's like expecting that the accidental shape taken by the splash when you upset a milk-jug should give you a correct account of how the jug was made and why it was upset.

Question 7.

Is it true that Christianity (especially the Protestant forms) tends to produce a gloomy, joyless condition of society which is like a pain in the neck to most people?

Lewis:

As to the distinction between Protestant and other forms of Christianity, it is very difficult to answer. I find by reading about the sixteenth century, that people like Sir Thomas More, for whom I have a great respect, always regarded Martin Luther's doctrines not as gloomy thinking, but as wishful thinking. I doubt whether we can make a distinction between Protestant and other forms in this respect. Whether Protestantism is gloomy and whether Christianity at all produces gloominess, I find it very difficult to answer, as I have never lived in a completely non-Christian society nor a completely Christian one, and I wasn't there in the sixteenth century, and only have my knowledge from reading books. I think there is about the same amount of fun and gloom in all periods. The poems, novels, letters, etc., of every period all seem to show that. But again, I don't really know the answer, of course. I wasn't there.

Question 8.

Is it true that Christians must be prepared to live a life of personal discomfort and self-sacrifice in order to qualify for 'Pie in the Sky'?

Lewis:

All people, whether Christian or not, must be prepared to live a life of discomfort. It is impossible to accept Christianity for the sake of finding comfort: but the Christian tries to lay himself open to the will of God, to do what God wants him to do. You don't know in advance whether God is going to set you to do something difficult or painful, or something that you will quite like; and some people of heroic mould are disappointed when the job doled out to them turns out to be something quite nice. But you must be prepared for the unpleasant things and the discomforts. I don't mean fasting, and things like that. They are a different matter. When you are training soldiers in manoeuvres, you practise in blank ammunition because you would like them to have practise before meeting the real enemy. So we must practise in abstaining from pleasures which are not in themselves wicked. If you don't abstain from pleasure, you won't be good when the time comes along. It is purely a matter of practise.

Voice.

Are not practices like fasting and self-denial borrowed from earlier or more primitive religions?

Lewis:

l can't say for certain which bits came into Christianity from earlier religions. An enormous amount did. I should find it hard to believe Christianity if that were not so. I couldn't believe that nine-hundred and ninety-nine religions were completely false and the remaining one true. In reality, Christianity is primarily the fulfilment of the Jewish religion, but also the fulfilment of what was vaguely hinted in all the religions at their best. What was vaguely seen in them all comes into focus in Christianity—just as God Himself comes into focus by becoming a Man. I take it that the speaker's remarks on earlier religions are based on evidence about modern savages. I don't think it is good evidence. Modern savages usually represent some decay in culture—you find them doing things which look as if they had a fairly civilized basis once, which they have forgotten. To assume that primitive man was exactly like the modern savage is unsound.

Voice.

Could you say any more on how one discovers whether a task is laid on one by God, or whether it comes in some other way? If we cannot distinguish between the pleasant and the unpleasant things, it is a complicated matter.

Lewis:

We are guided by the ordinary rules of moral behaviour, which I think are more or less common to the human race and quite reasonable and demanded by the circumstances. I don't mean anything like sitting down and waiting for a supernatural vision.

Voice.

We don't qualify for heaven by practice, but salvation is obtained at the Cross. We do nothing to obtain it, but follow Christ. We may have pain or tribulation, but nothing we do qualifies us for heaven, but Christ.

Lewis:

The controversy about faith and works is one that has gone on for a very long time, and it is a highly technical matter. I personally rely on the paradoxical text: 'Work out your own salvation . . . for it is God that worketh in you.'[2] It looks as if in one sense we do nothing, and in another case we do a damned lot. 'Work out your own salvation with fear and trembling,'[3] but you must have it in you before you can work it out. But I have no wish to go further into it, as it would interest no one but the Christians present, would it?

Question 9.

Would the application of Christian standards bring to an end or greatly reduce scientific and material progress? In other words, is it wrong for a Christian to be ambitious and strive for personal success?

Lewis:

It is easiest to think of a simplified example. How would the application of Christianity affect anyone on a desert island? Would he be less likely to build a comfortable hut? The answer is 'No.' There might come a particular moment, of course, when

2. Philippians ii. 12.
3. *Ibid.*

Christianity would tell him to bother less about the hut, i.e., if he were in danger of coming to think that the hut was the most important thing in the universe. But there is no evidence that Christianity would prevent him from building it.

Ambition! We must be careful what we mean by it. If it means the desire to get ahead of other people—which is what I think it does mean—then it is bad. If it means simply wanting to do a thing well, then it is good. It isn't wrong for an actor to want to act his part as well as it can possibly be acted, but the wish to have his name in bigger type than the other actors is a bad one.

Voice.

It's all right to be a General, but if it is one's ambition to be a General, then you shouldn't become one.

Lewis:

The mere event of becoming a General isn't either right or wrong in itself. What matters morally is your attitude towards it. The man may be thinking about winning a war; he may be wanting to be a General because he honestly thinks he has a good plan and is glad of a chance to carry it out. That's all right. But if he is thinking: 'What can I get out of the job?' or 'How can I get on the front page of the *Illustrated News?*' then it is all wrong. And what we call 'ambition' usually means the wish to be more conspicuous or more successful than someone else. It is this competitive element in it that is bad. It is perfectly reasonable to want to dance well or to look nice. But when the dominant wish is to dance better or look nicer than the others—when you begin to feel that if the others danced as well as you or looked as nice as you, that would take all the fun out of it—then you are going wrong.

Voice.

I am wondering how far we can ascribe to the work of the Devil those very legitimate desires that we indulge in. Some people have a very sensitive conception of the presence of the Devil. Others haven't. Is the Devil as real as we think he is? That doesn't trouble some people, since they have no desire to be good, but others are continually harassed by the Old Man himself.

Lewis:

No reference to the Devil or devils is included in any Christian Creeds, and it is quite possible to be a Christian without believing in them. I do believe such beings exist, but that is my own affair. Supposing there to be such beings, the degree to which humans were conscious of their presence would presumably vary very much. I mean, the more a man was in the Devil's power, the less he would be aware of it, on the principle that a man is still fairly sober as long as he knows he's drunk. It is the people who are fully awake and trying hard to be good who would be most aware of the Devil. It is when you start arming against Hitler that you first realize your country is full of Nazi agents. of course, they don't want you to believe in the

Devil. If devils exist, their first aim is to give you an anesthetic—to put you off your guard. Only if that fails, do you become aware of them.

Voice.

Does Christianity retard scientific advancement? Or does it approve of those who help spiritually others who are on the road to perdition, by scientifically removing the environmental causes of the trouble?

Lewis:

Yes. In the abstract it is certainly so. At a particular moment, if most human beings are concentrating only on material improvements in the environment, it may be the duty of Christians to point out (and pretty loudly) that this isn't the only thing that matters. But as a general rule it is in favour of all knowledge and all that will help the human race in any way.

Question 10.

The Bible was written thousands of years ago for people in a lower state of mental development than today. Many portions seem preposterous in the light of modern knowledge. In view of this, should not the Bible be re-written with the object of discarding the fabulous and re-interpreting the remainder?

Lewis:

First of all as to the people in a lower state of mental development. I am not so sure what lurks behind that. If it means that people ten thousand years ago didn't know a good many things that we know now, of course, I agree. But if it means that there has been any advance in *intelligence* in that time, I believe there is no evidence for any such thing. The Bible can be divided into two parts—the Old and the New Testaments. The Old Testament contains fabulous elements. The New Testament consists mostly of teaching, not of narrative at all: but where it *is* narrative, it is, in my opinion, historical. As to the fabulous element in the Old Testament, I very much doubt if you would be wise to chuck it out. What you get is something *coming gradually into focus.* First you get, scattered through the heathen religions all over the world—but still quite vague and mythical—the idea of a god who is killed and broken and then comes to life again. No one knows where he is supposed to have lived and died; he's not historical. Then you get the Old Testament. Religious ideas get a bit more focused. Everything is now connected with a particular nation. And it comes still more into focus as it goes on. Jonah and the Whale,[4] Noah and his Ark,[5] are fabulous; but the Court history of King David[6] is probably as reliable as the Court history of Louis XIV. Then, in the New Testament the *thing really happens.* The dying god really appears—as a historical Person, living in a definite place and time. If we *could* sort out all the fabulous elements in the earlier stages and separate

4. The Book of Jonah.
5. Genesis, chapters vi-viii.
6. II Samuel, ch. ii—I Kings, ch. ii.

them from the historical ones, I think we might lose an essential part of the whole process. That is my own idea.

Question 11.

Which of the religions of the world gives to its followers the greatest happiness?

Lewis:

Which of the religions of the world gives to its followers the greatest happiness? While it lasts, the religion of worshipping oneself is the best.

I have an elderly acquaintance of about eighty, who has lived a life of unbroken selfishness and self-admiration from the earliest years, and is, more or less, I regret to say, one of the happiest men I know. From the moral point of view it is very difficult! I am not approaching the question from that angle. As you perhaps know, I haven't always been a Christian. I didn't go to religion to make me happy. I always knew a bottle of Port would do that. If you want a religion to make you feel really comfortable, I certainly don't recommend Christianity. I am certain there must be a patent American article on the market which will suit you far better, but I can't give any advice on it.

Question 12.

Are there any unmistakable outward signs in a person surrendered to God? Would he be cantankerous? Would he smoke?

Lewis:

I think of the advertisements for 'White Smiles' Tooth Paste, saying that it is the best on the market. If they are true, it would follow that:

(1) Anyone who starts using it will have better teeth;

(2) Anyone using it has better teeth than he would have if he weren't using it.

But you can't test it in the case of one who has naturally bad teeth and uses it, and compare him with a healthy Negro who has never used tooth paste at all.

Take the case of a sour old maid, who is a Christian, but cantankerous. On the other hand, take some pleasant and popular fellow, but who has never been to Church. Who knows how much more cantankerous the old maid might be if she were *not* a Christian, and how much more likeable the nice fellow might be if he *were* a Christian? You can't judge Christianity simply by comparing the *product* in those two people; you would need to know what kind of raw material Christ was working on in both cases.

As an illustration, let us take a case of industrialism. Let us take two factories:

Factory A with poor and inadequate plant; and

Factory B with first-class modern plant.

You can't judge by the outside. You must consider the plant and methods by which they are run, and considering the plant at Factory A, it may be a wonder it does anything at all; and considering the new machinery at Factory B, it may be a wonder it doesn't do better.

Question 13.

What is your opinion about raffles within the plant—no matter how good the cause—which, not infrequently, is given less prominence than the alluring list of prizes?

Lewis:

Gambling ought never to be an important part of a man's life. If it is a way in which large sums of money are transferred from person to person without doing any good (e.g., producing employment, goodwill, etc.) then it is a bad thing. If it is carried out on a small scale, I am not sure that it is bad. I don't know much about it, because it is about the only vice to which I have no temptation at all, and I think it is a risk to talk about things which are not in my own make-up, because I don't understand them. If anyone comes to me asking to play bridge for money, I just say: 'How much do you hope to win? Take it and go away.'

Question 14.

Many people are quite unable to understand the theological differences which have caused divisions in the Christian Church. Do you consider that these differences are fundamental, and is the time now ripe for re-union?

Lewis:

The time is always ripe for re-union. Divisions between Christians are a sin and a scandal, and Christians ought at all times to be making contributions towards re-union, if it is only by their prayers. I am only a layman and a recent Christian, and I do not know much about these things, but in all the things which I have written and thought I have always stuck to traditional, dogmatic positions. The result is that letters of agreement reach me from what are ordinarily regarded as the most different kinds of Christians; for instance, I get letters from Jesuits, monks, nuns, and also from Quakers and Welsh Dissenters, and so on. So it seems to me that the 'extremist' elements in every Church are nearest one another and the liberal and 'broad-minded' people in each Body could never be united at all. The world of dogmatic Christianity is a place in which thousands of people of quite different types keep on saying the same thing, and the world of 'broad-mindedness' and watered-down 'religion' is a world where a small number of people (all of the same type) say totally different things and change their minds every few minutes. We shall never get re-union from them.

Question 15.

In the past the Church used various kinds of compulsion in attempts to force a particular brand of Christianity on the community. Given sufficient power, is there not a danger of this sort of thing happening again?

Lewis:

Yes, I hear nasty rumours coming from Spain. Persecution is a temptation to which all men are exposed. I had a postcard signed 'M.D.' saying that anyone who expressed and published his belief in the Virgin Birth should be stripped and flogged. That shows you how easily persecution of Christians by the non-Christians might come back. Of course, they wouldn't call it Persecution: they'd call it 'Compulsory re-education of the ideologically unfit', or something like that. But, of course, I have to admit that Christians themselves have been persecutors in the past. It was worse of them, because *they* ought to have known better: they weren't worse in any other way. I detest every kind of religious compulsion: only the other day I was writing an angry letter to *The Spectator* about Church Parades in the Home Guard!

Question 16.

Is attendance at a place of worship or membership with a Christian community necessary to a Christian way of life?

Lewis:

That's a question which I cannot answer. My own experience is that when I first became a Christian, about fourteen years ago, I thought that I could do it on my own, by retiring to my rooms and reading theology, and I wouldn't go to the churches and Gospel Halls; and then later I found that it was the only way of flying your flag; and, of course, I found that this meant being a target. It is extraordinary how inconvenient to your family it becomes for you to get up early to go to Church. It doesn't matter so much if you get up early for anything else, but if you get up early to go to Church it's very selfish of you and you upset the house. If there is anything in the teaching of the New Testament which is in the nature of a command, it is that you are obliged to take the Sacrament,[7] and you can't do it without going to Church. I disliked very much their hymns, which I considered to be fifth-rate poems set to sixth-rate music. But as I went on I saw the great merit of it. I came up against different people of quite different outlooks and different education, and then gradually my conceit just began peeling off. I realized that the hymns (which were just sixth-rate music) were, nevertheless, being sung with devotion and benefit by an old saint in elastic-side boots in the opposite pew, and then you realize that you aren't fit to clean those boots. It gets you out of your solitary conceit. It is not for me to lay down laws, as I am only a layman, and I don't know much.

Question 17.

If it is true that one has only to want God enough in order to find Him, how can I make myself want Him enough to enable myself to find Him?

---

7. John vi. 53–54: 'Except ye eat the flesh of the Son of man, and drink his blood, ye have no life in you. Whoso eateth my flesh, and drinketh my blood, hath eternal life; and I will raise him up at the last day.'

Lewis:

If you don't want God, why are you so anxious to want to want Him? I think that in reality the want is a real one, and I should say that this person has in fact found God, although it may not be fully recognized yet. We are not always aware of things at the time they happen. At any rate, what is more important is that God has found this person, and that is the main thing.

5
Myth Became Fact

MY FRIEND CORINEUS has advanced the charge that none of us are in fact Christians at all. According to him historic Christianity is something so barbarous that no modern man can really believe it: the moderns who claim to do so are in fact believing a modern system of thought which retains the vocabulary of Christianity and exploits the emotions inherited from it while quietly dropping its essential doctrines. Corineus compared modern Christianity with the modern English monarchy: the forms of kingship have been retained, but the reality has been abandoned.

All this I believe to be false, except of a few 'modernist' theologians who, by God's grace, become fewer every day. But for the moment let us assume that Corineus is right. Let us pretend, for purposes of argument, that *all* who now call themselves Christians have abandoned the historic doctrines. Let us suppose that modern 'Christianity' reveals a system of names, ritual, formulae and metaphors which persists although the thoughts behind it have changed. Corineus ought to be able to *explain* the persistence.

Why, on his view, do all these educated and enlightened pseudo-Christians insist on expressing their deepest thoughts in terms of an archaic mythology which must hamper and embarrass them at every turn? Why do they refuse to cut the umbilical cord which binds the living and flourishing child to its moribund mother? For, if Corineus is right, it should be a great relief to them to do so. Yet the odd thing is that even those who seem most embarrassed by the sediment of 'barbaric' Christianity in their thought become suddenly obstinate when you ask them to get rid of it altogether. They will strain the cord almost to breaking point, but they refuse to cut it. Sometimes they will take every step except the last one.

If all who professed Christianity were clergymen, it would be easy (though uncharitable) to reply that their livelihood depends on *not* taking that last step. Yet even if this were the true cause of their behaviour, even if all clergymen are intellectual prostitutes who preach for pay—and usually starvation pay—what they secretly believe to be false, surely so widespread a darkening of conscience among thousands of men not otherwise known to be criminal, itself demands explanation? And of course the profession of Christianity is not confined to the clergy. It is professed by millions of women and laymen who earn thereby contempt, unpopularity, suspicion, and the hostility of their own families. How does this come to happen?

Obstinacies of this sort are interesting. 'Why not cut the cord?' asks Corineus. 'Everything would be much easier if you would free your thought from this vestigial mythology.' To be sure: far easier. Life would be far easier for the mother of an invalid child if she put it into an Institution and adopted someone else's healthy baby instead. Life would be far easier to many a man if he abandoned the woman he has actually fallen in love with and married someone else because she is more suitable. The only defect of the healthy baby and the suitable woman is that they leave out the patient's only reason for bothering about a child or wife at all. 'Would not conversation be much more rational than dancing?' said Jane Austen's Miss Bingley. 'Much more rational,' replied Mr Bingley, 'but much less like a ball.'[1]

In the same way, it would be much more rational to abolish the English monarchy. But how if, by doing so, you leave out the one element in our State which matters most? How if the monarchy is the channel through which all the *vital* elements of citizenship—loyalty, the consecration of secular life, the hierarchical principle, splendour, ceremony, continuity—still trickle down to irrigate the dust-bowl of modern economic Statecraft?

The real answer of even the most 'modernist' Christianity to Corineus is the same. Even assuming (which I most constantly deny) that the doctrines of historic Christianity are merely mythical, it is the myth which is the vital and nourishing element in the whole concern. Corineus wants us to move with the times. Now, we know where times move. They move *away*. But in religion we find something that does not move away. It is what Corineus calls the myth, that abides; it is what he calls the modern and living thought that moves away. Not only the thought of theologians, but the thought of anti-theologians. Where are the predecessors of Corineus? Where is the epicureanism of Lucretius,[2] the pagan revival of Julian the Apostate?[3] Where are the Gnostics, where is the monism of Averroës,[4] the deism of Voltaire, the dogmatic materialism of the great Victorians? They have moved with the times. But the thing they were all attacking remains: Corineus finds it still there to attack. The myth (to speak his language) has outlived the thoughts of all its defenders and of all its adversaries. It is the myth that gives life. Those elements even in modernist Christianity which Corineus regards as vestigial, are the substance: what he takes for the 'real modern belief' is the shadow.

To explain this we must look a little closer at myth in general, and at this myth in particular. Human intellect is incurably abstract. Pure mathematics is the type of successful thought. Yet the only realities we experience are concrete—this pain, this pleasure, this dog, this man. While we are loving the man, bearing the pain, enjoying the pleasure, we are not intellectually apprehending Pleasure, Pain or Personality. When we begin to do so, on the other hand, the concrete realities sink to the level of mere instances or examples: we are no longer dealing with them, but with that which they exemplify. This is our dilemma—either to taste and not to know or to know and not to taste—or, more strictly, to lack one kind of knowledge because we are in an experience or to lack another kind because we are outside it. As thinkers we are cut off from what we think about; as tasting, touching, willing, loving, hating, we do not clearly understand. The more lucidly we think, the more we are cut off: the more deeply we enter into reality, the less we can think. You

---

1. *Pride and Prejudice*, ch. xi.
2. Titus Lucretius Carus (c. 99–55), the Roman poet.
3. Roman emperor, A.D. 361–3.
4. Averroës (1126–98), of Cordova, believed that only one intellect exists for the whole human race in which every individual participates, to the exclusion of personal immortality.

cannot *study* Pleasure in the moment of the nuptial embrace, nor repentance while repenting, nor analyse the nature of humour while roaring with laughter. But when else can you really know these things? 'If only my toothache would stop, I could write another chapter about Pain.' But once it stops, what do I know about pain?

Of this tragic dilemma myth is the partial solution. In the enjoyment of a great myth we come nearest to experiencing as a concrete what can otherwise be understood only as an abstraction. At this moment, for example, I am trying to understand something very abstract indeed—the fading, vanishing of tasted reality as we try to grasp it with the discursive reason. Probably I have made heavy weather of it. But if I remind you, instead, of Orpheus and Eurydice, how he was suffered to lead her by the hand but, when he turned round to look at her, she disappeared, what was merely a principle becomes imaginable. You may reply that you never till this moment attached that 'meaning' to that myth. Of course not. You are not looking for an abstract 'meaning' at all. If that was what you were doing the myth would be for you no true myth but a mere allegory. You were not knowing, but tasting; but what you were tasting turns out to be a universal principle. The moment we *state* this principle, we are admittedly back in the world of abstraction. It is only while receiving the myth as a story that you experience the principle concretely.

When we translate we get abstraction—or rather, dozens of abstractions. What flows into you from the myth is not truth but reality (truth is always *about* something, but reality is that *about which* truth is), and, therefore, every myth becomes the father of innumerable truths on the abstract level. Myth is the mountain whence all the different streams arise which become truths down here in the valley; *in hac valle abstractionis.*[5] Or, if you prefer, myth is the isthmus which connects the peninsular world of thought with that vast continent we really belong to. It is not, like truth, abstract; nor is it, like direct experience, bound to the particular.

Now as myth transcends thought, Incarnation transcends myth. The heart of Christianity is a myth which is also a fact. The old myth of the Dying God, *without ceasing to be myth,* comes down from the heaven of legend and imagination to the earth of history. It *happens*—at a particular date, in a particular place, followed by definable historical consequences. We pass from a Balder or an Osiris, dying nobody knows when or where, to a historical Person crucified (it is all in order) *under Pontius Pilate.* By becoming fact it does not cease to be myth: that is the miracle. I suspect that men have sometimes derived more spiritual sustenance from myths they did not believe than from the religion they professed. To be truly Christian we must both assent to the historical fact and also receive the myth (fact though it has become) with the same imaginative embrace which we accord to all myths. The one is hardly more necessary than the other.

A man who disbelieved the Christian story as fact but continually fed on it as myth would, perhaps, be more spiritually alive than one who assented and did not think much about it. The modernist—the extreme modernist, infidel in all but name—need not be called a fool or hypocrite because he obstinately retains, even in the midst of his intellectual atheism, the language, rites, sacraments, and story

---

5. 'In this valley of separation.'

of the Christians. The poor man may be clinging (with a wisdom he himself by no means understands) to that which is his life. It would have been better that Loisy[6] should have remained a Christian: it would not necessarily have been better that he should have purged his thought of vestigial Christianity.

Those who do not know that this great myth became Fact when the Virgin conceived are, indeed, to be pitied. But Christians also need to be reminded—we may thank Corineus for reminding us—that what became Fact was a Myth, that it carries with it into the world of Fact all the properties of a myth. God is more than a god, not less; Christ is more than Balder, not less. We must not be ashamed of the mythical radiance resting on our theology. We must not be nervous about 'parallels' and 'Pagan Christs': they *ought* to be there—it would be a stumbling block if they weren't. We must not, in false spirituality, withhold our imaginative welcome. If God chooses to be mythopoeic—and is not the sky itself a myth—shall we refuse to be *mythopathic?* For this is the marriage of heaven and earth: Perfect Myth and Perfect Fact: claiming not only our love and our obedience, but also our wonder and delight, addressed to the savage, the child, and the poet in each one of us no less than to the moralist, the scholar, and the philosopher.

6. Alfred Loisy (1857–1940), a French theologian and founder of the Modernist Movement.

6
'Horrid Red Things'

MANY THEOLOGIANS AND some scientists are ready now to proclaim that the nineteenth century 'conflict between science and religion' is over and done with. But even if this is true, it is a truth known only to real theologians and real scientists—that is, to a few highly educated men. To the man in the street the conflict is still perfectly real, and in his mind it takes a form which the learned hardly dream of.

The ordinary man is not thinking of particular dogmas and particular scientific discoveries. What troubles him is an all-pervading difference of atmosphere between what he believes Christianity to be and that general picture of the universe which he has picked up from living in a scientific age. He gathers from the Creed that God has a 'Son' (just as if God were a god, like Odin or Jupiter): that this Son 'came down' (like a parachutist) from 'Heaven', first to earth and later to some land of the dead situated beneath the earth's surface: that, still later, He ascended into the sky and took His seat in a decorated chair placed a little to the right of His Father's throne. The whole thing seems to imply a local and material heaven—a palace in the stratosphere—a flat earth and all the rest of those archaic misconceptions.

The ordinary man is well aware that we should deny all the beliefs he attributes to us and interpret our creed in a different sense. But this by no means satisfies him. 'No doubt', he thinks, 'once those articles of belief are there, they can be allegorised or spiritualised away to any extent you please. But is it not plain that they would never have been there at all if the first generation of Christians had had any notion of what the real universe is like? A historian who has based his work on the misreading of a document may afterwards (when his mistake has been exposed) exercise great ingenuity in showing that his account of a certain battle can still be reconciled with what the document records. But the point is that none of these ingenious explanations would ever have come into existence if he had read his documents correctly at the outset. They are therefore really a waste of labour; it would be manlier of him to admit his mistake and begin all over again.'

I think there are two things that Christians must do if they wish to convince this 'ordinary' modern man. In the first place, they must make it quite clear that what will remain of the Creed after all their explanations and reinterpretations will still be something quite unambiguously supernatural, miraculous, and shocking. We may not believe in a flat earth and a sky-palace. But we must insist from the beginning that we believe, as firmly as any savage or theosophist, in a spirit-world which can, and does, invade the natural or phenomenal universe. For the plain man suspects that when we start explaining, we are going to explain away: that we have mythology for our ignorant hearers and are ready, when cornered by educated hearers, to reduce it to innocuous moral platitudes which no one ever dreamed of denying. And there are theologians who justify this suspicion. From them we must part company absolutely. If nothing remains except what could be equally well stated without Christian formulae, then the honest thing is to admit that Christianity is untrue and to begin over again without it.

In the second place, we must try to teach something about the difference between thinking and imagining. It is, of course, a historical error to suppose that all, or even most, early Christians believed in the sky-palace in the same sense in which we believe in the solar system. Anthropomorphism was condemned by the Church as soon as the question was explicitly before her. But some early Christians may have done this; and probably thousands never thought of their faith without anthropomorphic imagery. That is why we must distinguish the core of belief from the attendant imagining.

When I think of London I always see a picture of Euston Station. But I do not believe that London *is* Euston Station. That is a simple case, because there the thinker *knows* the imagery to be false. Now let us take a more complex one. I once heard a lady tell her daughter that if you ate too many aspirin tablets you would die. 'But why?' asked the child. 'If you squash them you don't find any horrid red things inside them.' Obviously, when this child thought of poison she not only had an attendant image of 'horrid red things', but she actually believed that poison was red. And this is an error. But how far does it invalidate her thinking about poison? She learned that an overdose of aspirin would kill you; her belief was true. She knew, within limits, which of the substances in her mother's house were poisonous. If I, staying in the house, had raised a glass of what looked like water to my lips, and the child had said, 'Don't drink that. Mummie says it's poisonous,' I should have been foolish to disregard the warning on the ground that 'This child has an archaic and mythological idea of poison as horrid red things.'

There is thus a distinction not only between thought and imagination in general, but even between thought and those images which the thinker (falsely) believes to be true. When the child learned later that poison is not always red, she would not have felt that anything essential in her beliefs about poison had been altered. She would still know, as she had always known, that poison is what kills you if you swallow it. That is the essence of poison. The erroneous beliefs about colour drop away without affecting it.

In the same way an early peasant Christian might have thought that Christ's sitting at the right hand of the Father really implied two chairs of state, in a certain spatial relation, inside a sky-palace. But if the same man afterwards received a philosophical education and discovered that God has no body, parts, or passions, and therefore neither a right hand nor a palace, he would not have felt that the essentials of his belief had been altered. What had mattered to him, even in the days of his simplicity, had not been supposed details about celestial furniture. It had been the assurance that the once crucified Master was now the supreme Agent of the unimaginable Power on whom the whole universe depends. And he would recognise that in this he had never been deceived.

The critic may still ask us why the imagery—which we admit to be untrue—

should be used at all. But he has not noticed that any language we attempt to substitute for it would involve imagery that is open to all the same objections. To say that God 'enters' the natural order involves just as much spatial imagery as to say that He 'comes down'; one has simply substituted horizontal (or undefined) for vertical movement. To say that He is 're-absorbed' into the Noumenal is better than to say He 'ascended' into Heaven, only if the picture of something dissolving in warm fluid, or being sucked into a throat, is less misleading than the picture of a bird, or a balloon, going up. All language, except about objects of sense, is metaphorical through and through. To call God a 'Force' (that is, something like a wind or a dynamo) is as metaphorical as to call Him a Father or a King. On such matters we can make our language more polysyllabic and duller: we cannot make it more literal. The difficulty is not peculiar to theologians. Scientists, poets, psychoanalysts, and metaphysicians are all in the same boat—

Man's reason is in such deep insolvency to sense.

Where, then, do we draw the line between explaining and 'explaining away'? I do not think there is much difficulty. All that concerns the un-incarnate activities of God—His operation on that plane of being where sense cannot enter—must be taken along with imagery which we know to be, in the literal sense, untrue. But there can be no defence for applying the same treatment to the miracles of the Incarnate God. They are recorded as events on this earth which affected human senses. They are the sort of thing we can describe literally. If Christ turned water into wine, and we had been present, we could have seen, smelled, and tasted. The story that He did so is not of the same order as His 'sitting at the right hand of the Father'. It is either fact, or legend, or lie. You must take it or leave it.

7
Religion and Science

'MIRACLES,' SAID MY FRIEND. 'Oh, come. Science has knocked the bottom out of all that. We know that Nature is governed by fixed laws.'

'Didn't people always know that!' said I.

'Good Lord, no,' said he. 'For instance, take a story like the Virgin Birth. We know now that such a thing couldn't happen. We know there *must* be a male spermatozoon.'

'But look here', said I, 'St Joseph—'

'Who's he?' asked my friend.

'He was the husband of the Virgin Mary. If you'll read the story in the Bible you'll find that when he saw his fiancée was going to have a baby he decided to cry off the marriage. Why did he do that?'

'Wouldn't most men?'

'Any man would', said I, 'provided he knew the laws of Nature—in other words, provided he knew that a girl doesn't ordinarily have a baby unless she's been sleeping with a man. But according to your theory people in the old days didn't know that Nature was governed by fixed laws. I'm pointing out that the story shows that St Joseph knew *that* law just as well as you do.'

'But he came to believe in the Virgin Birth afterwards, didn't he?'

'Quite. But he didn't do so because he was under any illusion as to where babies came from in the ordinary course of Nature. He believed in the Virgin Birth as something *super*natural. He knew Nature works in fixed, regular ways: but he also believed that there existed something *beyond* Nature which could interfere with her workings—from outside, so to speak.'

'But modern science has shown there's no such thing.'

'Really,' said I. 'Which of the sciences?'

'Oh, well, that's a matter of detail,' said my friend. 'I can't give you chapter and verse from memory.'

'Rut, don't you see', said I, 'that science never could show anything of the sort?'

'Why on earth not?'

'Because science studies Nature. And the question is whether anything *besides* Nature exists—anything "outside". How could you find that out by studying simply Nature?'

'But don't we find out that Nature *must* work in an absolutely fixed way? I mean, the laws of Nature tell us not merely how things *do* happen, but how they *must* happen. No power could possibly alter them.'

'How do you mean?' said I.

'Look here,' said he. 'Could this "something outside" that you talk about make two and two five?'

'Well, no,' said I.

'All right,' said he. 'Well, I think the laws of Nature are really like two and two making four. The idea of their being altered is as absurd as the idea of altering the laws of arithmetic.'

'Half a moment,' said I. 'Suppose you put sixpence into a drawer today, and sixpence into the same drawer tomorrow. Do the laws of arithmetic make it certain you'll find a shilling's worth there the day after?'

'Of course', said he, 'provided no one's been tampering with your drawer.'

'Ah, but that's the whole point,' said I. 'The laws of arithmetic can tell you what you'll find, with absolute certainty, *provided that* there's no interference. If a thief has been at the drawer of course you'll get a different result. But the thief won't have broken the laws of arithmetic—only the laws of England. Now, aren't the laws of Nature much in the same boat? Don't they all tell you what will happen *provided* there's no interference?'

'How do you mean?'

'Well, the laws will tell you how a billiard ball will travel on a smooth surface if you hit it in a particular way—but only provided no one interferes. If, after it's already in motion, someone snatches up a cue and gives it a biff on one side—why, then, you won't get what the scientist predicted.'

'No, of course not. He can't allow for monkey-tricks like that.'

'Quite, and in the same way, if there was anything outside Nature, and if it interfered—then the events which the scientist expected wouldn't follow. That would be what we call a miracle. In one sense it wouldn't break the laws of Nature. The laws tell you what will happen if nothing interferes. They can't tell you whether something *is* going to interfere. I mean, it's not the expert at arithmetic who can tell you how likely someone is to interfere with the pennies in my drawer; a detective would be more use. It isn't the physicist who can tell you how likely I am to catch up a cue and spoil his experiment with the billiard ball; you'd better ask a psychologist. And it isn't the scientist who can tell you how likely Nature is to be interfered with from outside. You must go to the metaphysician.'

'These are rather niggling points,' said my friend. 'You see, the real objection goes far deeper. The whole picture of the universe which science has given us makes it such rot to believe that the Power at the back of it all could be interested in us tiny little creatures crawling about on an unimportant planet! It was all so obviously invented by people who believed in a flat earth with the stars only a mile or two away.'

'When did people believe that?'

'Why, all those old Christian chaps you're always telling about did. I mean Boethius and Augustine and Thomas Aquinas and Dante.'

'Sorry', said I, 'but this is one of the few subjects I do know something about.'

I reached out my hand to a bookshelf. 'You see this book', I said, 'Ptolemy's *Almagest*. You know what it is?'

'Yes,' said he. 'It's the standard astronomical handbook used all through the Middle Ages.'

'Well, just read that,' I said, pointing to Book I, chapter 5.

'The earth,' read out my friend, hesitating a bit as he translated the Latin, 'the earth, in relation to the distance of the fixed stars, has no appreciable size and must be treated as a mathematical point!'

There was a moment's silence.

'Did they really know that *then?*' said my friend. 'But—but none of the histories of science—none of the modern encyclopedias—ever mention the fact.'

'Exactly,' said I. 'I'll leave you to think out the reason. It almost looks as if someone was anxious to hush it up, doesn't it? I wonder why.'

There was another short silence.

'At any rate', said I, 'we can now state the problem accurately. People usually think the problem is how to reconcile what we now know about the size of the universe with our traditional ideas of religion. That turns out not to be the problem at all. The real problem is this. The enormous size of the universe and the insignificance of the earth were known for centuries, and no one ever dreamed that they had any bearing on the religious question. Then, less than a hundred years ago, they are suddenly trotted out as an argument against Christianity. And the people who trot them out carefully hush up the fact that they were known long ago. Don't you think that all you atheists are strangely unsuspicious people?'

8
The Laws of Nature

'POOR WOMAN,' SAID my friend. 'One hardly knows what to say when they talk like that. She thinks her son survived Arnhem because she prayed for him. It would be heartless to explain to her that he really survived because he was standing a little to the left or a little to the right of some bullet. That bullet was following a course laid down by the laws of Nature. It couldn't have hit him. He just happened to be standing off its line . . . and so all day long as regards every bullet and every splinter of shell. His survival was simply due to the laws of Nature.'

At that moment my first pupil came in and the conversation was cut short, but later in the day I had to walk across the Park to a committee meeting and this gave me time to think the matter over. It was quite clear that once a bullet had been fired from Point A in direction B, the wind being C, and so forth, it would pursue a certain path. But might our young friend have been standing somewhere else? And might the German have fired at a different moment or in a different direction? If men have free-will it would appear that they might. On that view we get a rather more complicated picture of the battle of Arnhem. The total course of events would be a kind of amalgam derived from two sources—on the one hand, from acts of human will (which might presumably have been otherwise), and, on the other, from the laws of physical nature. And this would seem to provide all that is necessary for the mother's belief that her prayers had some place among the causes of her son's preservation. God might continually influence the wills of all the combatants so as to allot death, wounds, and survival in the way He thought best, while leaving the behaviour of the projectile to follow its normal course.

But I was still not quite clear about the physical side of this picture. I had been thinking (vaguely enough) that the bullet's flight was *caused* by the laws of Nature. But is this really so? Granted that the bullet is set in motion, and granted the wind and the earth's gravitation and all the other relevant factors, then it is a 'law' of Nature that the bullet must take the course it did. But then the pressing of the trigger, the side wind, and even the earth, are not exactly *laws*. They are facts or events. They are not laws but things that obey laws. Obviously, to consider the pressing of the trigger would only lead us back to the free-will side of the picture. We must, therefore, choose a simpler example.

The laws of physics, I understand, decree that when one billiards ball (A) sets another billiards ball (B) in motion, the momentum lost by A exactly equals the momentum gained by B. This is a *Law*. That is, this is the pattern to which the movement of the two billiards balls must conform. Provided, of course, that something sets ball A in motion. And here comes the snag. The *law* won't set it in motion. It is usually a man with a cue who does that. But a man with a cue would send us back to free-will, so let us assume that it was lying on a table in a liner and that what set it in motion was a lurch of the ship. In that case it was not the law which produced the movement; it was a wave. And that wave, though it certainly moved *according* to the laws of physics, was not moved by them. It was shoved by other waves, and by winds, and so forth. And however far you traced the story back you would never find the *laws* of Nature causing anything.

The dazzlingly obvious conclusion now arose in my mind: *in the whole history of the universe the laws of Nature have never produced a single event.* They are the pattern to which every event must conform, provided only that it can be induced to happen. But how do you get it to do that? How do you get a move on? The laws of Nature can give you no help there. All events obey them, just as all operations with money obey the laws of arithmetic. Add six pennies to six and the result will certainly be a shilling. But arithmetic by itself won't put one farthing into your pocket. Up till now I had had a vague idea that the laws of Nature could make things happen. I now saw that this was exactly like thinking that you could increase your income by doing sums about it. The *laws* are the pattern to which events conform: the source of events must be sought elsewhere.

This may be put in the form that the laws of Nature explain everything except the source of events. But this is rather a formidable exception. The laws, in one sense, cover the whole of reality except—well, except that continuous cataract of real events which makes up the actual universe. They explain everything except what we should ordinarily call 'everything'. The only thing they omit is—the whole universe. I do not mean that a knowledge of these laws is useless. Provided we can take over the actual universe as a going concern, such knowledge is useful and indeed indispensable for manipulating it; just as, if only you have some money arithmetic is indispensable for managing it. But the events themselves, the money itself—that is quite another affair.

Where, then, do actual events come from? In one sense the answer is easy. Each event comes from a previous event. But what happens if you trace this process backwards? To ask this is not exactly the same as to ask where *things* come from— how there came to be space and time and matter at all. Our present problem is not about things but about events; not, for example, about particles of matter but about this particle colliding with that. The mind can perhaps acquiesce in the idea that the 'properties' of the universal drama somehow 'just happen to be there': but whence comes the play, the story?

Either the stream of events had a beginning or it had not. If it had, then we are faced with something like creation. If it had not (a supposition, by the way, which some physicists find difficult), then we are faced with an everlasting impulse which, by its very nature, is opaque to scientific thought. Science, when it becomes perfect, will have explained the connection between each link in the chain and the link before it. But the actual existence of the chain will remain wholly unaccountable. We learn more and more about the pattern. We learn nothing about that which 'feeds' real events into the pattern. If it is not God, we must at the very least call it Destiny—the immaterial, ultimate, one-way pressure which keeps the universe on the move.

The smallest event, then, if we face the fact that it occurs (instead of concentrating on the pattern into which, if it can be persuaded to occur, it must fit), leads us back to a mystery which lies outside natural science. It is certainly a possible supposition that behind this mystery some mighty Will and Life is at work. If so, any contrast between His acts and the laws of Nature is out of the question. It is His act alone that gives the laws any events to apply to. The laws are an empty frame; it is He who fills that frame—not now and then on specially 'providential' occasions, but at every moment. And He, from His vantage point above Time, can, if He pleases, take all prayers into account in ordaining that vast complex event which is the history of the universe. For what we call 'future' prayers have always been present to Him.

In *Hamlet* a branch breaks and Ophelia is drowned. Did she die because the branch broke or because Shakespeare wanted her to die at that point in the play? Either—both—whichever you please. The alternative suggested by the question is not a real alternative at all—once you have grasped that Shakespeare is making the whole play.

9
The Grand Miracle

ONE IS VERY often asked at present whether we could not have a Christianity stripped, or, as people who ask it say, 'freed' from its miraculous elements, a Christianity with the miraculous elements suppressed. Now, it seems to me that precisely the one religion in the world, or, at least, the only one I know, with which you could not do that is Christianity. In a religion like Buddhism, if you took away the miracles attributed to Gautama Buddha in some very late sources, there would be no loss; in fact, the religion would get on very much better without them because in that case the miracles largely contradict the teaching. Or even in the case of a religion like Mohammedanism, nothing essential would be altered if you took away the miracles. You could have a great prophet preaching his dogmas without bringing in any miracles; they are only in the nature of a digression, or illuminated capitals. But you cannot possibly do that with Christianity, because the Christian story is precisely the story of one grand miracle, the Christian assertion being that what is beyond all space and time, what is uncreated, eternal, came into nature, into human nature, descended into His own universe, and rose again, bringing nature up with Him. It is precisely one great miracle. If you take that away there is nothing specifically Christian left. There may be many admirable human things which Christianity shares with all other systems in the world, but there would be nothing specifically Christian. Conversely, once you have accepted that, then you will see that all other well-established Christian miracles—because, of course, there are ill-established Christian miracles; there are Christian legends just as much as there are heathen legends, or modern journalistic legends—you will see that all the well-established Christian miracles are part of it, that they all either prepare for, or exhibit, or result from the Incarnation. Just as every natural event exhibits the total character of the natural universe at a particular point and space of time; so every miracle exhibits the character of the Incarnation.

Now, if one asks whether that central grand miracle in Christianity is itself probable or improbable, of course, quite clearly you cannot be applying Hume's kind of probability. You cannot mean a probability based on statistics according to which the more often a thing has happened, the more likely it is to happen again (the more often you get indigestion from eating a certain food, the more probable it is, if you eat it again, that you will again have indigestion). Certainly the Incarnation cannot be probable in that sense. It is of its very nature to have happened only once. But then it is of the very nature of the history of this world to have happened only once; and if the Incarnation happened at all, it is the central chapter of that history. It is improbable in the same way in which the whole of nature is improbable, because it is only there once, and will happen only once. So one must apply to it a quite different kind of standard.

I think we are rather in this position. Supposing you had before you a manuscript of some great work, either a symphony or a novel. There then comes to you a person, saying, 'Here is a new bit of the manuscript that I found; it is the central passage of that symphony, or the central chapter of that novel. The text is incomplete without it. I have got the missing passage which is really the centre of the whole work.' The only thing you could do would be to put this new piece of the manuscript in that central position, and then see how it reacted on the whole of the rest of the work. If it constantly brought out new meanings from the whole of the rest of the work, if it made you notice things in the rest of the work which you had not noticed before, then I think you would decide that it was authentic. On the other hand, if it failed to do that, then, however attractive it was in itself, you would reject it.

Now, what is the missing chapter in this case, the chapter which Christians are offering? The story of the Incarnation is the story of a descent and resurrection. When I say 'resurrection' here, I am not referring simply to the first few hours, or the first few weeks of the Resurrection. I am talking of this whole, huge pattern of descent, down, down, and then up again. What we ordinarily call the Resurrection being just, so to speak, the point at which it turns. Think what that descent is. The coming down, not only into humanity, but into those nine months which precede human birth, in which they tell us we all recapitulate strange pre-human, sub-human forms of life, and going lower still into being a corpse, a thing which, if this ascending movement had not begun, would presently have passed out of the organic altogether, and have gone back into the inorganic, as all corpses do. One has a picture of someone going right down and dredging the sea-bottom. One has a picture of a strong man trying to lift a very big, complicated burden. He stoops down and gets himself right under it so that he himself disappears; and then he straightens his back and moves off with the whole thing swaying on his shoulders. Or else one has the picture of a diver, stripping off garment after garment, making himself naked, then flashing for a moment in the air, and then down through the green, and warm, and sunlit water into the pitch black, cold, freezing water, down into the mud and slime, then up again, his lungs almost bursting, back again to the green and warm and sunlit water, and then at last out into the sunshine, holding in his hand the dripping thing he went down to get. This thing is human nature; but, associated with it, all nature, the new universe. That indeed is a point I cannot go into tonight, because it would take a whole sermon—this connexion between human nature and nature in general. It sounds startling, but I believe it can be fully justified.

Now, as soon as you have thought of this, this pattern of the huge dive down to the bottom, into the depths of the universe and coming up again into the light, everyone will see at once how that is imitated and echoed by the principles of the natural world; the descent of the seed into the soil, and its rising again in the plants. There are also all sorts of things in our own spiritual life where a thing has to be killed, and broken, in order that it may then become bright, and strong, and splendid. The analogy is obvious. In that sense the doctrine fits in very well, so well in fact that immediately there comes the suspicion, Is it not filling in a great deal too well? In other words, does not the Christian story show this pattern of descent and re-ascent because that is part of all the nature religions of the world? We have read about it in *The Golden Bough*.[1] We all know about Adonis, and the stories of the rest of those rather tedious people; is not this one more instance of the same thing, 'the dying God'? Well, yes it is. That is what makes the question subtle. What the anthropological critic of Christianity is always saying is perfectly true. Christ *is* a figure of that sort. And here comes a very curious thing. When I first, after childhood, read the Gospels, I was full of that stuff about the dying God, *The Golden Bough*, and so on. It was to me then a very poetic, and mysterious, and quickening idea; and when I turned to the Gospels never will I forget my disappointment and repulsion at finding hardly anything about it at all. The metaphor of the seed dropping into the ground in this connexion occurs (I think) twice in the New Testament,[2] and for the rest hardly any notice is taken; it seemed to me extraordinary. You had a dying God, Who was always representative of the corn: you see Him holding the corn, that is, bread, in His hand, and saying, 'This is My Body',[3] and from my point of view, as I then was, He did not seem to realize what He was saying. Surely there, if anywhere, this connexion between the Christian story and the corn must have come out; the whole context is crying out for it. But everything goes on as if the principal actor, and still more, those about Him, were totally ignorant of what they were doing. It is as if you got very good evidence concerning the sea-serpent, but the men who brought this good evidence seemed never to have heard of sea-serpents. Or to put it in another way, why was it that the only case of the 'dying God' which might conceivably have been historical occurred among a people (and the only people in the whole Mediterranean world) who had not got any trace of this nature religion, and indeed seemed to know nothing about it? Why is it among *them* the thing suddenly appears to happen?

The principal actor, humanly speaking, hardly seems to know of the repercussions His words (and sufferings) would have in any pagan mind. Well, that is almost inexplicable, except on one hypothesis. How if the corn king is not mentioned in that Book, because He is here of whom the corn king was an image? How if the representation is absent because here, at last, the thing represented is present? If the shadows are absent because the thing of which they were shadows is here? The corn itself is in its far-off way an imitation of the supernatural reality; the thing dying, and coming to life again, descending, and re-ascending beyond all nature. The principle is there in nature because it was first there in God Himself. Thus one is getting in behind the nature religions, and behind nature to Someone Who is not explained by, but explains, not, indeed, the nature religions directly, but that whole characteristic behaviour of nature on which nature religions were based. Well, that is one way in which it surprised me. It seemed to fit in a very peculiar way, showing me something about nature more fully than I had seen it before, while itself remaining quite outside and above the nature religions.

Then another thing. We, with our modern democratic and arithmetical presuppositions would so have liked and expected all men to start equal in their search

1. By Sir James George Frazer.
2. John xii. 24; I Corinthians xv. 36.
3. Matthew xxvi. 26; Mark xiv. 22; Luke xxii. 19; I Corinthians xi. 24.

for God. One has the picture of great centripetal roads coming from all directions, with well-disposed people, all meaning the same thing, and getting closer and closer together. How shockingly opposite to that is the Christian story! One people picked out of the whole earth; that people purged and proved again and again. Some are lost in the desert before they reach Palestine; some stay in Babylon; some becoming indifferent. The whole thing narrows and narrows, until at last it comes down to a little point, small as the point of a spear—a Jewish girl at her prayers. That is what the whole of human nature has narrowed down to before the Incarnation takes place. Very unlike what we expected, but, of course, not in the least unlike what seems, in general, as shown by nature, to be God's way of working. The universe is quite a shockingly selective, undemocratic place out of apparently infinite space, a relatively tiny proportion occupied by matter of any kind. Of the stars perhaps only one has planets: of the planets only one is at all likely to sustain organic life. Of the animals only one species is rational. Selection as seen in nature, and the appalling waste which it involves, appears a horrible and an unjust thing by human standards. But the selectiveness in the Christian story is not quite like that. The people who are selected are, in a sense, unfairly selected for a supreme honour; but it is also a supreme burden. The People of Israel come to realize that it is their woes which are saving the world. Even in human society, though, one sees how this inequality furnishes an opportunity for every kind of tyranny and servility. Yet, on the other hand, one also sees that it furnishes an opportunity for some of the very best things we can think of—humility, and kindness, and the immense pleasures of admiration. (I cannot conceive how one would get through the boredom of a world in which you never met anyone more clever, or more beautiful, or stronger than yourself. The very crowds who go after the football celebrities and film-stars know better than to desire that kind of equality!) What the story of the Incarnation seems to be doing is to flash a new light on a principle in nature, and to show for the first time that this principle of inequality in nature is neither good nor bad. It is a common theme running through both the goodness and badness of the natural world, and I begin to see how it can survive as a supreme beauty in a redeemed universe.

And with that I have unconsciously passed over to the third point. I have said that the selectiveness was not unfair in the way in which we first suspect, because those selected for the great honour are also selected for the great suffering, and their suffering heals others. In the Incarnation we get, of course, this idea of vicariousness of one person profiting by the earning of another person. In its highest form that is the very centre of Christianity. And we also find this same vicariousness to be a characteristic, or, as the musician would put it, a *leit-motif* of nature. It is a law of the natural universe that no being can exist on its own resources. Everyone, everything, is hopelessly indebted to everyone and everything else. In the universe, as we now see it, this is the source of many of the greatest horrors: all the horrors of carnivorousness, and the worse horrors of the parasites, those horrible animals that live under the skin of other animals, and so on. And yet, suddenly seeing it in the light of the Christian story, one realizes that vicariousness is not in itself bad; that all these animals, and insects, and horrors are merely that principle of vicariousness twisted in one way. For when you think it out, nearly everything good in nature also comes from vicariousness. After all, the child, both before and after birth, lives on its mother, just as the parasite lives on its host, the one being a horror, the other being the source of almost every natural goodness in the world. It all depends upon what you do with this principle. So that I find in that third way also, that what is implied by the Incarnation just fits in exactly with what I have seen in nature, and (this is the important point) each time it gives it a new twist. If I accept this supposed missing chapter, the Incarnation, I find it begins to illuminate the whole of the rest of the manuscript. It lights up nature's pattern of death and rebirth; and, secondly, her selectiveness; and, thirdly, her vicariousness.

Now I notice a very odd point. All other religions in the world, as far as I know them, are either nature religions, or anti-nature religions. The nature religions are those of the old, simple pagan sort that you know about. You actually got drunk in the temple of Bacchus. You actually committed fornication in the temple of Aphrodite. The more modern form of nature religion would be the religion started, in a sense, by Bergson[4] (but he repented, and died Christian), and carried on in a more popular form by Mr Bernard Shaw. The anti-nature religions are those like Hinduism and Stoicism, where men say, 'I will starve my flesh. I care not whether I live or die.' All natural things are to be set aside: the aim is Nirvana, apathy, negative spirituality. The nature religions simply affirm my natural desires. The anti-natural religions simply contradict them. The nature religions simply give a new sanction to what I already always thought about the universe in my moments of rude health and cheerful brutality. The anti-nature religions merely repeat what I always thought about it in my moods of lassitude, or delicacy, or compassion.

But here is something quite different. Here is something telling me—well, what? Telling me that I must never, like the Stoics, say that death does not matter. Nothing is less Christian than that. Death which made Life Himself shed tears at the grave of Lazarus,[5] and shed tears of blood in Gethsemane.[6] This is an appalling horror; a stinking indignity. (You remember Thomas Browne's splendid remark: 'I am not so much afraid of death, as ashamed of it.')[7] And yet, somehow or other, infinitely good. Christianity does not simply affirm or simply deny the horror of death; it tells me something quite new about it. Again, it does not, like Nietzsche, simply confirm my desire to be stronger, or cleverer than other people. On the other hand, it does not allow me to say, 'Oh, Lord, won't there be a day when everyone will be as good as everyone else?' In the same way, about vicariousness. It will not, in any way, allow me to be an exploiter, to act as a parasite on other people; yet it will not allow me any dream of living on my own. It will teach me to accept with glad humility the enormous sacrifice that others make for me, as well as to make sacrifices for others.

---

4. Henri Bergson (1859–1941). His 'nature religion' is particularly evident in his *Matière et Mémoire* (1896) and *L'Evolution Créatrice* (1907).
5. John xi. 35.
6. Luke xxii. 44.
7. Browne's actual words are 'I am not so much afraid of death, as ashamed thereof.' *Religio Medici*, First Part, Section 40.

That is why I think this Grand Miracle is the missing chapter in this novel, the chapter on which the whole plot turns; that is why I believe that God really has dived down into the bottom of creation, and has come up bringing the whole redeemed nature on His shoulder. The miracles that have already happened are, of course, as Scripture so often says, the first fruits of that cosmic summer which is presently coming on.[8] Christ has risen, and so we shall rise. St Peter for a few seconds walked on the water;[9] and the day will come when there will be a re-made universe, infinitely obedient to the will of glorified and obedient men, when we can do all things, when we shall be those gods that we are described as being in Scripture. To be sure, it feels wintry enough still: but often in the very early spring it feels like that. Two thousand years are only a day or two by this scale. A man really ought to say, 'The Resurrection happened two thousand years ago' in the same spirit in which he says, 'I saw a crocus yesterday.' Because we know what is coming behind the crocus. The spring came slowly down this way; but the great thing is that the corner has been turned. There is, of course, this difference, that in the natural spring the crocus cannot choose whether it will respond or not. We can. We have the power either of withstanding the spring, and sinking back into the cosmic winter, or of going on into those 'high mid-summer pomps' in which our Leader, the Son of man, already dwells, and to which He is calling us. It remains with us to follow or not, to die in this winter, or to go on into that spring and that summer.

8. Romans viii. 23; xi. 16; xvi. 5; I Corinthians xv. 20; James i. 18; Revelation xiv. 4.
9. Matthew xiv. 29.

10
Christian Apologetics

SOME OF YOU are priests and some are leaders of youth organizations.[1] I have little right to address either. It is for priests to teach me, not for me to teach them. I have never helped to organize youth, and while I was young myself I successfully avoided being organized. If I address you it is in response to a request so urged that I came to regard compliance as a matter of Obedience.

I am to talk about Apologetics. Apologetics means of course Defence. The first question is—what do you propose to defend? Christianity, of course: and Christianity as understood by the Church in Wales. And here at the outset I must deal with an unpleasant business. It seems to the layman that in the Church of England we often hear from our priests doctrine which is not Anglican Christianity. It may depart from Anglican Christianity in either of two ways: (1) It may be so 'broad' or 'liberal' or 'modern' that it in fact excludes any real Supernaturalism and thus ceases to be Christian at all. (2) It may, on the other hand, be Roman. It is not, of course, for me to define to you what Anglican Christianity is—I am your pupil, not your teacher. But I insist that wherever you draw the lines, bounding lines must exist, beyond which your doctrine will cease either to be Anglican or to be Christian: and I suggest also that the lines come a great deal sooner than many modern priests think. I think it is your duty to fix the lines clearly in your own minds: and if you wish to go beyond them you must change your profession.

This is your duty not specially as Christians or as priests but as honest men. There is a danger here of the clergy developing a special professional conscience which obscures the very plain moral issue. Men who have passed beyond these boundary lines in either direction are apt to protest that they have come by their unorthodox opinions honestly. In defence of those opinions they are prepared to suffer obloquy and to forfeit professional advancement. They thus come to feel like martyrs. But this simply misses the point which so gravely scandalizes the layman. We never doubted that the unorthodox opinions were honestly held: what we complain of is your continuing your ministry after you have come to hold them. We always knew that a man who makes his living as a paid agent of the Conservative Party may honestly change his views and honestly become a Communist. What we deny is that he can honestly continue to be a Conservative agent and to receive money from one party while he supports the policy of another.

Even when we have thus ruled out teaching which is in direct contradiction to our profession, we must define our task still further. We are to defend Christianity itself—the faith preached by the Apostles, attested by the Martyrs, enbodied in the Creeds, expounded by the Fathers. This must be clearly distinguished from the

1. This paper was read to an assembly of Anglican priests and youth leaders at the 'Carmarthen Conference for Youth Leaders and Junior Clergy' of the Church in Wales at Carmarthen during Easter 1945.

whole of what any one of us may think about God and Man. Each of us has his individual emphasis: each holds, in addition to the Faith, many opinions which seem to him to be consistent with it and true and important. And so perhaps they are. But as apologists it is not our business to defend *them*. We are defending Christianity; not 'my religion'. When we mention our personal opinions we must always make quite clear the difference between them and the Faith itself. St Paul has given us the model in I Corinthians vii. 25: on a certain point he has 'no commandment of the Lord' but gives 'his judgement'. No one is left in doubt as to the difference in *status* implied.

This distinction, which is demanded by honesty, also gives the apologist a great tactical advantage. The great difficulty is to get modern audiences to realize that you are preaching Christianity solely and simply because you happen to think it *true*; they always suppose you are preaching it because you like it or think it good for society or something of that sort. Now a clearly maintained distinction between what the Faith actually says and what you would like it to have said or what you understand or what you personally find helpful or think probable, forces your audience to realize that you are tied to your data just as the scientist is tied by the results of the experiments; that you are not just saying what you like. This immediately helps them to realize that what is being discussed is a question about objective fact—not gas about ideals and points of view.

Secondly, this scrupulous care to preserve the Christian message as something distinct from one's own ideas, has one very good effect upon the apologist himself. It forces him, again and again, to face up to those elements in original Christianity which he personally finds obscure or repulsive. He is saved from the temptation to skip or slur or ignore what he finds disagreeable. And the man who yields to that temptation will, of course, never progress in Christian knowledge. For obviously the doctrines which one finds easy are the doctrines which give Christian sanction to truths you already knew. The new truth which you do not know and which you need must, in the very nature of things, be hidden precisely in the doctrines you least like and least understand. It is just the same here as in science. The phenomenon which is troublesome, which doesn't fit in with the current scientific theories, is the phenomenon which compels reconsideration and thus leads to new knowledge. Science progresses because scientists, instead of running away from such troublesome phenomena or hushing them up, are constantly seeking them out. In the same way, there will be progress in Christian knowledge only as long as we accept the challenge of the difficult or repellent doctrines. A 'liberal' Christianity which considers itself free to alter the Faith whenever the Faith looks perplexing or repellent *must* be completely stagnant. Progress is made only into a *resisting* material.

From this there follows a corollary about the Apologist's private reading. There are two questions he will naturally ask himself. (1) Have I been 'keeping up', keeping abreast of recent movements in theology? (2) Have I *stood firm (super monstratas vias)*[2] amidst all these 'winds of doctrine'?[3] I want to say emphatically that the sec-

2. The source of this is, I believe, Jeremiah vi. 16: '*State super vias et videte, et interrogate de semitis antiquis quae sit via bona, et ambulate in ea*' which is translated "Stand ye in the ways, and see, and ask for the old paths, where is the good way, and walk therein.'
3. Ephesians iv. 14.

ond question is far the more important of the two. Our upbringing and the whole atmosphere of the world we live in make it certain that our main temptation will be that of yielding to winds of doctrine, not that of ignoring them. We are not at all likely to be hidebound: we are very likely indeed to be the slaves of fashion. If one has to choose between reading the new books and reading the old, one must choose the old: not because they are necessarily better but because they contain precisely those truths of which our own age is neglectful. The standard of permanent Christianity must be kept clear in our minds and it is against that standard that we must test all contemporary thought. In fact, we must at all costs *not* move with the times. We serve One who said 'Heaven and Earth shall move with the times, but my words shall not move with the times.'[4]

I am speaking, so far, of theological reading. Scientific reading is a different matter. If you know any science it is very desirable that you should keep it up. We have to answer the current scientific attitude towards Christianity, not the attitude which scientists adopted one hundred years ago. Science is in continual change and we must try to keep abreast of *it*. For the same reason, we must be very cautious of snatching at any scientific theory which, for the moment, seems to be in our favour. We may *mention* such things; but we must mention them lightly and without claiming that they are more than 'interesting'. Sentences beginning 'Science has now proved' should be avoided. If we try to base our apologetic on some recent development in science, we shall usually find that just as we have put the finishing touches to our argument science has changed its mind and quietly withdrawn the theory we have been using as our foundation stone. *Timeo Danaos et dona ferentes*[5] is a sound principle.

While we are on the subject of science, let me digress for a moment. I believe that any Christian who is qualified to write a good popular book on any science may do much more by that than by any directly apologetic work. The difficulty we are up against is this. We can make people (often) attend to the Christian point of view for half an hour or so; but the moment they have gone away from our lecture or laid down our article, they are plunged back into a world where the opposite position is taken for granted. As long as that situation exists, widespread success is simply impossible. We must attack the enemy's line of communication. What we want is not more little books about Christianity, but more little books by Christians on other subjects—with their Christianity *latent*. You can see this most easily if you look at it the other way round. Our Faith is not very likely to be shaken by any book on Hinduism. But if whenever we read an elementary book on Geology, Botany, Politics, or Astronomy, we found that its implications were Hindu, that would shake us. It is not the books written in direct defence of Materialism that make the modern man a materialist; it is the materialistic assumptions in all the other books. In the same way, it is not books on Christianity that will really trouble him. But he would be troubled if, whenever he wanted a cheap popular introduction to some science, the best work on the market was always by a Christian. The

4. Matthew xxiv. 35; Mark xiii. 31; Luke xxi. 33.
5. 'I fear the Greeks even when they bear gifts', Virgil, *Aeneid*, bk. II, line 49.

first step to the re-conversion of this country is a series, produced by Christians, which can beat the *Penguin* and the *Thinkers Library* on their own ground. Its Christianity would have to be latent, not explicit: and *of course* its science perfectly honest. Science *twisted* in the interests of apologetics would be sin and folly. But I must return to my immediate subject.

Our business is to present that which is timeless (the same yesterday, today, and tomorrow)[6] in the particular language of our own age. The bad preacher does exactly the opposite: he takes the ideas of our own age and tricks them out in the traditional language of Christianity. Thus, for example, he may think about the Beveridge Report[7] and *talk* about the coming of the Kingdom. The core of his thought is merely contemporary; only the superficies is traditional. But your teaching must be timeless at its heart and wear a modern dress.

This raises the question of Theology and Politics. The nearest I can get to a settlement of the frontier problem between them is this:—that Theology teaches us what ends are desirable and what means are lawful, while Politics teaches what means are effective. Thus Theology tells us that every man ought to have a decent wage. Politics tells by what means this is likely to be attained. Theology tells us which of these means are consistent with justice and charity. On the political question guidance comes not from Revelation but from natural prudence, knowledge of complicated facts and ripe experience. If we have these qualifications we may, of course, state our political opinions: but then we must make it quite clear that we are giving our personal judgement and have no command from the Lord. Not many priests have these qualifications. Most political sermons teach the congregation nothing except what newspapers are taken at the Rectory.

Our great danger at present is lest the Church should continue to practise a merely missionary technique in what has become a missionary situation. A century ago our task was to edify those who had been brought up in the Faith: our present task is chiefly to convert and instruct infidels. Great Britain is as much part of the mission field as China. Now if you were sent to the Bantus you would be taught their language and traditions. You need similar teaching about the language and mental habits of your own uneducated and unbelieving fellow countrymen. Many priests are quite ignorant on this subject. What I know about it I have learned from talking in R.A.F.[8] camps. They were mostly inhabited by Englishmen and, therefore, some of what I shall say may be irrelevant to the situation in Wales. You will sift out what does not apply.

(1) I find that the uneducated Englishman is an almost total sceptic about History. I had expected he would disbelieve the Gospels because they contain miracles: but he really disbelieves them because they deal with things that happened 2000 years ago. He would disbelieve equally in the battle of Actium if he heard of it. To those who have had our kind of education, his state of mind is very difficult to

6. Hebrews xiii. 8.
7. Sir William H. Beveridge, *Social Insurance and Allied Services*, Command Paper 6404, Parliamentary Session 1942–43 (London: H. M. Stationery Office, 1942). The 'Beveridge Report' is a plan for the present Social Security system in Britain.
8. The Royal Air Force.

realize. To us the Present has always appeared as one section in a huge continuous process. In his mind the Present occupies almost the whole field of vision. Beyond it, isolated from it, and quite unimportant, is something called 'The Old Days'—a small, comic jungle in which highwaymen, Queen Elizabeth, knights-in-armour etc. wander about. Then (strangest of all) beyond The Old Days comes a picture of 'Primitive Man'. He is 'Science', not 'history', and is therefore felt to be much more real than The Old Days. In other words, the Pre-historic is much more believed in than the Historic.

(2) He has a distrust (very rational in the state of his knowledge) of ancient texts. Thus a man has sometimes said to me 'These records were written in the days before printing, weren't they? and you haven't got the original bit of paper, have you? So what it comes to is that someone wrote something and someone else copied it and someone else copied *that* and so on. Well, by the time it comes to us, it won't be in the least like the original.' This is a difficult objection to deal with because one cannot, there and then, start teaching the whole science of textual criticism. But at this point their real religion (i.e., faith in 'science') has come to my aid. The assurance that there is a 'Science' called 'Textual Criticism' and that its results (not only as regards the New Testament, but as regards ancient texts in general) are generally accepted, will usually be received without objection. (I need hardly point out that the word 'text' must not be used, since to your audience it means only 'a scriptural quotation'.)

(3) A sense of sin is almost totally lacking. Our situation is thus very different from that of the Apostles. The Pagans (and still more the *metuentes*[9]) to whom they preached were haunted by a sense of guilt and to them the Gospel was, therefore, 'good news'. We address people who have been trained to believe that whatever goes wrong in the world is someone else's fault—the Capitalists', the Government's, the Nazis', the Generals' etc. They approach God Himself as His *judges*. They want to know, not whether they can be acquitted for sin, but whether He can be acquitted for creating such a world.

In attacking this fatal insensibility it is useless to direct attention (a) To sins your audience do not commit, or (b) To things they do, but do not regard as sins. They are usually not drunkards. They are mostly fornicators, but then they do not feel fornication to be wrong. It is, therefore, useless to dwell on either of these subjects. (Now that contraceptives have removed the obviously *uncharitable* element in fornication I do not myself think we can expect people to recognize it as sin until they have accepted Christianity as a whole.)

I cannot offer you a water-tight technique for awakening the sense of sin. I can only say that, in my experience, if one begins from the sin that has been one's own chief problem during the last week, one is very often surprised at the way this shaft goes home. But whatever method we use, our continual effort must be to get their mind away from public affairs and 'crime' and bring them down to brass tacks— to the whole network of spite, greed, envy, unfairness and conceit in the lives of 'ordinary decent people' like themselves (and ourselves).

9. The *metuentes* or 'god-fearers' were a class of Gentiles who worshipped God without submitting to circumcision and the other ceremonial obligations of the Jewish Law. See Psalm cxviii. 4 and Acts x. 2.

(4) We must learn the language of our audience. And let me say at the outset that it is no use at all laying down *a priori* what the 'plain man' does or does not understand. You have to find out by experience. Thus most of us would have supposed that the change from 'may truly and indifferently minister justice' to 'may truly and impartially'[10] made that place easier to the uneducated; but a priest of my acquaintance discovered that his sexton saw no difficulty in *indifferently* ('It means making no difference between one man and another' he said) but had no idea what *impartially* meant.

On this question of language the best thing I can do is to make a list of words which are used by the people in a sense different from ours.

ATONEMENT. Does not really exist in a spoken modern English, though it would be recognized as 'a religious word'. In so far as it conveys any meaning to the uneducated I think it means *compensation*. No one word will express to them what Christians mean by *Atonement*: you must paraphrase.

BEING. (Noun) Never means merely 'entity' in popular speech. Often it means what we should call a 'personal being' (e.g., a man said to me 'I believe in the Holy Ghost but I don't think He is a being!').

CATHOLIC means Papistical.

CHARITY. Means (a) Alms (b) A 'charitable organization' (c) Much more rarely—Indulgence (i.e., a 'charitable' attitude towards a man is conceived as one that denies or condones his sins, not as one that loves the sinner in spite of them).

CHRISTIAN. Has come to include almost no idea of *belief*. Usually a vague term of approval. The question 'What do you call a Christian?' has been asked of me again and again. The answer they *wish* to receive is 'A Christian is a decent chap who's unselfish, etc.'.

CHURCH. Means (a) A sacred building, (b) The clergy. Does *not* suggest to them the 'company of all faithful people'.[11] Generally used in a bad sense. Direct defence of the Church is part of our duty: but use of the word *Church* where there is no time to defend it alienates sympathy and should be avoided where possible.

CREATIVE. Now means merely 'talented', 'original'. The idea of creation in the theological sense is absent from their minds.

CREATURE means 'beast', 'irrational animal'. Such an expression as 'We are only creatures' would almost certainly be misunderstood.

CRUCIFIXION, CROSS, etc. Centuries of hymnody and religious cant have so exhausted these words that they now very faintly—if at all—convey the idea of execution by torture. It is better to paraphrase; and, for the same reason, to say *flogged* for New Testament *scourged*.[12]

DOGMA. Used by the people only in a bad sense to mean 'unproved assertion delivered in an arrogant manner'.

IMMACULATE CONCEPTION. In the mouth of an uneducated speaker *always* means *Virgin Birth*.

10. The first quotation is from the prayer for the 'Whole state of Christ's Church' in the service of Holy Communion, Prayer Book (1662). The second is the revised form of that same phrase as found in the 1928 Prayer Book.
11. A phrase which occurs in the prayer of 'Thanksgiving' at the end of the service of Holy Communion.
12. Matthew xxvii. 26; Mark xv. 15; John xix. 1.

MORALITY means *chastity*.

PERSONAL. I had argued for at least ten minutes with a man about the existence of a 'personal devil' before I discovered that *personal* meant to him *corporeal*. I suspect this of being widespread. When they say they don't believe in a 'personal' God they may often mean only that they are not anthropomorphists.

POTENTIAL. When used at all is used in an engineering sense: *never* means 'possible'.

PRIMITIVE. Means crude, clumsy, unfinished, inefficient. 'Primitive Christianity' would not mean to them at all what it does to you.

SACRIFICE. Has no associations with temple and altar. They are familiar with this word only in the journalistic sense ('The Nation must be prepared for heavy sacrifices.').

SPIRITUAL. Means primarily *immaterial, incorporeal*, but with serious confusions from the Christian uses of πνεῦμα.[13] Hence the idea that whatever is 'spiritual' in the sense of 'non-sensuous' is somehow *better* than anything sensuous: e.g., they don't really believe that envy could be as bad as drunkenness.

VULGARITY. Usually means obscenity or 'smut'. There are bad confusions (and not only in uneducated minds) between: (a) The obscene or lascivious: what is calculated to provoke lust. (b) The indecorous: what offends against good taste or propriety. (c) The vulgar proper: what is socially 'low'. 'Good' people tend to think (b) as sinful as (a) with the result that others feel (a) to be just as innocent as (b).

To conclude—you must translate every bit of your Theology into the vernacular. This is very troublesome and it means you can say very little in half an hour, but it is essential. It is also of the greatest service to your own thought. I have come to the conviction that if you cannot translate your thoughts into uneducated language, then your thoughts were confused. Power to translate is the test of having really understood one's own meaning. A passage from some theological work for translation into the vernacular ought to be a compulsory paper in every Ordination examination.

I turn now to the question of the actual attack. This may be either emotional or intellectual. If I speak only of the intellectual kind, that is not because I undervalue the other but because, not having been given the gifts necessary for carrying it out, I cannot give advice about it. But I wish to say most emphatically that where a speaker has that gift, the direct evangelical appeal of the 'Come to Jesus' type can be as overwhelming today as it was a hundred years ago. I have seen it done, preluded by a religious film and accompanied by hymn singing, and with very remarkable effect. I cannot do it: but those who can ought to do it with all their might. I am not sure that the ideal missionary team ought not to consist of one who argues and one who (in the fullest sense of the word) preaches. Put up your arguer first to undermine their intellectual prejudices; then let the evangelist proper launch his

---

13. Which means 'spirit', as in I Corinthians xiv. 12.

appeal. I have seen this done with great success. But here I must concern myself only with the intellectual attack. *Non omnia possumus omnes.*[14]

And first, a word of encouragement. Uneducated people are not irrational people. I have found that they will endure, and can follow, quite a lot of sustained argument if you go slowly. Often, indeed, the novelty of it (for they have seldom met it before) delights them.

Do not attempt to water Christianity down. There must be no pretence that you can have it with the Supernatural left out. So far as I can see Christianity is precisely the one religion from which the miraculous cannot be separated. You must frankly argue for supernaturalism from the very outset.

The two popular 'difficulties' you will probably have to deal with are these. (1) 'Now that we know how huge the universe is and how insignificant the Earth, it is ridiculous to believe that the universal God should be specially interested in our concerns.' In answer to this you must first correct their error about *fact*. The insignificance of Earth in relation to the universe is not a modern discovery: nearly 2000 years ago Ptolemy (*Almagest*, bk. 1, ch. v) said that in relation to the distance of the fixed stars Earth must be treated as a mathematical point without magnitude. Secondly, you should point out that Christianity says what God has done for Man; it doesn't say (because it doesn't know) what He has or has not done in other parts of the universe. Thirdly, you might recall the parable of the one lost sheep.[15] If Earth has been specially sought by God (which we don't know) that may not imply that it is the most important thing in the universe, but only that it has *strayed*. Finally, challenge the whole tendency to identify size and importance. Is an elephant more important than a man, or a man's leg than his brain?

(2) 'People believed in miracles in the Old Days because they didn't then know that they were contrary to the Laws of Nature.' But they did. If St Joseph didn't know that a virgin birth was contrary to Nature (i.e., if he didn't know the normal origin of babies) why, on discovering his wife's pregnancy, was he 'minded to put her away'?[16] Obviously, no event would be recorded as a wonder *unless* the recorders knew the natural order and saw that this was an exception. If people didn't yet know that the Sun rose in the East they wouldn't be even interested in its once rising in the West. They would not record it as a *miraculum*—nor indeed record it at all. The very idea of 'miracle' presupposes knowledge of the Laws of Nature; you can't have the idea of an exception until you have the idea of a rule.

It is very difficult to produce arguments on the popular level for the existence of God. And many of the most popular arguments seem to me invalid. Some of these may be produced in discussion by friendly members of the audience. This raises the whole problem of the 'embarrassing supporter'. It is brutal (and dangerous) to repel him; it is often dishonest to agree with what he says. I usually try to avoid saying anything about the validity of his argument *in itself* and reply, 'Yes. That may do for you and me. But I'm afraid if we take that line our friend here on my left might say etc., etc.'

---

14. 'Not all things can we all do', Virgil, *Eclogues*, bk. VIII, line 63.
15. Matthew xviii. 11–14; Luke xv. 4–7.
16. Matthew i. 19

Fortunately, though very oddly, I have found that people are usually disposed to hear the divinity of Our Lord discussed *before* going into the existence of God. When I began I used, if I were giving two lectures, to devote the first to mere Theism; but I soon gave up this method because it seemed to arouse little interest. The number of clear and determined atheists is apparently not very large.

When we come to the Incarnation itself, I usually find that some form of the *aut Deus aut malus homo*[17] can be used. The majority of them start with the idea of the 'great human teacher' who was deified by His superstitious followers. It must be pointed out how very improbable this is among Jews and how different to anything that happened with Plato, Confucius, Buddha, Mohammed. The Lord's own words and claims (of which many are quite ignorant) must be forced home. (The whole case, on a popular level, is very well put indeed in Chesterton's *The Everlasting Man.)*

Something will usually have to be said about the historicity of the Gospels. You who are trained theologians will be able to do this in ways which I could not. My own line was to say that I was a professional literary critic and I thought I did know the difference between legend and historical writing: that the Gospels were certainly not legends (in one sense they're not *good* enough): and that if they are not history then they are realistic prose fiction of a kind which actually never existed before the eighteenth century. Little episodes such as Jesus writing in the dust when they brought Him the woman taken in adultery[18] (which have no *doctrinal* significance at all) are the mark.

One of the great difficulties is to keep before the audience's mind the question of Truth. They always think you are recommending Christianity not because it is *true* but because it is *good*. And in the discussion they will at every moment try to escape from the issue 'True—or False' into stuff about a good society, or morals, or the incomes of Bishops, or the Spanish Inquisition, or France, or Poland—or anything whatever. You have to keep forcing them back, and again back, to the real point. Only thus will you be able to undermine (a) Their belief that a certain amount of 'religion' is desirable but one mustn't carry it too far. One must keep on pointing out that Christianity is a statement which, if false, is of *no* importance, and, if true, of infinite importance. The one thing it cannot be is moderately important. (b) Their firm disbelief of Article XVIII.[19] Of course it should be pointed out that, though all salvation is through Jesus, we need not conclude that He cannot save those who have not explicitly accepted Him in this life. And it should (at least in my judgement) be made clear that we are not pronouncing all other religions to be totally false, but rather saying that in Christ whatever is true in all religions is consummated and perfected. But, on the other hand, I think we must attack wherever we meet it the nonsensical idea that mutually exclusive propositions about God can both be true.

17. 'Either God or a bad man.'
18. John viii. 3–8.
19. Article XVIII in the Prayer Book: *Of obtaining eternal Salvation only by the Name of Christ,* which says 'They also are to be had accursed that presume to say, That every man shall be saved by the Law or Sect which he professeth, so that he be diligent to frame his life according to that Law, and the light of Nature. For holy Scripture doth set out unto us only the Name of Jesus Christ, whereby men must be saved.'

For my own part, I have sometimes told my audience that the only two things really worth considering are Christianity and Hinduism. (Islam is only the greatest of the Christian heresies, Buddhism only the greatest of the Hindu heresies. Real Paganism is dead. All that was best in Judaism and Platonism survives in Christianity.) There isn't really, for an adult mind, this infinite variety of religions to consider. We may *salva reverentia*[20] divide religions, as we do soups, into 'thick' and 'clear'. By Thick I mean those which have orgies and ecstasies and mysteries and local attachments: Africa is full of Thick religions. By Clear I mean those which are philosophical, ethical and universalizing: Stoicism, Buddhism, and the Ethical Church are Clear religions. Now if there is a true religion it must be both Thick and Clear: for the true God must have made both the child and the man, both the savage and the citizen, both the head and the belly. And the only two religions that fulfil this condition are Hinduism and Christianity. But Hinduism fulfils it imperfectly. The Clear religion of the Brahmin hermit in the jungle and the Thick religion of the neighbouring temple go on *side by side*. The Brahmin hermit doesn't bother about the temple prostitution nor the worshipper in the temple about the hermit's metaphysics. But Christianity really breaks down the middle wall of the partition. It takes a convert from central Africa and tells him to obey an enlightened universalist ethic: it takes a twentieth-century academic prig like me and tells me to go fasting to a Mystery, to drink the blood of the Lord. The savage convert has to be Clear: I have to be Thick. That is how one knows one has come to the real religion.

One last word. I have found that nothing is more dangerous to one's own faith than the work of an apologist. No doctrine of that Faith seems to me so spectral, so unreal as one that I have just successfully defended in a public debate. For a moment, you see, it has seemed to rest on oneself: as a result, when you go away from that debate, it seems no stronger than that weak pillar. That is why we apologists take our lives in our hands and can be saved only by falling back continually from the web of our own arguments, as from our intellectual counters, into the Reality—from Christian apologetics into Christ Himself. That also is why we need one another's continual help—*oremus pro invicem*.[21]

20. 'Without outraging reverence.'
21. 'Let us pray for each other.'

11
Work and Prayer

EVEN IF I grant your point and admit that answers to prayer are theoretically possible, I shall still think they are infinitely improbable. I don't think it at all likely that God requires the ill-informed (and contradictory) advice of us humans as to how to run the world. If He is all-wise, as you say He is, doesn't He know already what is best? And if He is all-good won't He do it whether we pray or not?'

This is the case against prayer which has, in the last hundred years, intimidated thousands of people. The usual answer is that it applies only to the lowest sort of prayer, the sort that consists in asking for things to happen. The higher sort, we are told, offers no advice to God; it consists only of 'communion' or intercourse with Him; and those who take this line seem to suggest that the lower kind of prayer really is an absurdity and that only children or savages would use it.

I have never been satisfied with this view. The distinction between the two sorts of prayer is a sound one; and I think on the whole (I am not quite certain) that the sort which asks for nothing is the higher or more advanced. To be in the state in which you are so at one with the will of God that you wouldn't want to alter the course of events even if you could is certainly a very high or advanced condition.

But if one simply rules out the lower kind two difficulties follow. In the first place, one has to say that the whole historical tradition of Christian prayer (including the Lord's Prayer itself) has been wrong; for it has always admitted prayers for our daily bread, for the recovery of the sick, for protection from enemies, for the conversion of the outside world, and the like. In the second place, though the other kind of prayer may he 'higher' if you restrict yourself to it because you have got beyond the desire to use any other, there is nothing specially 'high' or 'spiritual' about abstaining from prayers that make requests simply because you think they're no good. It might be a very pretty thing (but, again, I'm not absolutely certain) if a little boy never asked for cake because he was so high-minded and spiritual that he didn't want any cake. But there's nothing specially pretty about a little boy who doesn't ask because he has learned that it is no use asking. I think that the whole matter needs reconsideration.

The case against prayer (I mean the 'low' or old-fashioned kind) is this. The thing you ask for is either good—for you and for the world in general—or else it is not. If it is, then a good and wise God will do it anyway. If it is not, then He won't. In neither case can your prayer make any difference. But if this argument is sound, surely it is an argument not only against praying, but against doing anything whatever?

In every action, just as in every prayer, you are trying to bring about a certain result; and this result must be good or bad. Why, then, do we not argue as the opponents of prayer argue, and say that if the intended result is good God will bring it to pass without your interference, and that if it is bad He will prevent it happening whatever you do? Why wash your hands? If God intends them to be clean, they'll come clean without your washing them. If He doesn't, they'll remain dirty (as Lady Macbeth found)[1] however much soap you use. Why ask for the salt? Why put on your boots? Why do anything?

We know that we can act and that our actions produce results. Everyone who believes in God must therefore admit (quite apart from the question of prayer) that God has not chosen to write the whole of history with His own hand. Most of the events that go on in the universe are indeed out of our control, but not all. It is like a play in which the scene and the general outline of the story is fixed by the author, but certain minor details are left for the actors to improvise. It may be a mystery why He should have allowed us to cause real events at all; but it is no odder that He should allow us to cause them by praying than by any other method.

Pascal says that God 'instituted prayer in order to allow His creatures the dignity of causality'. It would perhaps be truer to say that He invented both prayer and physical action for that purpose. He gave us small creatures the dignity of being able to contribute to the course of events in two different ways. He made the matter of the universe such that we can (in those limits) do things to it; that is why we can wash our own hands and feed or murder our fellow creatures. Similarly, He made His own plan or plot of history such that it admits a certain amount of free play and can be modified in response to our prayers. If it is foolish and impudent to ask for victory in a war (on the ground that God might be expected to know best), it would be equally foolish and impudent to put on a mackintosh—does not God know best whether you ought to be wet or dry?

The two methods by which we are allowed to produce events may be called work and prayer. Both are alike in this respect—that in both we try to produce a state of affairs which God has not (or at any rate not yet) seen fit to provide 'on His own'. And from this point of view the old maxim *laborare est orare* (work is prayer) takes on a new meaning. What we do when we weed a field is not quite different from what we do when we pray for a good harvest. But there is an important difference all the same.

You cannot be sure of a good harvest whatever you do to a field. But you can be sure that if you pull up one weed that one weed will no longer be there. You can be sure that if you drink more than a certain amount of alcohol you will ruin your health or that if you go on for a few centuries more wasting the resources of the planet on wars and luxuries you will shorten the life of the whole human race. The kind of causality we exercise by work is, so to speak, divinely guaranteed, and therefore ruthless. By it we are free to do ourselves as much harm as we please. But the kind which we exercise by prayer is not like that; God has left Himself a discretionary power. Had He not done so, prayer would be an activity too dangerous for man and we should have the horrible state of things envisaged by Juvenal: 'Enormous prayers which Heaven in anger grants.'[2]

---

1. Shakespeare, *Macbeth*, V, i, 34–57.
2. *Satires*, Bk. IV, Satire x, line 111.

Prayers are not always—in the crude, factual sense of the word—'granted'. This is not because prayer is a weaker kind of causality, but because it is a stronger kind. When it 'works' at all it works unlimited by space and time. That is why God has retained a discretionary power of granting or refusing it; except on that condition prayer would destroy us. It is not unreasonable for a headmaster to say, 'Such and such things you may do according to the fixed rules of this school. But such and such other things are too dangerous to be left to general rules. If you want to do them you must come and make a request and talk over the whole matter with me in my study. And then—we'll see.'

12
Man or Rabbit?

CAN'T YOU LEAD A GOOD LIFE without believing in Christianity?' This is the question on which I have been asked to write, and straight away, before I begin trying to answer it, I have a comment to make. The question sounds as if it were asked by a person who said to himself, 'I don't care whether Christianity is in fact true or not. I'm not interested in finding out whether the real universe is more like what the Christians say than what the Materialists say. All I'm interested in is leading a good life. I'm going to choose beliefs not because I think them true but because I find them helpful.' Now frankly, I find it hard to sympathise with this state of mind. One of the things that distinguishes man from the other animals is that he wants to know things, wants to find out what reality is like, simply for the sake of knowing. When that desire is completely quenched in anyone, I think he has become something less than human. As a matter of fact, I don't believe any of you have really lost that desire. More probably, foolish preachers, by always telling you how much Christianity will help you and how good it is for society, have actually led you to forget that Christianity is not a patent medicine. Christianity claims to give an account of *facts*—to tell you what the real universe is like. Its account of the universe may be true, or it may not, and once the question is really before you, then your natural inquisitiveness must make you want to know the answer. If Christianity is untrue, then no honest man will want to believe it, however helpful it might be: if it is true, every honest man will want to believe it, even if it gives him no help at all.

As soon as we have realised this, we realise something else. If Christianity should happen to be true, then it is quite impossible that those who know this truth and those who don't should be equally well equipped for leading a good life. Knowledge of the facts must make a difference to one's actions. Suppose you found a man on the point of starvation and wanted to do the right thing. If you had no knowledge of medical science, you would probably give him a large solid meal; and as a result your man would die. That is what comes of working in the dark. In the same way a Christian and a non-Christian may both wish to do good to their fellow men. The one believes that men are going to live for ever, that they were created by God and so built that they can find their true and lasting happiness only by being united to God, that they have gone badly off the rails, and that obedient faith in Christ is the only way back. The other believes that men are an accidental result of the blind workings of matter, that they started as mere animals and have more or less steadily improved, that they are going to live for about seventy years, that their happiness is fully attainable by good social services and political organisations, and that everything else (e.g., vivisection, birth-control, the judicial system, education) is to be judged to be 'good' or 'bad' simply in so far as it helps or hinders that kind of 'happiness'.

Now there are quite a lot of things which these two men could agree in doing for their fellow citizens. Both would approve of efficient sewers and hospitals and a healthy diet. But sooner or later the difference of their beliefs would produce differences in their practical proposals. Both, for example, might be very keen about education: but the kinds of education they wanted people to have would obviously be very different. Again, where the Materialist would simply ask about a proposed action 'Will it increase the happiness of the majority?', the Christian might have to say, 'Even if it does increase the happiness of the majority, we can't do it. It is unjust.' And all the time, one great difference would run through their whole policy. To the Materialist things like nations, classes, civilizations must be more important than individuals, because the individuals live only seventy odd years each and the group may last for centuries. But to the Christian, individuals are more important, for they live eternally; and races, civilizations and the like, are in comparison the creatures of a day.

The Christian and the Materialist hold different beliefs about the universe. They can't both be right. The one who is wrong will act in a way which simply doesn't fit the real universe. Consequently, with the best will in the world, he will be helping his fellow creatures to their destruction.

With the best will in the world . . . then it won't be his fault. Surely God (if there is a God) will not punish a man for honest mistakes? But was *that* all you were thinking about? Are we ready to run the risk of working in the dark all our lives and doing infinite harm, provided only someone will assure us that our own skins will be safe, that no one will punish us or blame us? I will not believe that the reader is quite on that level. But even if he were, there is something to be said to him.

The question before each of us is not 'Can *someone* lead a good life without Christianity?' The question is, 'Can *I*?' We all know there have been good men who were not Christians; men like Socrates and Confucius who had never heard of it, or men like J. S. Mill who quite honestly couldn't believe it. Supposing Christianity to be true, these men were in a state of honest ignorance or honest error. If their intentions were as good as I suppose them to have been (for of course I can't read their secret hearts) I hope and believe that the skill and mercy of God will remedy the evils which their ignorance, left to itself, would naturally produce both for them and for those whom they influenced. But the man who asks me, 'Can't I lead a good life without believing in Christianity?' is clearly not in the same position. If he hadn't heard of Christianity he would not be asking this question. If, having heard of it, and having seriously considered it, he had decided that it was untrue, then once more he would not be asking the question. The man who asks this question has heard of Christianity and is by no means certain that it may not be true. He is really asking, 'Need I bother about it? Mayn't I just evade the issue, just let sleeping dogs lie, and get on with being "good"? Aren't good intentions enough to keep me safe and blameless without knocking at that dreadful door and making sure whether there is, or isn't someone inside?'

To such a man it might be enough to reply that he is really asking to be allowed to get on with being 'good' before he has done his best to discover what *good* means.

But that is not the whole story. We need not inquire whether God will punish him for his cowardice and laziness; they will punish themselves. The man is shirking. He is deliberately trying not to know whether Christianity is true or false, because he foresees endless trouble if it should turn out to be true. He is like the man who deliberately 'forgets' to look at the notice board because, if he did, he might find his name down for some unpleasant duty. He is like the man who won't look at his bank account because he's afraid of what he might find there. He is like the man who won't go to the doctor when he first feels a mysterious pain, because he is afraid of what the doctor may tell him.

The man who remains an unbeliever for such reasons is not in a state of honest error. He is in a state of dishonest error, and that dishonesty will spread through all his thoughts and actions: a certain shiftiness, a vague worry in the background, a blunting of his whole mental edge, will result. He has lost his intellectual virginity. Honest rejection of Christ, however mistaken, will be forgiven and healed—'Whosoever shall speak a word against the Son of man, it shall be forgiven him.'[1] But to *evade* the Son of Man, to look the other way, to pretend you haven't noticed, to become suddenly absorbed in something on the other side of the street, to leave the receiver off the telephone because it might be He who was ringing up, to leave unopened certain letters in a strange handwriting because they might be from Him—this is a different matter. You may not be certain yet whether you ought to be a Christian; but you do know you ought to be a Man, not an ostrich, hiding its head in the sand.

But still—for intellectual honour has sunk very low in our age—I hear someone whimpering on with his question, 'Will it help me? Will it make me happy? Do you really think I'd be better if I became a Christian?' Well, if you must have it, my answer is 'Yes.' But I don't like giving an answer at all at this stage. Here is a door, behind which, according to some people, the secret of the universe is waiting for you. Either that's true, or it isn't. And if it isn't, then what the door really conceals is simply the greatest fraud, the most colossal 'sell' on record. Isn't it obviously the job of every man (that is a man and not a rabbit) to try to find out which, and then to devote his full energies either to serving this tremendous secret or to exposing and destroying this gigantic humbug? Faced with such an issue, can you really remain wholly absorbed in your own blessed 'moral development'?

All right, Christianity will do you good—a great deal more good than you ever wanted or expected. And the first bit of good it will do you is to hammer into your head (you won't enjoy *that!*) the fact that what you have hitherto called 'good'—all that about 'leading a decent life' and 'being kind'—isn't quite the magnificent and all-important affair you supposed. It will teach you that in fact you can't be 'good' (not for twenty-four hours) on your own moral efforts. And then it will teach you that even if you were, you still wouldn't have achieved the purpose for which you were created. Mere *morality* is not the end of life. You were made for something quite different from that. J. S. Mill and Confucius (Socrates was much nearer the reality) simply didn't know what life is about. The people who keep on asking if

1. Luke xii. 10.

they can't lead a decent life without Christ, don't know what life is about; if they did they would know that 'a decent life' is mere machinery compared with the thing we men are really made for. Morality is indispensable: but the Divine Life, which gives itself to us and which calls us to be gods, intends for us something in which morality will be swallowed up. We are to be re-made. All the rabbit in us is to disappear—the worried, conscientious, ethical rabbit as well as the cowardly and sensual rabbit. We shall bleed and squeal as the handfuls of fur come out; and then, surprisingly, we shall find underneath it all a thing we have never yet imagined: a real Man, an ageless god, a son of God, strong, radiant, wise, beautiful, and drenched in joy.

'When that which is perfect is come, then that which is in part shall be done away.'[2] The idea of reaching 'a good life' without Christ is based on a double error. Firstly, we cannot do it; and secondly, in setting up 'a good life' as our final goal, we have missed the very point of our existence. Morality is a mountain which we cannot climb by our own efforts; and if we could we should only perish in the ice and unbreathable air of the summit, lacking those wings with which the rest of the journey has to be accomplished. For it is *from* there that the real ascent begins. The ropes and axes are 'done away' and the rest is a matter of flying.

2. I Cor. xiii. 10.

13
On the Transmission
of Christianity[1]

DURING THE WAR we turn with quickened interest from the newspaper accounts of the fighting to the report of any man who has just returned from taking part in it himself. The manuscript of this little book when it was first put into my hands gave me a similar excitement. Discussions on education and on religious education are admirable things; but here we have something different—a first-hand record of the results which the existing system is actually producing while we discuss. Its value is enhanced by the fact that the author is not a minister of education, nor a headmaster, nor a clergyman, nor even a professional teacher. The facts he records are facts against which he ran his head unexpectedly, almost (you might say) accidentally, while doing a particular wartime job.

There are, of course, other things besides this in the book. But I emphasize its purely documentary value because that seems to me to be far the most important thing about it—the thing on which public attention ought to be focused. The abstracts of the author's lectures—or rather openings of discussions—are indeed full of interest, and many will wish to comment on them. They are the part of the book which it is easiest to discuss. But I insist that to concentrate on that part is an evasion.

When every allowance has been made for the possibility (delightfully unsuspected by himself) that the author has unusual talents as a teacher, two facts still emerge from his record unshaken. Firstly, that the content of, and the case for, Christianity, are not put before most schoolboys under the present system; and secondly, that when they are so put a majority find them acceptable. The importance of these two facts is that between them they blow away a whole fog of 'reasons for the decline of religion' which are often advanced and often believed. If we had noticed that the young men of the present day found it harder and harder to get the right answers to sums, we should consider that this had been adequately explained the moment we discovered that schools had for some years ceased to teach arithmetic. After that discovery we should turn a deaf ear to people who offered explanations of a vaguer and larger kind—people who said that the influence of Einstein had sapped the ancestral belief in fixed numerical relations, or that gangster films had undermined the desire to get right answers, or that the evolution of consciousness was now entering on its post-arithmetical phase. Where a clear and simple explanation completely covers the facts no other explanation is in court. If the younger generation have never been told what the Christians say and never

1. This paper was originally published as a Preface to B. G. Sandhurst's book, *How Heathen is Britain?* (London, 1946), in which Mr Sandhurst describes his work with a group of young men in an attempt to discover what their views were about Man and the Godhead of Christ.

heard any arguments in defence of it, then their agnosticism or indifference is fully explained. There is no need to look any further: no need to talk about the general intellectual climate of the age, the influence of mechanistic civilization on the character of urban life. And having discovered that the cause of their ignorance is lack of instruction, we have also discovered the remedy. There is nothing in the nature of the younger generation which incapacitates them for receiving Christianity. If any one is prepared to tell them, they are apparently ready to hear.

I allow, of course, that the explanation which our author has discovered merely puts the problem a generation further back. The young people today are un-Christian because their teachers have been either unwilling or unable to transmit Christianity to them. For the impotence or unbelief of their teachers larger and, no doubt, vaguer explanations are to be sought. But that, be it noted, is a historical problem. The schoolmasters of today are, for the most part, the undergraduates of twenty years ago—the products of the 'postwar' period. It is the mental climate of the Twenties that now dominates the form room class. In other words, the sources of unbelief among young people today do not lie in those young people. The outlook which they have—until they are taught better—is a backwash from an earlier period. It is nothing intrinsic to themselves which holds them back from the Faith.

This very obvious fact—that each generation is taught by an earlier generation—must be kept very firmly in mind. The beliefs which boys fresh from school now hold are largely the beliefs of the Twenties. The beliefs which boys from school will hold in the Sixties will be largely those of the undergraduates of today. The moment we forget this we begin to talk nonsense about education. We talk of the views of contemporary adolescence as if some peculiarity in contemporary adolescence had produced them out of itself. In reality, they are usually a delayed result—for the mental world also has its time-bombs—of obsolete adolescence, now middle-aged and dominating its form room. Hence the futility of many schemes for education. None can give to another what he does not possess himself. No generation can bequeath to its successor what it has not got. You may frame the syllabus as you please. But when you have planned and reported *ad nauseam,* if we are sceptical we shall teach only scepticism to our pupils, if fools only folly, if vulgar only vulgarity, if saints sanctity, if heroes heroism. Education is only the most fully conscious of the channels whereby each generation influences the next. It is not a closed system. Nothing which was not in the teachers can flow from them into the pupils. We shall all admit that a man who knows no Greek himself cannot teach Greek to his form: but it is equally certain that a man whose mind was formed in a period of cynicism and disillusion, cannot teach hope or fortitude.

A society which is predominantly Christian will propagate Christianity through its schools: one which is not, will not. All the ministries of education in the world cannot alter this law. We have, in the long run, little either to hope or fear from government.

The State may take education more and more firmly under its wing. I do not doubt that by so doing it can foster conformity, perhaps even servility, up to a point; the power of the State to de-liberalize a profession is undoubtedly very great. But all the teaching must still be done by concrete human individuals. The State has to use the men who exist. Nay, as long as we remain a democracy, it is men who give the State its powers. And over these men, until all freedom is extinguished, the free winds of opinion blow. Their minds are formed by influences which government cannot control. And as they come to be, so will they teach. Let the abstract scheme of education be what it will: its actual operation will be what the men make it. No doubt, there will be in each generation of teachers a percentage, perhaps even a majority, of government tools. But I do not think it is they who will determine the actual character of the education. The boy—and perhaps especially the English boy—has a sound instinct. The teaching of one true man will carry further and print deeper than that of a dozen white Babus. A minister of education (going back, unless I am mistaken, as far as Julian the Apostate[2] for his precedent) may banish Christian clergy from the schools. But if the wind of opinion is blowing in the Christian direction, it will make no difference. It may even do us good; and the minister will have been unknowingly 'the goddes boteler'.[3]

We are often told that education is a key position. That is very false in one sense and very true in another. If it means that you can do any great thing by interfering with existing schools, altering curricula and the like, it is very false. As the teachers are, so they will teach. Your 'reform' may incommode and overwork them, but it will not radically alter the total effect of their teaching. Planning has no magic whereby it can elicit figs from thistles or choke-pears from vines. The rich, sappy, fruit-laden tree will bear sweetness and strength and spiritual health: the dry, prickly, withered tree will teach hate, jealousy, suspicion, and inferiority complex— whatever you *tell* it to teach. They will do it unknowingly and all day long. But if we mean that to make adult Christians now and even beyond that circle, to spread the immediately sub-Christian perceptions and virtues, the rich Platonic or Virgilian *penumbra* of the Faith, and thus to alter the type who will be teachers in the future— if we mean that to do this is to perform the greatest of all services for our descendants, then it is very true.

So at least it seems to me: I do not know how far the author would agree with me. He has exposed the actual workings of modern education. To blame the schoolmasters of the last ten years for it would be ridiculous. The majority of them failed to hand on Christianity because they had it not: will you blame a eunuch because he gets no children or a stone because it yields no blood? The minority, isolated in a hostile environment, have probably done all they could, have perhaps done wonders: but little was in their power. Our author has also shown that the ignorance and incredulity of the pupils are very often removable—their roots far shallower than we had feared. I do not draw from this moral that it is now our business to 'get our teeth into the schools'. For one thing, I do not think we shall be allowed to. It is unlikely that in the next forty years England will have a government which would encourage or even tolerate any radically Christian elements in its State system of education. Where the tide flows towards increasing State control, Christianity, with its claims in one way personal and in the other way ecu-

2. See p. 342.
3. Chaucer, *The Hous of Fame*, bk. II, line 592.

menical and both ways antithetical to omnicompetent government, must always in fact (though not for a long time yet in words) be treated as an enemy. Like learning, like the family, like any ancient and liberal profession, like the common law, it gives the individual a standing ground against the State. Hence Rousseau, the father of the totalitarians, said wisely enough, from his own point of view, of Christianity, *Je ne connais rien de plus contraire à l'esprit social*.[4] In the second place, even if we were permitted to force a Christian curriculum on the existing schools with the existing teachers we should only be making masters hypocrites and hardening thereby the pupils' hearts.

I am speaking, of course, of large schools on which a secular character is already stamped. If any man, in some little corner out of the reach of the omnicompetent, can make, or preserve a really Christian school, that is another matter. His duty is plain.

I do not, therefore, think that our hope of re-baptising England lies in trying to 'get at' the schools. Education is not *in that sense* a key position. To convert one's adult neighbour and one's adolescent neighbour (just free from school) is the practical thing. The cadet, the undergraduate, the young worker in the C.W.U. are obvious targets: but any one and every one is a target. If you make the adults of today Christian, the children of tomorrow will receive a Christian education. What a society has, that, be sure, and nothing else, it will hand on to its young. The work is urgent, for men perish around us. But there is no need to be uneasy about the ultimate event. As long as Christians have children and non-Christians do not, one need have no anxiety for the next century. Those who worship the Life-Force do not do much about transmitting it: those whose hopes are all based on the terrestrial future do not entrust much to it. If these processes continue, the final issue can hardly be in doubt.

4. 'I know nothing more opposed to the social spirit.'

14

'Miserable Offenders'
An Interpretation of
Prayer Book Language

ONE OF THE ADVANTAGES of having a written and printed service, is that it enables you to see when people's feelings and thoughts have changed. When people begin to find the words of our service difficult to join in, that is of course a sign that we do not feel about those things exactly as our ancestors. Many people have, as their immediate reaction to that situation, the simple remedy—'Well, change the words'—which would be very sensible if you knew that we are right and our ancestors were wrong. It is always at least worth while to find out who it is that is wrong.

The Lenten season is devoted especially to what theologians call contrition, and so every day in Lent a prayer is said in which we ask God to give us 'contrite hearts'.[1] Contrite, as you know, is a word translated from Latin, meaning crushed or pulverized. Now modern people complain that there is too much of that note in our Prayer Book. They do not wish their hearts to be pulverized, and they do not feel that they can sincerely say that they are 'miserable offenders'.[2] I once knew a regular churchgoer who never repeated the words, 'the burden of them (i.e., his sins) is intolerable',[3] because he did not feel that they were intolerable. But he was not understanding the words. I think the Prayer Book is very seldom talking primarily about our feelings; that is (I think) the first mistake we're apt to make about these words 'we are miserable offenders'. I do not think whether we are feeling miserable or not matters. I think it is using the word miserable in the old sense—meaning an object of pity. That a person can be a proper object of pity when he is not feeling miserable, you can easily understand if you imagine yourself looking down from a height on two crowded express trains that are traveling towards one another along the same line at 60 miles an hour. You can see that in forty seconds there will be a head-on collision. I think it would be very natural to say about the passengers of these trains, that they were objects of pity. This would not mean that they felt miserable themselves; but they would certainly be proper objects of pity. I think that is the sense in which to take the word 'miserable'. The Prayer Book does not mean that we should feel miserable but that if we could see things from a sufficient height above we should all realize that we are in fact proper objects of pity.

As to the other one, about the burden of our sins being intolerable, it might be clearer if we said 'unbearable', because that still has two meanings: you say 'I can-

---

1. The Lenten Collect is appended at the end of this paper.
2. From the General Confession at Morning and Evening Prayer, which is appended.
3. The General Confession at the Holy Communion, also appended.

not bear it,' when you mean it gives you great pain, but you also say 'That bridge will not bear that truck'—not meaning 'That bridge will feel pain,' but 'If that truck goes on to it, it will break and not be a bridge any longer, but a mass of rubble.' I wonder if that is what the Prayer Book means; that, whether we feel miserable or not, and however we feel, there is on each of us a load which, if nothing is done about it, will in fact break us, will send us from this world to whatever happens afterwards, not as souls but as broken souls.

But are we really to believe that on each of us there lies something which, if not taken off us, will in fact break us? It is very difficult. No man has any natural knowledge of his own inner state and I think that at the beginning we probably find it much easier to understand and believe this about other people than about ourselves. I wonder, would I be safe in guessing that every second person has in his life a terrible problem, conditioned by some other person; either someone you work for, or someone who works for you, either someone among your friends or your relations, or actually someone in your own house, who is making, and has for years made, your life very much more difficult than it need be?—someone who has that fatal flaw in his character, on which again and again all your efforts have been wrecked, someone whose fatal laziness or jealousy or intolerable temper, or the fact that he never tells the truth, or the fact that he will always backbite and bear tales, or whatever the fatal flaw may be, which, whether it breaks him or not, will certainly break you.

There are two stages, I think, in one's approach to this problem. One begins by thinking that if only something external happened; if only after the war you could get a better job, if only you could get a new house or if only your mother-in-law or daughter-in-law was no longer living with you; if something like that happened, then things would really be better. But after a certain age you no longer think that, because you know for a fact, that even if all this happened, your husband would still be sulky and self-centred, your wife jealous or extravagant, or your employer a bully, or someone you employ and cannot dispense with, a cheat. You know, that if the war ended and you had a better job and a new house, and your mother-in-law or your daughter-in-law no longer lived with you, there would still be that final flaw in 'so and so's' character.

Perhaps in one's misery, one lets out to an intimate friend a little of what the real trouble is, and your intimate friend says, 'Why do you not speak to him or her? Why not have the matter out? They really cannot be as bad as you think.' But you say to yourself 'Oh! He doesn't know,' for of course you have tried again and again to have the matter out, and you know by bitter experience that it will not do the slightest good. You have tried it so often, and you know that any attempt to have it out will only produce either a scene or a total failure of understanding; or, perhaps worst of all, the other person will be kind and equable, and entirely agree with you, and promise to be different. And then in twenty-four hours everything will be exactly the same as it always has been!

Supposing you are not mistaken, misled by your own anger or something of that sort. Supposing you are fairly near the truth, then you are in one sense getting a glimpse of what God must see all the time, because in a certain sense He's up against these people. He is up against their problem as you are. He also has made excellent plans; He has also again and again done His part, by sending into the world prophets and wise men and at last Himself, His own Son. Again and again His plans too have been shipwrecked by that fatal flaw in people's character. And no doubt He sees much more clearly than we do; but even we can see in the case of other people, that unless something is done about their load it will break them. We can see that under the influence of nagging jealousy, or possessive selfishness, their character is day by day ceasing to be human.

Now take a step further. When God looks into your office, or parish, or school, or hospital, or factory, or home, He sees all these people like that, and of course, sees one more, the one whom you do not see. For we may be quite certain that, just as in other people, there is something on which our best endeavours have again and again been shipwrecked, so in us there is something quite equally fatal, on which their endeavours have again and again been shipwrecked. If we are beginners in the Christian life we have nothing to make the fatal flaw clear to ourselves. Does the person with a smelly breath know it smells? Or does the Club bore know he is a bore? Is there a single man or woman who believes himself or herself to be a bore or temperamentally jealous? Yet the world is pretty well sprinkled with bores and jealous people. If we are like that, everyone else will know it before we do. You ask why your friends have not told you about it. But what if they have? They may have tried again and again; but on every occasion, we thought they were being queer, that they were in a bad temper, or simply mistaken. They have tried again and again, and have probably now given it up.

What should be done about it? What is the good of my talking about the fatal flaw if one does not know about it? I think the first step is to get down to the flaws which one does know. I am speaking to Christians. Many of you, no doubt, are very far ahead of me in the Christian way. It is not for me to decide whether you should confess your sins to a priest or not (our Prayer Book leaves that free to all and demands it of none)[4] but if you do not, you should at least make a list on a piece of paper, and make a serious act of penance about each one of them. There is something about the mere words, you know, provided you avoid two dangers, either of sensational exaggeration—trying to work things up and make melodramatic sins out of small matters—or the opposite danger of slurring things over. It is essential to use the plain, simple, old-fashioned words that you would use about anyone else. I mean words like theft, or fornication, or hatred, instead of 'I did not mean to be dishonest,' or 'I was only a boy then,' or 'I lost my temper.' I think that this steady facing of what one does know and bringing it before God, without excuses, and seriously asking for Forgiveness and Grace, and resolving as far as in one lies to do better, is the only way in which we can ever begin to know the fatal thing which is always there, and preventing us from becoming perfectly just to our wife or husband, or being a better employer or employee. If this process is gone through, I do not doubt that most of us will come to understand and to share these old words like 'contrite', 'miserable' and 'intolerable'.

4. See the Exhortation in the service of Holy Communion.

Does that sound very gloomy? Does Christianity encourage morbid introspection? The alternative is much more morbid. Those who do not think about their own sins make up for it by thinking incessantly about the sins of others. It is healthier to think of one's own. It is the reverse of morbid. It is not even, in the long run, very gloomy. A serious attempt to repent and really to know one's own sins is in the long run a lightening and relieving process. Of course, there is bound to be a first dismay and often terror and later great pain, yet that is much less in the long run than the anguish of a mass of unrepented and unexamined sins, lurking in the background of our minds. It is the difference between the pain of the tooth about which you should go to the dentist, and the simple straight-forward pain which you know is getting less and less every moment when you have had the tooth out.

APPENDICES TO 'MISERABLE OFFENDERS'

1. *The Collect for Ash Wednesday (the first day of Lent), which is read every day in Lent after the Collect appointed for the Day:*
Almighty and everlasting God, who hatest nothing that thou hast made, and dost forgive the sins of all them that are penitent: Create and make in us new and contrite hearts, that we worthily lamenting our sins, and acknowledging our wretchedness, may obtain of thee, the God of all mercy, perfect remission and forgiveness; through Jesus Christ our Lord. *Amen.*

2. *The General Confession, which is said both at Morning and Evening Prayer:*
Almighty and most merciful Father, We have erred and strayed from thy ways like lost sheep, We have followed too much the devices and desires of our own hearts, We have offended against thy holy laws, We have left undone those things which we ought to have done, And we have done those things which we ought not to have done, And there is no health in us: But thou, O Lord, have mercy upon us miserable offenders; Spare thou them, O God, which confess their faults, Restore thou them that are penitent, According to thy promises declared unto mankind in Christ Jesus our Lord: And grant, O most merciful Father, for his sake, That we may hereafter live a godly, righteous, and sober life, To the glory of thy holy Name. *Amen*

3. *The General Confession, which is made at Holy Communion:*
Almighty God, Father of our Lord Jesus Christ, Maker of all things, Judge of all men: We acknowledge and bewail our manifold sins and wickedness, Which we from time to time most grievously have committed, By thought, word, and deed, Against thy Divine Majesty, Provoking most justly thy wrath and indignation against us. We do earnestly repent, And are heartily sorry for these our misdoings; The remembrance of them is grievous unto us; The burden of them is intolerable. Have mercy upon us, Have mercy upon us, most merciful Father; For thy Son our Lord Jesus Christ's sake, Forgive us all that is past; And grant that we may ever hereafter Serve and please thee in newness of life, To the honour and glory of thy Name; Through Jesus Christ our Lord. *Amen.*

15

The Founding of the
Oxford Socratic Club[1]

LIKE A QUIETLY efficient nurse arriving in a house confused by illness, or like the new general arriving at the siege of Ismail in Byron's *Don Juan*, our Chairman[2] broke in (if she will pardon the word) during the autumn of 1941 on that welter of discussion which even in war-time makes up five-eighths of the night life of the Oxford undergraduate. By stages which must have been very swift (for I cannot remember them), we found that a new society had been formed, that it was attempting the difficult programme of meeting once a week,[3] that it was actually carrying this programme out, that its numbers were increasing, and that neither foul weather nor crowded rooms (they were lucky who found seats even on the floor) would reduce the size of the meetings. This was the Socratic Club. Socrates had exhorted men to 'follow the argument wherever it led them': the Club came into existence to apply his principle to one particular subject-matter—the *pros* and *cons* of the Christian Religion.

It is a little remarkable that, to the best of my knowledge, no society had ever before been formed for such a purpose. There had been plenty of organizations that were explicitly Christian—the S.C.M.,[4] the Ark,[5] the O.U.C.H.,[6] the O.I.C.C.U.[7]— and there had been plenty of others, scientific or political, which were, if not explicitly, yet profoundly anti-Christian in outlook. The question about Christianity arose, no doubt, often enough in private conversation, and cast its shadow over the aesthetic or philosophical debates in many societies: but an arena specially devoted to the conflict between Christian and unbeliever was a novelty. Its value from a merely cultural point of view is very great. In any fairly large and talkative community such as a university there is always the danger that those who think alike should gravitate together into *coteries* where they will henceforth encounter opposition only in the emasculated form of rumour that the outsiders say thus and thus. The absent are easily refuted, complacent dogmatism thrives, and differences of opinion are embittered by group hostility. Each group hears not the best, but the worst, that the other group can say. In the Socratic all this was changed. Here a man could get the case for Christianity without all the paraphernalia of pietism

---

1. This is Lewis's Preface to the first *Socratic Digest*, vol. I (Oxford, 1942–1943). What is not mentioned here is the very important fact that Lewis was the Society's President from the time of its first meeting until he went to Cambridge in 1954.
2. Miss Stella Aldwinckle, who is still Chairman.
3. The first meeting was in Somerville College, Oxford, on the 26th January 1942.
4. The Student Christian Movement.
5. An Oxford Christian society.
6. Oxford University Church Union.
7. Oxford Intercollegiate Christian Union, now called The Christian Union.

and the the case against it without the irrelevant *sansculottisme* of our common anti-God weeklies. At the very least we helped to civilize one another; sometimes we ventured to hope that if our Athenian patron were allowed to be present, unseen, at our meetings he might not have found the atmosphere wholly alien.

We also learned, in those motley—and usually stifling—assemblies where English boys fresh from public schools rubbed shoulders with elderly European *Gelehrten* in exile, almost any type of opinion might turn up. Everyone found how little he had known about everyone else. We of the Christian party discovered that the weight of the sceptical attack did not always come where we expected it; our opponents had to correct what seemed to us their almost bottomless ignorance of the Faith they supposed themselves to be rejecting.

It is (theoretically) a difficulty in the British Constitution that the Speaker of the House of Commons must himself be a member of one of the Parties. There is a similar difficulty about the Socratic. Those who founded it do not for one moment pretend to be neutral. It was the Christians who constructed the arena and issued the challenge. It will therefore always be possible for the lower (the less Athenian) type of unbeliever to regard the whole thing as a cunningly—or not even so very cunningly—disguised form of propaganda. The Athenian type, if he had this objection to make, would put it in a paper and read that paper to the Socratic itself. He would be welcome to do so—though I doubt whether he would have the stomach if he knew with what pains and toil the committee has scoured *Who's Who* to find intelligent atheists who had leisure or zeal to come and propagate their creed. But when all is said and done, the answer to any such suspicion lies deeper. It is not here that the honesty of the Socratic comes in. We never claimed to be impartial. But argument is. It has a life of its own. No man can tell where it will go. We expose ourselves, and the weakest of our party, to your fire no less than you are exposed to ours. Worse still, we expose ourselves to the recoil from our own shots; for if I may trust my personal experience no doctrine is, for the moment, dimmer to the eye of faith than that which a man has just successfully defended. The arena is common to both parties and cannot finally be cheated; in it you risk nothing, and we risk all.

Others may have quite a different objection to our proceedings. They may protest that intellectual discussion can neither build Christianity nor destroy it. They may feel that religion is too sacred to be thus bandied to and fro in public debate, too sacred to be talked of—almost, perhaps, too sacred for anything to be done with it at all. Clearly, the Christian members of the Socratic think differently. They know that intellectual assent is not faith, but they do not believe that religion is only 'what a man does with his solitude'. Or, if it is, then they care nothing for 'religion' and all for Christianity. Christianity is not merely what a man does with his solitude. It is not even what God does with His solitude. It tells of God descending into the coarse publicity of history and there enacting what can—and must—be talked . about.

16
Religion Without Dogma?[1]

IN THIS PAPER on, 'The Grounds of Modern Agnosticism', Professor Price maintains the following positions: (1) That the essence of religion is belief in God and immortality; (2) that in most actual religions the essence is found in connection with 'accretions of dogma and mythology'[2] which have been rendered incredible by the progress of science; (3) that it would be very desirable, if it were possible, to retain the essence purged of the accretions; but (4) that science has rendered the essence almost as hard to believe as the accretions. For the doctrine of immortality involves the dualistic view that man is a composite creature, a soul in a state of symbiosis with a physical organism. But in so far as science can successfully regard man monistically, as a single organism whose psychological properties all arise from his physical, the soul becomes an indefensible hypothesis. In conclusion, Professor Price found our only hope in certain empirical evidence for the soul which appears to him satisfactory; in fact, in the findings of Psychical Research.

My disagreement with Professor Price begins, I am afraid, at the threshold. I do not define the essence of religion as belief in God and immortality. Judaism in its earlier stages had no belief in immortality, and for a long time no belief which was religiously relevant. The shadowy existence of the ghost in Sheol was one of which Jehovah took no account and which took no account of Jehovah. In Sheol all things are forgotten. The religion was centred on the ritual and ethical demands of Jehovah in the present life, and also, of course, on benefits expected from Him. These benefits are often merely worldly benefits (grandchildren and peace upon Israel), but a more specifically religious note is repeatedly struck. The Jew is athirst for the living God,[3] he delights in His Laws as in honey or treasure,[4] he is conscious of himself in Jehovah's presence as unclean of lips and heart.[5] The glory or splendour of God is worshipped for its own sake. In Buddhism, on the other hand, we find that a doctrine of immortality is central, while there is nothing specifically religious. Salvation from immortality, deliverance from reincarnation, is the very core of its message. The existence of the gods is not necessarily decried, but it is of no reli-

---

1. This paper was originally read to the Oxford Socratic Club on the 20th May 1946 as 'Religion without Dogma?', and later published in the *Phoenix Quarterly,* vol. I, No. I (Autumn 1946) under the title 'A Christian Reply to Professor Price'. It is an answer to 'The Grounds of Modern Agnosticism', a paper which Professor Price read to the Socratic Club on the 23rd October 1944, and which was published in the same issue of the *Phoenix Quarterly.* Though Lewis's paper was afterwards reprinted in *The Socratic Digest* [1948], it is obvious from the fact that many errors which appear in the *Socratic* version were corrected in the *Quarterly* version, that the *Quarterly* version represents Lewis's final revision. I have incorporated in the text given here all the marginal emendations which Lewis made in his copy of the *Phoenix Quarterly,* as well as those portions from the *Socratic* version which he had omitted in his revision.
2. H. H. Price, 'The Grounds of Modern Agnosticism', *Phoenix Quarterly*, vol. I, No. I (Autumn 1946), p. 25.
3. Psalm xlii. 2.
4. Psalm xix. 10.
5. Isaiah vi. 5.

gious significance. In Stoicism again both the religious quality and the belief in immortality are variables, but they do not vary in direct ratio. Even within Christianity itself we find a striking expression, not without influence from Stoicism, of the subordinate position of immortality. When Henry More ends a poem on the spiritual life by saying that if, after all, he should turn out to be mortal he would be

> ... *satisfide*
> *A lonesome mortall God t' have died.*[6]

From my own point of view, the example of Judaism and Buddhism is of immense importance. The system, which is meaningless without a doctrine of immortality, regards immortality as a nightmare, not as a prize. The religion which, of all ancient religions, is most specifically religious, that is, at once most ethical and most numinous, is hardly interested in the question. Believing, as I do, that Jehovah is a real being, indeed the *ens realissimum*, I cannot sufficiently admire the divine tact of thus training the chosen race for centuries in religion before even hinting the shining secret of eternal life. He behaves like the rich lover in a romance who woos the maiden on his own merits, disguised as a poor man, and only when he has won her reveals that he has a throne and palace to offer. For I cannot help thinking that any religion which begins with a thirst for immortality is damned, as a religion, from the outset. Until a certain spiritual level has been reached, the promise of immortality will always operate as a bribe which vitiates the whole religion and infinitely inflames those very self-regards which religion must cut down and uproot. For the essence of religion, in my view, is the thirst for an end higher than natural ends; the finite self's desire for, and acquiescence in, and self-rejection in favour of, an object wholly good and wholly good for it. That the self-rejection will turn out to be also a self-finding, that bread cast upon the waters will be found after many days, that to die is to live—these are sacred paradoxes of which the human race must not be told too soon.

Differing from Professor Price about the essence of religion, I naturally cannot, in a sense, discuss whether the essence as he defines it co-exists with accretions of dogma and mythology. But I freely admit that the essence as I define it always co-exists with other things; and that some of these other things even I would call mythology. But my list of things mythological would not coincide with his, and our views of mythology itself probably differ. A great many different views on it have, of course, been held. Myths have been accepted as literally true, then as allegorically true (by the Stoics), as confused history (by Euhemerus),[7] as priestly lies (by the philosophers of the enlightenment), as imitative agricultural ritual mistaken for propositions (in the days of Frazer).[8] If you start from a naturalistic philosophy, then something like the view of Euhemerus or the view of Frazer is likely to result. But I am not a naturalist. I believe that in the huge mass of mythology which

---

6. 'Resolution', *The Complete Poems of Dr Henry More*, ed. Alexander B. Grosart (Edinburgh, 1878), line 117, p. 176.
7. A Sicilian writer (c. 315 B.C.) who developed the theory that the ancient beliefs about the gods originated from the elaboration of traditions of actual historical persons.
8. James George Frazer, *The Golden Bough: A Study in Magic and Religion* (London, 1922).

has come down to us a good many different sources are mixed—true history, allegory, ritual, the human delight in story telling, etc. But among these sources I include the supernatural, both diabolical and divine. We need here concern ourselves only with the latter. If my religion is erroneous then occurrences of similar motifs in pagan stories are, of course, instances of the same, or a similar error. But if my religion is true, then these stories may well be a *preparatio evangelica,* a divine hinting in poetic and ritual form at the same central truth which was later focussed and (so to speak) historicised in the Incarnation. To me, who first approached Christianity from a delighted interest in, and reverence for, the best pagan imagination, who loved Balder before Christ and Plato before St Augustine, the anthropological argument against Christianity has never been formidable. On the contrary, I could not believe Christianity if I were forced to say that there were a thousand religions in the world of which 999 were pure nonsense and the thousandth (fortunately) true. My conversion, very largely, depended on recognizing Christianity as the completion, the actualization, the entelechy, of something that had never been wholly absent from the mind of man. And I still think that the agnostic argument from similarities between Christianity and paganism works only if you know the answer. If you start by knowing on other grounds that Christianity is false, then the pagan stories may be another nail in its coffin: just as if you started by knowing that there were no such things as crocodiles then the various stories about dragons might help to confirm your disbelief. But if the truth or falsehood of Christianity is the very question you are discussing, then the argument from anthropology is surely a *petitio.*

There are, of course, many things in Christianity which I accept as fact and which Professor Price would regard as mythology. In a word, there are miracles. The contention is that science has proved that miracles cannot occur. According to Professor Price 'a Deity who intervened miraculously and suspended natural law could never be accepted by Science';[9] whence he passes on to consider whether we cannot still believe in Theism without miracles. I am afraid I have not understood why the miracles could never be accepted by one who accepted science.

Professor Price bases his view on the nature of scientific method. He says that that method is based on two assumptions. The first is that all events are subject to laws, and he adds: 'It does not matter for our purpose whether the laws are "deterministic" or only "statistical."'[10] But I submit that it matters to the scientist's view of the miraculous. The notion that natural laws may be merely statistical results from the modern belief that the individual unit of matter obeys no laws. Statistics were introduced to explain why, despite the lawlessness of the individual unit, the behaviour of gross bodies was regular. The explanation was that, by a principle well known to actuaries, the law of averages levelled out the individual eccentricities of the innumerable units contained in even the smallest gross body. But with this conception of the lawless units the whole impregnability of nineteenth-century Naturalism has, as it seems to me, been abandoned. What is the use of saying that all events are subject to laws if you also say that every event which befalls the in-

9. Price, *op. cit.*, p. 20.
10. *Ibid.*

dividual unit of matter is *not* subject to laws. Indeed, if we define nature as the system of events in space-time governed by interlocking laws, then the new physics has really admitted that something other than nature exists. For if nature means the interlocking system, then the behaviour of the individual unit is outside nature. We have admitted what may be called the sub-natural. After that admission what confidence is left us that there may not be a supernatural as well? It may be true that the lawlessness of the little events fed into nature from the sub-natural is always ironed out by the law of averages. It does not follow that great events could not be fed into her by the supernatural: nor that they also would allow themselves to be ironed out.

The second assumption which Professor Price attributes to the scientific method is 'that laws can only be discovered by the study of publicly observable regularities.'[11] Of course they can. This does not seem to me to be an assumption so much as a self-evident proposition. But what is it to the purpose? If a miracle occurs it is by definition an interruption of regularity. To discover a regularity is by definition not to discover its interruptions, even if they occur. You cannot discover a railway accident from studying Bradshaw:[12] only by being there when it happens or hearing about it afterwards from someone who was. You cannot discover extra half-holidays by studying a school timetable: you must wait till they are announced. But surely this does not mean that a student of Bradshaw is logically forced to deny the possibility of railway accidents. This point of scientific method merely shows (what no one to my knowledge ever denied) that if miracles *did* occur, science, as science, could not prove, or disprove, their occurrence. What cannot be trusted to recur is not material for science: that is why history is not one of the sciences. You cannot find out what Napoleon did at the battle of Austerlitz by asking him to come and fight it again in a laboratory with the same combatants, the same *terrain*, the same weather, and in the same age. You have to go to the records. We have not, in fact, proved that science excludes miracles: we have only proved that the question of miracles, like innumerable other questions, excludes laboratory treatment.

If I thus hand over miracles from science to history (but not, of course, to historians who beg the question by beginning with materialistic assumptions) Professor Price thinks I shall not fare much better. Here I must speak with caution, for I do not profess to be a historian or a textual critic. I would refer you to Sir Arnold Lunn's book *The Third Day*.[13] If Sir Arnold is right, then the Biblical criticism which began in the nineteenth century has already shot its bolt and most of its conclusions have been successfully disputed, though it will, like nineteenth-century materialism, long continue to dominate popular thought. What I can say with more certainty is that that *kind of* criticism—the kind which discovers that every old book was made by six anonymous authors well provided with scissors and paste and that every anecdote of the slightest interest is unhistorical, has already begun to die out in the studies I know best. The period of arbitrary scepticism about the canon and text of Shakespeare is now over: and it is reasonable to expect that this method

11. *Ibid.*
12. George Bradshaw (1801–1853), who founded *Bradshaw's Railway Guide* which was published from 1839 to 1961.
13. (London, 1945).

will soon be used only on Christian documents and survive only in the *Thinkers Library* and the theological colleges.

I find myself, therefore, compelled to disagree with Professor Price's second point. I do not think that science has shown, or, by its nature, could ever show that the miraculous element in religion is erroneous. I am not speaking, of course, about the psychological effects of science on those who practise it or read its results. That the continued application of scientific methods breeds a temper of mind unfavourable to the miraculous, may well be the case, but even here there would seem to be some difference among the sciences. Certainly, if we think, not of the miraculous in particular, but of religion in general there is such a difference. Mathematicians, astronomers and physicists are often religious, even mystical; biologists much less often; economists and psychologists very seldom indeed. It is as their subject matter comes nearer to man himself that their anti-religious bias hardens.

And that brings me to Professor Price's fourth point—for I would rather postpone consideration of his third. His fourth point, it will be remembered, was that science had undermined not only what he regards as the mythological accretions of religion, but also what he regards as its essence. That essence is for him Theism and immortality. In so far as natural science can give a satisfactory account of man as a purely biological entity, it excludes the soul and therefore excludes immortality. That, no doubt, is why the scientists who are most, or most nearly, concerned with man himself are the most anti-religious.

Now most assuredly if naturalism is right then it is at this point, at the study of man himself, that it wins its final victory and overthrows all our hopes: not only our hope of immortality, but our hope of finding significance in our lives here and now. On the other hand, if naturalism is wrong, it will be here that it will reveal its fatal philosophical defect, and that is what I think it does.

On the fully naturalistic view all events are determined by laws. Our logical behaviour, in other words our thoughts, and our ethical behaviour, including our ideals as well as our acts of will, are governed by biochemical laws; these, in turn, by physical laws which are themselves actuarial statements about the lawless movements of matter. These units never intended to produce the regular universe we see: the law of averages (successor to Lucretius's *exiguum clinamen*)[14] has produced it out of the collision of these random variations in movement. The physical universe never intended to produce organisms. The relevant chemicals on earth, and the sun's heat, thus juxtaposed, gave rise to this disquieting disease of matter: organization. Natural selection, operating on the minute differences between one organism and another, blundered into that sort of phosphorescence or mirage which we call consciousness—and that, in some cortexes beneath some skulls, at certain moments, still in obedience to physical laws, but to physical laws now filtered through laws of a more complicated kind, takes the form we call thought. Such, for instance, is the origin of this paper: such was the origin of Professor Price's paper. What we should speak of as his 'thoughts' were merely the last link of a causal chain in which all the previous links were irrational. He spoke as he did because the matter

14. 'small inclination', *De Rerum Natura*, bk. II, line 292.

of his brain was behaving in a certain way: and the whole history of the universe up to that moment had forced it to behave in that way. What we called his thought was essentially a phenomenon of the same sort as his other secretions—the form which the vast irrational process of nature was bound to take at a particular point of space and time.

Of course it did not feel like that to him or to us while it was going on. He appeared to himself to be studying the nature of things, to be in some way aware of realities, even supersensuous realities, outside his own head. But if strict naturalism is right, he was deluded: he was merely enjoying the conscious reflection of irrationally determined events in his own head. It appeared to him that his thoughts (as he called them) could have to outer realities that wholly immaterial relation which we call truth or falsehood: though, in fact, being but the shadow of cerebral events, it is not easy to see that they could have any relation to the outer world except causal relations. And when Professor Price defended scientists, speaking of their devotion to truth and their constant following of the best light they knew, it seemed to him that he was choosing an attitude in obedience to an ideal. He did not feel that he was merely suffering a reaction determined by ultimately amoral and irrational sources, and no more capable of rightness or wrongness than a hiccup or a sneeze.

It would have been impossible for Professor Price to have written, or us to have read, his paper with the slightest interest if he and we had consciously held the position of strict naturalism throughout. But we can go further. It would be impossible to accept naturalism itself if we really and consistently believed naturalism. For naturalism is a system of thought. But for naturalism all thoughts are mere events with irrational causes. It is, to me at any rate, impossible to regard the thoughts which make up naturalism in that way and, at the same time, to regard them as a real insight into external reality. Bradley distinguished *idea-event* from *idea-making*,[15] but naturalism seems to me committed to regarding ideas simply as events. For meaning is a relation of a wholly new kind, as remote, as mysterious, as opaque to empirical study, as soul itself.

Perhaps this may be even more simply put in another way. Every particular thought (whether it is a judgment of fact or a judgment of value) is always and by all men discounted the moment they believe that it can be explained, without remainder, as the result of irrational causes. Whenever you know what the other man is saying is wholly due to his complexes or to a bit of bone pressing on his brain, you cease to attach any importance to it. But if naturalism were true then all thoughts whatever would be wholly the result of irrational causes. Therefore, all thoughts would be equally worthless. Therefore, naturalism is worthless. If it is true, then we can know no truths. It cuts its own throat.

I remember once being shown a certain kind of knot which was such that if you added one extra complication to make assurance doubly sure you suddenly found that the whole thing had come undone in your hands and you had only a bit of string. It is like that with naturalism. It goes on claiming territory after territory: first the inorganic, then the lower organisms, then man's body, then his emotions.

15. 'Spoken and Written English', *The Collected Papers of Henry Bradley*, ed. Robert Bridges (Oxford, 1928), pp. 168–93.

But when it takes the final step and we attempt a naturalistic account of thought itself, suddenly the whole thing unravels. The last fatal step has invalidated all the preceding ones: for they were all reasonings and reason itself has been discredited. We must, therefore, either give up thinking altogether or else begin over again from the ground floor.

There is no reason, at this point, to bring in either Christianity or spiritualism. We do not need them to refute naturalism. It refutes itself. Whatever else we may come to believe about the universe, at least we cannot believe naturalism. The validity of rational thought, accepted in an utterly non-naturalistic, transcendental (if you will), supernatural sense, is the necessary presupposition of all other theorizing. There is simply no sense in beginning with a view of the universe and trying to fit the claims of thought in at a later stage. By thinking at all we have claimed that our thoughts are more than mere natural events. All other propositions must be fitted in as best they can round that primary claim.

Holding that science has not refuted the miraculous element in religion, much less that naturalism, rigorously taken, can refute anything except itself, I do not, of course, share Professor Price's anxiety to find a religion which can do without what he calls mythology. What he suggests is simple Theism, rendered credible by a belief in immortality which, in its turn, is guaranteed by Psychical Research. Professor Price is not, of course, arguing that immortality would of itself prove Theism: it would merely remove an obstacle to Theism. The positive source of Theism he finds in religious experience.

At this point it is very important to decide which of two questions we are asking. We may be asking: (1) whether this purged minimal religion suggested by Professor Price is capable, as a historical, social and psychological entity, of giving fresh heart to society, strengthening the moral will, and producing all those other benefits which, it is claimed, the old religions have sometimes produced. On the other hand, we may be asking: (2) whether this minimal religion will be the true one; that is, whether it contains the only true propositions we can make about ultimate questions.

The first question is not a religious question but a sociological one. The religious mind as such, like the older sort of scientific mind as such, does not care a rap about socially useful propositions. Both are athirst for reality, for the utterly objective, for that which is what it is. The 'open mind' of the scientist and the emptied and silenced mind of the mystic are both efforts to eliminate what is our own in order that the Other may speak. And if, turning aside from the religious attitude, we speak for a moment as mere sociologists, we must admit that history does not encourage us to expect much envigorating power in a minimal religion. Attempts at such a minimal religion are not new—from Akhenaten[16] and Julian the Apostate[17] down to Lord Herbert of Cherbury[18] and the late H. G. Wells. But where are the saints,

16. Akhenaten (Amenhotep IV), king of Egypt, who came to the throne about 1375 B.C. and introduced a new religion, in which the sun-god Ra (designated as 'Aten') superseded Amon.
17. Roman emperor A.D. 361–3, who was brought up compulsorily as a Christian, but who on attaining the throne proclaimed himself a pagan, and made a great effort to revive the worship of the old gods.
18. Edward Herbert (1583–1648). He is known as the 'Father of Deism', for he maintained that among the 'common notions' apprehended by instinct are the existence of God, the duty of worship and repentance, and future rewards and punishment. This 'natural religion', he believed, had been vitiated by superstition and dogma.

the consolations, the ecstacies? The greatest of such attempts was that simplification of Jewish and Christian traditions which we call Islam. But it retained many elements which Professor Price would regard as mythical and barbaric, and its culture is by no means one of the richest or most progressive.

Nor do I see how such a religion, if it became a vital force, would long be preserved in its freedom from dogma. Is its God to be conceived pantheistically, or after the Jewish, Platonic, Christian fashion? If we are to retain the minimal religion in all its purity, I suppose the right answer would be: 'We don't know, and we must be content not to know.' But that is the end of the minimal religion as a practical affair. For the question is of pressing practical importance. If the God of Professor Price's religion is an impersonal spirituality diffused through the whole universe, equally present, and present in the same mode, at all points of space and time, then He—or it—will certainly be conceived as being beyond good and evil, expressed equally in the brothel or the torture chamber and in the model factory or the university common room. If, on the other hand, He is a personal Being standing outside His creation, commanding this and prohibiting that, quite different consequences follow. The choice between these two views affects the choice between courses of action at every moment both in private and public life. Nor is this the only such question that arises. Does the minimal religion know whether its god stands in the same relation to all men, or is he related to some as he is not related to others? To be true to its undogmatic character it must again say: 'Don't ask.' But if that is the reply, then the minimal religion cannot exclude the Christian view that He was present in a special way in Jesus, nor the Nazi view that He is present in a special way in the German race, nor the Hindu view that He is specially present in the Brahmin, nor the central African view that He is specially present in the thighbone of a dead English Tommy.

All these difficulties are concealed from us as long as the minimal religion exists only on paper. But suppose it were somehow established all over what is left of the British Empire, and let us suppose that Professor Price has (most reluctantly and solely from a sense of duty) become its supreme head on earth. I predict that one of two things must happen: (1) In the first month of his reign he will find himself uttering his first dogmatic definition—he will find himself saying, for example: 'No. God is not an amoral force diffused through the whole universe to whom suttee and temple prostitution are no more and no less acceptable than building hospitals and teaching children; he is a righteous creator, separate from his creation, who demands of you justice and mercy' or (2) Professor Price will not reply. In the second case is it not clear what will happen? Those who have come to his minimal religion from Christianity will conceive God in the Jewish, Platonic, Christian way; those who have come from Hinduism will conceive Him pantheistically; and the plain men who have come from nowhere will conceive Him as a righteous Creator in their moments of self-indulgence. And the ex-Marxist will think He is specially present in the Proletariat, and the ex-Nazi will think He is specially present in the German people. And they will hold world conferences at which they all speak the same language and reach the most edifying agreement: but they will all mean totally different things. The minimal religion in fact cannot, while it remains minimal, be acted on. As soon as you *do* anything you have assumed one of the dogmas. In practice it will not be a religion at all; it will be merely a new colouring given to all the different things people were doing already.

I submit it to Professor Price, with great respect, that when he spoke of mere Theism, he was all the time unconsciously assuming a particular conception of God: that is, he was assuming a dogma about God. And I do not think he was deducing it solely, or chiefly from his own religious experience or even from a study of religious experience in general. For religious experience can be made to yield almost any sort of God. I think Professor Price assumed a certain sort of God because he has been brought up in a certain way: because Bishop Butler and Hooker and Thomas Aquinas and Augustine and St Paul and Christ and Aristotle and Plato are, as we say, 'in his blood'. He was not really starting from scratch. Had he done so, had God meant in his mind a being about whom no dogma whatever is held, I doubt whether he would have looked for even social salvation in such an empty concept. All the strength and value of the minimal religion, for him as for all others who accept it, is derived not from it, but from the tradition which he imports into it.

The minimal religion will, in my opinion, leave us all doing what we were doing before. Now it, in itself, will not be an objection from Professor Price's point of view. He was not working for unity, but for some spiritual dynamism to see us through the black night of civilization. If Psychical Research has the effect of enabling people to continue, or to return to, all the diverse religions which naturalism has threatened, and if they can thus get power and hope and discipline, he will, I fancy, be content. But the trouble is that if this minimal religion leaves Buddhists still Buddhists, and Nazis still Nazis, then it will, I believe, leave us—as Western, mechanised, democratic, secularised men—exactly where we were. In what way will a belief in the immortality vouched for by Psychical Research, and in an unknown God, restore to us the virtue and energy of our ancestors? It seems to me that both beliefs, unless reinforced by something else, will be to modern man very shadowy and inoperative. If indeed we knew that God were righteous, that He had purposes for us, that He was the leader in a cosmic battle and that some real issue hung on our conduct in the field, then it would be something to the purpose. Or if, again, the utterances which purport to come from the other world ever had the accent which really *suggests* another world, ever spoke (as even the inferior actual religions do) with that voice before which our mortal nature trembles with awe or joy, then that also would be to the purpose. But the god of minimal Theism remains powerless to excite either fear or love: can be given power to do so only from those traditional resources to which, in Professor Price's conception, science will never permit our return. As for the utterances of the mediums . . . I do not wish to be offensive. But will even the most convinced spiritualist claim that one sentence from that source has ever taken its place among the golden sayings of mankind, has ever approached (much less equalled) in power to elevate, strengthen or correct even the second rank of such sayings? Will anyone deny that the vast majority of spirit messages sink pitiably below the best that has been thought and said even in this world?—that in most of them we find a banality and provincialism, a paradoxical union of the prim with the enthusiastic, of flatness and gush, which would suggest that the souls of the moderately respectable are in the keeping of Annie Besant[19] and Martin Tupper?[20]

I am not arguing from the vulgarity of the messages that their claim to come from the dead is false. If I did the spiritualist would reply that this quality is due to imperfections in the medium of communication. Let it be so. We are not here discussing the truth of spiritualism, but its power to become the starting point of a religion. And for that purpose I submit that the poverty of its contents disqualifies it. A minimal religion compounded of spirit messages and bare Theism has no power to touch any of the deepest chords in our nature, or to evoke any response which will raise us even to a higher secular level—let alone to the spiritual life. The god of whom no dogmas are believed is a mere shadow. He will not produce that fear of the Lord in which wisdom begins, and, therefore, will not produce that love in which it is consummated. The immortality which the messages suggest can produce in mediocre spirits only a vague comfort for our unredeemedly personal hankerings, a shadowy sequel to the story of this world in which all comes right (but right in how pitiable a sense!), while the more spiritual will feel that it has added a new horror to death—the horror of mere endless succession, of indefinite imprisonment in that which binds us all, *das Gemeine*.[21] There is in this minimal religion nothing that can convince, convert, or (in the higher sense) console; nothing, therefore, which can restore vitality to our civilization. It is not costly enough. It can never be a controller or even a rival to our natural sloth and greed. A flag, a song, an old school tie, is stronger than it; much more, the pagan religions. Rather than pin my hopes on it I would almost listen again to the drum-beat in my blood (for the blood is at least in some sense the life) and join in the song of the Maenads:

> Happy they whom the Daimons
> Have befriended, who have entered
> The divine orgies, making holy
> Their life-days, till the dance throbs
> In their heart-beats, while they romp with
> Dionysus on the mountains . . .[22]

Yes, almost; almost I'd sooner be a pagan suckled in a creed outworn.

Almost, but not, of course, quite. If one is forced to such an alternative, it is perhaps better to starve in a wholly secularised and meaningless universe than to recall the obscenities and cruelties of paganism. They attract because they are a distortion of the truth, and therefore, retain some of its flavour. But with this remark I have passed into our second question. I shall not be expected at the end of this paper to begin an apologetic for the truth of Christianity. I will only say something which

19. Annie Besant (1847–1933) was an ardent supporter of Liberal causes and became a member of the Theosophical Society in 1889.
20. Martin Tupper (1810–89) is probably best known for his *Proverbial Philosophy*—commonplace maxims and reflections couched in a rhythmical form.
21. Johann Wolfgang Goethe, *Epilog zu Schillers Glocke*, 1. 32. '*das Gemeine*' means something like 'that which dominates us all'.
22. Euripides, *Bacchae*, 1. 74.

in one form or another I have said perhaps too often already. If there is no God then we have no interest in the minimal religion or any other. We will not make a lie even to save civilization. But if there is, then it is so probable as to be almost axiomatic that the initiative lies wholly on His side. If He can be known it will be by self-revelation on His part, not by speculation on ours. We, therefore, look for Him where it is claimed that He has revealed Himself by miracle, by inspired teachers, by enjoined ritual. The traditions conflict, yet the longer and more sympathetically we study them the more we become aware of a common element in many of them: the theme of sacrifice, of mystical communion through the shed blood, of death and rebirth, of redemption, is too clear to escape notice. We are fully entitled to use moral and intellectual criticism. What we are not, in my opinion, entitled to do is simply to abstract the ethical element and set that up as a religion on its own. Rather in that tradition which is at once more completely ethical and most transcends mere ethics—in which the old themes of the sacrifice and rebirth recur in a form which transcends, though there it no longer revolts, our conscience and our reason—we may still most reasonably believe that we have the consummation of all religion, the fullest message from the wholly other, the living creator, who, if He is at all, must be the God not only of the philosophers, but of mystics and savages, not only of the head and heart, but also of the primitive emotions and the spiritual heights beyond all emotion. We may still reasonably attach ourselves to the Church, to the only concrete organization which has preserved down to this present time the core of all the messages, pagan and perhaps pre-pagan, that have ever come from beyond the world, and begin to practice the only religion which rests not upon some selection of certain supposedly 'higher' elements in our nature, but on the shattering and rebuilding, the death and rebirth, of that nature in every part: neither Greek nor Jew nor barbarian, but a new creation.

[NOTE: The debate between Lewis and Professor Price did not end here. In *The Socratic Digest*, No. 4 [1948], there follows a 'Reply' to Lewis's 'Religion without Dogma?' by Professor Price (pp. 94–102). Then, at a meeting of the Socratic Club on the 2nd February 1948, Miss G. E. M. Anscombe read a paper entitled 'A Reply to Mr C. S. Lewis's Argument that "Naturalism is Self-refuting"', afterwards published in the same issue of the *Digest* (pp. 7–15) as Professor Price's 'Reply'. Miss Anscombe criticised the argument found on pp. 136–38 of the paper printed above as well as chapter III, 'The Self-Contradiction of the Naturalist', of Lewis's book *Miracles* (London, 1947). The two short pieces that follow are (A) the Socratic minute-book account of Lewis's reply to Miss Anscombe and (B) a reply written by Lewis himself—both reprinted from the same issue of the *Digest* mentioned above (pp. 15–16). Aware that the third chapter of his *Miracles* was ambiguous, Lewis revised this chapter for the Fontana (1960) issue of *Miracles* in which chapter III is retitled 'The Cardinal Difficulty of Naturalism'.]

A

In his reply Mr C. S. Lewis agreed that the words 'cause' and 'ground' were far from synonymous but said that the recognition of a ground could be the cause of assent, and that assent was only rational when such was its cause. He denied that such words as 'recognition' and 'perception' could be properly used of a mental act among whose causes the thing perceived or recognized was not one.

Miss Anscombe said that Mr Lewis had misunderstood her and thus the first part of the discussion was confined to the two speakers who attempted to clarify their positions and their differences. Miss Anscombe said that Mr Lewis was still not distinguishing between 'having reasons' and 'having reasoned' in the causal sense. Mr Lewis understood the speaker to be making a tetrachotomy thus: (1) logical reasons; (2) having reasons (i.e., psychological); (3) historical causes; (4) scientific causes or observed regularities. The main point in his reply was that an observed regularity was only the symptom of a cause, and not the cause itself, and in reply to an interruption by the Secretary he referred to his notion of cause as 'magical'. An open discussion followed, in which some members tried to show Miss Anscombe that there was a connection between ground and cause, while others contended against the President [Lewis] that the test for the validity of reason could never in any event be such a thing as the state of the blood stream. The President finally admitted that the word 'valid' was an unfortunate one. From the discussion in general it appeared that Mr Lewis would have to turn his argument into a rigorous analytic one, if his notion of 'validity' as the effect of causes were to stand the test of all the questions put to him.

B

I admit that *valid* was a bad word for what I meant; *veridical* (or *verific* or *veriferous*) would have been better. I also admit that the cause and effect relation between events and the ground and consequent relation between propositions are distinct. Since English uses the word *because* of both, let us here use *Because* CE for the cause and effect relation ('This doll always falls on its feet *because* CE its feet are weighted') and *Because* GC for the ground and consequent relation ('A equals C *because* GC they both equal B'). But the sharper this distinction becomes the more my difficulty increases. If an argument is to be verific the conclusion must be related to the premises as consequent to ground, i.e., the conclusion is there *because* GC certain other propositions are true. On the other hand, our thinking the conclusion is an event and must be related to previous events as effect to cause, i.e., this act of thinking must occur *because* CE previous events have occurred. It would seem, therefore, that we never think the conclusion *because* GC it is the consequent of its grounds but only *because* CE certain previous events have happened. If so, it does not seem that the GC sequence makes us more likely to think the true conclusion than not. And this is very much what I meant by the difficulty in Naturalism.

17
Some Thoughts

AT FIRST SIGHT nothing seems more obvious than that religious persons should care for the sick; no Christian building, except perhaps a church, is more self-explanatory than a Christian hospital. Yet on further consideration the thing is really connected with the undying paradox, the blessedly two-edged character, of Christianity. And if any of us were now encountering Christianity for the first time he would be vividly aware of this paradox.

Let us suppose that such a person began by observing those Christian activities which are, in a sense, directed towards this present world. He would find that this religion had, as a mere matter of historical fact, been the agent which preserved such secular civilization as survived the fall of the Roman Empire; that to it Europe owes the salvation, in those perilous ages, of civilized agriculture, architecture, laws, and literacy itself. He would find that this same religion has always been healing the sick and caring for the poor; that it has, more than any other, blessed marriage; and that arts and philosophy tend to flourish in its neighbourhood. In a word, it is always either doing, or at least repenting with shame for not having done, all the things which secular humanitarianism enjoins. If our enquirer stopped at this point he would have no difficulty in classifying Christianity—giving it its place on a map of the 'great religions.' Obviously (he would say), this is one of the world-affirming religions like Confucianism or the agricultural religions of the great Mesopotamian city states.

But how if our enquirer began (as he well might) with quite a different series of Christian phenomena? He might notice that the central image in all Christian art was that of a Man slowly dying by torture; that the instrument of His torture was the world-wide symbol of the Faith; that martyrdom was almost a specifically Christian action; that our calendar was as full of fasts as of feasts; that we meditated constantly on the mortality not only of ourselves but of the whole universe; that we were bidden to entrust all our treasure to another world; and that even a certain disdain for the whole natural order (*contemptus mundi*) had sometimes been reckoned a Christian virtue. And here, once again, if he knew no more, the enquirer would find Christianity quite easy to classify; but this time he would classify it as one of the world-denying religions. It would be pigeon-holed along with Buddhism.

Either conclusion would be justified if a man had only the one or the other half of the evidence before him. It is when he puts both halves together and sees that Christianity cuts right across the classification he was attempting to make—it is then that he first knows what he is up against, and I think he will be bewildered.

Probably most of those who read this page have been Christians all their lives. If so, they may find it hard to sympathise with the bewilderment I refer to. To Christians the explanation of this two-edged character in their Faith seems obvious. They live in a graded or hierarchical universe where there is a place for everything and everything should be kept in its right place. The Supernatural is higher than the Natural, but each has its place; just as a man is higher than a dog, but a dog has its place. It is, therefore, to us not at all surprising that healing for the sick and provision for the poor should be less important than (when they are, as sometimes happens, alternative to) the salvation of souls; and yet very important. Because God created the Natural—invented it out of His love and artistry—it demands our reverence; because it is only a creature and not He, it is, from another point of view, of little account. And still more, because Nature, and especially human nature, is fallen it must be corrected and the evil within it must be mortified. But its essence is good; correction is something quite different from Manichaean repudiation or Stoic superiority. Hence, in all true Christian asceticism, that respect for the thing rejected which, I think, we never find in pagan asceticism. Marriage is good, though not for me; wine is good, though I must not drink it; feasts are good, though today we fast.

This attitude will, I think, be found to depend logically on the doctrines of the Creation and the Fall. Some hazy adumbrations of a doctrine of the Fall can be found in Paganism; but it is quite astonishing how rarely outside Christianity we find—I am not sure that we ever find—a real doctrine of Creation. In Polytheism the gods are usually the product of a universe already in existence—Keats' *Hyperion,* in spirit, if not in detail, is true enough as a picture of pagan theogony. In Pantheism the universe is never something that God made. It is an emanation, something that oozes out of Him, or an appearance, something He looks like to us but really is not, or even an attack of incurable schizophrenia from which He is unaccountably suffering. Polytheism is always, in the long run, nature-worship; Pantheism always, in the long run, hostility to nature. None of these beliefs really leaves you free *both* to enjoy your breakfast *and* to mortify your inordinate appetites—much less to mortify appetites recognised as innocent at present lest they should become inordinate.

And none of them leaves anyone free to do what is being done in the Lourdes Hospital every day: to fight against death as earnestly, skilfully, and calmly as if you were a secular humanitarian while knowing all the time that death is, both for better and worse, something that the secular humanitarian has never dreamed of. The world, knowing how all our real investments are beyond the grave, might expect us to be less concerned than other people who go in for what is called Higher Thought and tell us that 'death doesn't matter'; but we 'are not high minded',[1] and we follow One who stood and wept at the grave of Lazarus—not surely, because He was grieved that Mary and Martha wept, and sorrowed for their lack of faith (though some thus interpret) but because death, the punishment of sin, is even more horrible in His eyes than in ours. The nature which He had created as God, the nature which He had assumed as Man, lay there before Him in its ignominy; a foul smell, food for worms. Though He was to revive it a moment later, He wept at the shame; if I may here quote a writer of my own communion, 'I am not so much afraid

1. Psalm cxxxi. 1.

of death as ashamed of it.'[2] And that brings us again to the paradox. Of all men, we hope most of death; yet nothing will reconcile us to—well, its *unnaturalness.* We know that we were not made for it; we know how it crept into our destiny as an intruder; and we know Who has defeated it. Because Our Lord is risen we know that on one level it is an enemy already disarmed; but because we know that the natural level also is God's creation we cannot cease to fight against the death which mars it, as against all those other blemishes upon it, against pain and poverty, barbarism and ignorance. Because we love something else more than this world we love even this world better than those who know no other.

2. The reference is to Sir Thomas Browne's *Religio Medici,* First Part, Section 40, where he says 'I am not so much afraid of death, as ashamed thereof.'

18
'The Trouble with "X" . . .'

I SUPPOSE I may assume that seven out of ten of those who read these lines are in some kind of difficulty about some other human being. Either at work or at home, either the people who employ you or those whom you employ, either those who share your house or those whose house you share, either your in-laws or parents or children, your wife or your husband, are making life harder for you than it need be even in these days. It is to be hoped that we do not often mention these difficulties (especially the domestic ones) to outsiders. But sometimes we do. An outside friend asks us why we are looking so glum, and the truth comes out.

On such occasions the outside friend usually says, 'But why don't you tell them? Why don't you go to your wife (or husband, or father, or daughter, or boss, or landlady, or lodger) and have it all out? People are usually reasonable. All you've got to do is to make them see things in the right light. Explain it to them in a reasonable, quiet, friendly way.' And we, whatever we say outwardly, think sadly to ourselves, 'He doesn't know "X." ' We do. We know how utterly hopeless it is to make 'X' see reason. Either we've tried it over and over again—tried it till we are sick of trying it—or else we've never tried it because we saw from the beginning how useless it would be. We know that if we attempt to 'have it all out with "X" ' there will either be a 'scene,' or else 'X' will stare at us in blank amazement and say 'I don't know what on earth you're talking about'; or else (which is perhaps worst of all) 'X' will quite agree with us and promise to turn over a new leaf and put everything on a new footing—and then, twenty-four hours later, will be exactly the same as 'X' has always been.

You know, in fact, that any attempt to talk things over with 'X' will shipwreck on the old, fatal flaw in 'X's' character. And you see, looking back, how all the plans you have ever made always have shipwrecked on that fatal flaw—on 'X's' incurable jealousy, or laziness, or touchiness, or muddleheadedness, or bossiness, or ill temper, or changeableness. Up to a certain age you have perhaps had the illusion that some external stroke of good fortune—an improvement in health, a rise of salary, the end of the war—would solve your difficulty. But you know better now. The war is over, and you realise that even if the other things happened, 'X' would still be 'X', and you would still be up against the same old problem. Even if you became a millionaire, your husband would still be a bully, or your wife would still nag or your son would still drink, or you'd still have to have your mother-in-law to live with you.

It is a great step forward to realise that this is so; to face the fact that even if all external things went right, real happiness would still depend on the character of the people you have to live with—and that you can't alter their characters. And now comes the point. When you have seen this you have, for the first time, had a glimpse of what it must be like for God. For, of course, this is (in one way) just what God Himself is up against. He has provided a rich, beautiful world for people to live in. He has given them intelligence to show them how it can be used, and conscience to show them how it ought to be used. He has contrived that the things they need for their biological life (food, drink, rest, sleep, exercise) should be positively delightful to them. And, having done all this, He then sees all His plans spoiled—just as our little plans are spoiled—by the crookedness of the people themselves. All the things He has given them to be happy with they turn into occasions for quarrelling and jealousy, and excess and hoarding, and tomfoolery.

You may say it is very different for God because He could, if He pleased, alter people's characters, and we can't. But this difference doesn't go quite as deep as we may at first think. God has made it a rule for Himself that He won't alter people's character by force. He can and will alter them—but only if the people will let Him. In that way He has really and truly limited His power. Sometimes we wonder why He has done so, or even wish that He hadn't. But apparently He thinks it worth doing. He would rather have a world of free beings, with all its risks, than a world of people who did right like machines because they couldn't do anything else. The more we succeed in imagining what a world of perfect automatic beings would be like, the more, I think, we shall see His wisdom.

I said that when we see how all our plans shipwreck on the characters of the people we have to deal with, we are 'in *one* way' seeing what it must be like for God. But only in one way. There are two respects in which God's view must be very different from ours. In the first place, He sees (like you) how all the people in your home or your job are in various degrees awkward or difficult; but when He looks into that home or factory or office He sees one more person of the same kind— the one you never do see. I mean, of course, yourself. That is the next great step in wisdom—to realise that you also are just that sort of person. You also have a fatal flaw in your character. All the hopes and plans of others have again and again shipwrecked on your character just as your hopes and plans have shipwrecked on theirs.

It is no good passing this over with some vague, general admission such as 'Of course, I know I have my faults.' It is important to realise that there is some really fatal flaw in you: something which gives the others just that same feeling of *despair* which their flaws give you. And it is almost certainly something you don't know about—like what the advertisements call 'halitosis', which everyone notices except the person who has it. But why, you ask, don't the others tell me? Believe me, they have tried to tell you over and over again, and you just couldn't 'take it'. Perhaps a good deal of what you call their 'nagging' or 'bad temper' or 'queerness' are just their attempts to make you see the truth. And even the faults you do know you don't know fully. You say, 'I admit I lost my temper last night'; but the others know that you're always doing it, that you are a bad-tempered person. You say, 'I admit I drank too much last Saturday'; but every one else knows that you are an habitual drunkard.

That is one way in which God's view must differ from mine. He sees all the characters: I see all except my own. But the second difference is this. He loves the people in spite of their faults. He goes on loving. He does not let go. Don't say, 'It's all very well for Him; He hasn't got to live with them.' He has. He is inside them as well as outside them. He *is with* them far more intimately and closely and incessantly than we can ever be. Every vile thought within their minds (and ours), every moment of spite, envy, arrogance, greed and self-conceit comes right up against His patient and longing love, and grieves His spirit more than it grieves ours.

The more we can imitate God in both these respects, the more progress we shall make. We must love 'X' more; and we must learn to see ourselves as a person of exactly the same kind. Some people say it is morbid to be always thinking of one's own faults. That would be all very well if most of us could stop thinking of our own without soon beginning to think about those of other people. For unfortunately we *enjoy* thinking about other people's faults: and in the proper sense of the word 'morbid', that is the most morbid pleasure in the world.

We don't like rationing which is imposed upon us, but I suggest one form of rationing which we ought to impose on ourselves. Abstain from all thinking about other people's faults, unless your duties as a teacher or parent make it necessary to think about them. Whenever the thoughts come unnecessarily into one's mind, why not simply shove them away? And think of one's own faults instead? For there, with God's help, one *can* do something. Of all the awkward people in your house or job there is only one whom you can improve very much. That is the practical end at which to begin. And really, we'd better. The job has to be tackled some day: and every day we put it off will make it harder to begin.

What, after all, is the alternative? You see clearly enough that nothing, not even God with all His power, can make 'X' really happy as long as 'X' remains envious, self-centred, and spiteful. Be sure there is something inside you which, unless it is altered, will put it out of God's power to prevent your being eternally miserable. While that something remains there can be no Heaven for you, just as there can be no sweet smells for a man with a cold in the nose, and no music for a man who is deaf. It's not a question of God 'sending' us to Hell. In each of us there is something growing up which will of itself *be Hell* unless it is nipped in the bud. The matter is serious: let us put ourselves in His hands at once—this very day, this hour.

19
What Are We to Make
of Jesus Christ?

WHAT ARE WE to make of Jesus Christ? This is a question which has, in a sense, a frantically comic side. For the real question is not what are we to make of Christ, but what is He to make of us? The picture of a fly sitting deciding what it is going to make of an elephant has comic elements about it. But perhaps the questioner meant what are we to make of Him in the sense of 'How are we to solve the historical problem set us by the recorded sayings and acts of this Man?' This problem is to reconcile two things. On the one hand you have got the almost generally admitted depth and sanity of His moral teaching, which is not very seriously questioned, even by those who are opposed to Christianity. In fact, I find when I am arguing with very anti-God people that they rather make a point of saying, 'I am entirely in favour of the moral teaching of Christianity'—and there seems to be a general agreement that in the teaching of this Man and of His immediate followers, moral truth is exhibited at its purest and best. It is not sloppy idealism, it is full of wisdom and shrewdness. The whole thing is realistic, fresh to the highest degree, the product of a sane mind. That is one phenomenon.

The other phenomenon is the quite appalling nature of this Man's theological remarks. You all know what I mean, and I want rather to stress the point that the appalling claim which this Man seems to be making is not merely made at one moment of His career. There is, of course, the one moment which led to His execution. The moment at which the High Priest said to Him, 'Who are you?' 'I am the Anointed, the Son of the uncreated God, and you shall see Me appearing at the end of all history as the judge of the Universe.' But that claim, in fact, does not rest on this one dramatic moment. When you look into His conversation you will find this sort of claim running through the whole thing. For instance, He went about saying to people, 'I forgive your sins.' Now it is quite natural for a man to forgive something you do to *him*. Thus if somebody cheats *me* out of £5 it is quite possible and reasonable for me to say, 'Well, I forgive him, we will say no more about it.' What on earth would you say if somebody had done *you* out of £5 and *I* said, 'That is all right, I forgive him'? Then there is a curious thing which seems to slip out almost by accident. On one occasion this Man is sitting looking down on Jerusalem from the hill above it and suddenly in comes an extraordinary remark—'I keep on sending you prophets and wise men.' Nobody comments on it. And yet, quite suddenly, almost incidentally, He is claiming to be the power that all through the centuries is sending wise men and leaders into the world. Here is another curious remark: in almost every religion there are unpleasant observances like fasting. This Man suddenly remarks one day, 'No one need fast while I am here.' Who is this Man who remarks that His mere presence suspends all normal rules? Who is the person who can suddenly tell the School they can have a half-holiday? Sometimes the statements put forward the assumption that He, the Speaker, is completely without sin or fault. This is always the attitude. 'You, to whom I am talking, are all sinners,' and He never remotely suggests that this same reproach can be brought against Him. He says again, 'I am begotten of the One God, before Abraham was, I am,' and remember what the words 'I am' were in Hebrew. They were the name of God, which must not be spoken by any human being, the name which it was death to utter.

Well, that is the other side. On the one side clear, definite moral teaching. On the other, claims which, if not true, are those of a megalomaniac, compared with whom Hitler was the most sane and humble of men. There is no half-way house and there is no parallel in other religions. If you had gone to Buddha and asked him 'Are you the son of Bramah?' he would have said, 'My son, you are still in the vale of illusion.' If you had gone to Socrates and asked, 'Are you Zeus?' he would have laughed at you. If you had gone to Mohammed and asked, 'Are you Allah?' he would first have rent his clothes and then cut your head off. If you had asked Confucius, 'Are you Heaven?', I think he would have probably replied, 'Remarks which are not in accordance with nature are in bad taste.' The idea of a great moral teacher saying what Christ said is out of the question. In my opinion, the only person who can say that sort of thing is either God or a complete lunatic suffering from that form of delusion which undermines the whole mind of man. If you think you are a poached egg, when you are looking for a piece of toast to suit you, you may be sane, but if you think you are God, there is no chance for you. We may note in passing that He was never regarded as a mere moral teacher. He did not produce that effect on any of the people who actually met Him. He produced mainly three effects—Hatred—Terror—Adoration. There was no trace of people expressing mild approval.

What are we to do about reconciling the two contradictory phenomena? One attempt consists in saying that the Man did not really say these things, but that His followers exaggerated the story, and so the legend grew up that He had said them. This is difficult because His followers were all Jews; that is, they belonged to that Nation which of all others was most convinced that there was only one God—that there could not possibly be another. It is very odd that this horrible invention about a religious leader should grow up among the one people in the whole earth least likely to make such a mistake. On the contrary we get the impression that none of His immediate followers or even of the New Testament writers embraced the doctrine at all easily.

Another point is that on that view you would have to regard the accounts of the Man as being *legends*. Now, as a literary historian, I am perfectly convinced that whatever else the Gospels are they are not legends. I have read a great deal of legend and I am quite clear that they are not the same sort of thing. They are not artistic enough to be legends. From an imaginative point of view they are clumsy, they don't work up to things properly. Most of the life of Jesus is totally unknown to us, as is the life of anyone else who lived at that time, and no people building up a legend would allow that to be so. Apart from bits of the Platonic dialogues, there are no conversations that I know of in ancient literature like the Fourth Gospel. There is nothing, even in modern literature, until about a hundred years ago when the realistic novel came into existence. In the story of the woman taken in adultery we are told Christ bent down and scribbled in the dust with His finger. Nothing comes of this. No one has ever based any doctrine on it. And the art of *inventing* little irrelevant details to make an imaginary scene more convincing is a purely modern art. Surely the only explanation of this passage is that the thing really happened? The author put it in simply because he had *seen* it.

Then we come to the strangest story of all, the story of the Resurrection. It is very necessary to get the story clear. I heard a man say, 'The importance of the Resurrection is that it gives evidence of survival, evidence that the human personality survives death.' On that view what happened to Christ would be what had always happened to all men, the difference being that in Christ's case we were privileged to see it happening. This is certainly not what the earliest Christian writers thought. Something perfectly new in the history of the Universe had happened. Christ had defeated death. The door which had always been locked had for the very first time been forced open. This is something quite distinct from mere ghost-survival. I don't mean that they disbelieved in ghost-survival. On the contrary, they believed in it so firmly that, on more than one occasion, Christ had had to assure them that He was *not* a ghost. The point is that while believing in survival they yet regarded the Resurrection as something totally different and new. The Resurrection narratives are not a picture of survival after death; they record how a totally new mode of being has arisen in the Universe. Something new had appeared in the Universe: as new as the first coming of organic life. This Man, after death, does not get divided into 'ghost' and 'corpse'. A new mode of being has arisen. That is the story. What are we going to make of it?

The question is, I suppose, whether any hypothesis covers the facts so well as the Christian hypothesis. That hypothesis is that God has come down into the created universe, down to manhood—and come up again, pulling it up with Him. The alternative hypothesis is not legend, nor exaggeration, nor the apparitions of a ghost. It is either lunacy or lies. Unless one can take the second alternative (and I can't) one turns to the Christian theory.

'What are we to make of Christ?' There is no question of what we can make of Him, it is entirely a question of what He intends to make of us. You must accept or reject the story.

The things He says are very different from what any other teacher has said. Others say, 'This is the truth about the Universe. This is the way you ought to go,' but He says, '*I* am the Truth, and the Way, and the Life.' He says, 'No man can reach absolute reality, except through Me. Try to retain your own life and you will be inevitably ruined. Give yourself away and you will be saved.' He says, 'If you are ashamed of Me, if, when you hear this call, you turn the other way, I also will look the other way when I come again as God without disguise. If anything whatever is keeping you from God and from Me, whatever it is, throw it away. If it is your eye, pull it out. If it is your hand, cut it off. If you put yourself first you will be last. Come to Me everyone who is carrying a heavy load, I will set that right. Your sins, all of them, are wiped out, I can do that. I am Re-birth, I am Life. Eat Me, drink Me, I am your Food. And finally, do not be afraid, I have overcome the whole Universe.' That is the issue.

20

The Pains of Animals

A Problem in Theology[1]

The Inquiry by C. E. M. Joad

FOR MANY YEARS the problem of pain and evil seemed to me to offer an insuperable objection to Christianity. Either God could abolish them but did not, in which case, since He deliberately tolerated the presence in the universe of a state of affairs which was bad, I did not see how He could be good; or He wanted to abolish them but could not, in which case I did not see how He could be all-powerful. The dilemma is as old as St Augustine, and nobody pretends that there is an easy way of escape.

Moreover, all the attempts to explain pain away, or to mitigate its stark ferocity, or to present it as other than a very great evil, perhaps the greatest of evils, are palpable failures. They are testimonies to the kindness of men's hearts or perhaps to the queasiness of their consciences, rather than to the sharpness of their wits.

And yet, granting pain to be an evil, perhaps the greatest of evils, I have come to accept the Christian view of pain as not incompatible with the Christian concept of the Creator and of the world that He has made. That view I take to be briefly as follows: It was of no interest to God to create a species consisting of virtuous automata, for the 'virtue' of automata who can do no other than they do is a courtesy title only; it is analogous to the 'virtue' of the stone that rolls downhill or of the water that freezes at 32°. To what end, it may be asked, should God create such creatures? That He might be praised by them? But automatic praise is a mere succession of noises. That He might love them? But they are essentially unlovable; you cannot love puppets. And so God gave man free will that he might increase in virtue by his own efforts and become, as a free moral being, a worthy object of God's love. Freedom entails freedom to go wrong: man did, in fact, go wrong, misusing God's gift and doing evil. Pain is a by-product of evil; and so pain came into the world as a result of man's misuse of God's gift of free will.

So much I can understand; so much, indeed, I accept. It is plausible; it is rational; it hangs together.

But now I come to a difficulty, to which I see no solution; indeed, it is in the hope of learning of one that this article is written. This is the difficulty of animal pain, and, more particularly, of the pain of the animal world before man appeared upon

1. In his book *The Problem of Pain* one of the questions Lewis addressed himself to was: how to account for the occurrence of pain in a universe which is the creation of an all-good God, and in creatures who are not morally sinful. His chapter on 'Animal Pain' provoked a counter-inquiry from the late C. E. M. Joad, who was Head of the Department of Philosophy at the University of London. The result was this controversy.

the cosmic scene. What account do theologians give of it? The most elaborate and careful account known to me is that of C. S. Lewis.

He begins by making a distinction between sentience and consciousness. When we have the sensations *a*, *b*, and *c*, the fact that we have them and the fact that we know that we have them imply that there is something which stands sufficiently outside them to notice that they occur and that they succeed one another. This is consciousness, the consciousness to which the sensations happen. In other words, the experience of succession, the succession of sensations, demands a self or soul which is other than the sensations which it experiences. (Mr Lewis invokes the helpful metaphor of the bed of a river along which the stream of sensations flows.) Consciousness, therefore, implies a continuing *ego* which recognizes the succession of sensations; sentience is their mere succession. Now animals have sentience but not consciousness. Mr Lewis illustrates as follows:

> *This would mean that if you give such a creature two blows with a whip, there are. indeed, two pains: but there is no co-ordinating self which can recognise that 'I have had two pains.' Even in the single pain there is no self to say 'I am in pain'—for if it could distinguish itself from the sensation—the bed from the stream—sufficiently to say 'I am in pain', it would also be able to connect the two sensations as its experience.*[2]

(*a*) I take Mr Lewis's point—or, rather, I take it without perceiving its relevance. The question is how to account for the occurrence of pain (i) in a universe which is the creation of an all-good God; (ii) in creatures who are not morally sinful. To be told that the creatures are not really creatures, since they are not conscious in the sense of consciousness defined, does not really help matters. If it be true, as Mr Lewis says, that the right way to put the matter is not 'This animal is feeling pain' but 'Pain is taking place in this animal',[3] pain is nevertheless taking place. Pain is felt even if there is no continuing *ego* to feel it and to relate it to past and to future pains. Now it is the fact that pain is felt, no matter who or what feels it, or whether any continuing consciousness feels it, in a universe planned by a good God, that demands explanation.

(*b*) Secondly, the theory of sentience as mere succession of sensations presupposes that there is no continuing consciousness. No continuing consciousness presupposes no memory. It seems to me to be nonsense to say that animals do not remember. The dog who cringes at the sight of the whip by which he has been constantly beaten *behaves* as if he remembers, and behaviour is all that we have to go by. In general, we all act upon the assumption that the horse, the cat, and the dog with which we are acquainted remember very well, remember sometimes better than we do. Now I do not see how it is possible to explain the fact of memory without a continuing consciousness.

Mr Lewis recognizes this and concedes that the higher animals—apes, elephants, dogs, cats, and so on—have a self which connects experiences; have, in fact, what he calls a soul.[4] But this assumption presents us with a new set of difficulties.

---

2. *The Problem of Pain* (London, 1940), ch. ix, p. 120.
3. *Ibid.*, pp. 120–21.
4. *Ibid.*, p. 121.

(*a*) If animals have souls, what is to be done about their immortality? The question, it will be remembered, is elaborately debated in Heaven at the beginning of Anatole France's *Penguin Island* after the short-sighted St Mael has baptized the penguins, but no satisfactory solution is offered.

(*b*) Mr Lewis suggests that the higher domestic animals achieve immortality as members of a corporate society of which the head is man. It is, apparently, 'The-goodman-and-the-goodwife-ruling-their-children-and-their-beasts-in-the-good-homestead'[5] who survive. 'If you ask', he writes, 'concerning an animal thus raised as a member of the whole Body of the homestead, where its personal identity resides, I answer, "Where its identity always did reside even in the earthly life—in its relation to the Body and, specially, to the master who is the head of that Body." In other words, the man will know his dog: the dog will know its master and, in knowing him, will *be* itself.'[6]

Whether this is good theology, I do not know, but to our present inquiry it raises two difficulties.

(i) It does not cover the case of the higher animals who do not know man—for example, apes and elephants—but who are yet considered by Mr Lewis to have souls.

(ii) If one animal may attain good immortal selfhood in and through a good man, he may attain bad immortal selfhood in and through a bad man. One thinks of the overnourished lapdogs of idle overnourished women. It is a little hard that when, through no fault of their own, animals fall to selfish, self-indulgent, or cruel masters, they should through eternity form part of selfish, self-indulgent, or cruel superpersonal wholes and perhaps be punished for their participation in them.

(*c*) If the animals have souls and, presumably, freedom, the same sort of explanation must be adopted for pain in animals as is offered for pain in men. Pain, in other words, is one of the evils consequent upon sin. The higher animals, then, are corrupt. The question arises, who corrupted them? There seem to be two possible answers: (1) The Devil; (2) Man.

(1) Mr Lewis considers this answer. The animals, he says, may originally all have been herbivorous. They became carnivorous—that is to say, they began to prey upon, to tear, and to eat one another because 'some mighty created power had already been at work for ill on the material universe, or the solar system, or, at least, the planet Earth, before ever man came on the scene . . . If there is such a power . . . it may well have corrupted the animal creation before man appeared.'[7]

I have three comments to make:—

(i) I find the supposition of Satan tempting monkeys frankly incredible. This, I am well aware, is not a logical objection. It is one's imagination—or is it perhaps one's common sense?—that revolts against it.

(ii) Although most animals fall victims to the redness of Nature's 'tooth and claw', many do not. The sheep falls down the ravine, breaks its leg, and starves;

5. *Ibid.*, p. 127.
6. *Ibid.*, p. 128.
7. *Ibid.*, pp. 122–23 .

hundreds of thousands of migrating birds die every year of hunger; creatures are struck and not killed by lightning, and their seared bodies take long to die. Are these pains due to corruption?

(iii) The case of animals without souls cannot, on Mr Lewis's own showing, be brought under the 'moral corruption' explanation. Yet consider just one instance of nature's arrangements. The wasps, Ichneumonidae, sting their caterpillar prey in such a way as to paralyze its nerve centres. They then lay their eggs on the helpless caterpillar. When the grubs hatch from the eggs, they immediately proceed to feed upon the living but helpless flesh of their incubators, the paralyzed but still sentient caterpillars.

It is hard to suppose that the caterpillar feels no pain when slowly consumed; harder still to ascribe the pain to moral corruption; hardest of all to conceive how such an arrangement could have been planned by an all-good and all-wise Creator.

(2) The hypothesis that the animals were corrupted by man does not account for animal pain during the hundreds of million years (probably about 900 million) when the earth contained living creatures but did not contain man.

In sum, either animals have souls or they have no souls. If they have none, pain is felt for which there can be no moral responsibility, and for which no misuse of God's gift of moral freedom can be invoked as an excuse. If they have souls, we can give no plausible account (*a*) of their immortality—how draw the line between animals with souls and men with souls?—or (*b*) of their moral corruption, which would enable Christian apologists to place them in respect of their pain under the same heading of explanation as that which is proposed and which I am prepared to accept for man?

It may well be that there is an answer to this problem. I would be grateful to anyone who would tell me what it is.

THE REPLY
by C. S. Lewis

Though there is pleasure as well as danger in encountering so sincere and economical a disputant as Dr Joad, I do so with no little reluctance. Dr Joad writes not merely as a controversialist who demands, but as an inquirer who really desires, an answer. I come into the matter at all only because my answers have already failed to satisfy him. And it is embarrassing to me, and possibly depressing to him, that he should, in a manner, be sent back to the same shop which has once failed to supply the goods. If it were wholly a question of defending the original goods, I think I would let it alone. But it is not exactly that. I think he has perhaps slightly misunderstood what I was offering for sale.

Dr Joad is concerned with the ninth chapter of my *Problem of Pain*. And the first point I want to make is that no one would gather from his article how confessedly speculative that chapter was. This was acknowledged in my preface and repeatedly emphasized in the chapter itself. This, of course, can bring no ease to Dr Joad's difficulties; unsatisfactory answers do not become satisfactory by being tentative. I mention the character of the chapter to underline the fact that it stands on a rather different level from those which preceded it. And that difference suggests the place which my 'guesswork' about Beasts (so I called it at the time and call it still) had in my own thought, and which I would like this whole question to have in Dr Joad's thought too.

The first eight chapters of my book attempted to meet the *prima facie* case against theism based on human pain. They were the fruit of a slow change of mind not at all unlike that which Dr Joad himself has undergone and to which, when it had been completed, he at once bore honourable and (I expect) costly witness. The process of his thought differed at many points (very likely for the better) from the process of mine. But we came out, more or less, at the same place. The position of which he says in his article 'So much I understand; so much, indeed, I accept' is very close to that which I reached in the first eight chapters of my *Problem*.

So far, so good. Having 'got over' the problem of human pain, Dr Joad and I both find ourselves faced with the problem of animal pain. We do not at once part company even then. We both (if I read him correctly) turn with distaste from 'the easy speeches that comfort cruel men',[8] from theologians who do not seem to see that there is a real problem, who are content to say that animals are, after all, only animals. To us, pain without guilt or moral fruit, however low and contemptible the sufferer may be, is a very serious matter.

I now ask Dr Joad to observe rather closely what I do at this point, for I doubt if it is exactly what he thinks. I do not advance a doctrine of animal sentience as proved and thence conclude 'Therefore beasts are not sacrificed without recompense, and therefore God is just.' If he will look carefully at my ninth chapter he will see that it can be divided into two very unequal parts: Part One consisting of the first paragraph, and Part Two of all the rest. They might be summarized as follows:—

Part One. The data which God has given us enable us in some degree to understand human pain. We lack such data about beasts. We know neither what they are nor why they are. All that we can say for certain is that if God is good (and I think we have grounds for saying that He is) then the appearance of divine cruelty in the animal world must be a false appearance. What the reality behind the false appearance may be we can only guess.

Part Two. And here are some of my own guesses.

Now it matters far more whether Dr Joad agrees with Part One than whether he approves any of the speculations in Part Two. But I will first deal, so far as I can, with his critique of the speculations.

(1) Conceding *(positionis causa)*[9] my distinction between sentience and consciousness, Dr Joad thinks it irrelevant. 'Pain is felt', he writes, 'even if there is no continuing *ego* to feel it and to relate it to past and future pain,' and 'it is the fact that pain is felt, no matter who or what feels it . . . that demands explanation.' I agree that in one sense it does not (for the present purpose) matter 'who or what' feels it. That is, it does not matter how humble, or helpless, or small, or how removed from our spontaneous sympathies, the sufferer is. But it surely does matter how far the

8. G. K. Chesterton, 'A Hymn', line 11. The first line begins 'O God of earth and altar'.
9. 'for the sake of argument'.

sufferer is capable of what we can recognize as misery, how far the genuinely pitiable is consistent with its mode of existence. It will hardly be denied that the more coherently conscious the subject is, the more pity and indignation its pains deserve. And this seems to me to imply that the less coherently conscious, the less they deserve. I still think it possible for there to be a pain so instantaneous (through the absence of all perception of succession) that its 'unvalue', if I may coin the word, is indistinguishable from zero. A correspondent has instanced shooting pains in our own experience on those occasions when they are unaccompanied by fear. They may be intense: but they are gone as we recognize their intensity. In my own case I do not find anything in them which demands pity; they are, rather, comical. One tends to laugh. A series of such pains is, no doubt, terrible; but then the contention is that the series could not exist for sentience without consciousness.

(2) I do not think that behaviour 'as if from memory' proves memory in the conscious sense. A non-human observer might suppose that if we blink our eyes at the approach of an object we are 'remembering' pains received on previous occasions. But no memories, in the full sense, are involved. (It is, of course, true that the behaviour of the organism is modified by past experiences, and we may thus by metonymy say that the nerves remember what the mind forgets; but that is not what Dr Joad and I are talking of.) If we are to suppose memory in all cases where behaviour adapts itself to a probable recurrence of past events, shall we not have to assume in some insects an inherited memory of their parents' breeding habits? And are we prepared to believe this?

(3) Of course my suggested theory of the tame animals' resurrection 'in' its human (and therefore, indirectly, divine) context does not cover wild animals or illtreated tame ones. I had made the point myself, and added 'it is intended only as an illustration . . . of the general principles to be observed in framing a theory of animal resurrection.'[10] I went on to make an alternative suggestion, observing, I hope, the same principles. My chief purpose at this stage was at once to liberate imagination and to confirm a due agnosticism about the meaning and destiny of brutes. I had begun by saying that if our previous assertion of divine goodness was sound, we might be sure that *in some way or other* 'all would be well, and all manner of thing would be well'.[11] I wanted to reinforce this by indicating how little we knew and, therefore, how many things one might keep in mind as possibilities.

(4) If Dr Joad thinks I pictured Satan 'tempting monkeys', I am myself to blame for using the word 'encouraged'. I apologize for the ambiguity. In fact, I had not supposed that 'temptation' (that is, solicitation of the will) was the only mode in which the Devil could corrupt or impair. It is probably not the only mode in which he can impair even human beings; when Our Lord spoke of the deformed woman as one 'bound by Satan',[12] I presume He did not mean that she had been tempted into deformity. Moral corruption is not the only kind of corruption. But the word *corruption* was perhaps ill-chosen and invited misunderstanding. *Distortion* would have been safer.

---

10. *The Problem of Pain*, p. 128.
11. Lady Julian of Norwich, *Sixteen Revelations of Divine Love,* ch. xxvii.
12. Luke xiii. 16.

(5) My correspondent writes 'That even the severest injuries in most invertebrate animals are almost if not quite painless in the view of most biologists. Loeb collected much evidence to show that animals without cerebral hemispheres were indistinguishable from plants in every psychological respect. The instance readily occurs of the caterpillars which serenely go on eating though their interiors are being devoured by the larvae of some ichneumon fly. The Vivisection Act does not apply to invertebrates; which indicates the views of those who framed it.'

(6) Though Dr Joad does not raise the point, I cannot forbear adding some most interesting suggestions about animal fear from the same correspondent. He points out that human fear contains two elements: (a) the physical sensations, due to the secretions, etc.; (b) the mental images of what will happen if one loses hold, or if the bomb falls here, or if the train leaves the rails. Now (a), in itself, is so far from being an unmixed grief, that when we can get it without (b), or with unbelieved (b), or even with subdued (b), vast numbers of people like it: hence switchbacks, water-shoots, fast motoring, mountain climbing.

But all this is nothing to a reader who does not accept Part One in my ninth chapter. No man in his senses is going to start building up a theodicy with speculations about the minds of beasts as his foundation. Such speculations are in place only, as I said, to open the imagination to possibilities and to deepen and confirm our inevitable agnosticism about the reality, and only after the ways of God *to Man* have ceased to seem unjustifiable. We do not know the answer: these speculations were guesses at what it might possibly be. What really matters is the argument that there must be an answer: the argument that if, in our own lives, where alone (if at all) we know Him, we come to recognize the *pulchritudo tam antiqua et tam nova*,[13] then, in other realms where we cannot know Him (*connaître*), though we may know (*savoir*) some few things about Him—then, despite appearances to the contrary, He cannot be a power of darkness. For there were appearances to the contrary in our own realm too; yet, for Dr Joad as for me, they have somehow been got over.

I know that there are moments when the incessant continuity and desperate helplessness of what at least seems to be animal suffering make every argument for theism sound hollow, and when (in particular) the insect world appears to be Hell itself visibly in operation around us. Then the old indignation, the old pity arises. But how strangely ambivalent this experience is: I need not expound the ambivalence at much length, for I think I have done so elsewhere and I am sure that Dr Joad had long discerned it for himself. If I regard this pity and indignation simply as subjective experiences of my own with no validity beyond their strength at the moment (which next moment will change), I can hardly use them as standards whereby to arraign the creation. On the contrary, they become strong as arguments against God just in so far as I take them to be transcendent illumination to which creation must conform or be condemned. They are arguments against God only if they are themselves the voice of God. The more Shelleyan, the more Promethean my revolt, the more surely it claims a divine sanction. That the mere

13. St Augustine, *Confessions*, bk. X, ch. 27. 'Beauty so ancient and so new'.

contingent Joad or Lewis, born in an era of secure and liberal civilization and imbibing from it certain humanitarian sentiments, should happen to be offended by suffering—what is that to the purpose? How will one base an argument for or against God on such an historical accident!

No. Not in so far as we feel these things, but in so far as we claim to be right in feeling them, in so far as we are sure that these standards have an empire *de jure* over all possible worlds, so far, and so far only, do they become a ground for disbelief—and at the same moment, for belief. God within us steals back at the moment of our condemning the apparent God without. Thus in Tennyson's poem the man who had become convinced that the God of his inherited creed was evil exclaimed: 'If there be such a God, may the Great God curse him and bring him to nought.'[14] For if there is no 'Great God' behind the curse, who curses? Only a puppet of the little apparent 'God'. His very curse is poisoned at the root: it is just the same sort of event as the very cruelties he is condemning, part of the meaningless tragedy.

From this I see only two exits: either that there is a Great God, and also a 'God of this world',[15] a prince of the powers of the air, whom the Great God does curse, and sometimes curses through us; or else that the operations of the Great God are not what they seem to me to be.

14. 'Despair', xix, 106.
15. II Corinthians iv. 4.

21
Is Theism Important?[1]

I HAVE LOST the notes of what I originally said in replying to Professor Price's paper and cannot now remember what it was, except that I welcomed most cordially his sympathy with the Polytheists. I still do. When grave persons express their fear that England is relapsing into Paganism, I am tempted to reply, 'Would that she were.' For I do not think it at all likely that we shall ever see Parliament opened by the slaughtering of a garlanded white bull in the House of Lords or Cabinet Ministers leaving sandwiches in Hyde Park as an offering for the Dryads. If such a state of affairs came about, then the Christian apologist would have something to work on. For a Pagan, as history shows, is a man eminently convertible to Christianity. He is essentially the pre-Christian, or sub-Christian, religious man. The post-Christian man of our day differs from him as much as a *divorcée* differs from a virgin. The Christian and the Pagan have much more in common with one another than either has with the writers of the *New Statesman*; and those writers would of course agree with me. For the rest, what now occurs to me after re-reading Professor Price's paper is something like this.

1. I think we must introduce into the discussion a distinction between two senses of the word *Faith*. This may mean (a) a settled intellectual assent. In that sense faith (or 'belief') in God hardly differs from faith in the uniformity of Nature or in the consciousness of other people. This is what, I think, has sometimes been called a 'notional' or 'intellectual' or 'carnal' faith. It may also mean (b) a trust, or confidence, in the God whose existence is thus assented to. This involves an attitude of the will. It is more like our confidence in a friend. It would be generally agreed that Faith in sense A is not a religious state. The devils who 'believe and tremble'[2] have Faith-A. A man who curses or ignores God may have Faith-A. Philosophical arguments for the existence of God are presumably intended to produce Faith-A. No doubt those who construct them are anxious to produce Faith-A because it is a necessary pre-condition of Faith-B, and in that sense their ultimate intention is religious. But their immediate object, the conclusion they attempt to prove, is not. I therefore think they cannot be justly accused of trying to get a religious conclusion out of non-religious premises. I agree with Professor Price that this cannot be done: but I deny that the religious philosophers are trying to do it.

I also think that in some ages, what claim to be Proofs of Theism have had much more efficacy in producing Faith-A than Professor Price suggests. Nearly everyone I know who has embraced Christianity in adult life has been influenced by what

1. This is a reply to a paper Professor H. H. Price read to the Oxford Socratic Club. Professor Price's paper was published under the same title in *The Socratic Digest*, No. 5 (1962), pp. 39–47, and Lewis's answer was originally published in the same periodical.
2. James ii. 19.

seemed to him to be at least probable arguments for Theism. I have known some who were completely convinced by Descartes' Ontological Proof:[3] that is, they received Faith-A from Descartes first and then went on to seek and to find, Faith-B. Even quite uneducated people who have been Christians all their lives not infrequently appeal to some simplified form of the Argument from Design. Even acceptance of tradition implies an argument which sometimes becomes explicit in the form 'I reckon all those wise men wouldn't have believed in it if it weren't true.'

Of course Faith-A usually involves a degree of subjective certitude which goes beyond the logical certainty, or even the supposed logical certainty, of the arguments employed. It may retain this certitude for a long time, I expect, even without the support of Faith-B. This excess of certitude in a settled assent is not at all uncommon. Most of those who believe in Uniformity of Nature, Evolution, or the Solar System, share it.

2. I doubt whether religious people have ever supposed that Faith-B follows automatically on the acquisition of Faith-A. It is described as a 'gift'.[4] As soon as we have Faith-A in the existence of God, we are instructed to ask from God Himself the gift of Faith-B. An odd request, you may say, to address to a First Cause, an *Ens Realissimum*, or an *Unmoved Mover*. It might be argued, and I think I would argue myself, that even such an aridly philosophical God rather fails to invite than actually repels a personal approach. It would, at any rate, do no harm to try it. But I fully admit that most of those who, having reached Faith-A, pray for Faith-B, do so because they have already had something like religious experience. Perhaps the best way of putting it would be to say that Faith-A converts into religious experience what was hitherto only potentially or implicitly religious. In this modified form I would accept Professor Price's view that philosophical proofs never, by themselves, lead to religion. Something at least *quasi*-religious uses them before, and the 'proofs' remove an inhibition which was preventing their development into religion proper.

This is not exactly *fides quaerens intellectum*,[5] for these quasi-religious experiences were not *fides*. In spite of Professor Price's rejection, I still think Otto's account of the Numinous[6] is the best analysis of them we have. I believe it is a mistake to regard the Numinous as merely an affair of 'feeling'. Admittedly, Otto can describe it only by referring to the emotions it arouses in us; but then nothing can be described except in terms of its effects in consciousness. We have in English an exact name for the emotion aroused by the Numinous, which Otto, writing in German, lacked; we have the word Awe—an emotion very like fear, with the important difference that it need imply no estimate of danger. When we fear a tiger, we fear that it may kill us: when we fear a ghost—well, we just fear the ghost, not this or that mischief which it may do us. The Numinous or Awful is that of which we have this, as it were, objectless or disinterested fear—this awe. And 'the Numinous' is not a name for our own feeling of Awe, any more than 'the Contemptible' is a name for con-

---

3. This is briefly summed up in René Descartes' *Discours de la Méthode*, Part iv, in which he says 'I think, therefore I am.'
4. e.g., I Corinthians xii. 1–11; Ephesians ii. 8.
5. 'faith seeking understanding'.
6. Rudolf Otto, *The Idea of the Holy*, trans. John W. Harvey (London, 1923).

tempt. It is the answer to the question 'of what do you feel awe'. And what we feel awe of is certainly not itself awe.

With Otto and, in a sense, with Professor Price, I would find the seed of religious experience in our experience of the Numinous. In an age like our own such experience does occur but, until religion comes and retrospectively transforms it, it usually appears to the subject to be a special form of aesthetic experience. In ancient times I think experience of the Numinous developed into the Holy only in so far as the Numinous (not in itself at all necessarily moral) came to be connected with the morally good. This happened regularly in Israel, sporadically elsewhere. But even in the higher Paganism, I do not think this process led to anything exactly like *fides*. There is nothing credal in Paganism. In Israel we do get *fides* but this is always connected with certain historical affirmations. Faith is not simply in the numinous *Elohim*, nor even simply in the holy *Jahweh*, but in the God 'of our fathers', the God who called Abraham and brought Israel out of Egypt. In Christianity this historical element is strongly re-affirmed. The object of faith is at once the *ens entium*[7] of the philosophers, the Awful Mystery of Paganism, the Holy Law given of the moralists, and Jesus of Nazareth who was crucified under Pontius Pilate and rose again on the third day.

Thus we must admit that Faith, as we know it, does not flow from philosophical argument alone; nor from experience of the Numinous alone; nor from moral experience alone; nor from history alone; but from historical events which at once fulfil and transcend the moral category, which link themselves with the most numinous elements in Paganism, and which (as it seems to us) demand as their pre-supposition the existence of a Being who is more, but not less, than the God whom many reputable philosophers think they can establish.

Religious experience, as we know it, really involves all these elements. We may, however, use the word in a narrower sense to denote moments of mystical, or devotional, or merely numinous experience; and we may then ask, with Professor Price, how such moments, being a kind of *visio*, are related to faith, which by definition is 'not sight'. This does not seem to me one of the hardest questions. 'Religious experience' in the narrower sense comes and goes: especially goes. The operation of Faith is to retain, so far as the will and intellect are concerned, what is irresistible and obvious during the moments of special grace. By Faith we believe always what we hope hereafter to see always and perfectly and have already seen imperfectly and by flashes. In relation to the philosophical premises a Christian's faith is of course excessive: in relation to what is sometimes shown him, it is perhaps just as often defective. My faith even in an earthly friend goes beyond all that could be demonstratively proved; yet in another sense I may often trust him less than he deserves.

7. 'being of beings.'

22
Rejoinder
to Dr Pittenger

TO ONE OF the charges Dr Norman Pittenger makes in his 'Critique' in the October 1 *Christian Century*,[1] I must with shame plead guilty. He has caught me using the word 'literally' where I did not really mean it, a vile journalistic cliché which he cannot reprobate more severely than I now do myself.[2]

I must also admit some truth in his charge of Apollinarianism; there is a passage in my *Problem of Pain* which would imply, if pressed, a shockingly crude conception of the Incarnation. I corrected it by a footnote to the French edition but have not been able to do so elsewhere, save in so far as *Mere Christianity,* bk. IV, ch. 3, may provide an antidote.

This must not be taken to mean that my present conception would fully satisfy Dr Pittenger. He speaks about 'the validity of our Lord's unique place in Christian faith as that One in whom God was so active and so present that he may be called "God-Man"'.[3] I am not quite sure what this means. May I translate it, 'our Lord's actually unique place in the structure of utter reality, the unique mode, as well as degree, of God's presence and action in Him, make the formula "God-Man" the objectively true description of Him'? If so, I think we are very nearly agreed. Or must I translate it, 'the unique place which Christians (subjectively, in their own thoughts) gave to our Lord as One in whom God was present and active to a unique degree made it reasonable for them to call Him God-Man'? If so, I must demur. In other words, if Dr Pittenger's 'may be called' means anything less or other than 'is', I could not accept his formula. For I think that Jesus Christ is (in fact) the only Son of God—that is, the only original Son of God, through whom others are enabled to 'become sons of God'.[4] If Dr Pittenger wishes to attack that doctrine, I wonder he should choose me as its representative. It has had champions far worthier of his steel.

I turn next to my book *Miracles* and am sorry to say that I here have to meet Dr Pittenger's charges with straight denials. He says that this book 'opens with a definition of miracle as the "violation" of the laws of nature'.[5] He is mistaken. The passage (chapter 2) really runs: 'I use the word *Miracle* to mean an interference with

---

1. W. Norman Pittenger, 'A Critique of C. S. Lewis', *Christian Century*, vol. LXXV (1 October 1958), pp. 1104–07.
2. In *Broadcast Talks* (London, 1942), Part II, ch. 5, p. 60, Lewis had written that 'the whole mass of Christians are literally the physical organism through which Christ acts—that we are His fingers and muscles, the cells of His body.' The word 'literally', however, was deleted when *Broadcast Talks* was reprinted with two other short books as *Mere Christianity* (London, 1952) in which the phrase quoted above is found in bk. II, ch. 5, p. 51.
3. Pittenger, p. 1106.
4. John i. 12.
5. Pittenger, p. 1105.

Nature by supernatural power.'[6] If Dr Pittenger thinks the difference between the true text and his mis-quotation merely verbal, he has misunderstood nearly the whole book. I never equated nature (the spatio-temporal system of facts and events) with the laws of nature (the patterns into which these facts and events fall). I would as soon equate an actual speech with the rules of grammar. In chapter 8 I say in so many words that no miracle either can or need break the laws of Nature; that 'it is . . . inaccurate to define a miracle as something that breaks the laws of Nature';[7] and that 'The divine art of miracle is not an art of suspending the pattern to which events conform but of feeding new events into that pattern.'[8] How many times does a man need to say something before he is safe from the accusation of having said exactly the opposite? (I am not for a moment imputing dishonesty to Dr Pittenger; we all know too well how difficult it is to grasp or retain the substance of a book one finds antipathetic.)

Again, Dr Pittenger contrasts my view with that which makes miracles a sign of God's action and presence in creation. Yet in chapter 15 I say that the miracle at Cana manifests 'the God of Israel who has through all these centuries given us wine' and that in the miraculous feedings God 'does close and small . . . what He has always been doing in the seas, the lakes and the little brooks'.[9] Surely this is just what Dr Pittenger wanted me to say, and what Athanasius says *(De Incarnatione* xiv. 8, edited by F. L. Cross, 1939)?

It is very true that I make no use of the different words *(semeia, terata* and the rest) which New Testament writers use for miracles. But why should I? I was writing for people who wanted to know whether the things could have happened rather than what they should be called; whether we could without absurdity believe that Christ rose from the emptied tomb. I am afraid most of my readers, if once convinced that He did not, would have felt it of minor importance to decide whether, if He had done so, this nonexistent event would have been a *teras* or a *dunamis*. And (in certain moods) one does, after all, see their point.

Dr Pittenger thinks the Naturalist whom I try to refute in chapter 3 is a man of straw. He may not be found in the circles Dr Pittenger frequents. He is quite common where I come from; and, presumably, in Moscow. There is indeed a really serious hitch in that chapter (which ought to be rewritten), but Dr Pittenger has not seen it or has charitably kept silent about it.[10]

I now turn to the more difficult and interesting question of the Fourth Gospel. It is difficult because, here again, I do not quite understand what Dr Pittenger writes. He blames me for putting all four Gospels in the same category and especially for believing that Jesus claimed deity because the Fourth Gospel says He did. But this does not mean that Dr Pittenger rejects the fourth as simply untrue. According to him it gives that 'interpretation' of our Lord's 'significance' which the early Chris-

---

6. *Miracles: A Preliminary Study* (London, 1947). Because Lewis later revised chapter III of this book, all my text-references are to the 'revised' paperback edition of *Miracles* (Fontana Books, London, 1960), p. 9.
7. *Ibid.*, p. 63.
8. *Ibid.*, p. 64.
9. *Ibid.*, pp. 140, 141.
10. Lewis did, as just mentioned in a footnote above, revise chapter III of *Miracles*.

tians 'found', and 'rightly' found, 'to be true'.[11] Now in my language that significance of anything which is 'rightly found to be true' would be its true significance and those who found it would have found what the thing really meant. If the Fourth Gospel gives us what Jesus Christ really meant, why am I blamed for accepting it? But I am, and therefore Dr Pittenger's words must bear some other sense. Does he mean that what they 'rightly found to be true' was not true? Or that the significance which was rightly found to be true by them would be 'wrongly found' to be true by us? Or did they get the 'significance' right and go wrong about the 'interpretation of the significance'? I give it up.

I confess, however, that the problem of the Fourth Gospel raises in me a conflict between authority and private judgment: the authority of all those learned men who think that Gospel unhistorical, and my judgment as a literary critic which constrains me to think it at least as close to the facts as Boswell's *Johnson*. If I venture here to follow judgment in the teeth of authority, this is partly because I could never see how one escaped the dilemma *aut deus aut malus homo*[12] by confining oneself to the Synoptics. Moderns do not seem startled, as contemporaries were, by the claim Jesus there makes to forgive sins; not sins against Himself, just sins. Yet surely, if they actually met it, they would feel differently. If Dr Pittenger told me that two of his colleagues had lost him a professorship by telling lies about his character and I replied, 'I freely forgive them both', would he not think this an impertinence (both in the old and in the modern sense) bordering on insanity? And of course all three Synoptics tell the story of One who, at his trial, sealed His fate by saying He was the Son of God.

I am accused of attributing 'almost spatial transcendence' to God and of denying His continued presence within Nature because I speak of Him as 'invading' or 'intruding into' her.[13] This is really very hard of the Doctor. Of course the very word 'transcendence' contains a spatial image. So does 'immanence'. So does Dr Pittenger's 'God's action and *presence in* the creation'.[14] We must, after all, speak the language of men. (I have got much light on this problem from Edwyn Bevan's *Symbolism and Belief*.) But I freely admit that, believing both, I have stressed the transcendence of God more than His immanence. I thought, and think, that the present situation demands this. I see around me no danger of Deism but much of an immoral, naïve and sentimental pantheism. I have often found that it was in fact the chief obstacle to conversion.

Dr Pittenger says that I base the Faith on authority (which has 'grown up in the Church and won the assent of great doctors').[15] So does he; his authority is 'the total consentient witness of all Christians from the Apostles' time'.[16] I am not sure why he calls my authority 'mechanical'. Surely it differs from his mainly by being discoverable? The 'total consentient witness' would be grand if we had it. But of course the overwhelming majority of Christians, as of other men, have died, and are dying

---

11. Pittenger, p. 1106.
12. 'Either God or a bad man.'
13. Pittenger, p. 1105.
14. *Ibid.*
15. Pittenger, p. 1106, quoting Lewis's *Problem of Pain* (London, 1940), ch. v, p. 60.
16. Pittenger, p. 1106.

while I write, without recording their 'witness'. How does Dr Pittenger consult his authority?

Where he really hurt me was in the charge of callousness to animals. Surprised me too; for the very same passage is blamed by others for extreme sentimentality.[17] It is hard to please all. But if the Patagonians think me a dwarf and the Pygmies a giant, perhaps my stature is in fact fairly unremarkable.

The statement that I do not 'care much for' the Sermon on the Mount but 'prefer' the 'Pauline ethic' of man's sinfulness and helplessness[18] carries a suggestion of alternatives between which we may choose, where I see successive stages through which we must proceed. Most of my books are evangelistic, addressed to *tous exo*. It would have been inept to preach forgiveness and a Saviour to those who did not know they were in need of either. Hence St Paul's and the Baptist's diagnosis (would you call it exactly an *ethic?*) had to be pressed. Nor am I aware that our Lord revised it ('if ye, being evil. . .').[19] As to 'caring for' the Sermon on the Mount, if 'caring for' here means 'liking' or enjoying, I suppose no one 'cares for' it. Who can *like* being knocked flat on his face by a sledge-hammer? I can hardly imagine a more deadly spiritual condition than that of the man who can read that passage with tranquil pleasure. This is indeed to be 'at ease in Zion'.[20] Such a man is not yet ripe for the Bible; he had better start by learning sense from Islam: 'The heaven and the earth and all between, thinkest thou I made them *in jest?'*

And this illustrates what appears to me to be a weakness in the Doctor's critical method. He judges my books *in vacuo*, with no consideration of the audience to whom they were addressed or the prevalent errors they were trying to combat. The Naturalist becomes a straw man because he is not found among 'first-rate scientists' and readers of Einstein. But I was writing *ad populum*, not *ad clerum*. This is relevant to my manner as well as my matter. It is true, I do not understand why it is vulgar or offensive, in speaking of the Holy Trinity, to illustrate from plane and solid geometry the conception that what is self-contradictory on one level may be consistent on another.[21] I could have understood the Doctor's being shocked if I had compared God to an unjust judge or Christ to a thief in the night; but mathematical objects seem to me as free from sordid associations as any the mind can entertain.

But let all that pass. Suppose the image is vulgar. If it gets across to the unbeliever what the unbeliever desperately needs to know, the vulgarity must be endured. Indeed, the image's very vulgarity may be an advantage; for there is much sense in the reasons advanced by Aquinas (following Pseudo-Dionysius) for preferring to present divine truths *sub figuris vilium corporum*[22] (*Summa Theologica*, Qu. I, Art. 9 *ad tertium*).

When I began, Christianity came before the great mass of my unbelieving fellow-countrymen either in the highly emotional form offered by revivalists or in

17. The reference is to the chapter on 'Animal Pain' in *The Problem of Pain*.
18. Pittenger, P. 1106.
19. Matthew vii. 11. Luke xi. 13.
20. Amos vi. 1.
21. In *Mere Christianity*, bk. iv, ch. 2, p. 128, Lewis says 'In God's dimension, so to speak, you find a being who is three Persons while remaining one Being, just as a cube is six squares while remaining one cube.'
22. 'under the figures of vile bodies.'

the unintelligible language of highly cultured clergymen. Most men were reached by neither. My task was therefore simply that of a *translator*—one turning Christian doctrine, or what he believed to be such, into the vernacular, into language that unscholarly people would attend to and could understand. For this purpose a style more guarded, more *nuancé*, finelier shaded, more rich in fruitful ambiguities— in fact, a style more like Dr Pittenger's own—would have been worse than useless. It would not only have failed to enlighten the common reader's understanding; it would have aroused his suspicion. He would have thought, poor soul, that I was facing both ways, sitting on the fence, offering at one moment what I withdrew the next, and generally trying to trick him. I may have made theological errors. My manner may have been defective. Others may do better hereafter. I am ready, if I am young enough, to learn. Dr Pittenger would be a more helpful critic if he advised a cure as well as asserting many diseases. How does he himself do such work? What methods, and with what success, does he employ when he is trying to convert the great mass of storekeepers, lawyers, realtors, morticians, policemen and artisans who surround him in his own city?

One thing at least is sure. If the real theologians had tackled this laborious work of translation about a hundred years ago, when they began to lose touch with the people (for whom Christ died), there would have been no place for me.[23]

23. See Letter 11.

23
Must Our Image of God Go?[1]

THE BISHOP OF WOOLWICH will disturb most of us Christian laymen less than he anticipates. We have long abandoned belief in a God who sits on a throne in a localized heaven. We call that belief anthropomorphism, and it was officially condemned before our time. There is something about this in Gibbon. I have never met any adult who replaced 'God up there' by 'God out there' in the sense 'spatially external to the universe'. If I said God is 'outside' or 'beyond' space-time, I should mean 'as Shakespeare is outside *The Tempest*'; i.e., its scenes and persons do not exhaust his being. We have always thought of God as being not only 'in,' 'above', but also 'below' us: as the depth of ground. We can imaginatively speak of Father 'in heaven' yet also of the everlasting arms that are 'beneath'. We do not understand why the Bishop is so anxious to canonize the one image and forbid the other. We admit his freedom to use which he prefers. We claim our freedom to use both.

His view of Jesus as a 'window' seems wholly orthodox ('he that hath seen me hath seen the Father').[2] Perhaps the real novelty is in the Bishop's doctrine about God. But we can't be certain, for here he is very obscure. He draws a sharp distinction between asking 'Does God exist as a person?' and asking whether ultimate reality is personal. But surely he who says yes to the second question has said yes to the first? Any entity describable without gross abuse of language as God must be ultimate reality, and if ultimate reality is personal, then God is personal. Does the Bishop mean that something which is not 'a person' could yet be 'personal'? Even this could be managed if 'not a person' were taken to mean 'a person and more'—as is provided for by the doctrine of the Trinity. But the Bishop does not mention this.

Thus, though sometimes puzzled, I am not shocked by his article. His heart, though perhaps in some danger of bigotry, is in the right place. If he has failed to communicate why the things he is saying move him so deeply as they obviously do, this may be primarily a literary failure. If I were briefed to defend his position I should say 'The image of the Earth-Mother gets in something which that of the Sky-Father leaves out. Religions of the Earth-Mother have hitherto been spiritually inferior to those of the Sky-Father, but, perhaps, it is now time to readmit some of their elements.' I shouldn't believe it very strongly, but some sort of case could be made out.

1. This article, which first appeared in *The Observer* (24 March 1963), is a reply to the then Bishop of Woolwich, Dr J. A. T. Robinson's article 'Our Image of God Must Go', *The Observer* (17 March 1963), which is a summary of Dr Robinson's book *Honest to God* (London, 1963).
2. John xiv. 9.

PART II

1
Dangers of
National Repentance

THE IDEA OF national repentance seems at first sight to provide such an edifying contrast to that national self-righteousness of which England is so often accused and with which she entered (or is said to have entered) the last war, that a Christian naturally turns to it with hope. Young Christians especially—last-year undergraduates and first-year curates—are turning to it in large numbers. They are ready to believe that England bears part of the guilt for the present war, and ready to admit their own share in the guilt of England. What that share is, I do not find it easy to determine. Most of these young men were children, and none of them had a vote or the experience which would enable them to use a vote wisely, when England made many of those decisions to which the present disorders could plausibly be traced. Are they, perhaps, repenting what they have in no sense done?

If they are, it might be supposed that their error is very harmless: men fail so often to repent their real sins that the occasional repentance of an imaginary sin might appear almost desirable. But what actually happens (I have watched it happening) to the youthful national penitent is a little more complicated than that. England is not a natural agent, but a civil society. When we speak of England's actions we mean the actions of the British Government. The young man who is called upon to repent of England's foreign policy is really being called upon to repent the acts of his neighbour; for a Foreign Secretary or a Cabinet Minister is certainly a neighbour. And repentance presupposes condemnation. The first and fatal charm of national repentance is, therefore, the encouragement it gives us to turn from the bitter task of repenting our own sins to the congenial one of bewailing—but, first, of denouncing—the conduct of others. If it were clear to the young that this is what he is doing, no doubt he would remember the law of charity. Unfortunately the very terms in which national repentance is recommended to him conceal its true nature. By a dangerous figure of speech, he calls the Government not 'they' but 'we'. And since, as penitents, we are not encouraged to be charitable to our own sins, nor to give ourselves the benefit of any doubt, a Government which is called 'we' is *ipso facto* placed beyond the sphere of charity or even of justice. You can say anything you please about it. You can indulge in the popular vice of detraction without restraint, and yet feel all the time that you are practising contrition. A group of such young penitents will say, 'Let us repent our national sins'; what they mean is, 'Let us attribute to our neighbour (even our Christian neighbour) in the Cabinet, whenever we disagree with him, every abominable motive that Satan can suggest to our fancy.'

Such an escape from personal repentance into that tempting region

Where passions have the privilege to work
And never hear the sound of their own names[1]

would be welcome to the moral cowardice of anyone. But it is doubly attractive to the young intellectual. When a man over forty tries to repent the sins of England and to love her enemies, he is attempting something costly; for he was brought up to certain patriotic sentiments which cannot be mortified without a struggle. But an educated man who is now in his twenties usually has no such sentiment to mortify. In art, in literature, in politics, he has been, ever since he can remember, one of an angry and restless minority; he has drunk in almost with his mother's milk a distrust of English statesmen and a contempt for the manners, pleasures, and enthusiasms of his less-educated fellow countrymen. All Christians know that they must forgive their enemies. But 'my enemy' primarily means the man whom I am really tempted to hate and traduce. If you listen to young Christian intellectuals talking, you will soon find out who their real enemy is. He seems to have two names—Colonel Blimp and 'the business-man'. I suspect that the latter usually means the speaker's father, but that is speculation. What is certain is that in asking such people to forgive the Germans and Russians and to open their eyes to the sins of England, you are asking them, not to mortify, but to indulge, their ruling passion. I do not mean that what you are asking them is not right and necessary in itself; we must forgive all our enemies or be damned. But it is emphatically not the exhortation which your audience needs. The communal sins which they should be told to repent are those of their own age and class—its contempt for the uneducated, its readiness to suspect evil, its self-righteous provocations of public obloquy, its breaches of the Fifth Commandment.[2] Of these sins I have heard nothing among them. Till I do, I must think their candour towards the national enemy a rather inexpensive virtue. If a man cannot forgive the Colonel Blimp next door whom he has seen, how shall he forgive the Dictators whom he hath not seen?

Is it not, then, the duty of the Church to preach national repentance? I think it is. But the office—like many others—can be profitably discharged only by those who discharge it with reluctance. We know that a man may have to 'hate' his mother for the Lord's sake.[3] The sight of a Christian rebuking his mother, though tragic, may be edifying; but only if we are quite sure that he has been a good son and that, in his rebuke, spiritual zeal is triumphing, not without agony, over strong natural affection. The moment there is reason to suspect that he *enjoys* rebuking her—that he believes himself to be rising above the natural level while he is still, in reality, grovelling below it in the unnatural—the spectacle becomes merely disgusting. The hard sayings of our Lord are wholesome to those only who find them hard. There is a terrible chapter in M. Mauriac's *Vie de Jésus*. When the Lord spoke of brother

1. Wordsworth, *The Prelude*, bk. XI, line 230.
2. 'Honour thy father and thy mother; that thy days may be long in the land which the Lord thy God giveth thee.' Exodus xx. 12.
3. Luke xiv. 26: 'If any man come to me, and hate not his father, and mother, and wife, and children, and brethren, and sisters, yea, and his own life also, he cannot be my disciple.'

and child against parent, the other disciples were horrified. Not so Judas. He took to it as a duck takes to water: *'Pourquoi cetter stupeur?, se demande Judas. . . . Il aime dans le Christ cette vue simple, ce regard de Dieu sur l'horreur humaine.'*[4] For there are two states of mind which face the Dominical paradoxes without flinching. God guard us from one of them.

4. Francois Mauriac, *Vie de Jésus* (Paris, 1936), ch. ix. ' "Why this stupefaction?" asked Judas . . . He loved in Christ his simple view of things, his divine glance at human depravity.'

2
Two Ways with the Self

SELF-RENUNCIATION IS THOUGHT to be, and indeed is, very near the core of Christian ethics. When Aristotle writes in praise of a certain kind of self-love, we may feel, despite the careful distinctions which he draws between the legitimate and the illegitimate *Philautia*,[1] that here we strike something essentially sub-Christian. It is more difficult, however, to decide what we think of St François de Sales's chapter, *De la douceur envers nous-mêsmes*,[2] where we are forbidden to indulge resentment even against ourselves and advised to reprove even our own faults *avec des remonstrances douces et tranquilles*,[3] feeling more compassion than passion. In the same spirit, Lady Julian of Norwich would have us 'loving and peaceable', not only to our 'even-Christians', but to 'ourself'.[4] Even the New Testament bids me love my neighbour 'as myself',[5] which would be a horrible command if the self were simply to be hated. Yet Our Lord also says that a true disciple must 'hate his own life'.[6]

We must not explain this apparent contradiction by saying that self-love is right up to a certain point and wrong beyond that point. The question is not one of degree. There are two kinds of self-hatred which look rather alike in their earlier stages, but of which one is wrong from the beginning and the other right to the end. When Shelley speaks of self-contempt as the source of cruelty, or when a later poet says that he has no stomach for the man 'who loathes his neighbour as himself', they are referring to a very real and very un-Christian hatred of the self which may make diabolical a man whom common selfishness would have have left (at least, for a while) merely animal. The hard-boiled economist or psychologist of our own day, recognizing the 'ideological taint' or Freudian motive in his own make-up, does not necessarily learn Christian humility. He may end in what is called a 'low view' of all souls, including his own, which expresses itself in cynicism or cruelty, or both. Even Christians, if they accept in certain forms the doctrine of total depravity, are not always free from the danger. The logical conclusion of the process is the worship of suffering—for others as well as for the self—which we see, if I read it aright, in Mr David Lindsay's *Voyage to Arcturus*, or that extraordinary vacancy which Shakespeare depicts at the end of *Richard III*. Richard in his agony tries to turn to self-love. But he has been 'seeing through' all emotions so long that he 'sees through' even this. It becomes a mere tautology: 'Richard loves Richard; that is, I am I.'[7]

1. *Nicomachean Ethics*, bk. ix, ch. 8.
2. Pt. III, ch. ix 'Of Meekness towards Ourselves' in the *Introduction to the Devout Life* (Lyons, 1609).
3. 'with mild and calm remonstrances'.
4. *The Sixteen Revelations of Divine Love*, ch. xlix.
5. Matthew xix. 19; xxii. 39; Mark xii. 31, 33; Romans xiii. 9; Galatians v. 14; James ii. 8.
6. Luke xiv. 26; John xii. 25.
7. *Richard III*, V, iii, 184.

Now, the self can be regarded in two ways. On the one hand, it is God's creature, an occasion of love and rejoicing; now, indeed, hateful in condition, but to be
pitied and healed. On the other hand, it is that one self of all others which is called
I and *me*, and which on that ground puts forward an irrational claim to preference.
This claim is to be not only hated, but simply killed; 'never', as George MacDonald
says, 'to be allowed a moment's respite from eternal death'. The Christian must
wage endless war against the clamour of the *ego* as *ego*: but he loves and approves
selves as such, though not their sins. The very self-love which he has to reject is to
him a specimen of how he ought to feel to all selves; and he may hope that when
he has truly learned (which will hardly be in this life) to love his neighbour as himself, he may then be able to love himself as his neighbour: that is, with charity instead
of partiality. The other kind of self-hatred, on the contrary, hates selves as such. It
begins by accepting the special value of the particular self called *me*; then, wounded
in its pride to find that such a darling object should be so disappointing, it seeks
revenge, first upon that self, then on all. Deeply egoistic, but now with an inverted
egoism, it uses the revealing argument, 'I don't spare myself'—with the implication 'then *a fortiori* I need not spare others'—and becomes like the centurion in
Tacitus, *immitior quia toleraverat.*[8]

The wrong asceticism torments the self: the right kind kills the selfness. We must
die daily: but it is better to love the self than to love nothing, and to pity the self
than to pity no one.

8. *Annals*, Bk. I, sect. xx, line 14. 'More relentless because he had endured (it himself).'

3
Meditation on the Third Commandment

FROM MANY LETTERS to *The Guardian*,[1] and from much that is printed elsewhere, we learn of the growing desire for a Christian 'party', a Christian 'front', or a Christian 'platform' in politics. Nothing is so earnestly to be wished as a real assault by Christianity on the politics of the world: nothing, at first sight, so fitted to deliver this assault as a Christian Party. But it is odd that certain difficulties in this programme should be already neglected while the printer's ink is hardly dry on M. Maritain's *Scholasticism and Politics*.[2]

The Christian Party must either confine itself to stating what ends are desirable and what means are lawful, or else it must go further and select from among the lawful means those which it deems possible and efficacious and give to these its practical support. If it chooses the first alternative, it will not be a political party. Nearly all parties agree in professing ends which we admit to be desirable—security, a living wage, and the best adjustment between the claims of order and freedom. What distinguishes one party from another is the championship of means. We do not dispute whether the citizens are to be made happy, but whether an egalitarian or a hierarchical State, whether capitalism or socialism, whether despotism or democracy is most likely to make them so.

What, then, will the Christian Party actually do? Philarchus, a devout Christian, is convinced that temporal welfare can flow only from a Christian life, and that a Christian life can be promoted in the community only by an authoritarian State which has swept away the last vestiges of the hated 'Liberal' infection. He thinks Fascism not so much an evil as a good thing perverted, regards democracy as a monster whose victory would be a defeat for Christianity, and is tempted to accept even Fascist assistance, hoping that he and his friends will prove the leaven in a lump of British Fascists. Stativus is equally devout and equally Christian. Deeply conscious of the Fall and therefore convinced that no human creature can be trusted with more than the minimum power over his fellows, and anxious to preserve the claims of God from any infringement by those of Caesar, he still sees in democracy the only hope of Christian freedom. He is tempted to accept aid from champions of the *status quo* whose commercial or imperial motives bear hardly even a veneer of theism. Finally, we have Spartacus, also a Christian and also sincere, full of the prophetic and Dominical denunciations of riches, and certain that the 'historical Jesus', long betrayed by the Apostles, the Fathers, and the Churches, demands of us a Left revolution. And he also is tempted to accept help from unbelievers who profess themselves quite openly to be the enemies of God.

---

1. *The Guardian* was a weekly Anglican newspaper founded in 1846 to uphold Tractarian principles, and to show their relevance to the best secular thought of the day.
2. Jacques Maritain, *Scholasticism and Politics*, trans. M. J. Adler (London, 1950).

The three types represented by these three Christians presumably come together to form a Christian Party. Either a deadlock ensues (and there the history of the Christian Party ends) or else one of the three succeeds in floating a party and driving the other two, with their followers, out of its ranks. The new party—being probably a minority of the Christians who are themselves a minority of the citizens— will be too small to be effective. In practice, it will have to attach itself to the un-Christian party nearest to it in beliefs about means—to the Fascists if Philarchus has won, to the Conservatives if Stativus, to the Communists if Spartacus. It remains to ask how the resulting situation will differ from that in which Christians find themselves today.

It is not reasonable to suppose that such a Christian Party will acquire new powers of leavening the infidel organization to which it is attached. Why should it? Whatever it calls itself, it will represent, not Christendom, but a part of Christendom. The principle which divides it from its brethren and unites it to its political allies will not be theological. It will have no authority to speak for Christianity; it will have no more power than the political skill of its members gives it to control the behaviour of its unbelieving allies. But there will be a real, and most disastrous, novelty. It will be not simply a *part* of Christendom, but a *part claiming to be the whole*. By the mere act of calling itself the Christian Party it implicitly accuses all Christians who do not join it of apostasy and betrayal. It will be exposed, in an aggravated degree, to that temptation which the Devil spares none of us at any time—the temptation of claiming for our favourite opinions that kind and degree of certainty and authority which really belongs only to our Faith. The danger of mistaking our merely natural, though perhaps legitimate, enthusiasms for holy zeal, is always great. Can any more fatal expedient be devised for increasing it than that of dubbing a small band of Fascists, Communists, or Democrats 'the Christian Party'? The demon inherent in every party is at all times ready enough to disguise himself as the Holy Ghost; the formation of a Christian Party means handing over to him the most efficient make-up we can find. And when once the disguise has succeeded, his commands will presently be taken to abrogate all moral laws and to justify whatever the unbelieving allies of the 'Christian' Party wish to do. If ever Christian men can be brought to think treachery and murder the lawful means of establishing the *régime* they desire, and faked trials, religious persecution and organized hooliganism the lawful means of maintaining it, it will, surely, be by just such a process as this. The history of the late medieval pseudo-Crusader, of the Covenanters,[3] of the Orangemen,[4] should be remembered. On those who add 'Thus said the Lord' to their merely human utterances descends the doom of a conscience which seems clearer and clearer the more it is loaded with sin.

All this comes from pretending that God has spoken when He has not spoken. He will not settle the two brothers' inheritance: 'Who made Me a judge or a divider over you?'[5] By the natural light He has shown us what means are lawful: to find out which one is efficacious He has given us brains. The rest He has left to us.

3. The bodies of Presbyterians in Scotland who in the 16th and 17th centuries bound themselves by religious and political oaths to maintain the cause of their religion.
4. Members of the Orange Association (founded in 1795) who defended the cause of Protestantism in Ireland.
5. Luke xii. 14.

M. Maritain has hinted at the only way in which Christianity (as opposed to schismatics blasphemously claiming to represent it) can influence politics. Nonconformity has influenced modern English history not because there was a Nonconformist Party but because there was a Nonconformist conscience which all parties had to take into account. An interdenominational Christian Voters' Society might draw up a list of assurances about ends and means which every member was expected to exact from any political party as the price of his support. Such a society might claim to represent Christendom far more truly than any 'Christian Front'; and for that reason I should be prepared, in principle, for membership and obedience to be obligatory on Christians. 'So all it comes down to is pestering M.P.'s[6] with letters?' Yes: just that. I think such pestering combines the dove and the serpent. I think it means a world where parties have to take care not to alienate Christians, instead of a world where Christians have to be 'loyal' to infidel parties. Finally, I think a minority can influence politics only by 'pestering' or by becoming a 'party' in the new continental sense (that is, a secret society of murderers and blackmailers) which is impossible to Christians. But I had forgotten. There is a third way—by becoming a majority. He who converts his neighbour has performed the most practical Christian-political act of all.

6. Members of Parliament.

4
On the Reading of Old Books[1]

THERE IS A strange idea abroad that in every subject the ancient books should be read only by the professionals, and that the amateur should content himself with the modern books. Thus I have found as a tutor in English Literature that if the average student wants to find out something about Platonism, the very last thing he thinks of doing is to take a translation of Plato off the library shelf and read the *Symposium*. He would rather read some dreary modern book ten times as long, all about 'isms' and influences and only once in twelve pages telling him what Plato actually said. The error is rather an amiable one, for it springs from humility. The student is half afraid to meet one of the great philosophers face to face. He feels himself inadequate and thinks he will not understand him. But if he only knew, the great man, just because of his greatness, is much more intelligible than his modern commentator. The simplest student will be able to understand, if not all, yet a very great deal of what Plato said; but hardly anyone can understand some modern books on Platonism. It has always therefore been one of my main endeavours as a teacher to persuade the young that first-hand knowledge is not only more worth acquiring than second-hand knowledge, but is usually much easier and more delightful to acquire.

This mistaken preference for the modern books and this shyness of the old ones is nowhere more rampant than in theology. Wherever you find a little study circle of Christian laity you can be almost certain that they are studying not St Luke or St Paul or St Augustine or Thomas Aquinas or Hooker[2] or Butler,[3] but M. Berdyaev[4] or M. Maritain[5] or Mr Niebuhr[6] or Miss Sayers[7] or even myself.

Now this seems to me topsy-turvy. Naturally, since I myself am a writer, I do not wish the ordinary reader to read no modern books. But if he must read only the new or only the old, I would advise him to read the old. And I would give him this advice precisely because he is an amateur and therefore much less protected than the expert against the dangers of an exclusive contemporary diet. A new book is still on its trial and the amateur is not in a position to judge it. It has to be tested against the great body of Christian thought down the ages, and all its hidden implications (often unsuspected by the author himself) have to be brought to light. Often it cannot be fully understood without the knowledge of a good many other

---

1. This paper was originally written and published as an Introduction to St Athanasius' *The Incarnation of the Word of God,* trans. by A. Religious of C.S.M.V. (London, 1944).
2. Richard Hooker (c. 1554–1600), an Anglican divine.
3. Joseph Butler (1692–1752), Bishop of Durham.
4. Nicolas Berdyaev (1874–1948), a Russian philosopher and author.
5. Jacques Maritain (b. 1882), a French Thomist philosopher.
6. Reinhold Niebuhr (b. 1892), an American theologian.
7. Dorothy L. Sayers (1893–1957), author of several religious plays and many popular detective stories.

modern books. If you join at eleven o'clock a conversation which began at eight you will often not see the real bearing of what is said. Remarks which seem to you very ordinary will produce laughter or irritation and you will not see why—the reason, of course, being that the earlier stages of the conversation have given them a special point. In the same way sentences in a modern book which look quite ordinary may be directed 'at' some other book; in this way you may be led to accept what you would have indignantly rejected if you knew its real significance. The only safety is to have a standard of plain, central Christianity ('mere Christianity' as Baxter called it) which puts the controversies of the moment in their proper perspective. Such a standard can be acquired only from the old books. It is a good rule, after reading a new book, never to allow yourself another new one till you have read an old one in between. If that is too much for you, you should at least read one old one to every three new ones.

Every age has its own outlook. It is specially good at seeing certain truths and specially liable to make certain mistakes. We all, therefore, need the books that will correct the characteristic mistakes of our own period. And that means the old books. All contemporary writers share to some extent the contemporary outlook—even those, like myself, who seem most opposed to it. Nothing strikes me more when I read the controversies of past ages than the fact that both sides were usually assuming without question a good deal which we should now absolutely deny. They thought that they were as completely opposed as two sides could be, but in fact they were all the time secretly united—united *with* each other and *against* earlier and later ages—by a great mass of common assumptions. We may be sure that the characteristic blindness of the twentieth century—the blindness about which posterity will ask, 'But how *could* they have thought that?'—lies where we have never suspected it, and concerns something about which there is untroubled agreement between Hitler and President Roosevelt[8] or between Mr H. G. Wells and Karl Barth. None of us can fully escape this blindness, but we shall certainly increase it, and weaken our guard against it, if we read only modern books. Where they are true they will give us truths which we half knew already. Where they are false they will aggravate the error with which we are already dangerously ill. The only palliative is to keep the clean sea breeze of the centuries blowing through our minds, and this can be done only by reading old books. Not, of course, that there is any magic about the past. People were no cleverer then than they are now; they made as many mistakes as we. But not the *same* mistakes. They will not flatter us in the errors we are already committing; and their own errors, being now open and palpable, will not endanger us. Two heads are better than one, not because either is infallible, but because they are unlikely to go wrong in the same direction. To be sure, the books of the future would be just as good a corrective as the books of the past, but unfortunately we cannot get at them.

I myself was first led into reading the Christian classics, almost accidentally, as a result of my English studies. Some, such as Hooker, Herbert,[9] Traherne,[10] Tay-

8. This was written in 1943.
9. George Herbert (1593–1633), the English poet.
10. Thomas Traherne (1637–74), an English writer of religious works.

lor[11] and Bunyan,[12] I read because they are themselves great English writers; others, such as Boethius,[13] St Augustine, Thomas Aquinas and Dante, because they were 'influences'. George MacDonald I had found for myself at the age of sixteen and never wavered in my allegiance, though I tried for a long time to ignore his Christianity. They are, you will note, a mixed bag, representative of many Churches, climates and ages. And that brings me to yet another reason for reading them. The divisions of Christendom are undeniable and are by some of these writers most fiercely expressed. But if any man is tempted to think—as one might be tempted who read only contemporaries—that 'Christianity' is a word of so many meanings that it means nothing at all, he can learn beyond all doubt, by stepping out of his own century, that this is not so. Measured against the ages 'mere Christianity' turns out to be no insipid interdenominational transparency, but something positive, selfconsistent, and inexhaustible. I know it, indeed, to my cost. In the days when I still hated Christianity,[14] I learned to recognize, like some all too familiar smell, that almost unvarying *something* which met me, now in Puritan Bunyan, now in Anglican Hooker, now in Thomist Dante. It was there (honeyed and floral) in François de Sales;[15] it was there (grave and homely) in Spenser[16] and Walton;[17] it was there (grim but manful) in Pascal[18] and Johnson;[19] there again, with a mild, frightening, Paradisial flavour, in Vaughan[20] and Boehme[21] and Traherne. In the urban sobriety of the eighteenth century one was not safe—Law"[22] and Butler were two lions in the path. The supposed 'Paganism' of the Elizabethans could not keep it out; it lay in wait where a man might have supposed himself safest, in the very centre of *The Faerie Queene* and the *Arcadia*.[23] It was, of course, varied; and yet—after all—so unmistakably the same; recognizable, not to be evaded, the odour which is death to us until we allow it to become life:

an air that kills
From yon far country blows.[24]

We are all rightly distressed, and ashamed also, at the divisions of Christendom. But those who have always lived within the Christian fold may be too easily dispirited by them. They are bad, but such people do not know what it looks like from without. Seen from there, what is left intact, despite all the divisions, still appears

---

11. Jeremy Taylor (1613–67), an English divine, best known for his *Holy Living* and *Holy Dying*.
12. John Bunyan (1628–88), best known for his *Pilgrim's Progress*.
13. Boethius was born about 470 A.D. and wrote *The Consolation of Philosophy* .
14. Those who wish to know more about this period should read Lewis's autobiography, *Surprised by Joy* (London, 1955).
15. Francois de Sales (1567–1622) is best known for his *Introduction to the Devout Life* and the *Treatise on the Love of God*.
16. Edmund Spenser (1552?-99), author of *The Faerie Queene*.
17. Izaak Walton (1593–1683), best known for his *Compleat Angler*.
18. Blaise Pascal (1623–62), especially noted for his *Pensées*.
19. Dr Samuel Johnson (1709–84).
20. Henry Vaughan (1622–95), an English poet.
21. Jakob Boehme (1575–1624), a German Lutheran theosophical author.
22. William Law (1686–1761), whose *Serious Call to a Devout and Holy Life* much influenced Lewis.
23. By Sir Philip Sidney (1554–86).
24. A. E. Housman, *A Shropshire Lad* (London, 1896), stanza 40.

(as it truly is) an immensely formidable unity. I know, for I saw it; and well our enemies know it. That unity any of us can find by going out of his own age. It is not enough, but it is more than you had thought till then. Once you are well soaked in it, if you then venture to speak, you will have an amusing experience. You will be thought a Papist when you are actually reproducing Bunyan, a Pantheist when you are quoting Aquinas, and so forth. For you have now got on to the great level viaduct which crosses the ages and which looks so high from the valleys, so low from the mountains, so narrow compared with the swamps, and so broad compared with the sheeptracks.

The present book is something of an experiment. The translation is intended for the world at large, not only for theological students. If it succeeds, other translations of other great Christian books will presumably follow. In one sense, of course, it is not the first in the field. Translations of the *Theologia Germanica*,[25] the *Imitation*,[26] the *Scale of Perfection*,[27] and the *Revelations* of Lady Julian of Norwich,[28] are already on the market, and are very valuable, though some of them are not very scholarly. But it will be noticed that these are all books of devotion rather than of doctrine. Now the layman or amateur needs to be instructed as well as to be exhorted. In this age his need for knowledge is particularly pressing. Nor would I admit any sharp division between the two kinds of book. For my own part, I tend to find the doctrinal books often more helpful in devotion than the devotional books, and I rather suspect that the same experience may await many others. I believe that many who find that 'nothing happens' when they sit down, or kneel down, to a book of devotion, would find that the heart sings unbidden while they are working their way through a tough bit of theology with a pipe in their teeth and a pencil in their hand.

This is a good translation of a very great book. St Athanasius has suffered in popular estimation from a certain sentence in the 'Athanasian Creed'.[29] I will not labour the point that that work is not exactly a creed and was not by St. Athanasius, for I think it is a very fine piece of writing. The words 'Which Faith except every one do keep whole and undefiled, without doubt he shall perish everlastingly' are the offence. They are commonly misunderstood. The operative word is *keep*; not *acquire*, or even *believe*, but *keep*. The author, in fact, is not talking about unbelievers, but about deserters, not about those who have never heard of Christ, nor even those who have misunderstood and refused to accept Him, but of those who having really understood and really believed, then allow themselves, under the sway of sloth or of fashion or any other invited confusion to be drawn away into sub-Christian modes of thought. They are a warning against the curious modern assumption that all changes of belief, however brought about, are necessarily exempt from blame.[30] But this is not my immediate concern. I mention 'the creed

25. A late 14th century anonymous mystical treatise.
26. *The Imitation of Christ*, a manual of spiritual devotion first put into circulation in 1418. The authorship has traditionally been assigned to Thomas à Kempis (c. 1380–1471).
27. By Walter Hilton (d. 1396), an English mystic.
28. *The Sixteen Revelations of Divine Love* by Lady Julian of Norwich (c. 1342 -after 1413).
29. A profession of faith found in the English Prayer Book.
30. See Hebrews vi. 4 *et seq.*

(commonly called) of St Athanasius' only to get out of the reader's way what may have been a bogey and to put the true Athanasius in its place. His epitaph is *Athanasius contra mundum*, 'Athanasius against the world'. We are proud that our country has more than once stood against the world. Athanasius did the same. He stood for the Trinitarian doctrine, 'whole and undefiled', when it looked as if all the civilized world was slipping back from Christianity into the religion of Arius[31]— into one of those 'sensible' synthetic religions which are so strongly recommended today and which, then as now, included among their devotees many highly culti- vated clergymen. It is his glory that he did not move with the times; it is his reward that he now remains when those times, as all times do, have moved away.

When I first opened his *De Incarnatione* I soon discovered by a very simple test that I was reading a masterpiece. I knew very little Christian Greek except that of the New Testament and I had expected difficulties. To my astonishment I found it almost as easy as Xenophon; and only a master mind could, in the fourth century, have written so deeply on such a subject with such classical simplicity. Every page I read confirmed this impression. His approach to the Miracles is badly needed today, for it is the final answer to those who object to them as 'arbitrary and mean- ingless violations of the laws of Nature'.[32] They are here shown to be rather the re-telling in capital letters of the same message which Nature writes in her crabbed cursive hand; the very operations one would expect of Him who was so full of life that when He wished to die He had to 'borrow death from others'. The whole book, indeed, is a picture of the Tree of Life—a sappy and golden book, full of buoyancy and confidence. We cannot, I admit, appropriate all its confidence today. We can- not point to the high virtue of Christian living and the gay, almost mocking cour- age of Christian martyrdom, as a proof of our doctrines with quite that assurance which Athanasius takes as a matter of course. But whoever may be to blame for that it is not Athanasius.

The translator knows so much more Christian Greek than I that it would be out of place for me to praise her version. But it seems to me to be in the right tradition of English translation. I do not think the reader will find here any of that sawdusty quality which is so common in modern renderings from the ancient languages. That is as much as the English reader will notice; those who compare the version with the original will be able to estimate how much wit and talent is presupposed in such a choice, for example, as 'those wiseacres' on the very first page.

31. Arius (c. 250–c. 336), a champion of subordinationist teaching about the Person of Christ.
32. A few years after this was written, Lewis himself wrote an admirable defence of Miracles in his *Miracles: A Pre- liminary Study* (London, 1947) .

5
Two Lectures

'AND SO', SAID the lecturer, 'I end where I began. Evolution, development, the slow struggle upwards and onwards from crude and inchoate beginnings towards ever-increasing perfection and elaboration—that appears to be the very formula of the whole universe.

'We see it exemplified in everything we study. The oak comes from the acorn. The giant express engine of today comes from the Rocket. The highest achievements of contemporary art are in a continuous line of descent from the rude scratchings with which prehistoric man adorned the wall of his cave.

'What are the ethics and philosophy of civilized man but a miraculous elaboration of the most primitive instincts and savage taboos? Each one of us has grown, through slow prenatal stages in which we were at first more like fish than mammals, from a particle of matter too small to be seen. Man himself springs from beasts: the organic from the inorganic. Development is the key word. The march of all things is from lower to higher.'

None of this, of course, was new to me or to anyone else in the audience. But it was put very well (much better than it appears in my reproduction) and the whole voice and figure of the lecturer were impressive. At least they must have impressed me, for otherwise I cannot account for the curious dream I had that night.

I dreamed that I was still at the lecture, and the voice from the platform was still going on. But it was saying all the wrong things. At least it may have been saying the right things up to the very moment at which I began attending; but it certainly began going wrong after that. What I remembered on waking went like this: '. . . appears to be the very formula of the whole universe. We see it exemplified in everything we study. The acorn comes from a full-grown oak. The first crude engine, the Rocket, comes, not from a still cruder engine, but from something much more perfect than itself and much more complex, the mind of a man, and a man of genius. The first prehistoric drawings come, not from earlier scratchings, but from the hand and brain of human beings whose hand and brain cannot be shown to have been in any way inferior to our own; and indeed it is obvious that the man who first conceived the idea of making a picture must have been a greater genius than any of the artists who have succeeded him. The embryo with which the life of each one of us began did not originate from something even more embryonic; it originated from two fully-developed human beings, our parents. Descent, downward movement, is the key word. The march of all things is from higher to lower. The rude and imperfect thing always springs from something perfect and developed.'

I did not think much of this while I was shaving, but it so happened that I had no 10 o'clock pupil that morning, and when I had finished answering my letters I sat down and reflected on my dream.

It appeared to me that the Dream Lecturer had a good deal to be said for him. It is true that we do see all round us things growing up to perfection from small and rude beginnings; but then it is equally true that the small and rude beginnings themselves always come from some full-grown and developed thing. All adults were once babies, true: but then all babies were begotten and born by adults. Corn does come from seed: but then seed comes from corn. I could even give the Dream Lecturer an example he had missed. All civilizations grow from small beginnings; but when you look into it you always find that those small beginnings themselves have been 'dropped' (as an oak drops an acorn) by some other and mature civilization. The weapons and even the cookery of old Germanic barbarism are, so to speak, driftwood from the wrecked ship of Roman civilization. The starting point of Greek culture is the remains of older Minoan cultures, supplemented by oddments from civilized Egypt and Phoenicia.

But in that case, thought I, what about the first civilization of all? As soon as I asked this question I realised that the Dream Lecturer had been choosing his examples rather cautiously. He had talked only about things we can see going on around us. He had kept off the subject of absolute beginnings. He had quite correctly pointed out that in the present, and in the *historical* past, we see imperfect life coming from perfect just as much as *vice versa*. But he hadn't even attempted to answer the Real Lecturer about the beginnings of all life. The Real Lecturer's view was that when you got back far enough—back into those parts of the past which we know less about—you would find an absolute beginning, and it would be something small and imperfect.

That was a point in favour of the Real Lecturer. He at least had a theory about the absolute beginning, whereas the Dream Lecturer had slurred it over. But hadn't the Real Lecturer done a little slurring too? He had not given us a hint that his theory of the ultimate origins involved us in believing that Nature's habits have, since those days, altered completely. Her present habits show us an endless cycle—the bird coming from the egg and the egg from the bird. But he asked us to believe that the whole thing started with an egg which had been preceded by no bird. Perhaps it did. But the whole *prima facie* plausibility of his view—the ease with which the audience accepted it as something natural and obvious—depended on his slurring over the immense difference between this and the processes we actually observe. He put it over by drawing our attention to the fact that eggs develop into birds and making us forget that birds lay eggs; indeed, we have been trained to do this all our lives: trained to look at the universe with one eye shut. 'Developmentalism' is made to look plausible by a kind of trick.

For the first time in my life I began to look at the question with both eyes open. In the world I know, the perfect produces the imperfect, which again becomes perfect—egg leads to bird and bird to egg—in endless succession. If there ever was a life which sprang of its own accord out of a purely inorganic universe, or a civilization which raised itself by its own shoulder-straps out of pure savagery, then this event was totally unlike the beginnings of every subsequent life and every subsequent civilization. The thing may have happened; but all its plausibility is gone. On any view, the first beginning must have been outside the ordinary processes of nature. An egg which came from no bird is no more 'natural' than a bird which had existed from all eternity. And since the egg-bird-egg sequence leads us to no plausible beginning, is it not reasonable to look for the real origin somewhere outside sequence altogether? You have to go outside the sequence of engines, into the world of men, to find the real originator of the Rocket. Is it not equally reasonable to look outside Nature for the real Originator of the natural order?

6
Meditation in a Toolshed

I WAS STANDING today in the dark toolshed. The sun was shining outside and through the crack at the top of the door there came a sunbeam. From where I stood that beam of light, with the specks of dust floating in it, was the most striking thing in the place. Everything else was almost pitchblack. I was seeing the beam, not seeing things by it.

Then I moved, so that the beam fell on my eyes. Instantly the whole previous picture vanished. I saw no toolshed, and (above all) no beam. Instead I saw, framed in the irregular cranny at the top of the door, green leaves moving on the branches of a tree outside and beyond that, 90 odd million miles away, the sun. Looking along the beam, and looking at the beam are very different experiences.

But this is only a very simple example of the difference between looking at and looking along. A young man meets a girl. The whole world looks different when he sees her. Her voice reminds him of something he has been trying to remember all his life, and ten minutes casual chat with her is more precious than all the favours that all other women in the world could grant. He is, as they say, 'in love'. Now comes a scientist and describes this young man's experience from the outside. For him it is all an affair of the young man's genes and a recognised biological stimulus. That is the difference between looking *along* the sexual impulse and looking *at* it.

When you have got into the habit of making this distinction you will find examples of it all day long. The mathematician sits thinking, and to him it seems that he is contemplating timeless and spaceless truths about quantity. But the cerebral physiologist, if he could look inside the mathematician's head, would find nothing timeless and spaceless there—only tiny movements in the grey matter. The savage dances in ecstasy at midnight before Nyonga and feels with every muscle that his dance is helping to bring the new green crops and the spring rain and the babies. The anthropologist, observing that savage, records that he is performing a fertility ritual of the type so-and-so. The girl cries over her broken doll and feels that she has lost a real friend; the psychologist says that her nascent maternal instinct has been temporarily lavished on a bit of shaped and coloured wax.

As soon as you have grasped this simple distinction, it raises a question. You get one experience of a thing when you look along it and another when you look at it. Which is the 'true' or 'valid' experience? Which tells you most about the thing? And you can hardly ask that question without noticing that for the last fifty years or so everyone has been taking the answer for granted. It has been assumed without discussion that if you want the true account of religion you must go, not to religious people, but to anthropologists; that if you want the true account of sexual love you must go, not to lovers, but to psychologists; that if you want to understand some 'ideology' (such as medieval chivalry or the nineteenth-century idea of a 'gentleman'), you must listen not to those who lived inside it, but to sociologists.

The people who look *at* things have had it all their own way; the people who look *along* things have simply been brow-beaten. It has even come to be taken for granted that the external account of a thing somehow refutes or 'debunks' the account given from inside. 'All these moral ideals which look so transcendental and beautiful from inside', says the wiseacre, 'are really only a mass of biological instincts and inherited taboos.' And no one plays the game the other way round by replying, 'If you will only step inside, the things that look to you like instincts and taboos will suddenly reveal their real and transcendental nature.'

That, in fact, is the whole basis of the specifically 'modern' type of thought. And is it not, you will ask, a very sensible basis? For, after all, we are often deceived by things from the inside. For example, the girl who looks so wonderful while we're in love, may really be a very plain, stupid, and disagreeable person. The savage's dance to Nyonga does not really cause the crops to grow. Having been so often deceived by looking along, are we not well advised to trust only to looking at?—in fact to discount all these inside experiences?

Well, no. There are two fatal objections to discounting them *all*. And the first is this. You discount them in order to think more accurately. But you can't think at all—and therefore, of course, can't think accurately—if you have nothing to think *about*. A physiologist, for example, can study pain and find out that it 'is' (whatever *is* means) such and such neural events. But the word *pain* would have no meaning for him unless he had 'been inside' by actually suffering. If he had never looked *along* pain he simply wouldn't know what he was looking *at*. The very subject for his inquiries from outside exists for him only because he has, at least once, been inside.

This case is not likely to occur, because every man has felt pain. But it is perfectly easy to go on all your life giving explanations of religion, love, morality, honour, and the like, without having been inside any of them. And if you do that, you are simply playing with counters. You go on explaining a thing without knowing what it is. That is why a great deal of contemporary thought is, strictly speaking, thought about nothing—all the apparatus of thought busily working in a vacuum.

The other objection is this: let us go back to the toolshed. I might have discounted what I saw when looking along the beam (i.e., the leaves moving and the sun) on the ground that it was 'really only a strip of dusty light in a dark shed'. That is, I might have set up as 'true' my 'side vision' of the beam. But then that side vision is itself an instance of the activity we call seeing. And this new instance could also be looked at from outside. I could allow a scientist to tell me that what seemed to be a beam of light in a shed was 'really only an agitation of my own optic nerves'. And that would be just as good (or as bad) a bit of debunking as the previous one. The picture of the beam in the toolshed would now have to be discounted just as the previous picture of the trees and the sun had been discounted. And then, where are you?

In other words, you can step outside one experience only by stepping inside another. Therefore, if all inside experiences are misleading, we are always misled.

The cerebral physiologist may say, if he chooses, that the mathematician's thought is 'only' tiny physical movements of the grey matter. But then what about the cerebral physiologist's own thought at that very moment? A second physiologist, looking at it, could pronounce it also to be only tiny physical movements in the first physiologist's skull. Where is the rot to end?

The answer is that we must never allow the rot to begin. We must, on pain of idiocy, deny from the very outset the idea that looking *at* is, by its own nature, intrinsically truer or better than looking *along*. One must look both *along* and *at* everything. In particular cases we shall find reason for regarding the one or the other vision as inferior. Thus the inside vision of rational thinking must be truer than the outside vision which sees only movements of the grey matter; for if the outside vision were the correct one all thought (including this thought itself) would be valueless, and this is self-contradictory. You cannot have a proof that no proofs matter. On the other hand, the inside vision of the savage's dance to Nyonga may be found deceptive because we find reason to believe that crops and babies are not really affected by it. In fact, we must take each case on its merits. But we must start with no prejudice for or against either kind of looking. We do not know in advance whether the lover or the psychologist is giving the more correct account of love, or whether both accounts are equally correct in different ways, or whether both are equally wrong. We just have to find out. But the period of brow-beating has got to end.

7
Scraps

1

'YES,' MY FRIEND said. 'I don't see why there shouldn't be books in Heaven. But you will find that your library in Heaven contains only some of the books you had on earth.' 'Which?' I asked. 'The ones you gave away or lent.' 'I hope the lent ones won't still have all the borrowers' dirty thumb-marks,' said I. 'Oh yes they will,' said he. 'But just as the wounds of the martyrs will have turned into beauties, so you will find that the thumb-marks have turned into beautiful illuminated capitals or exquisite marginal woodcuts.'

2

'The angels', he said, 'have no senses; their experience is purely intellectual and spiritual. That is why we know something about God which they don't. There are particular aspects of His love and joy which can be communicated to a created being only by sensuous experience. Something of God which the Seraphim can never quite understand flows into us from the blue of the sky, the taste of honey, the delicious embrace of water whether cold or hot, and even from sleep itself.'

3

'You are always dragging me down,' said I to my Body. 'Dragging *you* down!' replied my Body. 'Well I like that! Who taught me to like tobacco and alcohol? You, of course, with your idiotic adolescent idea of being "grown-up". My palate loathed both at first: but you would have your way. Who put an end to all those angry and revengeful thoughts last night? Me, of course, by insisting on going to sleep. Who does his best to keep you from talking too much and eating too much by giving you dry throats and headaches and indigestion? Eh?' 'And what about sex?' said I. 'Yes, what about it?' retorted the Body. 'If you and your wretched imagination would leave me alone I'd give you no trouble. That's Soul all over; you give me orders and then blame me for carrying them out.'

4

'Praying for particular things', said I, 'always seems to me like advising God how to run the world. Wouldn't it be wiser to assume that He knows best?' 'On the same principle', said he, 'I suppose you never ask a man next to you to pass the salt, because God knows best whether you ought to have salt or not. And I suppose you never take an umbrella, because God knows best whether you ought to be wet or dry.' 'That's quite different,' I protested. 'I don't see why,' said he. 'The odd thing is that He should let us influence the course of events at all. But since He lets us do it in one way I don't see why He shouldn't let us do it in the other.'

8
The Decline of Religion

FROM WHAT I SEE of junior Oxford at present it would be quite easy to draw opposite conclusions about the religious predicament of what we call 'the rising generation', though in reality the undergraduate body includes men and women almost as much divided from one another in age, outlook, and experience as they are divided from the dons. Plenty of evidence can be produced to show that religion is in its last decline among them, or that a revival of interest in religion is one of their most noticeable characteristics. And in fact something that may be called 'a decline' and something that may be called 'a revival' are both going on. It will be perhaps more useful to attempt to understand both than to try our luck at 'spotting the winner'.

The 'decline of religion' so often lamented (or welcomed) is held to be shown by empty chapels. Now it is quite true that chapels which were full in 1900 are empty in 1946. But this change was not gradual. It occurred at the precise moment when chapel ceased to be compulsory. It was not in fact a decline; it was a precipice. The sixty men who had come because chapel was a little later than 'rollers'[1] (its only alternative) came no more; the five Christians remained. The withdrawal of compulsion did not create a new religious situation, but only revealed the situation which had long existed. And this is typical of the 'decline in religion' all over England.

In every class and every part of the country the visible practice of Christianity has grown very much less in the last fifty years. This is often taken to show that the nation as a whole has passed from a Christian to a secular outlook. But if we judge the nineteenth century from the books it wrote, the outlook of our grandfathers (with a very few exceptions) was quite as secular as our own. The novels of Meredith, Trollope, and Thackeray are not written either by or for men who see this world as the vestibule of eternity, who regard pride as the greatest of the sins, who desire to be poor in spirit, and look for a supernatural salvation. Even more significant is the absence from Dickens' *Christmas Carol* of any interest in the Incarnation. Mary, the Magi, and the Angels are replaced by 'spirits' of his own invention, and the animals present are not the ox and ass in the stable but the goose and turkey in the poulterer's shop. Most striking of all is the thirty-third chapter of *The Antiquary*, where Lord Glenallan forgives old Elspeth for her intolerable wrong. Glenallan has been painted by Scott as a life-long penitent and ascetic, a man whose every thought has been for years fixed on the supernatural. But when he has to

---

1. After there came to be a number of non-Anglican students in the Oxford colleges, those students who did not wish to attend the morning chapel service were required to report to the Dean five or ten minutes before the service and have their names put on his roll-call. Thus the 'rollers', who did not go to chapel, had to be up before those who did go. Neither chapel nor roll-call is compulsory now.

forgive, no motive of a Christian kind is brought into play: the battle is won by 'the generosity of his nature'. It does not occur to Scott that his facts, his solitudes, his beads and his confessor, however useful as romantic 'properties', could be effectively connected with a serious action which concerns the plot of the book.

I am anxious here not to be misunderstood. I do not mean that Scott was not a brave, generous, honourable man and a glorious writer. I mean that in his work, as in that of most of his contemporaries, only secular and natural values are taken seriously. Plato and Virgil are, in that sense, nearer to Christianity than they.

Thus the 'decline of religion' becomes a very ambiguous phenomenon. One way of putting the truth would be that the religion which has declined was not Christianity. It was a vague Theism with a strong and virile ethical code, which, far from standing over against the 'World', was absorbed into the whole fabric of English institutions and sentiment and therefore demanded church-going as (at best) a part of loyalty and good manners as (at worst) a proof of respectability. Hence a social pressure, like the withdrawal of the compulsion, did not create a new situation. The new freedom first allowed accurate observations to be made. When no man goes to church except because he seeks Christ the number of actual believers can at last be discovered. It should be added that this new freedom was partly caused by the very conditions which it revealed. If the various anti-clerical and anti-theistic forces at work in the nineteenth century had had to attack a solid phalanx of radical Christians the story might have been different. But mere 'religion'—'morality tinged with emotion', 'what a man does with his solitude', 'the religion of all good men'—has little power of resistance. It is not good at saying No.

The decline of 'religion', thus understood, seems to me in some ways a blessing. At the very worst it makes the issue clear. To the modern undergraduate Christianity is, at least, one of the intellectual options. It is, so to speak, on the agenda: it can be discussed, and a conversion may follow. I can remember times when this was much more difficult. 'Religion' (as distinct from Christianity) was too vague to be discussed ('too sacred to be lightly mentioned') and so mixed up with sentiment and good form as to be one of the embarrassing subjects. If it had to be spoken of, it was spoken of in a hushed, medical voice. Something of the shame of the Cross is, and ought to be, irremovable. But the merely social and sentimental embarrassment is gone. The fog of 'religion' has lifted; the positions and numbers of both armies can be observed; and real shooting is now possible.

The decline of 'religion' is no doubt a bad thing for the 'World'. By it all the things that made England a fairly happy country are, I suppose, endangered: the comparative purity of her public life, the comparative humanity of her police, and the possibility of some mutual respect and kindness between political opponents. But I am not clear that it makes conversions to Christianity rarer or more difficult: rather the reverse. It makes the choice more unescapable. When the Round Table is broken every man must follow either Galahad or Mordred: middle things are gone.

So much for the Decline of Religion; now for a Christian Revival. Those who claim that there is such a Revival would point to the success (I mean success in the sense that it can be tested by sales) of several explicitly and even violently Christian writers, the apparent popularity of lectures on theological subjects, and the brisk atmosphere of not unfriendly discussion on them in which we live. They point, in fact, to what I have heard described as 'the high-brow Christian racket'. It is difficult to describe the phenomenon in quite neutral terms: but perhaps no one would deny that Christianity is now 'on the map' among the younger *intelligentsia* as it was not, say, in 1920. Only freshmen now talk as if the anti-Christian position were self-evident. The days of 'simple un-faith' are as dead as those of 'simple faith'.

At this those who are on the same side as myself are quite properly pleased. We have cause to give thanks: and the comments which I have to add proceed, I hope, not from a natural middle-aged desire to pour cold water into any soup within reach, but only from a desire to forestall, and therefore to disarm, possible disappointments.

In the first place, it must be admitted by anyone who accepts Christianity, that an increased interest in it, or even a growing measure of intellectual assent to it, is a very different thing from the conversion of England or even of a single soul. Conversion requires an alteration of the will, and an alteration which, in the last resort, does not occur without the intervention of the supernatural. I do not in the least agree with those who therefore conclude that the spread of an intellectual (and imaginative) climate favourable to Christianity is useless. You do not prove munition workers useless by showing that they cannot themselves win battles, however proper this reminder would be if they attempted to claim the honour due to fighting men. If the intellectual climate is such that, when a man comes to the crisis at which he must either accept or reject Christ, his reason and imagination are not on the wrong side, then his conflict will be fought out under favourable conditions. Those who help to produce and spread such a climate are therefore doing useful work: and yet no such great matter after all. Their share is a modest one; and it is always possible that nothing—nothing whatever—may come of it. Far higher than they stands that character whom, to the best of my knowledge, the present Christian movement has not yet produced—the *Preacher* in the full sense, the Evangelist, the man on fire, the man who infects. The propagandist, the apologist, only represents John Baptist: the Preacher represents the Lord Himself. He will be sent— or else he will not. But unless he comes we mere Christian intellectuals will not effect very much. That does not mean we should down tools.

In the second place we must remember that a widespread and lively interest in a subject is precisely what we call a Fashion. And it is the nature of Fashions not to last. The present Christian movement may, or may not, have a long run ahead of it. But sooner or later it must lose the public ear; in a place like Oxford such changes are extraordinarily rapid. Bradley and the other idealists fell in a few terms, the Douglas scheme even more suddenly, the Vorticists overnight.[2] (Who now remembers Pogo? Who now reads *Childermass*?[3]) Whatever in our present success mere Fashion has given us, mere Fashion will presently withdraw. The real conversions

2. F. H. Bradley (1846–1924) was a Fellow of Merton College, Oxford, and the author of *Appearance and Reality* (London, 1893). Major C. H. Douglas, a socio-economist, wrote, among other works, *Social Credit* (London, 1933). The Vorticists were a school of artists of the 1920s.

3. No one, practically. As far as I can discover, Pogo, or the Pogo-stick, which was invented in 1922, is a stilt with a spring on which the player jumps about. *Childermass* is by P. Wyndham Lewis (London, 1928).

will remain: but nothing else will. In that sense we may be on the brink of a real and permanent Christian revival: but it will work slowly and obscurely and in small groups. The present sunshine (if I may so call it) is certainly temporary. The grain must be got into the barns before the wet weather comes.

This mutability is the fate of all movements, fashions, intellectual climates and the like. But a Christian movement is also up against something sterner than the mere fickleness of taste. We have not yet had (at least in junior Oxford) any really bitter opposition. But if we have many more successes, this will certainly appear. The enemy has not yet thought it worth while to fling his whole weight against us. But he soon will. This happens in the history of every Christian movement, beginning with the Ministry of Christ Himself. At first it is welcome to all who have no special reason for opposing it: at this stage he who is not against it is for it. What men notice is its difference from those aspects of the World which they already dislike. But later on, as the real meaning of the Christian claim becomes apparent, its demand for total surrender, the sheer chasm between Nature and Supernature, men are increasingly 'offended'. Dislike, terror, and finally hatred succeed: none who will not give it what it asks (and it asks all) can endure it: all who are not with it are against it. That is why we must cherish no picture of the present intellectual movement simply growing and spreading and finally reclaiming millions by sweet reasonableness. Long before it became as important as that the real opposition would have begun, and to be on the Christian side would be costing a man (at the least) his career. But remember. in England the opposition will quite likely be *called* Christianity (or Christo-democracy, or British Christianity, or something of that kind).

I think—but how should I know?—that all is going reasonably well. But it is early days. Neither our armour nor our enemies' is yet engaged. Combatants always tend to imagine that the war is further on than it really is.

9

Vivisection

IT IS THE rarest thing in the world to hear a rational discussion of vivisection. Those who disapprove of it are commonly accused of 'sentimentality', and very often their arguments justify the accusation. They paint pictures of pretty little dogs on dissecting tables. But the other side lie open to exactly the same charge. They also often defend the practice by drawing pictures of suffering women and children whose pain can be relieved (we are assured) only by the fruits of vivisection. The one appeal, quite as clearly as the other, is addressed to emotion, to the particular emotion we call pity. And neither appeal proves anything. If the thing is right—and if right at all, it is a duty—then pity for the animal is one of the temptations we must resist in order to perform that duty. If the thing is wrong, then pity for human suffering is precisely the temptation which will most probably lure us into doing that wrong thing. But the real question—whether it is right or wrong—remains meanwhile just where it was.

A rational discussion of this subject begins by inquiring whether pain is, or is not, an evil. If it is not, then the case against vivisection falls. But then so does the case for vivisection. If it is not defended on the ground that it reduces human suffering, on what ground can it be defended? And if pain is not an evil, why should human suffering be reduced? We must therefore assume as a basis for the whole discussion that pain is an evil, otherwise there is nothing to be discussed.

Now if pain is an evil then the infliction of pain, considered in itself, must clearly be an evil act. But there are such things as necessary evils. Some acts which would be bad, simply in themselves, may be excusable and even laudable when they are necessary means to a greater good. In saying that the infliction of pain, simply in itself, is bad, we are not saying that pain ought never to be inflicted. Most of us think that it can rightly be inflicted for a good purpose—as in dentistry or just and reformatory punishment. The point is that it always requires justification. On the man whom we find inflicting pain rests the burden of showing why an act which in itself would be simply bad is, in those particular circumstances, good. If we find a man giving pleasure it is for us to prove (if we criticise him) that his action is wrong. But if we find a man inflicting pain it is for him to prove that his action is right. If he cannot, he is a wicked man.

Now vivisection can only be defended by showing it to be right that one species should suffer in order that another species should be happier. And here we come to the parting of the ways. The Christian defender and the ordinary 'scientific' (i.e., naturalistic) defender of vivisection, have to take quite different lines.

The Christian defender, especially in the Latin countries, is very apt to say that we are entitled to do anything we please to animals because they 'have no souls'. But what does this mean? If it means that animals have no consciousness, then how is this known? They certainly behave as if they had, or at least the higher animals do. I myself am inclined to think that far fewer animals than is supposed have what we should recognise as consciousness. But that is only an opinion. Unless we know on other grounds that vivisection is right we must not take the moral risk of tormenting them on a mere opinion. On the other hand, the statement that they 'have no souls' may mean that they have no moral responsibilities and are not immortal. But the absence of 'soul' in that sense makes the infliction of pain upon them not easier but harder to justify. For it means that animals cannot deserve pain, nor profit morally by the discipline of pain, nor be recompensed by happiness in another life for suffering in this. Thus all the factors which render pain more tolerable or make it less totally evil in the case of human beings will be lacking in the beasts. 'Soullessness', in so far as it is relevant to the question at all, is an argument against vivisection.

The only rational line for the Christian vivisectionist to take is to say that the superiority of man over beast is a real objective fact, guaranteed by Revelation, and that the propriety of sacrificing beast to man is a logical consequence. We are 'worth more than many sparrows',[1] and in saying this we are not merely expressing a natural preference for our own species simply because it is our own but conforming to a hierarchical order created by God and really present in the universe whether any one acknowledges it or not. The position may not be satisfactory. We may fail to see how a benevolent Deity could wish us to draw such conclusions from the hierarchical order He has created. We may find it difficult to formulate a human right of tormenting beasts in terms which would not equally imply an angelic right of tormenting men. And we may feel that though objective superiority is rightly claimed for man, yet that very superiority ought partly to *consist in* not behaving like a vivisector: that we ought to prove ourselves better than the beasts precisely by the fact of acknowledging duties to them which they do not acknowledge to us. But on all these questions different opinions can be honestly held. If on grounds of our real, divinely ordained, superiority a Christian pathologist thinks it right to vivisect, and does so with scrupulous care to avoid the least dram or scruple of unnecessary pain, in a trembling awe at the responsibility which he assumes, and with a vivid sense of the high mode in which human life must be lived if it is to justify the sacrifices made for it, then (whether we agree with him or not) we can respect his point of view.

But of course the vast majority of vivisectors have no such theological background. They are most of them naturalistic and Darwinian. Now here, surely, we come up against a very alarming fact. The very same people who will most contemptuously brush aside any consideration of animal suffering if it stands in the way of 'research' will also, on another context, most vehemently deny that there is any radical difference between man and the other animals. On the naturalistic view the beasts are at bottom just the same *sort* of thing as ourselves. Man is simply the cleverest of the anthropoids. All the grounds on which a Christian might defend vivisection are thus cut from under our feet. We sacrifice other species to our own

1. Matthew x. 31.

not because our own has any objective metaphysical privilege over others, but simply because it is ours. It may be very natural to have this loyalty to our own species, but let us hear no more from the naturalists about the 'sentimentality' of anti-vivisectionists. If loyalty to our own species, preference for man simply because we are men, is not a sentiment, then what is? It may be a good sentiment or a bad one. But a sentiment it certainly is. Try to base it on logic and see what happens!

But the most sinister thing about modern vivisection is this. If a mere sentiment justifies cruelty, why stop at a sentiment for the whole human race? There is also a sentiment for the white man against the black, for a *Herrenvolk* against the non-Aryans, for 'civilized' or 'progressive' peoples against 'savage' or 'backward' peoples. Finally, for our own country, party, or class against others. Once the old Christian idea of a total difference in kind between man and beast has been abandoned, then no argument for experiments on animals can be found which is not also an argument for experiments on inferior men. If we cut up beasts simply because they cannot prevent us and because we are backing our own side in the struggle for existence, it is only logical to cut up imbeciles, criminals, enemies, or capitalists for the same reasons. Indeed, experiments on men have already begun. We all hear that Nazi scientists have done them. We all suspect that our own scientists may begin to do so, in secret, at any moment.

The alarming thing is that the vivisectors have won the first round. In the nineteenth and eighteenth century a man was not stamped as a 'crank' for protesting against vivisection. Lewis Carroll protested, if I remember his famous letter correctly, on the very same ground which I have just used.[2] Dr Johnson—a man whose mind had as much *iron* in it as any man's—protested in a note on *Cymbeline* which is worth quoting in full. In Act I, scene v, the Queen explains to the Doctor that she wants poisons to experiment on 'such creatures as We count not worth the hanging,—but none human.'[3] The Doctor replies:

> *Your Highness*
> *Shall from this practice but make hard your heart.*[4]

Johnson comments: 'The thought would probably have been more amplified, had our author lived to be shocked with such experiments as have been published in later times, by a race of men that have practised tortures without pity, and related them without shame, and are yet suffered to erect their heads among human beings.'[5]

The words are his, not mine, and in truth we hardly dare in these days to use such calmly stern language. The reason why we do not dare is that the other side has in fact won. And though cruelty even to beasts is an important matter, their

---

2. 'Vivisection as a Sign of the Times', *The Works of Lewis Carroll*, ed. Roger Lancelyn Green (London, 1965), pp. 1089–92. See also 'Some Popular Fallacies about Vivisection', *ib.*, pp. 1092–1100.
3. Shakespeare, *Cymbeline*, I, v, 19–20.
4. *Ibid.*, 23.
5. *Johnson on Shakespeare: Essays and Notes Selected and Set Forth with an introduction* by Sir Walter Raleigh (London, 1908), p. 181.

victory is symptomatic of matters more important still. The victory of vivisection marks a great advance in the triumph of ruthless, non-moral utilitarianism over the old world of ethical law; a triumph in which we, as well as animals, are already the victims, and of which Dachau and Hiroshima mark the more recent achievements. In justifying cruelty to animals we put ourselves also on the animal level. We choose the jungle and must abide by our choice.

You will notice I have spent no time in discussing what actually goes on in the laboratories. We shall be told, of course, that there is surprisingly little cruelty. That is a question with which, at present, I have nothing to do. We must first decide what should be allowed: after that it is for the police to discover what is already being done.

10
Modern Translations of the Bible

IT IS POSSIBLE that the reader who opens this volume[1] on the counter of a book-shop may ask himself why we need a new translation of any part of the Bible, and, if of any, why of the Epistles. 'Do we not already possess', it may be said, 'in the Authorised Version the most beautiful rendering which any language can boast?' Some people whom I have met go even further and feel that a modern translation is not only unnecessary but even offensive. They cannot bear to see the time-honoured words altered; it seems to them irreverent.

There are several answers to such people. In the first place the kind of objection which they feel to a new translation is very like the objection which was once felt to any English translation at all. Dozens of sincerely pious people in the sixteenth century shuddered at the idea of turning the time-honoured Latin of the Vulgate into our common and (as they thought) 'barbarous' English. A sacred truth seemed to them to have lost its sanctity when it was stripped of the polysyllabic Latin, long heard at Mass and at Hours, and put into 'language such as men do use'—language steeped in all the commonplace associations of the nursery, the inn, the stable, and the street. The answer then was the same as the answer now. The only kind of sanctity which Scripture can lose (or, at least, New Testament scripture) by being modernized is an accidental kind which it never had for its writers or its earliest readers. The New Testament in the original Greek is not a work of literary art: it is not written in a solemn, ecclesiastical language, it is written in the sort of Greek which was spoken over the Eastern Mediterranean after Greek had become an international language and therefore lost its real beauty and subtlety. In it we see Greek used by people who have no real feeling for Greek words because Greek words are not the words they spoke when they were children. It is a sort of 'basic' Greek; a language without roots in the soil, a utilitarian, commercial and administrative language. Does this shock us? It ought not to, except as the Incarnation itself ought to shock us. The same divine humility which decreed that God should become a baby at a peasant-woman's breast, and later an arrested field-preacher in the hands of the Roman police, decreed also that He should be preached in a vulgar, prosaic and unliterary language. If you can stomach the one, you can stomach the other. The Incarnation is in that sense an irreverent doctrine: Christianity, in that sense, an incurably irreverent religion. When we expect that it should have come before the World in all the beauty that we now feel in the Authorised Version we are as wide of the mark as the Jews were in expecting that the Messiah would come as a great earthly King. The real sanctity, the real beauty and sublimity of the New

1. This essay was originally published as an Introduction to J. B. Phillips' *Letters to Young Churches: A Translation of the New Testament Epistles* (London, 1947).

Testament (as of Christ's life) are of a different sort: miles deeper or _further in._

In the second place, the Authorised Version has ceased to be a good (that is, a clear) translation. It is no longer modern English: the meanings of words have changed. The same antique glamour which has made it (in the superficial sense) so 'beautiful', so 'sacred', so 'comforting', and so 'inspiring', has also made it in many places unintelligible. Thus where St Paul says 'I know nothing against myself,' it translates 'I know nothing by myself.'[2] That was a good translation (though even then rather old-fashioned) in the sixteenth century: to the modern reader it means either nothing, or something quite different from what St Paul said. The truth is that if we are to have translation at all we must have periodical re-translation. There is no such thing as translating a book into another language once and for all, for a language is a changing thing. If your son is to have clothes it is no good buying him a suit once and for all: he will grow out of it and have to be re-clothed.

And finally, though it may seem a sour paradox—we must sometimes get away from the Authorised Version, if for no other reason, simply _because_ it is so beautiful and so solemn. Beauty exalts, but beauty also lulls. Early associations endear but they also confuse. Through that beautiful solemnity the transporting or horrifying realities of which the Book tells may come to us blunted and disarmed and we may only sigh with tranquil veneration when we ought to be burning with shame or struck dumb with terror or carried out of ourselves by ravishing hopes and adorations. Does the word 'scourged'[3] really come home to us like 'flogged'? Does 'mocked him'[4] sting like 'jeered at him'?

We ought therefore to welcome all new translations (when they are made by sound scholars) and most certainly those who are approaching the Bible for the first time will be wise not to begin with the Authorised Version—except perhaps for the historical books of the Old Testament where its archaisms suit the saga-like material well enough. Among modern translations those of Dr Moffatt[5] and Monsignor Knox[6] seem to me particularly good. The present volume concentrates on the epistles and furnishes more help to the beginner: its scope is different. The preliminary abstracts to each letter will be found especially useful, and the reader who has not read the letters before might do well to begin by reading and reflecting on these abstracts at some length before he attempts to tackle the text. It would have saved me a great deal of labour if this book had come into my hands when I first seriously began to try to discover what Christianity was.

For a man who wants to make that discovery must face the epistles. And whether we like it or not, most of them are by St Paul. He is the Christian author whom no one can by-pass.

A most astonishing misconception has long dominated the modern mind on the subject of St Paul. It is to this effect: that Jesus preached a kindly and simple reli-

---

2. I Corinthians iv. 4.
3. John xix. 1.
4. Matthew xxvii. 29; Mark xv. 20; Luke xxii. 63; xxiii. 11, 36.
5. James Moffatt (1870–1944), whose translation of the New Testament appeared in 1913, his translation of the Old Testament in 1924, and the whole being revised in 1935.
6. Ronald A. Knox (1888–1957) published a translation of the New Testament in 1945, and a translation of the Old Testament in 1949.

gion (found in the Gospels) and that St Paul afterwards corrupted it into a cruel and complicated religion (found in the Epistles). This is really quite untenable. All the most terrifying texts come from the mouth of Our Lord: all the texts on which we can base such warrant as we have for hoping that all men will be saved come from St Paul. If it could be proved that St Paul altered the teaching of his Master in any way, he altered it in exactly the opposite way to that which is popularly supposed. But there is no real evidence for a pre-Pauline doctrine different from St Paul's. The Epistles are, for the most part, the earliest Christian documents we possess. The Gospels come later. They are not 'the gospel', the statement of the Christian belief. They were written for those who had already been converted, who had already accepted 'the gospel'. They leave out many of the 'complications' (that is, the theology) because they are intended for readers who have already been instructed in it. In that sense the Epistles are more primitive and more central than the Gospels—though not, of course, than the great events which the Gospels recount. God's act (the Incarnation, the Crucifixion, and the Resurrection) comes first: the earliest theological analysis of it comes in the Epistles: then, when the generation who had known the Lord was dying out, the Gospels were composed to provide for believers a record of the great Act and of some of the Lord's sayings. The ordinary popular conception has put everything upside down. Nor is the cause far to seek. In the earlier history of every rebellion there is a stage at which you do not yet attack the King in person. You say, 'The King is all right. It is his Ministers who are wrong. They misrepresent him and corrupt all his plans—which, I'm sure, are good plans if only the Ministers would let them take effect.' And the first victory consists in beheading a few Ministers: only at a later stage do you go on and behead the King himself. In the same way, the nineteenth-century attack on St Paul was really only a stage in the revolt against Christ. Men were not ready in large numbers to attack Christ Himself. They made the normal first move—that of attacking one of His principal ministers. Everything they disliked in Christianity was therefore attributed to St Paul. It was unfortunate that their case could not impress anyone who had really read the Gospels and the Epistles with attention: but apparently few people had, and so the first victory was won. St Paul was impeached and banished and the world went on to the next step—the attack on the King Himself. But to those who wish to know what St Paul and his fellow-teachers really said the present volume will give very great help.

11
Priestesses in the Church?

I SHOULD LIKE BALLS infinitely better', said Caroline Bingley, 'if they were carried on in a different manner . . . It would surely be much more rational if conversation instead of dancing made the order of the day.' 'Much more rational, I dare say,' replied her brother, 'but it would not be near so much like a Ball.'[1] We are told that the lady was silenced: yet it could be maintained that Jane Austen has not allowed Bingley to put forward the full strength of his position. He ought to have replied with a *distinguo*. In one sense conversation is more rational for conversation may exercise the reason alone, dancing does not. But there is nothing irrational in exercising other powers than our reason. On certain occasions and for certain purposes the real irrationality is with those who will not do so. The man who would try to break a horse or write a poem or beget a child by pure syllogizing would be an irrational man; though at the same time syllogizing is in itself a more rational activity than the activities demanded by these achievements. It is rational not to reason, or not to limit oneself to reason, in the wrong place; and the more rational a man is the better he knows this.

These remarks are not intended as a contribution to the criticism of *Pride and Prejudice*. They came into my head when I heard that the Church of England[2] was being advised to declare women capable of Priests' Orders. I am, indeed, informed that such a proposal is very unlikely to be seriously considered by the authorities. To take such a revolutionary step at the present moment, to cut ourselves off from the Christian past and to widen the divisions between ourselves and other Churches by establishing an order of priestesses in our midst, would be an almost wanton degree of imprudence. And the Church of England herself would be torn in shreds by the operation. My concern with the proposal is of a more theoretical kind. The question involves something even deeper than a revolution in order.

I have every respect for those who wish women to be priestesses. I think they are sincere and pious and sensible people. Indeed, in a way they are too sensible. That is where my dissent from them resembles Bingley's dissent from his sister. I am tempted to say that the proposed arrangement would make us much more rational 'but not near so much like a Church'.

For at first sight all the rationality (in Caroline Bingley's sense) is on the side of the innovators. We are short of priests. We have discovered in one profession after another that women can do very well all sorts of things which were once supposed to be in the power of men alone. No one among those who dislike the proposal is maintaining that women are less capable than men of piety, zeal, learning and

1. *Pride and Prejudice*, ch. xi.
2. Called the Episcopal Church in the United States.

whatever else seems necessary for the pastoral office. What, then, except prejudice begotten by tradition, forbids us to draw on the huge reserves which could pour into the priesthood if women were here, as in so many other professions, put on the same footing as men? And against this flood of common sense, the opposers (many of them women) can produce at first nothing but an inarticulate distaste, a sense of discomfort which they themselves find it hard to analyse.

That this reaction does not spring from any contempt for women is, I think, plain from history. The Middle Ages carried their reverence for one Woman to a point at which the charge could be plausibly made that the Blessed Virgin became in their eyes almost 'a fourth Person of the Trinity'. But never, so far as I know, in all those ages was anything remotely resembling a sacerdotal office attributed to her. All salvation depends on the decision which she made in the words *Ecce ancilla*,[3] she is united in nine months' inconceivable intimacy with the eternal Word; she stands at the foot of the cross.[4] But she is absent both from the Last Supper[5] and from the descent of the Spirit at Pentecost.[6] Such is the record of Scripture. Nor can you daff it aside by saying that local and temporary conditions condemned women to silence and private life. There were female preachers. One man had four daughters who all 'prophesied', i.e., preached.[7] There were prophetesses even in Old Testament times. Prophetesses, not priestesses.

At this point the common sensible reformer is apt to ask why, if women can preach, they cannot do all the rest of a priest's work. This question deepens the discomfort of my side. We begin to feel that what really divides us from our opponents is a difference between the meaning which they and we give to the word 'priest'. The more they speak (and speak truly) about the competence of women in administration, their tact and sympathy as advisers, their national talent for 'visiting', the more we feel that the central thing is being forgotten. To us a priest is primarily a representative, a double representative, who represents us to God and God to us. Our very eyes teach us this in church. Sometimes the priest turns his back on us and faces the East—he speaks to God for us: sometimes he faces us and speaks to us for God. We have no objection to a woman doing the first: the whole difficulty is about the second. But why? Why should a woman not in this sense represent God? Certainly not because she is necessarily, or even probably, less holy or less charitable or stupider than a man. In that sense she may be as 'God-like' as a man; and a given women much more so than a given man. The sense in which she cannot represent God will perhaps be plainer if we look at the thing the other way round.

Suppose the reformer stops saying that a good woman may be like God and begins saying that God is like a good woman. Suppose he says that we might just as well pray to 'Our Mother which art in heaven' as to 'Our Father'. Suppose he suggests that the Incarnation might just as well have taken a female as a male form,

3. After being told by the angel Gabriel that she has found favour with God and that she should bear the Christ Child, the Virgin exclaims 'Behold the handmaid of the Lord' (Luke i. 38). The *Magnificat* follows in verses 46–55.
4. Matthew xxvii. 55–6; Mark xv. 40–1; Luke xxiii. 49; John xix. 25.
5. Matthew xxvi. 26; Mark xiv. 22; Luke xxii. 19.
6. Acts ii. 1 *et seq.*
7. Acts xxi. 9.

and the Second Person of the Trinity be as well called the Daughter as the Son. Suppose, finally, that the mystical marriage were reversed, that the Church were the Bridegroom and Christ the Bride. All this, as it seems to me, is involved in the claim that a woman can represent God as a priest does.

Now it is surely the case that if all these supposals were ever carried into effect we should be embarked on a different religion. Goddesses have, of course, been worshipped: many religions have had priestesses. But they are religions quite different in character from Christianity. Common sense, disregarding the discomfort, or even the horror, which the idea of turning all our theological language into the feminine gender arouses in most Christians, will ask 'Why not? Since God is in fact not a biological being and has no sex, what can it matter whether we say *He* or *She*, *Father* or *Mother*, *Son* or *Daughter?'*

But Christians think that God Himself has taught us how to speak of Him. To say that it does not matter is to say either that all the masculine imagery is not inspired, is merely human in origin, or else that, though inspired, it is quite arbitrary and unessential. And this is surely intolerable: or, if tolerable, it is an argument not in favour of Christian priestesses but against Christianity. It is also surely based on a shallow view of imagery. Without drawing upon religion, we know from our poetical experience that image and apprehension cleave closer together than common sense is here prepared to admit; that a child who has been taught to pray to a Mother in Heaven would have a religious life radically different from that of a Christian child. And as image and apprehension are in an organic unity, so, for a Christian, are human body and human soul.

The innovators are really implying that sex is something superficial, irrelevant to the spiritual life. To say that men and women are equally eligible for a certain profession is to say that for the purposes of that profession their sex is irrelevant. We are, within that context, treating both as neuters. As the State grows more like a hive or an ant-hill it needs an increasing number of workers who can be treated as neuters. This may be inevitable for our secular life. But in our Christian life we must return to reality. There we are not homogeneous units, but different and complementary organs of a mystical body. Lady Nunburnholme has claimed that the equality of men and women is a Christian principle.[8] I do not remember the text in scripture nor the Fathers, nor Hooker, nor the Prayer Book which asserts it; but that is not here my point. The point is that unless 'equal' means 'interchangeable', equality makes nothing for the priesthood of women. And the kind of equality which implies that the equals are interchangeable (like counters or identical machines) is, among humans, a legal fiction. It may be a useful legal fiction. But in church we turn our back on fictions. One of the ends for which sex was created was to symbolize to us the hidden things of God. One of the functions of human marriage is to express the nature of the union between Christ and the Church. We have no authority to take the living and semitive figures which God has painted

8. Lady Marjorie Nunburnholme, 'A Petition to the Lambeth Conference', *Time and Tide*, vol. XXIX, No. 28 (10 July 1948), p. 720.

on the canvas of our nature and shift them about as if they were mere geometrical figures.

This is what common sense will call 'mystical'. Exactly. The Church claims to be the bearer of a revelation. If that claim is false then we want not to make priestesses but to abolish priests. If it is true, then we should expect to find in the Church an element which unbelievers will call irrational and which believers will call suprarational. There ought to be something in it opaque to our reason though not contrary to it—as the facts of sex and sense on the natural level are opaque. And that is the real issue. The Church of England can remain a church only if she retains this opaque element. If we abandon that, if we retain only what can be justified by standards of prudence and convenience at the bar of enlightened common sense, then we exchange revelation for that old wraith Natural Religion.

It is painful, being a man, to have to assert the privilege, or the burden, which Christianity lays upon my own sex. I am crushingly aware how inadequate most of us are, in our actual and historical individualities, to fill the place prepared for us. But it is an old saying in the army that you salute the uniform not the wearer. Only one wearing the masculine uniform can (provisionally, and till the *Parousia*)[9] represent the Lord to the Church: for we are all, corporately and individually, feminine to Him. We men may often make very bad priests. That is because we are insufficiently masculine. It is no cure to call in those who are not masculine at all. A given man may make a very bad husband; you cannot mend matters by trying to reverse the roles. He may make a bad male partner in a dance. The cure for that is that men should more diligently attend dancing classes; not that the ballroom should henceforward ignore distinctions of sex and treat all dancers as neuter. That would, of course, be eminently sensible, civilized, and enlightened, but, once more, 'not near so much like a Ball'.

And this parallel between the Church and the Ball is not so fanciful as some would think. The Church ought to be more like a Ball than it is like a factory or a political party. Or, to speak more strictly, they are at the circumference and the Church at the Centre and the Ball comes in between. The factory and the political party are artificial creations—'a breath can make them as a breath has made'. In them we are not dealing with human beings in their concrete entirety—only with 'hands' or voters. I am not of course using 'artificial' in any derogatory sense. Such artifices are necessary: but because they are our artifices we are free to shuffle, scrap and experiment as we please. But the Ball exists to stylize something which is natural and which concerns human beings in their entirety—namely, courtship. We cannot shuffle or tamper so much. With the Church, we are farther in: for there we are dealing with male and female not merely as facts of nature but as the live and awful shadows of realities utterly beyond our control and largely beyond our direct knowledge. Or rather, we are not dealing with them but (as we shall soon learn if we meddle) they are dealing with us.

---

9. The future return of Christ in glory to judge the living and the dead.

12
God in the Dock

I HAVE BEEN ASKED to write about the difficulties which a man must face in trying to present the Christian Faith to modern unbelievers. That is too wide a subject for my capacity or even for the scope of an article. The difficulties vary as the audience varies. The audience may be of this or that nation, may be children or adults, learned or ignorant. My own experience is of English audiences only, and almost exclusively of adults. It has, in fact, been mostly of men (and women) serving in the R.A F.[1] This has meant that while very few of them have been learned in the academic sense of that word, a large number of them have had a smattering of elementary practical science, have been mechanics, electricians or wireless operators; for the rank and file of the R.A.F. belong to what may almost be called 'the Intelligentsia of the Proletariat'. I have also talked to students at the Universities. These strict limitations in my experience must be kept in mind by the readers. How rash it would be to generalise from such an experience I myself discovered on the single occasion when I spoke to soldiers. It became at once clear to me that the level of intelligence in our army is very much lower than in the R.A.F. and that quite a different approach was required.

The first thing I learned from addressing the R.A.F. was that I had been mistaken in thinking materialism to be our only considerable adversary. Among the English 'Intelligentsia of the Proletariat', materialism is only one among many non-Christian creeds—Theosophy, Spiritualism, British Israelitism, etc. England has, of course, always been the home of 'cranks'; I see no sign that they are diminishing. Consistent Marxism I very seldom met. Whether this is because it is very rare, or because men speaking in the presence of their officers concealed it, or because Marxists did not attend the meetings at which I spoke, I have no means of knowing. Even where Christianity was professed, it was often much tainted with Pantheistic elements. Strict and well-informed Christian statements, when they occurred at all, usually came from Roman Catholics or from members of extreme Protestant sects (e.g., Baptists). My student audiences shared, in a less degree, the theological vagueness I found in the R.A.F., but among them strict and well-informed statements came from Anglo-Catholics and Roman Catholics; seldom, if ever, from Dissenters. The various non-Christian religions mentioned above hardly appeared.

The next thing I learned from the R.A.F. was that the English Proletariat is sceptical about History to a degree which academically educated persons can hardly imagine. This, indeed, seems to me to be far the widest cleavage between the learned and unlearned. The educated man habitually, almost without noticing it, sees the

---

1. Royal Air Force.

present as something that grows out of a long perspective of centuries. In the minds of my R.A.F. hearers this perspective simply did not exist. It seemed to me that they did not really believe that we have any reliable knowledge of historic man. But this was often curiously combined with a conviction that we knew a great deal about Pre-Historic Man: doubtless because Pre-Historic Man is labelled 'Science' (which is reliable) whereas Napoleon or Julius Caesar is labelled as 'History' (which is not). Thus a pseudo-scientific picture of the 'Cave-man' and a picture of 'the Present' filled almost the whole of their imaginations; between these, there lay only a shadowy and unimportant region in which the phantasmal shapes of Roman soldiers, stage-coaches, pirates, knights-in-armour, highwaymen, etc., moved in a mist. I had supposed that if my hearers disbelieved the Gospels, they would do so because the Gospels recorded miracles. But my impression is that they disbelieved them simply because they dealt with events that happened a long time ago: that they would be almost as incredulous of the Battle of Actium as of the Resurrection— and for the same reason. Sometimes this scepticism was defended by the argument that all books before the invention of printing must have been copied and re-copied till the text was changed beyond recognition. And here came another surprise. When their historical scepticism took that rational form, it was sometimes easily allayed by the mere statement that there existed a 'science called textual criticism' which gave us a reasonable assurance that some ancient texts were accurate. This ready acceptance of the authority of specialists is significant, not only for its ingenuousness but also because it underlines a fact of which my experiences have on the whole convinced me; i.e., that very little of the opposition we meet is inspired by malice or suspicion. It is based on genuine doubt, and often on doubt that is reasonable in the state of the doubter's knowledge.

My third discovery is of a difficulty which I suspect to be more acute in England than elsewhere. I mean the difficulty occasioned by language. In all societies, no doubt, the speech of the vulgar differs from that of the learned. The English language with its double vocabulary (Latin and native), English manners (with their boundless indulgence to slang, even in polite circles) and English culture which allows nothing like the French Academy, make the gap unusually wide. There are almost two languages in this country. The man who wishes to speak to the uneducated in English must learn their language. It is not enough that he should abstain from using what he regards as 'hard words'. He must discover empirically what words exist in the language of his audience and what they mean in that language: e.g., that *potential* means not 'possible' but 'power', that *creature* means not creature but 'animal', that *primitive* means 'rude' or 'clumsy', that *rude* means (often) 'scabrous', 'obscene', that the *Immaculate Conception* (except in the mouths of Roman Catholics) means 'the Virgin Birth'. A *Being* means 'a personal being': a man who said to me 'I believe in the Holy Ghost, but I don't think it is a being', meant: 'I believe there is such a Being, but that it is not personal.' On the other hand, *personal* sometimes means 'corporeal'. When an uneducated Englishman says that he believes 'in God, but not in a personal God', he may mean simply and solely that he is not an Anthropomorphist in the strict and original sense of that word. *Abstract* seems to have two meanings: (a) 'immaterial', (b) vague', obscure and unpractical.

Thus Arithmetic is not, in their language, an 'abstract' science. *Practical* means often 'economic' or 'utilitarian'. *Morality* nearly always means 'chastity': thus in their language the sentence 'I do not say that this woman is immoral but I do say that she is a thief,' would not be nonsense, but would mean: 'She is chaste but dishonest.' *Christian* has an eulogistic rather than a descriptive sense: e.g., 'Christian standards' means simply 'high moral standards'. The proposition 'So and so is not a Christian' would only be taken to be a criticism of his behaviour, never to be merely a statement of his beliefs. It is also important to notice that what would seem to the learned to be the harder of two words may in fact, to the uneducated, be the easier. Thus it was recently proposed to emend a prayer used in the Church of England that magistrates 'may truly and indifferently administer justice' to 'may truly and impartially administer justice'. A country priest told me that his sexton understood and could accurately explain the meaning of 'indifferently' but had no idea of what 'impartially' meant.

The popular English language, then, simply has to be learned by him who would preach to the English: just as a missionary learns Bantu before preaching to the Bantus. This is the more necessary because once the lecture or discussion has begun, digressions on the meaning of words tend to bore uneducated audiences and even to awaken distrust. There is no subject in which they are less interested than Philology. Our problem is often simply one of translation. Every examination for ordinands ought to include a passage from some standard theological work for translation into the vernacular. The work is laborious but it is immediately rewarded. By trying to translate our doctrines into vulgar speech we discover how much we understand them ourselves. Our failure to translate may sometimes be due to our ignorance of the vernacular; much more often it exposes the fact that we do not exactly know what we mean.

Apart from this linguistic difficulty, the greatest barrier I have met is the almost total absence from the minds of my audience of any sense of sin. This has struck me more forcibly when I spoke to the R.A.F. than when I spoke to students: whether (as I believe) the Proletariat is more self-righteous than other classes, or whether educated people are cleverer at concealing their pride, this creates for us a new situation. The early Christian preachers could assume in their hearers, whether Jews, *Metuentes* or Pagans, a sense of guilt. (That this was common among Pagans is shown by the fact that both Epicureanism and the Mystery Religions both claimed, though in different ways, to assuage it.) Thus the Christian message was in those days unmistakably the *Evangelium,* the Good News. It promised healing to those who knew they were sick. We have to convince our hearers of the unwelcome diagnosis before we can expect them to welcome the news of the remedy.

The ancient man approached God (or even the gods) as the accused person approaches his judge. For the modern man the roles are reversed. He is the judge: God is in the dock. He is quite a kindly judge: if God should have a reasonable defence for being the god who permits war, poverty and disease, he is ready to listen to it. The trial may even end in God's acquittal. But the important thing is that Man is on the Bench and God in the Dock.

It is generally useless to try to combat this attitude, as older preachers did, by dwelling on sins like drunkenness and unchastity. The modern Proletariat is not drunken. As for fornication, contraceptives have made a profound difference. As long as this sin might socially ruin a girl by making her the mother of a bastard, most men recognised the sin against charity which it involved, and their consciences were often troubled by it. Now that it need have no such consequences, it is not, I think, generally felt to be a sin at all. My own experience suggests that if we can awake the conscience of our hearers at all, we must do so in quite different directions. We must talk of conceit, spite, jealousy, cowardice, meanness, etc. But I am very far from believing that I have found the solution of this problem.

Finally, I must add that my own work has suffered very much from the incurable intellectualism of my approach. The simple, emotional appeal ('Come to Jesus') is still often successful. But those who, like myself, lack the gift for making it, had better not attempt it.

13
Behind the Scenes

WHEN I WAS TAKEN to the theatre as a small boy what interested me most of all was the stage scenery. The interest was not an aesthetic one. No doubt the gardens, balconies and palaces of the Edwardian 'sets' looked prettier to me than they would now, but that had nothing to do with it. Ugly scenery would have served my turn just as well. Still less did I mistake these canvas images for realities. On the contrary, I believed (and wished) all things on the stage to be more artificial than they actually were.

When an actor came on in ordinary modern clothes I never believed he was wearing a real suit with veritable waistcoat and trousers put on in the ordinary way. I thought he was wearing—and I somehow felt he ought to be wearing—some kind of theatrical overalls which were slipped on all in one piece and fastened invisibly up the back. The stage suit ought not to be a suit; it ought to be something quite different which nevertheless (that's where the pleasure comes) looked like a suit from the stalls. Perhaps this is why I continued, even after I was grown up, to believe in the Cold Tea theory; until a real actor pointed out that a man who played a leading part in a London theatre could afford to, and would certainly rather, provide real whisky (if need were) at his own charges than drink a tumbler of cold tea every evening shortly after his dinner.

No. I knew very well that the scenery was painted canvas; that the stage rooms and stage trees, seen from behind, would not look like rooms or trees at all. That was where the interest lay. That was the fascination of our toy theatre at home, where we made our own scenery. You cut out your piece of cardboard in the shape of a tower and you painted it, and then you gummed an ordinary nursery block on to the back to make it stand upright. The rapture was to dart to and fro. You went in front and there was your tower. You went behind and there—raw, brown cardboard and a block.

In the real theatre you couldn't go 'behind', but you knew it would be the same. The moment the actor vanished into the wings he entered a different world. One knew it was not a world of any particular beauty or wonder; somebody must have told me—at any rate I believed—it would be a rather dingy world of bare floors and whitewashed walls. The charm lay in the idea of being able thus to pass in and out of a world by taking three strides.

One wanted to be an actor not (at that age) for the sake of fame or applause, but simply that one might have this privilege of transition. To come from dressing rooms and bare walls and utilitarian corridors—and to come suddenly—into Aladdin's cave or the Darlings' nursery or whatever it was—to become what you weren't and be where you weren't—this seemed most enviable.

It was best of all when the door at the back of the stage room opened to show a little piece of passage—unreal passage, of course, its panels only canvas, intended to suggest (which one knew to be false) that the sham room on the stage was part of a whole house. 'You can just see a little *peep* of the passage in Looking-glass House . . . and it's very like our passage as far as you can see, only you know it may be quite different on beyond.' Thus Alice to the Kitten.[1] But the stage passage did not leave one to conjecture. One *knew* it was quite different 'on beyond', that it ceased to be a passage at all.

I envied the children in stage boxes. If one sat so far to the side as that, then by craning one's neck one might squint along the sham passage and actually see the point at which it ceased to exist: the joint between the real and the apparent.

Years afterwards I was 'behind'. The stage was set for an Elizabethan play. The back-cloth represented a palace front, with a practicable balcony on it. I stood (from one point of view) on that palace balcony; that is (from the other point of view) I stood on a plank supported by trestles looking out through a square hole in a sheet of canvas. It was a most satisfactory moment.

Now what, I wonder, is behind all this? And what, if anything, comes of it? I have no objection to the inclusion of Freudian explanations provided they are not allowed to exclude all others. It may, as I suppose someone will think, be mixed up with infantile curiosities about the female body. It doesn't feel at all like that. 'Of course not', they'll reply. 'You mustn't expect it to; no more than—let's see what would be a good parallel—why, no more than the stage rooms and forests look (from the front) like a collection of oddly shaped lath-and-canvas objects grouped in front of the dusty, draughty, whitewashed place "behind".'

The parallel is fairly exact. The complex, worming its way along in the unimaginable Unconscious, and then suddenly transforming itself (and gaining admission only by that transformation) as it steps into the only 'mind' I can ever directly know, is really very like the actor, with his own unhistrionic expression, walking along that bare, draughty 'off-stage' and then suddenly appearing as Mr Darling in the nursery or Aladdin in the cave.

But oddly enough we could fit the Freudian theory into the pleasure I started with quite as easily as we fit it into the Freudian theory. Is not our pleasure (even I take some) in Depth Psychology itself one instance of this pleasure in the contrast between 'behind the scenes' and 'on stage'? I begin to wonder whether that theatrical antithesis moves us because it is a ready-made symbol of something universal.

All sorts of things are, in fact, doing just what the actor does when he comes through the wings. Photons or waves (or whatever it is) come towards us from the sun through space. They are, in a scientific sense, 'light'. But as they enter the air they become 'light' in a different sense: what ordinary people call *sunlight* or *day*, the bubble of blue or grey or greenish luminosity in which we walk about and see. Day is thus a kind of stage set.

Other waves (this time, of air) reach my eardrum and travel up a nerve and tickle my brain. All this is behind the scenes, as soundless as the whitewashed passages are undramatic. Then somehow (I've never seen it explained) they step on to the

1. 'Lewis Carroll', *Through the Looking-Glass and What Alice Found There*, ch. 1.

stage (no one can tell me *where* this stage is) and become, say, a friend's voice or the *Ninth Symphony*. Or, of course, my neighbour's wireless—the actor may come on stage to play a drivelling part in a bad play. But there is always the transformation.

Biological needs, producing, or stimulated by, temporary physiological states, climb into a young man's brain, pass on to the mysterious stage and appear as 'Love'—it may be (since all sorts of plays are performed there) the love celebrated by Dante, or it may be the love of a Guido[2] or a Mr Guppy.[3]

We can call this the contrast of Reality and Appearance. But perhaps the fact of having first met it in the theatre will protect us from the threat of derogation which lurks in the word Appearance. For in the theatre of course the play, the 'appearance', is the thing. All the backstage 'realities' exist only for its sake and are valuable only in so far as they promote it. A good, neutral parable is Schopenhauer's story of the two Japanese who attend an English theatre. One devoted himself to trying to understand the play although he did not know a word of the language. The other devoted himself to trying to understand how the scenery, lighting and other machinery worked, though he had never been behind the scenes in a theatre. 'Here', said Schopenhauer, 'you have the philosopher and the scientist.'[4] But for 'philosopher' he might also have written 'poet', 'lover', 'worshipper', 'citizen', 'moral agent' or 'plain man'.

But notice that in two ways Schopenhauer's parable breaks down. The first Japanese could have taken steps to learn English; but have we ever been given any grammar or dictionary, can we find the teacher, of the language in which this universal drama is being performed? Some (I among them) would say Yes; others would say No; the debate continues. And the second Japanese could have taken steps—could have pulled wires and got introductions—to win admission behind the scenes and see the off-stage things for himself. At the very least he knew there were such things.

We lack both these advantages. Nobody ever can go 'behind'. No one can, in any ordinary sense, meet or experience a photon, a sound wave or the unconscious. (That may be one reason why 'going behind' in the theatre is exciting; we are doing what, in most cases, is impossible.) We are not even, in the last resort, absolutely sure that such things exist. They are constructs, things assumed to account for our experience, but never to be experienced themselves. They may be assumed with great probability; but they are, after all, hypothetical.

Even the off-stage existence of the actors is hypothetical. Perhaps they do not exist before they enter the scene. And, if they do, then, since we cannot go behind, they may, in their off-stage life and character, be very unlike what we suppose and very unlike one another.

---

2. One of the principal characters in Robert Browning's *The Ring and the Book.*
3. A character in Charles Dickens' *Bleak House.*
4. Lewis was probably recalling from memory the parable in Arthur Schopenhauer's *Studies in Pessimism* which runs: 'Two Chinamen travelling in Europe went to the theatre for the first time. One of them did nothing but study the machinery, and he succeeded in finding out how it was worked. The other tried to get at the meaning of the piece in spite of his ignorance of the language. Here you have the Astronomer and the Philosopher.' The parable is found in Schopenhauer's *Essays from the Parerga and Paralipomena,* trans. T. Bailey Saunders (London, 1951), pp. 80-1.

14
Revival or Decay?

BUT WOULD YOU DENY', said the Headmaster, 'that there is, here in the West, a great, even growing, interest in religion?'

It is not the sort of question I find easy to answer. *Great* and *growing* would seem more to involve statistics, and I had no statistics. I supposed there was a fairly widespread interest. But I didn't feel sure the Headmaster was interpreting it correctly. In the days when most people had a religion, what he meant by 'an interest in religion' could hardly have existed. For of course religious people—that is, people when they are being religious—are not 'interested in religion'. Men who have gods worship those gods; it is the spectators who describe this as 'religion'. The Maenads thought about Dionysus, not about religion. *Mutatis mutandis* this goes for Christians too. The moment a man seriously accepts a deity his interest in 'religion' is at an end. He's got something else to think about. The ease with which we can now get an audience for a discussion of religion does not prove that more people are becoming religious. What it really proves is the existence of a large 'floating vote'. Every conversion will reduce this potential audience.

Once the climate of opinion allows such a floating vote to form I see no reason why it should speedily diminish. Indecision, often very honest, is very natural. It would be foolish, however, not to realise that it is also no hardship. Floating is a very agreeable operation; a decision either way costs something. Real Christianity and consistent Atheism both make demands on a man. But to admit, on occasion, and as possibilities, all the comforts of the one without its discipline—to enjoy all the liberty of the other without its philosophical and emotional abstinences—well, this may be honest, but there's no good pretending it is uncomfortable.

'And would you, further, deny', said the Headmaster, 'that Christianity commands more respect in the most highly educated circles than it has done for centuries? The Intelligentsia are coming over. Look at men like Maritain, like Bergson, like—'

But I didn't feel at all happy about this. Of course the converted Intellectual is a characteristic figure of our times. But this phenomenon would be more hopeful if it had not occurred at a moment when the Intelligentsia (scientists apart) are losing all touch with, and all influence over, nearly the whole human race. Our most esteemed poets and critics are read by our most esteemed critics and poets (who don't usually like them much) and nobody else takes any notice. An increasing number of highly literate people simply ignore what the 'Highbrows' are doing. It says nothing to them. The Highbrows in return ignore or insult them. Conversions from the Intelligentsia are not therefore likely to be very widely influential. They may even raise a horrid suspicion that Christianity itself has become a part of the general 'Highbrow racket', has been adopted, like Surrealism and the pictures painted by chimpanzees, as one more method of 'shocking the bourgeois'. This would be dreadfully uncharitable, no doubt; but then the Intelligentsia have said a great many uncharitable things about the others.

'Then again', boomed the Headmaster, 'even where there is, or is as yet, no explicit religion, do we not see a vast rallying to the defence of those standards which, whether recognised or not, make part of our spiritual heritage? The Western—may I not say the Christian—values . . .'

We all winced. And to me in particular there came back the memory of a corrugated iron hut used as an R.A.F. chapel—a few kneeling airmen—and a young chaplain uttering the prayer, 'Teach us, O Lord, to love *the things Thou standest for.*' He was perfectly sincere, and I willingly believe that the *things* in question included something more and better than 'the Western values', whatever those may be. And yet . . . his words seemed to me to imply a point of view incompatible with Christianity or indeed with any serious Theism whatever. God is not, for it, the goal or end. He is (and how fortunate!) enlightened; has, or 'stands for', the right ideals. He is valued for that reason. He ranks, admittedly, as a leader. But of course a leader leads to something beyond himself. That something else is the real goal. This is miles away from 'Thou hast made us for Thyself and our heart has no rest till it comes to Thee.' The Maenads were more religious.

'And the substitutes for religion are being discredited,' continued the Headmaster. 'Science has become more a bogy than a god. The Marxist heaven on earth—'

And only the other day a lady told me that a girl to whom she had mentioned death replied 'Oh, but by the time I'm *that* age Science will have done something about it.' And then I remembered how often, in disputing before simple audiences, I had found the assured belief that whatever was wrong with man would in the long run (and not so very long a run either) be put right by 'Education'. And that led me to think of all the 'approaches' to 'religion' I actually meet. An anonymous postcard tells me that I ought to be flogged at the cart's tail for professing to believe in the Virgin Birth. A distinguished literary atheist to whom I am introduced mutters, looks away, and walks swiftly to the far end of the room. An unknown American writes to ask me whether Elijah's fiery chariot was really a Flying Saucer. I encounter Theosophists, British Israelites, Spiritualists, Pantheists. Why do people like the Headmaster always talk about 'religion'? Why not religions? We seethe with religions. Christianity, I am pleased to note, is one of them. I get letters from saints, who have no notion they are any such thing, showing in every line radiant faith, joy, humility, and even humour, in appalling suffering. I get others from converts who want to apologise for some small incivility they committed against me in print years ago.

These bits and pieces are all 'the West' I really know at first hand. They escape the Headmaster's treatment. He speaks from books and articles. The real sanctities, hatreds, and lunacies which surround us are hardly represented there. Still less, the great negative factor. It is something more than ignorance as he would understand the word. Most people's thinking lacks a dimension which he takes for granted. Two instances may make the distinction clear. Once, after I had said something on the air about Natural Law, an old Colonel (obviously *anima candida*)[1] wrote to say that this had interested him very much and could I just tell him of 'some handy little *brochure* which dealt with the subject fully'. That is ignorance, striking only in degree. Here is the other. A vet, a workman, and I were wearily stumbling about on a Home Guard patrol in the small hours. The vet and I got talking about the causes of wars and arrived at the conclusion that we must expect them to recur. 'But—but—but—' gasped the workman. There was a moment's silence, and he broke out, 'But then what's the good of the ruddy world going on?' I got a very clear impression of what was happening. For the first time in his life a really ultimate question was before him. The sort of thing we have been considering all our lives—the meaning of existence—had just broken upon him. It was a wholly new dimension.

Is there a homogeneous 'West'? I doubt it. Everything that can go on is going on all round us. Religions buzz about us like bees. A serious sex worship—quite different from the cheery lechery endemic in our species—is one of them. Traces of embryonic religions occur in science-fiction. Meanwhile, as always, the Christian way too is followed. But nowadays, when it is not followed, it need not be feigned. That fact covers a good deal of what is called the decay of religion. Apart from that, is the present so very different from other ages or 'the West' from anywhere else?

1. 'a candid, frank soul.'

15
Before We Can
Communicate

I HAVE BEEN ASKED to write about 'the problem of communication'; by which my inquirer meant 'communication under modern conditions between Christians and the outer world'. And, as usually happens to me when I am questioned, I feel a little embarrassed by the simplicity and unexcitingness of the answer I want to give. I feel that what I have to say is on a cruder and lower level than was hoped for.

My ideas about 'communication' are purely empirical, and two anecdotes (both strictly true) will illustrate the sort of experience on which they are based.

1. The old Prayer Book prayed that the magistrates might 'truly and indifferently administer justice'. Then the revisers thought they would make this easier by altering *indifferently* to *impartially*. A country clergyman of my acquaintance asked his sexton what he thought *indifferently* meant, and got the correct answer, 'It means making no difference between one chap and another.' 'And what', continued the parson, 'do you think *impartially* means?' 'Ah', said the sexton after a pause, 'I wouldn't know *that.*'

Everyone sees what the revisers had in mind. They were afraid that the 'man in the pew' would take *indifferently* to mean, as it often does, 'carelessly', without concern. They knew that this error would not be made by highly-educated people, but they thought it would be made by everyone else. The sexton's reply, however, reveals that it will not be made by the least educated class of all. It will be made only by those who are educationally in the middle; those whose language is fashionable (our elders would have said 'polite') without being scholarly. The highest and lowest classes are both equally safe from it; and *impartially*, which guards the 'middle' churchgoers from misunderstanding, is meaningless to the simple.

2. During the war I got into a discussion with a working man about the Devil. He said he believed in a Devil, but 'not a personal Devil'. As the discussion proceeded it grew more and more perplexing to both parties. It became clear that we were somehow at cross-purposes. Then, suddenly and almost by accident, I discovered what was wrong. It became obvious that he had, all along, been meaning by the word *personal* nothing more or less or other than *corporeal.* He was a very intelligent man, and, once this discovery had been made, there was no difficulty. Apparently we had not really disagreed about anything: the difference between us was merely one of vocabulary. It set me wondering how many of the thousands of people who say they 'believe in God but not in a personal God' are really trying to tell us no more than that they are not, in the strict sense, *anthropomorphists* and are, in fact, asserting, on this point, their perfect orthodoxy.

Where the revisers of the Prayer Book and I both went wrong was this. We both had *a priori* notions of what simple people mean by words. I assumed that the workman's usage was the same as my own. The revisers, more subtly but not more correctly, assumed that all would know the sense of *indifferently* which they were guarding against when they amended it. But apparently we must not decide *a priori* what other people mean by English words any more than what Frenchmen mean by French words. We must be wholly empirical. We must listen, and note, and memorise. And of course we must set aside every trace of snobbery or pedantry about 'right' or 'wrong' usages.

Now this is, I feel, very hum-drum and work-a-day. When one wants to discuss the problem of communication on a grand, philosophical level, when one wants to talk about conflicts of *Weltanschauung* and the predicament of modern, or urban, or crisis consciousness, it is chilling to be told that the first step is simply linguistic in the crudest sense. But it is.

What we want to see in every ordination exam is a compulsory paper on (simply) translation; a passage from some theological work to be turned into plain vernacular English. Just turned; not adorned, nor diluted, nor made 'matey'. The exercise is very like doing Latin prose. Instead of saying, 'How would Cicero have said that?', you have to ask yourself, 'How would my scout or bedmaker have said that?'

You will at once find that this labour has two useful by-products.

1. In the very process of eliminating from your matter all that is technical, learned, or allusive, you will discover, perhaps for the first time, the true value of learned language: namely, brevity. It can say in ten words what popular speech can hardly get into a hundred. Your popularisation of the passage set will have to be very much longer than the original. And this we must just put up with.

2. You will also discover—at least I, a copious 'translator', think I have discovered—just how much you yourself have, up to that moment, been understanding the language which you are now trying to translate. Again and again I have been most usefully humiliated in this way. One holds, or thinks one holds, a particular view, say, of the Atonement or Orders or Inspiration. And you can go on for years discussing and defending it to others *of your own sort*. New refinements can be introduced to meet its critics; brilliant metaphors can seem to illuminate its obscurities; comparisons with other views, 'placings' of it, are somehow felt to establish its position in a sort of aristocracy of ideas. For the others are all talking the same language and all move in the same world of discourse. All seems well. Then turn and try to expound this same view to an intelligent mechanic or a sincerely inquisitive, but superficially quite irreverent, schoolboy. Some question of shattering crudity (it would never be asked in learned circles) will be shot at you. You are like a skilled swordsman transfixed by an opponent who wins just because he knows none of the first principles. The crude question turns out to be fatal. You have never, it now appears, really understood what you have so long maintained. You haven't really thought it out; not to the end; not to 'the absolute ruddy end'.

You must either give it up, or else begin it all over again. If, given patience and ordinary skill, you cannot explain a thing to any sensible person whatever (provided he will listen), then you don't really understand it yourself. Here too it is very like doing Latin prose; the bits you can't get into Latin are usually the bits you haven't really grasped in the English.

What we need to be particularly on our guard against are precisely the vogue-words, the incantatory words, of our own circle. For your generation they are, perhaps, *engagement, commitment, over against, under judgment, existential, crisis,* and *confrontation.* These are, of all expressions, the least likely to be intelligible to anyone divided from you by a school of thought, by a decade, by a social class. They are like a family language, or a school slang. And our private language may delude ourselves as well as mystifying outsiders. Enchanted words seem so full of meaning, so illuminating. But we may be deceived. What we derive from them may sometimes be not so much a clear conception as a heart-warming sense of being at home and among our own sort. 'We understand one another' often means 'We are in sympathy.' Sympathy is a good thing. It may even be in some ways a better thing than intellectual understanding. But not the same thing.

16
Cross-Examination

[The following is an interview with C. S. Lewis, held on the 7th May 1963 in Lewis's rooms in Magdalene College, Cambridge. The interviewer is Mr. Sherwood E. Wirt of the Billy Graham Evangelistic Association Ltd.]

Mr Wirt:

Professor Lewis, if you had a young friend with some interest in writing on Christian subjects, how would you advise him to prepare himself?

Lewis:

I would say if a man is going to write on chemistry, he learns chemistry. The same is true of Christianity. But to speak of the craft itself, I would not know how to advise a man how to write. It is a matter of talent and interest. I believe he must be strongly moved if he is to become a writer. Writing is like a 'lust', or like 'scratching when you itch'. Writing comes as a result of a very strong impulse, and when it does come, I for one must get it out.

Mr Wirt:

Can you suggest an approach that would spark the creation of a body of Christian literature strong enough to influence our generation?

Lewis:

There is no formula in these matters. I have no recipe, no tablets. Writers are trained in so many individual ways that it is not for us to prescribe. Scripture itself is not systematic; the New Testament shows the greatest variety. God has shown us that he can use any instrument. Balaam's ass, you remember, preached a very effective sermon in the midst of his 'hee-haws'.[1]

Mr Wirt:

A light touch has been characteristic of your writings, even when you are dealing with heavy theological themes. Would you say there is a key to the cultivation of such an attitude?

Lewis:

I believe this is a matter of temperament. However, I was helped in achieving this attitude by my studies of the literary men of the Middle Ages, and by the writings of G. K. Chesterton. Chesterton, for example, was not afraid to combine seri-

1. Numbers xxii. 1–35.

ous Christian themes with buffoonery. In the same way, the miracle plays of the Middle Ages would deal with a sacred subject such as the nativity of Christ, yet would combine it with a farce.

Mr Wirt:
    Should Christian writers, then, in your opinion, attempt to be funny?

Lewis:
    No. I think that forced jocularities on spiritual subjects are an abomination, and the attempts of some religious writers to be humorous are simply appalling. Some people write heavily, some write lightly. I prefer the light approach because I believe there is a great deal of false reverence about. There is too much solemnity and intensity in dealing with sacred matters; too much speaking in holy tones.

Mr Wirt:
    But is not solemnity proper and conducive to a sacred atmosphere?

Lewis:
    Yes and no. There is a difference between a private devotional life and a corporate one. Solemnity is proper in church, but things that are proper in church are not necessarily proper outside, and vice versa. For example, I can say a prayer while washing my teeth, but that does not mean I should wash my teeth in church.

Mr Wirt:
    What is your opinion of the kind of writing being done within the Christian church today?

Lewis:
    A great deal of what is being published by writers in the religious tradition is a scandal and is actually turning people away from the church. The liberal writers who are continually accommodating and whittling down the truth of the Gospel are responsible. I cannot understand how a man can appear in print claiming to disbelieve everything that he presupposes when he puts on the surplice. I feel it is a form of prostitution.

Mr Wirt:
    What do you think of the controversial new book, *Honest to God*, by John Robinson, the Bishop of Woolwich?

Lewis:
    I prefer being honest to being 'honest to God'.

Mr Wirt:
    What Christian writers have helped you?

Lewis:

The contemporary book that has helped me the most is Chesterton's *The Everlasting Man.* Others are Edwyn Bevan's book, *Symbolism and Belief,* and Rudolf Otto's *The Idea of the Holy,* and the plays of Dorothy Sayers.[2]

Mr Wirt:

I believe it was Chesterton who was asked why he became a member of the church, and he replied, 'To get rid of my sins.'

Lewis:

It is not enough to want to get rid of one's sins. We also need to believe in the One who saves us from our sins. Not only do we need to recognize that we are sinners; we need to believe in a Saviour who takes away sin. Matthew Arnold once wrote, 'Nor does the being hungry prove that we have bread.' Because we are sinners, it does not follow that we are saved.

Mr Wirt:

In your book *Surprised by Joy* you remark that you were brought into the Faith kicking and struggling and resentful, with eyes darting in every direction looking for an escape.[3] You suggest that you were compelled, as it were, to become a Christian. Do you feel that you made a decision at the time of your conversion?

Lewis:

I would not put it that way. What I wrote in *Surprised by Joy* was that 'before God closed in on me, I was in fact offered what now appears a moment of wholly free choice.'[4] But I feel my decision was not so important. I was the object rather than the subject in this affair. I was decided upon. I was glad afterwards at the way it came out, but at the moment what I heard was God saying, 'Put down your gun and we'll talk.'

Mr Wirt:

That sounds to me as if you came to a very definite point of decision.

Lewis:

Well, I would say that the most deeply compelled action is also the freest action. By that I mean, no part of you is outside the action. It is a paradox. I expressed it in *Surprised by Joy* by saying that I chose, yet it really did not seem possible to do the opposite.[5]

2. Such as *The Man Born to Be King* (London, 1943; reprinted Grand Rapids, 1970).
3. (London, 1955), ch. xiv, p. 215.
4. *Ibid.,* p. 211.
5. *Ibid.*

Mr Wirt:

You wrote 20 years ago that 'A man who was merely a man and said the sort of things Jesus said would not be a great moral teacher. He would either be a lunatic—on a level with the man who says he is a poached egg—or else he would be the Devil of Hell. You must make your choice. Either this man was, and is, the Son of God: or else a madman or something worse. You can shut Him up for a fool, you can spit at Him and kill Him as a demon; or you can fall at His feet and call Him Lord and God. But let us not come with any patronizing nonsense about His being a great human teacher. He has not left that open to us. He did not intend to.'[6] Would you say your view of this matter has changed since then?

Lewis:

I would say there is no substantial change.

Mr Wirt:

Would you say that the aim of Christian writing, including your own writing, is to bring about an encounter of the reader with Jesus Christ?

Lewis:

That is not my language, yet it is the purpose I have in view. For example, I have just finished a book on prayer, an imaginary correspondence with someone who raises questions about difficulties in prayer.[7]

Mr Wirt:

How can we foster the encounter of people with Jesus Christ?

Lewis:

You can't lay down any pattern for God. There are many different ways of bringing people into His Kingdom, even some ways that I specially dislike! I have therefore learned to be cautious in my judgment.

But we can block it in many ways. As Christians we are tempted to make unnecessary concessions to those outside the Faith. We give in too much. Now, I don't mean that we should run the risk of making a nuisance of ourselves by witnessing at improper times, but there comes a time when we must show that we disagree. We must show our Christian colours, if we are to be true to Jesus Christ. We cannot remain silent or concede everything away.

There is a character in one of my children's stories named Aslan, who says, 'I never tell anyone any story except his own.'[8] I cannot speak for the way God deals with others; I only know how He deals with me personally. Of course, we are to pray for spiritual awakening, and in various ways we can do something toward it.

---

6. *Mere Christianity* (London, 1952), ch. iii, p. 42.
7. He is speaking of his *Letters to Malcolm: Chiefly on Prayer* (London, 1964).
8. Except for slight variations in the wording, Aslan says this to two children who ask Him about other people's lives in *The Horse and His Boy* (London, 1954), ch. xi, p. 147 and ch. xiv, p. 180.

But we must remember that neither Paul nor Apollos gives the increase.[9] As Charles Williams once said, 'The altar must often be built in one place so that the fire may come down in another place.'[10]

Mr Wirt:

Professor Lewis, your writings have an unusual quality not often found in discussions of Christian themes. You write as though you enjoyed it.

Lewis:

If I didn't enjoy writing I wouldn't continue to do it. Of all my books, there was only one I did not take pleasure in writing.

Mr Wirt:

Which one?

Lewis:

The Screwtape Letters. They were dry and gritty going. At the time, I was thinking of objections to the Christian life, and decided to put them into the form, 'That's what the devil would say.' But making goods 'bad' and bads 'good' gets to be fatiguing.

Mr Wirt:

How would you suggest a young Christian writer go about developing a style?

Lewis:

The way for a person to develop a style is (a) to know exactly what he wants to say, and (b) to be sure he is saying exactly that. The reader, we must remember, does not start by knowing what we mean. If our words are ambiguous, our meaning will escape him. I sometimes think that writing is like driving sheep down a road. If there is any gate open to the left or the right the readers will most certainly go into it.

Mr Wirt:

Do you believe that the Holy Spirit can speak to the world through Christian writers today?

Lewis:

I prefer to make no judgment concerning a writer's direct 'illumination' by the Holy Spirit. I have no way of knowing whether what is written is from heaven or not. I do believe that God is the Father of lights—natural lights as well as spiritual lights (James i. 17). That is, God is not interested only in Christian writers as such. He is concerned with all kinds of writing. In the same way a sacred calling is not

9. I Corinthians iii. 6.
10. 'Usually the way must be made ready for heaven, and then it will come by some other; the sacrifice must be made ready, and the fire will strike on another altar.' Charles Williams, *He Came Down from Heaven* (London, 1938), ch. ii, p. 25.

limited to ecclesiastical functions. The man who is weeding a field of turnips is also serving God.

Mr Wirt:

An American writer, Mr Dewey Beegle, has stated that in his opinion the Isaac Watts hymn, 'When I Survey the Wondrous Cross', is more inspired by God than is the 'Song of Solomon' in the Old Testament. What would be your view?

Lewis:

The great saints and mystics of the church have felt just the opposite about it. They have found tremendous spiritual truth in the 'Song of Solomon'. There is a difference of levels here. The question of the canon is involved. Also we must remember that what is meat for a grown person might be unsuited to the palate of a child.

Mr Wirt:

How would you evaluate modern literary trends as exemplified by such writers as Ernest Hemingway, Samuel Beckett and Jean-Paul Sartre?

Lewis:

I have read very little in this field. I am not a contemporary scholar. I am not even a scholar of the past, but I am a lover of the past.

Mr Wirt:

Do you believe that the use of filth and obscenity is necessary in order to establish a realistic atmosphere in contemporary literature?

Lewis:

I do not. I treat this development as a symptom, a sign of a culture that has lost its faith. Moral collapse follows upon spiritual collapse. I look upon the immediate future with great apprehension.

Mr Wirt:

Do you feel, then, that modern culture is being de-Christianized?

Lewis:

I cannot speak to the political aspects of the question, but I have some definite views about the de-Christianizing of the church. I believe that there are many accommodating preachers, and too many practitioners in the church who are not believers. Jesus Christ did not say 'Go into all the world and tell the world that it is quite right.' The Gospel is something completely different. In fact, it is directly opposed to the world.

The case against Christianity that is made out in the world is quite strong. Every war, every shipwreck, every cancer case, every calamity, contributes to making a *prima facie* case against Christianity. It is not easy to be a believer in the face of this surface evidence. It calls for a strong faith in Jesus Christ.

Mr Wirt:

Do you approve of men such as Bryan Green and Billy Graham asking people to come to a point of decision regarding the Christian life?

Lewis:

I had the pleasure of meeting Billy Graham once. We had dinner together during his visit to Cambridge University in 1955, while he was conducting a mission to students. I thought he was a very modest and a very sensible man, and I liked him very much indeed.

In a civilization like ours, I feel that everyone has to come to terms with the claims of Jesus Christ upon his life, or else be guilty of inattention or of evading the question. In the Soviet Union it is different. Many people living in Russia today have never had to consider the claims of Christ because they have never heard of those claims.

In the same way, we who live in English-speaking countries have never really been forced to consider the claims, let us say, of Hinduism. But in our Western civilization we are obligated both morally and intellectually to come to grips with Jesus Christ; if we refuse to do so we are guilty of being bad philosophers and bad thinkers.

Mr Wirt:

What is your view of the daily discipline of the Christian life—the need for taking time to be alone with God?

Lewis:

We have our New Testament regimental orders upon the subject. I would take it for granted that everyone who becomes a Christian would undertake this practice. It is enjoined upon us by Our Lord; and since they are His commands, I believe in following them. It is always just possible that Jesus Christ meant what He said when He told us to seek the secret place and to close the door.[11]

Mr Wirt:

What do you think is going to happen in the next few years of history, Mr Lewis?

Lewis:

I have no way of knowing. My primary field is the past. I travel with my back to the engine, and that makes it difficult when you try to steer. The world might stop in ten minutes; meanwhile, we are to go on doing our duty. The great thing is to be found at one's post as a child of God, living each day as though it were our last, but planning as though our world might last a hundred years.

We have, of course, the assurance of the New Testament regarding events to come.[12] I find it difficult to keep from laughing when I find people worrying about future destruction of some kind or other. Didn't they know they were going to die

---

11. Matthew vi. 5–6.
12. Matthew xxiv. 4–44; Mark xiii. 5–27; Luke xxi. 8–33.

anyway? Apparently not. My wife once asked a young woman friend whether she had ever thought of death, and she replied, 'By the time I reach that age science will have done something about it!'

Mr Wirt:

Do you think there will be wide-spread travel in space?

Lewis:

I look forward with horror to contact with the other inhabited planets, if there are such. We would only transport to them all of our sin and our acquisitiveness, and establish a new colonialism. I can't bear to think of it. But if we on earth were to get right with God, of course, all would be changed. Once we find ourselves spiritually awakened, we can go to outer space and take the good things with us. That is quite a different matter.

PART III

I

'Bulverism'

or, the Foundation of 20th Century Thought

IT IS A disastrous discovery, as Emerson says somewhere, that we exist. I mean, it is disastrous when instead of merely attending to a rose we are forced to think of ourselves looking at the rose, with a certain type of mind and a certain type of eyes. It is disastrous because, if you are not very careful, the colour of the rose gets attributed to our optic nerves and its scent to our noses, and in the end there is no rose left. The professional philosophers have been bothered about this universal black-out for over two hundred years, and the world has not much listened to them. But the same disaster is now occurring on a level we can all understand.

We have recently 'discovered that we exist' in two new senses. The Freudians have discovered that we exist as bundles of complexes. The Marxians have discovered that we exist as members of some economic class. In the old days it was supposed that if a thing seemed obviously true to a hundred men, then it was probably true in fact. Nowadays the Freudian will tell you to go and analyze the hundred: you will find that they all think Elizabeth [I] a great queen because they all have a mother-complex. Their thoughts are psychologically tainted at the source. And the Marxist will tell you to go and examine the economic interests of the hundred; you will find that they all think freedom a good thing because they are all members of the bourgeoisie whose prosperity is increased by a policy of *laissez-faire*. Their thoughts are 'ideologically tainted' at the source.

Now this is obviously great fun; but it has not always been noticed that there is a bill to pay for it. There are two questions that people who say this kind of things ought to be asked. The first is, Are *all* thoughts thus tainted at the source, or only some? The second is, Does the taint invalidate the tainted thought—in the sense of making it untrue—or not?

If they say that *all thoughts* are thus tainted, then, of course, we must remind them that Freudianism and Marxism are as much systems of thought as Christian theology or philosophical idealism. The Freudian and the Marxian are in the same boat with all the rest of us, and cannot criticize us from outside. They have sawn off the branch they were sitting on. If, on the other hand, they say that the taint need not invalidate their thinking, then neither need it invalidate ours. In which case they have saved their own branch, but also saved ours along with it.

The only line they can really take is to say that some thoughts are tainted and others are not—which has the advantage (if Freudians and Marxians regard it as an advantage) of being what every sane man has always believed. But if that is so, we must then ask how you find out which are tainted and which are not. It is no earthly use saying that those are tainted which agree with the secret wishes of the thinker. *Some* of the things I should like to believe must in fact be true; it is impossible to arrange a universe which contradicts everyone's wishes, in every respect, at every moment. Suppose I think, after doing my accounts, that I have a large balance at the bank. And suppose you want to find out whether this belief of mine is 'wishful thinking'. You can never come to any conclusion by examining my psychological condition. Your only chance of finding out is to sit down and work through the sum yourself. When you have checked my figures, then, and then only, will you know whether I have that balance or not. If you find my arithmetic correct, then no amount of vapouring about my psychological condition can be anything but a waste of time. If you find my arithmetic wrong, then it may be relevant to explain psychologically how I came to be so bad at my arithmetic, and the doctrine of the concealed wish will become relevant—but only *after* you have yourself done the sum and discovered me to be wrong on purely arithmetical grounds. It is the same with all thinking and all systems of thought. If you try to find out which are tainted by speculating about the wishes of the thinkers, you are merely making a fool of yourself. You must first find out on purely logical grounds which of them do, in fact, break down as arguments. Afterwards, if you like, go on and discover the psychological causes of the error.

In other words, you must show *that* a man is wrong before you start explaining *why* he is wrong. The modern method is to assume without discussion *that* he is wrong and then distract his attention from this (the only real issue) by busily explaining how he became so silly. In the course of the last fifteen years I have found this vice so common that I have had to invent a name for it. I call it Bulverism. Some day I am going to write the biography of its imaginary inventor, Ezekiel Bulver, whose destiny was determined at the age of five when he heard his mother say to his father—who had been maintaining that two sides of a triangle were together greater than the third—'Oh you say that *because you are a man.*' 'At that moment', E. Bulver assures us, 'there flashed across my opening mind the great truth that refutation is no necessary part of argument. Assume that your opponent is wrong, and then explain his error, and the world will be at your feet. Attempt to prove that he is wrong or (worse still) try to find out whether he is wrong or right, and the national dynamism of our age will thrust you to the wall.' That is how Bulver became one of the makers of the Twentieth Century.

I find the fruits of his discovery almost everywhere. Thus I see my religion dismissed on the grounds that 'the comfortable parson had every reason for assuring the nineteenth century worker that poverty would be rewarded in another world'. Well, no doubt he had. On the assumption that Christianity is an error, I can see early enough that some people would still have a motive for inculcating it. I see it so easily that I can, of course, play the game the other way round, by saying that 'the modern man has every reason for trying to convince himself that there are no eternal sanctions behind the morality he is rejecting'. For Bulverism is a truly democratic game in the sense that all can play it all day long, and that it gives no unfair privilege to the small and offensive minority who reason. But of course it gets us not one inch nearer to deciding whether, as a matter of fact, the Christian religion is true or false. That question remains to be discussed on quite different grounds—

a matter of philosophical and historical argument. However it were decided, the improper motives of some people, both for believing it and for disbelieving it, would remain just as they are.

I see Bulverism at work in every political argument. The capitalists must be bad economists because we know why they want capitalism, and equally the Communists must be bad economists because we know why they want Communism. Thus, the Bulverists on both sides. In reality, of course, either the doctrines of the capitalists are false, or the doctrines of the Communists, or both; but you can only find out the rights and wrongs by reasoning—never by being rude about your opponent's psychology.

Until Bulverism is crushed, reason can play no effective part in human affairs. Each side snatches it early as a weapon against the other; but between the two reason itself is discredited. And why should reason not be discredited? It would be easy, in answer, to point to the present state of the world, but the real answer is even more immediate. The forces discrediting reason, themselves depend on reasoning. You must reason even to Bulverize. You are trying to *prove* that all *proofs* are invalid. If you fail, you fail. If you succeed, then you fail even more—for the proof that all proofs are invalid must be invalid itself.

The alternative then is either sheer self-contradicting idiocy or else some tenacious belief in our power of reasoning, held in the teeth of all the evidence that Bulverists can bring for a 'taint' in this or that human reasoner. I am ready to admit, if you like, that this tenacious belief has something transcendental or mystical about it. What then? Would you rather be a lunatic than a mystic?

So we see there is justification for holding on to our belief in Reason. But can this be done without theism? Does 'I know' involve that God exists? Everything I know is an inference from sensation (except the present moment). All our knowledge of the universe beyond our immediate experiences depends on inferences from these experiences. If our inferences do not give a genuine insight into reality, then we can know nothing. A theory cannot be accepted if it does not allow our thinking to be a genuine insight, nor if the fact of our knowledge is not explicable in terms of that theory.

But our thoughts can only be accepted as a genuine insight under certain conditions. All beliefs have causes but a distinction must be drawn between (1) ordinary causes and (2) a special kind of cause called 'a reason'. Causes are mindless events which can produce other results than belief. Reasons arise from axioms and inferences and affect only beliefs. Bulverism tries to show that the other man has causes and not reasons and that we have reasons and not causes. A belief which can be accounted for entirely in terms of causes is worthless. This principle must not be abandoned when we consider the beliefs which are the basis of others. Our knowledge depends on our certainty about axioms and inferences. If these are the result of causes, then there is no possibility of knowledge. Either we can know nothing *or* thought has reasons only, and no causes.

[*The remainder of this essay, which was originally read to the Socratic Club before publication in the* Socratic Digest, *continues in the form of notes taken down by the Secretary of the Club. This explains why it is not all in the first-person, as is the text-proper.*]

One might argue, Mr Lewis continued, that reason had developed by natural selection, only those methods of thought which had proved useful surviving. But the theory depends on an inference from usefulness to truth, of which the validity would have to be *assumed*. All attempts to treat thought as a natural event involve the fallacy of excluding the thought of the man making the attempt.

It is admitted that the mind is affected by physical events; a wireless set is influenced by atmospherics, but it does not originate its deliverances—we'd take no notice of it if we thought it did. Natural events we can relate one to another until we can trace them finally to the space-time continuum. But thought has no father but thought. It is conditioned, yes, not caused. *My* knowledge *that* I have nerves is inferential.

The same argument applies to our values, which are affected by social factors, but if they are caused by them we cannot know that they are right. One can reject morality as an illusion, but the man who does so often tacitly excepts his own ethical motive: for instance the duty of freeing morality from superstition and of spreading enlightenment.

Neither Will nor Reason is the product of Nature. Therefore either I am self-existent (a belief which no one can accept) *or* I am a colony of some Thought and Will that are self-existent. Such reason and goodness as we can attain must be derived from a self-existent Reason and Goodness outside ourselves, in fact, a Supernatural.

Mr Lewis went on to say that it was often objected that the existence of the Supernatural is too important to be discernible only by abstract argument, and thus only by the leisured few. But in all other ages the plain man has accepted the findings of the mystics and the philosophers for his initial belief in the existence of the Supernatural. Today the ordinary man is forced to carry that burden himself. Either mankind has made a ghastly mistake in rejecting authority, or the power or powers ruling his destiny are making a daring experiment, and all are to become sages. A society consisting solely of plain men must end in disaster. If we are to survive we must either believe the seers or scale those heights ourselves.

Evidently, then, something beyond Nature exists. Man is on the border line between the Natural and the Supernatural. Material events cannot produce spiritual activity, but the latter can be responsible for many of our actions on Nature. Will and Reason cannot depend on anything but themselves, but Nature can depend on Will and Reason, or, in other words, God created Nature.

The relation between Nature and Supernature, which is not a relation in space and time, becomes intelligible if the Supernatural made the Natural. We even have an idea of this making, since we know the power of imagination, though we can create nothing new, but can only rearrange our material provided through sense data. It is not inconceivable that the universe was created by an Imagination strong enough to impose phenomena on other minds.

It has been suggested, Mr Lewis concluded, that our ideas of making and causing are wholly derived from our experience of will. The conclusion usually drawn is that there is no making or causing, only 'projection'. But 'projection' is itself a form of causing, and it is more reasonable to suppose that Will is the only cause we know, and that therefore Will is the cause of Nature.

A discussion followed. Points arising:

All reasoning assumes the hypothesis that inference is valid. Correct inference is self-evident.

'Relevant' (re evidence) is a *rational* term.

The universe doesn't claim to be *true*: it's just *there*.

Knowledge by revelation is more like empirical than rational knowledge.

Question: What is the criterion of truth, if you distinguish between cause and reason?

Mr Lewis: A mountainous country might have several maps made of it, only one of which was a *true* one, i.e., corresponding with the actual contours. The map drawn by Reason claims to be that *true* one. I couldn't get at the universe unless I could trust my reason. If we couldn't trust inference we could know nothing but our own existence. Physical reality is an *inference* from sensations.

Question: How can an axiom claim self-evidence any more than an empirical judgment on evidence?

[*The essay ends here, leaving this question unanswered.*]

2
First and Second Things

WHEN I READ in *Time and Tide* on June 6 [1942] that the Germans have selected Hagen in preference to Siegfried as their national hero, I could have laughed out loud for pleasure. For I am a romantic person who has frankly revelled in my Nibelungs and specially in Wagner's version of the story, ever since one golden summer in adolescence when I first heard the 'Ride of the Valkyries' on a gramophone and saw Arthur Rackham's illustrations to *The Ring*. Even now the very smell of those volumes can come over me with the poignancy of remembered calf-love. It was, therefore, a bitter moment when the Nazis took over my treasure and made it part of their ideology. But now all is well. They have proved unable to digest it. They can retain it only by standing the story on its head and making one of the minor villains the hero. Doubtless the logic of their position will presently drive them further, and Alberich will be announced as the true personification of the Nordic spirit. In the meantime, they have given me back what they stole.

The mention of the Nordic spirit reminds me that their attempted appropriation of *The Ring* is only one instance of their larger attempt to appropriate 'the Nordic' as a whole, and this larger attempt is equally ridiculous. What business have people who call might right to say they are worshippers of Odin? The whole point about Odin was that he had the right but not the might. The whole point about Norse religion was that it alone of all mythologies told men to serve gods who were admittedly fighting with their backs to the wall and would certainly be defeated in the end. 'I am off to die with Odin' said the rover in Stevenson's fable,[1] thus proving that Stevenson understood something about the Nordic spirit which Germany has never been able to understand at all. The gods will fall. The wisdom of Odin, the humorous courage of Thor (Thor was something of a Yorkshireman) and the beauty of Balder will all be smashed eventually by the *realpolitik* of the stupid giants and misshapen trolls. But that does not in the least alter the allegiance of any free man. Hence, as we should expect, real Germanic poetry is all about heroic stands, and fighting against hopeless odds.

At this stage it occurred to me that I had stumbled on a rather remarkable paradox. How is it that the only people in Europe who have tried to revive their pre-Christian mythology as a living faith should also be the people that shows itself incapable of understanding that mythology in its very rudiments? The retrogression would, in any case, be deplorable—just as it would be deplorable if a full-grown man reverted to the *ethos* of his preparatory school. But you would expect him at least to get the no-sneaking rule right, and to be quite clear that new boys ought

---

1. This is found in R. L. Stevenson's fable entitled 'Faith, Half-Faith, and No Faith', which was first published in *The Strange Case of Dr. Jekyll and Mr. Hyde with Other Fables* (London, 1896).

not to put their hands in their pockets. To sacrifice the greater good for the less and then not to get the lesser good after all—that is the surprising folly. To sell one's birthright for a mess of mythology and then to get the mythology all wrong—how did they do it? For it is quite clear that I (who would rather paint my face bright blue with woad than suggest that there is a real Odin) am actually getting out of Odin all the good and all the fun that Odin can supply, while the Nazi Odinists are getting none of it.

And yet, it seemed to me as I thought about it, this may not be such a paradox as it looks. Or, at least, it is a paradox which turns up so often that a man ought by now to be accustomed to it. Other instances began to come to mind. Until quite modern times—I think, until the time of the Romantics—nobody ever suggested that literature and the arts were an end in themselves. They 'belonged to the orna- mental part of life', they provided 'innocent diversion'; or else they 'refined our manners' or 'incited us to virtue' or glorified the gods. The great music had been written for Masses, the great picture painted to fill up a space on the wall of a noble patron's dining-room or to kindle devotion in a church; the great tragedies were produced either by religious poets in honour of Dionysus or by commercial poets to entertain Londoners on half-holidays.

It was only in the nineteenth century that we became aware of the full dignity of art. We began to 'take it seriously' as the Nazis take mythology seriously. But the result seems to have been a dislocation of the aesthetic life in which little is left for us but high-minded works which fewer and fewer people want to read or hear or see, and 'popular' works of which both those who make them and those who enjoy them are half ashamed. Just like the Nazis, by valuing too highly a real, but subor- dinate good, we have come near to losing that good itself.

The longer I looked into it the more I came to suspect that I was perceiving a universal law. *On cause mieux quand on ne dit pas Causons.*[2] The woman who makes a dog the centre of her life loses, in the end, not only her human usefulness and dignity but even the proper pleasure of dog-keeping. The man who makes alcohol his chief good loses not only his job but his palate and all power of enjoying the earlier (and only pleasurable) levels of intoxication. It is a glorious thing to feel for a moment or two that the whole meaning of the universe is summed up in one woman—glorious so long as other duties and pleasures keep tearing you away from her. But clear the decks and so arrange your life (it is sometimes feasible) that you will have nothing to do but contemplate her, and what happens? Of course this law has been discovered before, but it will stand re-discovery. It may be stated as follows: every preference of a small good to a great, or a partial good to a total good, involves the loss of the small or partial good for which the sacrifice was made.

Apparently the world is made that way. If Esau really got the pottage in return for his birthright,[3] then Esau was a lucky exception. You can't get second things by putting them first; you can get second things only by putting first things first. From which it would follow that the question, What things are first? is of concern not only to philosophers but to everyone.

---

2. 'One converses better when one does not say "Let us converse."'
3. Genesis xxvii.

It is impossible, in this context, not to inquire what our own civilization has been putting first for the last thirty years. And the answer is plain. It has been putting itself first. To preserve civilization has been the great aim; the collapse of civilization, the great bugbear. Peace, a high standard of life, hygiene, transport, science and amusement—all these, which are what we usually mean by civilization, have been our ends. It will be replied that our concern for civilization is very natural and very necessary at a time when civilization is so imperilled. But how if the shoe is on the other foot?—how if civilization has been imperilled precisely by the fact that we have all made civilization our *summum bonum?* Perhaps it can't be preserved in that way. Perhaps civilization will never be safe until we care for something else more than we care for it.

The hypothesis has certain facts to support it. As far as peace (which is one ingredient in our idea of civilization) is concerned, I think many would now agree that a foreign policy dominated by desire for peace is one of the many roads that lead to war. And was civilization ever seriously endangered until civilization became the exclusive aim of human activity? There is much rash idealization of past ages about, and I do not wish to encourage more of it. Our ancestors were cruel, lecherous, greedy and stupid, like ourselves. But while they cared for other things more than for civilization—and they cared at different times for all sorts of things, for the will of God, for glory, for personal honour, for doctrinal purity, for justice— was civilization often in serious danger of disappearing?

At least the suggestion is worth a thought. To be sure, if it were true that civilization will never be safe till it is put second, that immediately raises the question, second to what? What is the first thing? The only reply I can offer here is that if we do not know, then the first and only truly practical thing is to set about finding out.

3

The Sermon and the Lunch

AND SO', SAID the preacher, 'the home must be the foundation of our national life. It is there, all said and done, that character is formed. It is there that we appear as we really are. It is there we can fling aside the weary disguises of the outer world and be ourselves. It is there that we retreat from the noise and stress and temptation and dissipation of daily life to seek the sources of fresh strength and renewed purity. . .' And as he spoke I noticed that all confidence in him had departed from every member of that congregation who was under thirty. They had been listening well up to this point. Now the shufflings and coughings began. Pews creaked; muscles relaxed. The sermon, for all practical purposes, was over; the five minutes for which the preacher continued talking were a total waste of time—at least for most of us.

Whether I wasted them or not is for you to judge. I certainly did not hear any more of the sermon. I was thinking; and the starting-point of my thought was the question, 'How can he? How can *he* of all people?' For I knew the preacher's own home pretty well. In fact, I had been lunching there that very day, making a fifth to the Vicar and the Vicar's wife and the son (R.A.F.)[1] and the daughter (A.T.S.),[2] who happened both to be on leave. I could have avoided it, but the girl had whispered to me, 'For God's sake stay to lunch if they ask you. It's always a little less frightful when there's a visitor.'

Lunch at the vicarage nearly always follows the same pattern. It starts with a desperate attempt on the part of the young people to keep up a bright patter of trivial conversation: trivial not because they are trivially minded (you can have real conversation with them if you get them alone), but because it would never occur to either of them to say at home anything they were really thinking, unless it is forced out of them by anger. They are talking only to try to keep their parents quiet. They fail. The Vicar, ruthlessly interrupting, cuts in on a quite different subject. He is telling us how to re-educate Germany. He has never been there and seems to know nothing either of German history or the German language. 'But, father,' begins the son, and gets no further. His mother is now talking, though nobody knows exactly when she began. She is in the middle of a complicated story about how badly some neighbour has treated her. Though it goes on a long time, we never learn either how it began or how it ended: it is all middle. 'Mother, that's not quite fair,' says the daughter at last. 'Mrs Walker never said—' but her father's voice booms in again. He is telling his son about the organization of the R.A.F. So it goes on until either the Vicar or his wife says something so preposterous that the boy or the girl con-

1. Royal Air Force.
2. Auxiliary Territorial Service.

tradicts and insists on making the contradiction heard. The real minds of the young people have at last been called into action. They talk fiercely, quickly, contemptuously. They have facts and logic on their side. There is an answering flare up from the parents. The father storms; the mother is (oh, blessed domestic queen's move!) 'hurt'—plays pathos for all she is worth. The daughter becomes ironical. The father and son, elaborately ignoring each other, start talking to me. The lunch party is in ruins.

The memory of that lunch worries me during the last few minutes of the sermon. I am not worried by the fact that the Vicar's practice differs from his precept. That is, no doubt, regrettable, but it is nothing to the purpose. As Dr Johnson said, precept may be very sincere (and, let us add, very profitable) where practice is very imperfect,[3] and no one but a fool would discount a doctor's warnings about alcoholic poisoning because the doctor himself drank too much. What worries me is the fact that the Vicar is not telling us at all that home life is difficult and has, like every form of life, its own proper temptations and corruptions. He keeps on talking as if 'home' were a panacea, a magical charm which of itself was bound to produce happiness and virtue. The trouble is not that he is insincere but that he is a fool. He is not talking from his own experience of family life at all: he is automatically reproducing a sentimental tradition—and it happens to be a false tradition. That is why the congregation have stopped listening to him.

If Christian teachers wish to recall Christian people to domesticity—and I, for one, believe that people must be recalled to it—the first necessity is to stop telling lies about home life and to substitute realistic teaching. Perhaps the fundamental principles would be something like this.

1. Since the Fall no organization or way of life whatever has a natural tendency to go right. In the Middle Ages some people thought that if only they entered a religious order they would find themselves automatically becoming holy and happy: the whole native literature of the period echoes with the exposure of that fatal error. In the nineteenth century some people thought that monogamous family life would automatically make them holy and happy; the savage anti-domestic literature of modern times—the Samuel Butlers, the Gosses, the Shaws—delivered the answer. In both cases the 'debunkers' may have been wrong about principles and may have forgotten the maxim *abusus non tollit usum*:[4] but in both cases they were pretty right about matter of fact. Both family life and monastic life were often detestable, and it should be noticed that the serious defenders of both are well aware of the dangers and free of the sentimental illusion. The author of the *Imitation of Christ* knows (no one better) how easily monastic life goes wrong. Charlotte M. Yonge makes it abundantly clear that domesticity is no passport to heaven on earth but an arduous vocation—a sea full of hidden rocks and perilous ice shores only to be navigated by one who uses a celestial chart. That is the first point on which we must be absolutely clear. The family, like the nation, can be offered to God, can be converted and redeemed, and will then become the channel of particular blessings

3. James Boswell, *Life of Johnson*, ed. George Birkbeck Hill (Oxford, 1934), vol. IV, p. 397 (2 December 1784).
4. 'The abuse does not abolish the use.'

and graces. But, like everything else that is human, it needs redemption. Unredeemed, it will produce only particular temptations, corruptions, and miseries. Charity begins at home: so does uncharity.

2. By the conversion or sanctification of family life we must be careful to mean something more than the preservation of 'love' in the sense of natural affection. Love (in that sense) is not enough. Affection, as distinct from charity, is not a cause of lasting happiness. Left to its natural bent affection becomes in the end greedy, naggingly solicitous, jealous, exacting, timorous. It suffers agony when its object is absent—but is not repaid by any long enjoyment when the object is present. Even at the Vicar's lunch table affection was partly the cause of the quarrel. That son would have borne patiently and humorously from any other old man the silliness which enraged him in his father. It is because he still (in some fashion) 'cares' that he is impatient. The Vicar's wife would not be quite that endless whimper of self-pity which she now is if she did not (in a sense) 'love' the family: the continued disappointment of her continued and ruthless demand for sympathy, for affection, for appreciation has helped to make her what she is. I do not think this aspect of affection is nearly enough noticed by most popular moralists. The greed to be loved is a fearful thing. Some of those who say (and almost with pride) that they live only for love come, at last, to live in incessant resentment.

3. We must realize the yawning pitfall in that very characteristic of home life which is so often glibly paraded as its principal attraction. 'It is there that we appear as we really are: it is there that we can fling aside the disguises and be ourselves.' These words, in the Vicar's mouth, were only too true and he showed at the lunch table what they meant. Outside his own house he behaves with ordinary courtesy. He would not have interrupted any other young man as he interrupted his son. He would not, in any other society, have talked confident nonsense about subjects of which he was totally ignorant: or, if he had, he would have accepted correction with good temper. In fact, he values home as the place where he can 'be himself' in the sense of trampling on all the restraints which civilized humanity has found indispensable for tolerable social intercourse. And this, I think, is very common. What chiefly distinguishes domestic from public conversation is surely very often simply its downright rudeness. What distinguishes domestic behaviour is often its selfishness, slovenliness, incivility—even brutality. And it will often happen that those who praise home life most loudly are the worst offenders in this respect: they praise it—they are always glad to get home, hate the outer world, can't stand visitors, can't be bothered meeting people, etc.—because the freedoms in which they indulge themselves at home have ended by making them unfit for civilized society. If they practised elsewhere the only behaviour they now find 'natural' they would simply be knocked down.

4. How, then, *are* people to behave at home? If a man can't be comfortable and unguarded, can't take his ease and 'be himself' in his own house, where can he? That is, I confess, the trouble. The answer is an alarming one. There is *nowhere* this side of heaven where one can safely lay the reins on the horse's neck. It will never be lawful simply to 'be ourselves' until 'ourselves' have become sons of God. It is all there in the hymn—'Christian, seek not yet repose.' This does not mean, of course,

that there is no difference between home life and general society. It does mean that home life has its own rule of courtesy—a code more intimate, more subtle, more sensitive, and, therefore, in some ways more difficult, than that of the outer world.

5. Finally, must we not teach that if the home is to be a means of grace it must be a place of *rules*? There cannot be a common life without a *regula*. The alternative to rule is not freedom but the unconstitutional (and often unconscious) tyranny of the most selfish member.

In a word, must we not either cease to preach domesticity or else begin to preach it seriously? Must we not abandon sentimental eulogies and begin to give practical advice on the high, hard, lovely, and adventurous art of really creating the Christian family?

4
The Humanitarian
Theory of Punishment

IN ENGLAND WE HAVE lately had a controversy about Capital Punishment. I do not know whether a murderer is more likely to repent and make a good end on the gallows a few weeks after his trial or in the prison infirmary thirty years later. I do not know whether the fear of death is an indispensable deterrent. I need not, for the purpose of this article, decide whether it is a morally permissible deterrent. Those are questions which I propose to leave untouched. My subject is not Capital Punishment in particular, but that theory of punishment in general which the controversy showed to be almost universal among my fellow-countrymen. It may be called the Humanitarian theory. Those who hold it think that it is mild and merciful. In this I believe that they are seriously mistaken. I believe that the 'Humanity' which it claims is a dangerous illusion and disguises the possibility of cruelty and injustice without end. I urge a return to the traditional or Retributive theory not solely, not even primarily, in the interests of society, but in the interests of the criminal.

According to the Humanitarian theory, to punish a man because he deserves it, and as much as he deserves, is mere revenge, and, therefore, barbarous and immoral. It is maintained that the only legitimate motives for punishing are the desire to deter others by example or to mend the criminal. When this theory is combined, as frequently happens, with the belief that all crime is more or less pathological, the idea of mending tails off into that of healing or curing and punishment becomes therapeutic. Thus it appears at first sight that we have passed from the harsh and self-righteous notion of giving the wicked their deserts to the charitable and enlightened one of tending the psychologically sick. What could be more amiable? One little point which is taken for granted in this theory needs, however, to be made explicit. The things done to the criminal, even if they are called cures, will be just as compulsory as they were in the old days when we called them punishments. If a tendency to steal can be cured by psychotherapy, the thief will no doubt be forced to undergo the treatment. Otherwise, society cannot continue.

My contention is that this doctrine, merciful though it appears, really means that each one of us, from the moment he breaks the law, is deprived of the rights of a human being.

The reason is this. The Humanitarian theory removes from Punishment the concept of Desert. But the concept of Desert is the only connecting link between punishment and justice. It is only as deserved or undeserved that a sentence can be just or unjust. I do not here contend that the question 'Is it deserved?' is the only one we can reasonably ask about a punishment. We may very properly ask whether it is likely to deter others and to reform the criminal. But neither of these two last questions is a question about justice. There is no sense in talking about a 'just deterrent' or a 'just cure'. We demand of a deterrent not whether it is just but whether it will deter. We demand of a cure not whether it is just but whether it succeeds. Thus when we cease to consider what the criminal deserves and consider only what will cure him or deter others, we have tacitly removed him from the sphere of justice altogether; instead of a person, a subject of rights, we now have a mere object, a patient, a 'case'.

The distinction will become clearer if we ask who will be qualified to determine sentences when sentences are no longer held to derive their propriety from the criminal's deservings. On the old view the problem of fixing the right sentence was a moral problem. Accordingly, the judge who did it was a person trained in jurisprudence; trained, that is, in a science which deals with rights and duties, and which, in origin at least, was consciously accepting guidance from the Law of Nature, and from Scripture. We must admit that in the actual penal code of most countries at most times these high originals were so much modified by local custom, class interests, and utilitarian concessions, as to be very imperfectly recognizable. But the code was never in principle, and not always in fact, beyond the control of the conscience of the society. And when (say, in eighteenth-century England) actual punishments conflicted too violently with the moral sense of the community, juries refused to convict and reform was finally brought about. This was possible because, so long as we are thinking in terms of Desert, the propriety of the penal code, being a moral question, is a question on which every man has the right to an opinion, not because he follows this or that profession, but because he is simply a man, a rational animal enjoying the Natural Light. But all this is changed when we drop the concept of Desert. The only two questions we may now ask about a punishment are whether it deters and whether it cures. But these are not questions on which anyone is entitled to have an opinion simply because he is a man. He is not entitled to an opinion even if, in addition to being a man, he should happen also to be a jurist, a Christian, and a moral theologian. For they are not questions about principle but about matter of fact; and for such *cuiquam in sua arte credendum.*[1] Only the expert 'penologist' (let barbarous things have barbarous names), in the light of previous experiment, can tell us what is likely to deter: only the psychotherapist can tell us what is likely to cure. It will be in vain for the rest of us, speaking simply as men, to say, 'but this punishment is hideously unjust, hideously disproportionate to the criminal's deserts'. The experts with perfect logic will reply, 'but nobody was talking about deserts. No one was talking about *punishment* in your archaic vindictive sense of the word. Here are the statistics proving that this treatment deters. Here are the statistics proving that this other treatment cures. What is your trouble?'

The Humanitarian theory, then, removes sentences from the hands of jurists whom the public conscience is entitled to criticize and places them in the hands of technical experts whose special sciences do not even employ such categories as

---

1. 'We must believe the expert in his own field.'

rights or justice. It might be argued that since this transference results from an abandonment of the old idea of punishment, and, therefore, of all vindictive motives, it
will be safe to leave our criminals in such hands. I will not pause to comment on the
simple-minded view of fallen human nature which such a belief implies. Let us rather
remember that the 'cure' of criminals is to be compulsory; and let us then watch
how the theory actually works in the mind of the Humanitarian. The immediate
starting point of this article was a letter I read in one of our Leftist weeklies. The
author was pleading that a certain sin, now treated by our laws as a crime, should
henceforward be treated as a disease. And he complained that under the present
system the offender, after a term in gaol, was simply let out to return to his original
environment where he would probably relapse. What he complained of was not the
shutting up but the letting out. On his remedial view of punishment the offender
should, of course, be detained until he was cured. And of course the official straighteners are the only people who can say when that is. The first result of the Humanitarian theory is, therefore, to substitute for a definite sentence (reflecting to some
extent the community's moral judgment on the degree of ill-desert involved) an indefinite sentence terminable only by the word of those experts—and they are not
experts in moral theology nor even in the Law of Nature—who inflict it. Which of
us, if he stood in the dock, would not prefer to be tried by the old system?

It may be said that by the continued use of the word punishment and the use of
the verb 'inflict' I am misrepresenting Humanitarians. They are not punishing, not
inflicting, only healing. But do not let us be deceived by a name. To be taken without consent from my home and friends; to lose my liberty; to undergo all those
assaults on my personality which modern psychotherapy knows how to deliver;
to be re-made after some pattern of 'normality' hatched in a Viennese laboratory
to which I never professed allegiance; to know that this process will never end until
either my captors have succeeded or I grown wise enough to cheat them with
apparent success—who cares whether this is called Punishment or not? That it
includes most of the elements for which any punishment is feared—shame, exile,
bondage, and years eaten by the locust—is obvious. Only enormous ill-desert could
justify it; but ill-desert is the very conception which the Humanitarian theory has
thrown overboard.

If we turn from the curative to the deterrent justification of punishment we shall
find the new theory even more alarming. When you punish a man *in terrorem*,[2] make
of him an 'example' to others, you are admittedly using him as a means to an end;
someone else's end. This, in itself, would be a very wicked thing to do. On the classical theory of Punishment it was of course justified on the ground that the man
deserved it. That was assumed to be established before any question of 'making
him an example' arose. You then, as the saying is, killed two birds with one stone;
in the process of giving him what he deserved you set an example to others. But
take away desert and the whole morality of the punishment disappears. Why, in
Heaven's name, am I to be sacrificed to the good of society in this way?—unless, of
course, I deserve it.

2. 'to cause terror'.

But that is not the worst. If the justification of exemplary punishment is not to be based on desert but solely on its efficacy as a deterrent, it is not absolutely necessary that the man we punish should even have committed the crime. The deterrent effect demands that the public should draw the moral, 'If we do such an act we shall suffer like that man.' The punishment of a man actually guilty whom the public think innocent will not have the desired effect; the punishment of a man actually innocent will, provided the public think him guilty. But every modern State has powers which make it easy to fake a trial. When a victim is urgently needed for exemplary purposes and a guilty victim cannot be found, all the purposes of deterrence will be equally served by the punishment (call it cure' if you prefer) of an innocent victim, provided that the public can be cheated into thinking him guilty. It is no use to ask me why I assume that our rulers will be so wicked. The punishment of an innocent, that is, an undeserving, man is wicked only if we grant the traditional view that righteous punishment means deserved punishment. Once we have abandoned that criterion, all punishments have to be justified, if at all, on other grounds that have nothing to do with desert. Where the punishment of the innocent can be justified on those grounds (and it could in some cases be justified as a deterrent) it will be no less moral than any other punishment. Any distaste for it on the part of a Humanitarian will be merely a hang-over from the Retributive theory.

It is, indeed, important to notice that my argument so far supposes no evil intentions on the part of the Humanitarian and considers only what is involved in the logic of his position. My contention is that good men (not bad men) consistently acting upon that position would act as cruelly and unjustly as the greatest tyrants. They might in some respects act even worse. Of all tyrannies a tyranny sincerely exercised for the good of its victims may be the most oppressive. It may be better to live under robber barons than under omnipotent moral busybodies. The robber baron's cruelty may sometimes sleep, his cupidity may at some point be satiated; but those who torment us for our own good will torment us without end for they do so with the approval of their own conscience. They may be more likely to go to Heaven yet at the same time likelier to make a Hell of earth. Their very kindness stings with intolerable insult. To be 'cured' against one's will and cured of states which we may not regard as disease is to be put on a level with those who have not yet reached the age of reason or those who never will; to be classed with infants, imbeciles, and domestic animals. But to be punished, however severely, because we have deserved it, because we 'ought to have known better', is to be treated as a human person made in God's image.

In reality, however, we must face the possibility of bad rulers armed with a Humanitarian theory of punishment. A great many popular blue prints for a Christian society are merely what the Elizabethans called 'eggs in moonshine' because they assume that the whole society is Christian or that the Christians are in control. This is not so in most contemporary States. Even if it were, our rulers would still be fallen men, and, therefore, neither very wise nor very good. As it is, they will usually be unbelievers. And since wisdom and virtue are not the only or the commonest qualifications for a place in the government, they will not often be even the best unbelievers.

The practical problem of Christian politics is not that of drawing up schemes for a Christian society, but that of living as innocently as we can with unbelieving fellow-subjects under unbelieving rulers who will never be perfectly wise and good and who will sometimes be very wicked and very foolish. And when they are wicked the Humanitarian theory of punishment will put in their hands a finer instrument of tyranny than wickedness ever had before. For if crime and disease are to be regarded as the same thing, it follows that any state of mind which our masters choose to call 'disease' can be treated as crime; and compulsorily cured. It will be vain to plead that states of mind which displease government need not always involve moral turpitude and do not therefore always deserve forfeiture of liberty. For our masters will not be using the concepts of Desert and Punishment but those of disease and cure. We know that one school of psychology already regards religion as a neurosis. When this particular neurosis becomes inconvenient to government, what is to hinder government from proceeding to 'cure' it? Such 'cure' will, of course, be compulsory; but under the Humanitarian theory it will not be called by the shocking name of Persecution. No one will blame us for being Christians, no one will hate us, no one will revile us. The new Nero will approach us with the silky manners of a doctor, and though all will be in fact as compulsory as the *tunica molesta* or Smithfield or Tyburn, all will go on within the unemotional therapeutic sphere where words like 'right' and 'wrong' or 'freedom' and 'slavery' are never heard. And thus when the command is given, every prominent Christian in the land may vanish overnight into Institutions for the Treatment of the Ideologically Unsound, and it will rest with the expert gaolers to say when (if ever) they are to re-emerge. But it will not be persecution. Even if the treatment is painful, even if it is life-long, even if it is fatal, that will be only a regrettable accident; the intention was purely therapeutic. In ordinary medicine there were painful operations and fatal operations; so in this. But because they are 'treatment', not punishment, they can be criticized only by fellow-experts and on technical grounds, never by men as men and on grounds of justice.

This is why I think it essential to oppose the Humanitarian theory of punishment, root and branch, wherever we encounter it. It carries on its front a semblance of mercy which is wholly false. That is how it can deceive men of good will. The error began, perhaps, with Shelley's statement that the distinction between mercy and justice was invented in the courts of tyrants. It sounds noble, and was indeed the error of a noble mind. But the distinction is essential. The older view was that mercy 'tempered' justice, or (on the highest level of all) that mercy and justice had met and kissed. The essential act of mercy was to pardon; and pardon in its very essence involves the recognition of guilt and ill-desert in the recipient. If crime is only a disease which needs cure, not sin which deserves punishment, it cannot be pardoned. How can you pardon a man for having a gumboil or a club foot? But the Humanitarian theory wants simply to abolish Justice and substitute Mercy for it. This means that you start being 'kind' to people before you have considered their rights, and then force upon them supposed kindnesses which no one but you will recognize as kindnesses and which the recipient will feel as abominable cruelties. You have overshot the mark. Mercy, detached from Justice, grows unmerciful. That is the important paradox. As there are plants which will flourish only in mountain soil, so it appears that Mercy will flower only when it grows in the crannies of the rock of Justice: transplanted to the marshlands of mere Humanitarianism, it becomes a man-eating weed, all the more dangerous because it is still called by the same name as the mountain variety. But we ought long ago to have learned our lesson. We should be too old now to be deceived by those humane pretensions which have served to usher in every cruelty of the revolutionary period in which we live. These are the 'precious balms' which will 'break our heads'.[3]

There is a fine sentence in Bunyan: 'It came burning hot into my mind, whatever he said, and however he flattered, when he got me home to his House, he would sell me for a Slave.'[4] There is a fine couplet, too, in John Ball:

> *Be war or ye be wo;*
> *Knoweth your frend from your foo.*[5]

On Punishment: A Reply to Criticism
by C. S. Lewis

I have to thank the Editor for this opportunity of replying to two most interesting critiques of my article on the Humanitarian Theory of Punishment, one by Professor J. J. C. Smart[6] and the other by Drs N. Morris and D. Buckle.[7]

Professor Smart makes a distinction between questions of the First and of the Second Order: 'First' are questions like 'Ought I to return this book?'; Second, like 'Is promise-making a good institution?' He claims that these two Orders of question require different methods of treatment. The first can be answered by Intuition (in the sense which moral philosophers sometimes give that word). We 'see' what is 'right' at once, because the proposed action falls under a rule. But second-order questions can be answered only on 'utilitarian' principles. Since 'right' means 'agreeable to the rules' it is senseless to ask if the rules themselves are 'right'; we can only ask if they are useful. A parallel would be this: granted a fixed spelling we may ask whether a word is spelled correctly, but cannot ask whether the spelling system is correct, only if it is consistent or convenient. Or again, a form may be grammatically right, but the grammar of a whole language cannot be right or wrong.

Professor Smart is here, of course, treating in a new way a very ancient distinction. It was realised by all the thinkers of the past that you could consider either (a) Whether an act was 'just' in the sense of conforming to a law or custom, or (b) Whether a law or custom was itself 'just'. To the ancients and medievals, however, the distinction was one between (a) Justice by law or convention, *nomo (i)*, and (b) Justice 'simply' or 'by nature', *haplôs* or *physei*, or between (a) Positive Law,

---

3. Psalm cxli. 6.
4. *The Pilgrim 's Progress*, ed. James Blanton Wharey, second edition revised by Roger Sharrock, Oxford English Texts (Oxford, 1960), Part I, p. 70.
5. 'John Ball's Letter to the Peasants of Essex, 1381', lines 11–12, found in *Fourteenth Century Verse and Prose*, ed. Kenneth Sisam (Oxford, 1921), p. 161.
6. 'Comment: The Humanitarian Theory of Punishment', *Res Judicatae* vol. VI (February 1954), pp. 368–71.
7. 'Reply to C. S. Lewis', *Res Judicatae*, vol. VI (June 1953), pp. 231-237.

and (b) Natural Law. Both inquiries were about justice, but the distinction between them was acknowledged. The novelty of Professor Smart's system consists in confining the concept of justice to the First-order questions.

It is claimed that the new system (1) avoids a *petitio* inherent in any appeal to the Law of Nature or the 'simply' just; for 'to say that this is the Law of Nature is only to say that this is the rule we should adopt'; and (2) gets rid of dogmatic subjectivism. For the idea of desert in my article may be only 'Lewis's personal preference'.

I am not convinced, however, that Professor Smart's system does avoid these inconveniences.

Those rules are to be accepted which are useful to the community, utility being (I think) what will make that community 'happier'.* Does this mean that the happiness of the community is to be pursued *at all costs,* or only to be pursued in so far as this pursuit is compatible with certain degrees of mercy, human dignity, and veracity? (I must not add 'of justice' because, in Professor Smart's view, the rules themselves cannot be either just or unjust). If we take the second alternative, if we admit that there are some things, or even any one thing, which a community ought not to do however much it will increase its happiness, then we have really given up the position. We are now judging the useful by some other standard (whether we call it Conscience, or Practical Reason, or Law of Nature or Personal Preference). Suppose then, we take the first alternative: the happiness of the community is to be pursued at all costs. In certain circumstances the costs may be very heavy. In war, in some not improbable future when the world's food runs short, during some threat of revolution, very shocking things may be likely to make the community happier or to preserve its existence. We cannot be sure that frame-ups, witch-hunts, even cannibalism, would never be in this sense 'useful'. Let us suppose (what, I am very sure, is false) that Professor Smart is prepared to go the whole hog. It then remains to ask him why he does so or why he thinks we should agree with him. He of all men cannot reply that *salus populi suprema lex*[8] *is* the Law of Nature; firstly, because we others know that 'the people should be preserved' is not the Law of Nature but only one clause in that Law. What then could a pursuit of the community's happiness at all costs be based on if not on Professor Smart's 'personal preference'? The real difference between him and me would then be simply that we have different desires. Or, rather, that I have one more desire than he. For, like him, I desire the continuance and happiness of my country (and species),* but then I also desire that they should be people of a certain sort, behaving in a certain way. The second desire is the stronger of the two. If I cannot have both, I had rather that the human race, having a certain quality in their lives, should continue for only a few centuries than that, losing freedom, friendship, dignity, and mercy, and learning to be quite content without them, they should continue for millions of millennia. If it is merely a matter of wishes, there is really no further question for discussion.

---

*See the penultimate paragraph of Professor Smart's article.
8. Cicero, *De Legibus*, bk. III, pt. iii, sect. 8. 'The safety of the people is the highest law.'
* I am not sure whether for Professor Smart the 'community' means the nation or the species. If the former, difficulties arise about international morality, in discussing which I think Professor Smart would have to come to the species sooner or later.

Lots of people feel like me, and lots feel the other way. I believe that it is in our age being decided which kind of man will win.

And that is why, if I may say so without discourtesy, Professor Smart and I both matter so little compared with Drs Morris and Buckle. We are only dons; they are criminologists, a lawyer and a psychiatrist respectively. And the only thing which leads me so far off my own beat as to write about 'Penology' at all is my intense anxiety as to which side in this immensely important conflict will have the Law for its ally. This leads me to the only serious disagreement between my two critics and myself.

Other disagreements there are, but they mainly turn on misunderstandings for which I am probably to blame. Thus:

(1) There was certainly too little, if there was anything, in my article about the protection of the community. I am afraid I took it for granted. But the distinction in my mind would not be, as my critics suppose (Morris and Buckle, p. 232), one between 'subsidiary' and 'vital' elements in punishment. I call the act of taking a packet of cigarettes off a counter and slipping it into one's pocket 'purchase' or 'theft' according as one does or does not pay for it. This does not mean that I consider the taking away of the goods as 'subsidiary' in an act of purchase. It means that what legitimises it, what makes it purchase at all, is the paying. I call the sexual act chaste or unchaste according as the parties are or are not married to one another. This does not mean that I consider it as 'subsidiary' to marriage, but that what legitimises it, what makes it a specimen of conjugal behaviour at all, is marriage. In the same way, I am ready to make both the protection of society and the 'cure' of the criminal as important as you please in punishment, but only on a certain condition: namely, that the initial act of thus interfering with a man's liberty be justified on grounds of desert. Like payment in purchase, or marriage as regards the sexual act, it is this, and (I believe) this alone, which legitimises our proceeding and makes it an instance of punishment at all, instead of an instance of tyranny—or, perhaps, of war.

(2) I agree about criminal *children* (see Morris and Buckle, p. 234). There has been progress in this matter. Very primitive societies will 'try' and 'punish' an axe or a spear in cases of unintentional homicide. Somewhere (I think, in the Empire) during the later Middle Ages a pig was solemnly tried for murder. Till quite recently, we may (I don't know) have tried children as if they had adult responsibility. These things have rightly been abolished. But the whole question is whether you want the process to be carried further: whether you want us all to be simultaneously deprived of the protection and released from the responsibilities of adult citizenship and reduced to the level of the child, the pig, and the axe. I don't want this because I don't think there are in fact any people who stand to the rest of us as adult to child, man to beast, or animate to inanimate.* I think the laws which laid down a 'desertless' theory of punishment would in reality be made and administered by people just like the rest of us.

But the real disagreement is this. Drs Morris and Buckle, fully alive to dangers of the sort I dread and reprobating them no less than I, believe that we have a safe-

* This is really the same objection as that which I would make to Aristotle's theory of slavery (*Politics* 1254A *et seq.*). We can all recognize the 'natural' slaves (I am perhaps one myself) but where are the 'natural' masters?

guard. It lies in the Courts, in their incorruptible judges, their excellent techniques, and 'the controls of natural justice which the law has built up' (p. 233). Yes; if the whole tradition of natural justice which the law has for so long incorporated, will survive the completion of that change in our attitude to punishment which we are now discussing. But that for me is precisely the question. Our Courts, I agree, 'have traditionally represented the common man and the common man's view of morality' (p. 233). It is true that we must extend the term 'common man' to cover Locke, Grotius, Hooker, Poynet, Aquinas, Justinian, the Stoics, and Aristotle, but I have no objection to that; in one most important, and to me glorious, sense they were all common men.* But that whole tradition is tied up with ideas of free-will, responsibility, rights, and the law of nature. Can it survive in Courts whose penal practice daily subordinates 'desert' to therapy and the protection of society? Can the Law assume one philosophy in practice and continue to enjoy the safeguards of a different philosophy?

I write as the son of one lawyer and the lifelong friend of another,[9] to two criminologists one of whom is a lawyer. I believe an approximation between their view and mine is not to be despaired of, for we have the same ends at heart. I wish society to be protected and I should be very glad if all punishments were also cures. All I plead for is the *prior* condition of ill desert; loss of liberty justified on retributive grounds *before* we begin considering the other factors. After that, as you please. Till that, there is really no question of 'punishment'. We are not such poltroons that we want to be protected unconditionally, though when a man has deserved punishment we shall very properly look to our protection in devising it. We are not such busybodies that we want to improve all our neighbours by force; but when one of our neighbours has justly forfeited his right not to be interfered with, we shall charitably try to make his punishment improve him. But we will not presume to teach him (who, after all, are we?) till he has merited that we should 'larn him'. Will Dr Morris and Dr Buckle come so far to meet me as that? On their decision and on that of others in similar important offices, depends, I believe, the continued dignity and beneficence of that great discipline the Law, but also much more. For, if I am not deceived, we are all at this moment helping to decide whether humanity shall retain all that has hitherto made humanity worth preserving, or whether we must slide down into the subhumanity imagined by Mr Aldous Huxley and George Orwell and partially realised in Hitler's Germany. For the extermination of the Jews really would have been 'useful' if the racial theories had been correct; there is no foretelling what may come to seem, or even to be, 'useful', and 'necessity' was always 'the tyrant's plea'.[10]

*See also Lewis: *The Abolition of Man* (London, 1943), especially the Appendix.
9. Owen Barfield.
10. See Letter 12.

5
Xmas and Christmas
A Lost Chapter from Herodotus

AND BEYOND THIS there lies in the ocean, turned towards the west and north, the island of Niatirb which Hecataeus indeed declares to be the same size and shape as Sicily, but it is larger, though in calling it triangular a man would not miss the mark. It is densely inhabited by men who wear clothes not very different from the other barbarians who occupy the north-western parts of Europe though they do not agree with them in language. These islanders, surpassing all the men of whom we know in patience and endurance, use the following customs.

In the middle of winter when fogs and rains most abound they have a great festival which they call Exmas, and for fifty days they prepare for it in the fashion I shall describe. First of all, every citizen is obliged to send to each of his friends and relations a square piece of hard paper stamped with a picture, which in their speech is called an Exmas-card. But the pictures represent birds sitting on branches, or trees with a dark green prickly leaf, or else men in such garments as the Niatirbians believe that their ancestors wore two hundred years ago riding in coaches such as their ancestors used, or houses with snow on their roofs. And the Niatirbians are unwilling to say what these pictures have to do with the festival, guarding (as I suppose) some sacred mystery. And because all men must send these cards the market-place is filled with the crowd of those buying them, so that there is great labour and weariness.

But having bought as many as they suppose to be sufficient, they return to their houses and find there the like cards which others have sent to them. And when they find cards from any to whom they also have sent cards, they throw them away and give thanks to the gods that this labour at least is over for another year. But when they find cards from any to whom they have not sent, then they beat their breasts and wail and utter curses against the sender; and, having sufficiently lamented their misfortune, they put on their boots again and go out into the fog and rain and buy a card for him also. And let this account suffice about Exmas-cards.

They also send gifts to one another, suffering the same things about the gifts as about the cards, or even worse. For every citizen has to guess the value of the gift which every friend will send to him so that he may send one of equal value, whether he can afford it or not. And they buy as gifts for one another such things as no man ever bought for himself. For the sellers, understanding the custom, put forth all kinds of trumpery, and whatever, being useless and ridiculous, they have been unable to sell throughout the year they now sell as an Exmas gift. And though the Niatirbians profess themselves to lack sufficient necessary things, such as metal, leather, wood and paper, yet an incredible quantity of these things is wasted every year, being made into the gifts.

But during these fifty days the oldest, poorest and most miserable of the citizens put on false beards and red robes and walk about the market-place; being disguised (in my opinion) as *Cronos*. And the sellers of gifts no less than the purchasers become pale and weary, because of the crowds and the fog, so that any man who came into a Niatirbian city at this season would think some great public calamity had fallen on Niatirb. This fifty days of preparation is called in their barbarian speech the Exmas *Rush*.

But when the day of the festival comes, then most of the citizens, being exhausted with the *Rush*, lie in bed till noon. But in the evening they eat five times as much supper as on other days and, crowning themselves with crowns of paper, they become intoxicated. And on the day after Exmas they are very grave, being internally disordered by the supper and the drinking and reckoning how much they have spent on gifts and on the wine. For wine is so dear among the Niatirbians that a man must swallow the worth of a talent before he is well intoxicated.

Such, then, are their customs about the Exmas. But the few among the Niatirbians have also a festival, separate and to themselves, called Crissmas, which is on the same day as Exmas. And those who keep Crissmas, doing the opposite to the majority of the Niatirbians, rise early on that day with shining faces and go before sunrise to certain temples where they partake of a sacred feast. And in most of the temples they set out images of a fair woman with a new-born Child on her knees and certain animals and shepherds adoring the Child. (The reason of these images is given in a certain sacred story which I know but do not repeat.)

But I myself conversed with a priest in one of these temples and asked him why they kept Crissmas on the same day as Exmas; for it appeared to me inconvenient. But the priest replied, It is not lawful, O Stranger, for us to change the date of Crissmas, but would that Zeus would put it into the minds of the Niatirbians to keep Exmas at some other time or not to keep it at all. For Exmas and the *Rush* distract the minds even of the few from sacred things. And we indeed are glad that men should make merry at Crissmas; but in Exmas there is no merriment left. And when I asked him why they endured the *Rush*, he replied, It is, O Stranger, a *racket*; using (as I suppose) the words of some oracle and speaking unintelligibly to me (for a *racket* is an instrument which the barbarians use in a game called *tennis*).

But what Hecataeus says, that Exmas and Crissmas are the same, is not credible. For first, the pictures which are stamped on the Exmas-cards have nothing to do with the sacred story which the priests tell about Crissmas. And secondly, the most part of the Niatirbians, not believing the religion of the few, nevertheless send the gifts and cards and participate in the *Rush* and drink, wearing paper cars. But it is not likely that men, even being barbarians, should suffer so many and great things in honour of a god they do not believe in. And now, enough about Niatirb.

6
What Christmas Means to Me

THREE THINGS GO by the name of Christmas. One is a religious festival. This is important and obligatory for Christians; but as it can be of no interest to anyone else, I shall naturally say no more about it here. The second (it has complex historical connections with the first, but we needn't go into them) is a popular holiday, an occasion for merry-making and hospitality. If it were my business to have a 'view' on this, I should say that I much approve of merry-making. But what I approve of much more is everybody minding his own business. I see no reason why I should volunteer views as to how other people should spend their own money in their own leisure among their own friends. It is highly probable that they want my advice on such matters as little as I want theirs. But the third thing called Christmas is unfortunately everyone's business.

I mean of course the commercial racket. The interchange of presents was a very small ingredient in the older English festivity. Mr Pickwick took a cod with him to Dingley Dell; the reformed Scrooge ordered a turkey for his clerk; lovers sent love gifts; toys and fruit were given to children. But the idea that not only all friends but even all acquaintances should give one another presents, or at least send one another cards, is quite modern and has been forced upon us by the shopkeepers. Neither of these circumstances is in itself a reason for condemning it. I condemn it on the following grounds.

1. It gives on the whole much more pain than pleasure. You have only to stay over Christmas with a family who seriously try to 'keep' it (in its third, or commercial, aspect) in order to see that the thing is a nightmare. Long before December 25th everyone is worn out—physically worn out by weeks of daily struggle in overcrowded shops, mentally worn out by the effort to remember all the right recipients and to think out suitable gifts for them. They are in no trim for merry-making; much less (if they should want to) to take part in a religious act. They look far more as if there had been a long illness in the house.

2. Most of it is involuntary. The modern rule is that anyone can force you to give him a present by sending you a quite unprovoked present of his own. It is almost a blackmail. Who has not heard the wail of despair, and indeed of resentment, when, at the last moment, just as everyone hoped that the nuisance was over for one more year, the unwanted gift from Mrs Busy (whom we hardly remember) flops unwelcomed through the letter-box, and back to the dreadful shops one of us has to go?

3. Things are given as presents which no mortal ever bought for himself—gaudy and useless gadgets, 'novelties' because no one was ever fool enough to make their like before. Have we really no better use for materials and for human skill and time than to spend them on all this rubbish?

4. The nuisance. For after all, during the racket we still have all our ordinary and necessary shopping to do, and the racket trebles the labour of it.

We are told that the whole dreary business must go on because it is good for trade. It is in fact merely one annual symptom of that lunatic condition of our country, and indeed of the world, in which everyone lives by persuading everyone else to buy things. I don't know the way out. But can it really be my duty to buy and receive masses of junk every winter just to help the shopkeepers? If the worst comes to the worst I'd sooner give them money for nothing and write it off as a charity. For nothing? Why, better for nothing than for a nuisance.

7
Delinquents in the Snow

VOICES 'OFF', OUTSIDE the front door, annually remind us (usually at the most inconvenient moment) that the season of carols has come again. At my front door they are, once every year, the voices of the local choir; on the forty-five other annual occasions they are those of boys or children who have not even tried to learn to sing, or to memorize the words of the piece they are murdering. The instruments they play with real conviction are the door-bell and the knocker; and money is what they are after.

I am pretty sure that some of them are the very same hooligans who trespass in my garden, rob my orchard, hack down my trees and scream outside my windows, though everyone in the neighbourhood knows that there is serious illness in my family. I am afraid I deal with them badly in the capacity of 'waits'. I neither forgive like a Christian nor turn the dog on them like an indignant householder. I pay the blackmail. I give, but give ungraciously, and make the worst of both worlds.

It would be silly to publish this fact (more proper for a confessor's ear) if I did not think that this smouldering resentment, against which I win so many battles but never win the war, was at present very widely shared by law-abiding people. And Heaven knows, many of them have better cause to feel it than I. I have not been driven to suicide like Mr Pilgrim. I am not mourning for a raped and murdered daughter whose murderer will be kept (partly at my expense) in a mental hospital till he gets out and catches some other child. My greatest grievance is trivial in comparison. But, as it raises all the issues, I will tell it.

Not long ago some of my young neighbours broke into a little pavilion or bungalow which stands in my garden and stole several objects—curious weapons and an optical instrument. This time the police discovered who they were. As more than one of them had been convicted of similar crimes before, we had high hopes that some adequately deterrent sentence would be given. But I was warned: 'It'll all be no good if the old woman's on the bench.' I had, of course, to attend the juvenile court and all fell out pat as the warning had said. The—let us call her—Elderly Lady presided. It was abundantly proved that the crime had been planned and that it was done for gain: some of the swag had already been sold. The Elderly Lady inflicted a small fine. That is, she punished not the culprits but their parents. But what alarmed me more was her concluding speech to the prisoners. She told them that they must, they really must, give up these 'stupid pranks'.

Of course I must not accuse the Elderly Lady of injustice. Justice has been so variously defined. If it means, as Thrasymachus thought, 'the interest of the stronger', she was very just; for she enforced her own will and that of the criminals and they together are incomparably stronger than I.

But if her intention was—and I do not doubt that the road on which such justice is leading us all is paved with good ones—to prevent these boys from growing up into confirmed criminals, I question whether her method was well judged. If they listened to her (we may hope they did not) what they carried away was the conviction that planned robbery for gain would be classified as a 'prank'—a childishness which they might be expected to grow out of. A better way of leading them on, without any sense of frontiers crossed, from mere inconsiderate romping and plundering orchards to burglary, arson, rape and murder, would seem hard to imagine.

This little incident seems to me characteristic of our age. Criminal law increasingly protects the criminal and ceases to protect his victim. One might fear that we were moving towards a Dictatorship of the Criminals or (what is perhaps the same thing) mere anarchy. But that is not my fear; my fear is almost the opposite.

According to the classical political theory of this country we surrendered our right of self-protection to the State on condition that the State would protect us. Roughly, you promised not to stab your daughter's murderer on the understanding that the State would catch him and hang him. Of course this was never true as a historical account of the genesis of the State. The power of the group over the individual is by nature unlimited and the individual submits because he has to. The State, under favourable conditions (they have ceased), by defining that power, limits it and gives the individual a little freedom.

But the classical theory morally grounds our obligation to civil obedience; explains why it is right (as well as unavoidable) to pay taxes, why it is wrong (as well as dangerous) to stab your daughter's murderer. At present the very uncomfortable position is this: the State protects us less because it is unwilling to protect us against criminals at home and manifestly grows less and less able to protect us against foreign enemies. At the same time it demands from us more and more. We seldom had fewer rights and liberties nor more burdens: and we get less security in return. While our obligations increase their moral ground is taken away.

And the question that torments me is how long flesh and blood will continue to endure it. There was even, not so long ago, a question whether they ought to. No one, I hope, thinks Dr Johnson a barbarian. Yet he maintained that if, under a peculiarity of Scottish law, the murderer of a man's father escapes, the man might reasonably say, 'I am amongst barbarians, who . . . refuse to do justice . . . I am therefore in a state of nature . . . I will stab the murderer of my father.' (This is recorded in Boswell's *Journal of a Tour of the Hebrides* under 22 August 1773.)

Much more obviously, on these principles, when the State ceases to protect me from hooligans I might reasonably, if I could, catch and trash them myself. When the State cannot or will not protect, 'nature' is come again and the right of self-protection reverts to the individual. But of course if I could and did I should be prosecuted. The Elderly Lady and her kind who are so merciful to theft would have no mercy on me; and I should be pilloried in the gutter Press as a 'sadist' by journalists who neither know nor care what that word, or any word, means.

What I fear, however, is not, or not chiefly, sporadic outbreaks of individual vengeance. I am more afraid, our conditions being so like that of the South after the American Civil War, that some sort of Ku Klux Klan may appear and that this might eventually develop into something like a Right or Central revolution. For those who suffer are chiefly the provident, the resolute, the men who want to work, who have built up, in the face of implacable discouragement, some sort of life worth preserving and wish to preserve it. That most (by no means all) of them are 'middle class' is not very relevant. They do not get their qualities from a class: they belong to that class because they have those qualities. For in a society like ours no stock which has diligence, forethought or talent, and is prepared to practise self-denial, is likely to remain proletarian for more than a generation. They are, in fact, the bearers of what little moral, intellectual, or economic vitality remains. They are not nonentities. There is a point at which their patience will snap.

The Elderly Lady, if she read this article, would say I was 'threatening'—linguistic nicety not being much in her line. If by a *threat* you mean (but then you don't know much English) the conjectural prediction of a highly undesirable event, then I threaten. But if by the word *threat* you imply that I wish for such a result or would willingly contribute to it, then you are wrong. Revolutions seldom cure the evil against which they are directed; they always beget a hundred others. Often they perpetuate the old evil under a new name. We may be sure that, if a Ku Klux Klan arose, its ranks would soon be chiefly filled by the same sort of hooligans who provoked it. A Right or Central revolution would be as hypocritical, filthy and ferocious as any other. My fear is lest we should be making it more probable.

This may be judged an article unfit for the season of peace and goodwill. Yet there is a connection. Not all kinds of peace are compatible with all kinds of goodwill, nor do all those who say 'Peace, peace' inherit the blessing promised to the peacemakers.[1] The real *pacificus* is he who promotes peace, not he who gasses about it. Peace, peace . . . we won't be hard on you . . . it was only a boyish prank . . . you had a neurosis . . . promise not to do it again . . . out of this in the long run I do not think either goodwill or peace will come. Planting new primroses on the primrose path is no long-term benevolence.

There! They're at it again. 'Ark, the errol hygel sings.' They're knocking louder. Well, they come but fifty times a year. Boxing Day[2] is only two and a half weeks ahead; then perhaps we shall have a little quiet in which to remember the birth of Christ.

1. Jeremiah vi. 14; viii. 11 and Matthew v. 9.
2. The first week-day after Christmas.

8

Is Progress Possible?
Willing Slaves of the Welfare State

[*From the French Revolution to the outbreak of the First World War in 1914, it was generally assumed that progress in human affairs was not only possible but inevitable. Since then two terrible wars and the discovery of the hydrogen bomb have made men question this confident assumption. The Observer invited five well-known writers to give their answers to the following questions: 'Is man progressing today?' 'Is progress even possible?' This second article in the series is a reply to the opening article by C. P. Snow, 'Man in Society',* The Observer *(13 July 1958).*]

PROGRESS MEANS MOVEMENT in a desired direction, and we do not all desire the same things for our species. In 'Possible Worlds'[1] Professor Haldane pictured a future in which Man, foreseeing that Earth would soon be uninhabitable, adapted himself for migration to Venus by drastically modifying his physiology and abandoning justice, pity and happiness. The desire here is for mere survival. Now I care far more how humanity lives than how long. Progress, for me, means increasing goodness and happiness of individual lives. For the species, as for each man, mere longevity seems to me a contemptible ideal.

I therefore go even further than C. P. Snow in removing the H-bomb from the centre of the picture. Like him, I am not certain whether if it killed one-third of us (the one-third I belong to), this would be a bad thing for the remainder; like him, I don't think it will kill us all. But suppose it did? As a Christian I take it for granted that human history will some day end; and I am offering Omniscience no advice as to the best date for that consummation. I am more concerned by what the Bomb is doing already.

One meets young people who make the threat of it a reason for poisoning every pleasure and evading every duty in the present. Didn't they know that, Bomb or no Bomb, all men die (many in horrible ways)? There's no good moping and sulking about it.

Having removed what I think a red herring, I return to the real question. Are people becoming, or likely to become, better or happier? Obviously this allows only the most conjectural answer. Most individual experience (and there is no other kind) never gets into the news, let alone the history books; one has an imperfect grasp even of one's own. We are reduced to generalities. Even among these it is hard to strike a balance. Sir Charles enumerates many real ameliorations. Against these we must set Hiroshima, Black and Tans, Gestapo, Ogpu, brain-washing, the Russian slave camps. Perhaps we grow kinder to children; but then we grow less kind

---

1. One essay in J. B. S. Haldane's *Possible Worlds and Other Essays* (London, 1927). See also 'The Last Judgment' in the same book.

to the old. Any G.P.[2] will tell you that even prosperous people refuse to look after their parents. 'Can't they be got into some sort of Home?' says Goneril.[3]

More useful, I think, than an attempt at balancing, is the reminder that most of these phenomena, good and bad, are made possible by two things. These two will probably determine most of what happens to us for some time.

The first is the advance, and increasing application, of science. As a means to the ends I care for, this is neutral. We shall grow able to cure, and to produce, more diseases—bacterial war, not bombs, might ring down the curtain—to alleviate, and to inflict, more pains, to husband, or to waste, the resources of the planet more extensively. We can become either more beneficent or more mischievous. My guess is we shall do both; mending one thing and marring another, removing old miseries and producing new ones, safeguarding ourselves here and endangering ourselves there.

The second is the changed relation between Government and subjects. Sir Charles mentions our new attitude to crime. I will mention the trainloads of Jews delivered at the German gas-chambers. It seems shocking to suggest a common element, but I think one exists. On the humanitarian view all crime is pathological; it demands not retributive punishment but cure. This separates the criminal's treatment from the concepts of justice and desert; a 'just cure' is meaningless.

On the old view public opinion might protest against a punishment (it protested against our old penal code) as excessive, more than the man 'deserved'; an ethical question on which anyone might have an opinion. But a remedial treatment can be judged only by the probability of its success; a technical question on which only experts can speak. Thus the criminal ceases to be a person, a subject of rights and duties, and becomes merely an object on which society can work. And this is, in principle, how Hitler treated the Jews. They were objects; killed not for ill desert but because, on his theories, they were a disease in society. If society can mend, remake, and unmake men at its pleasure, its pleasure may, of course, be humane or homicidal. The difference is important. But, either way, rulers have become owners.

Observe how the 'humane' attitude to crime could operate. If crimes are diseases, why should diseases be treated differently from crimes? And who but the experts can define disease? One school of psychology regards my religion as a neurosis. If this neurosis ever becomes inconvenient to Government, what is to prevent my being subjected to a compulsory 'cure'? It may be painful; treatments sometimes are. But it will be no use asking, 'What have I done to deserve this?' The Straightener will reply: 'But, my dear fellow, no one's *blaming* you. We no longer believe in retributive justice. We're healing you.'

This would be no more than an extreme application of the political philosophy implicit in most modern communities. It has stolen on us unawares. Two wars necessitated vast curtailments of liberty, and we have grown, though grumblingly, accustomed to our chains. The increasing complexity and precariousness of our economic life have forced Government to take over many spheres of activity once

2. A general practitioner (doctor) .
3. In Shakespeare's *King Lear*.

left to choice or chance. Our intellectuals have surrendered first to the slave-philosophy of Hegel, then to Marx, finally to the linguistic analysts.

As a result, classical political theory, with its Stoical, Christian, and juristic key-conceptions (natural law, the value of the individual, the rights of man), has died. The modern State exists not to protect our rights but to do us good or make us good—anyway, to do something to us or to make us something. Hence the new name 'leaders' for those who were once 'rulers'. We are less their subjects than their wards, pupils, or domestic animals. There is nothing left of which we can say to them, 'Mind your own business.' Our whole lives *are* their business.

I write 'they' because it seems childish not to recognize that actual government is and always must be oligarchical. Our effective masters must be more than one and fewer than all. But the oligarchs begin to regard us in a new way.

Here, I think, lies our real dilemma. Probably we cannot, certainly we shall not, retrace our steps. We are tamed animals (some with kind, some with cruel, masters) and should probably starve if we got out of our cage. That is one horn of the dilemma. But in an increasingly planned society, how much of what I value can survive? That is the other horn.

I believe a man is happier, and happy in a richer way, if he has 'the freeborn mind'. But I doubt whether he can have this without economic independence, which the new society is abolishing. For economic independence allows an education not controlled by Government; and in adult life it is the man who needs, and asks, nothing of Government who can criticise its acts and snap his fingers at its ideology. Read Montaigne; that's the voice of a man with his legs under his own table, eating the mutton and turnips raised on his own land. Who will talk like that when the State is everyone's schoolmaster and employer? Admittedly, when man was untamed, such liberty belonged only to the few. I know. Hence the horrible suspicion that our only choice is between societies with few freemen and societies with none.

Again, the new oligarchy must more and more base its claim to plan us on its claim to knowledge. If we are to be mothered, mother must know best. This means they must increasingly rely on the advice of scientists, till in the end the politicians proper become merely the scientists' puppets. Technocracy is the form to which a planned society must tend. Now I dread specialists in power because they are specialists speaking outside their special subjects. Let scientists tell us about sciences. But government involves questions about the good for man, and justice, and what things are worth having at what price; and on these a scientific training gives a man's opinion no added value. Let the doctor tell me I shall die unless I do so-and-so; but whether life is worth having on those terms is no more a question for him than for any other man.

Thirdly, I do not like the pretensions of Government—the grounds on which it demands my obedience—to be pitched too high. I don't like the medicine-man's magical pretensions nor the Bourbon's Divine Right. This is not solely because I disbelieve in magic and in Bossuet's *Politique*.[4] I believe in God, but I detest theocracy. For every Government consists of mere men and is, strictly viewed,

4. Jacques Bénigne Bossuet, *Politique tirée des propres paroles de l'Écriture-Sainte* (Paris, 1709).

a makeshift; if it adds to its commands 'Thus saith the Lord', it lies, and lies dangerously.

On just the same ground I dread government in the name of science. That is how tyrannies come in. In every age the men who want us under their thumb, if they have any sense, will put forward the particular pretension which the hopes and fears of that age render most potent. They 'cash in'. It has been magic, it has been Christianity. Now it will certainly be science. Perhaps the real scientists may not think much of the tyrants' 'science'—they didn't think much of Hitler's racial theories or Stalin's biology. But they can be muzzled.

We must give full weight to Sir Charles's reminder that millions in the East are still half starved. To these my fears would seem very unimportant. A hungry man thinks about food, not freedom. We must give full weight to the claim that nothing but science, and science globally applied, and therefore unprecedented Government controls, can produce full bellies and medical care for the whole human race: nothing, in short, but a world Welfare State. It is a full admission of these truths which impresses upon me the extreme peril of humanity at present.

We have on the one hand a desperate need; hunger, sickness, and the dread of war. We have, on the other, the conception of something that might meet it: omnicompetent global technocracy. Are not these the ideal opportunity for enslavement? This is how it has entered before; a desperate need (real or apparent) in the one party, a power (real or apparent) to relieve it, in the other. In the ancient world individuals have sold themselves as slaves, in order to eat. So in society. Here is a witch-doctor who can save us from the sorcerers—a war-lord who can save us from the barbarians—a Church that can save us from Hell. Give them what they ask, give ourselves to them bound and blindfold, if only they will! Perhaps the terrible bargain will be made again. We cannot blame men for making it. We can hardly wish them not to. Yet we can hardly bear that they should.

The question about progress has become the question whether we can discover any way of submitting to the worldwide paternalism of a technocracy without losing all personal privacy and independence. Is there any possibility of getting the super Welfare State's honey and avoiding the sting?

Let us make no mistake about the sting. The Swedish sadness is only a foretaste. To live his life in his own way, to call his house his castle, to enjoy the fruits of his own labour, to educate his children as his conscience directs, to save for their prosperity after his death—these are wishes deeply ingrained in white and civilised man. Their realization is almost as necessary to our virtues as to our happiness. From their total frustration disastrous results both moral and psychological might follow.

All this threatens us even if the form of society which our needs point to should prove an unparalleled success. But is that certain? What assurance have we that our masters will or can keep the promise which induced us to sell ourselves? Let us not be deceived by phrases about 'Man taking charge of his own destiny'. All that can really happen is that some men will take charge of the destiny of the others. They will be simply men; none perfect; some greedy, cruel and dishonest. The more completely we are planned the more powerful they will be. Have we discovered some new reason why, this time, power should not corrupt as it has done before?

9

We Have No 'Right to Happiness'

AFTER ALL', SAID CLARE, 'they had a right to happiness.'

We were discussing something that once happened in our own neighbourhood. Mr A. had deserted Mrs A. and got his divorce in order to marry Mrs B., who had likewise got her divorce in order to marry Mr A. And there was certainly no doubt that Mr A. and Mrs B. were very much in love with one another. If they continued to be in love, and if nothing went wrong with their health or their income, they might reasonably expect to be very happy.

It was equally clear that they were not happy with their old partners. Mrs B. had adored her husband at the outset. But then he got smashed up in the war. It was thought he had lost his virility, and it was known that he had lost his job. Life with him was no longer what Mrs B. had bargained for. Poor Mrs A., too. She had lost her looks—and all her liveliness. It might be true, as some said, that she consumed herself by bearing his children and nursing him through the long illness that over-shadowed their earlier married life.

You mustn't, by the way, imagine that A. was the sort of man who nonchalantly threw a wife away like the peel of an orange he'd sucked dry. Her suicide was a terrible shock to him. We all knew this, for he told us so himself. 'But what could I do?' he said. 'A man has a right to happiness. I had to take my one chance when it came.'

I went away thinking about the concept of a 'right to happiness'.

At first this sounds to me as odd as a right to good luck. For I believe—whatever one school of moralists may say—that we depend for a very great deal of our happiness or misery on circumstances outside all human control. A right to happiness doesn't, for me, make much more sense than a right to be six feet tall, or to have a millionaire for your father, or to get good weather whenever you want to have a picnic.

I can understand a right as a freedom guaranteed me by the laws of the society I live in. Thus, I have a right to travel along the public roads because society gives me that freedom; that's what we mean by calling the roads 'public'. I can also understand a right as a claim guaranteed me by the laws, and correlative to an obligation on someone else's part. If I have a right to receive £100 from you, this is another way of saying that you have a duty to pay me £100. If the laws allow Mr A. to desert his wife and seduce his neighbour's wife, then, by definition, Mr A. has a legal right to do so, and we need bring in no talk about 'happiness'.

But of course that was not what Clare meant. She meant that he had not only a legal but a moral right to act as he did. In other words, Clare is—or would be if she thought it out—a classical moralist after the style of Thomas Aquinas, Grotius,

Hooker and Locke. She believes that behind the laws of the state there is a Natural Law.

I agree with her. I hold this conception to be basic to all civilization. Without it, the actual laws of the state become an absolute, as in Hegel. They cannot be criticized because there is no norm against which they should be judged.

The ancestry of Clare's maxim, 'They have a right to happiness,' is august. In words that are cherished by all civilized men, but especially by Americans, it has been laid down that one of the rights of man is a right to 'the pursuit of happiness'. And now we get to the real point.

What did the writers of that august declaration mean?

It is quite certain what they did not mean. They did not mean that man was entitled to pursue happiness by any and every means—including, say, murder, rape, robbery, treason and fraud. No society could be built on such a basis.

They meant 'to pursue happiness by all lawful means'; that is, by all means which the Law of Nature eternally sanctions and which the laws of the nation shall sanction.

Admittedly this seems at first to reduce their maxim to the tautology that men (in pursuit of happiness) have a right to do whatever they have a right to do. But tautologies, seen against their proper historical context, are not always barren tautologies. The declaration is primarily a denial of the political principles which long governed Europe: a challenge flung down to the Austrian and Russian empires, to England before the Reform Bills, to Bourbon France. It demands that whatever means of pursuing happiness are lawful for any should be lawful for all; that 'man', not men of some particular caste, class, status or religion, should be free to use them. In a century when this is being unsaid by nation after nation and party after party, let us not call it a barren tautology.

But the question as to what means are 'lawful'—what methods of pursuing happiness are either morally permissible by the Law of Nature or should be declared legally permissible by the legislature of a particular nation—remains exactly where it did. And on that question I disagree with Clare. I don't think it is obvious that people have the unlimited 'right to happiness' which she suggests.

For one thing, I believe that Clare, when she says 'happiness', means simply and solely 'sexual happiness'. Partly because women like Clare never use the word 'happiness' in any other sense. But also because I never heard Clare talk about the 'right' to any other kind. She was rather leftist in her politics, and would have been scandalised if anyone had defended the actions of a ruthless man-eating tycoon on the ground that his happiness consisted in making money and he was pursuing his happiness. She was also a rabid teetotaller; I never heard her excuse an alcoholic because he was happy when he was drunk.

A good many of Clare's friends, and especially her female friends, often felt—I've heard them say so—that their own happiness would be perceptibly increased by boxing her ears. I very much doubt if this would have brought her theory of a right to happiness into play.

Clare, in fact, is doing what the whole western world seems to me to have been doing for the last 40-odd years. When I was a youngster, all the progressive people were saying, 'Why all this prudery? Let us treat sex just as we treat all our other impulses.' I was simple-minded enough to believe they meant what they said. I have since discovered that they meant exactly the opposite. They meant that sex was to be treated as no other impulse in our nature has ever been treated by civilized people. All the others, we admit, have to be bridled. Absolute obedience to your instinct for self-preservation is what we call cowardice; to your acquisitive impulse, avarice. Even sleep must be resisted if you're a sentry. But every unkindness and breach of faith seems to be condoned provided that the object aimed at is 'four bare legs in a bed'.

It is like having a morality in which stealing fruit is considered wrong—unless you steal nectarines.

And if you protest against this view you are usually met with chatter about the legitimacy and beauty and sanctity of 'sex' and accused of harbouring some Puritan prejudice against it as something disreputable or shameful. I deny the charge. Foam-born Venus . . . golden Aphrodite . . . Our Lady of Cyprus . . . l never breathed a word against you. If I object to boys who steal my nectarines, must I be supposed to disapprove of nectarines in general? Or even of boys in general? It might, you know, be stealing that I disapproved of.

The real situation is skilfully concealed by saying that the question of Mr A.'s 'right' to desert his wife is one of 'sexual morality'. Robbing an orchard is not an offense against some special morality called 'fruit morality'. It is an offense against honesty. Mr A.'s action is an offense against good faith (to solemn promises), against gratitude (toward one to whom he wàs deeply indebted) and against common humanity.

Our sexual impulses are thus being put in a position of preposterous privilege. The sexual motive is taken to condone all sorts of behaviour which, if it had any other end in view, would be condemned as merciless, treacherous and unjust.

Now though I see no good reason for giving sex this privilege, I think I see a strong cause. It is this.

It is part of the nature of a strong erotic passion—as distinct from a transient fit of appetite—that it makes more towering promises than any other emotion. No doubt all our desires make promises, but not so impressively. To be in love involves the almost irresistible conviction that one will go on being in love until one dies, and that possession of the beloved will confer, not merely frequent ecstasies, but settled, fruitful, deep-rooted, lifelong happiness. Hence *all* seems to be at stake. If we miss this chance we shall have lived in vain. At the very thought of such a doom we sink into fathomless depths of self-pity.

Unfortunately these promises are found often to be quite untrue. Every experienced adult knows this to be so as regards all erotic passions (except the one he himself is feeling at the moment). We discount the world-without-end pretensions of our friends' amours easily enough. We know that such things sometimes last—and sometimes don't. And when they do last, this is not because they promised at the outset to do so. When two people achieve lasting happiness, this is not solely because they are great lovers but because they are also—I must put it crudely—good people; controlled, loyal, fair-minded, mutually adaptable people.

If we establish a 'right to (sexual) happiness' which supersedes all the ordinary rules of behaviour, we do so not because of what our passion shows itself to be in experience but because of what it professes to be while we are in the grip of it. Hence, while the bad behaviour is real and works miseries and degradations, the happiness which was the object of the behaviour turns out again and again to be illusory. Everyone (except Mr A. and Mrs B.) knows that Mr A. in a year or so may have the same reason for deserting his new wife as for deserting his old. He will feel again that all is at stake. He will see himself again as the great lover, and his pity for himself will exclude all pity for the woman.

Two further points remain.

One is this. A society in which conjugal infidelity is tolerated must always be in the long run a society adverse to women. Women, whatever a few male songs and satires may say to the contrary, are more naturally monogamous than men; it is a biological necessity. Where promiscuity prevails, they will therefore always be more often the victims than the culprits. Also, domestic happiness is more necessary to them than to us. And the quality by which they most easily hold a man, their beauty, decreases every year after they have come to maturity, but this does not happen to those qualities of personality—women don t really care twopence about our *looks*— by which we hold women. Thus in the ruthless war of promiscuity women are at a double disadvantage. They play for higher stakes and are also more likely to lose. I have no sympathy with moralists who frown at the increasing crudity of female provocativeness. These signs of desperate competition fill me with pity.

Secondly, though the 'right to happiness' is chiefly claimed for the sexual impulse, it seems to me impossible that the matter should stay there. The fatal principle, once allowed in that department, must sooner or later seep through our whole lives. We thus advance toward a state of society in which not only each man but every impulse in each man claims *carte blanche*. And then, though our technological skill may help us survive a little longer, our civilization will have died at heart, and will—one dare not even add 'unfortunately'—be swept away.

PART IV

Letters

[Though I have reprinted only Lewis's own letters here, I have attempted to place them in their context by citing the sources of the letters from the various correspondents which Lewis was answering, or who were answering him. Thus the subdivisions (a), (b), (c) and so forth.]

1
The Conditions for a Just War

(a) E. L. Mascall, 'The Christian and the Next War', *Theology*, vol. XXXVIII (January 1939), pp. 53–58.

(b) C. S. Lewis, 'The Conditions for a Just War', *ibid.* (May 1939), pp. 373–74:

Sir, In your January number Mr Mascall mentions six conditions for a just war which have been laid down by 'theologians'. I have one question to ask, and a number of problems to raise, about these rules. The question is merely historical. Who are these theologians, and what kind or degree of authority can they claim over members of the Church of England? The problems are more difficult. Condition 4 lays down that 'it must be morally certain that the losses, to the belligerents, the world, and religion, will not outweigh the advantages of winning'; and 6, that 'there must be a considerable probability of winning'. It is plain that equally sincere people can differ to any extent and argue for ever as to whether a proposed war fulfils these conditions or not. The practical question, therefore, which faces us is one of authority. Who has the duty of deciding when the conditions are fulfilled, and the right of enforcing his decision? Modern discussions tend to assume without argument that the answer is 'The private conscience of the individual,' and that any other answer is immoral and totalitarian. Now it is certain, in some sense, that 'no duty of obedience can justify a sin', as Mr Mascall says. Granted that capital punishment is compatible with Christianity, a Christian may lawfully be a hangman; but he must not hang a man whom he knows to be innocent. But will anyone interpret this to mean that the hangman has the *same* duty of investigating the prisoner's guilt which the judge has? If so, no executive can work and no Christian state is possible; which is absurd. I conclude that the hangman has done his duty if he has done his share of the general duty, resting upon all citizens alike, to ensure, so far as in him lies, that we have an honest judicial system; if, in spite of this, and unknowingly, he hangs an innocent man, then a sin has been committed, but not by him. This analogy suggests to me that it must be absurd to give to the private citizen the *same* right and duty of deciding the justice of a given war which rests on governments; and I submit that the rules for determining what wars are just were originally rules for the guidance of princes, not sub-jects. This does not mean that private persons must obey governments com-manding them to do what they know is sin; but perhaps it does mean (I write it with some reluctance) that the ultimate decision as to what the situation at a given moment is in the highly complex field of international affairs is one which must be delegated. No doubt we must make every effort which the constitu-tion allows to ensure a good government and to influence public opinion; but in the long run, the nation, as a nation, must act, and it can act only through its government. (It must be remembered that there are risks in both directions: if war is ever lawful, then peace is sometimes sinful.) What is the alternative? That individuals ignorant of history and strategy should decide for themselves whether condition 6 ('a considerable probability of winning') is, or is not, ful-filled?—or that every citizen, neglecting his own vocation and not weighing his capacity, is to become an expert on all the relevant, and often technical, problems?

Decisions by the private conscience of each Christian in the light of Mr Mascall's six rules would divide Christians from each other and result in no clear Christian witness to the pagan world around us. But a clear Christian witness might be attained in a different way. If all Christians consented to bear arms at the command of the magistrate, and if all, after that, refused to obey anti-Christian orders, should we not get a clear issue? A man is much more certain that he ought not to murder prisoners or bomb civilians than he ever can be about the justice of a war. It is perhaps here that 'conscientious objec-tion' ought to begin. I feel certain that one Christian airman shot for refusing to bomb enemy civilians would be a more effective martyr (in the etymologi-cal sense of the word) than a hundred Christians in jail for refusing to join the army.

Christendom has made two efforts to deal with the evil of war—chivalry and pacifism. Neither succeeded. But I doubt whether chivalry has such an unbro-ken record of failure as pacifism.

The question is a very dark one. I should welcome about equally refutation or development, of what I have said.

2
The Conflict in Anglican Theology

(a) Oliver C. Quick, 'The Conflict in Anglican Theology', *Theology*, vol. LXI (Octo-ber 1940), pp. 234–37.

(b) C. S. Lewis, *ibid.* (November 1940), p. 304:
Sir, In an admirable letter contributed to your October number Canon Quick remarks, '"Moderns" of every kind have one characteristic in common: they hate Liberalism.' Would it not be equally true to say, more shortly, '"Moderns" of every kind have one characteristic in common: they *hate*?' The matter de-serves, perhaps, more attention than it has received.

3
Miracles

(a) Peter May, 'Miracles', *The Guardian* (9 October 1942), p. 323.

(b) C. S. Lewis, *ibid.* (16 October 1942), p. 331:

Sir,—In answer to Mr May's question, I reply that whether the birth of St John Baptist were a miracle or no, it was not the same miracle as the birth of our Lord.[1] What was abnormal about St Elizabeth's pregnancy was that she was an elderly (married) woman, hitherto sterile. That Zacharias was the father of St John is implied in the text ('shall bear *thee* a son', Luke i. 13).

Of the natural conversion of water into wine, what I said was: 'God creates the vine and teaches it to draw up water by its roots and, *with the aid of the sun*, to turn that water into a juice *which will ferment* and take on certain qualities.'[2] For completeness I should, no doubt, have added 'with the aid of the soil', and perhaps other things; but this would not, from my point of view, have materially altered what I was saying. My answer to Mr May's question—where the other raw materials came from—would be the same, whether the list of raw materials be reduced to the mere vegetable and sunlight I mentioned, or extended to bring in all that the skilled botanist might add. I think they came from the same source at Cana whence they come in Nature. I agree with Mr May, of course, that on the hypothesis of the story being fiction, we can attach to it, as our ancestors did to the miracles in Ovid, any number of edifying *moralitates*. What I was doing was to combat that particular argument for its falsity which rests on the idea that, if it occurred, such an event would be arbitrary and meaningless.

4
Mr C. S. Lewis on Christianity

(a) W. R. Childe, 'Mr C. S. Lewis on Christianity', *The Listener*, vol. XXXI (2 March 1944), p. 245.

(b) C. S. Lewis, *ibid.* (9 March 1944), p. 273:

I agree with Mr W. R. Childe that it is no use to say 'Lord, Lord', if we do not do what Christ tells us: that, indeed, is one of the reasons why I think an aesthetic religion of 'flowers and music' insufficient.[3] My reason for thinking that a mere statement of even the highest ethical principles is not enough is precisely that to know these things is not necessarily to do them, and if Christianity brought no healing to the impotent will, Christ's teaching would not help us. I cannot blame Mr Childe for misunderstanding me, because I am naturally no judge

---

1. Mr May was criticizing the essay on 'Miracles' printed in this book. See page 313.
2. *Ibid.*, p. 316.
3. Mr Childe had taken exception to a passage in Lewis's B.B.C. broadcast 'The Map and the Ocean' in which he said, in speaking of a 'vague religion', that 'you will not get eternal life by just feeling the presence of God in flowers or music'. *The Listener*, vol. XXXI (24 February 1944), p. 216. The broadcast was later to become a chapter in Lewis's *Mere Christianity* (London, 1952), Bk. IV, ch. i, p. 122.

of my own lucidity; but I take it very hard that a total stranger whom I have never knowingly injured or offended, on the first discovery of a difference in theological opinion between us, should publicly accuse me of being a potential torturer, murderer and tyrant—for that is what Mr Childe's reference to faggots means if it means anything. How little I approve of compulsion in religion may be gauged from a recent letter of mine to the *Spectator* protesting against the intolerable tyranny of compulsory church parades for the Home Guard. If Mr Childe can find any passage in my works which favours religious or anti-religious compulsion I will give five pounds to any (not militantly anti-Christian) charity he cares to name. If he cannot, I ask him, for justice and charity's sake, to withdraw his charge.

(c) W. R. Childe, *ibid.* (16 March 1944), p. 301.

5
A Village Experience

C. S. Lewis, 'A Village Experience', *The Guardian* (31 August 1945), p. 335:

Sir,—I think your readers should, and will, be interested in the following extract from a letter I have just received; the writer is an invalid lady in a village:

'This used to be a God-fearing village with a God-fearing parson who visited and ran the Scouts ("Lovely troop we 'ad. *And* you should have 'eard our choir of a Sunday," says my bricklayer host). The young were polished up and sent to Sunday school, their parents filled the church to the brim. *Now* they have an octogenarian. No harm in that! My late uncle—at that age was going as strong as most two-year-olds. But this one—I noted for myself, seeing him pass—has been dead for years . . . He does not visit the sick, even if asked. He does nothing. And—listen—he stuck up a notice in the church: *No children admitted without their parents or an adult.* The village . . . went instantly Pagan. I must get away from it. Never before but in the vile pagan West Indies have I been without so much as an *extorted* Holy Sacrament. (*Can* one forbid the church to a Crissom child?—legally, I mean? Pass me a Bishop.)'

6
Correspondence with an Anglican Who Dislikes Hymns

(The 'correspondence' consists of two letters from Erik Routley to Lewis (an Anglican), and two letters from Lewis, all of which were published together in *The Presbyter*, vol. VI, No. 2 (1948), pp. 15–20. Lewis's letters appeared over the initials 'A. B.')

(a) Summary of a letter from Erik Routley to Lewis (dated 13 July 1946), p. 15:
'. . . The Hymn Society of Great Britain and Ireland is opening a file of new hymns to which modern hymn-writers are to be asked to contribute. I have been asked to write to you and ask if you will be a member of the panel to whom new hymns may be submitted in order that their merit may be assessed . . .'

(b) C. S. Lewis to Erik Routley (dated 16 July 1946), p. 15:

Dear Mr Routley,

The truth is that I'm not in sufficient sympathy with the project to help you. I know that many of the congregation like singing hymns: but am not yet convinced that their enjoyment is of a spiritual kind. It may be: I don't know. To the minority, of whom I am one, the hymns are mostly the dead wood of the service. Recently in a party of six people I found that all without exception would like *fewer* hymns. Naturally, one holding this view can't help you.

(c) Erik Routley to Lewis (dated 18 September 1946), pp. 15–?0.

(d) C. S. Lewis to Erik Routley (dated 21 September 1946), pp. 15–20:

I can't quite remember my own last letter; but I was wrong if I said or implied that (*a*) variables, (*b*) active participation by the people, or (*c*) hymns, were bad in principle. I would agree that anything the congregation *can do* may properly and profitably be offered to God in public worship. If one had a congregation (say, in Africa) who had a high tradition in sacred dancing and could do it really well I would be perfectly in favour of making a dance part of the service. But I wouldn't transfer the practice to a Willesden congregation whose best dance was a ballroom shuffle. In modern England, however, we can't sing—as the Welsh and Germans can. Also (a great pity, but a fact) the art of poetry has developed for two centuries in a private and subjective direction. That is why I find hymns 'dead wood'. But I spoke only for myself and a few others. If an improved hymnody—or even the present hymnody—does edify other people, of course it is an elementary duty of charity and humility for me to submit. I have never spoken in public *against* the use of hymns: on the contrary I have often told 'highbrow converts that a humble acquiescence in anything that may edify their uneducated brethren (however frightful it seems to the educated 'natural man') is the first lesson they must learn. The door is *low* and one must stoop to enter.

7

The Church's Liturgy, Invocation, and Invocation of Saints

(a) E. L. Mascall, 'Quadringentesimo Anno', *Church Times,* vol. CXXXII (6 May 1949), p. 282.

(b) C. S. Lewis, 'The Church's Liturgy', *ibid.* (20 May 1949), p. 319:

Sir,—If it is not harking back too far, I would like to make two layman's comments on the liturgical articles in your issue of May 6. Firstly, I would underline the necessity for uniformity, if in nothing else, yet in the time taken by the rite. We laymen may not be busier than the clergy but we usually have much less choice in our hours of business. The celebrant who lengthens the service by ten minutes may, for us, throw the whole day into hurry and confusion. It is difficult to keep this out of our minds: it may even be difficult to avoid some feeling of resentment. Such temptations may be good for us but it is not the celebrant's business to supply them: God's permission and Satan's diligence will see to that part of our education without his assistance.

Secondly, I would ask the clergy to believe that we are more interested in orthodoxy and less interested in liturgiology as such than they can easily imagine. Dr Mascall rightly says that variations are permissible when they do not alter doctrine. But after that he goes on almost casually to mention 'devotions to the Mother of God and to the hosts of heaven' as a possible liturgical variant. That the introduction of such devotions into any parish not accustomed to them would divide the congregation into two camps, Dr Mascall well knows. But if he thinks that the issue between those camps would be a liturgical issue, I submit that he is mistaken. It would be a doctrinal issue. Not one layman would be asking whether these devotions marred or mended the beauty of the rite; everyone would be asking whether they were lawful or damnable. It is no part of my object to discuss that question here, but merely to point out that it is the question.

What we laymen fear is that the deepest doctrinal issues should be tacitly and implicitly settled by what seem to be, or are avowed to be, merely changes in liturgy. A man who is wondering whether the fare set before him is food or poison is not reassured by being told that this course is now restored to its traditional place in the *menu* or that the tureen is of the Sarum pattern. We laymen are ignorant and timid. Our lives are ever in our hands, the avenger of blood is on our heels, and of each of us his soul may this night be required. Can you blame us if the reduction of grave doctrinal issues to merely liturgical issues fills us with something like terror?

(c) W. D. F. Hughes, *ibid.* (24 June 1949), p. 409.

(d) C. S. Lewis, *ibid.* (1 July 1949), p. 427:

Sir,—I agree with Dean Hughes that the connection of belief and liturgy is close, but doubt if it is 'inextricable'. I submit that the relation is healthy when liturgy expresses the belief of the Church, morbid when liturgy creates in the people by suggestion beliefs which the Church has not publicly professed, taught, and defended. If the mind of the Church is, for example, that our fathers erred in abandoning the Romish invocations of saints and angels, by all means let our corporate recantation, together with its grounds in scripture, reason and tradition be published, our solemn act of penitence be performed, the laity reinstructed, and the proper changes in liturgy be introduced.

What horrifies me is the proposal that individual priests should be encouraged to behave as if all this had been done when it has not been done. One correspondent compared such changes to the equally stealthy and (as he holds) irresistible changes in a language. But that is just the parallel that terrifies me, for even the shallowest philologist knows that the unconscious linguistic process is continually degrading good words and blunting useful distinctions. *Absit omen!* Whether an 'enrichment' of liturgy which involves a change of doctrine is allowable, surely depends on whether our doctrine is changing from error to truth or from truth to error. Is the individual priest the judge of that?

(e) Edward Every, 'Doctrine and Liturgy', *ibid.* (8 July 1949), pp. 445–46.

(f) C. S. Lewis, 'Invocation', *ibid.* (15 July 1949), pp. 463–64:

Sir,—Mr Every (quite legitimately) gives the word *invocation* a wider sense than I. The question then becomes how far we can infer propriety of *devotion* from propriety of *invocation?* I accept the authority of the *Benedicite*[4] for the propriety of *invoking (in* Mr Every's sense) saints. But if I thence infer the propriety of *devotions* to saints, will not an argument force me to approve devotions to stars, frosts and whales?

I am also quite ready to admit that I overlooked a distinction. Our fathers might disallow a particular mediaeval doctrine and yet not disallow some other doctrine which we laymen easily confuse with it. But if the issue is so much finer than I thought, this merely redoubles my anxiety that it should be openly and authoritatively decided.

If I feared lest the suggestions of liturgy might beguile us laymen on a simple issue, I am not likely to be comforted by finding the issue a subtle one. If there is one kind of devotion to created beings which is pleasing and another which is displeasing to God, when is the Church, as a Church, going to instruct us in the distinction?

Meanwhile, what better opportunity for the stealthy insinuation of the wrong kind than the unauthorized and sporadic practice of devotions to creatures before uninstructed congregations would our ghostly foe desire? Most of us laymen, I think, have a *parti pris* in the matter. We desire to believe as the Church believes.

(g) Edward Every, 'Invocation of Saints', *ibid.* (22 July 1949), pp. 481–82.

(h) C. S. Lewis, *ibid.* (5 August 1944), p. 513:

Sir,—I hope Mr Every has not misunderstood me. There is, I believe, a *prima facie* case for regarding devotions to saints in the Church of England as a controversial question (see Jewel,[5] *Apologia Ecclesiae Anglicanae,* Pt. II, ch. xxviii, *Homilies,* Bk. II, *Peril of Idolatry,* Pt. III; Laud,[6] *Conference with Fisher,* Sect. XXIII; Taylor,[7] *Dissuasive from Popery,* Pt. I, ch. ii, sect. 8). I merely claim that the controversy exists. I share Mr Every's wish that it should cease. But there are two ways in which a controversy can cease: by being settled, or by gradual and imperceptible change of custom. I do not want any controversy to cease in the second way.

I implore priests to remember what Aristotle tells us about unconscious revolution (πολλάκις λανθάνει μεγάλη γινομένη μετάβασις τῶν νομίμων *Politics* 1303 a 22).[8] When such unconscious revolution produces a result we like, we are all tempted to welcome it; thus I am tempted to welcome it when it leads to prayers for the dead. But then I see that the very same process can be used, and is used, to introduce modernist dilutions of the faith which, I am sure, Mr Every and I equally abominate. I conclude that a road so dangerous should never be trodden, whether the destination to which it seems to point is in itself good or bad. To write 'No Thoroughfare' over that road is my only purpose.

4. Found in the Prayer Book service of Morning Prayer, the original source of which is *The Song of the Three Holy Children* (vv. 35–66) in the Old Testament Apocrypha.
5. John Jewel (1522–7 1).
6. William Laud (1573–1645).
7. Jeremy Taylor (1613–67).
8. 'The occurrence of an important transition in customs often passes unnoticed.'

8
The Holy Name

(a) Leslie E. T. Bradbury, 'The Holy Name', *Church Times*, vol. CXXXIV (3 August 1951), p. 525.

(b) C. S. Lewis, *ibid.* (10 August 1951), p. 541:

Sir,—Having read Mr Bradbury's letter on the Holy Name, I have a few comments to make. I do not think we are entitled to assume that all who use this Name without reverential prefixes are making a 'careless' use of it; otherwise, we should have to say that the Evangelists were often careless. I do not think we are entitled to assume that the use of the word *Blessed* when we speak of the Virgin Mary is 'necessary'; otherwise, we should have to condemn both the Nicene and the Apostles' Creed for omitting it. Should we not rather recognize that the presence or absence of such prefixes constitutes a difference, not in faith or morals, but simply in style? I know that as their absence is 'irritating' to some, so their frequent recurrence is irritating to others. Is not each party innocent in its temperamental preference but grossly culpable if it allows anything so subjective, contingent. and (with a little effort) conquerable as a temperamental preference to become a cause of division among brethren? If we cannot lay down our tastes, along with other carnal baggage at the church door, surely we should at least bring them in to be humbled and, if necessary, modified, not to be indulged?

9
Mere Christians

(a) R. D. Daunton-Fear, 'Evangelical Churchmanship', *Church Times*, vol. CXXXV (1 February 1952), p. 77.

(b) C. S. Lewis, 'Mere Christians', *ibid.* (8 February 1952), p. 95:

Sir,—I welcome the letter from the Rural Dean of Gravesend, though I am sorry that anyone should have rendered it necessary by describing the Bishop of Birmingham as an Evangelical. To a layman, it seems obvious that what unites the Evangelical and the Anglo-Catholic against the 'Liberal' or 'Modernist' is something very clear and momentous, namely, the fact that both are thoroughgoing supernaturalists, who believe in the Creation, the Fall, the Incarnation, the Resurrection, the Second Coming, and the Four Last Things. This unites them not only with one another, but with the Christian religion as understood *ubique et ab omnibus.*[9]

The point of view from which this agreement seems less important than their divisions, or than the gulf which separates both from any non-miraculous version of Christianity, is to me unintelligible. Perhaps the trouble is that as supernaturalists, whether 'Low' or 'High' Church, thus taken together, they

---

9. 'everywhere and by all'. See St Vincent of Lérins, *Commonitorium* ii.

lack a name. May I suggest 'Deep Church'; or, if that fails in humility, Baxter's 'mere Christians'?

10
Canonization

(a) Eric Pitt, 'Canonization', *Church Times*, vol. CXXXV (17 October 1952), p. 743.

(b) C. S. Lewis, *ibid.* (24 October 1952), p. 763:

Sir,—I am, like Mr Eric Pitt, a layman, and would like to be instructed on several points before the proposal to set up a 'system' of Anglican canonization is even discussed. According to the *Catholic Encyclopaedia*, 'saints' are dead people whose virtues have made them 'worthy' of God's 'special' love. Canonization makes *dulia* 'universal and obligatory'; and, whatever else it asserts, it certainly asserts that the person concerned 'is in heaven'.

Unless, then, the word 'canonization' is being used in a sense distinct from the Roman (and, if so, some other word would be much more convenient), the proposal to set us a 'system' of canonization means that someone (say, the Archbishops) shall be appointed

(a) To tell us that certain named people are (i) 'in heaven', and (ii) are 'worthy' of God's 'special' love.

(b) To lay upon us (under pain of excommunication?) the duty of *dulia* towards those they have named.

Now it is very clear that no one ought to tell us what he does not know to be true. Is it, then, held that God has promised (and, if so, when and where?) to the Church universal a knowledge of the state of certain departed souls? If so, is it clear that this knowledge will discern varying degrees of kinds of salvation such as are, I suppose, implicit in the word 'special'? And if it does, will the promulgation of such knowledge help to save souls now *in viâ*? For it might well lead to a consideration of 'rival claims', such as we read of in the *Imitation of Christ* (Bk. III, ch. lviii), where we are warned, 'Ask not which is greater in the kingdom of heaven . . . the search into such things brings no profit, but rather offends the saints themselves.'

Finally, there is the practical issue: by which I do not mean the *Catholic Encyclopaedia's* neat little account of 'the ordinary actual expenses of canonization' (though that too can be read with profit), but the danger of schism. Thousands of members of the Church of England doubt whether *dulia is* lawful. Does anyone maintain that it is necessary to salvation? If not, whence comes our obligation to run such frightful risks?

11
Pittenger-Lewis and Version Vernacular

(a) W. Norman Pittenger, 'Pittenger-Lewis', *The Christian Century*, vol. LXXV (24 December 1958), pp. 1485–86.

(b) C. S. Lewis, 'Version Vernacular', *ibid.* (31 December 1958), p. 1515.

Sir: Thank you for publishing my 'Rejoinder to Dr Pittenger' (Nov. 26). Now would you, please, complete your kindness by publishing the statement that *'populam'* (p. 1360) is either my typist's or your printer's error for *'populum'*?

An article on 'translation' such as Dr Pittenger suggests in his letter in the Dec. 24 issue certainly needs doing, but I could not usefully do it for Americans. The vernacular into which they would have to translate is not quite the same as that into which I have translated. Small differences, in addressing proletarians, may be all-important.

In both countries an essential part of the ordination exam ought to be a passage from some recognized theological work set for translation into vulgar English—just like doing Latin prose. Failure on this paper should mean failure on the whole exam. It is absolutely disgraceful that we expect missionaries to the Bantus to learn Bantu hut never ask whether our missionaries to the Americans or English can speak American or English. Any fool can write *learned* language. The vernacular is the real test. If you can't turn your faith into it, then either you don't understand it or you don't believe it.

12
Capital Punishment and Death Penalty

(a) C. S. Lewis, 'Capital Punishment', *Church Times*, vol. CXLIV (1 December 1961), p. 7:

Sir,—I do not know whether capital punishment should or should not be abolished, for neither the natural light, nor scripture, nor ecclesiastical authority seems to tell me. But I am concerned about the grounds on which its abolition is being sought.

To say that by hanging a man we presumptuously judge him to be irredeemable is, I submit, simply untrue. My Prayer Book includes an exhortation to those under sentence of death which throughout implies the exact opposite. The real question is whether a murderer is more likely to repent and make a good end three weeks hence in the execution shed or, say, thirty years later in the prison infirmary. No mortal can know. But those who have most right to an opinion are those who know most by experience about the effect of prolonged prison life. I wish some prison chaplains, governors and warders would contribute to the discussion.

The suggestion of compensation for the relatives of the murdered man is in itself reasonable, but it ought not to be even remotely connected with the case for or against capital punishment. If it is, we shall be giving countenance to the archaic, and surely erroneous view that murder is primarily an offence not against society but against individuals.

Hanging is not a more irrevocable act than any other. You can't bring an innocent man to life: but neither can you give him back the years which wrongful imprisonment has eaten.

Other correspondents have pointed out that a theory of punishment which is purely exemplary or purely reformatory, or both, is shockingly immoral. Only the concept of desert connects punishment with morality at all. If deterrence is all that matters, the execution of an innocent man, provided the public think him guilty, would be fully justified. If reformation alone is in question, then there is nothing against painful and compulsory reform for all our defects, and a Government which believes Christianity to be a neurosis will have a perfectly good right to hand us all over to their straighteners for 'cure' to-morrow.

(b) Claude Davis, *ibid.* (8 December 1961), p. 14.

(c) C. S. Lewis, 'Death Penalty', *ibid.* (15 December 1961), p. 12:

Sir,—Dr Davis rightly reproves me for using the word *society* as I did. This hypostatised abstraction has already done harm enough. But I only meant 'all of us'. The absurdity of the view which treats murder as an offence against a single family is best illustrated by a case in the private speeches of Demosthenes (I can't turn it up at the moment, but your more scholarly readers no doubt can) .

A man, *A*, set free a female slave, *B*, his old nurse. *B* married. Her husband died without issue. Someone then murdered *B*. But under Athenian law no one could prosecute because there was no injured party. *A* could not act because *B*, when murdered, was no longer his property. There was no widower, and there were no orphans.

I am on neither side in the present controversy. But I still think the abolitionists conduct their case very ill. They seem incapable of stating it without imputing vile motives to their opponents. If unbelievers often look at your correspondence column, I am afraid they may carry away a bad impression of our logic, manners and charity.

INDEX

Abraham, 406
Actium, The Battle of, 363, 463
Acts of the Apostles, The, 364, 459
Adam, 311
Adler, M. J., 431
Adonis, 316, 356
Ahriman, 310, 311, 312
Akhenaten, 393
Aladdin, 466, 467
Alberich (in Wagner's *Ring*), 489
Aldwinckle, Stella, 385
Allah, 406
allegory, 320, 345
Amos, 422
Andromeda, 324
Anscombe, G. E. M., 306, 397–8
anthropology, 389
anthropomorphism, 346, 366, 424, 463, 472
Aphrodite (Venus), 358, 518
Apollinarianism, 419
Apollo, 317
Apollos of Alexandria, 479
apologetics, 360–9, 416
Apostles' Creed, The, 529
Aquinas, St Thomas, 349, 395, 422, 434, 436, 516
Arcadia, The, see Sir P. Sidney
Aristotle, 395, 429, 504, 528
Arius, 438
Ark (Society), The, 385
Arnhem, 351
Arnold, Matthew, 477, 390
Ascension, The, 320, 347
Aslan, 478
Athanasius, St, 306, 315, 320, 420, 434, 437, 438
Atonement, The, 365, 473
Augustine, St, 310, 349, 389, 395, 408, 414
Austen, Jane, 348, 458, 461
Austerlitz, 390
Auxiliary Territorial Service, 492
Averröes, 342

Babylon, 359
Bacchus, see Dionysus

Balaam's ass, 475
Balder, 343, 344, 389
Ball, John, 501
Bantus, The, 363, 464
Barfield, Owen, 308, 504
Barth, Karl, 435
Baxter, Richard, 435, 530
Beckett, Samuel, 480
Beegle, Dewey, 480
Berdyaev, Nicolas, 434
Bergson, Henri, 326, 358, 469
Besant, Annie, 396
Bevan, Edwyn, 421, 477
Beveridge, William H., 363
Beveridge Report, The, see W. H. Beveridge
Bingley, Caroline and Charles (in Austen's *Pride and Prejudice*), 342, 458
Blimp, Colonel, 427
Boehme, Jakob, 436
Boethius, 310, 349, 436
Bossuet, Jacques Bénigne, 514
Boswell, James, 301, 421, 510
Bowen, H. W., 329
Bradbury, Leslie E. T., 529
Bradley, F. H., 449
Bradley, Henry, 392
Bradshaw, George, 390
Bradshaw's Railway Guide, 390
Bramah, 406
Breakthrough, 307
Bridges, Robert, 392
Bristol Diocesan Gazette, 306
Browne, Thomas, 358, 401
Browning, Robert, 468
Buckle, Donald, 307, 501–4
Buddha, Gautama, 354, 368
Buddhism, 369, 387, 388, 395, 399
Bunyan, John, 436, 501
Butler, Samuel, 493
Byron, Lord, 385

Caesar, Julius, 463
Carroll, Lewis, 453, 467
Catholic Encyclopaedia, The, 530

533